Assessing and Correcting Classroom Reading Problems

Assessing and Correcting Classroom Reading Problems

J. Estill Alexander
University of Tennessee

Betty S. Heathington
University of Tennessee

Scott, Foresman/Little, Brown College Division
Scott, Foresman and Company
Glenview, Illinois   Boston   London

Library of Congress Cataloging-in-Publication Data

Alexander, J. Estill.
  Assessing and correcting classroom reading problems.

  Bibliography: p.
  Includes index.
  1. Reading disability. 2. Reading—Remedial teaching.
I. Heathington, Betty S. II. Title.
LB1050.5.A43 1988   372.4'3   87–23403
ISBN 0–673–39704–1

1 2 3 4 5 6 7 8 9 10 — RRC — 93 92 91 90 89 88 87

Printed in the United States of America

Preface

This text is intended for teachers and prospective teachers enrolled in a reading education course focused on assessing and correcting classroom reading problems. The text is appropriate for undergraduate and graduate students who have had a previous developmental reading course. It is viewed as appropriate for a second course in the study of reading for those who plan to teach in the elementary grades.

The content of the text is centered on corrective and remedial readers in the elementary classroom. A *corrective reader* is viewed as a student who is experiencing deficiencies in one or more areas in the cognitive or affective dimensions of reading. The deficiencies are generally not severe; instruction that meets the specific needs of these readers may be provided by the classroom teacher. *Remedial readers* are defined as students who have pronounced problems and are reading considerably below potential. These readers often receive instruction from others outside the classroom in addition to the classroom teacher.

This text focuses on how the classroom teacher can work with the corrective and remedial reader in the classroom. It is organized into four parts. Part I provides an introduction to reading problems in the schools, discusses possible correlates of these problems, and describes what the effective teacher of reading should do. The impact on the reader of such factors as affect, cognition, language, physical attributes, and culture is discussed.

Part II addresses formal and informal assessment of the student in the classroom to determine levels of reading proficiency and to gather information about reading problems. Basic guidelines for testing are provided.

Part III of the text is devoted to the types of reading problems seen in corrective or remedial readers and the skills they need to acquire to become effective readers. Readiness, word recognition, comprehension, study skills, and content reading are discussed as they relate to the student experiencing difficulty in reading. Materials are suggested for the corrective and remedial reader. A chapter to "put it all together" summarizes the classroom teacher's role in the corrective or remedial reader's instructional program in the classroom.

Part IV discusses extended clinical diagnosis and remediation outside the classroom. These chapters are intended to give the classroom teacher an awareness of what procedures may be used outside the classroom with remedial readers. Because these procedures affect the classroom teacher who has a remedial reader in her classroom, it is important for her to be aware of them.

The text has a strong focus on the affective domain as related to reading problems. A full chapter is devoted to the affective dimensions of reading, with assessment discussed and corrective strategies suggested. Parents also form a central part of the discussions in many chapters. Part IV, for example, describes how parents may help their children in many skill areas: readiness, word recognition, comprehension, study skills, and content reading.

"Questions to Guide Reading" is a special feature presented at the beginning of each major section of a chapter. Two types of questions are provided: *recall questions,* to which answers may be found in the text, and *thinking questions,* which enable the reader to think beyond the information presented. "Information to Consider," which follows each major section, summarizes in a few sentences the main ideas that were presented in the section. Also included at the end of each chapter are "Questions for Further Thought," that raises extended issues for the reader of this textbook and "Activities and Projects," which is designed to involve the student in a reading course in actual application of the material contained in each chapter. It is not intended that each student in a reading course will do all of the activities and projects suggested in this book.

The text is designed, as the title implies, to help the classroom teacher in assessing and correcting reading problems in the classroom setting. This book is intended to provide classroom teachers with the information they need to help problem readers. Research findings are presented to support much of the information that is given, but to provide *all* research on a particular topic would be beyond the scope of this textbook.

A great many people have helped us develop this text. Listing them all is impossible, but we do want to acknowledge several individuals. We are especially grateful to Mary Jane Hays, April Phillips, and Debbie Younger, who provided assistance in the preparation of the manuscript. Our thanks go also to Sabiha Aydelott, who developed Appendix E, and to Laura Rule Hendricks, who assisted with the preparation of Appendix D.

We wish to thank Mylan Jaixen for his assistance with the development of this text; Yvonne Mattershead and Billie Ingram of Little, Brown; and Christopher Jennison of Scott, Foresman. The following reviewers of the text also provided deeply appreciated and helpful comments: Mary Boehnlein, Cleveland State University; Beverly Bozsik, Norwich University; Judith Fortune, Seattle Pacific University; Janell Klesius, University of South Florida.

Contents

I

Readers and Factors Affecting Reading Proficiency

$\mathbf{M}$any children today are not reading as well as they could. The purpose of this text is to help classroom teachers assess and correct students' reading problems so that they may read at a level consistent with their reading potential.

Chapter 1 defines *reading* and *problem readers*. Attention is given to the incidence of reading problems and to classifications of problem readers. Chapters 2–4 focus on factors that may affect reading proficiency. The factors are generally referred to as *correlates,* since much of the research data are based on correlational studies.

Affective and cognitive correlates are presented in Chapter 2. The *affective correlates* discussed are attitudes toward reading, motivation, student interests, self-concept, and personality/emotional factors. *Cognitive correlates* include attention, perception (including discrimination), and the development of concepts and schemata. Attention is also given to metacognition and to intelligence (as it relates to the acquisition of reading skills).

Chapter 3 concerns language, cultural, and physical correlates of reading problems. Information is presented on language development and language variation. Among the cultural factors discussed are the home, socioeconomic status, and gender differences. Physical correlates of reading problems include visual and auditory acuity, speech problems, neurological and laterality problems, and general health.

Much attention is currently being given to what teachers do in an instructional setting that facilitates learning. In Chapter 4, the focus is on teacher effectiveness—both in personal characteristics and in behavior.

1

Readers with Problems

Today many people are concerned about the reading achievement of students in our schools; they feel that many students are leaving formal educational programs without acceptable reading proficiency. There is no disagreement that the graduates of our schools should be functionally literate; however, this worthy goal is not always reached. According to a study by Rosner et al. (1981), there are over 50 million adults in the United States who are functionally illiterate.

A good definition of functional literacy is difficult to establish, since kinds of reading skills and levels of proficiency may differ from one real-life endeavor to another. Kirsch and Guthrie (1977–78) state that the percentage of illiteracy in America varies from 1 percent to 20 percent. Such variation reflects differences in the definition and assessment of illiteracy. Even though functional literacy may be difficult to define, and thereby make its incidence difficult to measure, statistics such as those presented above should give educators cause for concern.

Important among these concerns is the question "How many of those persons defined as functionally illiterate could have learned to read better, given an appropriate learning environment?" An equally important question is "How many persons not defined as functionally illiterate could have attained a higher level of literacy?" The purpose of this text is to provide assistance to teachers so that they may help children achieve higher levels of literacy.

Toward a Definition of Reading and Readers Who Have Problems

QUESTIONS TO GUIDE READING

Recall Questions
1. What definition of reading is presented in this text?
2. How are problem readers defined?

Varying definitions of reading and reading problems can be found in the reading education literature. It is important to examine one's views on what is involved in the reading act. This section will present our beliefs about what the reading act entails and what constitutes reading problems.

READING

Many definitions of reading, both explicit and general, may be found in the literature. Since our knowledge of precisely how the brain functions when learners are processing print is not complete at this time, any definition is an approximation at best. Any definition of reading should address the influence of both the text and the reader on learning to read. It should focus on affect and cognition and on the skills involved in decoding and getting meaning. The definition should also suggest that the specific processes may vary among individuals and according to purpose. The definition of Robeck and Wilson (1974, p. 41) includes many of these factors: "Reading is a process of translating signs and symbols into meaning and incorporating the new meanings into existing cognitive and affective systems. Each reader defines reading in his own way, depending on the level at which he is functioning and the purpose he has for reading."

Several interacting variables other than those in the educational setting cause differences in the way a student learns to act on or process print. Among these factors are the affective, cognitive, language, cultural, and physical dimensions. (See Chapters 2–3 for discussions of research and theory on these variables.)

Certain specific beliefs about the reading act have guided the selection of content in this text to help teachers work with readers who have problems. They are listed as follows:

1. Affective systems influence the desire to learn to read, to comprehend, and to continue to read for recreation and life utilization. Affective systems are therefore basic to correcting reading problems. Teachers should be aware that important interactions occur among self-concept, attitude toward specific content, motivation, interest in given content, and personality characteristics.

2. Reading is an interactive process. It involves the interaction of the reader's background of information and interests with the information presented in the text and the type of reading task involved.

3. Storage systems that facilitate reading exist in the brain. These systems include semantic meanings, syntactic relationships, and graphophonic clues; they affect the ways the brain functions in interpreting, organizing, and retrieving information. Such functions are frequently referred to as *schemata*.

4. Attention, discrimination, and perception are essential to the reading act. The reader must know what to attend to, must be able to discriminate among sounds and symbols in varying combinations, and must be able to assign accurate meaning to that which has been discriminated.

5. Reading differs from individual to individual. For example, the strategies utilized for word recognition or recall of meaning may differ; thus, the processes involved differ.

6. Reading differs in focus from one developmental level to another. In beginning reading, for example, children spend a great amount of time mastering decoding techniques, while at more mature levels, readers may spend more time comprehending for specific purposes, reading critically, and considering applications of the material.

7. Learning effective decoding strategies is essential. Adequate comprehension will not occur until basic word recognition skills become automatic. There are various techniques using sight vocabulary, phonics, structural analysis, context clues, and dictionary aids to pronunciation that are helpful in identifying words on the printed page.

8. Thinking is necessary for comprehension. A proficient reader does more than pronounce words; he can interact with the text in predicting the author's intent and in critically judging the merit of the message. Children must have control over their own thinking and learning activities; that is, they must be aware of the skills, strategies, and resources needed to perform a given reading act and must be able to plan how best to use them.

9. Purpose is fundamental to skill development (as well as to overall comprehension). Those skills which are most important for reading for a given purpose or type of content should be taught and practiced in real-life situations. For example, the skills needed for skimming and scanning should be developed in conjunction with a purpose for skimming and scanning.

10. Reading of printed material involves more than words. Skills for interpreting pictures and graphic aids such as charts, graphs, and maps should be developed.

READING PROBLEMS

In this text, a reading problem will be said to exist if the learner is not reading up to his or her reading expectancy or potential. Reading problems occur when there are unfavorable interactions between the learning environment and the affective, cognitive, language, cultural, and physical dimensions that impinge on the learner.

The term *reading disability* is frequently found in the literature to refer to those students who are not reading to potential. This term has negative connotations and will generally not be used in this text. Instead, children who are not reading to potential will usually be referred to as "problem readers" or "readers with problems."

Several classifications and labels have been given to problem readers. These classifications and reactions to them are presented in the next section. Methods of determining reading problems are discussed in Chapter 13.

INFORMATION TO CONSIDER

1. Our knowledge about the processes involved in reading is not precise.
2. Different individuals may process print in different ways and for different purposes.
3. Children may be said to have reading problems when they do not read up to expectancy or potential.

Classifications and Labels

QUESTIONS TO GUIDE READING

Recall Questions
1. What are the typical classifications of reader "types"?
2. What are some identifying statements that can be made about each of these reader types?
3. How may learning disabilities be defined?
4. What is an underachiever as defined in this text?
5. Do all mentally retarded children necessarily have "reading problems" as defined in this text?
6. What are some reasonable expectations in reading for the borderline learner, the mildly retarded, and the moderately retarded?
7. What are four limitations of the use of classification and labels?

Thinking Questions
1. Why is it difficult to distinguish among developmental, corrective, and remedial readers?
2. When does a corrective reader become a remedial reader?

3. Why is it difficult to distinguish between children who have learning disabilities and those who have reading problems?
4. Could all readers be considered "developmental"?
5. Do you think the label "dyslexia" should continue to be used? Why or why not?

Various classifications of readers are found in the literature. A typical classification is in terms of "types" of readers—developmental, corrective, and remedial. These reader types will be briefly described below. This discussion will be followed by some additional classifications and labels. Limitations of classifications will also be discussed.

TYPICAL READER CLASSIFICATIONS

Developmental readers are those readers who are making normal progress in reading. They are progressing at a pace generally consistent with their age/grade level expectations and are using materials designed for their age/grade level. Instruction is provided by the regularly assigned classroom teacher and most frequently occurs in a group setting.

Corrective readers have some reading abilities but have deficiencies in one or more areas, cognitive or affective. The deficiencies are generally not severe; therefore, instruction that meets the specific needs of these learners may be provided by the classroom teacher, either as individual work or (more typically) in a small group setting in which the child works with children who have similar problems.

Corrective readers have the mental ability necessary to correct their deficiencies. Many such youngsters profit from short-term corrective programs. Students who have mastered some but not all of the "basic" minimum skill mandates typically found in many school systems may generally be classified as corrective readers. Chapters 5–12 of this text focus on this category of readers.

Remedial readers generally have pronounced problems and are reading at a level considerably below potential. Frequently there are skill deficiencies in many areas. In addition to educational causes, the problem may be related to affective, cognitive, language, cultural, and physical factors. (See Chapters 2–3.) Like corrective readers, children in this classification have the mental capacity to do considerably better than they are currently doing. Careful individual diagnosis should be made of such readers and instruction should be highly individualized, ideally on a one-to-one basis. The instruction should be provided by a person specially prepared to deal with severe reading problems.

Remedial readers are often removed from the classroom to receive instruction. Chapters 14–15 of this text explain some of the procedures used in diagnosis and remediation in clinics and other special programs.

The point at which a "corrective" reader becomes a "remedial" reader cannot be determined definitively. Teachers often need guidelines for suggesting which children may need special help. Guidelines for making this determination are suggested in Chapter 13.

ADDITIONAL CLASSIFICATIONS AND LABELS

Readers have been labeled or classified in ways other than those described above. One classification that often includes children who have reading problems is *learning disabilities* (LD). Teachers need to have an understanding of the similarities and differences in programs for the problem reader and the learning disabled child. Other labels with which teachers should be familiar as they relate to reading are the *bright underachiever*, the *slow learner*, the *language-different* child, and *dyslexia*.

Learning disabilities. Many children in classrooms today are said to have *learning disabilities*. Since children with learning disabilities often have a reading problem, there has been some difficulty in distinguishing between children who are problem readers and those who have learning disabilities. In fact, poor reading is the most frequently reported academic problem in children who are labeled as having learning disabilities (Lerner 1985, p. 349).

According to Lerner (1985, p. 2), the most widely used definition of learning disabilities is the one incorporated into Public Law 94–142 (U.S. Office of Education, August 23, 1977):

> "Specific learning disability" means a disorder in one or more of the basic psychological processes involved in understanding or in using language spoken or written, which may manifest itself in an imperfect ability to listen, think, speak, read, write, spell or to do mathematical calculations. The term includes such conditions as perceptual handicaps, brain injury, minimal brain dysfunction, dyslexia, and developmental aphasia. The term does not include children who have learning problems which are primarily the result of visual, hearing, or motor handicaps, of mental retardation, of emotional disturbance, or of environmental, cultural, or economic disadvantage.

Another influential definition is that proposed by the National Joint Committee on Learning Disabilities in 1981 (Hammill et al. 1981):

> Learning disabilities is a generic term that refers to a heterogeneous group of disorders manifested by significant difficulties in the acquisition and use of listening, speaking, reading, writing, reasoning, or mathematical abilities. These disorders are intrinsic to the individual and presumed to be due to central nervous system dysfunction. Even though a learning disability may occur con-

comitantly with other handicapping conditions (e.g. sensory impairment, mental retardation, social and emotional disturbance) or environmental influences (e.g. cultural differences, or inappropriate instruction, psycholinguistic factors), it is not the direct result of those conditions or influences.

Lerner (1985, p. 9) notes several common elements in the various definitions of learning disabilities: (1) neurological dysfunction, (2) uneven growth patterns, (3) difficulty in academic and learning tasks, (4) discrepancy between achievement and potential, and (5) exclusion of other causes. The reader will note that such definitions of learning disability include our concept of discrepancy between potential and achievement, but exclude many factors that we feel relate to reading development: visual and auditory acuity, emotions, culture, economic background, and instructional practices. Mental retardation, in our view, is not a determining factor in either learning disability or reading disability.

Both learning disabilities and reading education are established disciplines, represented by major national professional organizations and having major professional journals. Naturally, both are interested in helping children read better. The disciplines have evolved from different professional frameworks, however, and have differing certification programs.

Historically, learning disabilities specialists have been especially concerned with learning *processes*, while reading educators have focused primarily on the *product*, or content, of what was to be learned. That is, learning disabilities specialists gave considerable attention to central nervous system dysfunctions in perceptual and conceptual processing, whose causes may be organic or biochemical. Reading specialists, on the other hand, have been more concerned with reading skill defects and functional manifestations of problems with the reading act (Kaluger and Kolson 1978, p. 3).

In the late 1970s, Chall (1978) noted a trend toward the diminishing of differences between the two disciplines. Among learning disabilities specialists, there was a shifting away from a focus on diagnosing psychological process, such as visual and auditory perceptual abilities, toward considering specific reading problems. Such shifts tend to bring the two groups closer together, both in diagnosis and in instruction as it relates to reading. Thus, teachers nowadays may find many similar practices among reading specialists and learning disabilities specialists in regard to diagnosis and remediation of problem readers.

Within the disciplines of reading education and learning disabilities, there are differences in focus—both in theory and practice. Teachers should become familiar with the philosophy and practice of both groups in their school system.

Bright underachievers. A *bright underachiever* is a reader who may be achieving at or above age/grade level, yet has the potential to achieve at considerably higher levels. Bright underachievers do not generally receive special instruction outside the classroom, since they are meeting or surpassing the reading competency levels that have been established for them. However, they deserve assistance so that they may reach their full reading potential. More must be done with bright underachievers if our efforts to achieve acceptable levels of "literacy" are to be adequately realized.

Slow learners. *Slow learners* are those learners who are not mentally capable of reading at their designated age/grade levels. Some of these readers may be reading at "expectancy" level, while others may not. Formerly, these students were often segregated in special classrooms for the mentally retarded. Since the passage of Public Law 94–142, these students are functioning, partially at least, in regular classrooms. Their instructional programs need to be adapted to fit their ability and skill levels.

There have been many attempts to define mental retardation over the years. The American Association on Mental Deficiency (AAMD) defines it as shown in Table 1.1 (Grossman 1983, p. 13).

Using this classification scheme, learners with an IQ above 70 are not considered retarded. Kirk, Kliebhan, and Lerner (1978, pp. 2–4), in describing teaching reading to slow and disabled learners, posit a threefold classification as helpful in planning reading programs:

Borderline—IQ range of 68–85
Mildly Retarded—IQ range of 52–67
Moderately Retarded—IQ range of 36–51

In the Kirk, Kliebhan, and Lerner classification, the borderline learner is a dull-normal or dull-average learner who may read at the sixth to tenth grade level by age sixteen. For the "mildly retarded" classification, reading may begin sometime between the ages of nine and twelve, and the learner may make three or four grades' progress in six or seven years (assuming reading began at age nine). For the "moderately retarded" classification, they say little may be expected beyond the rote learning of some words.

In some areas, different definitions of mental retardation may be used.

Table 1.1. Level of Retardation Indicated by IQ Range Obtained on Measure of General Intellectual Functioning

Term	IQ Range for Classification Level
Mild mental retardation	50–55 to approx. 70
Moderate mental retardation	35–40 to 50–55
Severe mental retardation	20–25 to 35–40
Profound mental retardation	Below 20 or 25

Teachers should compare the definitions presented here with those used in their school system.

Language-different children. Children classified as *language-different* lack the language base necessary to deal with instruction in typical school settings. They also lack the language necessary to deal effectively with achievement or intelligence tests. Included in "language-different" classifications are the child who speaks no English; the ESL child (English as a Second Language), who is more proficient in another language than in English; and the child who speaks a nonstandard variety of English, which differs sufficiently from standard English in concepts, vocabulary, and/or syntax to affect comprehension in typical school settings.

Dyslexia. *Dyslexia* is a term frequently used in the professional literature, among lay groups, and in the media, but with various definitions, which has led to considerable confusion. According to the *Dictionary of Reading and Related Terms* (Harris and Hodges 1981, p. 95), the term "dyslexia" has three meanings, all of which focus on reading disability. One, a medical definition, regards dyslexia as a disease caused by a central nervous system dysfunction. A second definition, used by psychologists, suggests that it is a severe reading disability of unspecified origin. The third interpretation finds it synonymous with the presence of a reading problem regardless of severity, which is how the label is used by many educators and lay persons. In this sense, dyslexia is a symptom of a reading problem rather than a disease.

Harris and Hodges (1981, p. 95) state that "dyslexia has come to have so many incompatible connotations that it has lost any real value for educators, except as a fancy word for a reading problem. Consequently, its use may create damaging cause and effect assumptions for student, family, and teacher. Thus, in referring to a specific student, it is probably better that the teacher describe the actual reading difficulties, and make suggestions for teaching related to the specific difficulties, not apply a label which may create misleading assumptions by all involved."

The Harris and Hodges position seems to be appropriate; therefore, the term *dyslexia* will not be used in this text. Teachers may want to avoid using the term also, since it means different things to different people and thus is not particularly helpful when dealing with parents.

LIMITATIONS OF CLASSIFICATIONS AND LABELS

All classification schemes and labels have limitations to their usefulness. Teachers should be aware of these limitations and the potential negative impact that they may have on the child. Among the limitations are the following:

1. Arbitrary classifications sometimes result in children being placed in programs, tracks, or special classes in which limited expectations may inhibit student growth. A student may not be expected to achieve except in ways considered typical for that classification. The student may not be given the opportunity or encouragement to grow in other, equally important ways.

2. Some labels or classifications may actually be harmful to self-concept and to attitudes, because the student may come to believe that she can do no better than the label implies. When this happens, student effort is impaired.

3. Labels at times cause educators and parents to react in ways that are not conducive to learning on the part of the readers. The term "dyslexia," for example, may be used as an excuse for not making efforts to help the learner since, to some, the medical mystique of the term leads to a feeling that remediation efforts may be futile. Other labels such as *remedial readers* may lead anxious, concerned parents to apply undue pressure on the child in an attempt to ensure quick correction.

4. Arbitrary classifications may ignore the linguistic and cultural background of the learner. As we mentioned earlier, linguistic and cultural differences may prevent a learner from responding appropriately to tests designed to suggest potential.

Since classifications and labels often result in programmatic decisions for children that may be long-term in nature, they should be applied with great care. Classification schemes are justified only if they result in a comprehensive reading program that leads to an improved educational environment for all readers.

INFORMATION TO CONSIDER

1. Classroom teachers generally can work effectively with corrective readers.
2. Remedial readers generally need help from persons specially trained to work with severe reading problems.
3. Underachievers should receive special attention, as they are capable of achieving higher levels of literacy.
4. Slow learners *may* or *may not* be in need of corrective help, since some may have reached potential while others have not.
5. "Dyslexia" is not a useful label since it has so many interpretations.
6. Classifications and labels have limitations that may affect children adversely.

Status of Reading Problems in the United States

QUESTIONS TO GUIDE READING

Recall Questions
1. Why is it difficult to determine the incidence of reading problems with a reasonable degree of accuracy?
2. According to Downing and Leong, what is the percentage of remedial reading cases in this country?
3. What is the incidence of mental retardation?
4. What is the percentage of students who cannot learn to read at all?
5. According to data from the National Assessment of Educational Progress, what national trends are occurring in reading achievement?

Thinking Questions
1. Why do you think there are more boys than girls in lower level reading groups in classrooms? In remedial reading classes?
2. Why is there likely to be a high percentage of children with reading problems in disadvantaged areas?
3. Do you think students you know today are really reading better today than your peers were at their age? Why or why not?

It is difficult to state accurately how many learners are not reading as well as they should. Reasons for this difficulty include differences in definitions of what constitutes a reading problem, in the categorizations used to identify types of problems, in the populations assessed, and in the assessment techniques used. In this section, some estimates of the extent of reading problems are presented. The question of whether children are reading more poorly today than formerly is also addressed.

INCIDENCE OF READING PROBLEMS

In discussing the incidence of nonretarded children with reading disability, Downing and Leong (1982, p. 330) estimate that 10 to 12 percent of children in English-speaking countries experience reading problems. The number in disadvantaged areas may be considerably higher, reaching 50–100 percent according to Gilliland (1974, p. 3).

More boys than girls in the United States are reported to have reading problems. Asher (1977) reported that 70–75 percent of cases are boys. A lower boy-girl ratio (3:2) for *identified* reading problems was reported by

Naiden (1976) from a study in Seattle; however, the *referral* ratio remained at 3:1. Naiden suggests that teachers may refer more boys than girls because boys tend to be more disruptive in the classroom. Some teachers may also have expectations that boys need to achieve at high levels in our society and, thus, refer male problem readers more frequently for help.

The number of underachievers in our schools may also be higher than seems obvious. Many children in a given grade or school who score at or above grade level in reading may in fact have the potential to do significantly better.

THE SLOW LEARNER

Kirk, Kliebhan, and Lerner (1978, p. 5) state that the following percentages of our population may be labeled *slow learners* (recall that some of these learners may be reading up to potential while others may not):

Borderline	14%
Mildly Retarded	2%
Moderately Retarded	0.1%
Total Slow Learners	16%

Such figures vary, of course, from community to community and are partly dependent on socioeconomic levels. Kirk, Kliebhan, and Lerner (1978) also state that IQ tests tend to identify more borderline and mildly retarded children (IQ 52–85) in low socioeconomic status (SES) groups than in higher SES groups. However, this is not the case in the moderately retarded category (IQ 36–51).

Robeck and Wilson (1974, p. 86) maintain that only 0.5 percent of children are mentally retarded to the degree that they cannot learn to read. They also note that slow learners often do not reach their potential because of emotional barriers that come from repeated failure, unrealistic demands, and other negatively motivating experiences. Educators need to be aware that slow learners can attain some degree of reading ability and should consider the possibility that these learners may not be reaching their potential.

IS THE INCIDENCE OF READING PROBLEMS INCREASING?

It has been assumed by many lay persons, legislators, and some teachers that students are not reading as well today as they did formerly. Recent data challenge this assumption and suggest that the answer to the question is not a clearly delineated one.

Tuinman, Rowls, and Farr (1976) summarized data on this question in a study entitled *Reading Achievement in the United States: THEN and NOW*. The data were obtained from three major sources: statewide testing programs, research in large city systems, and commercial test publishing agencies. Although there are many limitations in comparing these data, such as a possible lack of representative populations, Tuinman, Rowls, and Farr make the following summarizing statement (pp. 462–63):

> We believe that, from the information we were able to gather, we would conclude first that there is no reason for *en masse* pessimism; second, that the gradual improvement in reading competency over the four decades prior to 1965 may have lessened or halted; and finally over the last ten years there may have been a very slight decline in reading achievement. Of all our hesitant interpretations, we feel least certain about the last one. We are convinced that anyone who says that he knows that literacy is decreasing is ignoring the data. Such a person is at best unscholarly and at worst dishonest.

Another source of information is the National Assessment of Educational Progress (NAEP) data. Nationwide assessments of reading achievement were conducted in 1970–71, 1974–75, 1979–80, and 1983–84. Nine-, thirteen-, and seventeen-year-old students were tested in the areas of literal comprehension, inferential comprehension, and reference skills.

Data from these NAEP assessments were summarized in *The Reading Report Card* (1985, pp. 9–10):

> *Nine-Year-Olds*. In the past 13 years, the reading proficiency of 9-year-old students has improved significantly. Although their reading proficiency increased steadily and dramatically over the 1970s, the most recent assessment shows no improvement since 1980.
>
> *Thirteen-Year-Olds*. Thirteen-year-olds too are reading significantly better than they were in 1971, but this improvement has not been as dramatic across assessments. Similar to the 9-year-olds, reading performance of 13-year-olds improved during the last half of the 1970s and leveled off after 1980.
>
> *Seventeen-Year-Olds*. Trends in achievement for 17-year-olds differ markedly from those for the other two age groups. Throughout the 1970s, the reading proficiency level of the 17-year-olds was remarkably constant, but this was followed by a significant improvement between 1980 and 1984.

These data suggest that reading scores have not declined as suggested by the media, some lay persons, and some professionals. However, there are still children with reading problems who are not reading to potential. As long as this situation exists, there will be a need for strong efforts to improve levels of reading ability.

Summary

There is concern today that students are not reading as well as they should. Although explicit definitions of functional literacy and reading expectancy are difficult to state, there seems little doubt that a segment of our school and adult populations is not reading as well as it could.

A definition of "reading" is difficult to formulate, since we have less than explicit information on what goes on in the brain when one reads. It seems that any adequate definition would be concerned with meaning—both the meaning that readers take to the printed page and the meaning they get from the printed page. As such, reading becomes an interactive, affective, and cognitive process among learner, text, and task that differs from individual to individual and from developmental level to developmental level.

There are interacting sets of factors—affective, cognitive, language, cultural, and physical—that impinge on learners as they learn to read. When these factors interact in unfavorable ways, students may develop a reading problem. The term "reading problems" in this text has been used to indicate children who are not reading up to expectancy or potential.

It is difficult to state accurately how many learners are not reading up to potential because definition parameters and assessment measures differ. A reasonable estimate would be that about 10–12 percent of the school population fall into this category, with boys comprising a large proportion of students so labeled. It is also reasonable to state that elementary school students are reading better today than they did fifteen years ago.

Questions for Further Thought

1. Should there be separate disciplines for reading education and learning disabilities? Why or why not?
2. Should all readers be classified as "developmental" readers if they are reading as well as they can? Why or why not?
3. What factors account for lack of reading up to potential among reading disability cases in your area?

Activities and Projects

1. Ask the principal of a nearby school how students with reading problems are identified in that school.
2. Study the National Assessment for Educational Progress (NAEP) data for ages thirteen and seventeen. What are the similarities and differences? How are these data similar to or different from the data for nine-year-olds?
3. Seek information about the incidence of reading problems in a school system with which you are familiar. What is the male-female ratio? What seems to account for the incidence data in this system?
4. Talk to a parent, a media person, a politician, and an educator about how they feel the status of reading proficiency is today compared to several years ago. How are their positions similar or different? How do you account for these similarities or differences?

2

Affective and Cognitive Correlates of Reading Problems

There are many possible reasons why children do not read as well as they could. In this text, factors related to reading problems are organized into six areas—affective, cognitive, language, cultural, physical, and effective instruction. These areas will be referred to as correlates in the following chapters since the information presented is based primarily on correlational studies.

Affective and cognitive correlates are discussed in Chapter 2; language, cultural, and physical correlates, in Chapter 3. Effective reading instruction is treated in Chapter 4. The selection of information for inclusion in Chapters 2–4 was based on personal experiences, research findings, theoretical positions, and the opinions of professionals working in the field.

In Chapters 2 and 3, information is provided about data obtained from remedial readers as well as from corrective readers. This seems reasonable since teachers will likely have some remedial readers in their classrooms, even though they may not be primarily responsible for instructing these children in reading. It is important that teachers understand why these readers may have developed problems and how such problems may interact with instruction. A problem in reading will, in all probability, affect the student in other curricular areas.

Some cautions about the relationship of the correlates to reading problems are in order. First, the presence in the learner of one or more of the *correlates* does not necessarily mean *causation*. In a correlational study, assessment procedures identify the presence or absence of the factor being assessed. The mere presence of a factor, such as a visual acuity problem or a language difference, for example, does not prove causation for given children.

Teachers should note that in some children the presence of a "factor" may be the effect of a prior reading problem rather than its cause. Some factors may arise concurrently with reading problems. Some may not affect reading to levels consistent with potential at all. In assessing the likely causes of given problems, however, teachers should not overlook the presence of any of the correlates, nor their possible interaction with the learner's reading problem. It seems reasonable to consider each of the correlates as potentially related until they are found not to be applicable. Otherwise, a crucial area may be overlooked.

A second caution relates to the research findings on the various correlates. Teachers often look for specific reasons that children do not read as well as they should, and are frustrated to hear some writers state that research in a given area is not definitive. There are legitimate reasons for such statements. This lack of definitiveness may be attributed to such factors as differences in definitions of problem readers and of the factors being studied, the types of research designs utilized in the investigations, differences in the ages of populations tested, lack of representativeness of samples used, the small number of children assessed in the study, differing achievement and ability levels of students tested, lack of precision in the test instruments and techniques employed, and experimenter bias in selecting factors to be investigated.

In Chapters 2 and 3, research findings are included in some areas that have been labeled "nondefinitive." This seems appropriate since there may possibly be a relationship between a reading problem and a specific factor for a given child; therefore, teachers should consider the factor as possibly, but not necessarily, contributing to the child's problem. Also, some of the correlates may have been overemphasized and said to be a major contributing factor when this is not necessarily true. Statements of "lack of definity" may help to correct this overemphasis.

A third caution involves the possible use of compensation strategies by the learner. Some children are better able to minimize the impact of a problem than others. For example, a visual acuity problem or a hearing loss may bother some children more than others because they have not learned effective coping strategies for dealing with the problem.

A fourth caution is that teachers should be aware of the probability of multiple causation of given reading problems. The possibility of multiple causation has been recorded in the literature for many years (Robinson 1946). Therefore, teachers should not expect to find a single cause that can be easily or quickly eliminated. Teachers should also be aware that it is frequently difficult to separate multiple causative forces. For example, a student's self-concept, emotional state, and level of achievement may all be interwoven. Improvement in one area may lead to improvement in another, even though no specific help has been given in the other area.

> ## QUESTIONS TO GUIDE READING
>
> ### Recall Questions
> 1. What are the components of Mathewson's affective model of the reading process?
> 2. What does research say about the relationship between attitudes and reading?
> 3. What are the four components of motivation, according to De Cecco and Crawford?
> 4. What does research say about students' interests?
> 5. On what two aspects of self-concept do most psychologists agree?
> 6. What does research say about the relationship between emotional or personality maladjustment and reading problems?
>
> ### Thinking Questions
> 1. Why should affective correlates be considered basic?
> 2. How do attitudes and interests differ?
> 3. How is self-concept related to attitudes?
> 4. How can a teacher determine an appropriate motivational level for a reading activity?
> 5. Why is there a potential relationship between emotional problems and reading achievement?

Affect provides the will or desire to learn to read and to continue using reading for pleasure and for gaining information. Affect is considered, in this text, to be a *basic* both in learning to read and in the prevention of reading problems. Affect is also considered basic to the improvement of reading ability once a child has developed reading problems.

In order to focus attention on its importance, affect will be the first correlate discussed in this text. This correlate fails to receive the attention it deserves in many instructional programs, due to current societal expectations that mandate that teachers spend most instructional time in assessing and developing cognitive skills.

There is a strong theoretical base for considering affect important. Mathewson (1985, p. 844) has proposed a theoretical, affective model of reading that focuses on four processes—attitudes, motivation, affect (pleasantness, unpleasantness, mood, sentiment, and emotion), and physical feelings (which convey pain or pleasure). The central construct of the model is attitude. Mathewson suggests that motivation and attitude may work together to create the conditions in which a learner attends to and performs the cognitive processes necessary to comprehend the material. Without appropriate affective conditions, efficient cognitive responses to print may not occur.

Several areas of the affective domain have been investigated relative to reading success, although research in this area has not received as high a priority as have the cognitive, language, cultural, or physical correlates. In this section information is presented on affective areas that have been shown to relate to reading: attitudes toward reading, motivation, student interests, self-concept, and personality or emotional factors.

ATTITUDES

Attitudes have been defined in various ways. One definition states that attitudes are feelings related to reading that cause the learner to approach or avoid a reading situation (Alexander and Filler 1976). According to another definition (Fishbein and Ajzen 1975), attitudes have three components—beliefs, feelings, and behaviors. This multidimensional view suggests that attitudes are more complex than simply a set of feelings.

Research on attitudes is difficult to synthesize because various investigators have defined them differently, measurement tools have varied, and measurement devices often lack precision. Moreover, attitudes are often situation-specific for given individuals, making variation in responses dependent somewhat on circumstances. Still another problem is that children sometimes respond to attitude assessment devices in ways they think teachers or others expect them to.

Davis (1978) made a comprehensive review of journal-published research on attitudes between 1900 and 1977. Only those studies which met criteria for good educational research were included. The conclusions from this review are shown in Figure 2.1.

Teachers should be aware of several myths regarding attitudes toward reading (Alexander and Filler 1976, p. 16). Combined, these myths suggest that white, bright girls from higher socioeconomic levels have more positive attitudes toward reading than do other students. While these beliefs may apply in given situations, such is not always the case. Teachers should avoid predetermined expectations about their students' attitudes. Such predetermination may result in the attitudes that are "expected."

Instructional practices *can* but not necessarily *will* make a difference in attitudes. Teachers must continually evaluate the impact of their methods, materials, strategies, and organizational procedures, and be ready to make changes when attitudes become negative.

The importance of the home in attitude formation should not be overlooked. Sartain (1981), reviewing research on the contribution of the family to reading attainment, generalized from the data that good readers come from home environments that foster positive attitudes toward reading and learning. Teachers of children who have reading problems may find that parent involvement programs emphasizing affect, in addition to cognitive skills, are important in effecting reading gains.

Figure 2.1. Davis's Conclusions from Research on Attitudes and Reading

1. Good comprehension is related to positive attitudes toward reading, while poor comprehension is related to poor attitudes.
2. Attitudes affect achievement. Attitudes become more positive with improved achievement.
3. Attitudes are more related to achievement than to ability; intelligence is not an accurate predictor of attitudes.
4. Attitudes toward reading are related to negative self-concepts.
5. Attitudes toward reading become less positive with an increase in the age of the students.
6. Class size is not related to attitudes toward reading.
7. Classroom organization may influence attitudes toward reading.
8. Content of textbooks and the instructional program may affect attitudes toward reading. This seems to be more true for boys than for girls. It is also possible that textbook content and instructional program type can be used to change attitudes toward reading.
9. Some studies reported that girls had more favorable attitudes toward reading than boys; others reported that boys had more favorable attitudes; still others reported no differences between boys and girls.
10. Socioeconomic status, race, and attitudes toward teachers are not related to students' reading attitudes.
11. What parents do in the home seems to affect attitudes toward reading more than father's occupation, socioeconomic status, educational level of the parents, or the number of books in the home.

MOTIVATION

Motivation is a key factor in helping children with reading problems reach their expectancy level. Progress is slow for those learners who are not concerned with improvement in reading or who do not enjoy reading.

In his affective model of the reading process, Mathewson (1985, pp. 842–43) states that motivation is "no less important" than attitude as an important construct in an affective model of the reading process. He feels that appropriate motivational processes need to be identified for learners, and lists the following as possible processes: belongingness and love, curiosity, competence, achievement, esteem, self-actualization, desire to know and understand, and aesthetic motivation. Such motives ensure that "a separate, energizing process" accompanies favorable attitudes toward reading. Motivation thus affects the decision to read.

De Cecco and Crawford (1974) identify four components of motivation: arousal, expectancy, incentive, and discipline.

1. *Arousal* refers to the initiation of an activity. The range of arousal is from very low (boredom) to high (emotional excitement), with the most conducive motivational level probably somewhere between these two ex-

tremes (Hebb 1955; Nuttin 1976). It may be difficult for learners or teachers to maintain very high levels of excitement over an extended period, even though there may be a motivational level sufficient to initiate an activity. The level may not be sufficient to continue the activity over time. It is important to attempt to keep the motivational level high enough so that the learner has more successes than failures.

2. *Expectancy* refers to the establishment of goals, objectives, and purposes that enable the learner to function with understanding. The processes involved in the reading act change with the purposes (Downing and Leong 1982, p. 254). Children need instruction in reading for different purposes. Practice is essential if children are to achieve flexibility in changing from one type of purpose to another.

3. *Incentive*—the rewarding of achievement in ways that encourage further learning and higher levels of achievement—may be *intrinsic* (satisfaction from within) or *extrinsic* (rewards provided by someone else). When incentives are used, they must be powerful enough to counterbalance any negativism associated with the stimulus situation (in our case, the reading environment). Behaviorists have placed more reliance on extrinsic motivators (material reinforcements such as gold stars or M&Ms) than have cognitive psychologists. Some authorities have warned that extrinsic motivators may undermine childrens' intrinsic interest in an activity (Lepper, Greene, and Nisbett 1973).

What is motivational for one individual or group may not be for another. Teachers must be constantly aware that different learners need different incentives to arouse and sustain proper levels of motivation. Incentives should only be used as long as the reader finds them rewarding. Change is often essential to maintain motivation.

4. *Discipline*—the management of behavior as the learner completes tasks in the instructional setting—must be appropriate for the student as an individual and within the classroom setting.

Attribution theory is a theory of motivation currently receiving attention. The theory is based upon the causes or reasons—"attributions"—that account for a learner's success or failure (Weiner 1979). The central assumption of attribution theory is that searching for understanding is a basic motivator.

An "attributional" question that readers may ask themselves when in a reading situation is "Why did I fail (or succeed) with this reading task?" Asking "why" questions about failure is more likely to lead to the identification of attributions than will questions about success.

Attributes can be categorized along several dimensions; two that are particularly relevant in reading situations are *locus of control* and *stability* (Winograd, Witte, and Smith 1986). *Locus of control* refers to whether the control is internal or external to the reader. *Stability* refers to whether the cause stays constant or varies over time. Weiner and his associates (1971) categorized four attributional causes along these dimensions: ability (internal and stable), effort (internal and unstable), task difficulty (external and stable), and luck (external and unstable). Winograd, Witte, and Smith (1986) cite research that emphasized the importance of viewing causal attributions from the student's perspective rather than from fixed assumptions. Ability, for example, may change with practice or with the learning of skills (as may effort, task difficulty, or luck).

It is important for teachers to try to understand the causes to which students themselves attribute their failure or success. This knowledge may be helpful in planning strategies to improve a student's perception of his reading ability or of the difficulty of the reading task. Success in developing reading skills and accomplishing reading tasks can affect the future effort a student devotes to such tasks. Teachers should also remember that students who have experienced failure over a period of time may have developed avoidance mechanisms that inhibit motivation. Change may come slowly, even with extensive and intensive efforts (Frymier 1968).

Parents are important motivators. Much of the motivation needed to learn to read comes from the home. Cooperative efforts between home and school are often necessary to ensure that readers with problems make progress.

Student interests, discussed in the following section, are also important in maintaining an adequate level of motivation. By tapping important intrinsic motivational processes, interests can be critical in helping children with reading problems reach potential.

INTERESTS

Interests affect reading in at least two ways—through the materials used and through the procedures used. Specific types of materials can often be key motivational factors in getting a student with reading problems to want to read. Estes and Vaughn (1973) found that interest was a potent factor in determining how well a child comprehends a passage. Belloni and Jongsma (1978) found that interests affected the reading comprehension of low-achieving adolescents and that "students transcended their frustrational levels when reading materials which were highly interesting to them" (p. 108). In yet another study, comprehension was improved when interests were considered (Asher and Markell 1974).

Children's interests do vary, with age (Taylor and Waynant 1978; Oliver 1977), gender (Norvell 1958; Meisel and Glass 1970; Heathington 1981), and ability. Gender is one of the most important determinants of student interests. Boys seem to have a narrower range of interests than girls (Stanchfield and Fraim 1979). Teachers may find it difficult to motivate boys unless the content is exciting and appeals to their specific interests.

In a comprehensive review of research on interests, Robinson and Weintraub (1973) drew several conclusions:

1. Reading interests change with the times. A popular topic for children in the elementary grades in the 1970s may not interest children of the same age in the 1980s.
2. Gender differences in reading interests are found even in early grades, and become more pronounced as children grow older.
3. Individuals show wide differences in reading interests.
4. Age, reading achievement, intelligence, and socioeconomic status affect the reading interests of children.

Although there is variation in children's interests, it is valuable for teachers to know general patterns of interest for assessment and program planning. Patterns of variation have been compiled by researchers such as Greenlaw (1983), who identified choices for primary and upper level students:

Primary Level

Rank	Category
1	Funny
2	Make-believe; about people; animals
3	Real things; rhyme; mystery

Upper Level

Rank	Category
1	Adventure; jokes/humor; information
2	Fantasy; mystery; sports; supernatural
3	How-to-do-it; biography; historical fiction; poetry

SELF-CONCEPT

Yawkey (1980, p. 4) defines self-concept as a

Conglomeration of unitary processes as well as a set of separate components— all of which reflect what a child knows about himself and how he feels about himself at given times and in various situations.

Quandt and Selznick (1984) describe two aspects of self-concept about which most psychologists agree:

1. The perceptions of self that individuals have include their views of themselves as compared to others (self-perception); their views of how others see them (self-other perception); and their views of how they wish they could be (self-ideal).
2. The perceptions of self that individuals have are largely based on the experiences they have had with those people who are important to them (significant others). Thus, such people can effect change in individuals' self-concept.

Children have a self-concept about reading, that is, they have perceptions about themselves in reading situations (Quandt and Selznick 1984, p. 2). These perceptions may be positive or negative. There is a strong relationship between self-concept and reading achievement; good readers tend to have more positive self-concepts than poor readers.

Determinants of self-concept may be situational, phenomenal, or internal (Shavelson, Hubner, and Stanton 1976). Reading *situations*, such as classroom groups, special reading groups or programs, content area classes, or reading aloud, determine in part whether students will perceive themselves as competent or incompetent in reading. The individual's perception of an experience or his point of view of an occurrence forms the *phenomenal* aspect. A student may actually read a passage aloud adequately; but if he perceives his performance as poor, his self-concept may be negative. *Internal* determinants of self-concept are those controlled by the student himself; they relate to the person's ideal of what his reading performance should be.

Children begin to lower their self-concepts as the result of learning problems at about the third-grade level. Preadolescents appear to be most susceptible to the effects of failure (Bingham 1980). How children feel about themselves can be critical to initial success in reading. In a study of how kindergarten children's self-concepts are related to beginning reading achievement, Wattenberg and Clifford (1966) found that children's feelings about themselves were more closely related to reading success than was intelligence.

Wigfield and Asher (1984) noted little difference in self-concept among socioeconomic (SES) levels, but found that the self-concept levels of low SES children declined more rapidly than in other SES groups. Spache (1976, p. 248) warns, however, that self-concepts of children from economically deprived homes may be relatively low. Teachers should be especially cognizant of this possibility. They should also remember that learners' reactions to failure are often more a function of the views that "significant others" have of them than of the failure experience itself (Maehr 1969). Teachers must make continual efforts to see that children feel they are being evaluated positively even though they may have a reading problem.

Relative to intelligence, Anastasiow (1964, 1967) found that bright children who were reading below expectations had lower self-concept scores than those who were reading as expected, and that girls with reading problems seem to be more affected by self-perceptions in reading than were boys with similar problems.

Children come to school feeling they will be able to learn to read. If this does not happen fairly quickly, feelings of inadequacy may develop. Lack of success leads to less success—and the self-fulfilling prophecy may become operable. Children with reading problems need successful experiences. These experiences should be as meaningfully related as possible to success in aspects of the curriculum other than reading.

When learners feel that they are regarded as incompetent by others who are important to them, they attempt to counteract in some way. For most children this involves disguising incompetency or withdrawing effort from those areas in which they think they are seen as incompetent. According to Quandt and Selznick (1984, p. 4), such withdrawal of effort may occur when the learners' efforts at reading are considered inadequate and may result in such behaviors as the "showing of apparent disinterest in reading, showing apparent lack of effort to learn to read, refusing to read assigned material and/or showing apparent carelessness or professed hatred of reading."

EMOTIONAL OR PERSONALITY MALADJUSTMENT

Many reading authorities feel that there is an important relationship between emotional problems or personality maladjustment and reading disability. The incidence of such problems in reading disability cases has been judged to be high.

The problem of cause or effect here is elusive, especially since assessment is generally made after both problems—reading and emotional—are present. It is difficult to say just what role emotional or personality problems had in such cases. The effects of such reading and emotional problems may be interactive (Downing and Leong 1982, p. 249); that is, one type of problem may intensify the other, to the detriment of the learner. Bond et al. (1984, p. 83), however, believe that the evidence makes it "fairly clear that emotional maladjustment is much more frequently the effect than the cause of reading disability."

Alexander (1971) identified several trends in research that focus on the relationship of personality maladjustment and reading problems:

1. No single personality pattern is characteristic of reading failure. Several types of emotional problems are potentially contributory, including conscious refusal to learn, overt hostility, negative conditioning to reading, displacement of hostility, resistance to pressure, clinging to dependency, quick discouragement, a feeling that success is dangerous, extreme distractibility or restlessness, absorption in a private world, and depression (Harris and Sipay 1985, pp. 313–25).

2. Although emotional problems are found frequently in learners with reading problems, reading problems are not always accompanied by a personality problem. Some learners are able to cope with their reading problems without developing emotional problems; these learners are generally easier to teach.

3. Good readers show some of the same symptoms of maladjustment as do poor readers; the difference seems to be one of degree rather than kind. Consistent group differences between good and poor readers are generally not found in the research literature.

4. There may be a decline in the impact of personality factors on reading problems as the learner gets older, although more empirical evidence is needed to support this statement. It seems reasonable to suggest that success with reading is a much more important developmental task for a beginning reader than for an older student, for whom peer relations or other factors may be more crucial.

Anxiety affects reading improvement. Downing and Leong (1982, p. 241) propose that anxiety "interferes with attentiveness because failure in reading constitutes a form of stress that causes the poor reader to perceive reading tasks as threats." Wigfield and Asher (1984), in addressing the role of anxiety, noted that research suggests that anxiety can affect learning in that anxious children may divide their attention between doing a task and a preoccupation with how well they are doing, rather than just focusing on the task at hand. Teachers must strive to reduce anxiety levels in problem readers for maximal growth.

Considering emotional and personality variables is also important in diagnostic and instructional procedures. Sampson (1966) suggests that instruction for problem readers will "fall flat" unless the teacher is fully aware of the potential interaction of emotions in the diagnostic and instructional setting. Emotional problems may interfere with the child's doing well in both assessment and instructional settings.

INFORMATION TO CONSIDER

1. Affect is basic to reading success.
2. Attitudes are highly individual and may be situation-specific.
3. What is motivational for one learner may not be for another.
4. Student interest is a potent factor in reading comprehension.
5. A child's reading self-concept is strongly related to his reading achievement.
6. Emotional problems are also strongly related to reading problems, but are probably an effect rather than a cause of the reading difficulties.

Cognitive Correlates

QUESTIONS TO GUIDE READING

Recall Questions
1. What cognitive correlates are said to be potentially related to reading problems?

2. What are definitions of cognition, attention, perception, intelligence, and modality?
3. What are the relationships (if any) between each cognitive correlate and reading problems?

Thinking Questions
1. Of the points mentioned in *Information to Consider*, which do you think most important for classroom teachers? Why? For special teachers of reading or clinicians? Why?
2. Which of the cognitive correlates do you consider most important for classroom teachers to include in the assessment process? Why? For special teachers of reading or clinicians? Why?

Cognition has been defined as *knowing*. Specifically, it is the process or result of recognizing, conceiving, judging, and reasoning. There is disagreement, however, about the specific components of cognition. Some psychologists consider perception to be a part of cognition; others do not (Harris and Hodges 1981, p. 54). Neisser (1976, p. 4), for example, states that "such terms as *sensation, perception, imagery, retention, recall, problem-solving,* and *thinking,* among others, refer to hypothetical stages or aspects of cognition." This explanation emphasizes the active, integrated nature of the cognitive processes that affect learning to read. Cognitive processes are central in all aspects of reading, from skill acquisition to the use of reading for pleasure or to gain knowledge.

Cognition is receiving much attention currently and is considered by some authorities to have considerable power in explaining why children do not read as well as they should. Aulls (1982) notes that there are authorities (Valtin 1978–79) who argue that theories of perception (as a specific, identifiable cognitive function) and physical etiological factors (vision, hearing, etc.) are currently in disfavor in explaining why children have reading problems. Other authorities also hold that differences in language functions seem particularly powerful in explaining why reading problems develop (Doehring et al. 1979; Ryan 1981; Vellutino 1977).

For purposes of discussion, information will be presented in this section on selected hypothetical stages of cognition, or *knowing:* attention, perception, and the development of concepts and schemata. Metacognition and the relationship between intelligence (as measured by intelligence or school ability tests) and the acquisition of reading skill will also be addressed.

Thinking is an important aspect of cognition. Thinking involves "the process(es), or product(s), of cognition" (Harris and Hodges 1981, p. 329), and as such relates to all aspects of cognition discussed in this section. Students need thinking or problem-solving skills as they attempt to decode and comprehend text. Athey (1983, p. 31) has linked thinking and reading by stating that to "promote thinking is to promote reading." Others point out that literacy instruction cannot logically be separated from higher thought processes (Yellin 1979) and that thinking is a prerequisite to and concomitant of reading at any level (Waller 1977). In Chapter 7, the theories of Piaget and of Feuerstein will be discussed.

ATTENTION

Attention is defined in *A Dictionary of Reading and Related Terms* (Harris and Hodges 1981, p. 24) as "the process, or result, of a selective, concentrated focus upon certain stimuli in perceiving, as *attention to text signals.*" Among the important attributes that are relevant for teachers are coming to attention, attending to the task, and maintaining attention over a period of time (Keogh and Margolis 1976). These attributes are partially independent, yet interactive.

Attention is the basis for both learning and memory (Robeck and Wilson 1974, p. 60). What is perceived depends on how the observer allocates attention. The cognitive anticipations that the learner develops through experience and the perceptual explorations that the learner carries out are involved in this process. Inadequate or inappropriate attention may be more important in contributing to the development of reading problems than some of the other correlates that have been widely researched. For example, Estes (1970) stated that the inability to focus attention was more useful in explaining rates of learning than were differences in intelligence.

There are limits to the amount of information a learner may attend to at a given time (LaBerge and Samuels 1985, p. 690). Children must, therefore, develop selective attention abilities to be efficient during the reading act. The learner must know what to attend to (selective attention) and must be able to sustain attention long enough for learning to take place. Just as learners must know what is important when attending to stimuli, they must also know what is irrelevant for their purposes (Gibson and Levin 1975, p. 26); otherwise, time is lost and comprehension may suffer.

Children must master certain aspects of the reading act in order to allocate their attention efficiently. For example, children cannot attend primarily to word recognition and at the same time achieve adequate comprehension. It is important to bring word recognition abilities to a fluent level so that attention may be given to the comprehension process. Otherwise, the child will be spending her learning time decoding at the expense of adequate comprehension.

The impact of attentional deficits, however, is viewed variously by authorities. According to Moore et al. (1982), readers with problems do not attend "selectively" as well as do good readers. Others feel that, in general, problem readers do not tend to show strong deficits in selective attention. Bauer (1982), for example, states that there is little support for an attentional deficit hypothesis as a major cause of reading problems.

There appear to be differences in what is critical information for given learners in accomplishing a reading task. What is critical for one learner may not be as important for another; for example, different students may utilize different cues to recognize words. Teachers and clinicians must know what information may help a child master a word recognition task. When students are helped to learn those features of words, for example, that may be useful in the decoding process, they can utilize this information at an earlier age than if left to discover such information for themselves (Lehman 1972).

The lack of ability to concentrate, or maintain sustained attention over a period of time, may be related to some reading problems. A short attention span occurs when attention is diverted by minor stimuli. The condition may be caused by physical, emotional, and educational factors such as distractibility, thyroid problems, nonstimulating learning environments, poor vision or hearing, the inability to understand what is taking place in school, and basic needs such as hunger.

The diagnostic process itself may be affected by lack of appropriate attention. Teachers should consider the possibility that poor performance on a test may be due to inattention rather than lack of ability to perform the task. Children should be observed carefully as they take tests; when possible, tests should be administered individually to children who have severe reading problems. By observing such children, the teacher may be able to determine whether the child was attending to the task.

PERCEPTION

Perception has been defined as "the extraction of information from sensory stimulation" (Harris and Hodges 1981, p. 232). They note that perception is "an active and selective process and so may be influenced by a person's attitude and by prior experience."

Since perception is active and selective, it involves learning. Perceptual learning is defined by Gibson and Levin (1975, p. 13) as learning to extract relevant information from the available stimuli. They state that the difference between skilled perceivers and the unskilled is that skilled perceivers obtain more information from the stimulus.

Perceptual learning is dependent on factors such as the child's attitudes and interests, innate abilities, physical abilities, and experiential background. The role of experience is especially important. What the learner knows in advance about the stimuli he is about to receive affects the perceptual process. Some learners from linguistically and culturally deprived environments may lack perceptual readiness for reading instruction and may not be able to make the necessary discriminations.

Research findings differ on the importance of perception to reading problems. As noted earlier, some authorities view deficits in perception as less important than language and cognition factors in explaining reading problems. Downing and Leong (1982, p. 309) state, based on an analysis of the literature, that perceptual factors cannot be the main cause of reading problems. Vernon (1969, p. 11) believes that when deficiencies are present they may be caused by maturational lag, state of language development, and/or personality characteristics.

Perceptual skills do seem to be important in learning to read, however, perhaps more so than some other highly researched factors such as intelligence. Gibson and Levin (1975, pp. 14–23) note three classes of perceptual learning that are particularly relevant for teachers of reading. The first consists of static elements; for example, the features that form sounds, letters, and words are sequenced in particular, unchanging ways in the English language. Another class relates to events that are invariant over time, such as the left-to-right direction of English print. The third pertains to higher-order variables (rules or generalizations) between features and events. Regular spelling patterns, phonic generalizations, and syntactic patterns are examples of this type of learning. Perceptual learning builds structures, called schemata, that direct further perceptual activity. (Schemata will be discussed more fully in later sections.)

The term *perceptual modality* refers to any of the sensory systems that are used to receive, process, or respond to sensation (Harris and Hodges 1981, p. 200). Of the perceptual modalities that have been investigated in relationship to reading problems, the visual and the auditory are more closely related than any other aspects of perception. Kinesthetic and tactile modalities are related to some degree; smell and taste perception are related only to a minor degree. Most authorities do not recommend matching a teaching method to a child's *preferred*, or strongest, perceptual modality as measured by a test of modal strength; the tests are inadequate assessment tools.

Visual perception. Visual perception may be defined as "the extraction of information about things, places, and events in the visible world; the process of seeing such characteristics of things as shape, color, size, distance, etc., and identifying them meaningfully" (Harris and Hodges 1981, p. 348). In learning to read, sighted persons need accurate perception of letters, words, phrases, and other perceptual units of meaning. The recent meta-analysis of visual perceptual studies done by Kavale (1982) concludes that visual perception is an important correlate of achievement in reading.

Visual perceptual skills are learned early from the learner's environment. Young children perceive their environment as a three-dimensional world in which objects keep their identity in space whether observed from top, front, bottom, sides, or otherwise. However, when learners confront the printed page, they find that sequence and position are invariant elements in English-language printing; that is, print is two-dimensional. This may cause problems at first with reversals of words (such as *saw* and *was*) or letters (such as *b* and *d*). These difficulties are normal in the early reading stages and do not generally signal perceptual handicaps. They are, rather, as yet unlearned adjustments to the two-dimensional world of print.

Visual discrimination, an important component of perception, refers to the process of perceiving likenesses and differences in visual stimuli. Children need to note those distinctive features that will help them discriminate one visual unit (letter, word, or phrase) from another as they master the decoding process. The letters *b* and *d*, mentioned above, are easily confused because they have very similar features. The distinctive feature in the discrimination of these letters is the location of the straight line in relationship to the curved line.

By age 6, children typically are adept at visual perception of simple forms and can perceive the distinctive characteristics of individual letters. Matching shapes as a visual perceptual readiness experience is therefore a waste of time for most five- and six-year-olds. Learners with perceptual problems at this age often have trouble with directionality and with knowing which features are significant in helping them make discriminations.

Gibson and Levin (1975, pp. 16, 195–97) have summarized information from empirical studies of visual perception which have instructional implications for sequencing and for selection of methodology. These are:

1. Lowercase letters can be read more quickly than uppercase letters. Children with visual discrimination problems should begin with lowercase letters.
2. Initial letters are perceived best visually, final letters next best, and medial letters least well. Support for the teaching of consonants before vowels may be found in these data.
3. Global form or contour is not effective in facilitating word perception. That is, teaching the overall shape of a word (look associated with

    ⌐‾‾‾⌐), is a poor word-recognition strategy.

4. Distinctive features, such as lines and curves in their various positions, are important in word perception. These need to be called to the attention of learners as they are taught to make discriminations.

Special attention needs to be given to many disadvantaged children, who may not have learned the visual perceptual skills necessary for success in reading. Disadvantaged learners tend to perform less well on tests of visual perception than more affluent children (Spache 1976, p. 12). It seems likely that these students have not learned from their environments what is needed for success with the tasks included on the tests, rather than that they are perceptually handicapped. Such deficiencies may, however, keep them from learning to read as rapidly as their more "advantaged" peers do. Some skills disadvantaged learners may have missed are the ability to make sharp discriminations among printed words and to retain the images of printed forms.

Auditory perception. Auditory perception refers to "the extraction of information from sounds"; *auditory discrimination,* an aspect of auditory perception, involves "the ability to hear likenesses and differences in the sounds of phonemes and words" (Harris and Hodges 1981, p. 26). Kavale's meta-analysis (1982) found auditory perception to be an important correlate of achievement in reading. Auditory discrimination, however, was found to be the only factor that was independent of intelligence in its relationship to reading ability.

There has been some concern with differences in auditory discrimination according to gender and socioeconomic level. Boys apparently do not learn auditory discrimination skills as readily as girls. Jean Robertson (1968) has suggested that instruction in auditory discrimination might be held separately for boys, who need more help than girls. Neuman (1981) cautions teachers that instruction on an auditory skill may strengthen the skill, as measured by tests, that skill may not transfer to reading achievement (again, as measured by tests).

Although black inner-city children tend to do quite poorly on most tests of phonemic (auditory) discrimination, the weight of the evidence is against poor auditory discrimination as a cause of poor reading among language-different speakers in general (Spache 1976, p. 93). Auditory discrimination in these children tends to be poorer when words are isolated, as in tests, than when presented in context; poor performance on isolated words does not necessarily affect comprehension of discourse.

Auditory discrimination is especially important in auditory perceptual processing if phonics is used as a dominant word recognition strategy. MacGinitie (1967) noted that the ability to discriminate sound parts in words is more important than IQ scores in relationship to reading success in first grade.

Kinesthetic and tactile perception. The *kinesthetic* sense is initiated by movement, such as writing or printing a letter or word. *Tactile* refers to perception by touch, as in tracing letters formed out of sandpaper or on a raised surface with the fingers. The relationship of these senses to reading problems is not yet clear; however, many educators recommend a combined kinesthetic and tactile approach in teaching word recognition to children with severe reading problems.

Some evidence exists that kinesthetic and tactile procedures provide reinforcement to learners who are having difficulty in other areas of perception. Roberts and Coleman (1958) found that learners who were inefficient in the use of visual cues were aided by the addition of kinesthetic reinforcement, while poor readers who had good visual perception were not. It may be the focused *attention* to details in sequence, rather than the sensation of movement or touch itself, that accounts for the success of the reinforcement (Ofman and Schaevitz 1963).

CONCEPTUALIZATION AND SCHEMATA

The ability to formulate concepts and schemata is basic to cognition. A concept can be viewed as "an abstract category of objects, ideas, and events that share certain attributes" (Ribovich 1979, p. 286). Central to Athey's view of reading as a thinking process is the "notion that concept development lies at the heart of the process" (1983, p. 26). Children with large numbers of concepts can probably learn more easily because they can relate new material to these concepts. Deficits in conceptual development are more likely to create problems with reading than are perceptual and memory deficits. Differences in the ability to think abstractly and to categorize are among the factors that differentiate good readers from poor ones (Dechant and Smith 1977, p. 46). (Chapter 10 will deal with comprehension differences of good and poor readers more fully.)

Concept formation is difficult to study precisely because concepts are abstractions, and researchers must therefore rely on inferences from observed behaviors. Dechant and Smith (1977, pp. 44, 46) have drawn the following conclusions from research on conceptualization:

1. The lower the mental age, the more specific the reaction of the learner to a word. Younger and less mature readers tend to perceive in the concrete rather than in the abstract.
2. The development of facility in conceptualization is a function of previous experience with forming concepts.
3. The greater the number of concepts that the learner has fixed through the use of words, the better the comprehension of the printed page.
4. The more specific the reader's reaction to words, the less effective is the comprehension of the printed text; the more general the reaction to words, the more effective the comprehension.
5. The better the ability to think in categories or in the abstract, the better the reading ability is likely to be.

As teachers provide instruction, they should not assume that children have even basic print-awareness concepts behind the words they use. Children frequently do not understand concepts such as *word*, *letter*, and *sound* (Reid 1966; Roberts 1981; Sanders 1981). Such concepts are basic to print awareness; they must be mastered before focusing on other concepts that incorporate these more basic ones.

Teachers also need to remember that conceptualization occurs on the affective as well as the cognitive level. Some students may find reading pleasurable and rewarding, while others find reading personally punishing. This punishment dimension can be related to lack of growth in reading.

Schema theory is a theory about knowledge. A *schema* is a "data structure for representing the generic concepts stored in memory. There are schemata representing our knowledge about all concepts: underlying objects, situations, events, sequences of events, actions, and sequences of actions" (Rumelhart 1984, p. 2). Schemata (plural of schema) are the building blocks of cognition (Rumelhart 1980). They are networks of interrelations that normally hold true among the features of a concept or concepts. Comprehension of the printed page is in terms of these networks. Anderson and Pearson (1984, p. 255) state that one has comprehended a text when he or she has found a "mental home" for the information in the text or has modified an existing mental home to accommodate the new information. Indeed, appropriate concepts and schemata are essential for all aspects of the reading act, including decoding.

Rumelhart (1981, p. 22) lists three explanations according to schema theory for the failure of students to comprehend a passage:

1. The reader may not have the appropriate schemata. In this case he/she simply cannot understand the concept being communicated.

2. The reader may have the appropriate schemata, but the clues provided by the author may be insufficient to suggest them. Here again the reader will not understand the text but, with appropriate additional clues, may come to understand it.

3. The reader may find a consistent interpretation of the text, but may not find the one intended by the author. In this case, the reader will "understand" the text, but will misunderstand the author.

Disadvantaged students often lack the concepts and schemata necessary to succeed in the typical school setting. This deficiency may be due to inadequate or inappropriate cognitive schemata (information, experiences, ideas, language, abstract thinking abilities, etc.) and/or to negative affective schemata (attitudes, interests, self-concept, for example). It is the teacher's task to develop both cognitive *and* affective concepts and schemata.

METACOGNITION

Metacognition refers to the "knowledge and control children have over their own thinking and learning activities" as they read. Two separate components are involved: (1) an awareness of those skills, strategies, and resources needed to perform a given task that involves reading, and (2) the ability to use self-regulatory mechanisms (such as checking, planning, evaluating, and revising plans) to complete the task successfully (Baker and Brown 1984b, p. 22).

Metacognitive skills are essential to the achievement of reading potential. Brown (1980, p. 456) has identified examples of reading skills and activities that involve metacognition:

1. Clarifying purposes of reading and understanding the implicit and explicit demands of a task.
2. Identifying important aspects of the message of a text.
3. Focusing on what is important in a message.
4. Monitoring ongoing activities to determine whether comprehension is taking place.
5. Self-questioning in order to determine whether goals are being achieved.
6. Taking corrective action when comprehension is not occurring.
7. Recovering from distractions and disruptions so that information gathering may be efficient.

Baker and Brown (1984a, pp. 374–76) have identified two classes of problems with metacognitive skills that may affect reading to potential. The first is the inefficient application of rules and strategies as one reads. The following research findings should be helpful to teachers: (1) making children aware that they should continue studying and self-testing will improve study performance in young children (Brown 1978); (2) instruction in self-questioning is an effective metacognitive strategy (André and Anderson 1978–79); and (3) developing a sense of logical structure of the text and of the inherent meaning in certain texts helps the less able student (Bransford et al. 1981).

The second class of problems concerns impoverished background knowledge. Children need to be instructed to fit current text messages into their background information. Teachers can help children accomplish this by tailoring the message to the child's level of understanding, continually focusing children's attention on main points, forcing comprehension monitoring through asking questions, and activating schemata by helping students see how new information is related to knowledge they already possess (Schallert and Kleiman 1979).

If children are not aware of their limitations and the complexity of the reading task, they will have difficulty in overcoming their problems. Failure to monitor one's own cognitive activities can lead to reading problems (Baker and Brown 1984a, p. 354). Proficient readers tend to engage in cognitive monitoring activities, while less experienced and less successful readers tend not to do so (Baker and Brown 1984b).

Brown (1978, p. 457) has identified several metacognitive areas that may be problem spots for children:

1. Recognizing that there has been an increase in the difficulty of the task.
2. Using inferential reasoning to assess the probability that a given assumption is based on prior knowledge.
3. Predicting the outcome of one's attempts to use given strategies.
4. Predicting task difficulty.
5. Planning ahead strategically for studying.
6. Knowing when one has succeeded or failed at a task so that new tasks can be initiated.

Metacognitive skills do not develop as early as many other cognitive skills, and the development is gradual. According to Armbruster and Brown (1984, p. 276), these skills can be systematically taught. Such instruction may help reduce reading problems. Learners at any age level are more likely to be actively involved cognitively when the tasks are of intermediate difficulty—neither too easy (resulting in boredom) nor too hard (resulting in frustration and giving up) (Baker and Brown 1984a, p. 354).

Intelligence

In the absence of universally accepted descriptions of intelligence, no attempt will be made to give a precise definition. In the research reported in this section, IQ may be assumed to be that which was measured by the tests given. While "intelligence" facilitates cognitive acts, high intelligence does not necessarily guarantee freedom from reading problems. Low intelligence, however, often impedes learning to read on grade level, and may lead to reading problems if teachers do not adjust instructional procedures to the child's level of intellectual functioning.

Some children with reading problems have average or above average intelligence; such learners are in special need of identification, since they have the potential for improved achievement. On the other hand, a high level of intelligence does not guarantee marked improvement in reading, even with remediation. Other factors such as self-concept, motivation, attitudes, and interests may interact in ways that negate achieving potential.

Low mental ability may affect reading in several ways. Children of lower intelligence have reduced reasoning power, which affects the ability to draw inferences, perceive relationships, and think critically. Observation of significant and distinctive features in recognizing words may be affected, as may recall of details.

Children with IQ scores between 75 and 90 can learn to read easy material, given adequate instruction with learning tasks appropriately spaced. Mildly retarded learners may achieve a level of literacy commensurate with their mental ability level in word recognition if instruction is planned appropriately (Carney 1979). Higher-level comprehension skills may pose more of a problem, however.

Intelligence test scores and reading achievement test scores are low or moderately correlated at primary grade levels and are more highly correlated at higher grade levels (Harris 1963, p. 48). Questions may be raised about the meaning of such correlations. Have the students had the opportunity to learn the concepts tested? Do they have the reading skills needed to function with the test? Are intelligence and reading achievement tests measuring aspects of the same ability or abilities? Both types of tests depend heavily on conceptual and vocabulary development. Intelligence tests may, in part, be measuring background information and reading skill rather than innate ability to learn.

IQ and school ability tests are often used in the diagnostic process as one measure of level of intellectual functioning and as one index for predicting achievement, although other factors may be more closely associated with reading problems than IQ. In his summary of research on IQ and reading, Farr (1969, p. 179) stated that language development, self-concept, and experiential background may be more closely related. Of course, intelligence may interact with these factors. Parental influence may also be a more effective predictor; for example, Dave (1963) found that such parental influences as aspirations for the learner's success, work orientation, academic guidance, and language models were better predictors of reading achievement than were IQ scores.

Lower socioeconomic students can perform better than usual on intelligence tests if they are sufficiently motivated (Cheyney 1976). Careful motivation in the testing process is often needed. Test results should therefore be interpreted cautiously when a low level of effort is suspected.

Despite the above cautions, intelligence tests (and school ability tests) do have a place in the diagnostic process: they provide one indicant of level of mental ability as it relates to schoolwork. When results are interpreted with caution, and when other indicants of ability to do schoolwork (such as language facility and listening ability) are considered, such tests can be an important diagnostic component.

Group IQ tests may produce two kinds of scores—verbal intelligence scores (based on written or spoken language) and performance, or nonverbal, scores (based on spatial and numerical relationships). Some reading educators have advocated the use of performance tests for learners with reading problems, in the belief that these tests were fairer to such children. However, these tests may be tapping different abilities from those required in the reading process. It is probably fairer, when giving a group IQ test, to administer both verbal and nonverbal forms. Both sets of data could then be considered when estimating the potential or probable level of mental functioning.

Individually administered IQ tests are more valid than group-administered tests in determining the probability that reading problems exist. According to Neville's (1965) study, a reading grade equivalency score of 4.0 is a critical minimum for obtaining reasonably valid IQ scores for intermediate-grade children when reading is required on the test. This suggests caution in interpreting group IQ test scores for children who have limited reading ability.

INFORMATION TO CONSIDER

1. Children may not know what is the most relevant information to attend to in performing a reading task. This deficit is amenable to instruction.

2. Critical information to which to attend may differ from one child to another.
3. Disadvantaged learners may not have the visual and auditory perceptual skills necessary for easy success with reading.
4. Boys may have more difficulty with auditory discrimination than girls.
5. Auditory perceptual skills are particularly important if intensive phonics instruction is used.
6. Kinesthetic and tactile procedures may provide the perceptual reinforcement necessary for some learners.
7. Concepts and schemata are essential for reading comprehension.
8. Conceptualization can be affective as well as cognitive.
9. Metacognitive skills are essential to the achievement of reading potential. These skills do not develop early, but they can be taught.
10. Lower-ability children can achieve success with many reading skills. Higher-level thinking is affected, however.
11. Individual intelligence tests are more valid than group tests for assessing problem readers.

Summary

The development of reading problems is influenced by several factors. Each reading problem generally has more than one impinging factor. Several groups of factors have been researched—affective, cognitive, language, cultural, physical, and the instructional environment. Affective and cognitive correlates were discussed in this chapter.

Much of the data for these correlates have been generated from correlational studies. Caution is needed in assuming cause-and-effect relationships from such data. The research and theory base, however, does permit some generalizations, which teachers should consider in the assessment and instruction.

Affect is basic in learning to read and in continuing to read for pleasure or information. Students' attitudes, motivational level, interests, and self-concepts are highly individual and should be considered in the diagnostic and instructional processes.

Emotional problems are frequently associated with reading difficulties. Such problems are more likely an effect than a cause, although in some instances emotional problems or personality maladjustment may be causal.

The cognitive factors discussed were attention, perception, conceptualization and schemata, metacognition, and intelligence. Reading teachers should consider each of these factors as possibly impinging on reading problems. The effects of cognitive functioning, cognitive control, and attention on attaining satisfactory levels of reading ability are receiving much consideration today; less emphasis is being placed on perceptual deficits.

Questions for Further Thought

1. Which factors of affect and cognition seem to have been overemphasized as impinging on reading problems? Why?
2. Are other factors underemphasized today? Why?
3. Which of the correlates discussed do you feel are most important for classroom teachers to consider? Why?
4. Should diagnostic attention to any of the factors be left to clinicians or to other specialists, rather than classroom teachers? Why?

Activities and Projects

1. Assume you are a special teacher of reading in your building and are discussing the affective correlates of reading problems with classroom teachers. What information would you include? Why? Do the same for the cognitive correlates.
2. Write a comprehensive paper synthesizing the research on one of the cognitive correlates discussed in this chapter. Compare your findings with those presented in the chapter.
3. Discuss any one of the correlates with a special teacher of reading or reading clinician. Summarize her thoughts and practices to present to the class.
4. Visit the reading supervisor in a school system. Find out what correlates receive attention in that school system and why. Do the same for the reading clinic at your college or university.

3

Language, Cultural, and Physical Correlates of Reading Problems

In addition to affective and cognitive correlates, discussed in the preceding chapter, language, cultural, and physical factors also affect a child's reading to potential. The manner in which a child develops language, the variations of his language, and his awareness of language affect his overall growth in reading. Teachers must explore possible relationships between a child's language and his problems in reading. Likewise, the child's culture can affect his reading ability; cultural aspects such as home factors, socioeconomic status, cultural differences, and gender differences have been shown to be possible reading correlates. Physical factors, such as visual and auditory acuity, speech production, neurological problems, and general health, may also affect reading development.

This chapter will focus on the correlates named above and on the impact of these factors on the child who is experiencing problems in reading.

Language Correlates

QUESTIONS TO GUIDE READING

Recall Questions
1. What is meant by the following terms: metalinguistic awareness, language variation, dialect, bilingualism, language registers, language instructional register, Black English, sociolect?
2. What are the general language characteristics of children, ages 3 months to 12 years, as summarized by Norton?
3. How may dialect "difference" interfere with learning to read?

Important relationships exist between language factors and achievement in reading. Recall that Aulls (1982, p. 579) cites research evidence that indicates that language factors are particularly significant in a child's learning to read as well as she can.

Language, as it relates to reading achievement, can be discussed in at least two very important ways—its development (including awareness of its use) and its variation. These dimensions interact with reading in several ways that affect achievement. For example, there may be a mismatch between the child's level of language development and the language used in books or other printed materials, thereby causing problems in the child's processing of print; or the language of the learner may differ from that of the teacher or other instructors, which can also affect a child's development in reading.

While a lack of proficiency with language may be a contributing factor for some children who are not reading to potential, teachers should remember that not all children whose language is different from that of the teacher or that used in the reading materials will have reading problems. If an appropriate instructional program is developed early for such children, reading problems can often be avoided.

LANGUAGE DEVELOPMENT

Most educators consider language development an important correlate of reading ability. According to Loban (1976), children who are slow in language development may also be low achievers in reading. Ruddell and Haggard (1985, p. 75) state that language development processes, both oral and written, are directly related to reading development and are interactive with the acquisition of reading proficiency. Early and Sawyer (1984, p. 82) feel that learning to read and write is an extension of learning to produce and comprehend oral language.

How well young children understand print depends on how well they understand how the oral language system operates. Children who learn to read easily are often those who speak fluently for a variety of purposes, who are familiar with print through the stories read to them, and who are eager to figure out what the words on the page say.

Research findings taken together suggest that a higher degree of relationship may exist between receptive oral language and reading than between expressive oral language and reading (Bond et al. 1984, p. 74). That is, the more concepts and language patterns a child understands, the greater the chances for reading success, even though the child may not be able to use all the language he or she understands.

Stages in language development. All children apparently go through similar stages of language development, but at varying rates. As we stated earlier, a child's proficiency with language interacts with his ability to process print. Therefore, teachers should be familiar with the typical stages of language development and should be able to see where children with reading problems are in the language development process.

The phonological (sound), morphological (meaning), and syntactic (sentence structure) systems that children bring to the reading act affect their processing abilities. Children who are entering school generally have control over much of the phonological system, and their morphological development is usually well along, though not complete. They also have control of syntactic patterning, although development continues throughout the elementary grades.

Ruddell and Haggard (1985, p. 75) identified five significant factors that characterize initial language acquisition and their link to the subsequent development of reading proficiency:

1. Children are active theory builders and hypothesis testers. The language rule system they have developed may not match that needed at school.
2. The driving force behind both language performance and reading growth is the need to get meaning and make sense of the world.
3. Language performance is directly related to the language environment in which the child finds himself. This environment includes both the models available and the opportunities for language interaction.
4. Oral and written language acquisition are both parallel and interactive in their development.
5. Reading acquisition and development are directly related to, and interact with, oral and written language development.

It is not possible to include in one chapter a complete description of the stages children typically pass through in language development, nor to discuss the strengths and weaknesses of theories of how language develops. Many other texts and college courses focus on this topic. In this chapter, a general guide only is given for teachers to use when observing the progress of given children through typical language development stages. Norton (1980, pp. 32–33) has briefly summarized the general language characteristics of children ages 3 months to 12 years to facilitate teachers' observations. Her useful summary, shown in Figure 3.1, is based on studies of Brown (1973) and Loban (1976) and a report by Bartel (1975).

If children are not proficient in a given stage of language development, teachers should not expect them to be able to process print that requires such development. For example, if children do not yet understand conditional clauses, then they will not be able to read complex sentences containing such clauses with full understanding. Teachers must make adjustments in programs until children have the language necessary to comprehend the text.

Metalinguistic awareness. Metalinguistic awareness may be defined as "the ability to reflect on and talk about language; specifically, language

Figure 3.1. General Language Characteristics (For Children Ages 3 Months to 12 Years)

Age	General Language Characteristics
3 months	The young child starts with all possible language sounds and gradually eliminates those sounds that are not used around him.
1 year	Many children are speaking single words (e.g., "mama"). Infants use single words to express entire sentences. Complex meanings may underlie single words.
18 months	Many children are using two or three word phrases (e.g., "see baby"). Children are developing their own language rule systems. Children may have a vocabulary of about 300 words.
2–3 years	Children use such grammatical morphemes as plural suffix /s/, auxiliary verb "is," and past irregular. Simple and compound sentences are used. Understands tense and numerical concepts such as "many" and "few." A vocabulary of about 900 words is used.
3–4 years	The verb past tense appears, but children may overgeneralize the "ed" and "s" markers. Negative transformation appears. Children understand numerical concepts such as "one," "two," and "three." Speech is becoming more complex, with more adjectives, adverbs, pronouns, and prepositions. Vocabulary is about 1500 words.
4–5 years	Language is more abstract and most basic rules of language are mastered. Children produce grammatically correct sentences. Vocabularies include approximately 2500 words.
5–6 years	Most children use complex sentences quite frequently. They use correct pronouns and verbs in the present and past tense. The average number of words per oral sentence is 6.8. It has been estimated that the child understands approximately 6,000 words.
6–7 years	Children are speaking complex sentences that use adjectival clauses, and conditional clauses beginning with "if" are beginning to appear. Language is becoming more symbolic. Children begin to read and write and understand concepts of time and seasons. The average sentence length is 7.5 words.

continued

Figure 3.1, continued

Age	General Language Characteristics
7–8 years	Children use relative pronouns as objects in subordinate adjectival clauses ("I have a cat which I feed every day"). Subordinate clauses beginning with "when," "if," and "because" appear frequently. The average number of words per oral sentence is 7.6.
8–10 years	Children begin to relate concepts to general ideas through use of such connectors as "meanwhile" and "unless." The subordinating connector "although" is used correctly by 50 percent of the children. Present participle active and perfect participle appear. The average number of words in an oral sentence is 9.0.
10–12 years	Children use complex sentences with subordinate clauses of concession introduced by "nevertheless" and "in spite of." The auxiliary verbs "might," "could," and "should" appear frequently. Children have difficulties distinguishing among past, past perfect, and present perfect tenses of the verb. The average number of words in an oral sentence is now 9.5.

From *The Effective Teaching of Language Arts*, by Donna E. Norton (Charles E. Merrill Pub. Co., 1980), pp. 32–33. Reprinted with permission.

awareness arising when a speaker or hearer begins consciously to think about the language being used" (Harris and Hodges 1981, p. 196). Metalinguistic awareness has developed when the student can talk about language. Some writers have questioned whether the speaker's ability to follow rules in producing speech are equivalent to the conscious knowledge of the rules of language (Fischer 1980; Ryan 1980). This conscious knowledge may be necessary for success in reading.

Metalinguistic knowledge seems to develop later than speaking and listening ability (Ryan 1980). Typical metalinguistic skills needed by students as they begin to learn to read include (1) the knowledge of distinctions among terms such as "words," "letters," "sounds," and "sentences"; and (2) the ability to divide simple sentences into their word units—for example, to segment "the store" into two word units (Blachowicz 1978).

Students' metalinguistic awareness is sometimes inadequate to deal with certain instructional materials used in classrooms (Blachowicz 1978). These materials are often developed on the assumption that students understand the meaning of such terms as "word," "letter," and "sound." When teachers use these materials and follow directions in guidebooks, they may be using terms that the learners do not understand.

LANGUAGE VARIATION

Languages develop and change in a variety of ways and for numerous reasons. A child may have a range of linguistic behaviors, including her own unique language patterns (idiolect) and a standard or a nonstandard dialect. A child's opportunity to learn language determines the patterns she speaks and understands.

Reading-related variations in language discussed in this section include language registers, bilingualism, and dialects (both social and ethnic). Teachers must consider carefully whether these language variations are related to problems a reader may be experiencing.

Language registers. A language register is a language variety that sets it apart from other registers by the social circumstance of its use (DeStefano 1978, p. 99). For example, the vocabulary and intonation patterns a teacher uses when talking to children may be different from those used when talking to colleagues in the teachers' lounge, even if the topics are the same. As the social circumstances change, so does the register. Changes in register occur in phonology, syntax, vocabulary, and in nonverbal behaviors (facial expression, use of hands, shrugs, etc.). Selection of an appropriate register from those available to an individual depends on whether the language user is speaking or writing and on the formality or informality of the situation.

A learner's repertoire of registers is a function of socioeconomic status, experience, age, gender, and special interests. Children differ in their ability to produce and comprehend registers. Some children may not be able to produce a given register in speech with skill, yet they may be able to comprehend that register when others use it. For example, a vernacular-speaking ghetto child may not be able to produce all the sounds of the words used by a commentator in a news broadcast, yet he may be able to understand what the commentator is saying (DeStefano 1978, p. 104).

A child's experience with language will determine whether he can use a given language register. For example, one child may be able to function well only on an informal oral level with parents or peers because his opportunities for learning language have been limited primarily to such groups, while another child may be able to function quite appropriately with formal written language in a school setting because his language learning opportunities have provided that preparation. Children's competence with registers should be taken into consideration when teachers give oral directions and when they select written materials to be read.

Figure 3.2 shows the types of registers identified by Ruddell and Haggard (1985, p. 70) as necessary within the school setting.

A special concern to teachers and clinicians should be the Language Instruction Register. As defined by DeStefano (1980), the Language Instruction Register (LIR) refers to the ways in which the teacher uses language in working with children. The important questions is, "How close is the match between the language used by the teacher as she teaches and the language that is understood by the students?" Unless students have a clear understanding of the vocabulary and syntactic patterns used by the teacher, they may not be able to understand the directions the teacher gives them.

Figure 3.2. Language Registers Needed in School

Language Function	Oral Form	Written Form
Informal Personal Exchange	Greetings	Personal notes to friends
	Communications of feelings	Unedited written experiences
	Control of others' behavior	Memos and directions
Formal Informational Exchange	Classroom discussion	Edited experience stories
	Classroom lectures	Edited academic reports
	Public speeches	School textbooks
Literary Exchange	Drama and theater	Poetry, narrative, drama

From *Theoretical Models and Processes of Reading,* ed. Harry Singer and Robert B. Ruddell, 3rd ed. (Newark, DE: International Reading Association, 1985), p. 70. Reprinted with permission of Robert Ruddell and Martha Rapp Haggard and the International Reading Association.

Bilingualism. Learners who speak more than one language (for example, Spanish and English) are said to be bilingual. In its broadest sense, bilingualism refers to the use of two languages without consideration as to the degree of proficiency in either language. However, a child may be more proficient in one than another. Mexican-Americans who speak Spanish and who have some proficiency in English are still considered bilingual.

Some children may enter school with little or no proficiency in English. These children need English-language instruction, not corrective or remedial reading instruction. Opportunities should be provided for them to learn English concepts and words prior to receiving reading instruction in written English.

Teaching non-English-speaking children is easier for teachers if the children already read in their native language. Teachers often find that these children gain proficiency in the recognition of English words before they can understand what they read. In such instances, teachers need to focus on the concepts that English words represent.

Non-English-speaking children who do not already read in their native language must be taught both to speak and to read the English language. If given appropriate instruction, these children generally do not have problems in reading. Teachers must recognize that progress may be slow, and tailor their expectations accordingly.

Many bilingual children who speak a little English have trouble understanding in school because their English vocabulary is of very limited depth. For example, they may know the word *run* as a physical activity, but not as a small stream of water. They may experience other problems related to English word order (such as placement of adjectives in relationship to nouns, for example) and to the complexity of English sentences (use and placement of prepositional phrases, for example). Bilingual speakers may also struggle with English phonemes that they have not learned to discriminate, or that do not exist, in their native language. An example is the short *i* and short *u* in patterns such as *bit, hit* and *but, hut* (Thonis 1976, pp. 2–5, 25).

Attitudes also significantly affect the learning of a second language. Some bilingual students may reject English because they see it as a threat to their native language and the cultural norms that have been associated with the mother tongue.

Thonis (1976, p. 1) has described conditions that impede reading achievement and create frustration for Spanish speakers:

1. a lack of experiences in the dominant culture from which concepts specific to the English-speaking community may be acquired;

2. an inadequate oral command of the English language which is the language of the instructional program;

3. a lowered sense of self-esteem resulting from repeated feelings of inadequacy; and

4. an unrealistic curriculum which imposes reading and writing English before listening comprehension and speaking fluency have been established.

These conditions may apply to other language speakers as well.

Dialects. A dialect is a subset of a language that differs from other subsets of that language in aspects of phonology, syntax, and vocabulary; it is variation *within* a language. Dialects are logical, rule-governed language varieties and should not be mistaken as indicants of cognitive deficits or inadequate language development. Dialect differences are merely differences, not inadequacies.

Geographical factors account for a large number of dialectal variations; for example, the speech patterns of educated Southerners and educated Bostonians differ in some aspects of phonology, syntax, and vocabulary. Such differences have minimal effects on reading. Another type of variation, determined by social context, is referred to as a *sociolect*. Sociolects include varieties attached to socioeconomic classes and to cultures, such as Black English and lower-class, nonstandard English (DeStefano 1978, Ch. 4).

Much research has been done on the effects of dialects on learning to read. According to Barnitz (1980), the question has not been fully answered; some studies show little or no interference (Rentel and Kennedy 1972), while other studies suggest that relationships may exist.

For instance, Bougere (1981) finds a correlation between dialect speaking and reading achievement and between dialects and socioeconomic status. Others reject a dialect-barrier hypothesis as accounting for reading problems. Goodman and Buck (1973, p. 6), for example, feel that "The only special disadvantage which speakers of low-status dialects suffer in learning to read is one imposed by teachers and schools. Rejection of their dialects and educators' confusion of linguistic deficiency interferes with the natural process by which reading is acquired and undermines the linguistic self-confidence of divergent speakers."

Lucas and Singer (1975) suggest that there is some evidence to support the position that dialect variation may interfere with oral reading on the syntactic level, but not on the phonological level. The effects of syntax may be transitory, however; as more English syntax is acquired, the interference lessens. Ruddell and Haggard (1985, p. 72), on the other hand, state that phonological differences may result in confusion of meaning when there are not enough contextual cues to clarify the intended meaning.

Black English variations have received considerable research attention, with a general conclusion that such variations do not necessarily interfere with the comprehension of Standard English. Copple and Suci (1974) found, for example, that dialect differences in black five- and seven-year-olds did not seem to interfere with their comprehension. Nevertheless, there is a disproportionate number of black children in remedial reading classes (Kachuck 1978). This may reflect teachers' lack of understanding of the reading competence of black children, or may betray the attitude that so-called nonstandard speech is somehow inadequate.

One attempt to minimize the impact of dialect on learning to read has been the use of "dialect readers," books written in the syntactic and spelling patterns that were felt to represent how the speakers of the dialect used oral English. However, there is no evidence that material written in a learner's dialect facilitates learning to read. It may be assumed that these children are accustomed to seeing English print in its standard form on TV, in signs, and elsewhere. That the pronunciation they give to these written forms may differ from the "standard" does not mean that children do not recognize and comprehend the printed forms in Standard English.

The attitudes of the teacher toward the learner's dialect may be of much greater significance in producing reading failure than a mismatch between the dialect and the materials and language of instruction. DeStefano (1978, p. 114) suggests that teachers are partially responsible for some of the problems encountered by students whose dialect varies from the norm accepted in school. She notes that "as a group teachers tend to hold normative, corrective views towards students' language" (p. 115). These views can cause students not to want to speak or write in class. Some research also suggests that teachers think that children who speak Black English dialects are less likely to read well (Crowl and MacGinitie 1974; Cunningham 1976–77).

Teachers should understand the dialect patterns of their students. Such understanding was mandated in the court case of *Martin Luther King Junior Elementary School Children, et al.* vs. *Ann Arbor School District Board* (1979). The court established that the language these children spoke in the home was not in itself a barrier to understanding in the classroom; their language became a barrier only when teachers did not take it into account in teaching Standard English. This void on the teachers' part may have contributed to the children's reading problems. The defendant Board was required to take steps to help its teachers recognize the home language of the students and to use that knowledge in their teaching of reading.

INFORMATION TO CONSIDER

1. Language development may affect reading achievement in school settings.
2. Children with language differences do not necessarily develop reading problems, if appropriate instructional programs are planned.
3. Teacher attitudes are more important than language variation in the development of reading problems.
4. The precise relationship between dialect and achievement is still open to research.
5. Speaking a Black English variety does not necessarily interfere with comprehension of Standard English.

Culture

QUESTIONS TO GUIDE READING

Recall Questions
1. How does the home environment interact with reading achievement?
2. What are some home activities that may lead to reading success?
3. What is the chief factor that may explain the relationship of socioeconomic status to reading achievement?
4. Why are children from low socioeconomic homes *less likely* to achieve in reading?
5. What are some cultural factors that interact with reading achievement?
6. What factors have been suggested as possible causes of gender differences in reading achievement?

Thinking Questions
1. Why is the affective dimension so important in the home environment?
2. Which of the cultural factors discussed relate most closely to program planning (in a practical sense)? Why?
3. How can teachers incorporate cultural correlates in the diagnostic process?

Culture refers to a total way of life that has been developed by groups of people and passed along from one generation to another. It includes customs, beliefs, traditions, values, and mores.

The influence of culture is pervasive. It affects students' success in school, including their reading achievement. Culture has an impact on the values that learners establish, their language development, the concepts and schemata they form, and the behavior patterns they set. Investigations into the effect of culture on reading achievement have focused on such correlates as home factors, socioeconomic status, cultural differences, and gender differences. Each of these correlates will be discussed in this section.

The Home

The home has a strong impact on reading achievement. According to Entwistle (1977, p. 80), the social influence of the family is greater than that of the school in causing achievement differences among learners.

It is in the home that language development is begun and that initial conceptual stimulation is provided. Children's values, attitudes, self-concept, and beliefs are also rooted in the home. The role model provided by the parents in literacy areas—recreational reading, library visits, or reading to children—influences the value children place on reading.

For some time research has shown marked differences between the home backgrounds of achievers and underachievers. Kurtz and Swenson (1951), found that in the homes of achieving students the parents read to the children, played with them, or attended school with them. These examples of positive support were less evident in homes of underachievers. Supplying reading materials for children may also make a difference. Almy's (1949) research indicated a relationship between certain home activities and children's reading success. Among the significant home activities mentioned by Almy were looking at books and magazines and taking an interest in letters and words. Parents' reading to their children also had a strong relationship to reading success.

The affective climate in the home is certainly relevant to reading problems. In early studies, Preston (1939) found that parents' attitudes toward their children became more negative once a reading problem arose; and Stewart (1950) found that mothers of retarded readers were somewhat hostile to their children, with accompanying guilt feelings that were manifested behaviorally as overindulgence or overprotectiveness. Affect in the home—love, support, understanding, a feeling of security—contributes to positive self-concepts and thus to achievement. On the other hand, negative parental reactions, such as excessive pressure on the child or comparing one child's reading ability with that of a more successful sibling, are counterproductive.

Conflict in the home or between home and school can create problems for students. More evidence of conflicts in the family relationships have been found in the homes of low achievers than in those of high achievers (Siegler and Gynther 1960). Conflict between home and school, with parents openly critical of the school, can undermine a child's learning (Klein et al. 1981). Programs for problem readers need parent support.

Cooperative planning with parents, bringing about active involvement of the home with the school, generally yields positive results. According to a review of research articles by Boehnlein and Hager (1985, p. 36), students whose parents became involved with their children's reading often showed increases in achievement. Schools must work toward strong, positive parent involvement programs including all faculty. This seems particularly true when children are having problems with reading.

Research on the effects of the home on reading achievement has been effectively summarized by Sartain (1981, p. 13):

1. Many children probably gain a somewhat greater amount of functional knowledge from the home and the community than they do from the school.
2. Good readers come from home environments that are psychologically comfortable, that foster positive attitudes toward reading and learning, and that provide stimulating cultural and language experiences.
3. Parents who are encouraged or are trained to do so can be effective in providing cultural experiences and many simple learning experiences.
4. Siblings, as well as aunts, uncles, and grandparents, can make valuable contributions through informal tutoring.

SOCIOECONOMIC STATUS

Socioeconomic status is a strong predictor of reading achievement. The chief factor that may explain this relationship is the language of the social class subculture (Downing and Leong 1982, p. 277). Other factors that may help explain why children from lower socioeconomic status achieve less well are "a harmful interaction among poverty, unemployment, mobility, and untreated physical handicaps; and conflict between the cultural mores and values of pupils and those of the middle-class teacher or middle-class-oriented school" (Spache 1976, p. 213).

Shannon (1985) interprets recent research to suggest that reading instruction may unintentionally perpetuate social-class differences. This occurs through ability-grouping practices and teachers' expectations for performance in such groups. He notes several studies suggesting that teachers have lower expectations for lower-class children than for middle- and upper-class children and treat them differently in instructional settings. Children's achievement in relationship to potential suffers accordingly.

The gap in reading achievement between children from lower SES groups and their peers tends to widen with time. In Barton's (1963) study, which showed particularly marked relationships between socioeconomic status and reading ability, the proportion of learners below grade level in lower socioeconomic classes increased progressively from grade 1 to grade 6. School failures were also significantly higher than in middle-class groups. These findings suggest that the school may not be adequately providing the experiences and instructional environment needed for these learners to make progress equivalent to other students whose general environments have provided a better match with the school experience.

From an analysis of research relating to socioeconomic status, Downing and Thackray (1975, p. 37) have concluded: "We may anticipate that children from lower socioeconomic class homes may tend to be ready for reading somewhat later than those from others, but this is due simply to the fact that certain types of experiences are *less likely* to be available to children in poorer homes. Books and other forms of written language are *less likely* to be in evidence. Parental attitudes are *less likely* to be positive toward intellectual activities such as reading." Note the qualifying phrase "less likely"; there are many children from lower socioeconomic homes whose parents have a positive attitude toward learning and who do receive much encouragement to succeed in school.

CULTURAL DIFFERENCES

"Culturally different" as used here refers to learners whose cultural values differ somewhat from those of the cultural mainstream. Prominent among such groups in this country are certain black, Mexican-American, Native American (Indian), and Appalachian cultures.

Cultural differences seem to have important relationships to reading achievement. A learner's world knowledge and her concepts and schemata are influenced by the cultural environment (Anderson and Barnitz 1984). When reading materials focus on areas for which students do not have the appropriate cultural schemata, they may have problems in comprehending those materials (Reynolds et al. 1982). Comprehension differences can occur both in particular word meanings and in the interpretation of stories (Rogers-Zegarra and Singer 1985).

McDermott (1985) further illustrates the impact of culture in his discussion of the importance of peer groups. Children may learn to attend to cues produced in peer groups and ignore those of the teacher and the mainstream school culture. Children tend to attend to cues that are consistent with their learned competence; in failing to attend to cues outside competence areas, they may appear to be learning disabled when indeed they are not.

Cultural differences may also occur in modes of responding to adults, in value systems, in desire for personal attention, in identification with family units, in achievement motivation, and in competitiveness. To illustrate this point, Kiefer and DeStefano (1985) note that Amish children are expected to be seen and not heard when in the presence of adults; that certain Native American children are also expected to remain silent in the presence of adults and to learn from observation rather than direct instruction; that native Hawaiian children do not like to be singled out for individual attention, and thus give minimal answers to questions (if they answer at all); and that Puerto Rican children tend to avoid eye contact when being reprimanded. Teachers of culturally different children should study those children's cultural values in order to develop an instructional program in which the students' cultural values are both understood and respected.

Rodrigues and White (1981, p. 3) offer several examples of questions that teachers should ask themselves about cultural factors. Knowing the answers to such questions can help teachers avoid unintended insults, facilitate cross-cultural communication, and make the school learning environment more acceptable to the culturally different student. Their questions are:

1. Does one point at a Navajo?
2. Does one pat Vietnamese children on their heads when praising them?
3. Does one point the soles of his or her shoes toward students of Arab descent?
4. Does the lowering of one's eyes indicate the same thing in all cultures?
5. How close does one stand to another when talking?
6. Under what conditions may one person touch another?

The impact of cultural differences on achievement may be minimized somewhat by an "open door policy" in school. Home/school involvement programs seem to be helpful. Comer (1980), in discussing the results of a five-year program involving substantial parental involvement in two inner-city schools, reports lasting achievement gains, improved attendance, and easing of behavior problems.

GENDER DIFFERENCES

Research done in the United States and Canada during the past century has confirmed differences in reading achievement between girls and boys (Lehr 1982). These differences have been found both in the acquisition of reading skills and in the incidence of reading problems.

Cultural expectations and maturational processes have been cited as reasons for the differences. While girls do mature physically more quickly than boys, there is some skepticism about the differential maturation hypothesis because in some cultures boys perform better in reading than girls (Downing and Leong 1982, p. 268).

The most probable hypotheses regarding causality are linked to cultural expectations (Kolczynski 1973; Lehr 1982). Teachers may expect girls to do better than boys (Johnson 1976); reading may be considered a more feminine activity (Downing and Thomson 1977); the structure of the school setting (with grouping and testing rather than individual tutoring as a norm) may not be conducive to boys' learning (Gross 1978); the predominance of female teachers in early school years may give girls more vivid role models (Preston 1962); and parental expectations, attitudes, and behaviors may favor the development of reading achievement in girls (Sheridan 1981, p. 11).

Regardless of the causes, the end result is that there are about three times as many boys as girls in remedial and corrective reading programs. A cultural basis for this ratio is supported by Preston (1962), who found that the incidence of reading problems was higher for German girls than boys. While teachers cannot overcome all the cultural expectations of society, they can adjust their expectations for boys' performance, and structure learning situations that might be more conducive to boys' learning preferences.

INFORMATION TO CONSIDER

1. The impact of the home environment on reading achievement is strong.
2. The chief factor in the relationship of socioeconomic status to reading achievement may be language competence in the school setting.
3. Children from lower socioeconomic homes may become progressively poorer in reading achievement than their peers unless there are strong and appropriate instructional programs for them.
4. Cultural differences can affect reading achievement. Teachers need to understand these differences and take them into account.
5. More boys than girls have problems with reading. The cause is more likely cultural than maturational.

Physical Correlates

QUESTIONS TO GUIDE READING

Recall Questions
1. What physical factors have been investigated in relationship to reading problems?
2. What is the relationship of each of these physical correlates to reading problems?

Reading is a complex act. There are several physical attributes that facilitate the processing of print. In this section, visual and auditory acuity, speech, neurological problems, laterality, and general health will be con-sidered. All of these areas have received considerable attention in the literature, although some are considered to be more closely related to reading problems than others.

VISUAL ACUITY

Visual acuity, as discussed in this section, is the physical ability to see. Visual perception, which is viewed as a cognitive act, is discussed in Chapter 2.

It is impossible to state precisely the impact of visual acuity on reading. Visual acuity *can* be a factor in the development of reading problems (Jobe 1976, p. 2) by interfering with a learner's appropriate response to instruc-tion. In general, visual acuity problems affect readers in two very real ways. The first is fatigue, which may result in laborious and inefficient efforts. A second reaction, avoidance of the reading act, may manifest itself in coping behaviors such as inattentiveness, daydreaming, or a general avoidance of nearpoint reading activities (Rouse and Ryan 1984).

A problem that may interfere with instruction or be harmful for one individual may not be for another, however; different people cope with visual problems in differing ways. Other factors, such as emotional dis-tress, may affect a person's ability to cope with acuity problems.

Rouse and Ryan (1984) state that in general school populations, only a small percentage of children have learning problems that can be attributed solely to visual acuity deficiencies. The incidence may be higher in clinical populations. Robinson (1946), for example, found that 63.4 percent of the clinical subjects (remedial readers) in her classic study had visual prob-lems that were considered causal.

Eye-care specialists are divided into two basic groups, ophthalmologists and optometrists, which usually disagree as to the role of vision in reading.

Ophthalmologists have medical degrees, can treat eye diseases, and tend to see vision in a physical, mechanical sense. Many ophthalmologists believe visual training is unscientific and thus ineffective in treating reading problems. They do not place as much importance on visual acuity factors as do optometrists, who are more likely to focus on the *process* of vision.

Optometrists are more concerned with the functioning of binocular vision, accommodation, convergence, and eye movement. They emphasize the value of visual training exercises in remediation that are designed to develop binocular visual skills.

Teachers frequently need to make referrals to eye-care specialists. In some states, teachers are prohibited by law from recommending one type of eye-care practitioner over another. Teachers should be able to explain the difference between the orientations of the two major eye-care groups, but should not make specific recommendations; that decision should be left to parents.

It does not seem necessary, in this text, to discuss the physiological mechanisms that permit humans to see, but reading teachers should have some knowledge of what constitutes good physical vision. Denby (1979) has briefly and cogently described the two major functions of the physical process of vision: the ability of the eye to see clearly and the ability of the two eyes to work together. Teachers should be aware of types of visual problems in these areas.

Several problems of the first type (clear vision) have been studied. Among these problems, as defined by Jobe (1976), are the following:

Accommodation—the act of changing the power of the crystalline lens of the eye so that objects can be seen clearly at different distances.

Astigmatism—a refractive condition of the eye in which the light from a point source is focused by the eye as two lines at right angles to each other and separated from each other along the line of light.

Hyperopia (farsightedness)—a refractive error of the eye in which a distant object can be seen clearly only by using some accommodation.

Myopia (nearsightedness)—a refractive error of the eye in which the image of a distant object is formed in front of the retina of the static eye. The far point of the myopic eye is at some finite distance (that is, less than 20 feet from the eye).

Anisometropia—a discrepancy between the refractive conditions in the two eyes.

The most common visual problems are hyperopia, myopia, and astigmatism. Rouse and Ryan (1984) summarize the research on these visual problems by stating that visual acuity has been found to have little correlation with reading ability. Hyperopia (farsightedness) is found more frequently in poor readers than in good readers. Myopia (nearsightedness) has been found more consistently in *good* readers than poor ones. Astigmatism, which causes blurring, has been found in poor readers, but the incidence is no higher than among children without reading problems.

Problems with the second type of acuity, binocular vision (concerning the ability of the eyes to work together), may interfere more with reading than deficiencies in clearness of vision. Binocular incoordination inhibits the inefficiency with which a child learns (Denby 1979), although it rarely interferes with the reader's ability to recognize letters or words (Strang 1969, p. 168).

Harris and Hodges (1981) have defined certain binocular problems that may interfere with reading:

Aniseikonia—a visual defect in which the size, and sometimes the shape, of retinal images from the two eyes are unequal. Aniseikonia is quite uncommon, but if present may contribute to reading problems by interfering with good binocular vision, which results in discomfort and fatigue. It is correctable with special lenses.

Heterophoria—a general term for oculomotor imbalance, or the tendency for the eyes to deviate from one another in their line of sight. Heterophoria may cause fusion to be broken and produce double vision (diplopia). Efforts to restore binocular vision may create fatigue, discomfort, and eyestrain.

Heterotropia—a general term for the deviation of one eye from the point of fixation of the other, as in exotropia (outward deviation) or esotropia (inward deviation). Heterotropia refers to all such deviate eye conditions in any direction, whether stemming from refractive, muscular, neurological, or hysterical causes, and whether present permanently or occasionally.

Since visual acuity defects may indeed affect reading, at least for some children, teachers must make sure that children are routinely screened for visual defects. Typical acuity assessment tools are discussed in Chapter 14.

AUDITORY ACUITY

Auditory acuity refers to the physical ability to hear; it is defined by Harris and Hodges (1981, p. 25) as the "keenness or sensitivity of hearing." Dechant and Smith (1977, p. 138) describe two kinds of auditory acuity deficiencies that may be important in learning to read: *tone deafness* and *intensity deafness*. A tone-deaf person lacks the ability to discriminate between pitches. A high-tone loss is more likely to affect a child's ability to hear and distinguish consonant speech sounds, while low-tone losses are more likely to affect the ability to hear vowel sounds. Articulation may be affected in either case. Obviously, such losses may interfere with learning that involves intensive phonics or other aural instruction.

Intensity deficiency may be of three types: central deafness, conductive loss, and nerve loss. Central deafness involves either damage to the auditory areas of the brain or a neurotic conversion reaction, known as hysteria. Conductive loss entails impairment in the conductive process in the middle ear. Nerve loss refers to an impairment of the auditory nerve, which affects clarity and thus the intelligibility of speech.

About 5 percent of schoolchildren have a serious hearing loss. Many more have lesser losses, which may become serious if untreated. Acuity losses may affect reading performance through defective discrimination, perception, blending, and auditory memory. Overall, the impact of auditory acuity problems on reading problems appears to be less than that of visual acuity, although it may be substantial if the hearing loss is extreme. The incidence of acuity problems, coupled with the dependence upon listening for learning through oral instruction, warrant attention to acuity in the diagnostic process.

Classroom teachers should refer for testing any children who appear to have hearing problems. Screening children for auditory acuity problems will be discussed in Chapter 14.

SPEECH

Four aspects of speech disorders that are often said to influence language (and ultimately reading) are articulation, fluency, voicing, and language difference (Downing and Leong 1982, pp. 130–34). Voicing problems, (the failure to vibrate the vocal cords for certain speech sounds, such as /d/ and /b/), are less common than articulatory and fluency problems and will not be discussed here. Language differences were discussed above.

In general, the relationship between speech disorders and reading difficulties is not clearcut. Speech problems may occur in combination with other factors, such as low intelligence and disadvantaged home environments, which interact with speech in their effect on reading.

All children with speech defects do not have problems with reading, nor does a speech defect necessarily cause a reading problem. Even pronounced speech problems may be present without causing problems with language or thought (Benson 1983). The possibility of an effect on reading is strong enough, however, to merit consideration in diagnostic and instructional procedures.

Articulation problems occur more frequently in children who have difficulty with reading than other types of speech problems. There is some evidence that articulatory defects in young children may be related to subsequent reading problems (Lyle 1970). Six types of articulation disorders are delineated by Downing and Leong (1982, pp. 130–31):

1. *Lack of maturity.* Children at an early age may not have mastered developmentally all speech sounds.
2. *Misordering of sounds.* This disorder may be caused by faulty perception in hearing or because another pattern is produced more easily; *aminal* for *animal*, for example.
3. *Omissions.* Phonemes are omitted from words, such as *do* for *dog*.
4. *Substitutions.* Phonemes are substituted one for another. Common substitutions are /k/ for /t/, /b/ for /v/, /f/ for /th/, /th/ for /s/, /w/ for /l/ or /r/.

5. *Distortions.* These sounds differ from substitutions in that they are not normally produced in the child's dialect group.
6. *Additions.* A phoneme is added, such as /furog/ for /frog/. This defect is less prevalent than other types of errors.

Articulation problems influence reading in that confusion occurs between what learners hear when they make given sounds and what they hear when others pronounce the same sounds. When articulation problems accompany reading problems, instructional procedures such as synthetic phonics (which require letter-by-letter sounding and blending) may need to be avoided.

Fluency problems involve *stuttering,* or stammering, and *cluttering.* Teachers are generally familiar with stuttering, which manifests itself as repetitions, prolongations, and hesitations that interfere with the normal flow of speech. Cluttering differs in that the speaker talks so fast that articulatory movements are not controlled with accuracy. This interference results in leaving out or transposing phonemes or syllables especially in medial and final positions.

Downing and Leong (1982, p. 131) cite research that suggests that stuttering may be an effect rather than a cause of reading problems. This finding should alert teachers to adjust their instructional practices when there is reason to believe that this has happened. Oral reading should be avoided unless the stutterer volunteers for it.

NEUROLOGICAL DYSFUNCTION

Neurological dysfunction has been used to refer to both serious brain dysfunctions (such as cerebral palsy, strokes, or aphasia, which make learning to read difficult if not impossible) and to mild brain damage. Several labels have also been given to *suspected* damage in the absence of confirmed pathological diagnoses. These include maturational lag, developmental dyslexia, minimal brain damage, primary retardation, and attentional deficit disorders.

The identification of brain damage is clearly the province of medically trained personnel. Teachers and clinicians are cautioned not to make such diagnoses; their role is to make referrals instead. Referrals may be made first to the child's pediatrician if he or she has had experience with both brain-damaged and normal children. This physician, in turn, may refer the child to a neurologist.

The decision of the classroom teacher to refer a child is generally made on the basis of direct observation and other available data. Harris and Sipay (1985, pp. 270–71) suggest that a referral may be based on evidence of "a history of difficult birth as indicated by prolonged labor, instrumental delivery, marked deformity of the head, difficulty in starting breathing, cyanosis, difficulty in sucking and swallowing, and so on; prematurity or low birth weight; poor equilibrium and general awkwardness; delayed speech development in the presence of otherwise normal mental ability; a history of convulsive seizures or lapses of consciousness; extreme restlessness; and distractibility."

Among the diagnostic procedures used by neurologists are the electroencephalogram (EEG) and its modifications. An EEG involves measuring electrical activity in the brain through electrodes placed at various points on the scalp. The electrical activity is recorded on moving graph paper. A specific relationship between EEG results and reading problems has not been specifically demonstrated (Benton 1975). Results of such procedures should be a part of the reading diagnostic process only when a neurologist specifically recommends it.

A modification of the EEG procedure is a brain electrical activity mapping (BEAM) procedure (Duffy et al. 1971), which has been said to be 80–90 percent accurate in distinguishing between normal children and those labeled dyslexic. The researchers state that measurements derived from topographic brain maps are consistent and can have diagnostic validity. They also note that the data may not be sufficiently specific to permit clinical differentiation of reading problems from other learning disabilities, but suggest that someday neurophysiological testing may prove as useful in learning disabilities as it now is in epilepsy.

A major problem for teachers is that specific remediation plans still must generally be made from an analysis of reading behaviors. In educational practice, this means that diagnoses of neurological problems are not precise enough to permit the development of specific remediation plans from the data. In fact, some writers such as Black (1976) state that remedial reading programs should not be based on a *probable* neurological condition, but rather on the reading skills needed by the learner.

This is not to suggest that neurological problems are not important; they may well be. Unless brain lesions are very severe, however, they often do not retard learning. Many children with verifiable brain damage make good progress in reading (Geneva Medico-Educational Service, 1968, pp. 158–71).

LATERALITY

Lateral dominance refers to the preferred use and superior functioning of one side of the body (including eye, hand, ear, and foot) over the other. Some persons exhibit crossed dominance. An example of crossed dominance is when the dominant hand and the dominant eye are on the opposite sides of the body. A few persons do not exhibit a preference for use of one side over the opposite side. Mixed handedness is an example of this phenomenon.

Extremely diverse positions about the supposed relationship between laterality and reading may be found in the literature. Some claim a relationship between laterality and reading problems (Orton 1937; Dearborne 1939). In contrast, Weintraub's (1968) review of laterality research based on nonclinical data shows little, if any, relationship between reading achievement and laterality. However, teachers may benefit from a statement by Downing and Leong (1982, p. 338): "While a poorly established laterality pattern . . . by itself does not explain fully reading retardation, this pattern of development in combination with other factors does make the child more vulnerable for learning disorders." The possibility of such a relationship should probably not be completely ruled out by teachers.

Directional confusion, rather than a pattern of lateral dominance, is a significant factor to consider. Directional confusion refers to uncertainty or inconsistency in left-right directionality; it can arise from either physiological or psychological factors and may be present with any pattern of lateral dominance. It is most likely to be present in learners with mixed hand dominance as measured by the Harris Tests of Lateral Dominance (Harris and Sipay, 1985, p. 290).

Directional confusion, accompanied by reversal tendencies, is common at the beginning reading ages. It is generally considered a problem if the child continues to have difficulties after considerable instruction in left-to-right direction in reading and writing has been given.

Teachers should check for mixed handedness, especially in beginning readers. This may be done by simple procedures such as handing the child a pencil or asking her to pick up a ball. The child must have an equal opportunity to respond with either hand. Decisions should be based on observation of several attempts.

General Health

The general state of a learner's health may, of course, affect learning to read. The correlation is not exact, since some learners can compensate for health problems better than others.

Children who are chronically ill (with asthma, heart problems, rheumatic fever, etc.) or malnourished are often unable to sustain attention sufficiently to master learning tasks because their vitality is diminished. Prolonged illness resulting in a child's missing school has obvious implications for reading achievement unless an effort is made to make up the work missed (especially skills that are prerequisites to future learning).

There are direct and indirect relationships between nutrition and learning. Direct relationships are those in which the central nervous system is affected by diet; indirect relationships are those in which the body's innate capacity to learn is affected by diet. Research in countries with severely deprived populations has shown that children who have protein-poor diets are less able to learn, have lower IQ scores, and exhibit poorer language than those children who have adequate protein (Pertz and Putnam 1982).

Glandular disturbances may affect success with reading. Thyroid problems are particularly debilitating. A thyroid deficiency may result in obesity and mental sluggishness; symptoms of excessive thyroid activity are weight loss, overactivity, irritability, and fatigue. Any learner suspected of having a glandular condition or other general health problem should be referred to a health care specialist. Often a good beginning place is the school nurse. Cooperation of parents or guardians is needed in order to make referrals to physicians.

Teachers are cautioned that health problems may often be found in children from disadvantaged homes and that children who are on drugs, whether prescribed or illicit, may be unable to function properly in the classroom.

INFORMATION TO CONSIDER

1. Although visual acuity defects may interfere with reading ability in some children, many children with visual defects learn to read as well and sometimes better than other children without visual problems.
2. The interaction of auditory acuity problems with reading is particularly significant if phonics is used as a major part of the instructional program.
3. When articulation problems are present, instructional procedures such as synthetic phonics (which requires letter-by-letter sounding and blending) should probably be avoided.
4. Speech defects are more significantly related to reading aloud than to silent reading. Instructional procedures should be modified to focus more on silent reading than on oral reading with students who have problems with speech, especially fluency.
5. It is possible for many children with verifiable brain damage to make good progress in reading.
6. Corrective and remedial programs for children with a neurological dysfunction should be based, in general, on the reading skill deficiency.
7. Teachers should give attention to problems of directional confusion.
8. Teachers should be cognizant of a child's general health. Nutrition, rest, medication, and glandular functions can affect performance in the classroom.

Summary

In this chapter, a discussion of language, culture, and physical correlates of reading problems has been presented. Much of the data for these correlates has been generated from correlational studies. Caution is needed in assuming cause-effect relationships from such data. The research and theory base, however, does permit some generalizations that teachers should consider in the diagnostic and instructional processes.

Language differences have a strong bearing on reading success. Children with language differences will generally not become problem readers if an appropriate instructional program is developed for them. Teachers' attitudes toward language differences are probably more significant in affecting learning than are the actual differences themselves.

The cultural milieu also affects reading achievement. The culture from which the child comes shapes his values, beliefs, mores, and traditions. Teachers need to understand how these factors may relate to reading success. For instance, the home environment bears a strong affective and cognitive influence on the child. Language competence, also related to reading achievement, may be the most important among the socioeconomic factors. More boys than girls in the United States and Canada have reading problems; the cause of this disparity is more likely cultural than maturational.

The physical factors presented in this chapter were visual acuity, auditory acuity, speech, neurological dysfunction, laterality, and general health. Research findings were generally mixed and were interpreted cautiously. However, each of these factors should be considered in diagnostic procedures, since they may be interfering with reading progress for some children.

Questions for Further Thought

1. Which of the correlates discussed in this chapter do you consider underemphasized by teachers in diagnostic and instructional processes?
2. Can teachers effectively assess language and cultural correlates? If so, how?
3. Which, if any, of the correlate areas need a stronger research base before the information will be valid enough to be used effectively by teachers?
4. If schools are contributing to the incidence of problem readers in lower socioeconomic classes, how can this situation be reversed?

Activities and Projects

1. Choose one of the correlate areas discussed in this chapter. Read the most recent research you can find on this correlate. Be prepared to discuss how your reading has refined your understanding.
2. Visit a reading supervisor in a school system. Find out how the correlates discussed in this chapter are assessed and what attention is given to the results.
3. Assume you are the special teacher of

reading for the school in which you teach. You are discussing with classroom teachers the relationship of language competence to the development of reading ability. What information would you include in your discussion?

4. Complete the task described in #3 above for any of the other correlates in this chapter.

5. Visit a remedial reading teacher. Find out what procedures are being utilized to maximize the effectiveness of the home support system for alleviating the reading problems of the children in the school.

4

Teachers and Teaching: Concepts of Effectiveness

In Chapters 2 and 3, affective, cognitive, language, cultural, and physical factors that affect a child's success in learning to read to potential were discussed. These factors are not the only determinants of reading success, however. There is no doubt that the teacher and the instructional environment also play an important role, one that should never be underestimated. As Wallace Ramsey (1962) has stated, "Given a good teacher, other factors in teaching reading tend to pale to insignificance." An effective teacher can maximize students' strengths and minimize their weaknesses in ways that reduce or eliminate the discrepancy between achievement and potential. Both what the teacher *is* and what the teacher *does* can make a difference in initial success in reading and in the correction of reading problems.

Research evidence has long suggested that teachers make a difference in instructional outcomes. In 1937, Gates concluded that correlations between mental age and achievement were highest in those classes that were identified as having good instruction and lowest in those in which the instruction was identified as the poorest. He also stated that the correlations seemed "to vary directly with the effectiveness of the provision for individual differences . . ." (p. 507). The United States Office of Education conducted extensive research on first-grade reading instruction in the 1960s. The major conclusion from this series of research studies, commonly referred to as the First Grade Studies (Bond and Dykstra 1967), was that the teacher was a more important factor in learning to read than were the methods, materials, and organizational practices used. There was a greater difference in achievement among the students of different teachers than there was among students who were instructed with different methods or materials (Bond and Dykstra 1967).

Although such evidence indicates that the teacher does indeed make a difference, the specific teacher characteristics that account for this are still being actively investigated. Teacher characteristics have been viewed several ways. Through the 1970s, much of the data have been based on correlational studies, with student achievement as the criterion; that is, the focus has been on the process-product of reading instruction (instructional practices, achievement tests, mastery tests, etc.) rather than on such topics as teachers' intentions, goals, judgments, and decision-making strategies (Rupley, Wise, and Logan 1986).

A pervasive problem of limited generalizability has surrounded much of the research on teacher effectiveness. Studies have often been based on limited populations (such as learners with reading or math problems), which may not be representative. In evaluating such research, current teachers should be aware of and concerned about the populations studied and about the interactions of teacher behaviors and the environmental contexts in which the studies were conducted.

After providing strong evidence that teachers affect instructional outcomes, Brophy (1979) suggests that there is no support for the notion of generic teaching skills, and that few, if any, of the behaviors identified in research are appropriate in all contexts. It is from this viewpoint that this chapter should be read. The concepts presented in this chapter should not be viewed as the basis for a checklist against which all teachers of reading should be evaluated. All concepts may not be appropriate to every reading instructional environment. Nevertheless, teachers should consider which of the concepts might relate to their particular teaching situation.

What Effective Reading Teachers *Are*

QUESTIONS TO GUIDE READING

Recall Question
1. What are twelve important personal teacher characteristics presented in this chapter as possible influences on student learning?

Thinking Question
1. Should affective characteristics of teachers and the learning environment be considered more important than the instructional strategies or techniques they use?

Several lists of positive teacher characteristics have been cited in the literature. These lists have tended to be general in nature and have combined both personal and institutional dimensions. Humphrey (1971) has listed the following necessary qualities for teachers of remedial readers:

- enthusiasm
- patience
- optimism
- sensitivity
- organization
- dedication
- confidence
- intelligence
- knowledge

These characteristics—many of them *affective* in nature—could be suggested for teaching any subject.

Ruddell and Haggard (1982) examined characteristics of teachers who had been identified as influential by former students. These teachers were asked what they believed to be the basis for the perceived influence on their former students. They found that the teachers listed personal characteristics as most important (48 percent). When these teachers were asked to identify the distinguishing traits of their own most significant teachers, personal characteristics again headed the list (44 percent). In examining what these influential teachers believed important to good teaching, Ruddell and Haggard categorized their responses in the following manner:

- personal characteristics   47%
- understands learner potential   18%
- attitude toward school   18%
- quality of instruction   16%
- life adjustment   1%

Note the high percentage of personal and affective characteristics.

Personal characteristics (what good teachers *are*) interact with teacher behavior; they are basic to good teaching in general and to the teaching of reading in particular. The effectiveness of specific strategies, techniques, and methods discussed in later chapters seem to be dependent, in part, on such characteristics.

The following twelve characteristics are vital to effective reading teachers:

Effective reading teachers are teachers who read. The importance of modeling (being seen reading, talking about what has been read) cannot be overemphasized. Liking to read can be contagious. If children feel positive toward the teacher and see the teacher reading, then reading may become a more valued activity for that child. Reading teachers should be seen reading by children, and should share what they are reading with them—but only if the teacher genuinely likes to read. If children perceive that the teacher is recommending an activity that he does not really like, then the end result could be negative rather than positive.

Effective reading teachers have a positive sense of self-worth, especially about helping others. Reading teachers must be good helpers if they are to aid children with reading problems. Combs, Avila, and Purkey (1971, p. 14) found several characteristics that distinguished good helpers from those less capable of helping others:

a. *Identification*—believing that one is identified with people rather than separated from them.

b. *Trustworthiness*—having faith in one's ability to be responsible and deal effectively with situations.

c. *Wanted*—believing that one is generally accepted by others and is likable and personable.

d. *Worthiness*—believing that one is worthy of respect and has dignity as a human being.

Effective reading teachers are knowledgeable. They understand what is involved in learning to read, how to teach reading, and how reluctant or problem readers may be motivated. They understand that reading is a skill that has both affective and cognitive bases. They are aware of the relationship of differing cultural and linguistic backgrounds to learning to read, and realize that physical and home problems may interfere with the learning process.

Effective reading teachers have a genuine affection for learners, apparent in both word and deed. Verbalized affection is useless if nonverbal behavior indicates a different attitude. Negative nonverbal behaviors, such as shrugging the shoulders, frowning, or delaying in providing assistance with a reading task, especially when a student has requested help, are all *read* by learners.

Effective reading teachers are enthusiastic and communicate their enthusiasm to problem readers. They have a lively, absorbing interest in what they are doing and they show it. Teacher enthusiasm has been found to be positively correlated with student achievement scores (Rosenshine and Furst 1971). Hamachek (1975, p. 303) has concluded from a comprehensive review of the literature that "teacher enthusiasm may be the most powerful characteristic when it comes to effective teaching."

Effective reading teachers accept learners as they are—their feelings, their emotional needs, and their values. Acceptance and understanding is often the most important step in working with problem readers. Most human beings want to be understood; readers with problems are no exception. Children tend to respond most positively when they feel they are accepted as worthwhile human beings. Accepting teachers recognize that value or belief systems for minorities, other ethnic groups, and various socioeconomic levels may differ from their own. They never denigrate these value or belief systems.

Effective reading teachers are open and flexible, giving learners the opportunity to make suggestions regarding their own welfare. Students may make more progress when they can make suggestions about methods, materials, and the correction of their own deficiencies. Good teachers avoid being too authoritarian, although they keep in mind that they are in charge and ultimately responsible for the learning environment.

Effective reading teachers are warm and cooperative. In today's classrooms, where drill on skills seems to be the order of the day, it is still possible to have a climate that is warm and comfortable rather than harsh and authoritarian. Classrooms in many of the institutions that have been identified as "effective schools" had warm, cooperative, convivial environments (Berliner and Rosenshine 1977).

Effective reading teachers have confidence in the learner's ability to improve her reading skill. Such teachers expect that their students will learn (Baumann 1984). A basic task of the teacher is to communicate his or her belief to the student with reading problems. Teachers should not be biased by the opinions of previous teachers or by remarks made in a child's cumulative folder. It is a rare child, indeed, who cannot make some progress.

Effective reading teachers are empathetic, not sympathetic. Students with reading problems do not need teachers who feel sorry for them and tell them so; they need teachers who understand their problems and who demonstrate their sincere care by helping students find solutions to their reading problems.

Effective reading teachers value diversity in learners. The effective teacher does not seek to make all learners alike in terms of reading skill development; such efforts breed mediocrity. Good teachers help each student reach his potential and help him develop proficiency in areas of special interest.

Effective reading teachers are structured and consistent in behavior. An orderly, teacher-directed instructional setting is important; such environments, however, should be tempered with warmth and praise (Solomon and Kendall 1976). In the Solomon and Kendall study, permissiveness, spontaneity, and pupil choice of activities were found to be negatively related to achievement and to pupil self-esteem. When teachers are structured and consistent in behavior, students know what to expect and what to do. They know what the routines are, and that once established they will be maintained with fairness. Pupil attitudes also tend to be more favorable in an orderly environment (Harris 1979).

INFORMATION TO CONSIDER

1. The personal characteristics of a teacher are vital for effective working relationships with children who have reading problems.
2. Teachers who *read* themselves serve as models for children.
3. Some important personal teacher characteristics are a positive self-concept, knowledge of the reading process and how to teach reading,

genuine liking for children, enthusiasm, acceptance of others, confidence in a learner's ability to achieve, empathy, and consistency in dealing with others.

What Effective Reading Teachers *Do*

QUESTIONS TO GUIDE READING

Recall Questions
1. What are the twenty "Do" characteristics that teachers who help problem readers should consider?
2. What are five motivational techniques that may be helpful when working with problem readers?
3. What are some specific competencies for effective diagnostic teachers of reading, according to Guszak?
4. How does Harris organize a 45-minute remedial lesson?

Thinking Questions
1. Why may a certain teacher behavior work well in general, but not always provide the needed spark for a given problem reader?
2. Why are students' attitudes so important in a corrective or remedial program?
3. Why is it important for reading teachers to work with parents and other members of the professional staff?
4. Why is the prevention of reading difficulties so important?
5. How may a teacher's personal characteristics interact with good teaching behaviors in ways that facilitate learning?

In addition to the personal and affective teacher characteristics discussed in the previous section, what the reading teacher *does* in the instructional setting can also make a significant difference in reading growth. In this section, teacher behaviors will be described that have been shown to help readers with problems. Teachers are cautioned that while a given behavior, strategy, or organizational pattern may work well with most children, it may not always provide the needed impetus for a specific student.

Effective reading teachers should consider attitudes basic to the improvement of reading problems. The assessment of pupil attitudes is a crucial first step in planning programs for problem readers. Pescosolido (1962) found that the determination of pupil attitudes toward reading had a significant relationship to growth in reading.

Effective classroom teachers must also demonstrate in their behavior that they have a commitment to developing positive attitudes toward reading. Heathington and Alexander (1984) found that primary grade teachers ranked the development of attitudes second in importance only to comprehension check as an activity in helping students read. However, data from the same study suggested that while attitudes are recognized by teachers as important, they are not always a priority in reading programs.

Effective reading teachers determine an appropriate instructional level for their readers in relationship to specific materials before they assign the materials to be read. If students are to make progress, instruction must be on a level that students can handle without feeling frustrated or bored. The material (both general reading and content area), the tasks assigned, and the instructional language of the teacher must be neither so difficult that students lose interest nor so easy that they feel they are not being challenged. The appropriateness of each task and each material assigned should be considered in terms of its fit with reader abilities. Ways teachers may approximate instructional level are presented in Chapter 5.

Effective reading teachers do only those assessments essential to getting instruction underway at the beginning of the instructional experience. That is, students should not be subjected to several days or weeks of testing prior to the beginning of instruction. Children can receive too much testing in a short period of time; such practice can harm attitudes and interests, particularly for those students who have had little prior success.

The amount of initial assessment will depend on whether the student is being diagnosed by the classroom teacher, reading teacher, or a clinician in a reading clinic. In the classroom setting, for example, the teacher may first determine proper "book fit" (that is, the book best suited for instructional use) and start students reading. Then, as instruction progresses, specific skill strengths and weaknesses can be assessed and attitudes and interests can be observed. The diagnostic teaching of lessons can also provide valuable information. Using such procedures, it is possible to consider students' feelings—their likes and dislikes about content, skills taught, and organizational patterns.

In a clinical setting, the diagnostician may only see the student two or three brief testing sessions. In such situations, it is necessary to complete all essential assessments during these sessions. It is possible, and often probable, that the diagnostician will not follow up with instruction but will make detailed recommendations for others. In this event the suggestions should be based on as complete a data base as possible.

Effective reading teachers diagnose both reading strengths and weaknesses. Students with reading problems are aware that they have shortcomings. Because these weaknesses have often been a focal point in their lives, they may understandably have a negative attitude toward corrective instruction. Diagnostic procedures are designed to point out weaknesses, but they can also be used to identify strengths. It is better to tell a child (or a parent) that he did well in several identified areas before describing other areas that need attention.

Areas of strength also provide a positive rather than a negative base on which to build an instructional program. A part of each corrective session should involve activities on a level at which the child can succeed. When this happens, the child is generally more willing to work on overcoming weaknesses.

Effective reading teachers establish manageable goals that can be measured. Establishing measurable goals and objectives was identified as a distinguishing feature of quality elementary reading programs by the American Institute for Research, an arm of the Right-to-Read Office of the U.S. Office of Education (Rupley 1976).

Goals should be challenging, obtainable, and clearly communicated to the child. Children with reading problems need a clear idea of what they are expected to accomplish, and they need to know when they have accomplished a goal. The goals set should relate to both strengths and weaknesses. Those relating to weaknesses should be chosen in terms of their immediate usefulness to school-related tasks and should, of course, be based on prerequisite skill and knowledge bases.

The number of goals set should be small, perhaps three to five. This number would enable the learner to concentrate attention on each goal frequently so that learning can be reinforced and skill performance can become automatic.

Effective reading teachers select materials appropriate to learner goals, needs, levels of performance, and interests. Materials should be viewed as instructional aids and not, as is sometimes the case, the curriculum. As teaching/learning aids, materials should be selected according to the student's attitudes and interests, the nature of the reading problem, the age and achievement level of the learner, the ease of use, and the content and readability of the materials.

Research suggests that when there is doubt about the appropriateness of various levels in graded materials, the easier of the levels should be chosen. Cooper (1952) found (in grades 2–6) that the easier a basal reader was for a child, the greater the progress made during that year. This finding was true for all ability levels. There is an affective advantage as well to choosing the easier of two levels: it is more positive to move a child up to a more difficult level than down to a lower level.

Effective reading teachers organize instructional time in ways that children can function efficiently in the instructional setting. According to Guthrie, Seifert, and Kline (1978), a reading program should be of sufficient length to yield permanent gains. In discussing program length for remedial situations, they noted that research indicates that a minimum of fifty contact hours is necessary (based on studies in which the pupil-teacher ratio was not more than 1:4). Gains come slowly for many problem readers, especially for those who have experienced much failure.

Scheduling of instruction should be flexible, with differing patterns emerging as the need arises. For example, with readers who have severe problems it may be necessary to give only individual attention in the beginning stages, later moving to a group situation of two students with similar needs and interests. A group of five or six may be a maximum for efficient learning when reading problems exist.

Teachers must also carefully determine the length of a reading session. Although a relationship has been found between length of reading period and achievement (Berliner 1981), more is not always better; children do become fatigued. Teachers need to determine the most effective time length for individual children or groups of children. Shorter, more frequent periods of instruction, possibly on a daily basis, may be more appropriate for younger children in the primary grades. Three remedial periods per week may produce adequate growth in the intermediate grades.

Effective reading teachers provide teacher-directed, task-oriented instruction. They utilize time well. Rosenshine and Furst (1971), summarizing research findings from approximately fifty studies on the relationship of teacher performance to student achievement, found that one of the teacher behaviors significantly correlated with achievement scores was the degree to which the teacher was task-oriented. When teachers are task-oriented, direct instruction on their part is the rule rather than the exception. Effective teachers are actively involved in helping students as they work both independently and in groups (Medley 1977).

Instructional time should be academic learning time; that is, the students should be paying attention to and participating in the task at hand. Such academic learning time has been found to be related to achievement (Berliner 1981).

Effective teachers provide minimal transition time between activities and keep the lesson at a brisk pace. Good and Beckerman (1978) found that teachers whose lessons were briskly paced obtained higher achievement gains. Such management behaviors as minimal transition time and pacing not only lead to greater achievement but also to fewer discipline problems (Baumann 1984).

Effective reading teachers often use a test-teach-retest-reteach (if necessary) model when working with children who have specific skills deficiencies. In this model, a diagnostic evaluation is made of the student's proficiency with a given skill, direct instructional teaching strategies are used to teach the skill, and follow-up evaluation is done to determine if the skill has been learned. If the skill has not been learned, reteaching should follow, with a second evaluation of instruction. In using this model, teachers need a variety of materials and techniques so that students may work at acquiring the skill with various materials and perhaps with modified techniques. Changes in materials and modification of techniques may, in themselves, serve as catalysts for improvement. It is also important that teachers pace skill instruction in a logical sequence of closely related steps, following drill with application in connected discourse.

Even if the student appears to master the skill after the first teaching sequence, a check on the skill at a later time is appropriate to assess for retention. This procedure is especially important for learners of lower mental ability.

Effective reading teachers plan strategies to correct specific reading problems. Such instruction must often be highly individualized. Planning for individual needs may mean setting up a program specifically for a given individual, or it may mean planning for a group when several students need work on the same skill or when interaction among students is desired.

In planning individualized programs, teachers should consider the learner's skill strengths and weaknesses; his attitudes and interests; the nature of the task to be completed; the instructional resources available; and the methods, strategies, and techniques to be used. There are no methods, strategies, or techniques that work well with *all* individuals or groups. Teachers should continually evaluate their instructional program, and be ready to make changes to ensure that both the cognitive and affective growth dimensions of learners are being addressed.

Effective reading teachers use diagnostic teaching procedures. Diagnosis in the instructional setting should be continuous and dynamic. In the diagnostic teaching process, the teacher gathers information on student strengths and weaknesses during each instructional session. On the basis of such information it may be necessary to modify instructional practices and materials.

Diagnostic teaching does not mean that teachers must be continually *testing;* rather, it implies an alertness of the part of the teacher to the performance and needs of the learner. While testing and behavioral observation are useful in determining learners' needs, they are more likely to uncover symptoms than to suggest the intrinsic reasons for a reading difficulty. Direct teaching of unlearned skills must follow testing and observation to help teachers determine whether the pupil is unable to learn the skill or whether her prerequisite information or instruction has been adequate.

Effective diagnostic teaching requires a high level of knowledge and hard work on the part of the teacher. Teachers need to know skill sequences, how affect relates to learning, and how to plan and evaluate each instructional session. Guszak (1978, Ch. 3) has identified some specific competencies for effective diagnostic teachers showing that they

- know the objectives of reading instruction;
- can utilize a sequence of relatively simple determiners of pupils' reading levels, their potential, and their skill needs;
- can prescribe instructional tasks and structure the learning environment in terms of the learner's goals and needs; and
- can organize materials, time, and learners in order to facilitate instruction.

Effective reading teachers use appropriate motivational techniques. These teachers ascertain the most efficient motivators for given learners in given situations. A motivator for one learner or group of learners in one situation may not work for other learners or in another situation.

Drill exercises are frequently viewed by readers with problems as dull, boring, or unnecessary. However, motivation can generally be heightened when the drill periods are short and interspersed with other types of reading activities, when they are individualized in terms of learner needs, and when the child knows he is making progress.

Effective reading teachers enable their students to be successful on a regular basis. This does not mean that the tasks should not be challenging, but rather that teachers should provide an opportunity for success, both with the amount of work to be done and with the task to be completed. Students do not progress satisfactorily when they are in a failure situation or when they are blamed in negative ways for their lack of success.

Effective reading teachers consider student error rates on assigned materials and tasks. Error rate should be low in guided or independent practice; in guided practice, Rosenshine and Stevens (1984, p. 788) recommend a success rate of 80 percent. Some children may need a higher rate to feel successful, while others may be able to tolerate a lower rate if they can see that they are making progress. Success rate seems to be particularly important in the primary grades (Rosenshine and Stevens 1984, p. 789).

The instructional context of the assigned task makes a difference also. For example, an error rate of 75 percent may be acceptable for comprehension of story material, while a rate of 90–100% may be more appropriate for practice on word recognition skills. Teachers should also remember that children can learn through making errors.

Effective reading teachers use praise and encouragement (Medley 1977). However, praise should always be *genuinely* deserved. Teachers lose credibility when they praise students for a poor or inadequate effort. Praise should not be overdone (Anderson et al. 1979), and should be focused on the child's acceptable performance of a given task. Negative teacher behaviors such as harsh criticism, sarcasm, and other signs of strong disapproval should be avoided.

Teachers are cautioned that students' perception of praise may differ. In Morine-Dershimer's (1982) study, for example, students' reactions to praise seemed to be a function of achievement level and level of participation in class activities. Praise was viewed as a reward by high achievement/high participation students, whereas children with low achievement/ low participation saw it as an instructional tool rather than as a reward.

Effective reading teachers provide appropriate feedback to students. Feedback is more effective when correct responses are followed by brief comments that affirm the correctness of the response. Feedback may be in the form of another question (Rosenshine and Stevens 1984, p. 788). With incorrect responses, the teacher may wish to ask sustaining questions that give hints or rephrase in simpler terms. They may also reteach the material through further explanation.

Effective reading teachers employ strategies that help learners cope with content-area materials. It is not enough to work with basic reading skills and with purely narrative, descriptive materials. Teachers must help students learn and apply the skills needed in other areas of the curriculum. It is important that special teachers of reading work with content-area teachers to help accomplish this goal. Chapter 12 provides information on working with study skills and content-area materials.

Effective reading teachers work toward preventing reading problems. A major goal of reading instruction should be the prevention of reading difficulties. When problems, or potential problems, are detected early and corrective measures are taken, more serious problems may be prevented. Prevention could lessen the need for remedial instruction in the intermediate grades, to the learner's personal and educational advantage. In addition, prevention can decrease expense and concern to the school, and spare the student emotional problems (and possibly the temptation to drop out.)

Considering the learner's readiness at *each* and *every* stage in the development of fluent reading is especially important in preventing problems. When there is a mismatch between the task and the student's readiness to perform it, a potential exists for the development of reading problems. The prevention of mismatches means that programs must be individualized.

Initial assessment, formal or informal, and diagnostic teaching are crucial to the prevention process. Where discrepancies exist between the reading program and the needs of the student, corrective procedures should be initiated immediately.

Effective reading teachers cooperate with other professionals who deal with problem readers. It is especially important that the classroom teacher and the special teacher of reading work together to maximize the effectiveness of instruction. Classroom teachers also need to cooperate with reading leaders (principals, supervisors, consultants, and building leaders) who assist them in their efforts. When the building leader is strong and knowledgeable, the chances for an effective school program is greater (Hoffman and Rutherford 1984).

Cooperation is not always found between reading specialists and classroom teachers. In Cohen, Intili, and Robbins's (1978) study of cooperation between these two groups, 49.3 percent of the teachers stated that special teachers of reading provided classroom teachers with no services other than instructing students. Only 20 percent of the classroom teachers reported receiving diagnostic feedback, suggestions, or materials from the special reading teacher at least once a week; and only 10 percent reported receiving help as often as twice a week.

Perhaps the most important cooperative effort is in developing mutually supportive goals among all professionals working with given problem readers. Common goals reduce duplication of effort and help ensure that the skills taught by one teacher are reinforced by another. Working together also helps eliminate conflicting methodologies and types of materials.

Cooperative planning is aided by having the special teacher of reading work in the classroom with the classroom teacher. This permits each to draw on the instructional strengths of the other, eliminates overlap in instruction, and permits joint evaluation of learner behaviors.

Effective reading teachers utilize parents in the prevention and correction of reading difficulties. Parents have long been overlooked as a valuable ally in the prevention and correction of reading problems. There should be a two-way flow of information between parents and the school.

Teachers should work cautiously and wisely with parents of children with reading problems, especially since attitudes toward school and toward teachers have a firm base in the home. Parents must not become negative toward their children and must not apply pressure on their children to the degree that the children become fearful or frustrated. Such feelings work in a negative way in the remediation process.

INFORMATION TO CONSIDER

1. Certain teacher behaviors can make a difference in helping children who have reading problems.
2. There are no teacher behaviors that are guaranteed to work with all students.
3. Teacher behaviors that often work include:
    a. considering students' attitudes toward reading
    b. determining appropriate instructional levels
    c. avoiding unnecessary assessments
    d. diagnosing pupils' strengths and weaknesses
    e. establishing manageable, measurable goals
    f. selecting appropriate materials
    g. organizing instructional time efficiently
    h. providing teacher-directed, task-oriented instruction that is appropriately paced
    i. using a test-teach-retest-reteach (if needed) method when working with specific skill deficiencies
    j. planning for correcting specific reading problems
    k. using diagnostic teaching procedures
    l. using effective motivational techniques
    m. ensuring success on a regular basis
    n. considering the effects of error rate
    o. using praise appropriately

p. providing effective feedback
q. helping students cope with content-area tasks
r. working to prevent reading difficulties
s. working with other professionals to solve children's reading problems
t. utilizing parents in working with children with reading problems.

Summary

There are many strategies and procedures that teachers may use to help make a difference in reading achievement. What works with one learner or group of learners or in one situation may not work with others.

In this chapter, two pervasive concepts affecting learning to read were discussed: what effective reading teachers *are* and what effective reading teachers *do*.

Among those factors related to what teachers *are*, the following were discussed: knowledge about reading, a genuine acceptance of children, optimism, acceptance of learners, openness and flexibility, warmth and cooperativeness, confidence in growth potential in learners, empathy, valuing diversity in learners, and consistency in behavior. The importance of the teacher's own self-concept and of his or her own reading behaviors were also highlighted.

Among the areas that were discussed in relation to what teachers *do* were: affect, instructional reading levels, amount of assessment, pupil strengths and weaknesses, goals that are manageable and measurable, use of appropriate materials, efficiently organized instructional time, attention to specific skill needs, consideration for error rates, teacher-directed instruction that is task-oriented, use of praise, appropriate feedback, brisk pacing, diagnostic teaching procedures, effective motivational strategies, provision for success on a regular basis, assistance with skills for content-area reading, and working with parents and other professionals in the prevention or correction of reading problems.

Questions for Further Thought

1. Are there additional characteristics of effective teachers that you think are important? Why?
2. Are there additional behaviors that effective reading teachers exhibit that might facilitate the prevention or correction of reading difficulties?
3. How can a teacher ensure that cooperation will take place among involved teachers and with parents?

Activities and Projects

1. Visit a reading teacher who you feel is successful. What characteristics does she possess? What does the teacher *do* in the instructional setting that seems to make a difference?
2. Visit a school with an effective parent involvement program. What are the components of the program? Why does it work?
3. Visit a school that uses a team approach to the prevention and/or correction of reading problems. How does the program work? Is it viewed as successful? Why?
4. Read "Classroom Instruction in Reading" by Barak Rosenshine and Robert Stevens, in *Handbook of Reading Research*, ed. P. David Pearson (New York: Longmans, 1984). Describe how this reading refined your understanding of the classroom instructional concepts presented in this chapter.
5. Read "Research in Effective Teaching: An Overview of Its Development" by William H. Rupley, Beth S. Wise, and John W. Logan, in *Effective Teaching of Reading: Research and Practice*, ed. James V. Hoffman (Newark, Del.: International Reading Association, 1986). Outline the current direction of teacher effectiveness research.

II
Classroom Assessment

If teachers are to help students with reading problems, they need knowledge of what those problems are. In this section of our book, we focus on ways teachers can assess reading strengths and weaknesses, both through informal classroom assessment and through norm- and criterion-referenced assessments.

Assessment refers to the act of gathering data in order to better understand an area of concern. Data gathering may be done through such means as observation, interviews, and tests. *Diagnosis* is a broader concept than assessment; it is a form of evaluation based on multiple assessments (of reading, for example, or reading-related behaviors). Diagnosis entails making judgments about the adequacy of performance and the factors that impinge on this performance; it involves data gathering and the formation of hypotheses. The assessment tools presented in this section are helpful in the diagnosis of reading problems.

Chapter 5 focuses primarily on informal classroom assessment. Considerable attention is given to ways that teachers may approximate instructional reading levels, using such tools as informal reading inventories, group reading inventories, and cloze and maze procedures. Commercial informal reading inventories and basal reader placement tests are also discussed.

In Chapter 6, the focus is on commercial tests that help teachers assess students' reading strengths and weaknesses. Two major categories are discussed—norm-referenced tests and criterion-referenced tests. Much attention is devoted to the selection of such tests, what the scores mean, and how the scores may be presented to parents.

5

Informal Classroom Assessment

Informal classroom assessment generally refers to the collecting of data for diagnosing reading strengths and weaknesses and for planning instructional programs to help overcome reading problems. Informal assessments include observation, interviewing, teacher-devised tests, checklists, and rating scales. These assessments provide data regarding "ecologically valid" behaviors; that is, behaviors in actual reading situations in the classroom. The information gathered here can be used in conjunction with, and often in lieu of, commercially developed norm-referenced and criterion-referenced tests. When well devised, informal assessments can provide a sound basis for many instructional decisions.

The first section of this chapter is devoted to a discussion of general principles that should guide teachers in assessing reading problems. The second section focuses on assessment of individual students' reading proficiency. The third section addresses procedures for group assessments.

The procedures discussed in this chapter will not provide all the data needed for effective assessment of reading proficiency. They often do not give enough information about specific skill strengths and weaknesses or about affective areas. Informal assessment procedures that assist in identifying specific skill strengths and weaknesses are discussed under the specific skills or areas in question (see Chapters 7–12). For example, ways to assess word recognition are presented in Chapter 9.

General Principles of Assessment

QUESTIONS TO GUIDE READING

Recall Question
1. What are the fourteen guidelines that should be considered in the assessment of reading problems?

Thinking Question

1. Which of the fourteen guidelines do you consider most crucial for the classroom teacher? Why? For the Chapter I teacher or reading clinician? Why?

The assessment of reading problems is a complex process, and should be guided by principles that help ensure the validity of the information gathering and decision making. The principles outlined below apply both to the informal procedures discussed in this chapter and to norm-referenced and criterion-referenced assessments, discussed in Chapter 6 and later.

1. Assessment should be made of both affective and cognitive factors since a child's reading potential is dependent on both. In schools, greater attention is generally given to cognitive factors, with little consideration (sometimes very little) of how students feel about reading or what they prefer to read.

2. Assessment should be continuous. Learners grow in reading abilities in different ways and at different rates. Without ongoing assessment, teachers may not be aware of important changes in their students and thus may not make instructional decisions that will maximally benefit them. Assessments should occur both prior to a new reading experience (to determine readiness) and during the learning situation (as a basis for further planning).

3. Assessment must entail more than measurement of specific reading skill development. Other areas such as language, culture, and physical factors also impinge on reading ability.

4. Every effort should be made to avoid biased assessments, especially in the choice of procedures. For example, one person may believe that most reading problems are related to educational defects; another may believe they stem mainly from emotional problems or perceptual problems. Such beliefs may limit the assessment process to the suspected cause. A variety of assessments are often needed to get a total picture of a child's reading problem.

5. Informal on-the-spot assessment is an appropriate teacher activity. Much can be learned about reading strengths and weaknesses in a natural, typical, ecologically valid setting that may not be available in a formal testing situation. Typical issues that can be addressed in on-the-spot assessment include:

Does the child really utilize specific word recognition strategies in actual practice?

Does the child really seem to like reading?

Is the child really interested in a *specific type* of content?

Such questions are often more easily or validly determined in the normal instructional setting than through special tests designed to assess these areas.

6. Assessments should be made from a variety of sources, both formal and informal. For example, one might ask whether the child who has trouble with inference skills on an informal reading inventory (IRI) also has trouble with these skills in his daily lessons. Or, from another angle, does there seem to be a consistent problem with vowel diphthongs both on tests and in routine daily work? The more instances of a given behavior, the stronger the base for making instructional decisions.

7. Assessment should be done in both individual and group situations. One does not always perform the same in private settings as in a group; teachers need to be aware of these differences in behavior. They should be especially alert to difficulties children have when working in groups. Group participation is an important skill for students to develop, since it is the standard situation for school instruction.

8. Assessments are not ends in themselves. They are justifiable only as an aid to and basis for the instructional decision-making process. Only those tests and procedures that are effective in such a process should be used, and only to the degree necessary to make a reliable determination of reading abilities. Excessive testing can create negative attitudes toward reading, especially if the student views such tests as part of a longstanding pattern of failure.

9. Assessments (tests, techniques, formats, etc.) should be as closely related to instructional procedures and formats as possible. Norm-referenced tests are often not reality-oriented (Ramsey 1967): comprehension on such tests, for example, is often checked by multiple-choice questions on very short passages in a timed situation, whereas in day-to-day classroom instruction comprehension is generally checked by recall questions following the reading of longer passages.

10. Assessments should be made of both strengths and weaknesses. Students should know what they do well and should be encouraged to build on their strengths while they work to overcome weaknesses. The focus on strengths often provides motivation that facilitates work on deficiencies.

11. In addition to assessments of the current status of affective and cognitive strengths and weaknesses, there should be an attempt to diagnose the reasons behind those abilities. Whenever possible, causes of problems should be alleviated or diminished to the point that progress can be made in overcoming the problem. Even though the causes are not always easy to determine precisely (see Chapters 2–3), they should not be ignored, nor should instruction designed to overcome the deficiencies be abandoned or delayed while causes are sought. Instruction to correct specific affective or cognitive deficiencies can begin while efforts continue to determine the underlying causes. Such determination will, of course, usually make correction easier.

12. Good rapport between the person doing the assessment and the student is essential, because rapport can affect test results. Rapport is sometimes easier to establish with the classroom teacher acting as evaluator than with an unfamiliar assessor. Outside clinicians and special teachers of reading should take some time to get to know a student before beginning testing procedures.

13. Assessment tools and procedures should be selected by those who make decisions about instruction rather than by a central administrative edict. Teachers and clinicians have greater insight into the needs of learners and the expectations for them than do "outside" persons, who often have little or no contact with direct instruction.

14. A team approach to assessment should be used when appropriate. Classroom teachers or special reading teachers may not be qualified to administer some prescribed tests, such as individual intelligence tests. Professionals such as school nurses, counselors, school psychologists, and social workers should be utilized to full advantage. A team approach is often particularly valuable in a clinical setting, where evaluations by psychologists, neurologists, and speech and hearing pathologists may contribute to an understanding of the child's problems.

INFORMATION TO CONSIDER

The assessment of reading problems is a complex process. Many factors need to be considered, requiring a variety of tools and procedures, to make valid judgments.

Individual Procedures for Estimating Reading Levels

QUESTIONS TO GUIDE READING

Recall Questions
1. What are five options teachers have for estimating students' reading levels?
2. What is an informal reading inventory (IRI)? How is each level defined?
3. What are the Betts criteria for determining each level of an IRI? Which miscues are counted in determining percentages?
4. What procedures are followed in administering an IRI?
5. What are five cautions that should be kept in mind when interpreting IRI data?

6. Why is it difficult to assess specific comprehension skills from a set of IRI questions?

Thinking Questions
1. Why is it important to look at IRI miscues qualitatively as well as quantitatively?
2. Why is it important not to be rigid when scoring an IRI?

One of the first priorities for classroom teachers is determining the most appropriate level at which to begin instruction for a given child. This determination enables a student to be given materials and tasks with which she can be successful early in the term. Once instruction is begun, a teacher can space further assessment procedures over time as she refines her decisions about a student's strengths, weaknesses, and needs. The teacher must remember that concentrated periods of testing may adversely affect students' attitudes toward reading.

Teachers have several options for estimating an appropriate instructional level, including placement tests provided by publishers of basal series, informal reading inventories, group reading inventories, cloze and maze procedures, and other quick (but less precise) on-the-spot assessment techniques. In this section three individual ways to estimate reading levels are presented—teacher-designed informal reading inventories (IRIs), commercial IRIs, and basal reader placement tests. Group reading inventories, cloze procedure, maze procedure, and other quick assessment procedures will be discussed in the following section.

Commercial IRIs and basal reader placement tests are not "informal" in the sense of being teacher-made; rather, they are commercially produced, criterion-referenced instruments (Farr and Carey 1986, p. 143). They will be briefly discussed here since they bear many similarities in construction, administration, and interpretation to teacher-made IRIs.

INFORMAL READING INVENTORIES

An informal reading inventory consists of sets of graded passages of text and sight word recognition lists. The text passages usually parallel book levels in a basal reading series. At each IRI level there is generally a list of twenty words to be recognized at sight, along with at least one passage of text to be read orally and one to be read silently. The graded passages are generally preceded by introductory statements and followed by four to ten questions that assess comprehension. There are generally IRI levels for preprimer, primer, first reader, second reader-I, second reader-II, third reader-I, third reader-II, and one level for each grade remaining in the series. IRIs may also be based on other types of instructional materials, such as content-area tests or high interest/controlled vocabulary materials. Since teacher-made and commercial IRIs are similar in format, the commercial IRI in Figure 5.9 (see p. 107) can give an idea of what parts of a teacher-made IRI look like.

Informal reading inventories serve two basic purposes: (1) identification of a student's reading levels (independent, instructional, and frustration), and (2) a beginning look at a student's strengths and weaknesses based on analyses of word recognition miscues and on the comprehension of passages read orally and/or silently. A child's listening comprehension level may also be assessed through an IRI.

As an assessment tool, IRIs possess high face validity. The procedure is very similar to instructional procedures used in many classrooms, as can be seen by comparing components of IRIs with those of basal reader lesson plans.

IRIs are considered by many reading educators to be one of the better assessment procedures. According to Powell (1970, p. 100), informal reading inventories "provide information pertinent to the assessment of reading ability to a degree far surpassing the quality and quantity of evaluation obtainable with standardized instruments." Farr and Carey (1986, p. 167) also note that IRIs are considered more valid than formal, norm-referenced testing procedures.

At the outset, teachers should note that an IRI from one type of material, such as a specific basal, may not predict how well a child will do on another type of material, such as content-area texts. Performance may not even be consistent between two basal reader series, since basals often differ in difficulty level and type of content.

Some classroom teachers will wish to construct their own IRIs even though such instruments are commercially available. Masztal and Smith (1984) found that 81 percent of the respondents in their study were familiar with the concept of an IRI; 78 percent knew how to administer one, and 54 percent had actually done so. Of those teachers who actually administered an IRI, 24 percent used those of their own construction, and an additional 5 percent used IRIs created by other teachers.

Although teachers may not develop IRIs on a regular basis, they should know how to construct, administer, and interpret an IRI. First, this knowledge will give them a better understanding of the strengths and limitations of the commercial IRIs they administer. Second, they will be better able to devise group procedures for estimating reading levels based on modifications of IRIs. Third, and perhaps most important, teachers will be better able to teach a basal reader lesson diagnostically by adapting procedures used in an IRI for day-to-day, on-the-spot assessments in classrooms.

In the sections that follow, information is presented on what IRIs are, the data they yield, and how they may be administered and interpreted. Information on constructing an IRI can be found in Appendix A.

IRI levels. Four performance levels are generally identified from the administration of a set of IRIs. These are the independent, instructional, and frustration reading levels and a listening comprehension level.

The *independent* reading level is the level at which a student can read without assistance from the teacher. Recreational reading and research-type reading in content areas are examples of reading activities appropriate for this level.

The *instructional* reading level is the level at which a student can function with the help of the teacher. Directed reading lessons in basals or content-area assignments for classroom discussion are types of reading activities appropriate for this level.

The *frustration* reading level is the level at which students make many oral reading errors and have inadequate comprehension, even with the assistance of the teacher. Assigned reading activities at this level should be avoided; students should be permitted to read materials at this level only if they evince a strong interest in the materials.

The *listening comprehension* level is the level at which students have acceptable comprehension of material that is read to them. When this level is higher than the instructional reading level, it is an indication that the student has the conceptual and language background needed for comprehension at higher reading levels. It may also suggest that the student has a reading skill deficiency that interferes with reaching his or her potential in reading.

Criteria for determining levels. In using an IRI to estimate reading levels, an evaluation is made of oral reading miscues and questions are asked to assess oral and silent reading comprehension. The presence or absence of tension signs as children read is also noted.

Several sets of criteria can be identified in the literature for evaluating oral reading miscues. Most are based on the number of scorable miscues made per hundred running words. Most authorities count omissions, substitutions, insertions, mispronunciations, reversals, and the words the reader fails to try to pronounce as scorable miscues. Some authorities count repetitions; others do not. Differing percentage criteria can also be found for evaluating acceptable levels of comprehension.

These sets of criteria are largely quantitative, in that they are based on a count of specific types of oral reading miscues and the number of comprehension questions missed. In some instances, they differ from each other in that they are based on different administration procedures and on the counting of different types of miscues.

According to Powell (1970, p. 100), there is a dearth of research evidence supporting the validity of any of the sets of criteria. Teachers should recall that the IRI procedure is "informal"; good teacher judgment will always be needed in interpreting data, regardless of the criteria used.

The most widely used set of criteria is that attributed to E. A. Betts (1946, pp. 438–85). These are outlined in Table 5.1.

The original Betts criteria were based on the oral reading of fourth graders who had already read the passage silently. Questions have been raised about using the Betts criteria for oral reading, since current practice is to have oral passages read at sight without the benefit of prior silent reading. More errors are likely to occur when passages are freshly read orally than when they are already familiar through silent reading. Oral reading at sight tends to give additional clues to the word recognition problems of the reader.

Among the authorities who have challenged the use of the Betts criteria are Powell and Dunkeld (1971), who found that younger children could tolerate more errors at the instructional level than indicated by the Betts criteria (95 percent accuracy) and still achieve a 70–75 percent level of comprehension. They have also stated that the word recognition criterion for the instructional level "appeared to be a function of the difficulty of materials and the age-grade of the child" (p. 638).

Teachers and clinicians who wish a set of criteria that is responsive to the difficulty of the material and the age/grade of the child may find the Powell (1980) criteria useful (see Fig 5.1). His criteria differ in both word recognition and comprehension scores and address both performance level and reading conditions. Powell names three reading functions: diagnostic, developmental, and lesson evaluation. The diagnostic function refers to oral reading done without prior silent reading. The developmental function refers to oral reading done after the material is read silently first. The lesson evaluation function refers to reading done after instruction has been provided. These varied criteria may provide a more accurate assessment of reading behavior.

Many teachers prefer criteria that are simpler and quicker to use than Powell's. Ekwall and Shanker (1983, p. 370) mention research that indicates the Betts criteria are acceptable if all repetitions are counted as scorable miscues. The Betts criteria seem reasonable if the following conditions are met:

1. The student does not read the passage silently before reading it aloud.
2. All repetitions are counted as scorable miscues.

Table 5.1. Betts's Criteria for Determining IRI Levels

	Word Recognition	Comprehension
Independent Level	99%	90%
Instructional Level	95%	75%
Frustration Level	90%	50%
Listening Level		75%

Figure 5.1. Informal Reading Inventory Scoring Criteria by Performance Level and Condition

	Diagnosis		Developmental Teaching		Lesson Evaluation	
	W/R	Comp. Percentage	W/R	Comp. Percentage	W/R	Comp. Percentage
Independent Level						
1–2	1/17+	80+	1/17+	80+	1/17+	80+
3–5	1/27+	85+	1/27+	85+	1/27+	85+
6+	1/35+	90+	1/35+	90+	1/35+	90+
Instructional Level						
1–2	1/8–1/16	55–80	1/12–1/16	70–80	Converted to	
3–5	1/13–1/26	60–85	1/20–1/26	75–85	independent	
6+	1/18–1/35	65–90	1/26–1/36	80–90	level	
Frustration Level						
1–2	1/7–	55–	1/11–	70–		
3–5	1/12–	60–	1/19–	75–		
6+	1/17–	65–	1/25–	80–		

From William R. Powell, "Measuring Reading Performance Informally," in *Journal of Children and Youth*, Vol. II (Winter 1980), Table 1, p. 28. Reprinted by permission.

3. The Powell word recognition criterion for instructional level at grades 1 and 2 (87 percent or more) is used. Experience has indicated that first and second graders can tolerate a lower word recognition percentage than indicated by Betts and still comprehend adequately, because the content of the instructional materials is generally familiar to most children.

Constructing an IRI. Masztal and Smith (1984) found that 24 percent of the elementary teachers they surveyed used IRIs that they had constructed. It is not easy to construct a valid IRI. Attention must be given to the selection of representative passages and a good word list, to the types and quality of questions asked, and to the affective or cognitive statements addressed to the child prior to reading. For those teachers who desire information on constructing an IRI, detailed information is given in Appendix A.

Administration of an IRI. Administration of an IRI usually takes from fifteen to thirty minutes. A longer time may be required depending on age, ability, length of passages, and the number of reading passages that must be administered before frustration and/or listening level criteria are met.

In administering an IRI, make the general atmosphere as little disruptive to the reader as possible. The room used should be free from distractions. In marking miscues, it is advisable to have the examiner sit across a table or at the side of a table, away from the student, so that errors may be marked as unobtrusively as possible. Examiners may hold the passage for marking on their laps to protect them from the student's view. For readers with severe problems who make many errors, the use of a tape recorder is recommended so that the examiner may replay the tape to check for accuracy in recording errors.

The following major steps represent a procedure examiners may follow in administering an IRI:

1. Establish rapport with the reader. This is especially important when the examiner and the student are not well known to each other.

2. Determine a good beginning point for administering the graded passages so that the reader's first efforts will be successful. In other words, try to set the first reading at the student's independent reading level. This beginning level may be established by two main methods:

a. Administer graded sight word lists, using the results to estimate the reader's independent reading level. When the word list is randomly taken from the entire text, begin the graded passages at the level on which the child misses no more than one sight word. When the list samples the new words in the text, find the highest level at which the child gets 80 percent of the words correct; then drop back one level to begin the reading of the graded passages. These procedures will generally yield the child's independent level.

Exposure time in presenting the sight words should be less than one second. The examiner may flash words printed on three-by-five-inch index cards, or use a hand tachistoscope. This is a small device with a narrow window, through which a list of words written on a strip of paper can be pulled to reveal one word at a time. With both procedures, the teacher will need a record sheet on which to record responses.

b. Teachers may use past records, former teacher opinions, and other assessment devices to make an "educated guess" of current reading levels. It should be noted that norm-referenced tests frequently overrate students, particularly at the primary grade levels. Dropping below the norm-referenced grade-equivalent score by one year in primary grades and two years in the intermediate grades is recommended if grade-equivalent scores are used as an indicator of reading level.

When teachers consider a student's records, they should be aware that the "successful" completion of a given level the previous year may not represent mastery of that level. It is often advisable to start an IRI one or two levels below the highest level previously completed according to school records.

3. If desired, administer an untimed word recognition test. This optional test is based on the graded sight word test used to determine the point at which to begin the graded passages. The child is shown the words missed

on the sight presentation and is asked to decode those words. This procedure provides information on the child's decoding skills independent of time pressure. It also provides the teacher with the opportunity to ask the child how she figured each word out, which gives an idea of which word recognition techniques the child can already use in decoding words. Untimed word recognition tests may be discontinued as soon as they have served their purpose.

4. Begin administering the graded passages at what you judge to be the reader's independent level (see step 2). If the student does not read the first set of passages at the independent level, administer passages at progressively lower levels until the independent level is reached. Then return to the beginning point and continue until the frustration level is reached. If the first reading is at the independent level, continue administering progressively harder passages until the frustration level is reached on both silent and oral passages (see step 5). The oral passage is generally administered first at each level, followed by the silent reading passage.

Introductory motivational statements are made before reading each passage. Oral reading miscues are marked as the child reads orally (see pp. 97–98). A desirable, though optional, component is a measure of the child's silent and oral reading rates. Teachers may use a stopwatch to ensure accuracy. When the child has finished reading a given passage, it is removed from his view and he is asked comprehension questions about the passage. The child is not permitted to look back at the text to find answers.

Examiners should generally not give help with decoding. If a child does not attempt to pronounce a word, the examiner should wait five seconds and then tell the child the word. If the examiner feels an answer to a comprehension question is incomplete, it is appropriate to ask the child to "tell you more" about the content being questioned.

5. Discontinue the reading of graded passages when the reader reaches the frustration level. That is, the oral reading passages should be discontinued when the child becomes frustrated with oral reading, and the silent reading passages should be discontinued when the child can no longer read with 75 percent comprehension. The frustration level will sometimes be different for silent and for oral reading.

6. Begin administering the listening passages at the next level higher than the child's instructional level. This procedure may require a third equivalent passage since the child may have already read an oral and a silent passage at this level. The listening passages should be approximately the same length as the silent reading passages.

Continue with the listening level passages until the listener can no longer comprehend at a 75 percent level. In some instances when a child is having more problems with listening than reading, passages at consecutively lower levels may be administered until a child can achieve 75 percent comprehension.

7. When the testing is complete, score, summarize, and interpret the data.

Scoring, summarizing, and recording IRI data. Three kinds of data are obtained from IRIs: oral reading miscues, answers to comprehension questions, and observation of related tension signs and behavioral characteristics as the child reads.

Recording and scoring oral reading miscues. Several types of miscues, or "errors," are recorded when analyzing oral reading behavior. Some are counted quantitatively in determining the word recognition percentages used in approximating levels. Others are not counted for determining percentages, but are used instead for qualitative assessment.

Nine oral reading miscue types are defined in Figure 5.2. When the Betts criteria are used, the first seven types are counted in calculating the percentages used in approximating levels, and the last two are noted for aiding a qualitative assessment. When applying the Powell criteria, the first six are scorable miscues in approximating levels; the last three are evaluated qualitatively. The main difference between the systems lies in the way repetitions are evaluated. The fact that repetitions were not counted in the scoring criteria by Powell suggests that they should be viewed as recordable miscues used for qualitative analyses.

A suggested system for marking oral miscues is also included in Figure 5.2. It is important for teachers to master a marking system that is comfortable for them. Modifications in the marking system presented may be made as long as they are consistent and intelligible, even at a later time. The examples of miscues come from the oral reading protocol in Figure 5.4.

In scoring miscues, even in a quantitative analysis, avoid counting miscues so as to penalize the reader unfairly. Guidelines for fair scoring are presented in Figure 5.3.

The protocol in Figure 5.4 illustrates the marking of an oral passage read by a fourth grader, using the system for marking and scoring miscues presented in Figures 5.2 and 5.3. A summary of the oral miscues recorded is found in Figure 5.5, offering a sample format for recording oral reading miscue data. An analysis of the reading of this passage may be found on pages 101–102.

Summarizing comprehension data. In determining reading or listening levels, count the number of questions answered correctly. Many teachers also take note of the different types of comprehension data; that is, how many literal, inferential, or vocabulary questions were answered correctly (see Fig. 5.6). The assumption is that the comprehension questions will reveal strengths and weaknesses in these various types of thinking. The validity of this assumption will be discussed in the section on interpreting comprehension data.

Recording behavioral characteristics. Behavioral characteristics and signs of tension are often helpful in assessing reading performance. When it is difficult to make decisions between instructional and frustration levels, the presence or absence of such characteristics may be highly useful in the decision-making process.

Figure 5.2. Oral Reading Miscue Types and How to Record Them

1. Omission—the skipping of one or more words at a single point in a text.

    To record: Draw an oval ⬭ around the omitted text.

    Example: ". . . into the (deep) water . . ."

2. Insertion—the addition of one or more extraneous words at a single point in a text.

    To record: Draw a caret ∧ at the point of insertion and write the word

    Example: ". . . help ^out^ ?"

3. Substitution—the replacement of one word or phrase by another.

    To record: Write the word or phrase substituted over the appropriate textual material.

    Example: "send ~~someone~~ *Somebody* . . ."

4. Mispronunciation—the incorrect sounding of a word or a part of a word.

    To record: Write the word as the child pronounces it above the mispronounced word. (If there is not enough time to write the word as the child says it, place a G above the word to denote a gross mispronunciation or a P over the mispronounced segment to denote a partial mispronunciation.)

    Example: ". . . in *\/daen ger\/* danger."

5. Reversal—the transposition of sounds within a word or of consecutive words.

    To record: Place a transposition mark ⌐⌐⌐ on or around the reversed material.

    Example: ". . . ⌐call⌐loudly⌐ . . ."

6. Words Aided—the supplying of a word by the examiner after the reader has made no oral attempt within five seconds to pronounce the word or after the reader has stated that she does not know the word.

    To record: Place an A over "aided" words.

    Example: ". . . grabs the ^A^object, . . ."

7. Repetition—the reiteration of a segment of text.

    To record: Draw a line under the material repeated.

    Example: ". . . grabs the object, . . ."

8. Spontaneous Correction—the correction of a miscue by the reader without prompting.

    To record: Place a ✓ by the miscue originally marked.

    Example: ". . . in a *pōle* ✓ pool."

9. Lack of Fluency—the reading of text slowly, haltingly, laboriously, or without attention to punctuation or appropriate pauses between phrases.

    To record: Place a slash / wherever there is choppy word-by-word reading or where punctuation is omitted.

    Examples: ". . . help/If . . ."

     ". . . jack/et . . ."

Figure 5.3. Guidelines for Scoring Oral Reading Miscues

1. Dialectal mispronunciations should not be counted. Such mispronunciations do no generally affect comprehension. In order to make this judgment, teachers need to be aware of their students' typical phonological patterns.
2. Mispronunciation of unfamiliar or deceptively spelled proper names, such as Juan or Juanita, should not be counted. However, common proper names such as Brown or White should be counted, since children with some reading skills would normally have appropriate decoding techniques for them.
3. Sometimes a reader follows a syntactic miscue with a second miscue that makes the syntax consistent with the first mistake: *the dog barks* for *the dogs bark*, for example. Count only one miscue when this happens (but mark both). Such miscues indicate a knowledge of how language functions.
4. Count only one miscue per word even though two types of miscues—such as a mispronunciation and the omission of a part of a word—may occur on a given word.
5. Insertions or omissions of more than one word in a single place in the text should count as one miscue. The omission of a full line would also be one miscue.
6. Whether a teacher should count a basic sight word substitution (example: *then* for *when*) as a miscue each time it occurs in a passage is a subject of disagreement. These errors may or may not interfere with comprehension. Repeated substitutions of one name for another (*Fred* for *Frank*) will probably not interfere with overall comprehension and should be counted only once; neither should *a* for *the* in a series be counted more than once. A basic word substitution that is syntactically or semantically incorrect and which would interfere with meaning should probably be counted each time it occurs.

Johnson and Kress (1965, pp. 3, 8) have listed behavioral characteristics in reading that are desirable or undesirable at the independent and instructional levels (see Fig. 5.7). A simple checklist may be devised for recording the presence of these behaviors.

Summarizing overall IRI data. The purpose of summarizing overall IRI data is to assess strengths and weaknesses easily for planning corrective strategies. The important point is to make the record-keeping simple, yet useful. Data must be *organized* in order to be readily available and meaningful. A sample format for an overall summary of IRI information is found in Figure 5.8.

Interpreting IRI data. The following paragraphs contain selected information that may assist teachers in interpreting IRI data. Attention is given to oral reading miscues, comprehension data, reading rate, and behavioral characteristics.

Comments on oral reading miscues. In estimating levels, the Betts and Powell criteria are applied quantitatively; each miscue is counted even though it may not seriously interfere with comprehension. It is desirable

Figure 5.4. Oral Reading Protocol

Suppose you see [*saw*] a child fall into the (deep) water in a pool [*pōle ✓*]. The child doesn't [*don't*] (seem to) know how to swim. What could you do to help? [*good how can ... out*]

If you see [*saw*] someone [*somebody*] in trouble [*trŏ bl̄e ✓*] in the water, (call loudly) for help. (If possible) send someone [*somebody*] (nearby) for adult help.

Never [*Don't*] jump into the water yourself [*by*]. By jumping in, you put your (own) life in danger [*dăn'gər ✓*]. (And) you may not (be able to) save (the other person) [*him*] Only trained (trained) lifeguards [*gōurds*] should go into the water to [*for*] help.

What can you do until help comes? [*come*] If the person [*he*] is just beyond reach, [*reaching*] try extending a towel, a pole [*toe/el*], or a tree branch [*brand*]. You can (also) use an oar [*a A*] or a fishing pole. When the person [*he*] grabs the object [*A*], pull him or her [*or her*] to safety. [*A*]

If you can't [*don't*] reach the person [*him*], throw something into the water that [*there ✓*] floats. Throw anything [*something*] that will support [*suppose*] the person. You might [*should*] throw a life jacket, a beach ball, a rubber tire [*running*], or a piece of wood. [*and*]

This is an edited version of a reading by a fourth-grade girl under the direction of Ms. Cleo Pace, graduate assistant in the University of Tennessee, Knoxville Reading Center. Excerpt from *Flying Hoofs*, Basics in Reading. Copyright © 1978 by Scott, Foresman and Company. Selection adapted from Julius B. Richmond and Eleanor T. Pounds in *You and Your Health*. Used with permission of Scott, Foresman and Company.

to look at miscues qualitatively as well. If errors do not really interfere with comprehension, a child may often read the materials without feeling frustration.

Research findings on oral miscues may aid a teacher in making qualitative evaluation of a child's oral reading. Those errors that interfere most with comprehension should be considered more seriously. The miscues that have the highest correlation with comprehension are mispronunciations, substitutions, words added, insertions, and reversals (Dunkeld 1970). These miscues require careful analysis to determine their effects on comprehension.

Figure 5.5. Summary of Oral Miscues

Omissions	17
Insertions	3
Substitutions	21
Mispronunciations	3
Reversals	1
Words Aided	5
Repetitions	4
Spontaneous Corrections	4
Lack of Fluency	9

Figure 5.6. Summarizing Comprehension Data

Main Idea	_3_ of _5_
Literal	—— of ——
Inferential	—— of ——
Vocabulary	—— of ——

While substitutions, the most frequent type of miscue, have been found to provide valuable diagnostic clues, the importance of omissions and insertions (the next most frequent types of miscues) has received less attention in the research literature, according to D'Angelo and Mahlios (1983). They studied the miscues of fifth graders and found that insertion and omission miscues caused very little syntactic or semantic distortion. Repetitions are often produced so that the reader can better process the text. That is, a reader may repeat to improve his oral reading fluency, or to stall for time in an attempt to process upcoming text.

Teachers should be aware that some miscues may be suggestive of good reading skills. For example, Beebe (1980), in a study of fourth-grade boys, found that corrections and acceptable miscues (substitutions that were syntactically or semantically correct) were *predictors* of reading compre-

Figure 5.7. Behavioral Characteristics in Reading

Desirable	Undesirable
Rhythmical, expressive oral reading	Lip movement
Accurate observation of punctuation	Finger pointing
Conversational tone	Head movement
Acceptable reading posture	Vocalization
Silent reading more rapid than oral	Subvocalization
Responses to questions in language equivalent to authors	Anxiety about performance

Figure 5.8. IRI Summary Sheet

IRI Summary

Name _Fred_   Grade _2_

Age _7_   School _Masonville_

Examiner _Irwin_   Date _Sept. 15, 1985_

Materials Used _____

| | **Word Recognition Data** | | **Level Information** | | | |
	Sight	Untimed	Oral WR	Oral Comp.	Silent Comp.	Listening Comp.
Preprimer	14 of 20	3 of 5				
Primer	10 of 20	3 of 10	90%	75%	79%	—
First						75%
Second						60%
Third						
Fourth						
Fifth						
Sixth						

Level Designations

     Independent _No independent level obtained_

     Instructional _Preprimer_

     Frustration _Primer_

     Listening _First grade_

Comments on comprehension _____

_____

Comments on behavioral characteristics _____

_____

_____

hension. Examples of this type of miscue from the protocol in Figure 5.4 are *can* for *could* and *somebody* for *someone*.

     Analyzing an oral reading protocol. Figure 5.4 shows a protocol of a fourth-grade girl reading from a basal reader at her assigned grade level. The summary of miscues in Figure 5.5 indicates that the reading of the material was very frustrating. A passage this difficult should not have been used for oral reading. If the procedures recommended earlier for administering an IRI had been followed, the student would probably have been stopped on the oral passages before reaching this level.

Some observations may be made from the protocol. The long pauses, hesitations, and omissions of words and phrases indicate that this reader hesitates to attack words unknown to her. Many substitutions are made, but they were usually logical. The reader appears to have had a general sense of the overall meaning of the passage (the main idea and some experiential knowledge of the topic), and thus was able to supply a reading that retained some sense of the text. She would probably be able to answer general-knowledge questions about helping someone in trouble in the water; in fact it would be difficult to construct text-dependent questions on this passage because the content is known to many children.

The reader obviously needs help with word recognition techniques—except for context, which already seems to be a strength. An additional check of sight vocabulary would be appropriate, along with a check on word endings to help pinpoint additional problems. Work on individual skill weaknesses should be followed by practice in applying these skills in connected text.

Interpreting comprehension data. IRIs may not reveal true strengths and weaknesses in comprehension skills (such as details, main idea, or sequence). Research suggests that skills may be influenced by general abilities such as vocabulary knowledge and the ability to reason in context (Schell and Hanna 1981). In addition, the questions asked in the IRI testing situation are limited in type; teachers will need to verify findings in the day-to-day teaching situation.

There are several questions a teacher may ask, however, when looking at a student's comprehension responses across several levels of an IRI (or, for that matter, in day-to-day teaching):

1. What types of vocabulary items were missed? Were they within the expected experiential background of the learner? Do these errors appear related to other comprehension mistakes; that is, did lack of vocabulary knowledge cause another question to be missed?

2. Was literal comprehension better than inferential or critical comprehension (or vice versa)? Many children have an easier time with factual recall than with inferences, especially at lower mental ability levels. This question is also related to general instructional practice. What kinds of questions predominate in your classes? Are children handling these types well?

3. Was comprehension better on oral or silent passages? Has oral reading been the predominant instructional mode in the classroom? If so, the child may perform better in that mode, particularly in the primary grades. In the intermediate grades, where more silent reading is done, children may exhibit better comprehension after silent reading.

4. Are there differences in types of comprehension errors as the difficulty of the passage increases? Pay particular attention to any error types at or below instructional level, since these are the levels at which school assignments are (or should be) made.

Question probes can be used in assessing children's responses to IRI comprehension questions. In this procedure, when a child misses a question, the teacher asks for more information or asks how the child arrived at the answer. The responses yield information about the child's thinking process in answering the questions.

Rate of reading IRI passages. Teachers may wish to time children as they read orally and silently, both for direct comparison and to measure each rate against the typical speed for children at their age/grade levels. Children may read accurately but at a laboriously slow rate, which can be frustrating. When a child performs slower than other group members, a lower group placement may be considered.

It is difficult to suggest typical reading rates, as they vary (or *should* vary) according to the type of material read. Better readers vary their rates according to material and purpose. Harris and Sipay (1985, p. 533), in reviewing the norms for several standardized silent reading tests, have found the highest, median, and lowest rates, based on test medians for silent reading in grades 2 through 6 (see Table 5.2).

Interpreting behavioral characteristics. Behavioral characteristics that children may exhibit as they work through an IRI were presented in Figure 5.7. The following paragraphs focus on information that is helpful in interpreting such behaviors.

Johnson and Kress (1965, p. 10) have reported the following behavioral characteristics at the frustration level: "abnormally loud or soft voice, arhythmical or word-by-word oral reading, lack of expression in oral reading, inaccurate observation of punctuation, finger pointing (at margin or every word), lip movement—head movement—subvocalization, frequent requests for examiner help, noninterest in the selection, yawning or obvious fatigue, [and] refusal to continue." Behavioral expectations listed

Table 5.2. Median Reading Rates for Grades 2–6

	Highest Test Rate WPM	Median Test Rate WPM	Lowest Test Rate WPM
Grade 2	118	86	35
Grade 3	138	116	75
Grade 4	170	155	120
Grade 5	195	177	145
Grade 6	230	206	171

Adapted from Albert J. Harris and Edward R. Sipay, *How to Increase Reading Ability*, 8th ed. (White Plains, N.Y.: Longman, 1985), p. 533, Table 14.1. Reprinted by permission of Longman, Inc.

in Figure 5.7 for independent and instructional levels may be too stringent for first and second graders. For example, arhythmical oral reading and finger pointing are often present in young readers. Some behaviors characteristic of the frustration level, such as lack of expression in oral reading at sight, may also be present in typical first- and second-grade readers.

Related behavioral characteristics may result from anxiety or from poor reading habits. Mangrum and Forgan (1979, pp. 88–89) recommend that behavioral characteristics associated with anxiety be considered in determining instructional level, as they will generally occur only when the material is too difficult or is becoming too difficult. On the other hand, when behavioral characteristics are the result of poor habits, they will be more generalized and often occur with both easier and harder material. In these instances, such characteristics may occur together with satisfactory word recognition and comprehension.

Determining reading levels. Mangrum and Forgan (1979, pp. 90–91) offer a set of guidelines that may be helpful to teachers as they use IRI data to determine reading levels:

1. When a reader scores at the independent level for word recognition and comprehension and is free of tension signs, the material may be said to be on the reader's independent level.
2. When a reader reaches the instructional level in word recognition and comprehension and displays two or fewer signs of anxiety, the material may be said to be on the reader's instructional level.
3. When a reader reaches the frustration level in word recognition and/or comprehension and/or there are four or more signs of anxiety, the material may be said to be on the frustration level.
4. When a reader scores at the independent level in word recognition and the instructional level in comprehension (or vice versa) and exhibits fewer than three signs of anxiety, the material may be considered on the instructional level (because the learner needs help with either word recognition or comprehension).

When it is difficult to make decisions between levels in borderline cases, observe whether the miscues interfere with meaning. If few of them do, less weight may be given to the total number of miscues. When the same error is repeated several times, such as a substitution of *then* for *when*, less weight may also be given to these miscues, especially if comprehension is not impaired.

When there is a discrepancy between silent and oral reading performance, the type of situation in which the reader typically functions should be considered. Does the instructional setting focus primarily on silent reading before oral reading? If so, silent reading performance should be given more consideration. The age/grade level of the student is also a consideration in interpreting discrepancies. Jacobs and Searfoss (1977, p. 28) claim that skill in silent reading should surpass that in oral reading at about mid-second grade and that the differential between the two should increase with successive grade levels.

A student may score at the instructional level on consecutive passages of varying difficulty. When this occurs, the highest passage level should be considered as the instructional level, unless there are several signs of tension present at this passage level (Sucher and Allred 1973, p. 37).

In summary, flexibility in the use and evaluation of an IRI should be maintained in determining levels.

Cautions in interpreting data. The following summary of cautions in interpreting IRIs should be recognized by teachers:

1. The criteria, as we have noted, are not precise; they are, rather, somewhat subjective and arbitrary. Good teacher judgment regarding their use is in order. Teachers need considerable knowledge about reading in order to make valid judgments (Farr and Carey 1986, p. 168).
2. Readability of texts varies from one area to another. The test passage may not reflect what the child can actually do with other portions of the text.
3. Data from IRIs are gathered in a short period of time. Children may differ from day to day in the number and type of errors made. Word recognition and comprehension patterns should be verified over time through diagnostic teaching of regular lessons.
4. The examiner may not be accurate in marking oral miscues. A study by Ladd (1961) indicated that examiners may miss 33 to 37 percent of errors, even after thirty hours of instruction in marking miscues.
5. IRI levels are not precise points. While they may be considered better guides than norm-referenced tests, they probably pinpoint a band or area in which a child may be appropriately placed, rather than a precise designation such as a 3–2 basal.
6. The use of oral reading miscues to make inferences about silent reading behaviors is based on the assumption that both processes are similar (Leu 1982). This may not be true; important differences exist between the two, although oral miscues are an important measure of what may be happening silently as a child reads. Both oral and silent reading should be tested at each level.
7. IRIs are not as useful at upper grade levels as they are at lower grade levels. There is less difference in the difficulty of the materials at upper levels, and background information plays a stronger role in comprehension. Oral and silent reading may be more dissimilar at these levels as well (Farr and Carey 1986, p. 168).

COMMERCIAL IRIS

Commercial IRIs are sometimes used by teachers to approximate reading levels and to give an initial indication of reading strengths and weaknesses. Masztal and Smith (1984) found that 27 percent of their respondents who used IRIs primarily used commercially produced tests.

Figures 5.9 and 5.10 show a passage from a commercial IRI and a summary sheet for data gathered from it.

Commercial IRIs have the advantage of saving time and of having been constructed by reading authorities; some have even been field tested. A major disadvantage frequently cited is that they are not based on specific instructional materials that a teacher may be planning to use, and so the results of the test may not match the texts to be used in the classroom. Caution is necessary in making a level placement based on the results of commercial IRIs.

Jongsma and Jongsma (1981) noted great variability in content, style, and length of passages among commercial IRIs. Some omitted silent reading passages, or suggested that they be optional. Differences also existed in directions to examiners, especially about types of miscues to score. Many relied heavily on literal questions. Validity seemed to relate more to readability estimates rather than to correspondence with classroom performance.

The question of reliability between two equivalent forms of given commercial IRIs has also been raised. Reliability between forms certainly is not perfect; however, in one study, reliability between forms was found not to be as bad as critics have suggested (Helgren-Lempesis and Mangrum 1986). These researchers found that reliability coefficients among alternate forms of the *Analytical Reading Inventory*, the *Basic Reading Inventory*, and the *Ekwall Reading Inventory* ranged from .60 to .78. The strength of these correlations suggests that teachers may expect some students to score at different levels on the two forms of a given test. Placement in materials should be made with caution.

Jongsma and Jongsma (1981) recommended that teachers choose carefully among IRIs in order to find the one that corresponds best to their regular instructional materials, to their philosophy about scoring miscues, and to their view of what types of comprehension questions are important.

The following is a selected list of commercially available IRIs:

1. Mary Lynn Woods and Alden J. Moe, *Analytical Reading Inventory*, 3rd ed. (Merrill, 1985). Three forms for students from primer level through grade 9. Summary sheets allow both qualitative and quantitative evaluations. General content.
2. Lois A. Bader, *Bader Reading and Language Inventory* (Macmillan, 1983). Three sets of passages: one for preprimary through eleventh or twelfth grade; one for use with children, adolescents, or adults; and one for adults who are beginning to read. Specific skills tests are also included.

Figure 5.9. Commercial IRI

○PP PASSAGE ━━━ FORM A ━━━ TEACHER PP○

MOTIVATIONAL STATEMENT: Read this story to find out what Joe found.

"I see a goat!" said Joe.

"Hello, Goat!
How are you?
I see you.
I like you.
Be my goat."

"Dad will like you.
So will Mom.
Come with me."

"Dad! Dad!
Look! Look!
See my goat!
Can I keep him?
Can he stay in my room?
Please!"

"A goat?" asked Dad.
"No! No!
Not a goat!
Not in the house.
Goats are not clean."

SCORING AID	
WORD RECOGNITION	
%—MISCUES	
99—1	
95—3	
90—6	
85—10	
COMPREHENSION	
%—ERRORS	
100—0	
87.5—1	
75—2	
62.5—3	
50—4	
37.5—5	
25—6	
12	0

64 WORDS

$$\frac{3900}{\text{WPM}}$$

COMPREHENSION QUESTIONS

— main idea
1. What would be a good title for this story? (Joe Finds a Goat; The Goat)

— sequence
2. What was the first thing that happened in the story? (Joe saw a goat.)

— detail
3. How did Joe feel about the goat he found? (He liked it.)

— detail
4. How did Joe think Dad and Mom would feel about the goat? (They would like it.)

— detail
5. Who did Joe call to see the goat? (Dad)

— detail
6. Where did Joe want the goat to stay? (in his room)

— inference
7. How did Dad feel about Joe keeping the goat in his room? (He didn't want him to.) What does the story say to make you believe that? (Dad says, "No! No!" and "Not in the house.")

— cause and effect/ detail
8. Why didn't Dad want the goat in the house? (Goats are not clean.)

[Note: Do not count as a miscue mispronunciation of the name Joe. You may pronounce this word for the student if needed.]

From Paul C. Burns and Betty D. Roe, *Informal Reading Inventory*, 2nd ed. (Boston: Houghton Mifflin, 1985), p. 44. Reprinted by permission of Houghton Mifflin Company.

Figure 5.10. Summary Sheet

SUMMARY ——————————————————————— TEACHER ———

NAME _____ GRADE _____ ORAL _____ SILENT _____ FORM _____

ADMINISTRATOR _____ DATE _____ RATE _____ HIGH _____ AVERAGE _____ LOW _____

INDEPENDENT LEVEL _____ INSTRUCTIONAL LEVEL _____ FRUSTRATION LEVEL _____ CAPACITY LEVEL _____

Strengths and weaknesses in word recognition: include information about use of or failure to use syntactic and graphic clues and about dialect-related miscues, which should not be considered serious recognition problems. Check items on chart. (Use back of form for additional space.)

Single consonants _____
Consonant blends _____
Single vowels _____
Vowel digraphs _____
Consonant digraphs _____
Diphthongs _____
Word beginnings _____

Word middles _____
Word endings _____
Prefixes _____
Suffixes _____
Inflectional endings _____
Compound words _____
Syllabication _____
Accent _____

Strengths and weaknesses in comprehension: include information about use of or failure to use semantic clues. (Use back of form for additional space.)

WORD RECOGNITION MISCUE ANALYSIS CHART

Miscue	PP	P	1	2	3	4	5	6	7	8	9	10	11	12	Total
Mispronunciation															
Substitution															
Refusal to pronounce															
Insertion															
Omission															
Repetition															
Reversal															
Total															

COMPREHENSION SKILL ANALYSIS CHART

Skill	Number of Questions	Number of Errors	Percent of Errors
Main idea			
Detail			
Sequence			
Cause and effect			
Inference			
Vocabulary			

SUMMARY TABLE OF PERCENTAGES

Level	Word Recognition	Oral Comprehension	Silent Comprehension	Average Comprehension
PP				
P				
1				
2				
3				
4				
5				
6				
7				
8				
9				
10				
11				
12				

From Paul C. Burns and Betty D. Roe, *Informal Reading Inventory*, 2nd ed. (Boston: Houghton Mifflin, 1985), p. 107. Reprinted by permission of Houghton Mifflin Company.

3. Jerry L. Johns, *Basic Reading Inventory*, 3rd ed. (Kendall/Hunt, 1985). Three forms for preprimer through grade 8. General content.
4. Morton Botel, *Botel Reading Inventory*, 2nd ed. (Follett, 1978). Four separate power tests: Decoding; Spelling Placement; Word Recognition (Forms A and B), designed to yield an estimate of oral reading ability; and Word Opposites (Forms A and B), designed as a group estimate of comprehension. Reading is of isolated words; no graded passages are included.
5. Nicholas J. Silvaroli, *Classroom Reading Inventory*, 5th ed. (Wm. C. Brown, 1986). Two forms for grades 1–6: one form for middle school and junior high, one for high school and adult. Content is general.
6. Eldon E. Ekwall, *Ekwall Reading Inventory*, 2nd ed. (Allyn and Bacon, 1986). Four forms (two oral and two silent) for preprimer through ninth grade. General content. Sight word and phonics surveys are also included.
7. Thomas A. Rakes, Joyce S. Chote, and Gayle Lane Waller, *Individual Evaluation Procedures in Reading* (Prentice-Hall, 1983). Two forms for primer level through grade 10; general content. Visual tests, auditory tests, and special word analysis and vocabulary tests are also included.
8. Paul C. Burns and Betty D. Roe, *Informal Reading Inventory*, 2nd ed. (Houghton Mifflin, 1985). Four forms for preprimer level through grade 12. General content.
9. Floyd Sucher, Ruel A. Allred, Wilson H. Lane, and Marjorie M. Lane, *Sucher-Allred Reading Placement Inventory* (Economy, 1986). Placement inventory for grades 1 to adult; reading skills survey test for grades 2–9; Lane Diagnostic Test of Word Perception Skills for grades 4–12.

Basal Reader Placement Tests

A widely used technique for estimating instructional level and for placing children in reading materials is that of initial placement inventories that are available with basal reader series. The types of assessment techniques used for basal reader placement vary from company to company.

Some placement tests are very similar to our concept of an IRI in that they test both word recognition and comprehension, with comprehension checks based on both oral and silent reading. Silent reading portions may be group administered, however, rather than individually administered. Some of the more comprehensive placement tests include tests for reading skills. Record-keeping forms are also provided.

The placement tests that accompany other basal series may not be as comprehensive as those described above. They may involve only a part of the IRI process, such as having the child read either orally or silently (but not both) in a group setting. Some are very limited and utilize only a ditto master sheet to check reading comprehension.

Figure 5.11 illustrates the placement inventories for *SERIES r: Macmillan Reading*.

Since basal reader placement tests are based on the series being used, they may save teachers considerable time. The tests are particularly valuable when they assess both oral and silent reading and are otherwise similar to an IRI. Cooper and Worden caution, however, that such tests tend to place students in materials that are too difficult (1983, p. 176). Teachers are advised to try the students out in books before making a definite placement. The group reading inventory procedure discussed below is valuable in this regard.

INFORMATION TO CONSIDER

1. Estimating a reading level is one of the first tasks in reading assessment.
2. Results of an initial assessment should be verified over time through diagnostic teaching.
3. An informal reading inventory is one of the most ecologically valid approaches for estimating reading levels and for obtaining initial diagnostic information, since it is closely related to good teaching methodology.
4. All informal assessment tools are just that—informal, imprecise tools; therefore, precise judgments should not be made from them.
5. A qualitative assessment of students' miscues is necessary for an adequate diagnosis.

Group Procedures for Estimating Reading Levels

QUESTIONS TO GUIDE READING

Recall Questions
1. What are three group approaches that may be used to estimate reading levels?
2. What are the major steps in administering the group reading inventory (GRI) described in this section?
3. What is cloze procedure? Maze procedure? What are the similarities and differences between the two? What are the criteria for the "level" determination for each?
4. What criteria should a teacher consider in selecting passages for the various group approaches to estimating levels?

Figure 5.11. Initial Placement Inventory

The Initial Placement Inventory is designed to aid the classroom teacher in determining the appropriate initial placement of the student for instruction in SERIES r: Macmillan Reading. The Initial Placement Inventory contains two types of tests: a group-administered, silent-reading inventory for selected levels of SERIES r for Grades 1-8, and an individually administered, oral-reading inventory for the same levels. An optional test of word recognition is included as a supplement to the oral-reading inventory. The accompanying manual for the Initial Placement Inventory provides instructions for administering the tests.

A portion of the Initial Placement Inventory appears on copying masters in the back of each Teacher's Edition for SERIES r, Grades 1-6. This abbreviated version offers limited capability for ascertaining placement and diagnosis. For more accurate placement of students in SERIES r, it is recommended that the complete Initial Placement Inventory be used.

Three levels of the Initial Placement Inventory are available in each Teacher's Edition of SERIES r, Grades 1-6.

Grade	Teacher's Edition	Portion of Initial Placement Inventory Available in Teacher's Editions
Grade 1	Preprimers Levels 4-6	Levels 4, 5, 6
	Primer Levels 7-8	Levels 6, 7, 9
	First Reader Levels 9-10	Levels 7, 9, 11
Grade 2	2-1 Reader Levels 11-12	Levels 9, 11, 13
	2-2 Reader Levels 13-14	Levels 11, 13, 15
Grade 3	3-1 Reader Levels 15-16	Levels 13, 15, 17
	3-2 Reader Levels 17-18	Levels 15, 17, 19
Grade 4	4th Reader Levels 19-21 Levels 22-24	Levels 17, 19, 25
Grade 5	5th Reader Levels 25-27 Levels 28-30	Levels 19, 25, 31
Grade 6	6th Reader Levels 31-33 Levels 34-36	Levels 25, 31, Grade 7

Each level of the Initial Placement Inventory consists of the following components:

Silent Reading Inventory (Group)	Oral Reading Inventory (Individual)	Word Recognition Test (Individual)
a. Reading Selection	**a.** Reading Selection	Graded word lists for teacher use with student
b. Multiple choice questions for independent student response	**b.** Questions for teacher use with student	

PLEASE NOTE: For teachers who use only the abbreviated version of the Initial Placement Inventory in the Teacher's Edition, it is mandatory that both group and individual inventories be administered for each student. The word-recognition test can be used to confirm the instructional level determined by the results of the silent and oral reading inventories.

From Carl B. Smith and Richard Wardhough, Teacher's Edition of *Secrets and Surprises*, *Series r: Macmillan Reading*, 1980 edition, Smith and Wardhough, Senior Authors, p. 427. Reprinted by permission of Macmillan Publishing Company.

This section focuses on group procedures for estimating reading levels. These procedures are more time-efficient than the individual procedures discussed above, but they do not provide as much diagnostic information. There is a trade-off between administration time and the amount of information available for diagnostic purposes. Discussed in this section are group reading inventories (GRIs) based on a Directed Reading Activity, on a modification of a Directed Reading-Thinking Activity, on cloze procedure, on maze procedure, and on quick class surveys.

GROUP READING INVENTORIES

The group reading inventory (GRI) procedures described in this section are designed for use with small groups of four to six students. They are ways of making an early approximation of instructional reading level and of identifying individual students who need more comprehensive assessment (such as an IRI). GRIs may be developed for both basal and content-area materials. The focus is not on teaching the material, but rather on assessing whether the children have the background knowledge and reading skills to handle the material. The format of a GRI should be similar to the format the teacher uses for instruction on a day-to-day basis; in fact, the validity of the procedure rests on its similarity to actual practice, since students may react differently to various formats.

The GRIs discussed here are based on "trying out" passages in texts, assuming that the teacher follows either a Directed Reading Activity (DRA) or Directed Reading-Thinking Activity (DRTA) format. Suggestions for selecting appropriate passages for GRIs are similar to those for selecting IRI passages (see Appendix A), with one possible difference: the passage should be long enough to yield several good questions, so that each pupil may have more than one or two chances to respond.

The groups selected for GRI assessments should be made up of students who the teacher has reason to believe are similar in their ability to handle reading materials. Judgments of probable similarity of children are based on information that may be gleaned from several sources: cumulative records; statements from former teachers; and observation of language facility, concept development, and affect.

When GRIs are based on DRAs, three phases are involved: background development, silent reading, and comprehension check (which includes oral rereading). Teacher preparation includes selection of an appropriate passage, consideration of the concepts and thinking abilities needed to understand the material, and anticipation of potential word recognition problems (Johnson and Kress 1965, p. 23).

In the background development phase, the teacher uses questioning to assess children's conceptual background for the story; determines students' grasp of needed vocabulary knowledge, again through questioning; evaluates interest in the material; evaluates how students are using thinking processes as they respond to the questioning; and notes their degree of attention. In this phase, the teacher stimulates group discussion and carefully observes individual students' reactions. Purposes for reading the material are also established. If a student has trouble functioning with the activities in this phase, it is quite likely that he cannot function adequately in an instructional setting in which that level of material is being used. Thus, the determination may already have been made that this material is not appropriate for this child.

The second phase involves silent reading of the passage. As students read, the teacher observes their behavior, noting those indicative characteristics suggested for observation during IRIs. Noted behaviors become a part of the final evaluation of the student's ability to function with the specified material.

A source of difficulty for the teacher during the second phase is remembering specific behaviors for given readers. These observations will necessarily be less precise than with an IRI. A simple checklist covering each aspect of the GRI may be helpful for recording information.

During phase three, the teacher checks comprehension, stimulates discussion, and has students read short passages orally. Before administering a GRI, the teacher should develop several potential questions for use in checking comprehension and guiding the discussion. The guidelines offered in Appendix A for developing questions for an IRI should be useful for GRIs as well. Questions supplied in teachers' manuals may also be used.

If there are four to six children in the group, more questions than the five to ten suggested for an IRI will be needed if each child's comprehension is to be sampled adequately through oral discussion. Each child should be asked about four questions for the assessment to be considered reasonable. The questions chosen should sample vocabulary knowledge and both literal and inferential comprehension. There may also be questions that assess a child's knowledge of skills needed to work through the text, such as questions on charts, graphs, or maps. As the comprehension check proceeds, the teacher should note which children can answer questions adequately and which types of questions (literal or inferential) seem to pose problems.

Children may write down their answers to comprehension questions if the teacher desires; this will enable each child to answer all questions. The teacher will gain more valuable information from written answers if the "test" is handled as an ungraded assignment and discussed in class. Discussion enables teachers to assess the thinking processes that were used in arriving at answers.

In assessing oral reading, the teacher may ask children to read sentences or paragraphs in response to questions or to support a point made in the discussion. As a child reads, the teacher notes any miscues. If the reader makes several errors on a paragraph, the material is probably too difficult, at least in terms of word recognition. Five errors in a short passage is suggestive of the frustration level. If a child has an opportunity to read thirty to fifty words orally, the assessment will have more validity.

If one child handles every phase spontaneously and independently, the material is probably too easy for her; the child should be involved in a GRI trial group at a higher level. Conversely, another child may have difficulty with each phase, suggesting that the material is too hard. This child should be placed in a GRI group at a lower level. For students who have a few difficulties with any phase, the material may be considered on their instructional level.

Such easy categorizations are not always possible, as a child may have considerable difficulty with one phase and none at all with another. For these children, the teacher may consider further assessment, possibly administering an IRI. In borderline cases, the teacher should probably first place the child in the lower of two levels. If this level proves too easy, "promotion" to a higher group almost always has a more positive impact on the child's affective development than dropping down from a more advanced group.

A Directed Reading-Thinking Activity (DRTA) format is outlined below by Stauffer, Abrams, and Pikulski (1978, p. 99). Note the differences from the DRA just described above, especially in step 2.

1. Group together five or six children who, based on available information, appear to have similar skills.
2. Have the group make predictions and set purposes. In addition to providing the information that is gathered in an individual IRI, these procedures allow observation of each child's behavior as part of a group.
3. Have the children read the designated selection silently.
4. Observe the silent reading.
5. Ask each child as many comprehension questions as can be reasonably devised from such a short selection.
6. Decide on the next steps. For children who appear to have been able to handle the material independently, retest them as a part of a group who will receive a group IRI [GRI] using more difficult material. For those who appear to be

at an instructional level, no further testing is needed. Those who had too much difficulty with the material should be retested with a group that will be exposed to easier material. Continue making these decisions after each group.

The GRI has more limitations than an IRI. The procedure is less precise and yields a narrower range of information to use in making diagnoses. Judgments are generally based on the teacher's necessarily imperfect recall of what happened as the GRI progressed. Record-keeping, when done, is also difficult, given the time constraints. Additional assessment will be needed if a more complete diagnosis of specific strengths and weaknesses seems warranted.

Cloze Procedure

Cloze procedure has both assessment and instructional uses. Cloze involves the systematic deletion of words from a passage, with readers then asked to replace the deleted item. The deletion scheme is generally every fifth, eighth, or tenth word. Cloze can be used to assess a child's interaction with a specific piece of material, to approximate instructional level, to test the reader's ability to respond to text syntactically and semantically, and to assess knowledge of content-area material (Bader 1980, p. 223). As an assessment tool, cloze is said to measure a reader's ability to handle linguistic structures. Since it requires a student to predict exact word replacements, it is also a measure of comprehension (Hittleman 1978, p. 136). Cloze results have positive correlations, ranging up to .90, with multiple-choice test results (Farr and Carey 1986, p. 36).

How accurately does cloze approximate instructional level? Jones and Pikulski (1974) studied cloze and IRI results with sixth-grade students and found 80 percent agreement on instructional level. They feel that if cloze can approximate instructional level on an IRI with 70 to 80 percent accuracy, it is an appropriate tool to use since it takes much less instructional time. As with a GRI, results should be viewed as tentative and verified through diagnostic teaching or with an IRI. Placement decisions should not be made on the basis of results from one assessment tool.

Experience has indicated that cloze is more appropriate for intermediate and upper grade levels than for lower primary grades. Many young children have difficulty with the cloze response mode, due to lack of experience with it in routine classroom instruction. Gove (1975) has found that with appropriate instruction, such as practice at filling in blanks, beginning readers can handle the cloze response mode. Remedial readers, when familiar with the response mode, are also able to handle cloze (Lopardo 1975).

Cloze passages are best selected from materials a teacher plans to use for regular instruction. Since readability varies from section to section in a text, care should be taken that passages are of average difficulty for the text. The guidelines for selecting a passage for an IRI (see Appendix A) are appropriate, with the exception of passage length. Directions for constructing, administering, and interpreting cloze tests to determine reading levels have been suggested by Earle (1976, pp. 64–65)*:

1. Select approximately 160 running words from required text material.
2. Print the first sentence in its entirety, unmutilated.
3. Select, at random, one of the next 5 words (i.e., one of the first 5 words in the second sentence). Delete this word and replace it with a blank of standard length. Continue to delete every fifth word until you have 50 blanks. End that sentence. Follow with a complete, unmutilated sentence.
4. Since most students will find the cloze a new experience, it is important to explain the purpose of the test, and to precede its administration by one or two similar very brief and easy exercises, completed with teacher guidance and/or peer collaboration. Administration rarely takes more than 30 minutes.
5. Since the test is not to be graded or returned to the students, the easiest means of scoring is to avoid the search for synonyms. Rather, mark as correct only those words or symbols which are exact replacements according to the original text material. Multiply each correct replacement by two to arrive at percent correct.
6. Research has shown the cloze to be a valid and reliable measure of reading comprehension. As with any test, however, your interpretation of the scores is most important. The research suggests that cloze scores of less than 30 to 35 percent are likely to indicate inadequate comprehension, while scores of greater than 55 to 60 percent are likely to indicate very high comprehension of the text in question.
7. Perhaps the best way to interpret your cloze scores, however, is to organize them in a single frequency distribution, i.e., arrange the scores in order to show that so many kids got 10 percent, so many got 12 percent, so many got 14 percent, and so on. This kind of organization will give a more graphic picture of how well individuals and groups in a particular class comprehended the text.

Thus, when approximating reading levels, scores of 55 to 60 percent may be said to represent independent level, scores of 35 to 55 percent the instructional level, and scores of less than 30 to 35 percent the frustration level.

Bader (1980, p. 224) says that passages shorter than 260 words may be used in primary grades. She suggests:

Preprimer	40–50 words
Primer	50–75 words
Grade 1	75–100 words
Grade 2	100–125 words
Grade 3	125–150 words

In primary grades, it may be better to permit students to write responses on the test sheet. Intermediate grade students can transfer their answers to another sheet of paper, thus enabling the cloze tests to be used again. For primary grades, deletion of every tenth word may be more appropriate; every fifth word may too formidable a task for young readers. Recall, however, that the percentage criteria for instructional levels have been based primarily on fifth-word deletions.

In scoring a cloze test to determine reading levels, only exact replacements should be counted as correct, as the research studies done to establish the percentages used only exact replacements. This method proved more efficient; it is difficult to get agreement on acceptable synonyms. Data from McKenna's study (1976) showed that for ordinary use with typical students, the verbatim score was virtually as valid as with the acceptance of reasonable synonyms; certainly it is simpler. Hargis (1972) found that slow-learning subjects score lower in relationship to normal subjects when synonyms were used.

Although cloze tests do not provide the diagnostic information that an IRI does, the procedure can be modified to yield some diagnostic information. One modification is to delete specific semantic or syntactic items, such as nouns or function words, so that teachers can see how well students can handle these linguistic elements. As students discuss reasons for their choices, teachers gain information on language competence. In this type of assessment procedure, reasonable synonyms that students can justify should be accepted. Warwick (1978) notes that it is more difficult to supply correct, verbatim content words than correct function words.

Categorization of errors made in this type of cloze test provides insight into the reading abilities of children. Are the errors correct syntactically but not semantically? This suggests that the child is utilizing language structure but may not be attending to overall meaning. If errors are semantically correct, it suggests that the child is comprehending overall, but may not be attending to specific words. When errors are both semantically and syntactically correct, the reader is using his knowledge of language and is also engaged in the overall comprehension of the material.

A commercially available cloze test, *The De Santi Cloze Inventory* (Allyn & Bacon, 1986), assesses reading performance in grades 3–12. It combines cloze procedure with Miscue Analysis to determine a reader's comprehension level and awareness of syntax and semantics. The inventory also permits the determination of independent, instructional, and frustration reading levels and assists in assessing students' reading strengths and weaknesses.

Maze Procedure

Another group device to determine reading levels is maze procedure (Guthrie et al. 1974). This technique is a modification of cloze in that a multiple-choice replacement is offered for the deleted words (usually every fifth word in a passage of about 120 words). Three choices are given to the reader for replacing the deleted word:

1. the correct word;
2. an incorrect word that is the same part of speech; and
3. an incorrect word that is a different part of speech.

Example: The boy and his dog ——————— home.
(went, store, seem)

Criterion scores for reading levels as developed by Bradley, Ackerson, and Ames (1978) are as follows:

Independent level	85% and above
Instructional level	50–85%
Frustration level	50% and below

Quick Assessment Procedures for Instructional Level

Harris and Sipay (1985, p. 172) have devised a quick check on comprehension, designed for preliminary screening or as a basis for organizing groups for GRIs:

> For a quick check on comprehension, one can choose a short selection (four or five pages) from near the beginning of the book and ask the children to read it silently. As each child finishes, he or she closes the book and looks up; in this way, the slowest readers are spotted quickly. When all have finished, the teacher can read a list of questions, to which the pupils write their answers. The children who score below 60% are likely to have difficulty understanding the book; the 60% scorers are marginal.

Word lists, though not as accurate as procedures such as the GRI, may give a rough estimate of instructional level. Refer back to the discussion of the IRI for information on the use of IRI word lists for estimating levels (pp. 94–95). Graded word lists, such as the *San Diego Quick Assessment List*, have also been recommended for this purpose (LaPray and Ross 1969). The word list procedure is less accurate than the other procedures discussed because it does not involve any assessment of comprehension of connected text.

Strengths and Limitations of Informal Assessment Procedures

As noted throughout this chapter, informal assessments themselves have strengths and limitations. Cautions have been suggested concerning their use. It is the task of the teacher to attempt to maximize the strengths when possible and to minimize the weaknesses. The following discussion summarizes some of the potential strengths and weaknesses.

STRENGTHS

First, informal assessments prepared and used by teachers tend to be more reality-oriented (Ramsey 1967) and thus more similar to instructional practice. The similarity to actual instructional procedures (format, response, mode, question types, etc.) tends to be considerably greater than with commercially produced procedures such as norm-referenced tests. An informal reading inventory is an example of an assessment that has ecological validity: the material used in IRIs (basal passages) and the response mode (free recall questions) are closer to a typical instructional procedure than on standardized tests, which often use short paragraphs followed by multiple-choice questions.

Second, informal assessments tend to have high content validity. That is, they include or sample the content that has been presented or is to be presented to the student during instruction. Thus, such procedures relate well to the specific curriculum in the school or classroom. They also enable teachers to determine whether children can apply reading skills they have learned in other classroom subjects.

Third, informal assessments can be devised and utilized as the need arises. Teachers do not have to wait for the go-ahead from a test selection committee, for purchasing approval, or for delivery.

Fourth, informal assessments usually involve little cost. The basal passages themselves, ditto sheets, chalkboards, interviews, conversations, and discussion are all inexpensive formats and procedures.

Fifth, assessments using informal tests are generally easy to administer and interpret. Teachers would obviously not construct tests that they could not give and interpret easily.

LIMITATIONS

First, the quality of informal assessments and tests is proportionate to the expertise of the teachers in preparing and utilizing them. For example, can the teacher select appropriate formats, choose the best materials for use in a testing situation, ask good questions, make quality observations, and sequence skills testing in an appropriate manner?

Second, informal assessments may lack validity; they may not really measure what the teacher thinks they measure. For example, does a test in phonics really measure phonic knowledge, or does it measure the words children already recognize by sight?

Third, the assessments may not be balanced in terms of items needed to measure skills or affect. For example, certain areas may be loaded with many items and other areas with few because some areas, such as literal understanding, are easier to construct test items for than others, such as inferential understanding or critical reasoning.

Fourth, with the exception of assessments designed to approximate a determination of instructional level (such as informal reading inventories and cloze and maze procedures), teachers may not be able to determine an adequate criterion level. That is, how much should a student know about a given skill area at a given point in time?

Fifth, the quality of the format or the reproduction process used for tests may be poor. Purple ditto sheets are frequently of poor quality. Type size may also be inappropriate; the page may be cluttered or poorly spaced; typographical errors may be present. All such factors may affect performance on tests.

INFORMATION TO CONSIDER

All informal assessment tests and procedures have strengths and limitations. Teachers must be cognizant of both when they select their assessment procedures.

Summary

This chapter has focused on selected informal assessment procedures that can be developed and utilized by teachers in diagnosing reading levels and reading behaviors. In making such assessments, the information-gathering procedures should be adequate, and at the same time efficient. Excessive or superfluous data collection should be avoided.

General guidelines for making the assessment process efficient and adequate were followed by discussion of the ways teachers can estimate students' reading levels. Much attention was given to the informal reading inventory (IRI), an individual assessment designed to determine students' reading and listening levels and to provide a beginning level of diagnostic information in word recognition and comprehension.

Teachers often prefer group assessment procedures, as they are less time-consuming than individual assessments; however, they provide less diagnostic information. Among the group procedures discussed were the group reading inventory (GRI), cloze procedure, maze procedure, and quick class surveys.

Informal assessments have strengths and limitations, which were set out so that teachers might judge the appropriateness of a given procedure for their own use.

Specific assessment procedures for reading skills (such as phonics) and affect (attitudes and interest) were not included in this chapter. These procedures will be presented in later chapters together with instructional strategies designed to enhance their efficiency.

Questions for Further Thought

1. Are there other sets of criteria for determining reading levels on an IRI that you consider valid? Why?
2. What are the major differences in the quality of data obtained from a group diagnostic procedure and an individual procedure?
3. What are appropriate guidelines for choosing assessment instruments to estimate reading levels?

Activities and Projects

1. Describe a classroom with which you are familiar. Then state what informal tests or procedures you would use for assessment. Give a reason for choosing each test or procedure. In what order would you consider administering these tests or procedures?
2. As you visit schools and talk to teachers, find out which of the general principles of assessment discussed in this chapter are operable. Which ones seem not to be operable? Why?
3. Construct one of the informal tests discussed in this chapter for a group or situation with which you are familiar. State how you attempted to maximize its strengths and minimize its limitations.
4. Construct a set of three consecutive levels of an IRI for a basal reader series, using the suggestions in Appendix A as a guide. Include a word list and three graded passages at each level.
5. Administer your IRI to a child. Describe what data you obtained.
6. Read *Approaches to the Informal Evaluation of Reading*, edited by John J. Pikulski and Timothy Shanahan (Newark, Del.: International Reading Association, 1982). Choose a type of test discussed in this chapter and state how Pikulski and Shanahan have refined your understanding of the concepts presented here.
7. Read "Informal Reading Inventories: A Review of the Issues" by Michael C. McKenna, in *The Reading Teacher*, vol. 36 (March 1983), pp. 670–79. Compare this critique with pages 94–116 in the reference cited in #6. Write a statement reflecting your perceptions of the validity and usefulness of an IRI.
8. Read *Reading Diagnosis and Remediation* by Don A. Brown (Prentice-Hall, 1982), pp. 120–29. What are the advantages and disadvantages of Brown's approach to a group reading inventory (GRI) as compared with those presented in this chapter?
9. Read *Reading: What Can Be Measured*, 2nd ed., by Roger Farr and Robert F. Carey (Newark, Del.: International Reading Association, 1986), pp. 166–73. State what you have learned about validity and reliability issues in informal assessments.

Addendum.

The following is a listing of the oral reading miscues for the fourth grader whose protocol appears in Figure 5.4. The listing generally follows the Betts criteria.

Written Text	Oral Response	Scoring
Suppose	did not attempt; examiner aided	scorable
see	substituted "saw"	scorable
into	omitted "to"	scorable
deep	omitted	scorable
pool	mispronounced as pōle, then corrected	recordable
doesn't	substituted "don't," then corrected	recordable
seem to	omitted	scorable
(after "swim")	inserted "good"	scorable
what	substituted "how"	scorable
could	substituted "can"	scorable
(after "could")	long pause	recordable
do to	omitted	scorable
(after "help")	inserted "out"	scorable
saw	substituted "see"	scorable
someone	substituted "somebody"	scorable
(after "someone")	long pause	recordable
trouble	mispronounced as "trōble," then corrected	recordable
call loudly	reversed to "loudly call"	scorable
"help./ If"	long pause	recordable
If possible	omitted	scorable
someone	substituted "somebody"	scorable
nearby	omitted	scorable
adult	did not attempt; examiner aided	scorable
for adult help	repeated phrase	scorable (Betts); recordable (Powell)
never	substituted "don't"	scorable
into	omitted "-to"	scorable
(after "water")	inserted "by"	scorable
own	omitted	scorable
(after "life")	long pause	recordable
danger	mispronounced as "daen/ger," then corrected	recordable
and	omitted	scorable
not/be	long pause between words	recordable
be able to	omitted	scorable
the other person	substituted "him"	scorable
trained	omitted "-ed"	scorable
lifeguards	mispronounced as "gōurds"	scorable
lifeguards/should	long pause between words	recordable

continued

Addendum. *(continued)*

Written Text	Oral Response	Scoring
into	omitted "-to"	scorable
to	substituted "for"	scorable
comes	substituted "come"	scorable, if not dialect
the person	substituted "he"	scorable
reach	substituted "reaching"	scorable
towel	mispronounced as "tōe/el"	scorable
a towel	repeated	scorable (Betts)
try extending a	repeated	scorable (Betts)
(after "a")	long pause	recordable
branch	mispronounced as "brand"	scorable
also	omitted	scorable
an	substituted "a"	scorable
car	did not attempt; examiner aided	scorable
fishing	omitted "-ing"	scorable
fishing	repeated	scorable (Betts)
(after "when")	long pause	recordable
person	substituted "he"	scorable
object	did not attempt; examiner aided	scorable
grabs the object	repeated	scorable (Betts)
or her	omitted	scorable
safety	did not attempt; examiner aided	scorable
can't	substituted "don't"	scorable
(after "reach")	long pause	recordable
the person	substituted "him"	scorable
throw	substituted "there," then corrected	recordable
into	omitted "-to"	scorable
anything	substituted "something"	scorable
support	substituted "suppose"	scorable
might	substituted "should"	scorable
jac/ket	paused between syllables	recordable
rubber	substituted "running"	scorable
or	substituted "and"	scorable

6

Norm- and Criterion-Referenced Tests

This chapter will focus on commercially produced norm- and criterion-referenced tests. Information from these tests is used in assessing reading achievement and in estimating potential for reading success. Norm-referenced tests (NRTs) systematically sample a body of information and provide a comparison of a given student's performance with that of a representative group of students. NRTs are often called "standardized" tests. Criterion-referenced tests (CRTs) enable teachers to compare students' performance against a standard of proficiency deemed to represent satisfactory performance at given age/grade levels.

The two types of tests do not represent totally discrete concepts, as the criterion levels established for a CRT are based on performance expectations for average children at given age/grade levels. The purpose for which a given test is used may determine the choice of type. For example, if a teacher wishes to compare the achievement of her class with the national average or to see how much change has occurred in her group over a period of time, an NRT is the appropriate choice; if she wishes to measure mastery of a specific reading objective, a CRT will better serve the purpose.

Using norm- and criterion-referenced tests is not necessarily the most valid way to gather data. According to Farr and Carey (1986, p. 3) these tests may not provide the best information. Informal assessments, as outlined in Chapter 5 and Chapters 7–12, may be more fruitful for assessing affect and specific skill strengths and weaknesses. Farr and Carey suggest that a test should meet three criteria if it is to be considered a good way to gather information:

1. Will this test provide the information that is really needed? That is, does the test sample from the domain of behaviors of pertinent interest and does the test provide a realistic context (one that is like the situation in which real reading behaviors occur)?

2. Does the test provide a convenient and nonthreatening means of collecting the needed information?
3. Does the sample of behaviors included on the test cover enough different situations to ensure that the results will be both valid and reliable?

Topics covered in this chapter on norm- and criterion-referenced tests include available types (with illustrative examples), how test results are interpreted and reported, criteria for selecting and evaluating tests, reporting test information to parents, guidelines for using test scores, and advantages and limitations.

There are many technical terms used in this chapter that are important in interpreting norm- and criterion-referenced tests. These concepts are often not well understood by teachers, administrators, legislators, or the lay public (Ruddell 1985), even though decisions are made affecting children's school careers (and ultimately their lives) based on the results of such tests. If readers are not familiar with the various technical terms and concepts, they are encouraged to study Appendix C, which presents many of the terms needed for an adequate understanding of this chapter. Selected key terms that are explained in Appendix C are asterisked the first time they are used in this chapter.

Norm-Referenced Tests

QUESTIONS TO GUIDE READING

Recall Questions
1. What are norm-referenced tests? Reading survey tests? Diagnostic reading tests? School ability tests?
2. What do the following terms or concepts mean: test norms, validity, reliability, standard error, grade-equivalent score, stanine, percentile, standard score?
3. What types of scores may be obtained from norm-referenced tests? What are their limitations?
4. In the test evaluation process, what questions should be asked?
5. What are the advantages and limitations of norm-referenced tests?

Thinking Questions
1. Why may tests designed to measure specific skills not really be measuring discrete abilities?
2. Why should (or should not) teachers consider out-of-level testing for children with reading problems?
3. How would you determine which type of validity is most important for a given test?

4. Why is it important to do an item analysis when evaluating content validity?
5. Why should a teacher be cautious in interpreting norm-referenced data? In reporting these data to parents?

Since norm-referenced tests are widely used in determining both students' reading achievement and their reading potential, teachers should understand something of their general nature, strengths, and limitations and how they should be selected.

TYPES OF NORM-REFERENCED TESTS

There are several types of norm-referenced tests used for assessment and diagnostic purposes. Prominent among these are group school ability tests, individually administered intelligence tests, survey reading achievement tests, and diagnostic reading tests.

Group school ability and individually administered intelligence tests are used to obtain an indication of the child's ability to succeed with school tasks. Survey tests indicate the overall level of achievement in reading by giving an estimate of how a child or a group compares to other children at given age/grade levels. A diagnostic reading test yields information on the child's ability to handle specific reading skills in comparison with his peers.

Group school ability tests. The purpose of group school ability tests is to predict success with cognitive, school-related tasks. They may be used as one indicator of whether a child is reading up to his potential.

There are several group school ability tests that teachers may consider for assessing academic aptitude. The *Otis-Lennon School Ability Test* (O–LSAT) (Psychological Corporation 1979, 1982) will be described below to give the reader an idea of what a school ability test is like. The O–LSAT is said to be a measure of abstract thinking and reasoning ability for students in grades 1–12. The test is a power test; that is, it is untimed.

There are five levels in each of two comparable forms (R and S):

Primary I: Grade 1
Primary II: Grades 2–3
Elementary: Grades 4–5
Intermediate: Grades 6–8
Advanced: Grades 9–12

A student known to be considerably more or less able than her age/grade peers may be given a higher or lower level of the test than normally given to her peers.

Scores are reported as percentile ranks,* stanines,* and school ability indexes (SAIs). A *percentile* indicates the percentage of examinees in the population on which the test was normed who scored lower than the student taking the test. A *stanine* places examinees in one of nine groups based on performance of a norming population. Stanines are related to the normal curve* (for a discussion of this relationship see Appendix C).

SAIs have replaced IQ as the basic way scores are reported for this test. SAIs have the same statistical characteristics as deviation IQs;* that is, they are based on the normal curve. The term SAI is used in reporting results rather than IQ to inhibit overinterpretation, as frequently happened with IQ scores. The following is a distribution of SAIs:

Above 132   2% of students
116–132   14% of students
84–132   68% of students
68–84   14% of students
Below 68   2% of students

Figure 6.1 shows O–LSAT norms for performance by age: percentile ranks and stanines for SAIs.

All NRTs should be *reliable*. Reliability* refers to the extent to which the test measures consistently. Reliability is reported in *coefficients*, which are measures of the degree of a relationship. Split-half reliability coefficients* for the various levels range from .91 to .94 when scores are considered by grade and from .94 to .95 when scores are considered by age. Test-retest reliability* by test levels ranges from .84 to .92. These reliability scores are all good.

NRTs should also be *valid*. Validity* refers to the extent to which the test measures what it is supposed to measure. One way O–LSAT validity data are reported is in terms of correlations* with subject-matter grades. These correlations have a median of .49, and are considered low according to most guides for evaluating correlations.

A test should have a low standard error of measurement* if individual scores are to have meaning. Standard error is an estimate of how much an obtained score differs from a hypothetical true score. Standard error tells what percentage of the time an individual's hypothetically true score would fall between certain points or scores. The standard error for most age groups on the O–LSAT is 4 SAI points. This means that if a student obtained a score of 90, 68 percent of the time his hypothetically true score would range from 86 to 94; the range would be wider the other 32 percent of the time. Thus, it can be seen that SAIs, like IQ scores, should not be interpreted as precise measures.

Figure 6.1. Norms for Performance by Age Percentile Ranks and Stanines for Otis-Lennon School Ability Indexes

SAI	%ile Rank	Sta-nine	SAI	%ile Rank	Sta-nine	SAI	%ile Rank	Sta-nine	SAI	%ile Rank	Sta-nine
150	99		127	95		103	57		79	10	
149	99		126	95		102	55		78	9	
148	99		125	94		101	52		77	8	
147	99		124	93		100	50	5	76	7	
146	99		123	92	8	99	48		75	6	2
145	99		122	91		98	45		74	5	
144	99		121	90		97	43		73	5	
143	99		120	89		96	40		72	4	
142	99		119	88		95	38		71	4	
141	99		118	87		94	35				
			117	86		93	33		70	3	
140	99	9	116	84		92	31	4	69	3	
139	99		115	83	7	91	29		68	2	
138	99		114	81		90	27		67	2	
137	99		113	79		89	25		66	2	
136	99		112	77		88	23		65	1	
135	99		111	75		87	21		64	1	
134	98		110	73		86	19		63	1	1
133	98		109	71		85	17		62	1	
132	98		108	69	6	84	16	3	61	1	
131	97		107	67		83	14		60	1	
130	97		106	65		82	13		59	1	
129	96		105	62		81	12		58 and below	1	
128	96		104	60		80	11				

An important feature of the test is its relationship to the *Metropolitan Achievement Tests* (MAT6) survey battery, discussed later in this chapter. When these tests are given at approximately the same time, ability/achievement comparisons can be determined. A child's actual achievement may be compared with his achievement potential, based on how well children in the norming population scored on both tests. This information could help a teacher identify students who might not be reading up to potential. Achievement/ability comparisons are also possible with the *Stanford Achievement Test*, 7th ed.

Another school ability test that permits comparisons with achievement is the *Test of Cognitive Skills* (California Test Bureau/McGraw-Hill 1982). Anticipated achievement scores are available when the test is administered in conjunction with either the *Comprehensive Tests of Basic Skills, Forms U and V* (CTBS) or the *California Achievement Tests, Forms C and D* (CAT). In reviewing the CTBS, Schell (1984) notes that a difference between achievement and expectation based on the *Test of Cognitive Skills* is reported only if the difference is statistically significant* at the .20 level; teachers should not assume that such differences necessarily indicate that the child is a remedial reader.

Additional group tests of mental ability may be found in Appendix D. A list of publishers is given in Appendix F.

In summary, *group school ability tests* have strengths and limitations. They can be given, scored, and interpreted by classroom teachers. They provide one measure of scholastic aptitude, enabling them to be used (with caution) in estimating reading expectancy. Among their limitations are that they may be culturally or linguistically biased and that the examinee's ability to read may affect results on those tests for which reading is required.

Individual intelligence tests. Intelligence tests also purport to assess general mental ability or scholastic aptitude. Some intelligence tests are designed for administration to groups, others to individuals only. Tests administered by classroom teachers are generally group tests, while those administered in a clinic are generally individual tests. Test items may be either *verbal*, relying heavily on language items, or *nonverbal*, involving the manipulation of numbers or objects and geometric designs in spatial arrangements. Both verbal and nonverbal scores should be considered in assessing remedial readers.

Individual intelligence tests are generally considered more valid than group tests in assessing mental ability. Among the available individual tests that classroom teachers may give, score, and interpret are the *Slosson Intelligence Test—Revised* (SIT) and the *Peabody Picture Vocabulary Test— Revised* (PPVT–R).

The *Slosson Intelligence Test—Revised*, 1984 edition (Slosson Educational Publications) is intended to be helpful in predicting reading achievement and in screening students who have reading problems. It covers ages from infancy to adulthood and has an administration time of ten to twenty minutes. Deviation IQs are reported, as are percentiles, stanine categories, and NCEs (normal curve equivalents*). Data provided by the publisher indicate a high correlation (.979) with the *Revised Stanford-Binet Intelligence Scale*. King and Henk (1985) examined the relationship of the SIT with the *Weschler Intelligence Scale for Children—Revised* among students referred to the University of Georgia Reading Clinic. They found the correlation between the two tests in providing reading expectancy estimates to be .96.

The PPVT–R (American Guidance Service 1981) is a measure of receptive vocabulary for Standard English and provides an estimate of verbal ability or scholastic aptitude. It does not purport to be a comprehensive test of intelligence. As a measure of a student's receptive vocabulary, it is in a sense an achievement test. It is useful as an initial screening device for identifying bright, low-ability, or language-impaired children. An important function of the test is assistance in identifying problem readers (Dunn and Dunn 1981, pp. 1–3).

The PPVT–R has two forms, L and M. It can be administered quickly, is untimed, and requires no reading or writing. The stimulus situation for the test is a series of 175 plates, each of which contains four pictures. The examiner says a stimulus word and the examinee points to the picture that best illustrates the stimulus (see Fig. 6.2).

The norming population closely matches the national census on standardization variables such as region of the country and type of community. Figure 6.3 shows the location of the communities used in the norming process. Raw scores are converted to standard scores,* percentile ranks, stanines, and age equivalents.*

The median* standard error on the PPVT–R for the various age levels is six raw-score points. A raw score is the number of items the examinee got right. The test was normed on 4,200 subjects across the United States, using a stratified random sampling* plan. The median split-half reliability coefficients were .80 for Form L and .81 for Form M. Median alternate form* reliability for raw scores was .82 for immediate retest and .78 for delayed retest. Validity is based on high correlations with measures of

Figure 6.2. PPVT–R Stimulus Training Plate

A

Training Plate A, Form L, Regular Edition of *Peabody Picture Vocabulary Test–Revised*, by Lloyd M. Dunn and Leota M. Dunn. © 1981. Reproduced by permission of American Guidance Service. All rights reserved.

Figure 6.3. Locations of the 25 Communities Included in the PPVT–R Standardization Sample, Ages 2½ Through 18

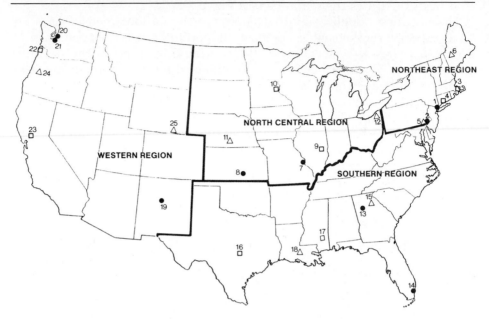

Legend

● Central city (population ≥ 50,000)

□ Suburb or small town (population 2,500 to 49,999)

△ Rural area (population < 2,500)

Northeast Region

1. New York, New York
2. Philadelphia, Pennsylvania
3. Ipswich, Massachusetts
4. New Haven, Connecticut[a]
5. Exton, Pennsylvania[b]
6. Farmington, Maine[b]

North Central Region

7. St. Louis, Missouri
8. Wichita, Kansas
9. Charleston, Illinois
10. Minneapolis & St. Paul, Minnesota[a]
11. Kearny, Nebraska[b]
12. Kent, Ohio[b]

Southern Region

13. Atlanta, Georgia
14. Miami, Florida
15. Athens, Georgia[b]
16. Austin, Texas[a]
17. Hattiesburg, Mississippi
18. Lafayette, Louisiana[b]

Western Region

19. Albuquerque, New Mexico
20. Seattle, Washington
21. Tacoma, Washington
22. Astoria, Oregon
23. Sacramento, California[a]
24. Eugene, Oregon[b]
25. Laramie, Wyoming[b]

[a]Testing was done in one or more suburban areas near this city.

[b]Testing was done in one or more rural areas near this city.

vocabulary, moderate correlations with other tests of verbal intelligence, (for example, the WISC–R) and a reasonable correlation with measures of school achievement.

Special teachers of reading or clinicians may wish a more precise measure, such as that afforded by the *Weschler Intelligence Scale for Children—Revised* (WISC–R) or the *Revised Stanford-Binet Intelligence Scale* (see Ch. 14 for discussion of these tests). These tests should be administered only by specially trained personnel.

In summary, individual intelligence tests that teachers may administer aid in assessing mental ability and in predicting whether children are reading to potential. The major disadvantage is that individual administration is time-consuming, particularly if given to large numbers of children.

Additional individual mental ability tests are discussed in Chapter 14; a few others are briefly annotated in Appendix D.

Reading survey achievement tests. Survey achievement tests in reading generally measure a broad range of reading skills and abilities. These tests often yield grade-equivalent scores in word recognition (or vocabulary) and comprehension, and an average grade-equivalent score (combining word recognition and comprehension scores) is also generally available. Survey tests are more meaningful for group comparisons than for diagnosing individuals, since they generally do not yield enough information on specific skills to permit an adequate diagnosis.

Among the leading survey tests of reading achievement are:

California Achievement Tests, Forms E & F (California Test Bureau/McGraw-Hill, 1985). Eleven levels, ranging from K.0 to 12.9.

Comprehensive Tests of Basic Skills, Forms U and V (California Test Bureau/McGraw-Hill, 1985). Eleven levels (A–K), ranging from K.0 to 12.9.

Gates-MacGinitie Reading Tests (Riverside Publishing Company, 1978). Seven levels, ranging from Readiness through grades 10–12. All levels except Readiness have at least two forms. Levels D and E, for grades 4–9, have three forms.

Iowa Tests of Basic Skills (Riverside Publishing Company, 1982). Ten levels, for grades K–9.

Metropolitan Achievement Tests, 6th ed. (Psychological Corporation, 1985). Norm-referenced and criterion-referenced. Two forms with eight levels, ranging from K.0 to 12.9.

Stanford Achievement Test Series (Psychological Corporation, 1982). Ten levels, ranging from K.0 to 13; alternate forms available for levels from 2.5 to 13.

As a representative example, the reading portion of the *Metropolitan Achievement Test*, 6th ed. (MAT6) will be briefly discussed. The MAT6 tests are designed to measure achievement in major skill and content areas of school curricula, including reading. The tests, designed with eight overlapping batteries for K–12.9, consist of both survey and diagnostic tests, which can be used independently or together depending on the information needed. Both norm-referenced and criterion-referenced information are available.

Test levels and instructional grade levels for the survey tests are as follows:

Preprimer	K.0–K.5
Primer	K.5–1.4
Primary 1	1.5–2.4
Primary 2	2.5–3.4
Elementary	3.5–4.9
Intermediate	5.0–6.9
Advanced 1	7.0–9.9
Advanced 2	10.0–12.9

In levels spanning K.5–4.9, word recognition, vocabulary, and comprehension are assessed. In levels spanning 5.0–12.9, only vocabulary and comprehension are assessed. Figure 6.4 shows a sample format used in the survey tests. Norm-referenced scores available include percentile ranks, stanines, grade equivalents, scaled scores,* normal curve equivalents, and achievement/ability comparisons.

A special feature of the MAT6 is a criterion-referenced score obtained from the Reading Comprehension test that enables teachers to match performance to a specific basal reading series. This score, called Instructional Reading Level (IRL), gives an instructional reading level similar to an IRI. At lower grade levels, the match is with basal series and with skill needs; in upper grades, the match is with subject areas such as science and social studies. The MAT6 has Basal Textbook Resource Guides available for the leading basal reading series. These guides provide a match between test objectives and the basal series.

Teachers are often concerned whether obtained test results such as the IRL are accurate in estimating instructional level. In a study of the fifth edition of the MAT, Smith and Beck (1980) found the IRL to be an acceptable determiner of instructional level for children in grades 1 through 6.

The reading diagnostic tests for K.5–1.9 measure skills such as visual discrimination, letter recognition, auditory discrimination, sight vocabulary, phoneme/grapheme: consonants, phoneme/grapheme: vowels, vocabulary in context, and reading comprehension. For 1.5–2.9, visual discrimination and letter recognition are dropped, and a test for word-part clues is added. For 2.5–3.9, auditory discrimination is dropped, with

Figure 6.4. Page from MAT6 Elementary Form Parent Pretest Information Folder

READING

Reading items for the Elementary level are grouped into three tests: Vocabulary, Word Recognition Skills, and Reading Comprehension. The Vocabulary Test measures how well your child knows the meaning of words in context. Items in the Word Recognition Skills Test measure how well pupils match spoken word sounds to printed words and understand more difficult words by studying their parts. The Reading Comprehension Test measures your child's understanding of short stories. Some children taking MAT6 at this level will mark their answers in the test booklet; others will use a separate answer sheet.

Vocabulary

What To Do
Read the sentence. **Pick** the word that best completes the sentence. **Mark** the letter for that word.

1   He wanted a _____ for his birthday.

    Ⓐ red   Ⓒ wagon

    Ⓑ pretty   Ⓓ again

Word Recognition Skills

What To Do
Read the KEY WORD. **Then** read the four words next to it. One of the words has the **same sound** as the underlined part of the KEY WORD. **Mark** the letter for that word.

1		2	
	Ⓐ belt		Ⓔ bet
gr<u>ee</u>n	Ⓑ belong	st<u>e</u>p	Ⓕ feat
	Ⓒ bend		Ⓖ brief
	Ⓓ center		Ⓗ herb

What To Do
Read the sentence. **Pick** the word that best completes the sentence. **Mark** the letter for that word.

3   Every _____ of the puzzle must be found.

    Ⓐ parted   Ⓒ parts

    Ⓑ part   Ⓓ parting

Reading Comprehension

What To Do
Look at the story. In a box at the top of the story there is a purpose question. **Read** the purpose. It will help you when reading the story. **Next,** read the story. **Then** answer each question that follows. **Mark** the letter for each answer.

> How did Bill fool Betty
> and her pet bird?

Betty has a pet bird called Tom. Tom likes cake. Her friend Bill put a peanut in Tom's cage. When Betty <u>saw</u> the peanut she laughed. She did not think Tom would eat the peanut.

The next day the peanut was gone. She thought she had been wrong. But Bill told her he had taken the peanut out of the cage.

1   Tom likes to eat —

    Ⓐ peanuts

    Ⓑ cake

    Ⓒ birds

    Ⓓ candy

2   In this story, the word <u>saw</u> means —

    Ⓔ a cutting tool

    Ⓕ lost

    Ⓖ an old saying

    Ⓗ noticed

no new tests added. For 3.5–4.9, sight vocabulary is dropped, and a test for rate of comprehension is added. Skimming and scanning is added for 5.0–6.9; phoneme/grapheme tests and word-part clues are dropped for 7.0–9.9.

In addressing the issue of validity of the MAT6, content objectives were determined from analyses of textbook series, state guidelines, and school system syllabi. These were then reviewed by panels of curriculum experts from across the country. Test items were written by curriculum and measurement experts and then edited by people with classroom experience. Test items were also reviewed by advisers representing various ethnic groups, in an attempt to avoid ethnic bias.

In summary, group reading achievement tests provide information for comparing groups with norm groups, for evaluating overall effectiveness of instruction, and for identifying those children who need further testing. They are easy to administer, but many such tests lack diagnostic information and content depth, and may often overrate students' instructional level. The MAT6 tests, with both norm-referenced and criterion-referenced portions, seem to overcome some of the limitations commonly associated with survey tests.

Additional reading survey tests may be found in Appendix D.

Diagnostic reading tests. Diagnostic reading tests purport to measure specific skills involved in processing print. That is, they are intended to measure areas such as phonic analysis, auditory discrimination, and literal comprehension. As such, they have the potential of providing more information to a teacher than survey achievement tests. However, it is difficult to document the existence of discrete skills in the reading process. Farr and Carey (1986, p. 150) state that most research on the discriminant validity of subtests on specific skills does not support the contention that they can be assessed validly.

An example of a diagnostic reading test is the widely used *Stanford Diagnostic Reading Test* (SDRT), 3rd ed. (The Psychological Corporation 1984). Its primary purpose is to identify pupils' strengths and weaknesses in reading. The SDRT places more emphasis on the low achiever than do survey tests by including more easy questions.

Four major areas of reading skills are covered on the SDRT: decoding, vocabulary, comprehension, and rate. There is a changing focus on skills as one moves through levels of the test, with decoding receiving stronger attention at primary levels and a concentration on comprehension, vocabulary, and rate at higher levels. There are four levels of diagnostic testing (Red, Green, Brown, and Blue), with two parallel forms (G and H) at each level.

The Red Level is designed for use at the end of grade 1, in grade 2, and for extremely low achievers in grade 3. The tests assess auditory discrimination, phonetic analysis, auditory vocabulary, word recognition, and comprehension of short sentences and paragraphs.

The Green Level is designed for use in grades 3 and 4 and for very low achieving pupils in grade 5. It assesses auditory discrimination, phonetic and structural analysis, auditory vocabulary, and literal and inferential comprehension.

The Brown Level is intended for use in grades 5 through 8 and with very low achieving high school students. It assesses phonetic and structural analysis, auditory vocabulary, literal and inferential comprehension of textual, functional, and recreational reading material, and reading rate.

The Blue Level is designed for use from the end of grade 8 through community college with students who have reading problems from grade 8 on. It assesses phonetic and structural analysis; knowledge of word meanings and word parts; reading rate, including skimming and scanning; and literal and inferential comprehension of textual, functional, and recreational reading materials. Figure 6.5 shows the subtests and skills measured on the *Stanford Diagnostic Reading Test*, 3rd ed.

Two categories of scores are available: content-referenced and norm-referenced. Content-referenced scores provide data on specific sets of questions and yield useful diagnoses of specific strengths and weaknesses. Scores available are raw scores and Progress Indicator cutoff scores. Progress Indicator scores identify students who have demonstrated a competence level such that they can succeed in regular school programs.

Norm-referenced scores compare students' scores with the norming population; they are best used to compare students' performance across subtests or in relationship to peers. Scores available include percentile ranks, stanines, grade equivalents, scaled scores, and normal curve equivalents. *Scaled scores* express performance on a single scale across forms and levels of the same subtest. *Normal curve equivalent* scores are derived from percentile rank. They are a linear transformation of normalized Z-scores* and are used almost exclusively in research studies. Score types and recommendations for their use can be found in Figure 6.6.

High reliability coefficients are reported for subtests at each level. For example, reliability coefficients on the Brown Level for grade 5, based on raw scores, range from .87 to .94.

Validity on the SDRT is said to reflect the objectives of the content of reading programs across the country. One indicator of validity is whether the test measures the curricular content of a particular school. Individual schools are asked to compare the items of the test with the objectives of the local curriculum to determine its validity.

The Manuals for Interpreting Results contain valuable information on organizing classes for prescriptive teaching, determining students' instructional needs, motivating pupils, and planning instruction to meet specific skill needs.

In summary, group diagnostic reading tests can assist a teacher in obtaining helpful information in a short period of time. They do provide more information for teachers to use than most survey tests. There is some question about whether these tests really measure subskills; also, given

Figure 6.5. Subtests and Skills of *Stanford Diagnostic Reading Test*

Decoding			
RED LEVEL	**GREEN LEVEL**	**BROWN LEVEL**	**BLUE LEVEL**
TEST 2: Auditory Discrimination Consonants (15 Items) Vowels (15 Items)	TEST 2: Auditory Discrimination Consonants (15 Items) Vowels (15 Items)		
TEST 3: Phonetic Analysis Consonants (24 Items) Vowels (16 Items)	TEST 3: Phonetic Analysis Consonants (15 Items) Vowels (15 Items)	TEST 3: Phonetic Analysis Consonants (15 Items) Vowels (15 Items)	TEST 4: Phonetic Analysis Consonants (15 Items) Vowels (15 Items)
	TEST 4: Structural Analysis Word Division (24 Items) Blending (24 Items)	TEST 4: Structural Analysis Word Division (48 Items) Blending (30 Items)	TEST 5: Structural Analysis Affixes (15 Items) Syllables (15 Items)

Vocabulary			
RED LEVEL	**GREEN LEVEL**	**BROWN LEVEL**	**BLUE LEVEL**
TEST 1: Auditory Vocabulary (36 Items)	TEST 1: Auditory Vocabulary (40 Items)	TEST 1: Auditory Vocabulary (40 Items)	TEST 2: Vocabulary (30 Items) TEST 3: Word Parts (30 Items)

Comprehension			
RED LEVEL	**GREEN LEVEL**	**BROWN LEVEL**	**BLUE LEVEL**
TEST 4: Word Reading (30 Items) TEST 5: Reading Comprehension Sentence Reading (28 Items) Paragraph Comprehension (20 Items)	TEST 5: Reading Comprehension Literal Comprehension (24 Items) Inferential Comprehension (24 Items)	TEST 2: Reading Comprehension (Items measure two skills) Literal Comprehension (30 Items) Inferential Comprehension (30 Items) and Textual Reading (20 Items) Functional Reading (20 Items) Recreational Reading (20 Items)	TEST 1: Reading Comprehension (Items measure two skills) Literal Comprehension (30 Items) Inferential Comprehension (30 Items) and Textual Reading (20 Items) Functional Reading (20 Items) Recreational Reading (20 Items)

Rate			
RED LEVEL	**GREEN LEVEL**	**BROWN LEVEL**	**BLUE LEVEL**
			TEST 6: Scanning and Skimming (32 Items)
		TEST 5: Reading Rate (33 Items)	TEST 7: Fast Reading (30 Items)

From *Manual for Interpreting SDRT*, Table 1, p. 7. Reproduced by permission from the *Stanford Diagnostic Reading Test*, 3rd Edition. Copyright © 1984 by Harcourt Brace Jovanovich, Inc. All rights reserved.

Figure 6.6. Score Types for SDRT: Their Characteristics and Applications

Score	Recommended Uses	Subtests	Comparable Across: Forms	Levels	Grades
Raw Scores	Deriving other scores; instructional purposes; statistical analysis when on same subtest, form, and level.	No	No	No	Only on same subtest, form, and level.
Progress Indicators	Skill-based diagnosis; instructional purposes; curriculum evaluation.	No	Yes	No	No
Percentile Ranks	Comparing across subtests; comparing with national or local performance; reporting scores.	Yes	Yes	Yes	No
Stanines	Comparing across subtests; grouping.	Yes	Yes	Yes	No
Normal Curve Equivalents (NCEs)	Comparing across subtests; comparing with national or local performance; reporting scores.	Yes	Yes	Yes	No
Grade Equivalents	Comparing with national sample.	No	Yes	Yes	Yes
Scaled Scores	Growth studies; out-of-level or mixed-form testing; statistical analysis when on same subtest.	No	Yes	Yes	Yes

From *Manual for Interpreting SDRT*, Table 4, p. 15. Reproduced by permission from the *Stanford Diagnostic Reading Test*, 3rd Edition. Copyright © 1984 by Harcourt Brace Jovanovich, Inc. All rights reserved.

diagnostic reading tests may not measure specific curricular objectives in given schools.

Selected individual diagnostic reading tests are discussed in Chapter 14. A listing of additional diagnostic tests may be found in Appendix D.

Out-of-level tests. Some teachers feel that it is fairer to give students who have reading problems a standardized test that matches their achievement level rather than one on their age/grade level, believing that this procedure gives the child an opportunity to be reasonably successful with the task. Teachers should be aware of certain problems inherent in this procedure. First, there may not be a content or format match with the reader. Second, great care must be taken in interpreting results. The stanines, percentiles, and grade-equivalent scores have been determined on age/grade peers and are not appropriate for use unless the publisher has also developed out-of-level norms. Even when out-of-level norms are available, teachers should study the population on which these norms were developed to determine whether there is a match with their children.

One norm-referenced group survey reading test that provides out-of-level norms is the *Gates-MacGinitie Reading Tests*, 2nd ed. (Riverside, CA, 1978). There are seven levels of the tests, from Readiness through Survey F (grades 10–12). All but the Readiness level have two forms, except for levels D and

E for grades 4–9, which have three forms. Available scores include percentile ranks, normal curve equivalents, stanines, grade equivalents, and scaled scores. Norms available for each test level (including out-of-level) may be seen in Figure 6.7.

The test was normed on a national stratified sample of approximately 100,000 students. Reliability coefficients are high, ranging from .88 to .95. Teachers should make their own validity assessment, using a series of questions provided for the purpose.

There is some evidence to support the use of out-of-level tests. For example, Smith et al. (1983) studied on-level and out-of-level results on the *Gates-MacGinitie Reading Tests* of fourth graders who were reading below grade level and enrolled in compensatory programs. They generalized from their data on these students that the out-of-level testing might provide a more accurate assessment of achievement than on-level testing.

Figure 6.7. Norms Available for Each Test Level of the Gates-MacGinitie Reading Test

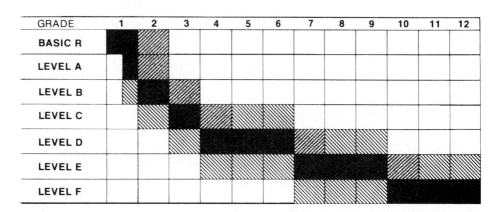

Intended grade range for average classes

Out-of-level use

Out-of-level use

Administering Norm-Referenced Tests

Teachers should follow the directions for administration precisely in order that the data may be interpreted meaningfully. Deviations from suggested procedures can affect test results. When deviations occur, teachers should not interpret the results according to the information presented in the manual. They may look at responses to individual test items to help in determining strengths and weaknesses, but should not use the tables that compare test performance with the norming group.

In certain situations, it may be desirable not to follow the suggested procedures. Teachers may wish to obtain specific diagnostic information about a given child without comparison to the students on whom the test was normed. For example, the teacher may wish to see how many items a student knows on a given test, without concern for the speed with which the child can answer the items; or the teacher may wish to see how many items a child could have answered if he had adequate time. In these cases, the teacher allows the student to finish a test after time is called. The child should mark clearly the last item that was attempted while being timed. Perhaps a different colored pencil could be used for the remainder of the test. If the tests are to be machine scored for system use, a felt-tipped pen or another type of pen that is not read by the machine should be used. Teachers would then analyze the responses before the response sheets are sent for machine scoring.

Providing unlimited time enables the teacher to determine whether speed is a factor in the test results. It also provides an opportunity to secure a larger sample of items for item analysis. As noted earlier, norms should not be applied to such scores since they are not secured under the conditions required by the norming process.

How Norm-Referenced Reading Test Results Are Reported

Several ways that norm-referenced test results are reported have been identified in previous sections. Among the scores most frequently listed in manuals are the following: raw scores, grade-equivalent scores, percentile ranks, stanines, and types of scaled scores. *Raw scores*, the number of items to which correct responses were given on the test, are used to derive each of the other scores.

A *grade-equivalent score* (GEs) is an indicant of performance expressed in months of a grade (i.e., 3.5 or 5.6). A reader who obtains a GEs of 3.1 on a test of reading comprehension can answer as many comprehension questions correctly as the average third grader in the first month of school who was tested when the norms were developed. Grade-equivalent scores have limited diagnostic value in working with problem readers because they do not suggest specific reading strengths and weaknesses.

Some grade-equivalent scores are *projected*. Many tests are normed, or standardized, only once in a given school year. Thus only one grade equivalent score (in terms of months) per school year is based on the actual performance of students in the norming population. For example, a test given during the second month of school to fifth graders would result in a score of 5.2, which would be assigned to those students obtaining a score at the mean level. All other grade-equivalent scores for that year's level, such as 5.8, would be statistically projected by a process known as interpolation.* Grade-equivalent scores are, at times, projected for grades not included in the norming population through a process called extrapolation.* For example, a score of 9.5 may be given when the highest level of students included in the test were eighth graders.

In interpreting a grade-equivalent score, it is important to consider the standard error of measure on the test from which the score was derived. A grade-equivalent score is not something a student "has." Recall that standard error is an estimate of how much an obtained score deviates from a hypothetical true score. The standard error of the SDRT, Brown Level, Reading Comprehension test for grade 6 is 3.1 raw score points. This means that 68 percent of the time an examinee's hypothetically true score will be within a range from 3.1 raw points above the obtained score to 3.1 points below that score, a margin of 6.2 raw score points out of a potential 40. The other 32 percent of the time the obtained score may deviate further from the "true" score.

Many reading educators object to the use of grade-equivalent scores. The International Reading Association, the world's largest professional association of reading educators, passed a resolution at its Delegates Assembly in April 1981 recommending that educators abandon the practice of reporting grade-equivalent scores to various parents and the media and that test authors and publishers eliminate grade-equivalent score interpretation tables from their test manuals. This resolution was based on the assumption that such scores are often misunderstood by many persons and are used for making instructional decisions about children that are not valid.

A *percentile rank* is a score that indicates how many examinees scored below a given examinee. The percentile range is from 1 to 99. A percentile rank of 50 indicates that the examinee scored at the average level, based on the scores of students in the norming population; a percentile rank of 96 means that the child scored higher than 96 percent of the students who took the test.

As with grade-equivalent scores, there is the possibility of random error with percentile ranks. The ranks are not precise and should not be interpreted as such; neither do they represent equal units of ability. Percentile ranks tend to "bunch up" around the middle of the range and spread out at the ends of the range. Therefore, a small score difference may not have the same meaning at the middle of the range of percentile ranks as it does at the extremes. It may take only one or two raw score points to make a difference in rank at the upper and lower range, while it may take several raw score points to move a child up or down in rank toward the middle of the range.

Percentile ranks are best used for reporting scores in relationship to the norming group. They are not that helpful in pinpointing particular reading strengths and weaknesses. They are less likely to be misunderstood and cause anxiety in parents than are grade-equivalent scores, however, because they bear no specific grade level designation.

Stanines (short for standard nine-point scale) are among the most widely used scores. A stanine places an examinee in one of nine groups based on the performance of the norming population (see Appendix C for a listing of the nine specific categories). Stanines from a survey test can suggest the need for more thorough diagnostic procedures (Estes and Vaughn 1978, p. 57). Students who score in stanines 1–3 or 7–9 deviate enough from the average to warrant such attention.

Stanines seem less precise than grade-equivalent scores to many teachers; but it is this apparent lack of precision that makes their use more appropriate. They cover a broader range of obtained scores than grade-equivalent scores and percentile ranks, thus eliminating much of the inaccuracy of these scores.

Stanines are mathematically and statistically the most acceptable scores to report to parents. Of the scores discussed here, they are among the easiest to understand and are the safest to use in terms of accuracy.

Scaled scores permit comparisons of a child's score from different levels or forms of a given test. These scores eliminate some of the weaknesses of grade-equivalent scores and percentiles. They are a valid way of looking at change in a child, since the difference between two scaled scores at one part of the scale represents the same difference in performance as between two scores at another part of the scale. That is, the scale is continuous, making comparisons in student growth more meaningful. Comparisons using scaled scores should be done only for specific tests; they are meaningless for comparing tests from different publishers and for comparing subtests of a diagnostic battery since each subtest has its own system of scaled scores.

REPORTING TO PARENTS

Parents are entitled to information about their children. They want to know how their child compares with others and how much progress he or she has made. They often misinterpret norm-referenced scores, however, and are then hesitant to admit that they misunderstood and are not entirely pleased with the type and amount of information given them (Dreher and Singer 1985).

Information given to parents should be provided in understandable terms, with an attempt to eliminate as much anxiety as possible. Grade-equivalent scores and IQ scores often cause such anxiety because parents think these scores are more precise and meaningful than they really are.

It is probably best, when possible, to refrain from reporting a specific IQ score to parents, as such scores are frequently used to label children or to compare one child with another. The newer school ability tests that have dropped the concept of IQ, use scores such as School Ability Indices instead, which one hopes will not be as widely misinterpreted.

When specific IQ scores are reported to the parent, it is a good practice to identify a level of functioning, such as high average or low average, rather than focusing on a specific score. Before interpreting scores to parents, teachers should consider the effects of the standard error of the test on the score, the validity information on the test, the effort the child put forth on the test, and possible physical and emotional factors present when the test was taken. All of these variables can affect the obtained scores.

Ideally, grade-equivalent scores should not be reported to parents since they too are often misunderstood. Parents tend to feel that they represent a precise, measurable level of achievement in months and years, which is an inaccurate concept. If grade-equivalent scores are reported to parents, efforts should be made to ensure that parents understand what such scores may or may not mean. The possibility of error on the test should be mentioned.

Percentile ranks are sometimes reported to parents. Again, these scores may be misinterpreted in that they may seem to be more precise than they are. Parents should be advised that it takes several score points to change percentile ranks in the middle range, while it may take only a few raw score points to change ranks significantly at the extremes of the range.

Stanines are probably the best scores to report to parents. Such scores are more dependable because they are broader in nature. In conducting parent conferences in which stanines are the scores reported, the teacher may wish to follow the guidelines recommended by Durost (1961):

1. Do not talk about the normal curve. Teachers should talk instead about variability in height and weight and indicate that there are more persons in the average category than at the extremes. Parents should understand that the same holds true for tests and that stanines are a way of transforming raw scores into nearly equal ranges of ability or achievement.
2. Encourage parents to think of each stanine as representing ranges of achievement or ability. Stanines 1, 2, and 3 represent performance below average; stanines 4, 5, and 6 represent average performance; and stanines 7, 8, and 9 represent above-average performance.
3. Explain how stanines are used in grouping, in diagnosing strengths and weaknesses, and in comparing achievement to potential.

4. Advise parents that stanines are the best way of interpreting intelligence tests since the results are more stable than IQ scores. Parents should understand, however, that a given stanine level is based on only one test and may vary somewhat from test to test.

ADVANTAGES AND LIMITATIONS OF NORM-REFERENCED TESTS

Norm-referenced tests have advantages and limitations. Teachers should weigh the potential advantages of a given test against its potential limitations when deciding whether to use that test as a part of the diagnostic process.

Advantages. Among the advantages of norm-referenced tests are the following:

1. The tests are carefully developed by professionals with expertise in the fields of test construction and reading education. Great care is normally taken in their construction.
2. They have statistically determined reliability and some indication of why they are valid for what they purport to measure.
3. Norm-referenced tests have precise administration procedures that are generally easy to follow, and which have been subjected to scrutiny for clarity when the test was normed. They may therefore be clearer to students than the directions that teachers may provide for their own informal tests.
4. Norm-referenced tests are appropriate for comparing general levels of achievement, particularly for groups of students. That is, teachers may wish to see how their group compares in achievement with the norm group, with another group using differing methods or materials, or with another group they have previously taught. Norm-referenced tests are probably better suited for this purpose than informal or criterion-referenced tests. Comparable forms are generally available, making possible pre- and post-comparisons of growth. Such tests are more appropriate for comparing ranges of achievement than teacher-made or criterion-referenced tests, as they are generally constructed to span more than one grade level.
5. Norm-referenced tests are useful as a screening device in determining whether further testing is needed. That is, when a child scores below what the teacher feels should be appropriate for his age/grade level, he may be selected for more intensive assessment procedures to determine his potential and his reading strengths and weaknesses.

Limitations. Norm-referenced tests have limitations, some considered quite serious by certain reading educators. Teachers are urged to consider these limitations as they decide what assessment procedures to use, make instructional decisions based on the results, and report the results to parents.

1. Norm-referenced tests often do not assess reading behaviors in ways that approximate actual day-to-day instruction. Children may, therefore, not respond on the test as they would in the classroom. For instance, a test may sample very short passages with children using response modes (such as multiple choice or cloze) not used in typical instructional practice. Some children may have difficulty because they do not have facility with the response mode. Ramsey (1967, p. 67) feels that the tests that meet a "reality" criterion are best for assessing reading behaviors. A test should assess reading abilities and behaviors in ways similar to the ways these abilities are used in the classroom.

2. Norm-referenced tests represent only one sample of reading behaviors, at one point in time, under a specific set of testing conditions. Students may perform differently under other sets of conditions or at other times. A good example is a child's performance under a timed testing situation. Students may exert a level of effort for this short period of time that they would not be able to continue throughout the school day. No important diagnostic decision should be based on one sample of behaviors.

3. The diagnostic value of many norm-referenced tests is often limited. Survey reading achievement tests are not designed to serve a diagnostic function; rather, they measure a limited number of broadly defined reading skills such as "vocabulary" and "comprehension." Tests labeled as "diagnostic" may also be limited, as was stated earlier. Diagnostic tests often include subtests, which may sample a limited number of skills with a relatively few items. Such subtests may not cover the specific objectives of the school's curriculum in a given area. Teachers should examine specific items in subtests in order to determine whether the test or subtest is valid for their situation.

4. Subtests may not measure skills discretely. In determining whether subtests measure different skills, teachers should consult the statistical data for the correlations between subtests. Intercorrelations between subtests should be low (below .65). When the intercorrelations are high, there is a possibility that the subtests are measuring the same skill or ability.

   Some authorities see no evidence that subtests are really valid measures of separate and discrete skills. Farr and Carey (1986, p. 17) state that "[R]esearch on the reading process indicates that reading cannot be fractionated into a set of separate skills; to do so is to misunderstand reading behavior." Teachers need to examine test items in order to determine if the items on subtests really seem to measure the skill as children in their classrooms use it.

5. Norm-referenced tests are appropriate only for students who are similar to the norming population on which the test was standardized

and who have been exposed to instructional situations similar to the testing format.

The validity of such norm-referenced tests is particularly suspect for students who are culturally or linguistically different from the sample used to establish norms. Tests that sample a range of knowledge and experiences to which given students have not been exposed will hardly yield useful results. Items can offend the culturally different student emotionally. Ethnic pride may also be a factor. More data are needed from large samples of linguistically and culturally different students in order to learn more precisely how these students function in given testing situations. A further caution: older tests may not be appropriate for current use, as educational practices and student characteristics may have changed.

6. Behavior sampling may be limited. In order to produce a test with a reasonable time for administration, test makers are often forced to choose between breadth and depth. A test may have a few items that sample a wide range of behaviors, or several samples of a narrower range of behaviors. The latter can be an advantage for diagnostic purposes. Teachers need to be knowledgeable about the range of behaviors sampled in a given test.

7. The grade-equivalent score, a frequently used score obtained from a norm-referenced test, does not necessarily represent an examinee's hypothetical "true" score. Neither are percentile ranks precise scores. Both lead to misinterpretation.

8. Norm-referenced test results rarely suggest an actual instructional level, and should not be used for this purpose. Grade-equivalent scores are often inflated in terms of the student's actual performance in a classroom. Scores that fall at the upper and lower ends of a range of scores are not as valid as those which fall in the middle of the range, due to problems with test construction and statistical treatments (Karlin 1973). Norm-referenced tests also tend to give artificially high grade-equivalent scores for low students in the intermediate grades because chance in a multiple choice format can inflate a grade-equivalent score.

Another possible reason that tests may overestimate instructional level is that many students try harder in a brief, timed testing situation but cannot sustain that performance for longer periods of time.

9. Comprehension scores may not actually represent information gained from reading the test items because some questions may be passage-independent for some children; that is, the items may be answered from general knowledge rather than from the student's having read the test. Results of studies done by Preston (1964) and Pyrczak (1979) indicate a substantial number of passage-independent items in norm-referenced tests. Teachers need to ask themselves whether given students might have answered specific questions without having read the passage.

10. While not a limitation of a test per se, machine scoring can be a limitation in the diagnostic value of the test unless the data returned to the teacher indicates the specific types of items the child got right or wrong. Teachers frequently need to look at student responses for each item in order to get usable information. Often machine-scored results do not provide enough such specific information.

EVALUATING AND SELECTING NORM-REFERENCED TESTS

The first step in selecting and evaluating norm-referenced tests is to identify the goals and objectives for reading instruction. A decision must be made as to what is important in the reading curriculum, which students should receive what types of instruction, what levels of performance in given areas are needed, and what feelings or beliefs about reading are desirable. These decisions will determine the content of the tests and their use.

Second, a search should be made for tests that are appropriate for the established goals and objectives. This may involve tests for groups and individuals, tests of achievement and of school academic potential, survey tests, and diagnostic tests. In making this search, teachers may seek assistance from publishers, testing specialists in school systems, or university professors knowledgeable in reading education and in testing.

Third, once potentially useful tests have been identified, they should be critically evaluated. In this evaluation process, several questions need to be asked:

1. Is the test valid?

Validity is the most critical consideration in evaluating and selecting a norm-referenced test. Farr and Carey (1986, pp. 15–22) have identified four critical issues surrounding test validity—whether the test actually assesses a particular reading behavior, whether a single test can tell us all we need to know about a child's reading behavior, how the test results are to be used, and whether the test results will be misunderstood or misused by educators or the public.

Validity is determined by test makers in several ways. A common method is to include items that recognized authorities feel measure the skill or sample the quality being assessed. Another common way is to examine curriculum guides from across the country and to sample those skills and abilities found most frequently. A third way is to correlate the test with another test that is felt to measure the same content or construct.

Several types of validity may be relevant for consideration, depending on the purpose for which the test is to be used. These are content, construct, criterion (concurrent and predictive), and face validity.

Content validity refers to whether the test samples reading behavior and skills that have been taught or are to be taught in the reading program. Teachers need to check tests item by item to make this determination. A good way to begin this process is for the teacher to take the test herself. This will call attention to the content and to potential problems that students may have with the format, directions, and so on. In taking the test, Rupley and Blair (1983, pp. 20–21) suggest that teachers:

1. look for items that are poorly written;
2. assess the difficulty level of the items being considered;
3. determine whether a sufficient number of items are used to sample the behaviors being tested;
4. determine whether there are items that do not really relate to the behaviors being tested; and
5. assess the amount of time required to complete the items.

Construct validity refers to whether a test is measuring a psychological quality that theory and common sense assumes to be in existence. Construct validity is especially important for tests that purport to measure intelligence, academic aptitude, or global reading comprehension. The test should include items that attempt to measure these qualities. Again, an inspection of test items seems appropriate. Gronlund (1976) suggests that evidence for construct validity can be obtained in four ways:

1. through an analysis of the mental processes required by the items on the test [the "inspection" referred to above];
2. through a look at the scores of groups known to the teacher [readers with problems, superior readers, slow learners, etc.];
3. through a look at pre- and post-treatment data; and
4. through correlations with other tests felt to measure the same construct.

Criterion validity is concerned with whether test results correlate with some independent measure. There are two types of criterion validity about which teachers should know—predictive and concurrent.

Predictive validity refers to how well the test predicts future behavior. Reading readiness tests, for example, should have high predictive validity; there should be a positive relationship between the way students perform on the readiness test and how well they do with the reading instructional program.

Concurrent validity refers to how well performance on a given test compares with performance on another measure that is assumed to be valid. Even if a given test correlates highly with some other measure that has established validity, teachers may still wish to check the content or construct validity of the other measure in order to assess whether it measures what they wish to measure. This will help establish the validity of the test they are considering using.

Face validity refers to whether a test visually appears to be measuring that which it is intended to measure. For example, if the test measures reading achievement, it should appear to the students to assess reading achievement. Students may try harder and have more faith in the results when the test has high face validity.

2. Is the test reliable?

A test is reliable if it measures consistently over time so that the results are dependable. A test can be reliable even if it is not valid: students in a course in reading education might perform consistently on a test in chemical engineering, but such a test would not be a valid measure of what they learned about reading education. Therefore, both validity and reliability must be considered.

Several factors contribute to reliability. One important factor is test length. In a short test, missing one item has a greater effect than on a test with a large number of items measuring the same skill. A second factor is the number of response options. Where there are two possible answers from which to choose rather than four or five, the chances of guessing right increase dramatically. Test-taking skills may also affect reliability.

Test-retest and alternate form reliability coefficients are often lower than split-half reliability, which is determined from the same administration of a given test. Alternate form and test-retest procedures are closer to actual classroom assessment practices. (See Appendix C for a discussion of types of reliability.)

In general, a reliability coefficient of .80 and above (on a test that measures a range of several grades) is acceptable for assessing groups of students; a coefficient of .90 is acceptable for a test designed for individual administration. For a test measuring a single grade only, coefficients should be in the high .70s or low .80s for measuring individuals (Spache 1976, p. 286). Smith and Fisher (1978, p. 13) state that a test with a reliability coefficient under .80 is of limited use, and for diagnostic purposes, a reliability coefficient of at least .90 is necessary.

3. Was the norming population similar to the students who are to be tested?

Unless there are similarities between the norming population and the students to be tested, the norms may be relatively meaningless for the tested child or group. A description of the norming population can generally be found in the examiner's manual that accompanies the test.

4. Is the test practical to use?

Practicality is concerned with such factors as ease of administration, scoring, and interpretation; testing time; mode of administration; and cost. Teachers should have the expertise to administer and interpret the tests if the results are to be meaningful.

Ease of scoring is sometimes a concern. Scoring is often done with machines, which seems to save teachers time; however, it should be stated that again much useful diagnostic information is obtained when teachers score their students' tests themselves and note answers to specific items.

The time required for completing a test should be weighed against the results. The test should yield the most diagnostic information (with validity and reliability being considered) in the shortest testing time.

Mode of administration—whether the test must be given individually or whether it may be given to groups—may also be a practical factor worth considering. More diagnostic information is generally available from tests that are administered individually. Teachers have an opportunity to observe the individual child closely and, if appropriate, to probe reasons for their answers. However, the time required for a large number of children to be tested individually may be prohibitive. Teachers must balance the need for in-depth diagnostic information against the time required to secure the information.

The cost of a given test also needs to be considered. Tests that are less expensive yet valid and reliable, would naturally be given preference over more costly ones.

Teachers and clinicians can profit from developing, or adapting, a checklist for evaluating tests that is appropriate for their situation. Kavale (1979) has developed a checklist that is appropriate for consideration; see the Addendum at the end of this chapter.

INFORMATION TO CONSIDER

1. Norm-referenced tests can be useful in making diagnostic decisions.
2. Teachers should understand as much as possible about how NRTs are constructed, how to administer them so that as much information as possible is obtained, how scores are statistically developed, how valid the tests really are, how scores may be interpreted, and how scores should be reported to parents.
3. NRTs have strengths and limitations, both of which should be considered for each test before it is used as an assessment tool.
4. Caution should be used in interpreting data from NRTs and in reporting interpretations to parents.

Criterion-Referenced Tests

QUESTIONS TO GUIDE READING

Recall Questions
1. What are criterion-referenced tests?
2. What are the advantages and limitations of criterion-referenced tests?
3. What is a useful set of criteria for evaluating criterion-referenced tests?

Thinking Questions
1. Why is it important to evaluate the content validity of criterion-referenced tests?
2. Are the assumptions on which criterion-referenced tests are built defensible? Why?
3. Why is it difficult to delineate a specific scope and sequence of reading skills?

Criterion-referenced tests (CRTs) are measures of the extent to which a student can perform a desired reading behavior. CRTs are designed to analyze reading strengths and weaknesses in individual children with regard to a particular standard, or criterion. There are two commonly used types of CRTs—mastery tests and minimum competency tests. *Mastery tests* assess whether the student has mastered given reading skills or levels of material. Such tests frequently accompany basal reading series, and are used to assess the skills taught and whether the book level has been "mastered." *Minimum competency* tests are used to assess whether students have a desired level of reading skill in order to perform tasks routinely encountered in life. Minimum competency tests are also used in making pass/fail decisions or graduation decisions. In many states, such minimum competency tests are mandated.

Criterion-referenced tests may be used as an integral part of a diagnostic program along with teacher-made tests, observation, and norm-referenced tests. Criterion-referenced tests are valuable for measuring the skills they were designed to measure, and can be used profitably when they are congruent with the curriculum.

CRTs are generally prepared in one of two ways: (1) by developing a set of objectives with accompanying test items (objectives-based assessment) or (2) by carefully defining a domain of performance, such as reading, with a set of test items that measures the domain (domain-referenced assessment) (Popham 1978).

Criterion-referenced tests relate a student's performance to an absolute standard, or criterion. Many teacher-made tests have this characteristic. There is an acceptable level of performance, or a satisfactory-unsatisfactory point on a continuum of possible points. CRTs are unlike norm-referenced tests in that there are no comparison scores (grade equivalents, percentiles, scaled scores, or stanines) by which to compare the student with a norming population.

Criterion-referenced tests are based on certain assumptions (Kavale 1979). One assumption is that a defensible hierarchy of skills can be delineated, based on a consensus among teachers and reading educators across schools and systems about the relative importance of various skills. Other assumptions are that the items chosen for a CRT are valid for measuring particular skills and that a given level of mastery represents an acceptable level of knowledge ability or performance.

REPRESENTATIVE CRITERION-REFERENCED TESTS

There are many types of criterion-referenced tests, including teacher-made tests. CRTs also accompany basal reader series, and are appropriate in those classrooms in which a given basal reading series is the basic curriculum. Sets of CRTs also form a part of management systems that utilize various materials.

A representative sample of the most widely used commercially available criterion-referenced tests follows:

The Fountain Valley Teacher Support System (Zweig Associates, Huntington Beach, CA). Seventy-seven one-page tests covering 367 behavioral objectives, for grades 1–6.

PRI Reading Systems (CTB/McGraw-Hill, 1980). Five levels (A–E) with a total of 171 specific objectives, for grades K–9. Four skill clusters are assessed—oral language, word attack and usage, comprehension, and applications. This test is described more fully below to furnish a detailed example of criterion-referenced tests.

Reading Yardsticks (Riverside Publishing Company, 1981). Nine levels, for grades K–8. The test measures decoding, vocabulary, comprehension, and rate, with emphasis varying from level to level. Each skill area has 4 to 8 subtests, covering 17 to 46 objectives.

Wisconsin Tests of Reading Skills Development (Learning Multi-systems, Inc., Madison, WI, 1972). Two forms, for grades K–6. The tests measure word attack (K–3), comprehension (K–6), and study skills (K–6).

Three types of assessment are possible. *Skill-area assessment* tests broad reading skills such as word analysis. *Category-objectives assessment* refers to terminal reading objectives, such as sound-symbol correspondences. *Instructional-objectives assessment* focuses on specific skills such as the mastery of individual vowels and consonants. Figure 6.8 shows the objectives structure of the PRI systems, including levels, skill clusters, skill areas, category objectives, and instructional objectives.

The PRI provides supplementary instructional materials, such as lesson plans and activities, to help students with skills they have not mastered. According to the publisher, the PRI should enable teachers to:

- place students at instructional level
- diagnose reading strengths and individual needs
- prescribe appropriate materials and activities

Figure 6.8. The Objective Structure of the PRI

The Objectives Structure

Levels

Skill Clusters	A PRE-K—1 7 Cat. Obj., 13 Inst. Obj.	B 1—2 19 Cat. Obj., 39 Inst. Obj.	C 2—3 18 Cat. Obj., 43 Inst. Obj.	D 4—6 17 Cat. Obj., 42 Inst. Obj.	E 7—9 14 Cat. Obj., 34 Inst. Obj.
Oral Language 10 Category Obj. 12 Instructional Obj.	1 Sound Seg/Comparison 2 Single Words 2 Syllables 2 Vocabulary 4 Word Meaning 3 Syntax 6 Sentence Structure 7 Negatives	1 Sound Seg/Comparison 2 Syllables 3 Initial, Ending Consonants 2 Vocabulary 4 Word Meaning 5 Multimeaning Words 3 Syntax 6 Sentence Structure 7 Negatives 8 Variant Word Orders			
Oral Comprehension 4 Category Obj. 9 Instructional Obj.	4 Literal Meaning 9 Basic Facts-Oral 10 Event Sequence-Oral 5 Inferred Meaning 11 Character Analysis-Oral 12 Future Events-Oral	4 Literal Meaning 9 Basic Facts-Oral 10 Event Sequence-Oral 5 Inferred Meaning 11 Character Analysis-Oral 12 Future Events-Oral 13 Main Idea-Oral			
Word Analysis 10 Category Obj. 24 Instructional Obj.	6 Letter Recognition 14 Letter Names 15 Uppercase, Lowercase Letters 16 Alphabetical Order 7 Word Recognition 17 Sight Words in Context	7 Word Recognition 18 High-Frequency Sight Words 19 Word-Sound Correspondence 8 Symbol/Sound Correspondence 20 Single Vowels 21 Word Completion 22 Vowel Digraphs/Diphthongs 23 Syllabication 9 Structural Analysis 25 Compound Words 26 Root Words 28 Affix Usage	7 Word Recognition 18 High-Frequency Sight Words 8 Symbol/Sound Correspondence 20 Single Vowels 21 Word Completion 22 Vowel Digraphs/Diphthongs 23 Syllabication 9 Structural Analysis 25 Compound Words 26 Root Words 27 Contractions 28 Affix Usage	8 Symbol/Sound Correspondence 21 Word Completion 22 Vowel Digraphs/Diphthongs 23 Syllabication 24 Diacritical Marks 9 Structural Analysis 28 Affix Usage	
Vocabulary 10 Category Obj. 19 Instructional Obj.	10 Word Picturing 29 Word Illustration 11 Word Matching 30 Categorization 31 Antonyms 32 Synonyms 12 Word Meaning 33 Word Definition	10 Word Picturing 29 Word Illustration 11 Word Matching 30 Categorization 31 Antonyms 32 Synonyms 12 Word Meaning 33 Word Definition	10 Word Picturing 29 Word Illustration 11 Word Matching 30 Categorization 31 Antonyms 32 Synonyms 12 Word Meaning 33 Word Definition 34 Multimeaning Words in Context	11 Word Matching 31 Antonyms 32 Synonyms 12 Word Meaning 33 Word Definition 34 Multimeaning Words in Context	11 Word Matching 31 Antonyms 32 Synonyms 12 Word Meaning 33 Word Definition 34 Multimeaning Words in Context

Skill Area

Category Objective

Instructional Objective

Oral Language

Attack & Usage

Word

Word Usage
11 Category Obj.
32 Instructional Obj.

Column 1	Column 2	Column 3	Column 4
13 Language Mechanics 35 Plurals 36 Capitalization 37 Punctuation **14 Sentence Parts** 39 Prepositional Phrases 40 Pronouns 41 Modifier Usage **15 Syntax** 44 Context Clues 45 Verb Tense, Agreement	**13 Language Mechanics** 35 Plurals 36 Capitalization 37 Punctuation **14 Sentence Parts** 39 Prepositional Phrases 40 Pronouns 41 Modifier Usage 42 Connectors **15 Syntax** 44 Context Clues 45 Verb Tense, Agreement	**13 Language Mechanics** 36 Capitalization 37 Punctuation **14 Sentence Parts** 42 Connectors 43 Subjects, Predicates **15 Syntax** 44 Context Clues 45 Verb Tense, Agreement 46 Modifier Placement 47 Complete Sentences	**13 Language Mechanics** 36 Capitalization 37 Punctuation 38 Possessives **15 Syntax** 44 Context Clues 45 Verb Tense, Agreement 46 Modifier Placement 47 Complete Sentences

Comprehension

Literal Comprehension
8 Category Obj.
15 Instructional Obj.

Column 1	Column 2	Column 3	Column 4
16 Story Detail 48 Subject Details 49 Action Details **17 Paraphrasing** 53 Sentence Paraphrasing	**16 Story Detail** 48 Subject Details 49 Action Details 50 Story Setting 51 Event Sequence **17 Paraphrasing** 53 Sentence Paraphrasing	**16 Story Detail** 50 Story Setting 51 Event Sequence 52 Motivation **17 Paraphrasing** 54 Paragraph Paraphrasing	**16 Story Detail** 51 Event Sequence 52 Motivation **17 Paraphrasing** 54 Paragraph Paraphrasing

Interpretive and Critical Comprehension
12 Category Obj.
24 Instructional Obj.

Column 1	Column 2	Column 3	Column 4
18 Main Idea 55 Topic **19 Inference** 57 Future Events 58 Character Analysis **20 Figurative/Descriptive Lang.** 61 Metaphors/Similes	**18 Main Idea** 55 Topic **19 Inference** 57 Future Events 58 Character Analysis 59 Cause and Effect **20 Figurative/Descriptive Lang.** 61 Metaphors/Similes	**18 Main Idea** 56 Passage Summary **19 Inference** 57 Future Events 58 Character Analysis 59 Cause and Effect 60 Drawing Conclusions **61 Metaphors/Similes** 62 Idiomatic Expressions	**18 Main Idea** 56 Passage Summary **19 Inference** 57 Future Events 58 Character Analysis 59 Cause and Effect 60 Drawing Conclusions **61 Metaphors/Similes** 62 Idiomatic Expressions 63 Tone/Mood

Applications

Study Skills
5 Category Obj.
9 Instructional Obj.

Column 1	Column 2	Column 3	Column 4
22 Reference Skills 66 Front, Back Matter		**21 Information Organization** 64 Paragraph Structure 65 Outlines **22 Reference Skills** 67 Bibliography 69 Library Resources	**21 Information Organization** 64 Paragraph Structure 65 Outlines **22 Reference Skills** 69 Library Resources

Content Area Reading
9 Category Obj.
27 Instructional Obj.

Column 1	Column 2	Column 3	Column 4
23 Social Studies 70 Directions 71 Vocabulary 72 Graphic Displays **24 Science** 73 Directions 74 Vocabulary 75 Graphic Displays **25 Mathematics** 76 Directions 77 Vocabulary 78 Graphic Displays	**23 Social Studies** 70 Directions 71 Vocabulary 72 Graphic Displays **24 Science** 73 Directions 74 Vocabulary 75 Graphic Displays **25 Mathematics** 76 Directions 77 Vocabulary 78 Graphic Displays	**23 Social Studies** 70 Directions 71 Vocabulary 72 Graphic Displays **24 Science** 73 Directions 74 Vocabulary 75 Graphic Displays **25 Mathematics** 76 Directions 77 Vocabulary 78 Graphic Displays	**23 Social Studies** 70 Directions 71 Vocabulary 72 Graphic Displays **24 Science** 73 Directions 74 Vocabulary 75 Graphic Displays **25 Mathematics** 76 Directions 77 Vocabulary 78 Graphic Displays

- teach critical reading skills
- monitor progress toward mastery
- reinforce and enrich mastered skills

Additional criterion-referenced tests are described in Appendix D. A list of publishers can be found in Appendix E.

ADVANTAGES AND LIMITATIONS

Significant among the advantages of criterion-referenced tests is their potentially close relationship to the objectives of instruction, especially those objectives that lend themselves to expression in behavioral terms. CRTs are effective diagnostic tools in teaching programs with highly specific objectives because the tests can be selected to correspond with those objectives. Criterion-referenced tests are more likely to be valid measures of skill-based "basics" programs than norm-referenced tests.

Criterion-referenced tests have limitations, however. Some goals and objectives do not lend themselves well to this type of assessment, especially in affective areas and in critical and creative reading.

A second limitation is that CRTs measure mastery of specific skills in relationship to the format and material used in learning those skills. They do not necessarily measure success with other formats or types of materials.

A third limitation is that skills are generally measured in isolation; therefore, the ability of a student to apply these specific skills in processing running text for everyday purposes is not measured. In addition to determining students' mastery levels, teachers need to know how well they can think about reading material, how they feel about the act of reading itself, and how well they can actually use the material they read.

A further limitation is that CRTs are only as good as the objectives on which they were based and the sequence of skills from which they were determined. Whether the objectives and sequence are congruent with the student's instructional program is a determination that should be made before selection. Otherwise, there is a danger that the test will determine the curriculum.

Although it is not possible at the present time to delineate a specific set of skills related to the reading act or to state a defensible sequence in which such skills are best learned, criterion-referenced tests behave as if this were possible. This is a problem with CRTs.

Still another potential problem is that of reliability. The larger the number of items used to test a given skill or objective, the greater the potential reliability of the test. Some CRTs may have too few items to assure confidence in the results.

Perhaps the most significant limitation relates to the criterion levels of mastery. Whether such a standard can be determined outside a given curriculum is questionable. What is an acceptable criterion level: 100 percent, 90 percent, 70 percent? Otto (1973) offers some guidelines for establishing criteria of mastery. He states that performance should be nearly perfect (the student should score close to 100%) if:

1. the skill is important for future learning,
2. the objective calls for mastery, and
3. if guessing is a possibility, (e.g. if multiple-choice formats are used).

SELECTING CRITERION-REFERENCED TESTS

Commercial criterion-referenced tests should be evaluated carefully before selection. The following questions should be asked:

1. How closely does the test measure what is taught in the curriculum?
2. How close is the sequence of skills tested to the instructional sequence?
3. Are the skills tested really necessary for success with reading?
4. Does the test assess skills in a manner similar to that used in the teaching process?
5. Are as many areas of reading covered as possible? Do the authors acknowledge that there are important areas, such as affect and critical thinking, that cannot be tested well using this format?
6. Is there an effective, efficient record-keeping system?

INFORMATION TO CONSIDER

1. Criterion-referenced tests (CRTs) can have a valid place in assessment and diagnostic processes.
2. CRTs do not measure all important aspects of reading.
3. CRTs have strengths and limitations that should be understood by teachers before they are interpreted.

Guidelines for Using Test Scores

QUESTIONS TO GUIDE READING

Recall Question
1. What are six guidelines that may be helpful in using test results effectively?

Chapter 13 will focus on putting together assessment information from several sources, of which test scores will be one. Canney (1979) has suggested a set of guidelines for avoiding poor decisions based on incomplete or inaccurate test results:

1. Validate the content of test items. Evaluate specific test items to determine whether they actually are measuring the content and skills you want to measure.
2. Keep equilibrium in the assessment program. Consider the diagnostic value of observation, teacher-made tests, norm-referenced tests, and criterion-referenced tests; decide how each can best contribute to your needs.
3. Review progress frequently in order to check judgments based on the diagnostic measures that were used. A most helpful way to do this is through diagnostic teaching discussed earlier (see Chapter 4).
4. Investigate discrepancies between performance on tests and performance in day-to-day instruction. Recall that students may not perform over time as they did on one specific test at a given moment. Consider reasons why this may be true.
5. Formulate instructional plans together with students and share general test results with them. In interpreting test results, focus on broad levels (such as stanines) rather than specifics (such as grade equivalents), which probably carry less relevance.
6. Interpret all data in terms of the student and the curriculum in which the student is functioning. The child and the curriculum, not a test prepared for general populations, should be the basis for instructional decisions. Do not evaluate solely in terms of performance on a given test.

INFORMATION TO CONSIDER

Teachers should avoid making poor instructional decisions based on incomplete or inaccurate test results.

Summary

This chapter has focused on two assessment tools that may be used by teachers in assessment and diagnostic processes: norm-referenced tests and criterion-referenced tests. Norm-referenced tests compare students' performance with other students across the country at the same age/grade levels. Criterion-referenced tests compare students' performance against a standard of proficiency.

Norm-referenced tests have been widely used in making educational decisions, often by persons who lacked knowledge of how they were constructed and how the scores obtained should be interpreted. This chapter offered information on test validity, reliability, types of scores and their interpretation, and reporting scores to parents. Strengths and limitations of NRTs were discussed, along with criteria for evaluation and selection.

Commercial criterion-referenced tests are newer than norm-referenced tests, although since many teacher-made tests are criterion-referenced, the concept is certainly not new. CRTs have a valid place in assessing reading skill strengths and weaknesses, even though, like NRTs, they have strengths and limitations. The selection and use of CRTs was featured prominently in this chapter.

The chapter concluded with a set of guidelines for using test scores. It is important that teachers only use data that are meaningful for given children in their specific instructional environment.

Questions for Further Thought

1. What are some problems in comparing results from different tests?
2. What are some of the difficulties involved in putting together data from different sources (such as observation and norm-referenced tests)?
3. How would you attempt to assess the impact of noneducational factors (such as language and culture) on test results?
4. What is the impact of teacher attitude on the role of various assessment techniques in diagnosis?
5. Why is it important to consider the development of local norms (rather than national ones) to be used in interpreting norm-referenced tests?

Activities and Projects

1. Apply the criteria for evaluating norm-referenced tests presented in this chapter to a diagnostic reading test. Report the results to the class.

2. Apply the criteria for evaluating criterion-referenced tests suggested in this chapter to one such test. Discuss the problems you encountered.
3. Visit a special teacher of reading. Determine how the teacher reports test results to students and to parents.
4. Examine a norm-referenced test and a criterion-referenced test that purport to measure the same skill. What are the similarities and differences?
5. Read "Validity and Reliability in Reading Assessment" in Roger Farr and Robert F. Carey, *Reading: What Can Be Measured?*, 2nd ed. (Newark, Del.: International Reading Association, 1986), Ch. 5. State how your reading has refined your understanding of this chapter.

Addendum. Test Selection Checklist by Kenneth Kavale

I. What is your purpose for evaluating this test?
  A. Why do I need a test?
  B. What information do I require?
II. Test Overview
  A. Test information
    1. Name of test—what does name imply about purpose?
    2. Author.
    3. Publisher.
    4. Date of publication and last revision.
  B. Target population
    1. Age level—appropriate for your situation?
    2. Grade level—appropriate for your situation?
    3. Individual or group administration.
    4. Number of available forms—is another form available for future use?
  C. What construct or quality is this test designed to measure?
III. Practical features
  A. Time considerations
    1. Time required to administer total test.
    2. Could the time requirement be handled in your situation?
    3. Time required to score—how involved and time-consuming is the scoring procedure?
    4. Who could score the test in your situation? Does scoring involve judgment or simply tallying right and wrong responses?
    5. Is machine scoring available?
  B. Financial considerations
    1. Cost of test booklet.
    2. Cost of answer sheets.
    3. Cost of test manuals.
    4. Cost of replacement materials.
    5. Cost of scoring services.
  C. General considerations
    1. Are the directions for administering clear and is the language appropriate for the students in your class?
    2. Are the directions for scoring clear?
    3. Are answer sheets appropriate for age and ability level of students?
    4. What training is required to administer the test?

D. Format design
    1. Are illustrations current?
    2. Is print size adequate?

IV. Validity
  A. What evidence of validity is given?
  B. Does reported validity appear adequate in relation to intended purposes?
  C. Subtest validity
    1. Does the name adequately describe the subject?
    2. Does the subtest seem logically related to the test as a whole?

V. Reliability
  A. What evidence for reliability is given?
  B. Do the reported reliabilities appear adequate?
  C. Subtest reliability
    1. Are reported coefficients adequate?
    2. Are subtests sufficiently long?

VI. Norms (when appropriate)
  A. Are the norms provided adequate and appropriate?
  B. Does the normative sample seem truly representative?
    1. Up-to-date?
    2. Age—does the sample cover age range in your class?
    3. Sex—were appropriate numbers of boys and girls included?
    4. Socioeconomic level—does sample cover SES found in your class?
    5. Range of ability—does the sample include ability levels found in your class?
  C. Are the norms relevant for your class and purposes?

VII. Bias
  A. Is there evidence in the test content of sex stereotyping?
  B. Is there evidence in the test content of racial or ethnic bias?

VIII. General evaluation
  A. What is your general evaluation of the test?
  B. For what purpose and group would you recommend this test?

From Kenneth Kavale, "Selecting and Evaluating Reading Tests," in *Reading Tests and Teachers: A Practical Guide*, ed. Robert Schreiner, pp. 15–17. Copyright 1979 International Reading Association. Reprinted with permission of Kenneth Kavale and the International Reading Association.

III
Corrective Strategies for the Classroom

The classroom teacher has responsibility for understanding the reading problems that students in his class may have. The teacher should know how to assess such problems and then provide experiences designed to improve reading skills. This part of the book focuses on corrective strategies in the classroom for teachers of corrective and remedial readers.

Chapter 7 focuses on affective factors related to reading, such as attitudes toward reading, reading interests, motivation related to reading, and reading self-concept. These factors are considered basic to improving the skills of the corrective or remedial reader.

Chapter 8 covers readiness for reading. The readiness skills considered necessary for effective reading include skills in thinking, language, and print awareness. The classroom teacher may encounter corrective and remedial readers who are at the readiness stage of reading; they must provide instruction for these students at that level.

Strategies in word recognition for the corrective or remedial reader are the central theme of Chapter 9. Four word-recognition skills receive attention: sight words, phonics, context, and structural analysis. Strategies for the classroom teacher are suggested in each of these skill areas.

Chapter 10 concentrates on comprehension strategies for the corrective and remedial reader. Many activities can be implemented in the classroom setting to help the problem reader overcome deficiencies in comprehension. Because comprehension is viewed as a basic requirement for effective reading, the classroom teacher must be able to plan effective strategies in this area.

Strategies in study skills and content reading serve as the focus of Chapter 11. The classroom teacher can provide corrective and remedial readers with activities designed to improve the way they study. Such study usually involves content-area reading; thus, study skills and content reading are combined in this chapter as skills to be promoted by the classroom teacher for the corrective or remedial reader.

In Chapter 12, the emphasis is on materials to be used by the classroom teacher in providing instruction for the corrective and remedial reader. Appendix E serves as an extension of Chapter 12, providing a list of specific materials in the eight major categories discussed in the chapter: reading programs, computerized reading materials, taped and talking books, magazines, high interest/low vocabulary books, skill books, games, and newspapers.

The final chapter in this part, Chapter 13, is intended to help the classroom teacher pull together the information in Chapters 7–12. An outline of how the classroom teacher can be involved in the instructional program of both corrective and remedial readers is provided.

Part III should serve as an overall guide to the types of strategies teachers may use in the classroom with corrective and remedial readers. The teacher needs strategies that may be used in a busy classroom to help an individual student with a specific reading problem. In this way, she can help the student gain skills in becoming an effective reader.

7

Affect

In Chapter 2, affect was shown to be a correlate of reading problems. Consideration is often not given to this vital dimension. A student with a reading problem that shows up in low reading-achievement scores or inadequate reading skills usually receives some type of corrective or remedial instruction in the schools; her skills are assessed and a plan is established to improve her reading. Rarely, however, is such attention given to the student who dislikes reading, has little interest in reading, is unmotivated to read, or has a poor self-concept of himself as a reader. The student may or may not have a problem with reading skills, yet he does have a problem with reading: he chooses not to read. Charlotte Huck (1973, p. 203) has declared:

> If we teach a child to read, yet develop not the taste for reading, all our teaching is for naught. We shall have produced a nation of "illiterate literates"— those who know how to read, but do not read.

Directing attention to the same situation, Estes (1971, p. 135) has aptly stated:

> Certainly, how students feel about reading is as important as whether they are able to read, for, as is true with most abilities, the value of reading ability is in its use rather than its possession.

Throughout the years, many other people have stated the situation in similar words:

> The person who doesn't read isn't much better off than the one who can't.

Statements such as these clearly indicate that the affective domain is basic to reading success, as it provides students with the desire to read for pleasure and information. Teachers need to be aware of corrective and remedial readers who feel negative about reading, exhibit little motivation to read, have few reading interests, or possess a negative concept of themselves as readers. Instructional activities must be planned for these students that focus on the affective dimension of reading. Of course, teachers must also be conscious of these same problems in those readers who have adequate reading skills.

This chapter will address reading problems students may have in four dimensions of the affective domain: attitudes toward reading, reading interests, motivations for reading, and self-concept related to reading.

Positive attitudes toward reading indicate that a student likes to read, enjoys engaging in reading activities, and finds pleasure in the act of reading. In the section on attitudes, general information is provided about attitudes; indicators of positive and negative attitudes toward reading are described; ways to assess students' attitudes toward reading are discussed; and instructional activities are suggested for students with negative attitudes toward reading.

Reading interests vary by grade level and gender. They may be directed at a topic (science, animals, sports) or a format (comic books, newspapers, paperback books). In the section on interests, ways of assessing interests are discussed, along with methods of developing instructional programs for corrective and remedial readers based on their interests.

Motivation serves as the energizing force for the affective domain, and is therefore of particular importance to the corrective or remedial reader. The section of this chapter on motivation includes a discussion of the various types of motivation, how teachers can work with students who have problems with motivation, and instructional strategies to help motivate students to read. Motivation plays a crucial role in helping corrective or remedial readers become actively involved in reading.

Self-concept is a critically important affective factor. Many readers with poor reading skills will have correspondingly poor self-concepts; they do not view themselves as competent in reading, nor do they think that significant others see them as effective readers. Such self-concepts can be debilitating to students who encounter problems in gaining reading skills. The section on self-concept includes a discussion of assessment measures that can be used to explore self-concept regarding reading and what teachers and parents can do to promote feelings of adequacy about reading.

Attitudes Toward Reading

QUESTIONS TO GUIDE READING

Recall Questions
1. What characteristics apply to attitudes toward reading?
2. What behaviors indicate negative attitudes toward reading?
3. What types of assessments may be used to measure attitudes toward reading?

4. What types of instructional strategies can be used to improve reading attitudes?

5. How can parents help improve children's attitudes toward reading?

Thinking Questions

1. Why do you think attitudes should (or should not) be the central component of affect related to reading?

2. Why does (or does not) the tripartite components of attitude cover all essential aspects of a student's attitude toward reading?

3. Why is (or is not) reading attitude situation-specific (why, for instance, may a student enjoy reading at home but not at school)?

4. What activities to promote positive attitudes in the classroom can be applicable to reading in the home environment?

Mathewson (1985), in describing an affective model of reading, has stated that the central component should be attitude. Teachers may therefore want to consider this dimension as a beginning step in an overall assessment of affect. To provide a general background, some of the characteristics of attitude will be discussed before specific methods of assessment are described.

Understanding Attitudes Toward Reading

Attitude has been described as a tripartite, as multidimensional, as situational, as experience-based, and as changeable. Many authorities believe it is more than "feelings." Rather, it arises from a student's experiences, can vary with the purpose for reading and the reading environment, and may be changed if appropriate actions are taken.

Just as "trust" or "freedom" cannot be viewed directly, neither can attitudes be "seen." However, positive or negative attitudes are inferred through a person's actions. While there is much we do not understand about attitudes, some basic characteristics are suggested by research.

Tripartite components. Attitude is often viewed as tripartite with components of belief, feeling, and behavior (Fishbein and Ajzen 1975, p. 340). Related to reading, the tripartite encompasses a student's knowledge about reading (beliefs), evaluation of reading (feelings), and actions involving reading (behaviors).

The *belief* component reveals the thoughts, ideas, knowledge, or opinions the student holds with respect to reading. Belief links reading to some attribute such as "worthiness," "boredom," or "getting a good job," as reflected in statements such as the following:

- Reading is a worthwhile activity.
- Reading is boring.
- Being a good reader helps you get a good job.

As a second component of the tripartite, *feelings* reflect a student's evaluation of reading on a continuum from negative to positive, expressed in such terms as "liking," "disliking," "enjoying," or "being uncomfortable." Sample statements showing feelings toward reading include the following:

- I like to read.
- I dislike reading.
- I enjoy reading stories.

The third component of attitude is *behavior*, showing the actual involvement of the student in a reading activity. When the student reads in free time or chooses reading over other activities, she is demonstrating a positive attitude through her behavior. The following statements show reading-related behaviors:

- I read during free time.
- I read on vacation.
- I read at bedtime.

Multidimensionality. According to Lewis and Teale (1980), attitude toward reading is multidimensional, having three factors:

1. *Individual development*—the value placed on reading as a means of gaining insight into self, others, and life in general.
2. *Utility*—the value placed on reading for attaining educational or vocational success or for managing in life.
3. *Enjoyment*—the pleasure derived from reading.

Lewis and Teale use this multidimensional concept of attitudes to show that students may have differing emphases in their attitudes. For instance, one student may view reading primarily as an enjoyable activity; another student sees it as having utility; and still another student sees reading as a way to gain insight into life. All of these students may have an overall favorable attitude toward reading, but they vary in the emphasis they place on the various factors.

Situation. Heathington (1975) has stated that attitudes may vary depending on various reading situations: free reading at school, organized reading at school, reading in the library, reading at home, and recreational reading. While a student may hold a positive attitude about reading at home, he may have a negative attitude about reading in the organized reading class at school.

Since reading attitude may be situation-specific, a teacher may approach assessment of attitude from this viewpoint. He may examine the student's attitudes in the various reading situations and then plan corrective or remedial strategies focused on a particular environment or situation.

Experience. Attitudes are formed as a result of the experiences, direct or indirect, that a student has had in the past (Fishbein and Ajzen 1975, p. 217). Direct experiences relate to the child's actual encounters with reading: learning to read, reading in a group, having parents read to her, or engaging in numerous other reading activities. Some children enter school having experienced a multitude of reading encounters; others have had extremely limited associations with reading. Whether these experiences have been pleasant or not will affect a child's attitude toward reading.

Indirect experiences for a child may consist of comments made or experiences related by adults or peers about reading. If significant people in a child's life make negative or disparaging statements about reading or relate unpleasant encounters with reading, the child's attitude will often be influenced in a detrimental way.

Capability of being changed. Research in social psychology has demonstrated that attitudes can change (Fishbein and Ajzen 1975, p. 387). While limited research has been done with respect to reading, Bullen (1970) did find that a special "books exposure" program involving the use of volunteers to promote reading appreciation improved students' attitudes toward reading. Instructional practices and special programs may have an impact on attitudes, but will not necessarily do so (Alexander and Filler 1976). Therefore, teachers must realize that their instructional practices may affect attitudes toward reading, in either a negative or positive way. With corrective and remedial readers, teachers must constantly question whether their instructional methods are contributing to positive or negative attitudes toward reading.

Brown, Wallbrown, and Engin (1979) suggest that attitudes are influenced by task variables, situation variables, and subject variables. Task variables include instructional materials, situation variables refer to teaching style and methods, and subject variables reflect the characteristics and background of the students.

RECOGNIZING NEGATIVE ATTITUDES TOWARD READING

Teachers often use two techniques for assessing a student's attitudes toward reading: observation and self-report instruments. Both of these methods will provide important data for the teacher to use in working with a corrective or remedial reader.

Observation of attitudes. Some of the behaviors that researchers (Heath-ington and Alexander 1978; Rowell 1972) note as indicative of poor atti-tudes toward reading are:

Does not read during free time.
Does not talk about books read at home.
Does not select reading over other recreational activities.
Does not volunteer to read aloud in class.
Does not ask to go to the library.
Does not finish books she starts.
Does not ask for books as presents.
Does not ask to share books in class.
Does not read during vacation time.
Does not express an interest in coming to reading group.
Does not volunteer answers to questions during reading class.
Does not request that the teacher read a story to the class.
Does not listen attentively when someone reads.

Teachers must be alert to a pattern of such behaviors. While a few of the behaviors exhibited at isolated times may not be a cause for concern, a consistent negative behavior pattern should be a signal to the teacher that the student's attitude may be a problem.

Observation of attitudes toward reading should be comprehensive and structured. Students' behavior should be viewed over a period of time and in a variety of reading situations. Specified behaviors to be observed should be outlined in advance of the actual observation, preferably through the use of a structured observational checklist. Two sample checklists are described below.

The checklist shown in Figure 7.1 was developed based on interviews with students (Heathington and Alexander 1978). It is designed as a quick assessment of attitudes toward reading, although the authors recommend that observation extend over at least a two-week period of time. Checks in the "no" column alert the teacher to possible problems in various read-ing activities: reading aloud in class, reading during free time, reading at home, choosing reading over other activities, and using the library.

The authors find several benefits in their checklist:

1. It is a listing of behaviors that children themselves have indicated are representative of positive and negative attitudes toward reading.
2. It is concise and quick to use.
3. It can be used to diagnose reading attitudes in various situations or environments.
4. It views reading behaviors over time.

Rowell's observation scale, shown in Figure 7.2, measures children's behaviors toward reading in three categories: reading for pleasure, reading

Figure 7.1. Observation Checklist to Assess Reading Attitudes

In the two-week period, has the child:

	yes	no
1. Seemed happy when engaged in reading activities?	_____	_____
2. Volunteered to read aloud in class?	_____	_____
3. Read a book during free time?	_____	_____
4. Mentioned reading a book at home?	_____	_____
5. Chosen reading over other activities (playing games, coloring, talking, etc.)?	_____	_____
6. Made requests to go to the library?	_____	_____
7. Checked out books at the library?	_____	_____
8. Talked about books he/she has read?	_____	_____
9. Finished most of the books she/he has started?	_____	_____
10. Mentioned books she/he has at home?	_____	_____

From Betty S. Heathington and J. Estill Alexander, "A Child-Based Observation Checklist to Assess Attitudes Toward Reading," *The Reading Teacher*, April 1978, p. 770. Copyright 1978 International Reading Association. Reprinted with permission of The International Reading Association.

in the content areas, and reading as it takes place in reading class (Rowell 1972). The teacher uses five ratings to document each of 16 behaviors: always occurs, often occurs, occasionally occurs, seldom occurs, and never occurs. An overall score is obtained for the student by assigning a number to each of the five ratings: 1 for "never occurs" to 5 for "always occurs." An overall score below 48 indicates an attitude problem toward reading. The scale is a useful way for the teacher not only to explore a student's current attitudes toward reading but also to measure changes in attitudes by using the scale at various intervals during the year.

Self-report instruments. In recent years a number of scales have been developed to measure attitudes toward reading. Epstein (1980) has collected many of these scales into a volume on reading attitude measurement. A common characteristic of many of the scales is that they use self-report to determine a student's attitudes.

Self-report scales for reading attitude sometimes consist of a series of statements or questions to which children must respond "yes" or "no" or "agree" or "disagree" (the range is often extended to include "strongly agree," "strongly disagree," and "neutral"). Students may be asked to complete a partial sentence or to select between two statements about reading.

Two attitude scales that use self-report are shown in Figures 7.3 and 7.4. Both scales were developed on a common characteristic of attitudes: that they are situational. The situations or reading environments include:

Figure 7.2. A Scale of Reading Attitude Based on Behavior

Name of student _____ Grade _____ Date _____

School _____ Observer _____

Directions: Check the most appropriate of the five blanks by each item below. Only one blank by each item should be checked.

	Always Occurs	Often Occurs	Occasionally Occurs	Seldom Occurs	Never Occurs
1. The student exhibits a strong desire to come to the reading circle or to have reading instruction take place.	_____	_____	_____	_____	_____
2. The student is enthusiastic and interested in participating once he comes to the reading circle or the reading class begins.	_____	_____	_____	_____	_____
3. The student asks permission or raises his hand to read orally.	_____	_____	_____	_____	_____
4. When called upon to read orally the student eagerly does so.	_____	_____	_____	_____	_____
5. The student very willingly answers a question asked him in the reading class.	_____	_____	_____	_____	_____
6. Contributions in the way of voluntary discussions are made by the student in the reading class.	_____	_____	_____	_____	_____
7. The student expresses a desire to be read to by you or someone else, and he attentively listens while this is taking place.	_____	_____	_____	_____	_____
8. The student makes an effort to read printed materials on bulletin boards, charts, or other displays having writing on them.	_____	_____	_____	_____	_____

Figure 7.2. *(continued)*

	Always Occurs	Often Occurs	Occasionally Occurs	Seldom Occurs	Never Occurs
9. The student elects to read a book when the class has permission to choose a "free-time" activity.	____	____	____	____	____
10. The student expresses genuine interest in going to the school's library.	____	____	____	____	____
11. The student discusses with you (the teacher) or members of the class those items he has read from the newspaper, magazines, or similar materials.	____	____	____	____	____
12. The student voluntarily and enthusiastically discusses with others the book he has read or is reading.	____	____	____	____	____
13. The student listens attentively while other students share their reading experiences with the group.	____	____	____	____	____
14. The student expresses eagerness to read printed materials in the content areas.	____	____	____	____	____
15. The student goes beyond the textbook or usual reading assignment in searching for other materials to read.	____	____	____	____	____
16. The student contributes to group discussions that are based on reading assignments made in the content areas.	____	____	____	____	____

From C. Glennon Rowell, "An Attitude Scale for Reading," *The Reading Teacher*, February 1972, p. 444. Reprinted with permission of C. Glennon Rowell and The International Reading Association.

Figure 7.3. Heathington Primary Scale

The Primary Scale consists of 20 questions which are to be read to the respondent. After listening to a question beginning with the words "How do you feel. . . ," the respondent is asked to mark one of five faces (very unhappy, unhappy, neutral, happy, very happy) which shows how he feels about the question. A score of 5 is given for each very happy face chosen, a 4 for a happy face, a 3 for a neutral face, a 2 for an unhappy face, and a 1 for a very unhappy face. The possible range of scores is 5 × 20 (100) to 1 × 20 (20).

Sample of Partial Answer Sheet

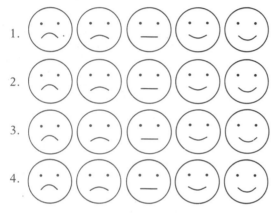

The following directions should be followed in administering the primary scale:

Your answer booklet is made up of two pages. Page one goes from number 1 to number 10, and page two goes from number 11 to number 20. Beside each number are five faces: a very unhappy face, an unhappy face, a face that's neither happy nor unhappy, a happy face, and a very happy face. I will ask you how you feel about certain things and you will put an X on the face that shows how you feel. Suppose I said, "How do you feel when you eat chocolate candy? Which face shows how you feel?" Someone may have chosen an unhappy face because he doesn't like chocolate candy: someone else may have chosen a happy face bacause he likes chocolate candy. Now, I'll read some questions to you and you mark the face that shows how you feel about what I read. Remember to mark how *you* feel because everyone does not feel the same about certain things. I'll read each question two times. Mark only one face for each number. Are there any questions? Now listen carefully. "Number 1. . . ."

Certain groupings of questions can be considered broadly diagnostic. That is, they indicate specific areas of a child's reading environment toward which he may feel positively or negatively. The following groupings are suggested:

1. Free reading in the classroom (items 3, 17)
2. Organized reading in the classroom (items 4, 7, 8, 13)
3. Reading at the library (items 1, 18)
4. Reading at home (items 6, 12, 15, 19)
5. Other recreational reading (items 2, 5, 9, 16)
6. General reading (items 10, 11, 14, 20).

Primary Scale

How do you feel . . .

1. when you go to the library?
2. when you read instead of playing outside?
3. when you read a book in free time?
4. when you are in reading group?
5. when you read instead of watching TV?
6. when you read to someone at home?
7. about the stories in your reading book?
8. when you read out loud in class?
9. when you read with a friend after school?
10. when you read stories in books?
11. when you read in a quiet place?
12. when you read a story at bedtime?
13. when it's time for reading circle (group)?
14. when you read on a trip?
15. when you have lots of books at home?
16. when you read outside when it's warm?
17. when you read at your desk at school?
18. when you find a book at the library?
19. when you read in your room at home?
20. when you read instead of coloring?

From J. Estill Alexander and Ronald C. Filler, *Attitudes and Reading*, pp. 28–32. Copyright 1976 International Reading Association. Reprinted with permission of The International Reading Association.

Figure 7.4. Heathington Intermediate Scale

The Intermediate Scale is composed of 24 statements about reading. The respondent is asked to mark whether he strongly disagrees, disagrees, is undecided, agrees, or strongly agrees with the statement read by the teacher. A score of 5 is given for a very positive response, a 4 for a positive response, a 3 for a neutral or undecided response, a 2 for a negative response, and a 1 for a very negative response.

On 9 of the items (numbers 2, 6, 10, 14, 15, 16, 20, 21, 23), a response of "strongly agree" indicates a very positive attitude and receives a score of 5. On the remaining 15 items, a response of "strongly disagree" indicates a very positive attitude and receives a score of 5. The possible range of scores is 5 × 24 (120) to 1 × 24 (24).

The following directions can be used in administering the intermediate scale:

On your answer sheet, numbers on the right-hand column go from number 1 to number 12. Numbers on the left-hand column go from number 13 to number 24. Beside each number are five boxes. Over each box are one or two letters. *SD* stands for strongly disagree, *D* for disagree, *U* for undecided, *A* for agree, and *SA* for strongly agree. I will read certain statements to you and you are to mark an X in the box that shows how you feel. Suppose I said, "You enjoy eating chocolate candy." What box would you mark? Someone might love chocolate candy and would mark "strongly agree"; another person might enjoy it and mark "agree." Remember that everyone may not feel the same about the statements so make sure you mark how *you* feel. Mark only one box for each number. I'll read each statement two times. Are there any questions? Now listen carefully. 'Number 1 . . .' ."

The Intermediate Scale also has groups of questions which can be used by classroom teachers to diagnose specific areas of reading attitudes. They are as follows:

Sample of Full Answer Sheet

1. Free reading in the classroom (items 5, 6, 15)
2. Organized reading in the classroom (items 1, 24)
3. Reading in the library (items 3, 4, 9, 17, 21)
4. Reading at home (items 7, 10, 11, 20)
5. Other recreational reading (items 12, 13, 23)
6. General reading (items 2, 8, 14, 16, 18, 19, 22)

Intermediate Scale

1. You feel uncomfortable when you're asked to read in class.
2. You feel happy when you're reading.
3. Sometimes you forget about library books that you have in your desk.
4. You don't check out many library books.
5. You don't read much in the classroom.
6. When you have free time at school, you usually read a book.
7. You seldom have a book in your room at home.
8. You would rather look at the pictures in a book than read the book.

continued

Figure 7.4. *(continued)*

9. You check out books at the library but never have time to read them.	17. Most of the books you choose are not interesting.
10. You wish you had a library full of books at home.	18. You don't read very often.
11. You seldom read in your room at home.	19. You think reading is work.
12. You would rather watch TV than read.	20. You enjoy reading at home.
13. You would rather play after school than read.	21. You enjoy going to the library.
14. You talk to friends about books that you have read.	22. Often you start a book, but never finish it.
15. You like the room to be quiet so you can read in your free time.	23. You think that adventures in a book are more exciting than TV.
16. You read several books each week.	24. You wish you could answer the questions at the end of the chapter without reading it.

From J. Estill Alexander and Ronald C. Filler, *Attitudes and Reading*, pp. 28–32. Copyright 1976 International Reading Association. Reprinted with permission of The International Reading Association.

- school-related reading (free reading and organized reading)
- reading at the library
- reading at home
- other recreational reading
- general reading

The scale shown in Figure 7.3 is designed for primary students; the one in Figure 7.4 is for intermediate students. If assessment shows that a student has problems in one of the situations identified on the scales, the teacher may want to use some of the suggestions outlined below.

For school-related activities

1. Use instructional materials that the student has a need or purpose for reading. While a basal reader may be used effectively for part of a student's program, teachers frequently should use reading materials that relate to a child's needs or purposes.
2. Use flexible grouping for reading. Not only do children become bored with the sameness of ability grouping, but those students in the low reading group often feel they are the "dumb" reading group. Corrective and remedial readers are usually in the low reading group in their class and thus fail to be grouped with good readers at any time.
3. Monitor your behavior carefully as you teach each reading group organized by ability. Ensure that *all* groups and each individual in the group have opportunities for thinking-type discussions and for creative extension activities. Sometimes only the high-ability group or the highly verbal individual has such opportunities.

4. Provide time in the classroom for individualized, free reading. Skill drills can be overdone. Classroom reading should not consist entirely of basal readers and workbooks; let children read often in self-selected materials.

For home activities

1. Relate any negative attitudes the child may have toward reading at home to parents during conferences. Suggest activities for parents to help their children enjoy reading.
2. Stress to parents the importance of their serving as a role model for reading. Suggest that a family reading time be set aside each day, even if only a few minutes can be devoted to it. The establishment of the reading *habit* is vital.
3. Collect and share with parents articles focusing on reading in the home.

For library activities

1. Encourage and allow students to go to the school library as often as possible. Establishing a library habit is important even if it is only to browse through the books, looking at pictures and examining the contents.
2. Spend time familiarizing students with the library, making sure they know where to find different types of reading materials.
3. Add a few books each week to the classroom library collection. Highlighting these special additions will often encourage children to want to read them.
4. Have a special library time each week, encouraging a child to share the book he is currently reading. He may share only one special event from the book to entice others to read it.

For recreational reading

1. Send home suggestions for activity packets for vacation time. Include the titles of recommended books and where they may be purchased or borrowed from the library.
2. Recommend that parents establish a summer reading chart, listing all of the books the children read during summer vacation. Suggestions for making a chart may be developed by the teacher to send home at the beginning of summer vacation. Children should be encouraged to drop by after returning to school in the fall to show the "old" teacher what they read during vacation.
3. Suggest the newspaper as a daily reading activity.

INSTRUCTIONAL STRATEGIES

The teacher's behavior and the instructional strategies he uses can have a profound impact on students' attitudes toward reading. Bruckerhoff (1977) conducted a study asking students to describe experiences in school that helped to establish their feelings about reading. Students mentioned many teacher activities that created positive feelings about reading. For example, the teacher:

- was excited about books
- liked to read
- read to students
- helped students find appropriate books
- talked to students about books
- encouraged the use of the library
- allowed free time reading
- had a supply of books available to use

In contrast, Bruckerhoff found that other actions of the teacher made students feel negative about reading. For example, the teacher:

- gave long lists of questions at the end of stories
- did not allow students to read the books they wanted to read
- did not explain how to use a library
- over-dissected a story
- required outlines or book reports to be written concerning a book or story
- did not give enough time for reading
- did not give students a chance to discuss a book
- required students to read aloud
- grouped students by ability
- required books that were too difficult for students

Estes and Johnstone (1979, pp. 5–13) have suggested twelve ways to make students hate reading:

1. Fail children who do not read up to grade level.
2. Define reading ability as scores on a standardized test.
3. Drill skills.
4. Separate learning to read from reading to learn.
5. Read aloud in groups, round-robin.
6. Insist on careful reading for detail.
7. Follow the lesson plan in the manual to the letter.
8. Don't skip stories in the basal, and do not switch children from one basal series to another.

9. For vocabulary development, have children copy definitions from the dictionary.
10. Do not let children read ahead in the story to find out how it is organized or told.
11. Do not have ungraded materials around, like paperback books, magazines, or newspapers.
12. Always set children's purposes for them.

Teachers can often benefit from a careful review of their own practices or behaviors. Alexander and Filler (1976) have developed a checklist that allows the teacher to examine her expectations, biases, assessment, classroom environment, and other relevant aspects needed to provide a positive atmosphere for helping students develop an appropriate attitude toward reading (see Fig. 7.5).

Figure 7.5. Checklist for Teachers

	Yes	No
1. Have I considered relevant factors that may affect positive attitude development and maintenance?	_____	_____
a. Do the achievement levels and self-concepts of my students affect reading positively or negatively?	_____	_____
b. Are there negative attitudes toward my students present on the part of parents and other important individuals?	_____	_____
c. Is it apparent to my students that I like reading?	_____	_____
d. Do I expect my students to have certain attitudes toward reading?	_____	_____
e. Am I biased in my beliefs about the effects of sex, intelligence, and socioeconomic status on attitudes?	_____	_____
2. Have I accurately assessed the attitudes of my students?	_____	_____
a. Have I chosen the assessment technique that will yield the most information in my situation?	_____	_____
b. Have I sampled behaviors that are appropriate indicators of attitudes toward reading?	_____	_____
c. Have I attempted to ensure that my students have responded honestly to my assessment techniques?	_____	_____
d. Have I gathered information over time in order that consistent patterns may be noted?	_____	_____
e. Have I kept appropriate records in order that all relevant information may be considered?	_____	_____
3. Have I considered aspects of the reading environment that may affect attitude development and maintenance?	_____	_____

continued

Figure 7.5. *(continued)*

	Yes	No
a. Is my classroom atmosphere conducive to positive attitudes?	_____	_____
b. Do I help my students develop and maintain positive self-concepts?	_____	_____
c. Do I consider the interests and reading achievement levels of my students when I select materials?	_____	_____
d. Do I help students see a need for reading?	_____	_____
e. Do I give students purposes for reading that are relevant for them?	_____	_____
f. Do I reinforce successful reading behaviors?	_____	_____
g. Do I read myself and read to children?	_____	_____
h. Do I make books available and provide time for my students to read?	_____	_____
i. Do I teach those skills that enable my students to read material that is important to them?	_____	_____
j. Do I let my students make choices from among appropriate materials?	_____	_____
k. Do I help my students learn those skills that help them in reading in the content areas?	_____	_____
l. Do I encourage my students to use the information gained from reading in creative ways?	_____	_____
m. Do I utilize instructional programs and strategies about which I am enthusiastic and in which my students are interested?	_____	_____
n. Are my grouping practices conducive to positive attitude development and maintenance?	_____	_____
o. Do I work with parents in order that they may assist with positive attitude development and maintenance in their children?	_____	_____

From J. Estill Alexander and Ronald C. Filler, *Attitudes and Reading*, pp. 66–67. Copyright 1976 International Reading Association. Reprinted with permission of The International Reading Association.

INFORMATION TO CONSIDER

1. Attitudes toward reading may serve as the central component in an affective model of reading.
2. Attitudes toward reading may be described as tripartite, multidimensional, situational, experience-based, and capable of being changed.

3. Teachers may determine students' attitudes toward reading through structured observation and self-report instruments.
4. Teachers should plan instructional activities that focus on the specific areas of students' attitudes that have been determined to be negative toward reading.
5. A teacher's behavior has a tremendous influence on a student's attitude toward reading.

Interests

QUESTIONS TO GUIDE READING

Recall Questions
1. What categories can be used to describe children's reading interests?
2. How may reading interests of corrective and remedial readers be assessed?
3. What activities may a teacher use to focus on the interests of students with reading problems?

Thinking Questions
1. How might the teacher use the categorization of books to advantage besides simply grouping books by interest areas in the classroom?
2. Why would teachers assess interests differently for different children?

Teachers can use the reading interests of corrective and remedial students to advantage in instruction. Interests are potential motivators. Students give special attention to reading materials that interest them. Such materials stimulate students' curiosity, answer their questions, or relate to purposes they have for reading. If teachers consider the interests of their students as they plan instructional activities, they will satisfy one of the primary needs of their students: to read materials in which they have an interest. A goal of teachers should be to bring a student together with just the right book at the right time.

To focus on the interests of corrective and remedial readers, teachers must consider several factors: the categorization of interests, the influence of interests on comprehension, the assessment of reading interests, and methods by which interests may be used in instruction. This section addresses each of these factors, with emphasis on the ways teachers and parents can use students' interests in everyday reading activities.

Categorization of Reading Interests

Reading interests may be categorized in many different ways, such as topic, style of writing or genre, and format. These categories may be used to probe the interests of corrective and remedial readers.

Topic relates to the subject or content of the reading material. For example, science is a topic, as are sports, animals, plants, and sewing. Corrective and remedial readers are no different than other students in that some topics are much more appealing to them than others. They are much more likely to read materials if the topics are interesting to them.

Style of writing or *genre* refers to a distinctive type or category of literary composition such as fiction, nonfiction, or biography. One student may like to read primarily mysteries, while another prefers historical fiction. Teachers may investigate students' interests based on these various types of writing.

Format refers to the presentation of material, the size, shape, and general makeup of a piece of written material. For example, the general arrangement or organization of a magazine is different from a paperback novel. The magazine usually has illustrations or pictures, a variety of short articles, a soft cover, and a variety of print types and sizes. The paperback novel usually has fewer illustrations or pictures, one continuing story, a consistent type of print, and a harder cover than a magazine. One student may prefer the layout or organization of the magazine; another may prefer the format of the paperback book.

Manning, Manning, and Wolfson (1982) classify subject-matter interests as follows:

- fantasy
- adventure
- sports
- personal problems
- social studies
- machines and applied science
- animals
- physical science
- famous people
- multiethnic
- family life and children
- fine and applied arts
- plants

Stanchfield and Fraim (1979), in examining boys' interests, not only looked at *content*, such as outdoor life, explorations and expeditions, sports and games, war, automobiles, motorcycles, science fiction, sea adventure, humor, mystery and detective, occupations, music, travel, and animal adventure; they also considered characteristics of style, such as unusual experiences, excitement, suspense, liveliness and action, surprise and un-expectedness, funny incidents, frightening or scary incidents, family love and closeness, happiness, heroism, and familiar experience.

INFLUENCE ON COMPREHENSION

Teachers of corrective and remedial readers should be aware that several research studies indicate that comprehension of material is affected by content. Since comprehension of text is the foremost goal of reading instruction, teachers should address this important relationship as they work with students who have reading problems.

Because interests do affect comprehension, Belloni and Jongsma (1978) offer the following cautions for teachers:

- Assessment, both standardized and informal, may be affected by a student's interest in the passages used in the assessment instrument.
- Instruction in comprehension may be more effective when high-interest materials are used.
- Students may be able to benefit from recreational reading in difficult materials if they find the materials highly interesting.

ASSESSING INTERESTS

Teachers may use various instruments or inventories to assess aspects of reading interests in their students. In assessing interests, teachers may consider topic, style or genre, and format. Both informal observation and structured self-report may be used to assess interests.

Some corrective and remedial students express their reading interests easily. These individuals often verbalize their likes and dislikes strongly, with such comments as "I don't like books about animals," "I want a book about dinosaurs," "Books about plants are boring," "I like books with lots of pictures," or "I like comic books." For these students, the teacher merely has to listen to them, jotting down their expressed interests so that he may refer to them when selecting books for the students. Informal observation will provide the teacher with sufficient information about the interests of these students.

Other students may be less able to explain what types of books interest them. However, when presented with a list of choices, they are able to state the topics, styles, and formats they prefer. The teacher will probably want to use a more structured instrument to determine the interests of these students, such as a self-report questionnaire or interest inventory.

Self-report has been shown to be a valid way to assess students' reading interests (Baldwin, Johnson, and Peer 1981). Figure 7.6 shows one type of self-report inventory to use to assess students' interests (Alexander 1988).

Figure 7.6. Alexander Interest Inventory

Name _____ Room _____

1. In my free time, I like to _____.
2. My father and I like _____.
3. My mother and I like _____.
4. I have _____ brother(s) and _____ sister(s).
   My _____ and I like to _____.
5. My friends and I like _____.
   We play at _____.
6. I like to help at home by _____.
   But I do not like to _____.
7. I (like-do not like) to play with toys and games.
   My favorite toys and games are _____.
8. I (like-do not like) TV. My favorite programs are _____
   _____.
9. I (like-do not like) to go to the movies. My favorite movies are _____
   _____.
10. I (like-do not like) pets. My favorite pets are _____
    _____.
11. I go to scouts (yes-no); church (yes-no); clubs (yes-no). My favorite clubs are
    _____.
12. I (like-do not like) to take trips. I have visited _____
    _____.
    I would like to visit _____.
13. I (like-do not like) to collect things. My favorite collections are _____
    _____.
14. I (like-do not like) to make things. I have made_____
    _____.
15. I (like-do not like) to read. I read storybooks (yes-no); newspapers (yes-no);
    magazines (yes-no); comic books (yes-no). My favorites are _____
    _____.
16. I do not like to read about _____.
17. I (like-do not like) to go to the library.
18. I (like-do not like) to read at home. My parents like for me to read at home
    (yes-no).
19. If I could have any three things I could wish for, I would like _____
    _____ , _____
    _____ , and _____.
20. When I grow up, I think I would like to _____
    _____
    _____.

From J. Estill Alexander, "Affective Dimensions" in J. Estill Alexander, General Ed., *Teaching Reading*, 2nd ed., p. 381. Copyright © 1983 by Little, Brown and Company (Inc.). Reprinted with permission.

It is an open-ended questionnaire that examines many aspects of a student's life, such as leisure activities, family interactions, TV and movies, clubs, pets, trips, the library, wishes, and (if appropriate for age level) career preferences.

As a teacher surveys the interests of a student, she should use not only a structured reading interest inventory, but also information about non-reading activities. For example, knowing that a student is going on a trip to England may be a cue for the teacher to suggest books about that country; hearing that a student has a stamp collection allows the teacher to suggest books on that topic.

Another structured way to assess reading interests is to use an inventory, such as the one for upper level elementary students shown in Figure 7.7 (Heathington 1979). This inventory probes both topic and format interests of students.

In addition, teachers may use the following activities to ascertain their students' reading interests:

- observe what kinds of objects they bring to school
- keep a record of the library books they check out
- observe what sports they enjoy
- listen to their conversations about vacation times
- ask them to keep a log of daily activities
- ask about their favorite types of TV characters or stories
- listen to their casual conversations regarding what's current

It is suggested that teachers of corrective and remedial readers establish some type of system for recording the interests of their students, whether the interest is determined through informal observation or a questionnaire or inventory. One suggestion is to make a card for each student; as a teacher notes various interests, she can enter them on the card. She may want to have the card accessible during classroom sharing sessions so that she can easily jot down interests that the student mentions.

The teacher can also use the card to assist in expanding a student's interests. For example, a student may have a very narrow focus, wanting to read only books on the topic of dinosaurs, comic books, mysteries, or books by one author. The teacher could use a "Possible Interest" category on the card to list possibilities for expanding the students' interests. For example, if a student likes only books by one author, the teacher may try to interest the student in other books by an author with a similar style.

ACTIVITIES FOCUSING ON STUDENTS' INTERESTS

Teachers can focus instructional activities on students' interests. In one study of why students in middle grades did not read more often, students reported some of their concerns about reading interests (Heathington 1979):

1. There are not enough books on topics of interest to them.
2. The respondents were unable to find "good books," "more books on a certain topic," "the right book," or "an interesting book." Students

Figure 7.7. Reading Interest Checklist

Your feelings can be shown by circling the appropriate number beside each item. For "very little," circle the number 1. For "very much," circle the number 5. If your "likes" are somewhere between, circle the appropriate number.

I like to read about	very little				very much
a. adventures	1	2	3	4	5
b. animals	1	2	3	4	5
c. art/music/dance	1	2	3	4	5
d. boys/girls my age	1	2	3	4	5
e. comedy	1	2	3	4	5
f. famous people	1	2	3	4	5
g. food	1	2	3	4	5
h. history	1	2	3	4	5
i. human body/health	1	2	3	4	5
j. make-believe characters	1	2	3	4	5
k. mysteries	1	2	3	4	5
l. romance/love	1	2	3	4	5
m. science	1	2	3	4	5
n. science fiction	1	2	3	4	5
o. space	1	2	3	4	5
p. sports	1	2	3	4	5
q. transportation	1	2	3	4	5
r. war/armed services	1	2	3	4	5

I like to read					
a. comic books	1	2	3	4	5
b. encyclopedias	1	2	3	4	5
c. funnies	1	2	3	4	5
d. hardbacks	1	2	3	4	5
e. library books	1	2	3	4	5
f. magazines	1	2	3	4	5
g. newspapers	1	2	3	4	5
h. novels	1	2	3	4	5
i. paperbacks	1	2	3	4	5
j. textbooks	1	2	3	4	5
k. TV guides	1	2	3	4	5

From Betty S. Heathington, "What To Do About Reading Motivation in the Middle Schools," *Journal of Reading*, May 1979, p. 711. Copyright 1979 International Reading Association. Reprinted with permission of The International Reading Association.

sometimes mentioned specific topics; they wanted more science fiction; "juicier" books; more sports books or magazines; more funny books; books about sex; more mysteries; more "tender" books; more books about teenage problems.

3. They want to select their own books. The following comments are typical: "I want to read books I choose." "I would read more if teachers

would not push me into reading certain books." "I would read more if I could read any book I wanted."

These concerns of middle graders are typical of students at many ages. Among the most positive actions a teacher can take to promote interest in reading is to make books available that have features students prefer and to allow students control over their own selections.

Another way teachers can use students' interests to advantage is to provide nonstandard reading materials. Urell (1976) specifies some of these types of materials:

- baseball and football cards
- athletic programs (local teams)
- matchbooks
- greeting cards
- joke books
- cereal and other food boxes
- comic strips
- menus from local restaurants
- Guinness Book of World Records
- old catalogs
- travel brochures
- maps
- pins and buttons from election campaigns
- bumper stickers
- driver's manual
- texts of songs accompanying tapes and records

The parents of corrective and remedial readers may provide assistance to the classroom teacher by suggesting topics about which their children like to read. The teacher may want to send a questionnaire such as the one in Figure 7.6 home with the student, to be completed jointly by parents and child. This gets the parents involved in the discussion of interests. When the parent comes for a conference, discussion can center around the child's reading interests and how to expand and promote them.

Teachers can also promote reading by setting up interest areas in the classroom. Possible ways to categorize interest areas might be by author, topic, format (such as paperback books or magazines), or style (such as mysteries or poetry).

Students need someone with whom to share their reading experiences. Adults realize that after reading a book or seeing a movie, they enjoy discussing it with someone who has had the same experience; children need the same thing. Teachers should read books their students are reading so that they can discuss them together. Students may also pair with peers who have read the same book, sharing details they each enjoyed or found interesting about the book.

McCool (1979, p. 11), in a list of facetious suggestions for how to make students hate reading, included three items related to reading interests:

1. Force the student to read only classics. Insist each finish at least 18 by the end of the year or receive a failing grade. Remind the students that contemporary books have no place in school.
2. Prohibit skinny or picture books. Books should always be filled with words only. Pictures and illustrations take up too much space in a book.
3. Confiscate any improper materials brought into the room, such as magazines, comics, newspapers. Remind the students that they aren't capable of making proper choices about good reading materials.

INFORMATION TO CONSIDER

1. Reading interests may be categorized by topic, style of writing or genre, and format.
2. Comprehension is affected by content of the reading material.
3. Observation and self-report instruments may be used to assess students' reading interests.
4. Teachers should address students' reading interests in instructional activities.

Motivation

QUESTIONS TO GUIDE READING

Recall Questions
1. What are some motives that Mathewson specifies for reading?
2. What is the difference between extrinsic and intrinsic motivation for reading?
3. How may a teacher determine what is motivating corrective or remedial reading students to read?
4. What are some activities that might motivate students to read?

Thinking Questions
1. Why is the motive of curiosity and exploration the most important one for problem readers?
2. Why would extrinsic motivation be more important for the corrective or remedial reader than for the student making normal progress in reading?
3. What are possible disadvantages of using reading logs or diaries to determine students' motives for reading?

Teachers should consider not only the attitudes of their students toward reading and the reading interests of their students, but also their students' motives for reading. Why do children read? What do they gain from the act of reading that is significant to them? What is the value they see in reading?

Mathewson (1976, p. 657) views motivation as the energizing force in his affective model of reading. He states that a child "will need not only a favorable attitude toward reading materials, but also an appropriate motivation." A child can have positive feelings about reading but fail to engage in reading activities because he is not motivated to read. Motivation, then, becomes an important link in the affective domain as it relates to reading.

Because motivation is such a key element, teachers may well question what motivates students to read. Little basic information is available to guide them. Except for Mathewson's (1976; 1985) important model of the affective domain, which includes motivation as a component, most information for teachers on the topic of motivation relates to practical suggestions for activities to motivate children to read. Teachers, especially of corrective and remedial readers, need more information about why their students choose to read or why they choose to engage in some other activity.

Among the motives for reading that Mathewson (1976; 1985) identifies are: curiosity and exploration, achievement, self-actualization, activity, and anxiety. As teachers become more aware of each of these motives, they will be able to analyze quickly the reading activities that they plan for their students. As they learn more about what motivates each student, they will be able to match the appropriate reading activities to the individual student's motives at various times.

This section contains a discussion of five of the motives for reading outlined by Mathewson that are particularly important in corrective situations. The use of a reading log or diary is suggested to determine students' motives for reading. Several reading activities that teachers and parents can use to help corrective and remedial readers are categorized by motivation type.

MOTIVES FOR READING

Motivation can be either intrinsic or extrinsic. *Extrinsic motivation* may include either praise or punishment; in either case, it comes from outside sources, such as parents, teachers, or peers. Because it depends on others, extrinsic motivation for reading is not as satisfactory as *intrinsic motivation*, which comes from within oneself. Teachers should strive to have the student depend on herself to sustain reading behavior. The student should want to read to find needed information or because she enjoys reading, not because she receives praise from the teacher or such items as stars or candy. Therefore, while teachers may use extrinsic motivation to promote reading activities, they should be striving for intrinsic motivation as a final accomplishment for their students.

Curiosity and exploration. Teachers would like for their corrective and remedial reading students to be curious about books, to want to find out what is inside the covers. Reading for information is included in this motive. Students who want to know how to build a model airplane, who won the 1974 World Series, or more about Russia will be driven by their curiosity to read about these topics. If we want students to read because they are curious and want to explore new ideas, they must be allowed to select their own books. Students often find it difficult to get interested in books that teachers or parents have determined they should read.

Although curiosity and exploration are intrinsic motivations for reading, teachers can promote them by making interesting books available. Teachers can set the stage for students to be curious about books by arranging displays of books known to be of interest to students. The displays should be changed often, both in location in the room and in type of books; otherwise, they will become overly familiar and children will cease to notice them.

Teachers also can read a book to a group of students, stopping at a thrilling or exciting part. Students must then finish reading the book themselves to find out what happens at the end. This type of activity combines the natural curiosity of the child with the instructional activity of the teacher; the result can be a more motivated student.

Achievement. Achievement motivation receives a great deal of attention in research studies. It refers to the need of students to succeed in order to obtain something of value to them.

Achievement is a common part of school life. Grades or scores on exams are the most often used measures of achievement. From the early grades onward, students attempt to score well on tests, homework, and various other school projects. Sometimes achievement is related to physical accomplishments such as number of push-ups, points scored in a basketball game, or field goals kicked. However, most school accomplishments relate primarily to cognitive achievement.

Corrective and remedial readers have not been able to achieve at the rate of their peers. Often they have not been able to make good grades in reading. They may not read well enough to answer questions the teacher asks after a story has been read.

Some problem readers have withdrawn from situations that involve achievement because they have never been able to reach the preset standards for performance. The ability to achieve seems constantly to elude these students, even though they see others around them who seem to reach their reading goals easily. Teachers must be careful to set achievement standards that are attainable for corrective and remedial students; only in this way can achievement be used as a motive for reading. There must be a realistic expectation of success if achievement is to serve as an effective motivator.

Achievement is usually extrinsically motivated: teachers or parents set the goals. A certain performance is required for a grade of "A," or certain facts must be known for a passing grade on an exam. However, many students work hard to achieve at a level that will please their teachers and parents. For these students, achievement can be a powerful motivator.

Self-actualization. Some students read because they find the content of books helps them become what they want to become. Through stories about big-league baseball players or firefighters, reading can provide a sense of direction in children's lives. Biographies of famous people serve as examples of those who have attained their dreams and life goals. Such reading materials inspire many students to reach for similar standards of excellence. Information about careers and life pursuits is also found in the pages of books. Students read to make decisions about this career or that career, weighing the values of becoming a police officer, an army officer, or a doctor.

More fundamental to some older students is printed self-help information about the best way to hit a tennis ball, the most nutritious meals for healthy skin, or the best way to take care of one's teeth. As students mature, they find that many popular magazines will provide the materials to satisfy some of their needs at that age. They read to find out how to reach their "ideal," whether it is as an athlete, musician, or artist.

Reading for self-actualization is primarily an intrinsically motivated endeavor, in that the student usually has a self-established purpose for his reading. However, teachers who are aware of their students' interests can also help them by making such materials available.

Activity. Some children read because it is an activity, something to do. Neuman (1980, p. 334) states that one reason children read is for relief from boredom. Children in her study were motivated to read for the following specific purposes:

"It gives me something to do."
"It makes the time go by."
"I read when I have nothing to do."

Neuman attributes all of these statements to reading for relief from boredom.

Today, television is a strong competitor for children's choice of an activity, especially since it requires less effort on the part of the student than reading. Children whose parents allow unlimited television may spend much less leisure time reading than in front of the TV.

Corrective and remedial readers have an especially difficult choice. Television requires few skills; reading requires many, some of which are difficult for poor readers. In order to make reading attractive enough to lure these students away from the TV, materials must be found that are not only interesting but also easy to read.

Children read in a variety of places. Teachers and parents can take advantage of some of these places to motivate reading as an activity. They may place reading materials in these places so that children will read as an activity to keep themselves occupied. Reading might then become a "habit" in these particular places.

Children find many places to read outside of school. In a study probing where they read, Heathington (1975) found the following places were mentioned most often:

- In their bedroom at home
- In the living room of their home
- At friends' or relatives' homes
- Outside (under a tree, on a swing, in a tree fort)
- In the kitchen of their home
- In cars or buses
- On trips

Anxiety. The motive for some children's reading is anxiety: fear of failing an exam or not performing well on a task. Fear of negative comments from teachers, parents, or peers may create anxiety, resulting in a negative motive for reading.

Escape reading may be motivated by anxiety (Mathewson 1976). The child may read to withdraw from unpleasant or overwhelming situations. Neuman (1980) also sees escape as a motive for reading. In her study, students reported that reading allows them to be in their "own little world," takes them away from their "pains and worries," and keeps their "mind off things."

While teachers want students to read, they want them to have varied interests. If carried to excess, escape reading may be a problem for some readers. However, it is usually not a problem for corrective and remedial readers. Their motivation related to anxiety is much more likely to be due to fears about grades or approval from others.

Anxiety is associated with extrinsic motivation. Pressure from significant others is likely to create anxiety that motivates a student to read. Anxiety is a negative motivator, therefore one that teachers should try to avoid.

OTHER FACTORS RELATED TO MOTIVATION

As teachers plan instruction for students, they may want to consider other information related to motivation and reading:

1. Motivation differs from time to time. One motive may be operating at one time, another motive at another time, and perhaps multiple motives at some times. Teachers must recognize when to stress one motive over another. They are encouraged to use multiple motivation, such as curiosity and exploration or self-actualization, to promote reading.

2. Subject-area reading often presents little motivation for students because it seems to have little direct bearing on their present or future lives. Reading historical dates in social studies, seemingly irrelevant scientific facts, or novels with abstract ideas and circumstances may not be motivating for some students.

3. Materials may be a significant factor in students' lack of motivation. Roggenbuck (1977) states that many children are not motivated to spend time reading books because they do not see themselves or their families reflected either frequently or accurately in their reading texts. She suggests that reading materials must have relevance and reality to motivate children to read.

4. Emotional or personality problems may have an impact on motivation to read. Classroom teachers rarely have the expertise needed to deal with these types of problems; referral to school psychologists or counselors is usually necessary. However, classroom teachers should be able to recognize potential emotional or personality problems in order to make timely referrals. The following questions may be helpful in noting potential problems in this area.

Does the student:

- refuse to participate in reading activities?
- show hostility toward you in reading class or toward reading materials (by maliciously abusing books, for example)?
- become abusive in language or action when asked to read or complete a reading assignment?
- quickly lose patience in trying to complete a reading assignment?
- seem unable to focus on reading for a reasonable period of time?
- seem to daydream constantly rather than focus on reading?
- continually make statements about her inability ever to become a good reader?

- seem overly anxious about completing reading assignments?
- seek constant reassurance that her participation in reading activities is acceptable?

Whether emotional or personality problems are a cause or an effect of poor reading, the classroom teacher has a responsibility to notice students who seem to have problems in this area and to make appropriate referral to specialists. In the classroom, the teacher may benefit from several general guidelines regarding the corrective or remedial reader with emotional problems:

- Avoid open confrontation with the student in front of other class members regarding his refusal to participate in reading activities.
- Talk with the student privately about his refusal to participate in classroom activities or his hostility toward reading class or reading materials, asking him to describe his actions.
- Maintain a calm manner in all discussions with the student.
- Assign a reasonable amount of reading so that he is not frustrated.
- Monitor the student's involvement; when he daydreams or withdraws, pull him back into classroom activities by saying his name or commenting positively about some aspect of his work or behavior.
- Try to reassure him that he can improve his reading ability, pointing out his accomplishments.
- Structure tasks so that he can be successful.
- Show a genuine interest in him as an individual by asking him about his hobbies and interests in reading.

ASSESSING CHILDREN'S MOTIVES FOR READING

It is helpful for teachers to be aware of their students' motives for reading. One way to assess their motivations is to ask students to keep a reading log or diary, in which they record their after-school reading activities, the amount of time spent in reading, the type of materials read, and their reason for reading the materials. Examination of the log will give teachers a clearer understanding of students' reasons or motives for reading.

ACTIVITIES TO MOTIVATE READERS

After teachers have an overall view of their students' various motives for reading, they can determine if students have multiple motives for reading. Multiple positive motives for reading should be encouraged. One motive may be important at one time, while another will be a priority at another time.

While teachers cannot forcibly motivate students to read, they can organize time, materials, and circumstances to capitalize on students' motives for reading. Below are listed typical activities that teachers may use to help students become more actively involved in reading by promoting certain motives.

To promote curiosity and exploration, a teacher can use the following ideas:

- Change book displays in the classroom often. Students will notice "new" books, especially those with appealing covers or titles.
- Read a portion of a book. At a strategic point, stop and suggest that the students finish the book on their own.
- Bring in objects that relate to a book and display these objects with the book. For example, seashells could be used in a display with several books about the sea.
- Encourage students to share books they are reading. They can tell a portion of the story or some significant event or fact in the book. This will encourage others to read the book.
- Cover the title of a book. Ask students to read the book and suggest a title for it.

To promote self-actualization as a motive, teachers can try the following:

- Have popular magazines available on topics students want to know more about.
- Show a movie about a famous person, and then set up displays of books about the person.
- Have displays of books arranged by careers, for children to think about what they would like to become when they grow up.

INFORMATION TO CONSIDER

1. Among the chief motives for reading are curiosity and exploration, achievement, activity, anxiety, and self-actualization.
2. Motivation may be either extrinsic or intrinsic.
3. Motivation differs with time and circumstances.
4. Teachers may plan activities that facilitate motivation for reading.
5. Reading logs or diaries can reveal students' motives for reading.
6. Emotional or personality problems may affect motivation to read.

Self-Concept

QUESTIONS TO GUIDE READING

Recall Questions
1. How does self-perception, self-other perception, and self-ideal perception relate to a student's self-concept?
2. What can cause a student's self-concept to change?
3. How can a teacher assess a student's self-concept?
4. How can the teacher facilitate development of positive self-concepts in corrective and remedial reading students?
5. How do parents influence their children's self concepts?

Thinking Questions
1. If the reading experiences of a student continue to be negative, will he always have a poor self-concept?
2. Why would the role of the teacher be more crucial than that of parents in changing a child's reading self-concept?
3. How much success must a child experience before she changes her negative view of herself as a reader?
4. Must a child always have positive experiences with reading to have a positive view of himself as a reader?

Quandt and Selznick (1984) have pointed out that a corrective or remedial reader's own view of her reading ability (self-perception) may be drawn from comparisons with her classmates, siblings, or other significant individuals. She may view her ability as inferior to that of these other individuals; her self-concept is low. Or the reader may perceive that others think her reading ability is poor (self-other perception); this, too, affects her self-concept. Finally, the reader may wish she could read as well as a certain classmate, a sister, or a babysitter (self-ideal). The reading level of these individuals is her ideal. All three of these perceptions, as described by Quandt and Selznick, affect the student's self-concept related to reading.

As with other affective dimensions, self-concept is based on experience. As they develop, children try to do many different things. Sometimes they are successful, and sometimes they fail. They get varying reactions from others around them about their efforts. Children learn that if they act a certain way, they will get a certain reaction.

Often the corrective or remedial reader has tried to learn to read but has experienced difficulties. Classmates may have laughed at his mistakes; teachers may have admonished him to "try harder" or berated him for "not trying." The child fears that if he attempts the act of reading again, he will get similar responses; it is to be expected that he will avoid reading in order to escape the negative consequences. His need to preserve his self-esteem forces him to withdraw from reading-related situations.

A student's inability to keep up in the early grades has much to do with forming her self-concept. She usually begins the task of learning to read with enthusiasm and eagerness. However, as she encounters difficulties while others around her learn to read easily, she becomes fearful. At first, she works hard, thinking she can overcome her inadequacies. Later, she seems to quit trying, either passively withdrawing from reading activities or countering with aggressive behavior. Both reactions are focused on preserving her self-concept.

Self-concept can change. If the people whose views are important to the student, such as teachers and parents, change their attitude and behaviors toward him, the student's views of himself may change.

ASSESSING SELF-CONCEPT

Self-concept may be inferred from a student's behavior in reading activities as well as from general comments he and others make about his reading competency. Situations or comments that might indicate a problem regarding a student's reading self-concept include the following:

- The student hesitates to volunteer to read aloud.
- The student makes negative comments about his ability to read orally.
- Other students make negative comments about the student's reading ability.
- The student makes little or no attempt to complete reading assignments.
- The student makes comments such as "I can't do that page" or "I can't understand that story."

In contrast, the student who has a positive self-concept demonstrates behaviors such as the following:

- She is eager and willing to read independently, sure in the knowledge that she will know the words and succeed in the task.
- She accepts new tasks in reading, confident of success.
- She is able to maintain a sense of positive self-concept even when she fails. She knows that she is a worthwhile person even if she cannot easily accomplish every task.

Teachers may recognize, through such situations or comments, those corrective or remedial readers who have negative self-concepts. Because they have had difficulties in reading, these students are likely candidates for having poor self-concepts.

Observation allows the teacher to determine which students have a positive reading self-concept—who are eager to read, learn new words, and discover new books. The student with a positive reading self-concept is sure that he can be successful in all of these encounters with reading. In contrast, the student with a negative reading self-concept avoids reading, procrastinates completing reading assignments, and is afraid to learn new words or read new types of books. She is afraid she will fail in these endeavors.

A revealing activity for the teacher to perform is to jot down the comments a student may hear about his reading from peers, teachers, and parents, such as the following:

"Mary is still in that baby book." (peer)
"Mary, you're not trying to figure out that word." (teacher)
"Mary just seems to be a real slow reader." (parent)
"Mary never has the place when we're reading." (peer)
"Mary's in the low reading group." (peer)
"Mary, you should remember that word." (teacher)
"Mary doesn't read as well as her younger sister Beth." (parent)

Certainly such comments do little to promote a positive self-concept of oneself as a reader. It seems unlikely that any student's self-concept can remain high with exposure to such statements.

ACTIVITIES TO PROMOTE POSITIVE SELF-CONCEPT

Teachers must overcome past negative experiences a child may have had with reading and help him replace them with positive interactions. He must be placed in situations where not only the teacher, but classmates also see him as a successful reader. If he is always grouped by ability in the lowest reading group, he may think of himself as a failure. Grouping by interests or some other way may overcome some of the negative feelings that the child has about his reading ability. Even though his skills in reading may not be on a level with others in his class, he can feel good about the reading he can do. Teachers constantly must try to work with students in such ways that they are not looked upon as the "low" group.

Teachers must also be cautious of their nonverbal responses to students as well as their verbal behaviors. Failure to make eye contact, to smile, or to attend to a student's comments can be detrimental to a student's self-concept.

McDonald (1980) lists several ways to enhance positive self-concept in a classroom:

- Recognize, respect, and encourage individual differences.
- Teach the child to be pleased about the good fortune of others.
- Capitalize on a child's strengths.
- Provide a comprehensive range of activities for children.
- Separate a child's behavior from the person he is.
- Be consistent.

The teacher may also find the following principles to be helpful in working with readers who have poor self-concepts:

1. The teacher must be aware of each student's reading level and provide instruction at that level. All students do not progress at the same pace; there will be some who cannot move as quickly as others.
2. The teacher should demonstrate interest in the reading activities of each student. He should inquire about the books the student is reading, her reactions to the books, and what significant ideas the student found in reading the books.
3. Reading instruction must be organized so that all students can achieve. When rewards can be attained only by a few, children are treated unfairly. Classroom prizes, competitions, rewards, and grades must be structured so that all can attain levels of success.
4. A student must be shown that he can read fluently. Using a tape recorder and an easy reader, the teacher can ask the student to practice on the book until she has mastered it. She then can read the book to others in the class, demonstrating her fluency in reading. The positive comments made by the teacher and other students will counter the negative comments that the student has been experiencing.
5. When a child remembers a difficult word, reads a passage fluently, or remembers significant aspects about a story, the teacher should reinforce this positive endeavor through spoken approval, written comments, happy faces drawn on the student's paper, or other such rewards.
6. Teachers must be honest in using compliments. They can show a student that his reading is better than before without having to call it "perfect" or "extraordinary."

There are several ways parents can help improve a child's reading self-concept:

1. Parents must refrain from comparing their child's reading performance with that of classmates or siblings. Instead, they should stress the improvement their child is making.
2. Parents should encourage their child to try reading new words, and to see the task as achievable. When the child succeeds, the parent should emphasize that he can do this again in the future.

3. Parents, too, must recognize when a book is too difficult. They should encourage reading in books that the child finds comfortable.
4. Parents must always help their children "bounce back" in the event of failure. Assurances that they have succeeded before and can do so again can offset negative perceptions resulting from failure in a reading activity.

INFORMATION TO CONSIDER

1. Self-concept is experience-based.
2. Self-concept can be changed.
3. Reading self-concept may be determined by observation.
4. Both teacher and parents play an important role in helping children establish positive reading self-concepts.

Summary

The affective domain is basic to reading success for all students, especially corrective and remedial students, because it determines whether they will want to read and will continue to read throughout their lives. This chapter has addressed four dimensions of the affective domain related to reading: attitudes toward reading, reading interests, motivations for reading, and self-concept related to reading.

Indicators of positive and negative attitudes toward reading, ways to assess students' attitudes, and suggestions for instructional activities to promote positive attitudes were described. Assessment of reading interests was discussed, together with instructional strategies for making use of the interests of corrective and remedial readers. Various types of motivation were outlined and activities suggested for motivating students. Ways teachers and parents can help promote positive reading self-concepts were discussed. The focus of the chapter was on ways to assess the various affective dimensions and plan instruction to help corrective and remedial readers in these areas.

Questions for Further Thought

1. Which of the four dimensions of affect discussed in this chapter (attitudes, interests, motivation, self-concept) is most important to corrective and remedial readers? Why?
2. Why do teachers tend to give less attention to affect than to cognitive aspects of reading?
3. How could more attention be given to affective dimensions of reading in teacher education programs?
4. In what situations would a teacher give primary consideration to cognitive aspects of reading rather than affective aspects?

Activities and Projects

1. Administer a reading interest inventory to a group of corrective and remedial readers. Select books for the students based on their interests.
2. Determine the attitudes of a corrective or remedial reader, using one of the reading attitude scales. Plan activities for the student based on his diagnosed needs.
3. Ask a corrective or remedial reader to keep a reading log of her reasons for reading. Determine her primary motives for reading.
4. Develop a parent workshop to suggest ways for them to promote a positive self-concept related to reading for their children.

8

Readiness

Before an individual begins the formal process of learning to read, there are certain prerequisite skills that seem to facilitate the process; these have been called readiness or prereading skills. Readiness instruction is not limited to kindergarten or first-grade pupils. Students of any age may need such instruction; teachers and clinicians may encounter third graders, seventh graders, or even adults who lack readiness skills. To be able to help students, teachers must be knowledgeable about the various types of readiness skills, possible causes of failure to acquire them, procedures for assessing specific needs in this area, and instructional strategies and materials to use with students. This chapter will provide information about these aspects of readiness.

Readiness is defined in *A Dictionary of Reading and Related Terms* (Harris and Hodges 1981, pp. 263–64) as "preparedness to cope with a learning task . . . determined by a complex pattern of intellectual, motivational, maturational, and experiential factors in the individual which may vary from time to time and from situation to situation." Specifically, *reading* readiness is defined in the same document as "readiness to profit from beginning reading instruction" (p. 269).

The readiness skills presented in this chapter combine and integrate the intellectual, maturational, and experiential factors referred to by Harris and Hodges. The motivational factor, or the entire dimension of affect, was the focus of Chapter 7. The authors consider the affective dimension to be basic to readiness and the primary consideration of teachers who are working with corrective or remedial readers. This chapter will focus on thought, language, and print awareness as additional factors to be addressed in determining readiness for reading.

Thinking skills are necessary for learning to read. If a student does not have adequate concepts, reading will have little meaning even if the student is able to decode the words. Some writers have even suggested that a priority should be placed on the development of thinking skills in the early grades of school, with formal reading instruction postponed to later grades. While there is a lack of agreement on this idea, there is general consensus that the development of thinking skills is of utmost importance to reading.

Language skills are also viewed as vital. Since reading is a concentrated involvement with language, the importance of understanding and using language seems evident. Some students exhibit limited development of language, either in their ability to communicate effectively through oral language or in their ability to predict language patterns. Such students may be unable to cope with the language demands of the reading process.

Print awareness is the final readiness skill discussed in this chapter. Knowledge that print is meaningful, the distinction between pictures and print, orientation skills (left-to-right, top-to-bottom), concepts of word boundaries, and visual and auditory discriminations are some of the important aspects of print awareness. Increasing attention is being given to print awareness as an important skill needed by students to engage successfully in beginning reading activities.

The following sections will describe in more detail the thinking, language, and print awareness skills needed by corrective or remedial reading students. The focus will be on descriptions of the various skills, assessment, and instructional activities to promote the development of each skill.

Thinking Skills

QUESTIONS TO GUIDE READING

Recall Questions
1. How do the theories of Piaget and Feuerstein relate to readiness for reading?
2. What problems are identified as related to thinking?
3. How can thinking be assessed?
4. What kinds of activities can promote thinking skills?

Thinking Questions
1. Do you agree with Furth that thinking skills rather than reading skills should be stressed in the early grades? Why or why not?
2. Why do you think some parents provide few mediated experiences for their children?
3. Do all children with reading problems have inadequate concepts?
4. Is observation adequate for assessing thinking skills?

The early years in a child's life provide an excellent time to develop thinking skills. For some children, however, there is a void in the experiences that could facilitate the development of these skills. These students may become corrective or remedial readers because they lack the necessary thinking skills to make reading meaningful.

Some educators have emphasized the importance of thinking skills in the early years of a child's life by advocating that in the early grades, a school should concentrate on thinking skills, not on reading (Furth 1970). Furth believes that concentration on thinking skills at these early stages will enable children to move easily into formal reading instruction. Hoffman and Fillmer (1979, p. 290) warn that reading programs "that attempt to teach reading before children have developed adequate problem solving skills may be responsible for producing children who learn not to read." Many others disagree, as evidenced by the general introduction of formal reading to students in most first grades in the United States. However, educators generally share the belief that thinking skills are essential to reading.

Teachers may encounter corrective or remedial reading students who have been pressured to begin formal reading instruction before they possessed the thinking skills needed to be intelligent readers. To help these students get ready for reading instruction, teachers should direct attention to the maximum development of thinking skills. Furth (1970, p. 3) has noted that while "the development of intelligence proceeds spontaneously, it can be helped or hindered by the environment." Environment and experiences can influence cognitive development (Kirkland 1978). Teachers can play an important role in establishing the proper environment to foster the development of thinking.

THEORIES REGARDING THINKING

The theories of Jean Piaget and Reuven Feuerstein may provide insight into the relationship between thinking and reading. The ideas of both men concern general cognitive development and are based on years of observation of how children learn.

Jean Piaget. Piaget (Phillips 1969; Furth 1970) contended that cognitive development consists of the formation of and changes in structural units called *schemes*. The development of such structures involves two aspects: (1) *assimilation*, which occurs when a person experiences something in the environment and incorporates it into his existing schemes; and (2) *accommodation*, which occurs when the schemes are changed because of the incoming experience. Cognitive structures or schemes are preserved through assimilation or modified by accommodation (Murray 1978).

Piaget proposed periods or stages that children pass through in an unvarying sequence, though not necessarily at the same ages. These periods have implications for learning to read (Kirkland 1978):

1. *Sensorimotor period (ages 0–2 years).* The child cannot use an image or word to represent an object or event unless the object or event is actually present.

2. *Preoperational period (ages 2–7 years)*. During this period, the child begins to differentiate a word from what it stands for: the marks in a book
represent words. The child, however, focuses on only one feature of a
situation. She cannot reverse her thinking to the starting point (reversibility); she can only deal with concrete events; she is very egocen-
tric; and she reasons transductively, going from one particular to another
particular.
3. *Concrete operations period (ages 7–11 years)*. The child is developing
reversibility, seeing another's viewpoint, reasoning inductively and de-
ductively, classifying events and objects, placing events in series, and
relating one event to another.
4. *Formal operations period (ages 11–15 years)*. Abstract thinking is possible.

While Piaget did not address reading per se, his theories have been
related to reading through the following generalizations (Cleland 1980;
Cleland 1981):

1. Experiences are necessary for forming the schemes, or cognitive structures, necessary for reading.
2. Each student has unique schemes; these result from experiences and
the organization of those experiences. How a student interprets text is
dependent on his schemes.
3. If a student is in a concrete period, the teacher should provide concrete
learning experiences.
4. The student probably must be in the concrete operations period to learn
to read, because many reading tasks require such thinking skills as the
ability to reverse operations, to classify, to see another's point of view,
and to sequence events.

Reuven Feuerstein. Feuerstein's theories on thinking also have significant
implications for readiness for reading. Feuerstein does not believe that
cognitive functioning is "set" but rather that there are things which teachers can do to improve thinking skills. Feuerstein's teaching process has
five aspects (Harth 1982, p. 6):

1. Regulation of behavior through inhibition and control of impulsivity.
2. Improvement of deficient cognitive functions.
3. Enrichment of the repertoire of mental operations.
4. Enrichment of the task-related contentual repertoire.
5. Creation of reflective, insightful thought processes.

Harth (1982) describes Feuerstein's ideas regarding how each of these
five aspects can be improved:

1. Regarding inhibition and impulsivity, the teacher can impose a latency in responding. For example, the student may be cautioned against blurting out answers; the teacher may require that he write out the answers instead to encourage more thoughtful behavior.
2. A student with deficient cognitive functioning seems to have no organized approach to a task, but rather jumps into it without prior planning. The teacher must help the student identify a plan of attack before he begins a task. For example, the teacher may ask the student to plan his day when he arrives at school.
3. Enrichment of the student's repertoire of mental operations means adding such operations as analogies, categorizations, progressions, and seriations. Feuerstein emphasizes that these operations should be taught free of curriculum content, as curriculum content has its own structure, which will diminish the intensity of the response.
4. For enrichment of task-related contentual repertoire, the student must have certain categories of concepts: orientation (such as left, right, up, down); relationships between objects and events (such as identical, opposite, common); and labels for specific objects or events, along with their characteristics.
5. For the student to have insightful, reflective thought processes, he must be aware of his own problem-solving behaviors. He must analyze behaviors to determine why they were successful or unsuccessful, and identify the processes he used to solve a problem successfully.

To promote thinking skills, Feuerstein calls for *mediated experiences*, in which a more knowledgeable person (a parent or teacher) intervenes between the student and the environment so as to order and clarify the environment. For example, a parent using this technique would give reasons for various phenomena in the world:

> "The baby is crying *because* she is hungry."
> "You cannot have a cookie *because* you will not be hungry at dinner when healthy foods are served."
> "Don't go across the street *because* a car might hit you and hurt you."

Feuerstein feels that parents who have not provided such mediated experiences before the child comes to school may have limited their child's thinking skills. The teacher's task is to provide such experiences.

It is not enough for the teacher to provide a stimulating environment such as books or games; the teacher must mediate between the materials and the child, explaining and making the materials meaningful. The teacher should be an active, dynamic mediator: instructing, prompting, and asking for explanations.

Reading Problems Related to Thinking

The teacher may encounter students with reading problems that can be directly associated with inadequate thinking skills. The theories of Piaget and Feuerstein, as well as ideas expressed by others, clearly become relevant when teachers view these problems from the perspective of thinking skills. Some of these problems are discussed below.

Limited concept development. Tolstoy (quoted in Vygotsky 1962, p. 7) believes that "children often have difficulty in learning a new word not because of its sound but because of the concept to which the word refers." Some reading materials contain concepts unknown to the student and unrelated to her life. There is no background of experience that can be drawn upon as the student attempts to comprehend the materials. The student from a disadvantaged background who must deal with middle-class stories in a basal reader is an illustration of such a mismatch between the student's concepts and those presented in a text.

Vygotsky (1962, p. 55) emphasizes that "memorizing words and connecting them with objects does not in itself lead to concept development." Reading must be a meaningful process, rather than just a mechanical one. The student who does not understand that the words on a page have meaning may not be ready to read. When a student reads the word "buffalo," she must have some meaning attached to the word. Films, pictures, and direct observation are some of the ways used to allow students to build experiences.

Teachers need to relate new materials to things students already know. Children with large numbers of concepts can probably learn more easily because they can relate new material to these concepts (Seng 1970). A reading program tied in to students' verbal descriptions of their experiences is an appropriate one for most students. The language experience approach provides opportunities in reading for the teacher to build on concepts children already have. (See Ch. 15 for a description of the language experience approach with corrective or remedial students.)

Limited symbolic functions. The student may be unaware that the letters *d-o-g* stand for an animal. These students cannot deal with the abstract in letting various marks or lines stand for a concrete object.

Limited classification skills. Some students are not able to find common characteristics in the words they are trying to learn. Students must be able to know that the letter *a* could be classified as a vowel, a letter, or an adjective. When students are able to generalize that *take, make,* and *lake* can be classified together, they can generalize that *-ake* represents certain sounds. When they can sort *butterfly, banana,* and *beautiful* together, they can generalize that *b* represents a certain sound. Students must recognize that letters can be written in different forms, such as capitals, lowercase, or italics, and that an *a* in all of these situations is still an *a*.

Limited decentration concepts. A problem in this area suggests the student's inability to examine more than one aspect of a word. She may concentrate on one feature of a word to the exclusion of other features. For example, the student may confuse two words such as *that* and *there* because she focuses only on the *th* without paying attention to the rest of the word; or she may be unable to distinguish between *wash* and *wish* or *came* and *come* because she is focusing only on the aspect they have in common. The student may also be unable to see the word *set* and understand that it could have one meaning in one situation ("He *set* the vase down") and another meaning in a different context ("He had a *set* of dishes").

Limited relational concepts. Limitations in this area in reading may be seen in the student who does not realize that there is a relationship between the beginning of a story and the ending; or the student may not realize that the words in a passage are related in a particular way. The ability to predict what word or phrases may go together is lacking. Such a student can be seen guessing wildly at a word, rather than using prediction skills to anticipate what word would relate to others in the story.

Students with a problem in relational concepts may not recognize that events of today are related to those of yesterday and tomorrow. They may focus only on the present or one part of a story, not recognizing the gestalt of the passage. In the early stage of learning to read, these students may not relate the various parts of a word, i.e., letters, to each other. They may see each letter as standing alone.

Limited development of part-whole concepts. When a student lacks part-whole concepts, he cannot break words into smaller parts, decode the smaller part, and then reassemble the parts into a word which he can pronounce.

Limited seriation concepts. The inability to see the sequence or order of letters in a word indicates a problem in this area. Not recognizing the importance of a specific order of letters, such a student may read *saw* for *was*.

Limited ability to plan actions. A plan of action for "attacking" an unknown word is often difficult for a student. When faced with an unknown word, the student stops; she does not realize she can use prediction, context, or phonics to figure out the unknown word. She lacks a knowledge of what she is doing as she reads. This knowledge, described as metacognition, has particular application to word attack. (See Chapter 10 for a discussion of metacognition.)

Assessment of thinking skills can be done through observation, with the teacher asking questions such as the following:

1. Does the student demonstrate an understanding of words and phrases used in conversation and in printed materials read to him?
2. Is the student aware that lines on paper can represent a concrete object?
3. Can the student sort objects by shape, size, or color?
4. Can the student focus on more than one aspect of a situation?
5. Does the student understand that events today relate to yesterday and tomorrow?
6. Does the student realize that parts make up a whole?
7. Can the student arrange objects in a sequence from smallest to largest?
8. Can the student identify a problem and describe how to solve it?

The questions above illustrate some of the problems that a teacher may observe in his classroom. As several educators stress, the teacher may want to foster cognitive development before attempting to stress formal reading skills. This can often reduce the conflict the student faces as he strives to achieve a skill for which he is not yet ready.

ACTIVITIES TO PROMOTE THINKING SKILLS

The teacher can structure the environment so that the student has many opportunities to engage in activities that promote thinking. Some suggestions follow:

1. Encourage students to discuss various types of objects that they bring to school.
2. Take students on many field trips.
3. Invite community individuals to share their travel experiences and special hobbies.
4. Have students make a collage of all forms of the letters *a, b,* and so on that they find in a magazine.
5. Have students decide whether two written words are alike or different: *wash—wash* or *wash—wind.*
6. Read a portion of a story to students, and then ask them to predict the ending. Have students describe why their solution is feasible.
7. Cut students' name tags into individual letters; ask them to reassemble their own names. Do the same with other words with which the children are familiar.
8. Have a series of similar objects that are of different sizes. Have students arrange them in order.
9. Have students explain why they did something: "I sharpened my pencil *because* . . ." or "I wore my coat today *because* . . . ."
10. Help students plan and list what they are to do that day.

Parents can promote thinking skills in a variety of ways. Teachers should encourage parents of their corrective or remedial readers to help their child. The teacher may suggest that parents:

1. Talk to the child, identifying by name objects and people in the environment, in books, and on television.
2. Identify the beginning and ending of a story.
3. Ask the child to predict a word when reading a story to her.
4. Let the child explain the sequence of activities she will do that day.
5. Ask the child to tell how one word is different from another.
6. Suggest that the child sort things in different ways, such as the laundry by color or the silverware by type of item.
7. Mediate experiences by explaining the reasons behind various activities, such as "I'm washing the clothes because they are dirty."
8. Ask the child how certain words differ from each other in shape, length, and other visual characteristics.

The teacher should strive to provide classroom activities in stimulating surroundings, with a mediator to explain things and events in the environment. Increased thinking skills will lead to increased readiness for reading.

INFORMATION TO CONSIDER

1. Thinking skills are prerequisite to formal reading instruction.
2. The theories of Piaget and Feuerstein offer insights into developing the thinking skills of corrective or remedial reading students.
3. Inadequate thinking skills can hinder the acquisition of reading skills.
4. Teachers may assess students' thinking skills through observation.
5. Activities may be planned by teachers to promote thinking skills of corrective or remedial reading students.

Language

QUESTIONS TO GUIDE READING

Recall Questions
1. What is metalinguistic awareness?
2. What are the metalinguistic skills identified by Blachowicz as needed by students?

3. What problems are encountered in reading by the nonstandard language user?
4. What are the three ways Pickert and Chase have recommended to assess language abilities?
5. What do the authors suggest for improving language skills?
6. What does Gonzales suggest that teachers *do* and *not do* relative to language abilities of students?

Thinking Questions
1. Are language experience materials the *best* materials for students with language problems?
2. What can a teacher do when students in her class are unaccepting of a particular student's nonstandard language?
3. Do you agree that retelling is the best way to assess a student's use of language? Why or why not?
4. What can teachers do if parents are unable to provide experiences with language for their children?
5. What are the advantages of Nurss's suggestion of one-to-one interactions between adults and children relative to language development?

Language is vital to readiness for reading. In a recent survey of early childhood reading educators' perceptions of reading readiness, Wilson and Thrower (1985) found that among many divergent views, one area of support from all of these educators was the importance of a strong language base for young children. Teachers must consider both the oral language usage and the oral language understanding of their students; a lack of appropriate development in either of these skills may lead to problems in reading. Oral language usage will help students see the match between spoken words and print. In the *language experience approach* to teaching reading, the student produces language by dictating experiences to the teacher, who writes them down. For a student who does not have facility in English (a native foreign speaker, for instance), such a task can be difficult. While concepts in the student's primary language may be complete, these concepts have yet to be related to English symbols.

Even though some children begin school with well developed speech or oral language in English, they may not have adequate understanding of language. Some researchers have questioned whether the speaker's ability to follow rules in producing speech is equivalent to a conscious knowledge of the grammatical rules underlying language (Fischer 1980; Ryan 1980). This conscious knowledge, or *metalinguistic awareness*, may be necessary for reading. Teachers should be aware that not only a student's inadequate oral language in English, but also a lack of metalinguistic awareness can be a cause for concern.

Research in psycholinguistics also stresses the contribution of language understanding to learning to read. Psycholinguistics, merging psychology and linguistics, focuses on the student's use and understanding of language.

Special attention is placed on the sounds, meaning, and word order (phonology, semantics, and syntax) of language.

When a student is aware of language, he can draw inferences concerning sounds; for example, five words beginning with the grapheme *m* sound alike, therefore, that sound may be generalized to be associated with other written words beginning with *m*. The student who can anticipate or predict what word would follow "She played the _____" can more easily engage in reading as a meaningful process.

Students generate rules of language by hearing it, either in conversation or as it is read to them from a book. Students who have had limited experiences in hearing such language patterns may experience difficulties in making generalizations. Children who have had little exposure to rhymes or language games ("Who can think of a word that begins like butterfly?") may be at a disadvantage in learning to read.

ASSESSING LANGUAGE

Pickert and Chase (1978) have proposed three ways to assess language abilities: (1) informal teacher's observation of children's use of language in the classroom; (2) comprehension questions after children have heard something read or spoken orally or after they have read; and (3) story retelling. Of these three methods, Pickert and Chase favor retelling because they feel that this technique focuses on the student's ability to comprehend, organize, and express connected speech. The teacher would evaluate the student's language by noting the complexity of grammatical forms and vocabulary; the level of organizational skills, including logical or sequential recall of information; and the presence of fluent, grammatical, meaningful speech.

IMPROVING LANGUAGE SKILLS

The materials used to teach reading can be important for the student experiencing language problems. Materials using natural, meaningful language are recommended. Language experience stories are natural materials since they use the student's own language. This language, however, while natural, may not be simple. For example, the language of the student used in language experience stories may be more complex than the language found in basal readers. Using a computation of syntactic complexity and the Fry readability formula, Garman (1981) found that language experience stories of children were at a higher level than the basals in which they were reading.

Some stress that metalinguistic awareness is enhanced by the language experience approach, since the student is actively involved in the transcription of dictated language to print (Blachowicz 1978). They are aware of the match between their spoken language and what is written down.

Cunningham (1983) has described a structured language experience approach that can be used with students who have limited oral language facility. Because such students sometimes have difficulty responding individually to a teacher's request to tell a story that can be written down, Cunningham suggests organizing students in groups of three to five. The small group then shares some common experience, such as looking at pictures of various foods, culminating in a collective meeting with the teacher. The teacher provides a "starter" for responses growing out of the experience, such as "I like to eat _____." Various students are asked to complete the starter, resulting in a language experience story such as the following:

"I like to eat *candy.*" (Jane)
"I like to eat *beans.*" (Paul)
"I like to eat *popcorn.*" (Mary)

In this approach, the student with limited oral language skills may participate actively in the language experience story.

An approach to use with second-language learners may involve surrounding the student with a written environment as natural as an aural environment (Past, Past, and Guzman 1980). The teacher structures the classroom so that written words are evident throughout, with labels on objects and the student's name on his belongings such as his desk or pencil. The classroom is meaningful since the student is involved actively with it and the labels provide the written identifier of spoken words.

Pictures may also be used effectively to provide second-language students with a situational context for developing language (Sinatra 1981). Students may already have adequately developed concepts in their first language; the picture serves as a concrete representation. As the student verbally describes the picture using his second language, he gains facility in the use of oral language. Sinatra stressed that the visual element may be personalized further by using actual photographs of the student and events in his life. The second language is used to describe and narrate events depicted in the photographs.

Smith (1983) feels that the language awareness of students can be influenced greatly by teachers or other adults who read aloud to them. He feels that the teacher who spends ample time reading to his students during the prereading period is providing them with the vital opportunities of sharing and becoming accustomed to the language of books. This understanding of the language of books seems to be a key element in readiness for reading.

Language development requires that the teacher provide many opportunities for students to use a range of discourse functions such as explaining, narrating, or instructing (Cazden 1983). Describing how to dribble a basketball or paint a picture, telling about a surprise birthday party, and giving step-by-step directions for baking cookies are all effective means of developing language facility. Students need to develop language skills in sequencing ideas, staying on the topic, and expanding a point to be able to communicate their ideas to others. To provide feedback about the adequacy or completeness of their discourse, students need a listener. The teacher can serve both as a listener and as a model for various types of discourse.

Wordless picture books can serve as excellent resources for language development, with the student supplying an oral description of what is happening in the pictures. The teacher and students in a small group can prompt expansion of language as they become interested in the narration.

The teacher's behavior must be accepting and helpful in relation to a student's language. The student's language is personal, a part of her culture and heritage. The teacher must respect the language, expanding and developing it to help the student respond to all possible environments and situations.

A list of do's and don't's regarding language activities may be summarized from an article by Gonzales (1980).

Do provide opportunities for children to hear language.

Do stimulate children to use language.

Do provide an accepting environment for language usage.

Do allow ample opportunities for children to engage in conversations.

Do concentrate on communicative language activities, not artificial language studies.

Do allow students to develop language through trial and error.

Do, as the teacher, accept the responsibility of providing the appropriate environment and facilitating spontaneous talk.

Don't promote mechanistic language activities, such as studying grammar or correcting pronunciations.

Don't try to develop language through formal, artificial activities that have no relevance to students' everyday lives (such as teaching grammatical structures).

Don't rely completely on basal reader materials, since their language is often artificial and unnatural.

Don't, as a teacher, do all the talking. Students need time to try out language as well as listening to language.

Parents can play a crucial role in the language development of children in the early years. Greaney (1986) suggests two ways in which the home environment can contribute to the language development of children: (1) parents' verbal interactions with their children, which help develop the child's linguistic cognitive skills; and (2) parent-child reading, which helps the child in understanding written words and labeling of objects and supports language development.

By reading to their children, parents can instill a knowledge of the language of books and the concept of *story*. Children who have had books and stories read to them develop a sense of structure of what a story includes—its framework; they are thus prepared for predicting how a story will unfold. This ability to predict is important in the development of reading skills because it helps with both word recognition and comprehension; students can predict what word would "fit," or what might be a likely outcome in the story. If students have not yet developed this concept of story, the teacher will need to read extensively to them so that they can.

Parents can also help by talking to their children, serving both as a model for language usage and as a listener for the children as they use language. Children need this essential experience of communicating with others.

One study of interactions in a day-care center found that the children there had insufficient opportunities to use expressive language; their responses to adults' questions were typically only "yes" or "no." (Nurss, Hough, and Goodson 1981). It was felt that more one-on-one interaction between the child and an adult or an adult with a small group of children was needed. The suggestion was made that teachers should encourage children to expand on an idea or a description they have expressed, developing the oral language skills of students to a higher level.

Language is an important prereading skill. The more that children are surrounded by the world of language and become aware of its functions, the more impact such events will have on their enjoyment and success in learning to read. For children who have not had extensive language involvement prior to coming to school or in the early years of school, the teacher must provide language experiences that will enrich and develop these children's language.

INFORMATION TO CONSIDER

1. Both oral language usage and oral language understanding are important prereading skills.
2. The nonstandard language user may experience difficulties in acquiring reading skills.
3. Teachers may use observation probe questioning and story retelling to assess language skills of corrective and remedial students.
4. Language experience stories can be used effectively for language development of poor readers.
5. Teachers and parents influence the child's language awareness and usage.

Print Awareness

QUESTIONS TO GUIDE READING

Recall Questions
1. What is meant by the term "print awareness"?
2. What are the five print awareness skills described in this chapter?
3. Do children always understand terms such as "word," "letter," or "long word"?
4. What is Morris and Henderson's five-step instructional plan for developing the concept of "word"?
5. What aspects of print awareness are assessed on Clay's Sand Test?

Thinking Questions
1. How do teachers show that they recognize the importance of the print awareness of their corrective or remedial reading students?
2. Should teachers emphasize writing as a means of developing print awareness? Why or why not?
3. Do you agree that some children may find print aversive and boring? Why or why not?
4. Do you agree that a test such as Clay's Sand Test is the best assessment of print awareness? Why or why not?

The United States may be regarded as a print-oriented society. People are expected to read their monthly bills, their insurance policies, the labels on cans on the supermarket shelves, the driver's manual, bus schedules, and countless other printed pieces of information. Many children develop an early awareness of print in their environment: television makes the words "McDonald's" or "Coke" part of their sight vocabulary. As they recognize familiar symbols, they become active participants in the use of print. Some children, however, lack stimulation concerning print. They have little curiosity about written symbols around them, and often have problems learning to read in school.

Print awareness is a necessary prereading skill. Remedial readers, who are unable to participate in formal reading activities, need experiences that will help them achieve greater consciousness of print. Various skills are linked to print awareness: distinction between pictures and words, orientation (left-to-right and top-to-bottom), concept of boundaries for words and sentences, concept of print as meaningful, and visual and auditory discrimination. This section will focus on these types of print awareness and what teachers can do to help children gain competency in this area.

PICTURE AND WORD DISTINCTIONS

The earliest books parents read to their children typically have few words and many colorful pictures. These pictures help children develop concepts about things around them. At a certain point, the child will recognize that the words are separate from the picture: in essence, the words represent the ideas expressed in the picture. The same thing happens when the child recognizes the word "McDonald's" or "Coke" in a context other than the golden arches or the bottle. The child is then learning that words alone can be used to describe people, places, and actions. This basic distinction between pictures and words is the first step in developing print awareness.

ORIENTATION

Children must learn that English print starts at the left and moves to the right. Not all languages have this type of orientation. English print moves from left to right, makes a return sweep to the next line, and continues down the page of text. Children whose parents have read to them, pointing out the words as they move along the printed page, may have adequate orientation to print in books. However, for children who have not had the benefit of such an introduction to the direction of print, instructional activities may be needed to help them develop the skill.

Print orientation can often be facilitated by the introduction of writing. As a student forms his name, which is such an important, personal word for him, he learns how to form letters in a left-to-right direction.

Vogel (1980) has found that children at times do not seem to realize that left-to-right orientation is relevant to identifying symbols. Even when this realization comes, left-to-right orientation is sometimes a low priority and less likely to be noticed than other characteristics.

WORD/SENTENCE BOUNDARIES

Morris and Henderson (1981) point to the "concept of word" as the awareness that spoken words are represented in print bounded by spaces. Some children do not have a stable concept of "letter" or "word." In one study, children showed confusion about such terms as "a letter," "a long word," "a string of words," and "a new word" (Sanders 1981). Directions in teacher guidebooks commonly include such terms, and teachers often take it for granted that their students are comprehending such directions.

Ehri (1978) states that print marks boundaries better than such boundaries are marked in speech. For example, dialect or other speech patterns often result in several words being "run together" in speech. This does not happen in print: words are separated by blank spaces and sentence units are separated by punctuation marks. Children who have always heard "You hafta go" may have a problem when they attempt to match what sounds like three words with four printed words: "You have to go."

Morris and Henderson (1981) provide a five-step instructional plan for teachers to use in developing the concept of *word:*

1. The student learns to recite a four-line rhyme or poem.
2. A printed copy of the rhyme is given to the student, with the explanation that this is a written version of the rhyme. The teacher models reading the rhyme and points out individual words.
3. The teacher and child read the rhyme together.
4. The teacher then points to individual words in the rhyme, asking the student to pronounce the word.
5. The printed copy is removed and the student is presented with isolated words.

This sequence is very similar to the language experience approach. However, the first step is different in that the student, because the rhyme has been memorized, can recall all of the words even without the printed version in front of her.

VISUAL AND AUDITORY DISCRIMINATION

Reading requires certain visual and auditory discriminations between words. Some children experience difficulty in readiness for reading because they have not developed these discriminations. Because formal reading instruction later will require such skills, teachers should be attuned to children who may be experiencing problems in auditory or visual discrimination.

Visual discrimination. As they get ready for reading, children need to be able to discriminate first between words and then between letters. Visual discrimination should proceed from the gross to the refined. For example, after the child realizes that words are separated by "white spaces," he must then begin to recognize that these words look different from each other. This is the beginning stage of visual discrimination.

At this stage, the teacher can assess readiness in visual discrimination by asking the child to circle the two identical words in a selection of three. For example, the child would circle as indicated below:

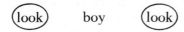

This is a global response to visual differences in words.

Further refinement occurs when the child moves to letter discrimina-tions. For example, the child circles the two words that are alike in a series of three very similar ones:

(read)   real   (read)

Visual discrimination proceeds from initial to final to medial letters, as shown in the three illustrations below:

1. initial letters

(meat)   seat   (meat)

2. final letters

meat   (meal)   (meal)

3. medial letters

(meet)   meat   (meet)

Some educators believe that extensive training in visual discrimination of pictures, shapes, or numbers should precede word or letter discrimi-nations. This position has not been supported adequately by research. Others believe that children learn to read by reading (Smith 1983), and that extensive practice in nonreading materials can turn children off to reading.

Teachers must use caution in giving extensive visual discrimination exercises to students who have problems in this area before their vision has been checked. These children may well be unable to distinguish words and letters because of physical visual problems. Once such problems are ruled out, attention directed at visual discrimination of words and letters should help children become ready for reading instruction.

Auditory discrimination. Children who cannot discriminate one word or one sound from another may have problems in formal reading programs, especially if phonics instruction plays a prominent role in these programs. Phonics focuses on word identification through the use of sounds; therefore, if the child cannot differentiate among sounds, problems are likely to occur.

As with visual discrimination, the teacher should focus on activities that progress from gross to refined. For example, the teacher may pronounce three words and ask the child to say which two are alike:

cat   tap   cat

The student learns to discriminate differences in beginning sounds, then ending sounds, and finally medial sounds:

1. initial sounds
   bat cat bat
2. final sounds
   bad bag bad
3. medial sounds
   bad bud bad

Whether or not auditory discrimination training in nonsense words is worthwhile is questionable. Many educators feel that discrimination activities should concentrate on real words.

As with visual discrimination, physical problems must be addressed first if a child seems to have an auditory discrimination problem. The teacher should request that parents have their child's hearing checked to determine any physical problems.

Fun activities in the form of rhymes can be used to sharpen children's auditory discriminations. Thinking of rhyming words is a pleasurable activity for most children.

PRINT MEANINGFULNESS

Frank Smith (1983) has stated that children who see print as purposeless or nonsensical will find it aversive and boring. Children must come to the learning situation in reading with an appreciation that the activity is meaningful to them.

The purpose of print is communication. If reading is viewed as rote decoding, then students may not realize that the purpose is to transmit ideas from the writer of the text to the reader.

It is not necessary for every word to be in a sentence for it to have meaning; it must simply be in context. For example, word labels attached to classroom objects such as a chalkboard or desk are in a meaningful context, even if the word is isolated on a card.

RELATION OF PRINT AWARENESS TO OTHER SKILLS

Print awareness seems to be related to many of the other skills discussed in this chapter. They relate and integrate to form a general readiness for the formal introduction of reading.

Hiebert (1980) found that the development of print awareness seems to be related to a set of three predictors: logical reasoning, oral language comprehension, and home experiences. It is evident that the roles of affect, thinking, language, and print awareness are highly related. Students experiencing problems in one area will often experience difficulties in other areas.

ASSESSING PRINT AWARENESS

Marie Clay (cited in Morris and Henderson 1981) claims that reading readiness should be judged through observation of children's attempts to read written text, rather than on the traditional readiness tests. Clay's Sand Test examines aspects of print awareness discussed in this section. Information from such a test provides the well-trained teacher with specific information about her students' readiness for reading.

The Sand Test (Clay 1979) measures several skills, including the following:

Child can show the front of the book.
Child realizes that print carries the message, not the picture.
Child can show where reading is to begin.
Child knows that reading goes from left to right.
Child realizes there is a return sweep to left.
Child knows where the first and last parts of the story are found.
Child knows a left page is read before a right page.
Child knows the meaning of punctuation.
Child knows the concept of *word*.

PARENTAL ACTIVITIES

Parents can help develop their child's print awareness through some of the following activities:

1. Ask the child to show them the front of a book, the back of the book, or where the story begins.
2. Indicate that they are reading from left to right.
3. Start the story by commenting, "This is the beginning of the story," and finish by saying, "That was the end of the story."
4. Point out punctuation marks and explain what they tell the reader.
5. Play word games with the child, asking her to tell whether words are alike or different.
6. Ask the child to point to a certain word that has appeared a number of times.

INFORMATION TO CONSIDER

1. Print awareness is an important prereading skill.
2. Print awareness skills include distinction between pictures and words, orientation, word boundaries, meaningfulness of print, and visual and auditory discrimination.
3. Print awareness skills are related to affective, thinking, and language skills.
4. Print awareness may be assessed through observation or a test such as Clay's Sand Test.

Summary

Some corrective and remedial readers may be at the readiness stage of reading. Teachers must provide instruction for them at this level. This chapter has presented information to help teachers understand the skills needed at the readiness level. Three readiness skills prerequisite to reading instruction have been discussed: thought, language, and print awareness. Each of these skills seems to make an important contribution to a child's success in reading. For each skill area, assessment and instructional procedures have been suggested.

The influence that both parents and teachers exert on children has been pointed out. Suggestions have been made for both teachers and parents to help corrective and remedial readers get ready for formal reading instruction.

Questions for Further Thought

1. Is it possible for teachers to mediate experiences, as suggested by Feuerstein?
2. How can teachers promote the extensive experiences children need to hear varied language patterns?
3. Why would some children have little print awareness, even though print seems to be all around them?
4. What other concepts about print are needed by students in addition to those discussed in this chapter?

Activities and Projects

1. Observe one or more teachers as they interact with children. Note the instances when they serve as a mediator of experiences.
2. Use Cunningham's structured language experience approach with a small group of corrective or remedial readers.
3. Develop five activities that parents may use to help their children develop their language skills.
4. Give Clay's Sand Test to a corrective or remedial reader. Draw conclusions from the results.

9

Word Recognition

Word recognition, word attack, decoding, and word analysis are terms often used interchangeably to denote skills students use as they attempt to identify words. Slight differences in the meaning of these terms may be noted in the literature: word recognition is sometimes viewed as the instant identification of words, while word attack, word analysis, and decoding may be seen more as skills used to "figure out" an unknown word. However, in this chapter, the term *word recognition* will be used in a comprehensive way to describe skills that give students the overall ability to identify words; either by instant recognition or after using various strategies for identification. Four word-recognition skills will be discussed: sight words, phonics, context, and structural analysis. Each of these skills may be used by students who are experiencing difficulties in reading to improve their reading ability.

Sight words provide a base for word recognition because they are recognized instantly by students. Lack of adequate facility with sight words is often a problem for remedial reading students. Teachers may encounter students who do not have the necessary sight word vocabulary to read fluently enough to understand the text easily. The reading pace of these students is so slow, word by word, that they fail to gain meaning from a passage; therefore, they cannot see reading as a meaningful activity. In addition, students may not know enough sight words to be able to make generalizations about words, such as common beginning or ending sounds or word parts. The section on sight words in this chapter will focus on some basic sight word lists and methods that teachers may use to help students increase their number of sight words.

The second word-recognition skill to be discussed is phonics, or the ability to "sound out" new words. For some students, phonics can provide considerable assistance in improving word recognition. Included in this section are recommendations for teachers about strategic phonic skills that may be stressed in a remedial reading program, and some cautions regarding drill activities in phonics.

Context is the third word-recognition skill to be addressed. Poor readers often pay little attention to the larger text; instead, they focus only on the word "under attack." The section on using context will provide suggestions for procedures and activities that teachers may use to promote a student's use of context to gain proficiency in word recognition.

Structural analysis of words, or morphemic analysis, is the final word-recognition skill to be discussed in this chapter. Students sometimes fail to see significant word units in larger words, or to break a word down into manageable parts. Suggested activities in this section should help teachers plan instruction for students who lack this important word-recognition skill.

Process of Word Recognition

QUESTIONS TO GUIDE READING

Recall Questions
1. What are the steps Cunningham has suggested for her compare/contrast theory of word recognition?
2. What are the five stages in Samuels's theory of word recognition?
3. What are the basic word-recognition skills identified as necessary by Dahl and Samuels?

Thinking Questions
1. What influence does the student's background have on the compare/contrast theory of word recognition?
2. What may determine which cue a student uses in the recognition of a word?
3. Do you think a student must have competency in all of the word-recognition skills identified by Dahl and Samuels?

As the teacher attempts to assess and remediate word-recognition problems, it may be helpful to examine some of the processes in which students engage as they identify an unfamiliar word. As a new word is encountered, what does the student do to identify it correctly? Several theories have been proposed.

Cunningham (1980) has suggested a compare/contrast theory, with multisteps in which the reader, as he encounters an uknown word,

- searches through a store of known words, comparing the unknown word with the store of known words,
- segments the unknown word into parts if the word as a whole cannot be recognized,
- compares each part of the word to known words, word parts, and fragments, and

- recombines the word parts into a unit that seems to be meaningful and that he seems to remember hearing.

As the student engages in the process, he will form various generalizations or rules, unique to his experience, that can be used as he encounters other unfamiliar words in the future.

In another theory, Samuels (1976) has provided a five-stage model of word recognition:

1. The printed stimulus (word) is presented.
2. The reader selects some aspect of this total stimulus (such as a letter, group of letters, or word length) as a cue, to which a response is attached.
3. The reader must be able to recognize the cue again.
4. The appropriate response is available to hook up with the cue.
5. The appropriate response and the cue are linked.

The emphasis in this model is on the associative stage, when the cue and response are linked together. This seems to be a function of long-term memory.

Dahl and Samuels (1977) have stated that in word recognition, the reader

- uses information in the passage to make a prediction of what a word will be,
- compares the printed word to the predicted word, and
- either accepts or rejects the prediction.

Dahl and Samuels have identified certain basic word-recognition skills that are needed to accomplish this task:

1. The learner must be able to respond with a word when given an initial letter. (Example: When asked to say a word that begins with the letter *m*, the student can come up with an answer such as "man" or "moon" or "mommy.")
2. The learner should be able to identify the first letter in a spoken word. (Example: When the teacher says the word "dog," the student can identify the initial letter as *d*.)
3. When a word is presented to him orally, the learner can recognize the initial letter visually from among several printed letters. (Example: When the teacher shows a written *b*, *g*, and *m* and then says the word "man," the student should be able to point to the letter *m*.)
4. The learner can use the auditory context to predict words. (Example: When the teacher speaks the sentence, "My dog likes to chase _____," the student can orally supply an appropriate word, such as "cars" or "cats."

5. The learner can use auditory context to predict words after hearing the initial sound. (Example: When the teacher says the sentence, "My sister plays the p _____," the student can orally give the remainder of a suitable word, such as "piano" or "piccolo.")
6. The learner can use visual context to predict words. (Example: When the teacher gives the student the printed sentence, "The dog ran __ ," the student can orally provide a word such as "fast" or "far.")
7. The learner can use visual context and the first letter to predict a word. (Example: When the teacher gives the student the printed sentence, "The man drove the car down the h _____," the student can supply a word such as "hill.")

The information given above provides the teacher with important information about what is happening as the student attempts to process unknown words.

INFORMATION TO CONSIDER

1. Theories of word recognition help teachers understand the process their students use in recognizing a word.
2. Skills involved in word recognition should relate to a theory of word recognition.

Informal Assessment of Word-Recognition Problems

QUESTIONS TO GUIDE READING

Recall Questions
1. What behaviors may indicate to a teacher that a student has problems in the area of word recognition?
2. What types of word-recognition skills are assessed on the IRI?

Thinking Questions
1. How may a teacher determine if a negative attitude toward reading is related to a problem in word recognition?
2. What might be the advantages of using an informal assessment, such as an IRI, as opposed to informal observation by the teacher?

The classroom teacher's first indication that a student may have a word-recognition problem may come through everyday observation or informal testing. Continuous monitoring of certain behaviors may alert the teacher to a problem before it becomes a serious one. It is vital that problems be recognized as early as possible. As certain behaviors are noted, more extensive assessment may be called for to verify that a problem really exists. While one behavior may not be a sufficient cause for concern, a pattern of behaviors should be a signal to the teacher that special attention is needed.

INFORMAL OBSERVATION

The teacher may informally observe students' behaviors in seven areas related to word recognition: changes in attitude toward reading, failure to read materials on grade level, reading word by word, repeating words, identifying a word impulsively, omitting words, and inability to recognize common word parts. Such observation is done both during the reading class and during the remainder of the school day, for instance during content-area instruction. Comments that the student makes about reading are also noted.

Negative change in attitude. A primary indication that a student is experiencing difficulty in word recognition is a change in the student's attitude toward reading. He may start avoiding the reading situation, even though he began the class with enthusiasm. On entering a reading situation with a new teacher, a student usually makes a serious attempt to do well. However, when faced with difficulties, he will often lose his enthusiasm. Prolonged periods of frustration and failure often result in the student's disinterest even in a new reading situation: he may expect to experience failure again and will not put forth effort.

The student may procrastinate in performing assigned reading tasks. As he attempts to engage in activities other than the reading tasks assigned to him, his behavior may be interpreted as aggressive. A persistent negative attitude or a change in attitude from positive to negative is a likely signal to the teacher that a student is having problems; these problems may be related to word-recognition skills.

Failure to read material on grade level. The teacher may recognize that a problem exists when the student cannot effectively read materials on her grade level. She may have a problem with the reading text or with social studies, science, or other content materials. A student who fails to understand the text, to respond to comprehension questions, or to retell a passage accurately may be unable to recognize enough of the words for the passage to have meaning.

Reading word by word. A particular student may tend to read a passage haltingly, using a word-by-word approach. The student seems to be merely "word calling," saying each word alone as if it had no relation to the rest of the phrase or sentence. At times, the student may try to use phonics to sound out a word, but does so too slowly to maintain the fluency needed to comprehend the passage. The poor reader may analyze a word on a letter-by-letter basis, in contrast to the fluent reader who looks at word units quickly to identify an unknown word. The student with a word-recognition problem often seems unable to concentrate on more than one element of a word at a time.

Repeating words. When a poor reader cannot identify an unknown word, she may repeat words preceding the unknown word. For example, in the sentence, "She saw the red helicopter," the student may continue to repeat "the red" several times, trying to give herself time to identify the unknown word "helicopter." Teachers will often note a pattern of repetition of words for students with poor word-recognition skills.

Identifying a word impulsively. A student may seem to guess wildly at a word, substituting an incorrect word or even a nonword. The substituted word may have no relation to the rest of the passage and probably confounds the student's attempts to make sense of the passage; yet the student seems unable to delay an impulsive response when more careful analysis of the word is needed.

Omitting words. At times, a student may simply skip one or more words when reading orally. The meaning of the text may or may not be changed by the omission of the word(s). It may be that the student is being too hurried in reading the passage. Some reading specialists feel that if the meaning is not affected, omissions are not a serious problem, as long as the student can correctly identify the omitted word when it is presented, either in isolation or in another context. However, a student may omit words because he does not have the word-recognition skills needed for identifying the word, which is a serious problem.

Inability to recognize common word parts. Proficient readers realize that words have many common parts. Prefixes, suffixes, and other word parts such as *-ite, -ack,* or *-ame* are illustrations of some of the frequently occurring parts of words. Good readers are able to recognize these parts in unknown words, using this technique as a way to decode them. Poor readers are unable to see these common or familiar parts in new words, and so cannot use this strategy in attacking an unknown word.

Informal Assessment Using the IRI

The informal reading inventory (IRI) provides an excellent assessment of word-recognition problems (see Ch. 5). Assessment on the IRI reveals problems in word substitution or mispronunciation, omission, repetition, and addition. Teachers may either develop their own informal reading inventory or use a commercial one.

INFORMATION TO CONSIDER

1. Informal observation of reading behaviors and informal assessment using an IRI can provide the teacher with information about the student's word-recognition skills.

Sight Words

QUESTIONS TO GUIDE READING

Recall Questions
1. What are some of the basic sight word lists mentioned in this chapter?
2. What are four methods for teaching sight words?
3. What are high-imagery words?
4. What is the context plus isolation procedure for teaching sight words? The natural language procedure?

Thinking Questions
1. What factors would determine whether a teacher would use a basic sight word list, such as the Dolch Basic Sight Word List or the Fry Instant Word List, or develop his own list?
2. How would student characteristics influence the way sight words are taught?
3. Why is the teacher's role considered important in teaching sight words?
4. What are some possible disadvantages associated with using games to teach sight words?

Most teachers realize that students need a set of words that they recognize instantly. These *sight words* should be ones that students will encounter most frequently as they read. They should be in the student's speaking vocabulary or frequently heard in his environment, especially since these much-used words are often irregular in spelling or pronunciation.

As students accumulate a store of sight words, they can begin the process of reading, using the known words to generalize about unknown words and to predict words in passages. The first step for many remedial readers is to build this base of known words.

Two approaches may be used by the teacher in providing a list of sight words for students: she may develop her own list from materials her students will be reading, or she may use a basic sight word list developed by researchers. In developing her own list, the teacher merely compiles words that are found in books the student reads or in experience stories that he dictates. Words that occur most frequently in the materials might be the first choices. If the teacher decides to use an existing basic sight word list, the following descriptions may be helpful.

BASIC SIGHT WORD LISTS

Several basic sight word lists have been compiled by researchers. They vary to some extent, depending on the source of materials and procedures used in their development. Teachers may want to seek out further information about a particular list before selecting it for their corrective or remedial readers.

Dolch basic sight word list. This list, first published in 1936, contains 220 basic sight words. There are no nouns on this list; a separate Dolch list contains 95 common nouns. Although the Dolch list is over fifty years old, it is still widely used by many researchers as a standard of comparison to other lists that have been developed more recently. The list continues to be mentioned prominently in discussions concerning basic sight words.

Fry instant word list. In 1980, Edward Fry provided an updated version of his Instant Word List (see Fig. 9.1). This list of 300 words is based on 5 million running words in library books and magazines in twelve subject-matter areas. Fry has emphasized that

- the first 10 words in his list make up approximately 24 percent of all written material,
- the first 100 words make up approximately 50 percent of all written material, and
- the first 300 words make up about 65 percent of all written material.

A teacher can easily recognize the value of a student's knowing half the words in a passage with 100 basic sight words.

Figure 9.1. Fry Instant Words

The Instant Words: First Hundred

First 25 Group 1a	Second 25 Group 1b	Third 25 Group 1c	Fourth 25 Group 1d
the	or	will	number
of	one	up	no
and	had	other	way
a	by	about	could
to	word	out	people
in	but	many	my
is	not	then	than
you	what	them	first
that	all	these	water
it	were	so	been
he	we	some	call
was	when	her	who
for	your	would	oil
on	can	make	now
are	said	like	find
as	there	him	long
with	use	into	down
his	an	time	day
they	each	has	did
I	which	look	get
at	she	two	come
be	do	more	made
this	how	write	may
have	their	go	part
from	if	see	over

Common suffixes: *s, ing, ed*

The Instant Words: Second Hundred

First 25 Group 2a	Second 25 Group 2b	Third 25 Group 2c	Fourth 25 Group 2d
new	great	put	kind
sound	where	end	hand
take	help	does	picture
only	through	another	again
little	much	well	change
work	before	large	off
know	line	must	play
place	right	big	spell
year	too	even	air
live	mean	such	away
me	old	because	animal

Figure 9.1. *(continued)*

The Instant Words: Second Hundred

First 25 Group 2a	Second 25 Group 2b	Third 25 Group 2c	Fourth 25 Group 2d
back	any	turn	house
give	same	here	point
most	tell	why	page
very	boy	ask	letter
after	follow	went	mother
thing	came	men	answer
our	want	read	found
just	show	need	study
name	also	land	still
good	around	different	learn
sentence	form	home	should
man	three	us	America
think	small	move	world
say	set	try	high

Common suffixes: *s, ing, ed, er, ly, est*

The Instant Words: Third Hundred

First 25 Group 3a	Second 25 Group 3b	Third 25 Group 3c	Fourth 25 Group 3d
every	left	until	idea
near	don't	children	enough
add	few	side	eat
food	while	feet	face
between	along	car	watch
own	might	mile	far
below	close	night	Indian
country	something	walk	real
plant	seem	white	almost
last	next	sea	let
school	hard	began	above
father	open	grow	girl
keep	example	took	sometimes
tree	begin	river	mountain
never	life	four	cut
start	always	carry	young
city	those	state	talk
earth	both	once	soon
eye	paper	book	list
light	together	hear	song
thought	got	stop	leave

continued

Figure 9.1. *(continued)*

The Instant Words: Third Hundred

First 25 Group 3a	Second 25 Group 3b	Third 25 Group 3c	Fourth 25 Group 3d
head	group	without	family
under	often	second	body
story	run	late	music
saw	important	miss	color

Common suffixes: *s, ing, ed, er, ly, est*

From Edward Fry, "The New Instant Word List," *The Reading Teacher*, December 1980, pp. 286–288. Copyright 1980 International Reading Association. Reprinted with permission of Edward Fry and The International Reading Association.

American Heritage High Frequency Word List. Walker (1979) has presented the American Heritage High Frequency Word List. These 1000 words accounted for 84.6 percent of the running text in several subject-matter areas specified by 90 school systems as required and recommended reading for students in grades 3–9. The list is available arranged either alphabetically or in order of frequency.

Johns's list of nouns. Johns (1975) has developed a list of 30 nouns that he believes are of particular value to beginning readers. In comparing nouns found in four published word lists (American Heritage Intermediate Corpus, Durr's 188 Words, Kucera-Francis 500 Frequent Words, and Murphy's 727 Words), Johns found 20 nouns common to all four word lists and 26 common to at least three. He then compared these 46 nouns with Dolch's list of 95 common nouns, finding 30 concordances. Johns has stated that these 30 words "seem worthy of being taught as sight words" (p. 540). Johns (1983, p. 83) also offers a list of thirteen words that "will usually account for one-fourth of the words in print":

> a   for in it that to you
> and he is of the was

TEACHING SIGHT WORDS

Several methods may be used for teaching sight words. Four possibilities have been proposed:

1. Present the printed sight word alone.
2. Present the printed sight word along with a picture representing the word.
3. Present the printed sight word in a phrase or sentence.

4. Present the printed sight word in a phrase or sentence along with a representative picture.

Singer (1980, p. 291) believes that beginning readers will be "more accurate in identifying words at sight when they focus upon printed words alone because only then could they derive cues from the printed words and associate them with the spoken form of the word." The association between seeing the printed word alone and hearing it pronounced seems to be important, at least in the view of some reading authorities.

Other researchers have noted, after examining readers' learning of function words (such as "might," "which," "enough"), that those students who were taught words in isolated units learned more about the spelling of the word and the manner in which the orthographic forms represent the pronunciation (Ehri and Wilce 1980).

Ceprano (1981, p. 321) has reviewed the relevant research on methods of teaching sight words, specifically examining the question of whether to teach words in context or in isolation. She has concluded:

> Teaching procedures which emphasize the distinctive features of words do enhance learning of individual words. Thus, during any one teaching session it may be helpful to present a selection of words that differ in shape, length, and letter characteristics and to call attention to those features as each word is introduced.

Ceprano also cautions that words that students learn in isolation may not transfer to reading in context.

Hoskisson (Groff 1979) has recommended that the entire sentence be used to teach a word, rather than presenting an individual word in isolation. He has used the analogy of learning to speak, in which an entire sentence is used to convey meaning and to serve as a model for the child. Krieger (1981) has found that poor readers identified more high-frequency words in context than in isolation. She has stated that if poor readers consistently are given reading in context so that they can use their linguistic knowledge, they will become better readers.

In evaluating research evidence concerning which method is preferable, the teacher should be aware that the effectiveness of a method seems to be dependent on the standard used to measure its success. For example, several research studies have pointed to the superiority of the word-alone method, evaluating success in terms of accuracy on a word list reading task (Singer 1980). However, when semantic and syntactic knowledge of words was used as the measurement criterion, words in a meaningful sentence were more effective (Ehri and Wilce 1980). Rather than view the decision as an either/or situation, the teacher should consider that the several methods available may each be of benefit to different students in her classroom. She should remember the uniqueness of the learner: what is effective with one student may not be effective with another.

Specific Procedures for Instruction

Several reading experts have formulated procedures for teaching sight words; two of these are presented below. Teachers may want to try some of these procedures with their corrective or remedial reading students.

Context plus isolation procedure. McNinch (1981) has recommended first presenting the word in a sentence and then isolating the word. His procedure includes the following steps:

1. Choosing an unknown sight word that is in the student's oral vocabulary, the teacher uses the word orally in a sentence.
2. The teacher then presents a written sentence containing the word. (All other words in the sentence should already be in the student's sight vocabulary.) The teacher reads the sentence and underlines the unknown sight word.
3. The teacher writes the new word in isolation, comparing it to the one in the sentence. He points to various discriminating features of the word, such as the beginning letter or the number of letters, as a comparison is made between the word in the sentence and the word in isolation.
4. The student then reads the word in another sentence or phrase, which, like the first one, contains no other unknown words.
5. A transfer is then made to other reading materials, such as having the student read a library book containing the unknown word.
6. The student is then provided practice on the word in the form of games designed to achieve mastery of the word.

Natural language procedure. Hoskisson's method (Groff 1979) stresses the development of a sight vocabulary through the use of natural language, that is, phrases or sentences, so that words are not isolated apart from their context. His procedure includes these steps:

1. The teacher reads a printed sentence or phrase to the student.
2. The student reads after the teacher, phrase by phrase or sentence by sentence.
3. The teacher then reads the phrase or sentence aloud but leaves out words, which are supplied by the student.
4. As a final step, the student reads the phrase or sentence by himself.

Suggestions for Teaching Sight Words

Several strategies have been shown to be effective in teaching sight words: using high-imagery words, a word-family approach, games, or word cards.

Teachers should consider these strategies as they work with students who cannot readily accumulate a store of basic sight words.

High-imagery words. High-imagery words, such as "house," "tree," and "car," lend themselves easily to visual clues (pictures) as reinforcement. By contrast, low-imagery words, such as "day," "mile," or "time," are extremely difficult to represent pictorially. In a research study, Hargis and Gickling (1978) found that high-imagery words were more readily learned as sight words than low-imagery words, and also remained in memory storage better. Kolker and Terwilliger (1981) found that first and second graders learned high-imagery nouns in fewer trials than low-imagery nouns.

Word-family approach. McCabe (1978) has suggested that 170 of the 220 Dolch words can be taught using a word-family approach. The teacher can help the student write a Dolch word on the front of a card and then write other words in the same family (not Dolch words) on the back of the card.

Games. Games using sight words can be very effective with corrective and remedial reading students. Word bingo uses sight words in the squares, giving students exposure to the words while providing the competition of a game. Games can either be purchased commercially or constructed by the teacher.

Word cards. Student-made word cards can be used to help students develop their sight word vocabulary. The student can print a word on the front of the card. On the back, she can print a sentence using the word in context. The student may work with the card in several ways:

1. Under the word on the front of the card, she can write all the words she can think that rhyme with it. For example, she could write "cat," "rat," and "bat" under the word "fat."
2. Under the word on the front of the card, she can write words that are formed by adding a suffix. For example, she could write "running," "runner," and "runs" under the word "run."
3. Under the sentence on the back of the card, she can write other sentences using the target word.
4. Under the sentence on the back of the card, she can write other sentences using the word plus a suffix.

THE TEACHER'S ROLE

Singer (1980) and others have emphasized the crucial role of the teacher in sight word learning. Singer has stated that the teacher should show the student the printed word, asking the student to say the word. It is important that the teacher indicate to the student whether the response is right or wrong. If the student gives a wrong response, the teacher should immediately give the correct response, while the student is still looking at the word. Then the teacher should have the student repeat the correct response.

Since a sight word vocabulary serves as a base on which to build further word-recognition skills, the teacher must work diligently with remedial reading students to improve their sight word vocabulary. The teacher must be resourceful in trying the various procedures and methods discussed in this section to find those which work best with each student.

INFORMATION TO CONSIDER

1. Teachers may use existing basic sight word lists or ones that they develop themselves to teach sight words.
2. Several methods can be used to teach sight words.
3. The success of a method for teaching sight words may depend on the characteristics of the student.
4. The use of high-imagery words, word-family approach, games, and word expansions have been found to be effective techniques in teaching sight words.

Phonics

QUESTIONS TO GUIDE READING

Recall Questions
1. How may consonant sounds be assessed? Vowel sounds? Consonant clusters or digraphs? Diphthongs?
2. What cautions must be recognized by the teacher in assessing phonic skills?
3. Is it necessary for a student to be able to define phonic terms?
4. What are the most useful phonic generalizations, according to Burmeister?
5. What are three steps in Johnson and Lehnert's instructional model for teaching phonics?

Thinking Questions
1. Should a teacher assess all of the phonic skills, such as consonants, vowels, and consonant clusters, when testing a student?

2. What may affect a teacher's decision to use a group or individual phonic test?
3. What are alternative instructional models to the Johnson and Lehner model for teaching phonics?
4. How may a teacher determine when to reteach a sound-symbol relationship?

Phonics is the association of specific sounds with specific symbols. As students gain a body of sight words, they should begin to notice that certain words have the same sound at the beginning, middle, or end of a word. They should then generalize that a certain printed letter represents a certain sound; they will try that sound as they attempt to attack an unknown word containing the same letter.

Phonics has been proclaimed by some as the answer to every student's reading problem. Others view it as only one of several skills that can help a student identify an unknown word. The history of reading instruction reveals periods of time when phonics was stressed to the exclusion of other skills, and other times when phonics was virtually ignored.

Teachers of corrective and remedial students especially ponder the question, "How much phonics instruction should I provide for my corrective or remedial reading students?" The solution seems to have been aptly stated by Heilman (1972, p. 200): "In the final analysis, the optimum amount of phonics instruction for every child is the minimum he needs to become an independent reader." Teachers must realize that the amount of phonics needed to deal effectively with unknown words varies from one student to another. Only sound professional judgments by teachers can determine when "too much" phonics is producing too little gain to make it worthwhile for students. Teachers must always be aware that too many drill activities in any word-recognition skill may create negative attitudes toward reading and thereby defeat the primary objective of reading instruction.

To work with poor readers in developing their phonic skills, teachers should be aware of how these skills can be assessed, what activities are appropriate for increasing various phonic skills, and how they should deal with the question of the usefulness of phonic generalizations. These topics are discussed in the following section.

ASSESSMENT OF PHONIC SKILLS

Phonic tests usually assess a student's ability to correlate the sounds and symbols of consonants and vowels. In addition, students are often assessed on their ability to blend two or more sounds into one unit or word. Some assessment procedures are described below.

Consonants. One way to measure consonant ability is to have the teacher pronounce either a real or a nonsense word and ask the student to point to the printed letter that represents the beginning or ending sound in the word. For example, the teacher would say "lat" and ask the student to point to the printed letter which represents the final sound; the student would point to the letter *t*.

Another way to measure a student's ability in consonant sounds is to ask him to form a new word verbally by substituting a different initial consonant for the one in a given printed word. For example, the student might be shown the word "mat" followed by a *c* [*mat (c)*]. The student would be asked what the word would be if *m* were changed to *c*.

A third way that ability in consonant sound-symbol association is assessed is simply to have the student look at individually printed consonant letters and ask her to give the sound associated with the letter. Since it is impossible to produce some consonant sounds free of the following / ə / sound, it is acceptable to have this sound in the response.

Vowels. Skill in vowel sound-symbol association may be assessed by visually presenting the student with the various vowel letters and asking him to make the short sound corresponding to each letter or to give a word beginning with that sound. The student would then be asked to do the same for the long sound of the vowels.

Nonsense words may also be used to assess vowel sound-symbol ability. The student may be shown a printed nonsense word such as "rit." He is asked to pronounce the word with a long *i* sound and then to pronounce it with a short *i* sound.

Consonant clusters and digraphs. A consonant cluster is a combination of two or three consonants together. Each consonant sound is heard, though pronounced quickly. Consonant clusters may be combinations with /r/ (*cr, str, tr,* or *br*), with /1/ (*sl, bl, cl,* or *fl*), or beginning with /s/ (*sn, sm,* or *sc*). A consonant digraph is also a combination of two consonant letters together; however, they have a new sound unlike either of the individual sounds that the letters generally represent. Common consonant digraphs are /sh/,/wh/,/th/,/ch/,/ph/,/gh/, and /nk/.

Often a list of clusters is shown to the student, and he is asked to point to the printed letters that are at the beginning of a word pronounced by the teacher. For example, the student might be shown a list of *cr, pl, str, cl,* and *dr.* When the teacher says the word "street," the student should point to the *str.* A similar task would be used for consonant digraphs.

In another assessment task for consonant clusters, the student might be asked first to recognize both a consonant cluster and a word part and then to blend them together. The student might be shown a printed *cr* and *uck* and asked to blend them together into one nonsense word, "cruck."

Diphthongs. A diphthong is a combination of two vowels, both being sounded. Examples of diphthongs are *ow, oi, ou*, and *oy* in such words as "cow," "oil," "house," and "toy." To assess a student's skill in using diphthongs, the teacher may present the student with a series of nonsense words, such as "floy," containing various diphthongs, and ask the student to pronounce each word.

ASSESSMENT CAUTIONS

The teacher must address the question, "How much phonics?" The authors stress the need for a balanced corrective or remedial word recognition program, which incorporates not only phonics but sight words, context, and structural analysis. Time limitations in a student's program must also be taken into consideration: developing positive attitudes and improving comprehension, for example, must be given appropriate attention. If too much time is given to any word-recognition skill, a student may be denied instruction in another skill that will give her increased proficiency and enjoyment in reading.

In assessing phonic knowledge through various tests, teachers should be aware that the type of assessment may have an impact on the results. Pikulski and Shanahan (1978) have pointed out that results may vary with

- a group versus an individual assessment,
- a required production response (oral or written) versus a recognition response, or
- different types of materials, such as individual letters versus syllables or real words versus nonsense words.

Varied types of probes may be needed to make accurate assessments. The teacher should realize that each test is only one piece of information in assessing the overall reading skills of students.

DEFINING PHONIC TERMS

Many terms are involved in the study of phonics: consonants, vowels, clusters, digraphs, and diphthongs, to name only a few. Teachers, as well as students, are often frustrated by the terminology, and the jargon can be intimidating to students.

Students may have difficulty in defining phonic terms. The important point is not whether they can define the terms but how they use phonic principles. Investigations of this issue have shown that students can apply phonic principles in their word attack even when they have difficulty in verbalizing definitions of terms (Tovey 1980). While there seems to be some evidence of a relationship between use of phonic generalizations and reading ability, students do not necessarily need to be able to verbalize the generalizations for a correlation to exist (Rosso and Emans 1981). Excessive teaching of terminology may be a poor use of a teacher's time; the ability to use the generalizations is the important skill students need to attain.

USEFULNESS OF PHONIC GENERALIZATIONS

An issue basic to any discussion of phonics is the usefulness of phonic generalizations or rules. For many years students learned the rules and attempted to apply them, and were often frustrated when they did not work. They then had to learn that there were exceptions to the rules.

Beginning in the 1950s, and especially in the 1960s, several significant studies were conducted to determine the usefulness of these phonic generalizations. Burmeister (1968) examined seven of these research studies and developed a list of fourteen "especially useful" phonic generalizations. This list should be a significant guideline for corrective or remedial reading teachers as they determine which rules they should use in instructional plans for their students. Burmeister's recommendations (shown in Fig. 9.2) are divided into categories: consonant sounds; vowel sounds—single vowels; vowel sounds—final "vowel-consonant-e"; and vowel sounds—adjacent vowels. Teachers should be cautious in extending this list; other rules may seem helpful, but have actually been proven to have a low utility rate when applied to the many words that students will encounter in their daily reading.

AN INSTRUCTIONAL MODEL

In planning activities for students with problems in phonic skills, teachers may find an instructional model developed by Johnson and Lehnert (1983) to be useful (see Fig. 9.3). It is one way to approach both the assessment and the remediation of phonics with students. Using a "natural way to learn phonics" (p. 288), Johnson and Lehnert propose a model that uses a language experience story dictated by students as a beginning step. Phonics is incorporated in this step as the teacher writes and speaks each word that has been dictated, emphasizing initial, medial, and final sounds.

During the second step, which is creative writing, students have the opportunity to experiment with sound-symbol relationships as they use "invented" spellings to write the words in their stories. Students are not told how to spell words; instead, they are encouraged to "listen to the sounds they hear in the word and associate the appropriate letters to make

Figure 9.2. Burmeister's Recommended Phonic Generalizations

Consonant Sounds
1. *C* followed by *e, i,* or *y* sounds soft; otherwise *c* is hard (omit *ch*). (certain, city, cycle; attic, cat, clip; success)
2. *G* followed by *c, i,* or *y* sounds soft; otherwise *g* is hard (omit *gh*). (gell, agile, gypsy; gone, flag, grope; suggest)
3. *Ch* is usually pronounced as it is in "kitchen," not like *sh* as in "machine."
4. When a word ends in *ck,* it has the same last sound as in "look."
5. When *ght* is seen in a word, *gh* is silent. (thought, night, right)
6. When two of the same consonants are side by side, only one is heard. (dollar, paddle)

Vowel Sounds—Single Vowels
1. If the only vowel letter is at the end of a word, the letter usually stands for a long sound (one-syllable words only). (be, he, she, go)
2. When *consonant* + *y* are the final letters in a one-syllable word, the *y* has a long *i* sound; in a polysyllabic word the *y* has a short *i* (long *e*) sound. (my, by, cry; baby, dignity)
3. A single vowel in a closed syllable has a short sound, except that it may be modified in words in which the vowel is followed by an *r.* (club, dress, at, car, pumpkin, virgin)
4. The *r* gives the preceding vowel a sound that is neither long nor short. (car, care, far, fair, fare) [single or double vowels]

Vowel Sounds—Final Vowel–Consonant–e
When a word ends in *vowel–consonant–e,* the *e* is silent, and the vowel may be long or short. (cape, mile, contribute, accumulate, exile, line, have, prove, encourage, ultimate, armistice, come, intensive, futile, passage)

Vowel Sounds—Adjacent Vowels
1. Digraphs: When the following double vowel combinations are seen together, the first is usually long and the second is silent: *ai, ay, ea, ee, oa, ow* (*ea* may also have a short *e* sound, and *ow* may have an *ou* sound) [main, pay; eat, bread; see, oat, sparrow, how]
2. Diphthongs (or blends): The following double vowel combinations usually blend: *au, aw, ou, oi, oy, oo* (*oo* has two common sounds). [auto, awful, house, coin, boy, book, rooster]
3. *io* and *ia*: *io* and *ia* after *c, t,* or *s* help to make a consonant sound: vic*io*us, par*tia*l, musi*cia*n, vi*sio*n, atten*tio*n (even o*cea*n).

From Lou Burmeister, "Usefulness of Phonic Generalizations," *The Reading Teacher,* January 1968, pp. 353–354. Reprinted with permission of the International Reading Association.

these sounds" (p. 290). Through this experimentation and usage, students develop generalizations about sound-symbol relationships.

In the third step, the teacher analyzes the invented spellings in the creative writing to determine each student's skills and needs in phonics. This analysis provides an indication of proficiency in initial, medial, and

Figure 9.3. Johnson and Lehnert's Instructional Model for Phonics

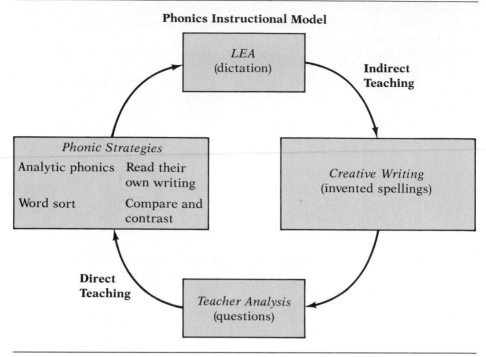

Phonics Instructional Model

From Ken Vander Meulen, *Reading Horizons: Selected Readings*. (Kallamazoo, MI: Western Michigan University, 1983), p. 289. Reprinted by permission.

final sounds. The teacher then plans appropriate strategies to help with any problem area.

Implementation of the planned strategies is the fourth and final step. In this step, activities include sorting words, using analytic phonics, using compare and contrast phonics, and reading their own writing.

Other Instructional Activities

Specific instructional activities for problem areas in phonics are listed below by type of problem. These are illustrative of the types of tasks that can be of value to students following an assessment of a specific problem.

Problems with consonant sounds. The problem may be with initial, medial, or final consonant sounds. Activities must be adapted to fit the specific needs of the student.

Activity: The teacher reads a sentence such as, "I like my new ball," and then asks the student to supply another word which would begin like "ball." The student might suggest "book," "bat," or "belt."

Activity: The teacher pronounces three words, two of which begin or end alike. The student must say which words are alike. For example, "bat," "meat," and "butterfly" might be read; the student indicates that "bat" and "butterfly" begin alike.

Activity: A bingo game can be used effectively in a small group situation. Bingo cards are given to each student. As the teacher calls out a word, the student places a token on a letter written on the card that corresponds to the initial letter of the word the teacher has read.

Activity: The teacher asks the student to name objects in the room that begin or end like a certain word. Pictures could also be used to find objects that have the same beginning or ending sound as the identified word.

Activity: Using several wooden clothespins, the teacher marks a consonant letter on each one. The student finds pictures in magazines of objects whose names begin with each of the consonants written on the clothespins. The student cuts out the pictures and clips them in the appropriate clothespin.

Problems with vowel sounds. Students need to become proficient in both the long and short sounds of vowels. Assessment may reveal problems in one or both areas.

Activity: The teacher helps students learn an identifying word for each short vowel sound. (Example: *a—apple; e—elephant.*)

Activity: Students sort known words (written on cards) into piles by those that have two or three letters and end with a vowel. The student makes a generalization about the words in each pile. For example, "he," "she," "me," and "so" might be grouped together because they are all words of two or three letters that end with a vowel. The student would generalize that at the end of a short word, a vowel often has the long sound.

Activity: The teacher writes on a card a word with a missing vowel. The student's task is to see how many words she can write on the card, using varying vowels to fill in the blank. For example, "m—t" would be given; the student could write "mat," "mit," and "met."

Activity: Students sort pictures according to similar beginning vowel sounds.

Activity: To help to identify the various vowels visually, a student can cut out words from magazines that contain the letters *a,e,i,o,* and *u.* He can group similar letters together. As the teacher helps him pronounce each word, the student further sorts them into piles, one for long and one for short sounds.

Problems with clusters and digraphs. Similar activities can be developed for both of these phonic skill areas.

Activity: The teacher can fold a sheet of paper into six parts (three on the back and three on the front). At the top of each part, he writes a word that has a consonant cluster or digraph at the beginning of the word. The cluster or digraph is underlined. The student then finds pictures of objects whose names begin with the same cluster or digraph printed at the top of each section of the paper, and pastes them in the appropriate place.

Activity: The teacher can show a word card with flaps in which the word "train," for instance, could be changed to "brain" when a *br* on the flap is moved to cover the *tr*. Numerous changes could be made with flaps with other letters.

Problems with diphthongs. For students who have difficulty with diphthongs, activities such as the following can be used.

Activity: The teacher can construct flash cards which show the printed diphthong together with a picture illustrating a word using that letter combination.

Activity: A list such as the following can be given to the student, who is asked to make words using the diphthongs provided:

_oi_	ou_	_ou_
_oy	oi_	_ow

Activity: The teacher can ask students to collect words containing diphthongs from magazines. Students can then paste like diphthongs together on a half-sheet of construction paper, labeling each sheet with the identified diphthong.

A CAUTION FOR TEACHERS

Teachers are often frustrated by the student who seems to know the sound-symbol relations in a given word but is unable to decode the word. Cohn and D'Alessandro (1978) have stated that "only in a small percentage of cases is it true that poor word analysis performance in decoding a list of words is attributable to a lack of knowledge of the sound-symbol relationship involved" (p. 343). When a teacher attempts to reteach sound-symbol relationships, she may be trying to correct a condition that does not exist. Rather than continued drill on sound-symbol relationships, the teacher should help the student understand what he is doing. Questions which she should ask include the following:

Is he using a variety of word-recognition skills? He should learn to move from one to another to decode a word: from context to phonics to known word parts or sight words in the unknown word.

Is he quickly moving from one attack skill to another?

Is he aware of the types of attack he is using?

This type of instructional activity and discussion will generally be of more benefit than merely reteaching something that is already known.

Context

Context helps the reader in identifying an unknown word and in deciding which pronunciation of a word to use in a sentence. For example, in the sentences, "I read yesterday" and "I will read today," the context helps the reader in selecting the correct pronunciation of "read." Context is a word-recognition skill that takes advantage of the student's background of experiences, knowledge of language structure, and attention to the text to promote fluent reading. Context involves the reader in using his skills to name words in his speaking vocabulary, or those known aurally from his daily experiences that are not yet recognized in printed form.

In using context, the reader examines surrounding words, phrases, and sentences to assist him in decoding an unfamiliar word. Often a student does not know a particular word in a passage; however, by understanding the overall events in the passage, she can predict the correct word. The student who carefully attends to a passage increases her ability to predict an unknown word. She can read faster and more fluently as she makes predictions and anticipates what words will come next in the text.

A reader's awareness or knowledge of language has a significant influence on his ability to use context as a word-recognition skill. Students who know language patterns and have a good understanding of syntax have a better background for using context to figure out an unknown word. A student whose knowledge of syntactical structures has taught him that a verb often follows a noun can narrow his alternatives when encountering an unknown word following a noun. For example, in the sentence, "The man _____ a fish," the student could anticipate a verb such as "caught."

The overall vocabulary, concepts, and prior experiences of the reader facilitate the use of context. A student who has a large speaking vocabulary or encounters many words in her daily experiences will more likely be able to identify those words when she sees them in print. A student who does not have a word in his speaking or listening vocabulary will have a poor chance of being able to decode the word in a printed passage. By the same token, when a student has had experiences similar to those in a particular reading passage, he will be better able to predict what words will occur in the text. Therefore, it is very important that a passage be interesting and relevant to the student if he is expected to use context as a word-recognition clue.

Pictures, graphs, tables, and other similar items may also be used to provide context cues for an unknown word. Students are often unaware of the cues these types of aids can provide in word identification.

Using context is not simply taking a "wild guess" at an unknown word. It involves the use of prior experiences, knowledge of language structures, attention to surrounding text, and aids such as pictures or graphs. Context usage involves intelligent predictions of a word that would be appropriate in a passage. The reader can then use other word-recognition skills, such as phonics and known word parts, to narrow the range of viable alternatives to the exact word.

The reader who uses context effectively is constantly aware that the text or passage she is reading should make sense. She knows that reading is a meaningful process; if a passage does not make sense, she recognizes that she is making mistakes in word identification.

Teachers must teach readers to use context automatically to self-correct any errors made while reading. As the reader samples the printed page, she may make incorrect predictions. However, as she proceeds through the text, she realizes she has incorrectly identified a particular word that has appeared many times. For example, in the following passage, the reader missed the word "dragon" twice before self-correcting it the third time it was encountered in the passage. By the third repetition, enough cues had been given to enable her to identify the word correctly.

A big dragon lives by the sea.
Puff is the dragon's name.
Puff is a magic dragon.
Puff is a good dragon.

In using context to decode an unknown word, the reader makes a prediction, tries out the word in the passage, and then either accepts the word if it makes sense or rejects it to move on to another prediction.

RECOGNIZING THE PROBLEM

Through informal classroom observation, the classroom teacher can often recognize a student who is having difficulty using context. Several behaviors indicate problems in using context to identify an unfamiliar word:

Failure to verbalize context as a strategy. A teacher may informally ask a student what she does when she comes to an unknown word. The student should be able to state that she sounds out the word, or that she examines known parts, or that she figures out what word would make sense in the passage. If she does not realize that context is an available strategy, it is unlikely that she will use that strategy in unlocking unknown words.

Word-by-word reading. While word-by-word oral reading may be a symptom of other word-recognition problems, such as a limited sight word vocabulary, it may also result from a failure to use context. The student may not be using prediction and his knowledge of language structures to read an entire phrase fluently; rather, he reads every word as if it had no relationship to the words before or after it. Because of this slow word-by-word pace, he may forget what was said in the beginning of a passage before he reaches the end.

Refusal to predict. Some students refuse to use their experience and knowledge of sentence structure to predict a word. Instead, when they get to an unknown word, they stop, expecting the teacher or another child in the group to supply the unfamiliar word. The observant teacher will notice such a student who seems unwilling or unable to make a sensible prediction for an unfamiliar word.

Low comprehension scores. The student who does not use context may score higher on the vocabulary test portion of a standardized test than she does on the comprehension portion of the test. The vocabulary section is a list of words in isolation, while the comprehension section has words in a meaningful context. If a student has facility in context, reading scores should be higher on the comprehension section, since the student has more information available to identify the word.

Syntactical and semantic errors. Failure to use context will often be revealed by syntactical or semantic mistakes in oral reading. As the student reads, he substitutes words that do not retain the meaning or syntax of the sentence. The following is an example of a syntactical error made by a student:

      rain
The boy ran down the hill.

"Rain" is not the same part of speech as "ran." The student should have been expecting a verb to follow the noun; instead, he probably used phonics for the first letter only. Knowledge of language structure would have helped to correctly identify "ran."

The following illustration demonstrates a student who does not use semantic context:

         dig
The boy saw the dog.

"Dig" does not fit the meaning of the sentence.

A careful analysis of a student's syntactical and semantic errors on the reading passages of an informal reading inventory will reveal students who do not use context to attack unfamiliar words.

Failure to self-correct. A student often fails to correct miscues, even though the passage as read is making no sense at all. He proceeds through the passage, usually word by word, seemingly with no concern that what he is reading carries no meaning. He does not stop to comment that the passage is not making sense, but struggles on just to get to the end.

CAUSES OF CONTEXT PROBLEMS

Possible causes of the behaviors outlined above may be linked to the student's background or experiences. Inadequate use of context may be due to the following factors:

Beliefs about reading. If a child has only seen reading as a drill in decoding isolated words, he may fail to use context because he does not realize that all the words in a passage contribute to and develop ideas on a certain topic. Parents, teachers, and others who read to children in early childhood usually help children develop the idea that printed words tell a story or provide information. Children without this experience may not approach the reading task to gain meaning from it; they may simply try to decode the words.

Poor concept formation. Children with limited experiences have limited concepts. When they encounter reading materials by commercial publishers, they may not understand terms and events in the story if these events are not in their conceptual framework. Such students will often have difficulty in using context because they do not have a repertoire of possible words or events for the story that could serve as possible choices in using context. The words are not familiar from daily experience; therefore, they cannot make predictions even if they attend closely to the text.

Material not matched to experience. Closely associated with the lack of concept development is the failure of the teacher to match the reading materials to the student's background. The language experience story is often advocated, as it can be directly related to the student's experiences and matched to his oral language. If language experience materials are not used, the teacher should be careful to provide materials for students that are suited to their background and oral language.

Discouragement of prediction. A student will usually eliminate behaviors that are not rewarded positively. If a teacher discourages a student from predicting by providing negative verbal or nonverbal feedback for such an action, the reader is likely to stop predicting what word will make sense in a passage. The student may learn that it is better to avoid making a prediction than to take a chance of being wrong.

Predicting what will come next in a passage entails a risk: the student may be wrong in her prediction. If she cannot feel comfortable in taking a risk, she will fall into a pattern of word-by-word reading to ensure that she is correct. Smith (1983, p. 17) has stated, "Learning cannot take place without error." Therefore, if teachers want students to learn, they must allow them to make mistakes.

Instead of looking unfavorably on a student's prediction, a teacher should plan activities that encourage prediction as a strategy. Students who have not had such training may be at a disadvantage when analyzing an unknown word.

Overemphasis on phonic cues. Some students do not use context because they have been taught exclusively by an intensive phonics method. Having become overly dependent on phonic cues, they carefully try to "sound out" every word, letter by letter. It is a slow procedure in which fluency and, consequently, comprehension are often lost. For these students, phonics has been the foremost and only automatic strategy to use when they come across an unknown word.

ACTIVITIES TO PROMOTE CONTEXT

It is fortunate when parents and preschool teachers begin early to promote the use of context. They can do this by letting children complete a line in a favorite nursery rhyme or supply the ending of a sentence in a book that is being read to them. Letting children finish familiar phrases can be a worthwhile activity.

The classroom teacher cannot assume that students will learn to use context on their own. Discussions with students are needed to point out the various strategies to use when an unknown word is encountered. Possibilities include using their backgrounds of experience and their knowledge of language structure to help them anticipate appropriate words.

The teacher should demonstrate to students how they can use context combined with other word-recognition skills. While all word-recognition skills are important in helping a student analyze an unknown word in a passage, context is probably the most appropriate one for a student to try first. Context emphasizes the purpose of reading: to gain meaning from a printed passage. Context helps the reader realize that what comes before and after the unknown word influences his ability to figure out the word.

After the student has generated possibilities for the unknown word by using context cues, he can then refine the possibilities through other word-recognition strategies. This movement to other strategies should become automatic, so that the reader will not lose fluency in reading a passage. Phonic cues are a good second strategy to use to add preciseness to the selection from alternatives. The beginning letter or letters can help in narrowing the choices from the predicted alternatives. Phonics can give preciseness to the possibilities generated by the context.

A combination of word-recognition skills, and the automatic response to go from one to another, will help a student become a more fluent reader. The teacher's task is to help the student understand what he is doing as he reads a passage and what strategies he can use to increase his ability to figure out an unfamiliar word.

Context-plus method. Spiegel, Reck, and Fitzgerald (1983) found that a context-plus-phonics strategy was effective in increasing second-grade students' use of context as a word-recognition skill. In their study, students engaged in the following activities over a period of time:

1. Students first practiced predicting an obvious word which was omitted from a sentence. (Example: Santa Claus brings _____ at Christmas.)

2. Students then completed practice exercises in which they were taught to skip an unknown word, read on to the end of the sentence, and then go back to put in a word that would make sense and that had the first letter of the unknown word.
3. Students were taught to ask themselves three questions when they predicted a certain word for a sentence:
   Does it make sense?
   Could you say it that way?
   Does that word begin with the right first letter?

4. Students monitored and corrected the teacher when she orally read sentences on chart paper. As the teacher made errors that either did not make sense or did not begin with the right first letter, students would explain why she was wrong.
5. Students played a game in which they could move a token if they correctly identified an underlined word that was in a rich context.

Hierarchy of cues. In providing written exercises for students to practice decoding an unfamiliar word using context, the reader should keep in mind that certain exercises seem to be more difficult for students than others. Emans and Fisher (1967) investigated the difficulty of six types of fill-in-the-blank exercises and developed the following hierarchy: number 1 is easiest for students and number 6 is the most difficult.

1. All consonants are given in an underlined word.
   The _l _ph _nt was in the circus.
2. Four word choices are given.
   The _____was in the circus.
      book
      elephant
      name
      pail
3. Beginning and ending letters are given.
   The e_____ t was in the circus.
4. The length of the word is given.
   The _____was in the circus.
5. The beginning letter is given.
   The e_____ was in the circus.
6. No clue is given.
   The _____was in the circus.

Other activities. Teachers can plan activities using semantic and syntactic clues to increase a student's awareness and use of context. The emphasis in semantic clues is on obtaining meaning from surrounding words and ideas and prior experiences related to the material being read. The emphasis in syntactical clues is on the structure of language, that is, the relationship between nouns and verbs, descriptors (adjectives) and nouns, and articles (such as "the," "a," or "an") and the subsequent nouns. The following five activities will be appropriate for many students.

Activity: After having a student fill in a missing word in a spoken sentence, the teacher can then give written sentences with a word missing.

Activity: The teacher can develop cloze passages for students. Chapter 5 contains a description of how to construct such a passage. Special cloze passages could be designed so that the deleted words carry the primary meaning of the passage. The teacher should make sure the materials are easy for the student; he should not have to deal with too many unknown words.

Activity: Three word cards can be attached together with a ring in the upper left corner. A sentence with one word missing is written on the first card. The student must predict the missing word. After the prediction is made, the student flips to the second card, which has the first letter of the missing word written on it. The student then confirms her prediction or makes another. Finally, she flips to the third card, which shows the correct word.

Activity: The student is asked to retell a story. This will help him to see how words in a narrative fit together.

Activity: Provide extensive time for students to try out the skills they may have learned on reading materials that they select themselves. This is extremely necessary if they are to view reading as meaningful.

A NOTE TO TEACHERS

The teacher must provide opportunities for students to self-correct. When the teacher rushes to supply an unknown or mispronounced word, the student is denied the opportunity to self-correct as he proceeds through the text. The teacher should allow time for the student to figure out the word on his own.

Students must be given opportunities to read in context. Teachers often become so concerned about the lack of skills in corrective or remedial readers that they focus almost all their activities on isolated word drill. In an informal survey of remedial and corrective reading sessions, Allington (1977) found that students were doing very little actual reading: no student read more than 100 words in context in a reading session.

Allington stated that "reading is not responding to flashcards, nor is it filling in blanks, marking vowel values, or responding to graphemes presented in isolation" (p. 58). He suggested that teachers

- assess the amount of reading in context that occurs in their reading class,
- set a goal of 500 words in context for each lesson,

- avoid having a mini-lesson in word analysis during the context reading, and
- chart the number of words a student reads in context during a session.

Frank Smith (1983, p. 16) has stated that good readers "do not read words, they read meanings" and that "reading without anticipating is not reading at all." In encouraging students to use context, teachers promote the ideas of reading for meaning, of actively engaging in the prediction of events in the passage, and of letting their past experiences unite with events or information in the passage to help them understand more of the world around them. Figuring out the word is not the end product of reading: getting meaning is the ultimate goal.

INFORMATION TO CONSIDER

1. The use of context clues may facilitate word recognition.
2. Language awareness, vocabulary, concepts, and prior experiences affect a reader's use of context.
3. Prediction using context is not "wild guessing" and should be encouraged.
4. Teacher observation of certain student behaviors can be used to note those students who fail to use context.
5. Teachers and parents should encourage children to use context very early in their experiences with reading.

Structural Analysis

QUESTIONS TO GUIDE READING

Recall Questions
1. What component skills are included in the category of structural analysis?
2. What is a word family?
3. What is the procedure Graves and Hammond have recommended for teaching prefixes?
4. What syllabic generalizations have been recommended by Burmeister as being useful?
5. What types of assessments could be used for structural analysis skills?

Thinking Questions
1. Why is the use of structural analysis as a word-recognition skill dependent upon a student's repertoire of sight words and phonic skills?
2. Do you agree with Groff's statement that syllable-phoneme correspondence should be taught before letter-phoneme correspondence? Why or why not?
3. What could be possible disadvantages to instructing students in using structural analysis for facilitating word recognition?

In this section, structural analysis will be discussed as a word-recognition skill. This skill involves breaking down an unknown word into parts to make recognition possible. If Cunningham's (1980) compare/contrast theory of mediated word recognition is correct, the student's word-recognition skills will be enhanced by instruction in the use of word parts. Cunningham has suggested that in word recognition, a student segments an unknown word into the largest manageable units. These units are compared to known words, nonwords, or fragments and then recombined into a word the student has heard or that is meaningful. In such a procedure, the repertoire of known words and word parts becomes important. The greater the store of words and word parts, the greater the likelihood that the student can find a match between the store and an unknown word.

For the student who is having difficulty in identifying words, especially polysyllabic ones, the teacher may decide that instruction and attention to word parts would be worthwhile. The teacher will sometimes notice students who seem to use only the first letter of a word in identification; they do not visually survey the word to pick up cues other than the beginning letter. If the student can develop a strategy of looking through an unknown word for consistent, known word parts, his word-recognition skills may improve.

Analyzing a word letter by letter can be extremely time-consuming. Corrective or remedial reading students sometimes develop this strategy for decoding a word. To attach a sound to each symbol in a word and then recombine all the sounds into an identifiable word is probably the most inefficient of all strategies. If a reader can move away from smaller units, such as letters, to word parts, she should be able to increase her reading fluency.

Structural analysis as a word-recognition skill is dependent on sight words. It is not feasible to begin instruction in word parts until the student has acquired a basic sight word vocabulary. Phonic skills should also be developed prior to instruction in word parts; because only part of an unknown word may be in a student's store of words, he may need to use phonic clues to identify some parts of a word.

Included in the category of structural analysis are several component skills: word families, root words, prefixes, suffixes, syllables, and compound words. While there is overlapping among these components, each one has a certain approach to the study of structural analysis that makes it worthy of individual attention. A student may not need instruction in every component; the teacher must judge which structural analysis components are necessary to provide the student with adequate skills to make word recognition efficient.

In describing the use of structural analysis, Otto and Smith (1980) have stressed attention to the *morpheme*, the smallest unit of a word that carries meaning. While a word may have only one morpheme, such as "make," "tall," or "see," some words contain more than one morpheme, such as "maker," "taller," and "seeing." Otto and Smith have recommended that the student

- be aware that words may contain more than one morpheme,
- gain an expanding corpus of morphemes, and
- search for known morphemes in new words.

They have pointed out that teachers should be cautious about asking students to find "little words" in "big words," pointing to the problem created by "fat" in "father" and "the" in "mother." The *root word*, or base word, is a much more stable unit, and the term should cause less confusion for the student.

WORD FAMILIES

A word family typically has almost all letters in common. The following groups represent common families:

kite   bite   site   smite

train   brain   gain   main

tame   lame   same   blame

McCabe (1978) has provided a list of phonic families within the Dolch sight word list (Fig. 9.4). Using these words, word families and sight word learning can be combined.

For the student who needs remediation practice in recognizing word families, the following activities could be used:

Activity: Print a list of words on index cards and place them in one pile. Ask a student to sort the cards into categories by similar endings.

Activity: Ask a student to circle words in the comics section of the newspaper that have common endings.

Root Words

The root word is the base of a word: it carries the primary meaning. Knowledge and identification of root words not only helps a student in word recognition, but also helps him understand how several words can have a common element; for example, "helps," "helper," "helpful," "helping," "helpfulness," "helped," and "helpers" all share a common base, "help." If the one root word is known, it provides a cue for recognizing seven other words.

If a teacher determines that a student would benefit from instruction in recognizing root words, the activities below may be helpful:

Activity: Ask the student to form as many words as possible from a given root word. This may be done as a game, with two competing groups vying to make the most words in a specified time period.

Activity: Have the student circle the roots within a list of words:

working   reading
teacher   boyish
laughing   keeper

Prefixes and Suffixes

An understanding of prefixes and suffixes can assist a student in both the identification of a word and its meaning. Prefixes are word parts attached to the beginning of a word that affect the meaning, such as:

bi-   multi-   re-
dis-   pre-   sub-
in-   pro-   un-

Prefixes are attached to root words to form such words as:

biweekly   disenchantment   invalid
multicolor   prearrange   procreate
return   subcontract   undone

Suffixes affect meaning just as prefixes do; however, they are affixed to the ending of a word. Typical suffixes are:

Figure 9.4. Examples of Phonic Families Among Dolch Sight Words, for Diagnostic/Prescriptive Learning of Patterns

Base Word	Other Members of the Family
had*	bad sad dad lad Tad mad fad
black*	lack back sack rack crack
after*	raft rafter craft aft
am	Sam ham dam mam jam ram cram
an*	man ban bran fan Jan pan plan
and*	band sand land brand hand
door*	floor doorway backdoor doors
duck	luck tuck stuck puck truck muck
eggs	beg keg peg Peg Meg leg
would	should could
good*	wood hood stood brotherhood
all*	tall stall install wall ball
saw*	raw draw law slaw flaw claw jaw
because	cause pause clause
toys	toy joy enjoy enjoys Roy annoy
box	ox fox sox boxer
book*	look took shook nook rook crook
coat*	oat goat float moat throat boat
white*	bite kite invite polite unite write
birthday	birth girth mirth
	day lay play pay clay stay may
us	bus pus plus thus
up*	pup cup sup "whup"
upon	up pup cup sup
	on Don con Ron bonfire
under*	thunder blunder plunder

*Word from harder half of Dolch Basic Sight Vocabulary of 220 Words

From Don McCabe, "220 Sight Words Are Too Many for Students with Memories like Mine," *The Reading Teacher*, April 1978, p. 792. Copyright 1978 International Reading Association. Reprinted with permission of Don McCabe and The International Reading Association.

-er	-est	-ful
-less	-ment	-ness
-ship	-tion	-ure

When added to a base, the following words would result:

warmer	cleanest	helpful
careless	enjoyment	happiness
ownership	contribution	closure

Figures 9.5 and 9.6 contain lists developed by Ives, Bursuk, and Ives (1979) of prefixes and suffixes that children may encounter.

Graves and Hammond (1980) have recommended a procedure for teaching prefixes to students as a way of unlocking new words. The procedure is equally applicable to teaching suffixes.

1. Select four words containing the same prefix to present to students.
2. Have the students determine the meaning of those four words.
3. Have the students identify the common prefix in all four words and determine its meaning.
4. Help students realize how the prefix contributed to the meaning of the four words.
5. Have students examine four sentences, each with a different word containing the prefix; have them identify the meaning of the word and the effect of the prefix on the word.

The student who has a problem in recognizing prefixes and suffixes may increase his skill through the following exercises:

Activity: Have the student circle the prefixes or suffixes in all the words that appear in the sports section of the newspaper. Compile a master list of prefixes or suffixes using these words. Group them in categories.

Activity: Name a particular prefix or suffix. Have a contest to see which student can write the most words using the particular affix. (Students may be given a list of root words as a reference.)

Figure 9.5. List of Prefixes

Easily Identified Prefixes

Prefix	Example	Common Meaning
⟨a-⟩	atypical	not, without
⟨ab-⟩	abnormal	away, from
⟨ad-⟩	admit	to, toward, near
	accord	
⟨ante-⟩	anteroom	before, prior to
⟨auto-⟩	autobiography	self
⟨bi-⟩	biangular	two
⟨circum-⟩	circumnavigate	around
⟨com-⟩	commingle	together, jointly
	collaborate	
	coauthor	
⟨counter-⟩	counterattack	opposition
⟨de-⟩	defrost	opposition

Figure 9.5. *(continued)*

Easily Identified Prefixes

Prefix	Example	Common Meaning
⟨dis-⟩	disappear	opposition
	dishonest	not
⟨en-⟩	enslave	cause to
⟨ex-⟩	ex-president	former
⟨extra-⟩	extramarital	outside, beyond
⟨fore-⟩	forejudge	before
⟨hyper-⟩	hyperactive	overly, beyond
⟨in-⟩	indirect	not
	illegal	
	immeasurable	
	irrational	
⟨inter-⟩	interstate	between
⟨intra-⟩	intrastate	within
⟨mal-⟩	malfunctioning	poorly, badly
⟨micro-⟩	microwave	small
⟨mid-⟩	midyear	middle
⟨mis-⟩	miscount	wrongly, badly
⟨mono-⟩	monotone	one
⟨multi-⟩	multicolored	many
⟨neo-⟩	neoclassical	new
⟨non-⟩	nonliving	not
⟨per-⟩	permeate	thoroughly, through
⟨poly-⟩	polysyllabic	many
⟨post-⟩	postwar	after
⟨pre-⟩	prewar	before
⟨pro-⟩	pro-American	for, favoring
⟨pseudo-⟩	pseudoscience	false
⟨re-⟩	rewrite	again, repeat
⟨retro-⟩	retroactive	back
⟨semi-⟩	semirigid	partly
⟨sub-⟩	subsoil	under, beneath
⟨super-⟩	superhuman	above, beyond
⟨syn-⟩	syndrome	together, with
	symbiosis	
⟨trans-⟩	transoceanic	across
⟨tri-⟩	triangular	three
⟨ultra-⟩	ultramodern	above, extremely
⟨un-⟩	unhappy	not
	untie	do opposite action
⟨uni-⟩	unicolor	one
⟨vice-⟩	vice-consulate	subordinate

From Josephine P. Ives, Lauren Z. Bursuk, and Sumner A. Ives, *Word Identification Techniques* (Boston: Houghton Mifflin Company, 1979), pp. 110–111. Reprinted with the permission of Houghton Mifflin Company.

Figure 9.6. List of Suffixes

Noun- and Adjective-Marking Suffixes

Suffix	Noun Example	Adjective Example
⟨-able⟩		breakable
⟨-acy⟩	primacy	
⟨-age⟩	orphanage	
⟨-al⟩	arrival	fictional
⟨-an⟩	republican	
⟨-ian⟩	Iranian	Iranian
⟨-n⟩	American	American
⟨-ance⟩	acceptance	
⟨-ancy⟩	ascendancy	
⟨-ant⟩	claimant	determinant
⟨-ar⟩	scholar	
⟨-ary⟩	commentary	budgetary
⟨-ate⟩	consulate	
⟨-ation⟩	affirmation	
⟨-cal⟩		historical
⟨-dom⟩	freedom	
⟨-ed⟩		cultured
⟨-ee⟩	appointee	
⟨-eer⟩	auctioneer	
⟨-en⟩		golden
⟨-ence⟩	preference	
⟨-ency⟩	consistency	
⟨-ent⟩	deterrent	abhorrent
⟨-er⟩	driver	
⟨-or⟩	sailor	
⟨-ery⟩	bravery	
⟨-ese⟩	journalese	
⟨-esque⟩		statuesque
⟨-ess⟩	authoress	
⟨-et⟩	floweret	
⟨-ette⟩	cigarette	
⟨-iferous⟩		odoriferous
⟨-fold⟩		tenfold
⟨-ful⟩		peaceful
⟨-ing⟩	meeting	
⟨-graph⟩	radiograph	
⟨-hood⟩	childhood	
⟨-ible⟩	convertible	
⟨-ic⟩		poetic
⟨-ice⟩	service	
⟨-ics⟩	athletics	
⟨-ile⟩		infantile
⟨-ine⟩	heroine	elephantine
⟨-ion⟩	regulation	
⟨-ish⟩		foolish
⟨-ism⟩	alcoholism	

Figure 9.6. *(continued)*

Noun- and Adjective-Marking Suffixes

Suffix	Noun Example	Adjective Example
⟨-ist⟩	racist	
⟨-ity⟩	civility	
⟨-ive⟩		creative
⟨-kin⟩	lambkin	
⟨-less⟩		witless
⟨-let⟩	booklet	
⟨-like⟩		childlike
⟨-ling⟩	weakling	
⟨-ly⟩		kindly
⟨-ment⟩	development	
⟨-ness⟩	kindness	
⟨-ology⟩	etymology	
⟨-ory⟩	depository	compensatory
⟨-ous⟩		joyous
⟨-ry⟩	citizenry	
⟨-ship⟩	friendship	
⟨-some⟩		burdensome
⟨-ster⟩	youngster	
⟨-ty⟩	certainty	
⟨-ude⟩	definitude	
⟨-ule⟩	molecule	miniscule
⟨-ulent⟩		fraudulent
⟨-ure⟩	failure	
⟨-y⟩	honesty	messy

Verb-Marking Suffixes

Suffix	Example
⟨-ate⟩	activate
⟨-en⟩	shorten
⟨-esce⟩	convalesce
⟨-fy⟩	beautify
⟨-ify⟩	solidify
⟨-ize⟩	terrorize

Adverb-Marking Suffixes

Suffix	Example
⟨-fold⟩	tenfold
⟨-ly⟩	slowly
⟨-most⟩	topmost
⟨-ward(s)⟩	westward(s)
⟨-wise⟩	clockwise

From Josephine P. Ives, Lauren Z. Bursuk, and Sumner A. Ives, *Word Identification Techniques* (Boston: Houghton Mifflin Company, 1979), pp. 112–115. Reprinted with permission of Houghton Mifflin Company.

Syllables

Burmeister (1968) has compiled a list of especially useful syllabic generalizations. This list, shown in Figure 9.7, is a distillation of several research studies. If a teacher wants to provide instruction in the division of words into syllables, these are the generalizations that seem most essential.

In practice activities, it is helpful for students to spend some time practicing dividing unfamiliar or nonsense words. If they divide a word that is already known, little is gained from the activity.

Compound Words

When two or more root words are combined, the new word is called a *compound word*. Examples include:

storybook	cookbook	handball
cowboy	baseball	busload
meatball	worksheet	topside

Figure 9.7. Burmeister's List of Useful Syllabication Generalizations

Syllabication—Determination of a Syllable
Every single vowel or vowel combination means a syllable (except a "final *e*" in a "vowel-consonant-*e*" ending).

Syllabication—Structural Syllabication
These generalizations take precedence over phonic syllabication generalizations.
1. Divide between a prefix and a root.
2. Divide between two roots.
3. Usually divide between a root and a suffix.

Syllabication—Phonic Syllabication
1. When two vowel sounds are separated by two consonants, divide between the consonants but consider *ch*, *sh*, *ph*, and *th* to be single consonants (assist, convey, bunny, Houston, rustic).
2. When two vowel sounds are separated by one consonant, divide either before or after the consonant. Try dividing before the consonant first. (Consider *ch*, *sh*, *ph*, and *th* to be single consonants). [alone, select, ashame, Japan, sober; comet, honest, ever, idiot, modest, agile, general]
3. When a word ends in a "consonant-*l-e*" divide before the consonant. (battle, treble, tangible, kindle).

From Lou Burmeister, "Usefulness of Phonic Generalizations," *The Reading Teacher*, January 1968, pp. 354–355. Reprinted with permission of The International Reading Association.

Some corrective and remedial readers seem unable to see that there are two distinct words in each compound word; they merely see one global word. Even though they know both these words, they may not see the relationship between them.

The following exercises could be useful in working with students with problems in analyzing compound words:

Activity: Have students circle each base word in a list of compound words.

Activity: Cut an index card into two parts. Write one part of a compound word on one part and the other on the second part. Using several divided compound words, ask a student to assemble the cards so as to form as many compound words as he can.

ASSESSMENT OF STRUCTURAL ANALYSIS SKILLS

The teacher has several possibilities for assessing students' skills in structural analysis. Oral reading is one way, either of graded passages on an informal reading inventory or of an appropriate passage or word list in the classroom.

Paper and pencil tests can also be used. The student usually circles the parts of a word or places slash marks between the parts:

   pre/plan

Various mastery tests accompanying a basal reading series or competency skills tests of a school system usually assess the ability to recognize word parts. Teachers can easily construct their own tests.

Failure to recognize word parts visually can be seen in the behavior of students who seem to have no strategy to break a multisyllable word into manageable parts for identification. The problem is usually noted as students encounter longer words in their reading; however, the ability to see word families is a skill needed even in the beginning phase of learning to read.

INSTRUCTIONAL PROCEDURES

The sample activities suggested in this section usually group themselves into certain types:

- circling common word parts
- creating a list of words that have a common word part
- circling or placing slashes between each part of a multisyllabic word
- using given word parts to create a word made of several parts

Teachers can use these basic guides to create games and activities specific to the particular skill needed by the student.

Wilson (1981) has outlined a procedure that can be applied to exercises with prefixes, suffixes, or compound words. He provides the following illustration using the prefix *un-*:

- Present the word "happy" in a sentence.   John is happy.
- Change the word to "unhappy."   John is unhappy.
- Have the students generalize the difference in meaning.
- Present several other words using *un-* in a similar manner.
- Have the students generalize by answering the question, "What does *un-* generally do to the meaning of a word to which it is prefixed?"
- Collect word patterns of this type and see if they apply to the generalization.
- Note that *un-* has a consistent sound and that it changes the meaning of the words to which it is attached.
- As the students read, their attention should be called to words prefixed by *un-*. They should determine if these words fit the generalization.

Cunningham (1980) tested the following word-recognition strategy in a research study and found it to be of benefit:

1. Students were given six polysyllabic words and asked to write them on separate index cards. Most of these words were familiar to the students.
2. Students were told these were clue words and that they would be given other words to decode by using parts of the six clue words.
3. Students used the clue words in sentences and were asked to pronounce them.
4. Students were then shown unknown polysyllabic words that contained portions of the six clue words. They were to decode the unknown word by comparing it to the clue words.
5. The number of clue words and unknown words was gradually increased.

RECOMMENDATIONS CONCERNING STRUCTURAL ANALYSIS

The use of structural analysis to increase the word-recognition skills of corrective and remedial reading students seems to offer benefits. However, it should not be seen as the sole, isolated skill for students to use; rather it is recommended as one of several skills that should be sharpened to increase the student's ability to read.

Further recommendations concerning instruction in structural analysis are offered below:

1. Word parts should be taught in context as much as possible. While teaching students to analyze a word visually by circling the various parts may be done using isolated words, the teacher needs to provide extensive time for the student to practice this skill in a story context. Once the awareness has been established that she should break an unidentifiable word into parts, the student should be given ample opportunity to try out this newly learned principle. Teachers sometimes spend too much time on skill practice when the student has already learned the principle and simply needs adequate time to read materials containing words to which the principle can be applied.

2. A teacher may teach word parts through either an inductive or a deductive approach. Using the *inductive approach*, the teacher could ask students to sort all of the words together that had a common characteristic, such as a certain prefix. After noting the similarity of the words grouped together, the students then make a generalization about the sound or influence of the group of word parts. In the *deductive approach* the teacher presents the generalization and asks the students to find representative examples.

3. If the student has no problems in analyzing multisyllabic words, there is no need to teach these skills. Each of the specific structural analysis skills should be diagnosed as a need of a particular student. If he already has these skills, his time could better be spent in reading for enjoyment or information.

The use of structural analysis can facilitate fluency for many students. It is a skill some corrective and remedial readers may be lacking; teachers can do much to promote the use of this skill in students.

INFORMATION TO CONSIDER

1. Instruction in structural analysis may facilitate a student's word-recognition skills.
2. Included in structural analysis skills are word families, root words, prefixes/suffixes, syllables, and compound words.
3. Word parts may be assessed through oral reading, paper and pencil tests, and mastery tests.
4. Word parts should be taught in context as much as possible.
5. Structural analysis may be taught through an inductive or a deductive approach.
6. Instruction in structural analysis should be done only when there is a need on the student's part.

Strategies to Improve Word-Recognition Skills

QUESTIONS TO GUIDE READING

Recall Questions
1. What is "context reading time"?
2. What are the procedures used in the method of repeated reading?
3. What questions should a student ask herself in the multipronged approach to word recognition?

Thinking Questions
1. How much time in a reading program should be devoted to context reading?
2. Is it appropriate for students to rate their own reading in the method of repeated reading? Under what conditions?
3. Do you agree that a multipronged approach to word recognition is superior to concentration on one skill?

Certain strategies seem especially appropriate for increasing the word-recognition skills of corrective or remedial students. Three such strategies, appropriate for classroom use, are: context reading time, repeated reading, and a multipronged attack.

CONTEXT READING TIME

Foremost in any reading program should be the provision of time for students to read materials they select themselves. Students often choose not to read if they are not allowed to read books and materials of interest to them and do not have time set aside in the school day for such reading (Heathington 1979). It seems that school should be the one place to provide time for and encourage independent reading activities.

Some activities referred to as reading are actually skill drills. While there should be a place in every reading program for word-recognition instruction, the teacher must monitor the amount of time devoted to skill activities versus that devoted to self-selected context reading. Teachers are sometimes unaware of how much time they plan for skill activities as opposed to self-selected reading. They must schedule context reading time as an important part of each class day.

REPEATED READING

Repeated reading is recommended as a method to improve corrective or remedial reading students' word-recognition skills (Samuels 1979). Repeated reading involves having the student reread a passage orally until he is reading it smoothly and fluently. The passage should be short (50–200 words, depending on the reading level of the student) and contain concepts familiar to the student. Often the reading is tape-recorded, with accuracy and reading time noted for each reading. A chart or graph may be plotted to show the relationship of accuracy and speed to the number of repetitions. To summarize:

1. The teacher selects a short passage of interest to the student.
2. She has the student read the passage orally as she times the reading and records the number of word-recognition errors.
3. She asks the student to reread the passage orally until fluency is achieved, recording accuracy and time for each reading.
4. The teacher provides another passage and continues the process.

Repeated reading has the advantage of allowing students to be exposed to the same words often enough to make the response automatic and give them a sense of fluency in reading. This helps in building their store of words needed to decode unfamiliar words.

Repeated reading as a classroom technique for students with reading problems has been adapted for use with a partner by Blum and Koskinen (1984). The following guidelines are offered for the classroom teacher:

1. Before the student reads the passage aloud to a partner, ask him to read it silently.
2. One student of each pair will be the reader and one will be the listener. Allow the two students to decide who will be the first reader; later they will exchange roles.
3. As the reader reads aloud to the listening partner, ask the listener to record the time in seconds for each reading (see Fig. 9.8).
4. Ask the reader to mark the self-evaluation sheet (shown in Fig. 9.9) after the first reading.
5. After the second reading, ask the reader to mark the evaluation sheet again.
6. After the third reading, ask the reader once more to mark the evaluation sheet.
7. Ask the reader to look at the evaluation sheet to determine whether his reading has improved.
8. When the first reader is finished, the listening partner then becomes the reader, following the same steps described above.

Blum and Koskinen have suggested that teachers ask students to evaluate their reading in two ways: (1) by rereading the passage while their partners time them, and (2) by rating their own reading after each passage on the self-evaluation scale.

Figure 9.8. Repeated Reading Rating Sheet for Partner's Time Recording

Name _____ Date _____

Dog Gone Good Reading Chart

```
No. of Sec.
    25   ____  ____  ____  ____
    30   ____  ____  ____  ____
    35   ____  ____  ____  ____
    40   ____  ____  ____  ____
    45   ____  ____  ____  ____
( . . . 130)  ____  ____  ____  ____
          #1    #2    #3    #4
                Readings
```

From Irene H. Blum and Patricia S. Koskinen, "Adapting Repeated Reading for Use in the Classroom." In Linda B. Gambrell, ed. *Reading: Process, Instruction and Assessment*, Yearbook of the State of Maryland International Reading Association, 1984, p. 17. Reprinted by permission.

MULTIPRONGED ATTACK

Frenzel (1978) has stressed that students need a multipronged attack in word recognition, using all four skills: sight words, phonics, structural analysis, and context clues. Students must master all four and know when to use them.

In the multipronged approach, students use several word-recognition skills as they approach a reading passage. They need to know how to relate the various skills to each other. For example, when a student comes to a word he does not know, he should ask himself several questions:

- What word would make sense in this passage? (context)
- What beginning sound does the first letter represent? (phonics)
- What parts of this word are familiar or common to words I already know? (structural analysis and sight words)

INFORMATION TO CONSIDER

1. Teachers should provide a time for reading in context in their classroom.
2. The method of repeated reading helps students experience fluent, smooth reading.

Figure 9.9. Repeated Reading Rating Sheet for Reader Self-Evaluation

Name _____ Date _____

Dog Gone Good Reading Sheet

Directions: Circle the dog that shows how you read.

Reading #1
How well did you read?

fantastic   good   fair   not so good   terrible

Reading #2
How well did you read?

fantastic   good   fair   not so good   terrible

Reading #3
How well did you read?

fantastic   good   fair   not so good   terrible

Did reading your passage a few times help you understand it better?   Yes   No
Did reading your passage a few times help you read it more smoothly?   Yes   No

Dog drawing selected from "Reading Attitude Inventory," Campbell, P. Livonia Public Schools, Livonia, Michigan, 1966.

From Irene H. Blum and Patricia S. Koskinen, "Adapting Repeated Reading for Use in the Classroom." In Linda B. Gambrell, ed., *Reading: Process, Instruction and Assessment*, Yearbook of the State of Maryland International Reading Association, 1984, p. 18. Reprinted by permission.

3. Four word-recognition skills—sight words, phonics, structural analysis, and context—can be used together to gain proficiency in word recognition.

Parents as Helpers

QUESTIONS TO GUIDE READING

Recall Questions
1. What are the word-recognition skills with which parents can help their children?
2. Why is the teacher's role in providing guidelines to parents important?

Thinking Questions
1. Should the teacher encourage parents to help with basal reading lessons?
2. What are some possible disadvantages of having parents assist their children in improving their reading?

There are important ways in which parents can influence and assist their children in gaining word-recognition skills. Teachers should recognize the important role of parents and enlist their help to work with students who have word-recognition problems. Parents can help students with sight words, phonics, structural analysis, and context. However, teachers must emphasize certain guidelines, or some parents may become so overzealous that students who are experiencing difficulties in word recognition will be further discouraged by excessive drills at home. Teachers should try to focus parents' attention on helping children find pleasure in words and ideas found in books and other reading materials. The following section contains general suggestions from a booklet for parents entitled *Helping Hands* (Heathington and Gambrell 1980).

HELPING WITH SIGHT WORDS

Teachers do not want to encourage parents to become drill sergeants who lead their children through long periods of drill each night on a list of sight words. Instead, parents should be encouraged to point out words children encounter in daily life. The following activities are typical of those which parents should be encouraged to use:

Breakfast circles. Have your child find one new word every day on the package of a breakfast product that is used for several days (such as a cereal box or milk carton). Circle the first word with a red pen. On the second day, let your child read the word from the previous day and circle one more word. Continue each day with a review of previous words circled in red and the selection of a new word.

Vegetable cut-ups. When cooking a meal using frozen or canned vegetables, let your child cut the picture from the label. Have her glue or tape it onto a 3" x 5" card and write the name of the product (beans, corn, tomatoes) underneath the picture. On the back of the card, let her write a sentence about the product. (Example: I like beans.) Help with printing and spelling if needed.

Teachers may want to send a list or booklet or similar suggestions home to parents. Many parents want to help their children who are experiencing problems in reading, but they often do not know what they can do to help.

Helping with Phonics

Children can experience the fun of exploring the sounds of words with their parents. Many parents have played a game with their children in which each one named a word that began like "butterfly" (or some other word) until they had exhausted their store of *b* words. Many children's books, such as nursery rhymes or Dr. Seuss, appeal to children because of their patterned sounds.

Teachers can help parents foster an awareness and enjoyment of sounds. The activities below are recommended to parents of corrective and remedial reading children:

Rhyme time. Car trips are a good time to play Rhyme Time. Think of a word ("bake") and say, "Let's see how many words we can think of that rhyme with *bake*, and let's make sentences with them. Here's one: I will *bake* a cake. Now you think of a word that rhymes with *bake*." Your child would say something like "take," and then perhaps: "I want to *take* my dog for a walk." Then it is your turn. The winner is the one who thinks of the last rhyming word. The person who loses gets to choose a new word to begin another rhyming game.

Word for the day. As your child prepares for bed, ask him to recall a special word he heard that day. If he cannot recall a word, suggest one that you heard that day. Let your child think of other words he knows that sound like the word for the day, either in the initial or in the ending sounds.

HELPING WITH CONTEXT

Perhaps the most beneficial way a parent can help with context is to let the child fill in an omitted word while reading out loud to him. Nursery rhymes are especially good for this: "Jack and Jill ran up the _____." However, prediction can be used in stories as well. The parent should simply stop and let the child finish the thought, such as: "Suddenly the old man saw a _____."

HELPING WITH STRUCTURAL ANALYSIS

Parents can point out to children that certain words share common parts. Activities related to word families are perhaps the easiest word-part skill for parents to use with their children. The following word family activities may be suggested for parents:

Comic capers. Read the comics to your child. Afterward let her circle two or more words in the comics that share a common part. Ask your child to circle the common parts as you say the words.

Silly sayings. Ask your child to find three to four words that have common parts. Write the words on a sheet of paper. Then ask your child to make a funny sentence with the words. For example, the words "cake," "make," and "lake" could make the silly saying, "A cake can make a lake."

Parents can be an important resource for teachers. The time and effort they will often devote to interactions with their children are well worth the teacher's efforts in enlisting their help. However, parents need suggestions and guidelines from teachers to make the experiences positive.

INFORMATION TO CONSIDER

1. Parents can be valuable resources to classroom teachers in helping students with word-recognition problems.
2. Teachers must provide structure to parents in helping their children with reading through suggested guidelines and activities.

Summary

This chapter has provided information on four types of word-recognition skills: sight words, phonics, context, and structural analysis. Sight words are needed by corrective and remedial readers so that they may develop enough fluency to facilitate comprehension and to make generalizations about words. Phonic skills allow students to "sound out" words, providing them with a way to attack unknown words. Context aids in word recognition and can be utilized effectively by poor readers if they understand its importance. Structural analysis skills permit students to examine words by parts.

Assessment procedures have been recommended in this chapter to help teachers determine whether a student has a word-recognition problem. Possible types of activities and procedures to facilitate development of word-recognition skills have been suggested. Specific information about teaching each word-recognition skill has been given. The overall aim was to provide enough guidance for the classroom teacher to remediate problems adequately that his students may have in the area of word recognition.

Questions for Further Thought

1. Do you think that sight words, phonics, context, and structural analysis are the four most basic word-recognition skills?
2. What other behaviors besides those named by the authors may be indicative of a student with problems in word recognition?
3. Is a store of sight words the most basic word-recognition skill?

Activities and Projects

1. After observing a student in a classroom, state why you feel he does or does not have a word-recognition problem.
2. After collecting information about two or three other basic sight word lists in addition to those described in this chapter, select the one that is most appropriate for a specified student. Justify the selection.
3. Examine a basal reading series. Determine if phonic generalizations with high utility have been selected for inclusion in the series.
4. Observe reading activities in several classrooms, comparing the amounts of time spent in isolated word analysis and in context-type reading.
5. Construct an informal assessment checklist for determining skills in prefixes, suffixes, syllables, and compound words.

10

Comprehension

In the chapter on word recognition, various skills needed for identifying a word were described. One cannot ignore the importance of word identification: it is a prerequisite to reading comprehension. Comprehension, however, should always be central to the reading act. It cannot be assumed that just because a student can decode words, she understands what those words mean. Teachers are often perplexed by students who can recognize the words in a passage but are unable to comprehend what is meant by the strings of words they have just read. These students often lack the awareness that reading should be a meaningful process, that proficiency in reading is not measured only by the ability to "call the words."

If students used only materials in learning to read that served an independent purpose of their own for reading, they might see more readily that meaning is the primary purpose of reading. However, our system of formal instruction in reading often involves the use of controlled or teacher-initiated materials such as basal reading series, language experience stories, and linguistic readers. Teachers must then lead children to set purposes for reading; this is sometimes a difficult task. If children had a firmly established purpose of their own for reading and understood the importance of what they were reading, they would not have to be shown that reading is a meaningful process.

Most people agree that reading must be meaningful, that the purpose of reading is for information or enjoyment, and that reading time is wasted if the material has not been comprehended. If a child does not understand the written directions for building a model airplane, he is frustrated. If he reads a story in a book that he does not understand, he does not enjoy it. The student knows he has not understood the directions for the model airplane because he cannot proceed in putting all the parts together. When he fails to enjoy the story in the book because it makes no sense, he also knows he has not grasped the material. In both cases, the reader is aware of his inability to comprehend, but he may not know what strategies to use to increase his comprehension.

At other times, the reader is not aware that he has not understood. He may put the entire model airplane together incorrectly, not realizing how the model could have been improved if the directions had been correctly interpreted. He may read the entire story in the book without realizing he has made incorrect inferences about several of the characters or the plot. In these two situations, the reader thinks he has understood, but has not.

Some students do not seem to be aware that reading has a meaningful purpose. These students often focus exclusively on decoding the words, thinking this is the essence of the reading act. They are not aware that the goal of reading is to comprehend the printed material.

Teachers must recognize another aspect of comprehension: when another person, such as a teacher, tries to determine if a student has understood specified events or details in a reading passage, the task becomes more complex. Three viewpoints exist: what the author is saying, what the teacher thinks the author is saying, and what the student thinks the author is saying. Because the teacher and student each come to the same written passage with differing experiences, expectations, and purposes, their specific interpretations of the text may differ. Comprehension assessment then becomes a complex process.

For teachers, the problem is to understand what is involved in comprehension and to determine how to help students who are experiencing difficulties in comprehension. Therefore, the purposes of this chapter are to provide descriptive information about comprehension, to discuss ways teachers can recognize comprehension problems, to state some possible causes, and to outline instructional strategies that teachers may use with students who seem unable to gain skills in comprehending written text.

Understanding Comprehension

QUESTIONS TO GUIDE READING

Recall Questions
1. What factors influence comprehension?
2. What are the levels of comprehension described by Huus?
3. According to the results of Durkin's research, what aspect of comprehension was receiving primary attention by the teachers in her study?
4. According to Durkin, do basal reading manuals emphasize comprehension instruction?

Thinking Questions
1. How would you define comprehension?
2. Do you agree with Durkin's definition of comprehension instruction?

3. Should teachers use basal reading manuals as they teach comprehension?
4. Why do teachers of corrective and remedial readers need a well-developed information base concerning comprehension instruction?

Defining comprehension is not an easy task. Most reading educators and researchers conclude that it is much easier to define phonics, sight words, or context clues. Yet teachers must proceed with as much information on the topic as possible, which includes some type of understanding of the various aspects included in a definition of comprehension.

Most people will agree that three elements are involved: the reader, the text, and the meaning or ideas gained from the text. McNeil (1984, p. 2) has defined comprehension as "an interaction between reader and text by which meaning is created." Communication of some type occurs between the writer and the reader: the reader interprets the written message, integrating the information into her own knowledge structures. Lapp and Flood (1984, p. 274) have stated that "comprehension occurs when the reader extracts meaning from the written text rather than when he merely names the words in the text." Many corrective and remedial readers see reading primarily as code breaking; they focus only on the identification of words. When teachers question them about what they have read, they cannot recall any message that the writer shared. These readers are not communicating with the writer.

Johnston (1983) has said that comprehension has occurred when the reader understands the logical connections found in a reading passage. Ideas expressed in the text relate to each other; the reader who has comprehended has reached logical conclusions about these relationships. Johnston has further explained that reading is "the process of using the cues provided by the author and one's prior knowledge to infer the author's intended meaning" (p. 9). The reader who can easily recognize those cues will be better able to understand the author's printed message. Likewise, the reader who has a rich background of knowledge and experiences will also be better able to interpret the author's meaning. Johnston's definition of reading points to the importance of two aspects of comprehension: the reader's ability in recognizing the writer's cues to meaning and the reader's background knowledge and experiences. Using these two elements, the reader establishes what he believes to be the meaning of the text.

As the reader interacts with the printed passage, his focus may vary from concentration on "getting the author's message straight" to "predicting what the author's message ought to be" (Pearson 1984, p. 2). According to Pearson, this variability of focus may be due to purpose for reading, familiarity with the topic, interest and motivation, and complexity of the discourse. These factors account for the varying degrees of comprehension students may display when assessed. If a student is asked to read a passage in which he is not interested, this will affect his comprehension. Total unfamiliarity with the topic will also affect comprehension. Each of these factors influences comprehension independently; their interaction is an additional influence. Because of these various factors which influence comprehension, the teacher faces a complex problem.

It must also be noted that comprehension is a *process*, which cannot be observed easily. *Products* resulting from an assessment of comprehension can be observed: the answers students give to questions, their written responses to questions, or their retelling of a written passage they have read. However, teachers must be aware of not only the products but also the processes of comprehension as they plan instruction for students with comprehension problems.

LEVELS OF COMPREHENSION

Huus (1972) has described several levels of comprehension using the terms literal, interpretive, and psychological integration. At the *literal level*, the reader "grasps the work as a whole" (p. 223). This is illustrated when the student, after completing the reading of a passage, can summarize, paraphrase, or outline the writer's ideas. At the *interpretive level*, the reader can use several text elements to derive meaning, such as "context, sequence, time, place, theme, character development, mood and tone, style, and relationships of various types, such as cause-effect, fact-fancy, agents-events, part-whole, conclusions, and predictions" (p. 224). At the *assimilative* or *psychological integration level*, the reader questions what the text means to her. This level provides a personal connection between the text and the reader as she absorbs the ideas she has acquired through reading and makes them a part of her total knowledge.

Comprehension levels have also been described as "reading the lines" (literal); "reading between the lines" (inferential); and "reading beyond the lines" (critical).

COMPREHENSION INSTRUCTION

Although it is difficult to define precisely, some educators believe that comprehension can be taught. Others believe that comprehension cannot be taught directly, but that it can be facilitated by providing appropriate reading experiences. Durkin (1978–79) has provided details to help teachers recognize characteristics of comprehension instruction. She has stated that comprehension instruction includes efforts "to teach children the meaning of a unit that is larger than a word" and "to teach them how to work out the meaning of such units" (p. 487). Durkin uses a definition by Golinkoff to further refine her description of comprehension instruction (p. 488):

Comprehension: instruction—Teacher does/says something to help children understand or work out the meaning of more than a single, isolated word.

Basal reading series purport to contain activities to increase comprehension skills. These series usually list such skills as "recognizing the main idea and details in a passage" and "understanding the sequence of events in a passage" as comprehension skills. Since the majority of teachers use these materials, one would assume that comprehension is taught in schools. However, this assumption has been questioned recently in an observational study by Durkin (1978-79), who found that almost no comprehension instruction, according to her definition, occurred in the classrooms she observed. Durkin found that teachers were primarily assessing comprehension, not teaching it. The teachers she observed asked many questions, but rarely did any follow-up of wrong answers; students were not asked to prove why they responded as they did. Much of the time in the classroom was devoted to giving, completing, and checking written assignments.

More recently, Durkin (1981) has examined basal reading manuals to determine what suggestions they give for comprehension instruction. She found the manuals also focus more on assessment and practice than on comprehension instruction. When instruction in certain comprehension skills is mentioned, there seems to be little connection demonstrated between the skill and how to read.

More information is needed on instructional procedures to use in teaching comprehension, especially to students whose comprehension is poor. Increased attention in the reading field has been devoted to comprehension in recent years. It has received high priority in research studies, and implications for practice are following much of this research. This trend should result in more definitive information for teachers on what is involved in comprehension instruction.

INFORMATION TO CONSIDER

1. Defining comprehension is difficult.
2. Most people agree that the reader, the text, and the meaning or ideas gained from the text are involved in comprehension.
3. There seem to be varying levels of comprehension, with literal, interpretive, and psychological integration being the levels described by Huus.
4. Durkin found that teachers in her study were primarily assessing comprehension rather than teaching it, and that basal manuals focused more on assessment and practice than on comprehension instruction.

Theories and Models of Comprehension

How does comprehension occur? What happens as the reader tries to communicate with the writer of a text? What factors are involved in this process? These questions arise as teachers attempt to understand how their students comprehend and what they as teachers can do to facilitate comprehension in students who are experiencing difficulties. Several theories or models of various aspects of comprehension have implications for teachers as they plan instructional strategies for their students. Included in this chapter are schema theory, metacognition, psycholinguistics, affective dimensions, and vocabulary; all of these have particular relevance to an understanding of comprehension. Knowledge about these elements should help the teacher in the practical instruction of corrective and remedial reading students.

Pointing to the need for theories of reading comprehension, Strange (1980, p. 391) has stated:

> In teaching, a theory becomes useful when it allows us to interpret what children do as well as make judgments concerning appropriate instruction that

children may need. In addition, a theory becomes useful when it allows us to plan meaningful instructional episodes and provide appropriate practice activities.

Strange has further stated that a theory of comprehension is useful in several ways:

- It explains something using the knowledge we think we have.
- It is dynamic, changing as we acquire more knowledge.
- It provides a structure that can be used in observing and evaluating events.
- It allows predictions to be made about something happening in a certain way.
- It helps teachers interpret what children do.
- It assists teachers in planning meaningful instruction for students.

In the following discussion of some of the theories regarding various aspects of comprehension, attention has been directed toward helping the teacher view the theory in a way that will allow him to make his instruction more meaningful. The suggested applications are especially relevant for students experiencing problems in comprehension.

SCHEMA THEORY

Schema theory, as defined by Rumelhart (1981), is a "theory about how knowledge is represented and about how that representation facilitates the use of knowledge in particular ways" (p. 4). As applied to reading, Rumelhart has explained that clues the reader gets from a written passage suggest certain interpretations. These interpretations are evaluated and refined as sentence after sentence in the passage is read. Finally, the reader comes to believe he has discovered the correct interpretation of the passage, one that is consistent with the clues that have been provided.

A *schema* (schemata is the plural form) is a pattern of organized ideas that the reader possesses. For example, as a student reads the story of the Three Billy Goats Gruff, she may use several existing schemata as she reads: schemata for goats, bridges, green grass, walking across bridges, and trolls. Her schemata for goats may include their colors, their horns, and their eating habits. Her schemata for walking across bridges may include personal experiences of walking across several types of bridges.

As the student reads the story, she interprets the text using her existing schemata. As the story unfolds, she evaluates her interpretations of goats, trolls, and walking across bridges. The student must constantly integrate her prior experiences and knowledge with what she is currently reading. Her schemata for trolls may have included only "good" characteristics: now she realizes a troll may be a "bad" character.

Strange (1980) has suggested several applications of schema theory to instruction in the classroom:

1. Recognize the importance of alerting students to relevant schemata for a story before asking them to read. For example, before reading the story of the Three Billy Goats Gruff, the teacher would encourage students to describe their existing ideas of goats, trolls, and walking across bridges. The students would predict how their schemata of these concepts will interact with the story they are about to read.

2. Provide adequate vocabulary instruction. The student's knowledge of words is tied to labels for schemata. He may know the word "goat" but not have the term "billy goat" in his vocabulary. Instruction in this new term will expand his vocabulary and inventory of labels.

3. Use textually explicit, textually implicit, and schema-implicit questions. Strange has described these as requiring literal recall, text-to-text inferences, and text-to-schema reference, respectively. He has provided the following definitions, patterning them after those of Pearson:

> *textually explicit*: both question and answer are derived from the text and the relationship between them is grammatically cued in the text
> *textually implicit*: both question and answer are derived from the text but the relationship between them is not grammatically cued in the text
> *schema-implicit*: a question derived from the text is asked and a plausible response is given that is not found in the text

4. Analyze miscomprehension. Strange has pointed out that much can be learned from the incorrect answers that students give. The teacher should try to determine possible explanations for the incorrect responses; she should probe to determine the student's thinking and rationale for an answer.

The relationship of a student's schemata to the text is crucial. Extensive research has been conducted in recent years concerning the effect of the organization of text on the reader's comprehension. Terms used for this type of inquiry include discourse analysis, text structure, story structure, and story grammar, each having somewhat different definitions but focusing overall on the way text is organized. Also included in the examination of text structure are such elements as word or phrase placement within a sentence and sentence placement within a paragraph. The arrangement of words and ideas in text influences their comprehension by the reader.

The difference in structure between various types of text has also received attention. A short story has one type of structure; poetry has another type. Lapp and Flood (1984) have recommended that students be exposed to many types of writings so that they can develop strategies for comprehending diverse types. They have listed and illustrated seven types of writings (p. 282):

- *narrative writings*—tales, fables, short stories, novelettes
- *poetry writings*—poetry, song lyrics, nursery rhymes, proverbs
- *textual writings*—textbooks; science, social studies
- *dramatic writings*—dramas, plays
- *editorial writings*—magazines, newspapers, diaries, journals
- *representational writings*—charts, graphs, tables, figures, maps
- *functional literacy writings*—cartoons, propaganda, advertisements, applications, schedules

Story grammars are often used to illustrate the basic elements of stories and the relationships between the various elements. Readers need a story schema, an expectation of what is included in a typical story. Whaley (1981) has pointed out that "an individual's knowledge of story components appears to facilitate comprehension and memory of stories." She has cited Mandler and Johnson's six major story elements (p. 763):

- *setting*—introduces the protagonist or main character of the first episode; may include statements about time, locale, or props
- *beginning*—some precipitating event occurs
- *reaction*—the protagonist's internal simple reaction to the beginning and his or her formulation of a goal
- *attempt*—the planned effort to achieve a goal
- *outcome*—the success or failure of the attempt
- *ending*—the long-range consequence of the action, the final response of a story character, or an emphatic statement

Bower (reported by Guthrie 1977) has provided a similar structure for stories, with some accompanying rules:

Rule 1: A story usually has a setting, theme, plot, and resolution. These elements usually occur in that order.

Rule 2: The setting usually includes a description of characters, location, and time.

Rule 3: The theme usually includes the main goal of the main character. There is often a series of episodes, each designed to enable the main character to reach her goal. An outcome provides the final resolution.

Catterson (1979) has explained that "readers will make correct responses to reading material only if they approach that material from the perspective of its overall 'writing pattern,' that is, its form of discourse [or rhetoric]" (p. 3). This explains why some students are unable to answer questions posed by teachers after reading certain types of discourse.

Catterson has admonished that students need knowledge of various forms of discourse, such as narration, explanation, classification, description, and argument. She has recommended that teachers survey materials to determine what form of discourse they are, and then ask questions appropriate to the specific form of discourse. The following is Catterson's list of questions for narrative, classification patterns, and explanation patterns (p. 4):

Questions for Reading Narrative (Chronological Pattern)

1. What is the sequence of main events of the story?
2. Who are the main characters and what does each do?
3. Where and when does the story take place?

Questions for Reading Classification Patterns (Topical Outline Pattern)

1. What is the name of the main classification of the selection? (Title)
2. What are the names of the main subclassifications of the selection? (Titles of sections)
3. Are there subtopics under each subclassification?
4. What are the major details related to each subtopic?

Questions for Reading Explanation Patterns

1. What main question is the overall explanation designed to answer?
2. What "subexplanations" must be understood in sequence?

METACOGNITION

In recent years, the concept of *metacognition* has been given attention in comprehension research. It seems to have important implications for the classroom.

Metacognitive skill in reading has been defined "as the ability to detect failure of comprehension processing" (Hosslini and Ferrell 1982, p. 263) and as "readers' awareness and self-control of their understanding and of strategies that facilitate comprehension" (Fitzgerald 1983, p. 249). Fitzgerald has further explained: "Understanding the text is called comprehension. Knowing you understand the text is called metacomprehension" (p. 251).

It is important for readers to know when they have and have not understood the contents of a reading passage. When a reader has well-developed metacognitive skills, he is able to realize when he is comprehending and when not; he is also aware of strategies to use to improve his comprehension.

Guthrie (1982) has noted that effective readers seem to show more metacognitive processing then poor readers. Poor readers do not seem to realize when they have not comprehended a reading selection. In addition, they do not seem to know what to do to increase their comprehension. Poor readers do not seem to have the control over their reading that good readers do.

The student who displays metacognition rereads a passage when the meaning is unclear, raises questions to clarify a passage, and adjusts his reading rate to the difficulty of the material (Babbs and Moe 1983). As the student reads, he monitors his understanding. Pearson has summarized a description of comprehension monitoring as a series of questions the reader asks herself:

Am I understanding what I read?
If not, why not?
What can I do to understand what I am reading?

PSYCHOLINGUISTIC THEORY

Goodman (1976) has stated that the purpose of reading is to reconstruct meaning—specifically, the meaning the writer had in mind as she wrote. Meaning is in the minds of both reader and writer. The reader's ability to determine the writer's meaning depends on the reader's prior experiences in reconstructing meaning in text through the use of language. Goodman has characterized reading as a *psycholinguistic* process, in which thought and language interact.

The reader's knowledge of language is central to psycholinguistic theory. Goodman, illustrating with the sentence, "John hit Bill," has stated that meaning is derived from these symbols by the way we structure them. The difference in meaning between "John hit Bill" and "Bill hit John" is in the way the sentence is patterned, that is, in its *syntax*. When the reader is a competent language user, he knows the difference between the two sentences. The order of the words, or syntax, indicates to the reader whether Bill is doing the hitting or is receiving the hits. The language competence of the reader affects his reading ability through comprehension of text.

Goodman has indicated that both syntactic and semantic information are necessary in gaining meaning from text. *Syntactic information* includes sentence patterns—the sequences and interrelationships of language; pattern markers, such as function words, inflections, and punctuation; and transformational rules, which are linked to the deep structure of a text. *Semantic information* includes a reader's prior experiences, his existing concepts, and his vocabulary.

Psycholinguistic theory has important implications for teachers who are working with students with comprehension problems. If the reader is not a competent language user, he may have trouble in interpreting text appropriately. Teachers should analyze whether students have had the relevant experiences necessary to understand a particular reading passage.

Affective Dimension

Tuinman (1984) has stated that discussion of the theoretical nature of comprehension should include consideration of the role of affect, not only as it relates to characters in a passage, but also as it relates to the reader: how her goals for reading influence her interpretation of the text. Tuinman has pointed out that readers can vary in their affective states going into the reading situation, just as they differ in terms of their prior knowledge. The effect of emotional states on information processing is important.

Mathewson (1985) has assigned affect a determining role in the comprehension of text. He explains this by pointing out that if an individual lacks the appropriate attitude and motivation, she will make the decision not to read at all, thereby negating *any* comprehension that might result from reading the passage. According to Mathewson, motivation and attitude combine to make the student attentive to the reading passage. He reasons that if the reader's attitude is positive and motivation is appropriate, comprehension will be more efficient. Conversely, if attitude is negative and motivation is inappropriate, comprehension will suffer.

Knowledge about the affective influences on comprehension will enable the teacher to consider carefully the effects of proper attitudes and motivation on reading comprehension. Chapter 7 provides an in-depth discussion of the affective dimensions of reading.

Role of Vocabulary

The relationship between good vocabulary and success in reading has been strongly suggested in research and in theoretical positions of reading authorities. Davis (1968), for example, found that the factor that correlated most highly with comprehension was a knowledge of word meanings. Anderson and Freebody (1979) have stated that the number of words a reader knows is predictive of his ability to comprehend text.

Anderson and Freebody (1979) offer three hypotheses to explain the strong relationship between vocabulary knowledge and reading comprehension: the instrumental hypothesis, the aptitude hypothesis, and the knowledge hypothesis. The *instrumental hypothesis* holds that specific vocabulary knowledge contributes to comprehension simply because the prospective reader knows more words. The *aptitude hypothesis* suggests that individuals with large vocabularies comprehend better because they have better innate verbal ability. The *knowledge hypothesis* suggests that the more knowledge (in the form of concepts or schemata) a student has about a topic, the more words he knows related to that topic. Anderson and Freebody (p. 89) note that no serious scholar in reading education accepts any single one of these hypotheses as an adequate explanation of the relationship between word meanings and reading comprehension. Any one or more of the hypotheses may apply in a given situation.

IMPACT OF THEORIES AND MODELS

While there is considerable overlapping in many of these theories and models that help explain comprehension, each has been presented separately for the teacher to form a schema for each one. In the remaining discussions of comprehension, the teacher should note how many characteristics are shared by the various theories and models and how much they relate to each other to account for the way readers gain meaning from text.

INFORMATION TO CONSIDER

1. A theory of comprehension is useful to the classroom teacher as he plans instructional activities.
2. Schema theory provides explanations of why students fail to comprehend written text.
3. Organization of the text itself can influence a corrective or remedial reader's comprehension.
4. Metacognition allows the student to be aware of her reading performance and to use self-regulatory mechanisms in guiding her reading.
5. Psycholinguistics allows the poor reader to use language and thought to improve his comprehension.
6. Affective dimensions have an impact on a student's comprehension of text.

Comprehension Skills

QUESTIONS TO GUIDE READING

Recall Questions
1. What are the five categories of comprehension skills discussed by the authors?
2. What questions has Sadow suggested for sequencing materials?
3. How may teachers help expand students' vocabularies?
4. What four reasons for prediction are given by Smith?

Thinking Questions
1. Is the determination of the main idea of a passage the most important skill for corrective or remedial readers in organizing information?
2. How can corrective or remedial students be encouraged to ask questions to increase their comprehension?

3. Is reading impossible without prediction, as suggested by Smith?
4. Why would children of nine or ten benefit more from induced imagery than younger children?
5. Why is background important in making inferences?
6. What words can a writer use to enable a reader to predict the mood of a passage?

Each of the theories of comprehension which we have just examined suggests the need for certain skills to achieve competence in comprehension. Five major skill areas will be discussed in this section: organizing information; self-monitoring/self-directing; using prior experiences and language; understanding text structure; and using affect to promote comprehension. A modeling strategy that teachers can use to teach these skills is also provided in this section.

Teachers need to know which skills are necessary for readers to interact effectively with print and gain information and meaning from the ideas writers have to share. Instructional strategies can then be planned to promote those skills. When a teacher realizes a student is not comprehending, she can diagnose which skill or combination of skills the student needs to develop.

ORGANIZING INFORMATION

Schema theory reflects the need for skills in the organization and labeling of information in retrievable, facilitating structures. Organization can be achieved through skills in focusing on main ideas and associated details, sequencing, summarizing, and stating conclusions. Through these skills, corrective and remedial students can improve their organization of the thoughts and ideas expressed in written text. Skills in vocabulary or word knowledge are useful as they serve as labels for schemata. Existing schemata are enriched and expanded as vocabulary is increased.

Determining main ideas and details. The ability to organize information around a main idea is an important comprehension skill. Schemata are organized around main ideas and their supports, using appropriate labels. The student who can sort through all the ideas in a reading passage and determine which are relevant has achieved skill in finding the essence of the writer's message.

A corrective or remedial student should try to anticipate the main ideas in a story before he begins to read. When he is asked, "What do you think this story will be about?" he should be able to predict a main idea. As he reads, his original prediction of the main idea will be either confirmed, rejected, or modified. At the end of the story, an overall idea should have crystallized.

In this process, the reader not only develops a feeling for the essence of the reading passage, but also examines the supporting details that led him to choose the idea that seemed to dominate the entire passage. Students who are never asked to defend their choice of a main idea are missing opportunities to realize the impact of supporting details on the overall meaning of a passage. Teachers should not ask only for the main idea but should also inquire about the instances and details that led to the determination of the main idea. This is especially vital for poor readers.

Often two fluent adult readers are amazed that one got one "messge" (or main idea) from a certain novel while the other got a different message. Detailed discussion of how and why each arrived at a certain idea can often resolve and clarify differing interpretations. Teachers should realize that students experiencing difficulties in reading need such discussion.

Sequencing. Sequencing is another important organizational skill that helps the reader pursue a line of reasoning in a story. The sequence of events often has a great impact on the outcome of a story; sequencing helps the reader anticipate what may happen.

Knowledge of story structure (setting, theme, plot, resolution) helps the reader recall events in a story in an organized, sequential manner. The reader uses her existing schema of a story structure, integrating the people and events in the present reading passage into the existing schema so that she has a logical, sequential framework of the story.

Sadow (1982, p. 520) has developed five generic questions, based on Rumelhart's story grammar, that should help a reader in sequencing material in a story:

1. Where and when did the events in the story take place, and who was involved in them? (Setting)
2. What started the chain of events in the story? (Initiating event)
3. What was the main character's reaction to this event? (Reaction)
4. What did the main character do about it? (Action)
5. What happened as a result of what the main character did? (Consequence)

By teaching corrective and remedial students to examine the major elements of a story through these questions, teachers can help students attend to the sequence in the story.

Sequencing is equally important in reading social studies or science materials. Students should be taught how to increase their awareness of sequence in these reading selections as well as in narrative passages.

Summarizing. Students are often asked to summarize a passage they have read. Some individuals can do this in a clear, coherent manner; others seem to recall events haphazardly. Whether the summarization is in verbal or written form, ideas must be organized so as to capture the main ideas, details, and sequence of the reading passage.

Teachers must help poor readers become skillful in summarizing what they have read. This not only allows them to comprehend the material more effectively, but also helps them gain skills in communicating with others.

Stating conclusions. This skill involves drawing appropriate conclusions from the details that have been provided in a reading selection. The reader must often work with both literal and inferential information in a passage. Corrective and remedial students must have practice in establishing facts and inferences and in drawing conclusions. They must be shown where their reasoning has been correct or faulty. Discussion serves as a way of drawing conclusions and possibly searching for further ones. Students need experiences in defending a conclusion they have drawn from a reading passage.

Vocabulary or word meaning. Well-developed schemata require a large store of words to lend preciseness and elaboration to each schema. For example, if the student knows the word "dog," her schema for the word might include four legs; colors, such as brown, black, or white; size; and barking characteristics. Imagine how much this student's schema is enlarged, however, when she also knows the terms Pekingese, dachshund, beagle, and cocker spaniel. She then can have a schema for each of these dogs regarding color, size, and barking characteristics. When reading a passage about a certain type of dog, the reader who has the more precise or expanded vocabulary will be at an advantage in understanding the text.

Teachers should plan activities to expand the vocabulary of their corrective and remedial students.[1] It should not be done by asking students to memorize the definition of a certain number of words, but rather in a meaningful way that incorporates their existing word knowledge with the new words.

Morrison (1979) has suggested that word-meaning skills can be taught using context. Context gives the reader keys to the meaning of an unknown word. Students can be taught to look at words that appear in print before and after the unknown word as clues to the meaning of the unknown word. Morrison has provided a list of context clues to be used in determining the meaning of words:

Context Clues

Explicit	*Implicit*
synonyms	cause-effect
definition	contrast
equivalent phrase	example
summary	modifying phrase

---

[1]Activities for teaching vocabulary may be found in Chapter 6 of J. Estill Alexander, ed., *Teaching Reading*, 3rd ed. (Boston: Little, Brown and Co., 1988).

Words can be presented in both explicit and implicit ways. Morrison defines several types of explicit clues: synonym (one or two words), definition (phrase or sentence), equivalent phrase (one or two sentences), and summary (two or three sentences). The meaning of words can also be determined implicitly through cause-effect, contrast, example, or modifying phrase.

Studies of prefixes and suffixes can also expand a student's word knowledge. Using the student's existing knowledge of words such as "unhappy," "untrue," or "unable," the teacher can help a student recognize that when *un-* is before a base word, it usually means "not." When the student then encounters the word "unrealistic," he will know that this means "not realistic."

Many corrective or remedial students have comprehension difficulties in content-area reading. Terms are often abstract, unique, and technical. Before reading, teachers must make sure that students have the appropriate labels and names for the ideas presented in the reading selection.

Vocabulary skills are especially necessary with abstract words. A schema a student might have for the word "free" might be vague because of its abstractness. Included in the schema might be illustrations such as "free-flying bird," "a free Coke," "a free ticket to a baseball game." As a new story is introduced about the freedom achieved through the American Revolution, the teacher should help students see the relation between their schema of "free" and the freedom described in the story—how political freedom is like a free-flying bird. This allows students to integrate the new ideas of "free" into their existing ideas, expanding and refining the structures.

Figurative language can often create a comprehension problem for corrective and remedial students. What does it mean when someone talks about "eating your head off" or "a bull in a china shop"? Students can miss some of the meaning of a passage as a result of their inability to understand an author's use of figurative language. Only through studying such terms and relating them to existing ideas can poor readers comprehend the figurative language used in many passages.

SELF-MONITORING/SELF-DIRECTING

The reader's awareness and control of the reading process is recognized in the theory of metacognition. Skills associated with metacognition, such as purpose setting, self-questioning, monitoring, and using imagery, stress this individual, self-directing role of the reader. Each of these skills promotes the idea of the reader's active, guiding participation in the reading process. Rather than seeing reading as an encounter with abstract, impersonal printed material, the reader views his role as a participant who determines what is to be gained from the text.

Setting purposes. The Directed Reading Activity has long been used to help the reader set a purpose for reading. The teacher should help the corrective and remedial student develop the skill of setting purposes. The student should pose questions before each reading:

Why am I reading this?
What will I gain from reading this?

DuBois and Stice (1981, p. 174) have outlined various purposes for reading:

- to improve one's reading
- to learn about the world across time and space
- to complete work tasks
- for enjoyment

At times, children may read simply to improve their reading, doing workbook pages or practicing fluency using a technique such as repeated reading. Purposes set for reading will usually relate to "finding out about _____," something suggested by the picture on the first page or the title of the story.

Self-questioning. Both before and during reading, the poor reader should develop skills in asking herself questions. This encourages her active involvement in monitoring the text.

It is important for the teacher to use appropriate questioning as she works with corrective and remedial students, as students often model the teacher's types of questions. Teachers should use both literal and nonliteral questions. The three classes of questions and responses, as categorized by Pearson and Johnson (1978), can be used: textually explicit, which requires "reading the lines"; textually implicit, which requires "reading between the lines"; and scriptally implicit, which requires "reading beyond the lines," or the use of prior knowledge.

In the past, teachers have typically been the ones to ask questions of students, as in the directed reading lesson of a basal reading series. When poor readers ask their own questions, however, they become more involved in directing their own learning. They can become skilled in automatically asking their own questions when they begin a story: "What is happening in this picture?" or "What does this title mean?"

Using imagery. Imagery involves drawing mental pictures of events in a story. Poor readers can be asked to form images or pictures in their minds of events or objects in a reading selection. These are called *induced images*, as opposed to pictures that are provided.

Some studies have shown that imagery facilitates comprehension of text. In one study, when students were asked to visualize the information in a passage, they were able to draw more inferences (Steingart and Glock 1979). A comprehensive review of several research studies was done by Pressley (1977), who stated that by the time children reach the age of nine or ten, they can benefit from the use of induced images. Those students who do not "spontaneously integrate text" seem to benefit the most from the use of mental imagery.

Correcting miscomprehension. Corrective and remedial readers need to develop skill in recognizing when they have not understood material and finding strategies they can use to correct miscomprehension. Rereading, looking up words in the dictionary, and examining context are all ways to correct miscomprehension. The poor reader should continually be monitoring as he reads, asking himself, "Is this making sense?"

USING PRIOR EXPERIENCES AND LANGUAGE

Psycholinguistics stresses the reader's use of cognition and language in the reading process. Skills in predicting, inferring, and understanding sentence patterns and in punctuation can provide the corrective or remedial reader with many clues to meaning in text. As the student gains skills in these areas, she becomes aware of the role language plays in reading. Using her prior experiences and understanding of language, the student is able to select the minimal clues from the printed page that will allow her to comprehend the writer's message. Psycholinguistics stresses that only a small part of the information that the reader uses in reading comes from the printed page. The fluent reader comprehends without reading the individual words, that is, without decoding to the level of spoken language.

Predicting. As corrective or remedial students read, they should anticipate events. They can use existing schemata to predict how events might proceed, what the outcome might be, or what the reaction of various characters might be.

Smith (1983) has stated that "reading is impossible without prediction" (p. 26). When the reader predicts, he is actively interacting with the meaning of the text. Prediction involves the elimination of alternatives so that reading can be more efficient. Smith has listed four reasons for predicting (p. 27):

1. Individual words have too many meanings.
2. The spellings of words do not always indicate how they should be pronounced.
3. There is a limit to how much of the "visual information" of print the brain can process during reading.
4. The capacity of short-term memory (or "working memory") is limited.

The reader's past experiences with language play an important role in predicting. Students use their semantic knowledge in predicting that certain words will occur together. For example, they expect words like "snow," "winter," and "white" to occur together, but do not expect "summer," "cold," and "ice" to be together in a reading passage.

Making inferences. Hansen and Hubbard (1984) have theorized that students have problems in making inferences because of their lack of background experiences related to the material they are reading and because they have not had practice in inferential thinking. Poor readers must not be tied to the literal levels or explicitly stated ideas in a story often described as "reading the lines." They need to develop skills in "reading between the lines," inferring cause-effect relationships of ideas and objects present in the text.

Trabasso (1981) has stated that a reader does one of two things when he makes an inference: "he either finds semantic and/or logical relations between propositions or events which are expressed in the narrative or he fills in missing information which is necessary to making connections between events" (p. 56). He has explained that inferencing involves "translating a series of sentences into a causal chain of underlying conceptualizations" (p. 57). He has given several functions of inference:

1. To resolve problems in lexical ambiguity. For example, in the sentence, "Mary had a little lamb," "had" could mean "owned a possession," "ate," or "gave birth to"; "lamb" could mean "a living animal" or "a prepared meal." Inference allows the reader to choose the most logical alternative.
2. To clarify nominal and pronominal references. Again using the illustration, "Mary had a little lamb. Its fleece was white as snow," Trabasso has pointed out that "its" refers to the lamb, not to Mary. Inference provides the reader with this information.
3. To establish context. Writers do not always provide exact details about the context of a story. The setting of a story can be established through inference, using context.

Inference, according to Trabasso, requires the following elements: background knowledge, vocabulary (conceptualization), text structure (settings, events that create goals for the protagonist, plans for achieving goals, actions, consequences or goal realizations, and reactions by the protagonist), knowledge of social and personal interaction (motives and actions), and knowledge of causal relationships between events (causal chain).

Understanding sentence patterns. Sentence organization skills seem to be related to comprehension. These skills are usually measured by a sentence anagram task, in which a jumbled set of words is arranged to form a proper sentence.

In one study, Greenewald and Pederson (1983) found that students developed skills in sentence organization and improved their comprehension through practice in organizing jumbled words into sentences. Students first began their practice with jumbled phrases, and then worked on jumbled single words. They were instructed to locate the action word first; after that they were to ask themselves a series of "wh-" questions (who, what, when, where, why) in order to put the words in a coherent order.

Understanding punctuation. Poor readers often pay no attention whatsoever to periods, commas, or question marks. They cannot, therefore, use these marks as clues to meaning in the reading passage. If students can learn to use these marks to determine when to pause, when to stop, and what ideas belong together, their comprehension can be improved. Many children never realize that punctuation serves an important purpose in both reading and writing—that they can use it as clues to meaning.

Understanding Text Structure

Skills related to the text itself provide another category of comprehension skills. The reader uses his awareness and knowledge of the organization of text to gain meaning. He uses the cues that an author provides in the text to determine appropriate relationships between ideas in the passage.

An awareness of the ways an author can arrange a certain type of discourse is valuable to the corrective or remedial reader. This knowledge promotes other skills such as the ability to predict, self-question, or understand the sequence in a reading selection.

The reader should be able to recognize some of the basic types of discourse, both narrative and expository. These materials include poetry, plays, magazines, charts, advertisements, and a variety of other genres. The teacher should provide instruction to corrective and remedial students that will help them in understanding how these various materials are organized.

Using Affect

Affect can play a vital role in comprehension. The corrective or remedial reader's awareness of his own attitudes and motives for reading are essential. As he asks himself, "How do I feel about reading this passage?" he relates the affective aspects of reading to the purposes he sets for the task. He becomes aware that his attitude toward the reading passage will affect his comprehension.

The reader's skill in detecting the mood of a written text is also valuable in understanding a reading passage. Cues the writer provides to allow the reader to sense the mood of a passage can help in the interpretation of text. The description of crying, boisterous talking, or other mood setting allows the reader to infer the emotional states of certain characters in the story.

The writer's use of loaded words, propaganda, and bandwagon techniques can influence the reader's interpretation of the text. Corrective and remedial reading students must be skillful in determining when some words are being used to create a certain mood in a passage or to manipulate his feelings about a character in the story.

INFORMATION TO CONSIDER

1. The corrective or remedial reader needs skills in organizing and labeling information to improve her comprehension.
2. Poor readers can improve their comprehension through self-monitoring and self-directing their reading.
3. Skills in using prior experiences and language can enhance the corrective or remedial reader's comprehension of reading materials.
4. Teachers must help students become skillful in understanding text structures.
5. The reader's own awareness of his attitudes and motives as well as the mood of the reading passage can affect comprehension.

Possible Causes of Comprehension Problems

QUESTIONS TO GUIDE READING

Recall Questions
1. How do good and poor comprehenders differ?
2. What are the three categories of possible causes of poor comprehension outlined by the authors?
3. What possible causes of poor comprehension are related to the reader? The text? The instructional program?
4. What guidelines should a teacher remember as he instructs corrective or remedial readers in comprehension?

Thinking Questions
1. What other possible causes might be associated with the reader? The text? The instructional program?

Why do some students attain competency in the comprehension skills just outlined while others are unable to achieve these skills, which are needed for efficient, meaningful reading? Some of the reasons seem obvious after reviewing various theories of comprehension; researchers have sug-gested other reasons. In a review of several research studies of good and poor comprehenders, Steig (1979) has stated that they differ in several aspects:

1. Good comprehenders are faster decoders than poor comprehenders.
2. Good comprehenders can hold more "just-read" words in memory than poor comprehenders; therefore, good comprehenders can integrate new information being read to that already read and remembered.
3. The errors made by good comprehenders do not distort the meaning of the passage as much as those of poor comprehenders.
4. Good comprehenders tend to correct their errors more than poor com-prehenders.
5. Good comprehenders adjust their approach to a reading task according to the purpose; poor comprehenders do not.

Golinkoff (1975–76) has also made a comparison of the reading com-prehension processes of good and poor comprehenders. He has stated that good comprehenders:

- are capable of rapid and accurate word recognition
- seem to read in units at least as large as phrases
- are adaptable and flexible, changing their approach to a reading task as needed to attend to the information most relevant to their purpose for reading
- know what good comprehension includes and can correct their errors
- treat reading as a way of gaining meaning

In contrast, Golinkoff has listed the following as characteristics of poor comprehenders:

- They have inadequate decoding skills.

- They have a slow reading rate.
- They have less ability to organize text.
- They are inflexible.
- They use a minimum size word unit.

He has concluded that the poor comprehender is a "slave to the actual printed word" (p. 656).

The causes of poor comprehension can be grouped into three categories: those related to the reader, those related to the textual material, and those related to instructional practices. Causes associated with the reader himself include inadequate prior experiences, lack of awareness of reading as a meaningful process, poor memory usage, inadequate decoding skills, and lack of flexibility. Causes of comprehension problems related to the text include structural organization that makes it impossible for the reader to communicate with the ideas the writer is trying to share. The instructional program can cause comprehension problems when there is inappropriate or insufficient instruction in comprehension, or when there is a mismatch between the materials used for instruction and those that the reader needs and prefers.

READER

The following possible causes of poor comprehension are associated with the reader.

Inadequate prior experiences. Children's backgrounds have a tremendous influence on their comprehension abilities. Even a fluent reader has problems comprehending some reading materials. Without a background in chemistry, the reader may have trouble comprehending the ideas in the following paragraph and the relationships between them:

> The free radicals that initiate the polymerization of unsaturated compounds can be generated in the mixture by the interaction of oxidizing and reducing agents (redox initiation). In fact, when a peroxidic catalyst is employed with a mercaptan modifier, the initiation of polymerization may occur only by the way of the mercaptide radicals. These may form by interaction of the modifier with the catalyst as well as in the chain-transfer process.

Prior knowledge and background make a difference in comprehension. The richer the background the reader brings to the printed page through his knowledge of content and language, the more he can integrate new information in a reading passage with the existing information he possesses. This idea relates to schema theory and the integration of new ideas into existing schema; it also relates to psycholinguistics and the minimal sampling that the fluent reader needs to be able to reconstruct meaning.

Students lacking adequate background experiences in content and language will not comprehend as well as those with rich, elaborated background structures. The teacher of corrective or remedial readers must recognize this as a cause of many students' poor comprehension of text.

Little awareness of reading as a meaningful process. The reader may be unable to comprehend ideas in a reading selection because he has never realized that reading has a purpose: to find meaning in the printed words on the page. Because this reader does not realize that reading should make sense, he will often encounter problems in comprehension. Such a reader will not self-correct a garbled passage as he reads because he is unaware that the text needs to be meaningful.

Poor memory usage. As the student with decoding problems plods along on a word-by-word basis, problems in memory storage develop. Because she fails to sample the text, selecting only those relevant cues needed to create meaning, the poor comprehender's memory storage is packed with each and every word in a reading passage.

Smith (1983) has pointed out that it is "impossible to store the first words of a sentence while waiting to get to its end before making a decision about meaning. By the time the end of the sentence is reached, the beginning will have been forgotten." The student who has never learned to sample print, who feels every word must be read, is not using memory properly.

Inadequate decoding skills. The reader must have adequate decoding skills to read the text effectively for meaning. Many students have not achieved a level of automaticity in decoding words so that they can concentrate on meaning. The inability to read fluently is a major cause of some students' problems in comprehension.

The technique of repeated reading (see Ch. 9) has been designed to aid children who have not been able to achieve the decoding necessary for reading fluency. This strategy allows the poor reader to experience fluent reading while being exposed to only a limited number of words that must be recognized. Repeated reading provides the automaticity and decoding experiences to help the student who cannot comprehend because he cannot decode words fluently.

Inflexibility. The poor comprehender is often inflexible. He reads at a certain rate no matter what the purpose for reading. He may have only needed to skim the material for specific information; instead, he slowly reads all the words. His idea of reading is to decode every word. The poor comprehender often has only one rate and one approach to reading a passage.

Text

The type and arrangement of text can cause problems in comprehension. While reading educators cannot easily write their own materials for corrective or remedial students, they can be selective in choosing texts that promote ease in comprehension. Previous discussion has focused on certain structures for narrative and expository writing. Texts whose structures diverge from the traditional structures or that make comprehension difficult should be avoided. If a text is poorly arranged, comprehension can be affected.

Instructional Program

The instructional program provided for a student can affect comprehension. Teachers should be particularly interested in these points because they exert a strong influence over the type of instructional program students receive.

Failure to attend to interests. Students often feel they do not get to read what they want to read (Heathington 1979). They feel they are constantly reading what the teacher assigns or books that happen to be available, rather than topics or books in which they are interested. They do not feel they have control over the topics and books they can use in reading time.

Research has shown that comprehension is related to the interests of the reader. This may be because readers prefer to read about topics about which they have some background experience, and can integrate new information from the text into a large store of existing information. Mathewson's model (1985) has shown that a lack of interest in the content, form, or format of the reading materials influences comprehension.

Mismatch of reading materials. Instructional programs often fail to match the reading level of the materials to that of the student. This mismatching can cause comprehension problems. A student who is placed in a reading text that is too difficult will struggle with decoding, unable to read fluently, gradually assuming that the word-by-word pace she is using is the only rate used in reading.

If the student had been given reading materials at her independent reading level for free-time reading, she would have been able to maintain a fluency in reading that would promote comprehension.

Limited types of questions. If a teacher constantly asks only literal questions, students may approach a text only for the purpose of reading exactly what is printed on the page, rather than reading between or beyond the lines. The teacher can serve as a model for questions that students generate themselves. This model should include all levels of comprehension questions.

Questions teachers ask can also help children develop a story structure. When a teacher asks questions that follow story structures, the reader should develop a sense of "story."

Teacher's Role

The classroom teacher may help the comprehension of her corrective and remedial readers by using a model of direct instruction. Cooper (1986, p. 39) has presented such a model. He states that in direct instruction, the teacher helps students by:

- demonstrating what is to be learned
- arranging opportunities to use what was learned
- providing corrective feedback and monitoring

Cooper provides the following specific steps in his model for direct instruction:

1. Teaching
   a. Let students know what is to be learned and help them relate it to prior experiences.
   b. Model the skill or process and verbalize the thinking that takes place.
      Teacher models for students.
      Students model for teacher.
   c. Provide guided practice in the use of the skill or process.
   d. Summarize what was learned and verbalize how and when to use it.
2. Practicing
   Provide students with independent practice in the skill or process.
3. Applying
   a. Remind students of the skill, process, or strategy that is to be applied.
   b. Have students read the text selection to determine its intent.
   c. Discuss the text
      (1) to check students' understanding of the selection.
      (2) to check students' application of the skill or process taught.
   d. Summarize what was learned and how it was used in reading.

Using such a modeling process, the teacher can help corrective and remedial readers comprehend text material. The teacher may also find the following guidelines helpful:

1. Make reading a meaningful encounter between the reader and the text.
2. Allow students to use rapid decoding in their free-time reading by matching the materials to their independent reading level.

3. Stress that reading is for meaning, not to decode every word.
4. Encourage students to read at different rates for different purposes.
5. Give students the responsibility of monitoring their own comprehension.
6. Provide students with as many experiences as possible through concrete objects, films, reading, and other media.
7. Enrich students' vocabularies with new words.
8. Select texts organized in patterns that can be easily comprehended.
9. Ask many types of questions, encouraging students to ask questions as well.
10. Let students select reading materials on topics in which they are interested as often as possible.

INFORMATION TO CONSIDER

1. Good and poor comprehenders differ in several ways.
2. Reading comprehension problems may result from causes associated with the reader: inadequate prior experiences, little awareness of reading as a meaningful process, poor memory usage, inadequate decoding skills, and inflexibility.
3. The type and arrangement of text can cause problems for corrective or remedial readers.
4. The instructional program provided for students can affect their comprehension.
5. The teacher can work more effectively with readers with comprehension problems if she follows certain guidelines.

Assessing Comprehension Problems

QUESTIONS TO GUIDE READING

Recall Questions
1. What are some examples of product assessment of comprehension? Process assessment?
2. What guidelines do Neilsen and Braun recommend for constructing comprehension questions for assessment?
3. What is Clark's technique for assessing taped free recall?
4. How does Durkin define comprehension assessment?
5. What problems do the authors outline as occurring in comprehension assessment?

Comprehension may be assessed through *product* or *process* measures, although most comprehension measurement is done using product assessment (Johnston 1983). Product assessment occurs after reading has taken place, through such means as probe questions, multiple-choice questions, and retelling or recalling the story or reading passage. Process assessment is much more difficult because it involves an attempt to understand and measure comprehension as it is occurring. Two measures may provide assessment of process comprehension: miscue analysis and cloze procedures.

QUESTIONING

The teacher often assesses comprehension by asking questions after the student has read a selection. Such questioning may require various levels of thinking, such as literal or nonliteral recall.

Several taxonomies of questioning are available. Basically, a taxonomy has levels that aim both at literal interpretation of the text and interpretation beyond the information provided in the text. Sanders (1966) has developed a widely used one containing seven levels of questions:

1. Memory: recognizing or recalling information given in the text
2. Translations: expressing ideas in a different form or language
3. Interpretation: seeing relationships among facts or ideas
4. Application: solving a problem using generalizations or facts
5. Analysis: applying logic to the solution of a problem
6. Synthesis: using creative thinking to solve a problem
7. Evaluation: making judgments based on defined standards

Questioning related to IRI. The comprehension questioning part of an informal reading inventory usually contains multiple levels of questions. These questions may be labeled according to type, such as "F" for factual or "I" for inferential.

Questioning related to story grammar. Marshall (1984) has advocated the use of questioning as an informal assessment of comprehension. Such responses are superior to standardized tests, in her opinion, because analysis of these responses "allows us to gain insight into the ways in which an individual organizes information and can be used to help guide instruction designed to promote better ways of organizing information" (p. 80). However, Marshall has recommended specific criteria for the teacher to use to determine the appropriateness of students' responses.

For assessing narrative discourse, Marshall (p. 85) has recommended the following questions, based on story grammar:

Setting:	Where (or when) did the story happen?
	How would the story change if the setting changed?
Character:	What is _____ like?
	What does _____ do and say that makes him/her like _____?
	Why did _____ do _____?
Topic:	What is the moral of the story?
	What is the author's opinion about _____?
Conflict:	What is the problem _____ faces?
	How might _____ solve this problem?
Reaction 1:	How does _____ feel about the problem?
	What does _____ think about the problem?
Attempts:	What does _____ do first, second, etc.?
	Why does _____ fail to solve the problem?
	What might _____ do next?
Resolution:	What did _____ do to solve the problem?
	How was the problem solved?
	Who solved _____'s problem?
Reaction 2:	How does _____ feel about the solution?
	How do you feel about the solution?
	How would you solve the problem?

The checklist shown in Figure 10.1 was suggested by Marshall as a way of monitoring students' success in responding to the various story structure questions. She has also pointed out that the same set of questions and checklist could be used in assessing a student's retelling of a story.

Questioning guidelines. The teacher usually plays an active role in questioning to assess comprehension. He has the responsibility of selecting types of questions and examining the responses. He will need to plan his questions carefully. Neilsen and Braun (1980) have provided four guidelines for the construction of comprehension questions:

1. Determine which type of comprehension the question is intended to measure (literal, inferential, or creative).

Figure 10.1. Marshall's Checklist for Questions About Narration

+ excellent
√ satisfactory
— unsatisfactory

Name _____

story/date	questions							
	setting	character	topic	conflict	reaction	attempts	solution	reaction
XXX	√	√	—	√	—	√	√	√
XXX	√	√	—	√	√	√	√	√
XXX	+	√	—	√	√	√	√	√
XXX	+	√	√	√	+	√	√	√
XXX	√	√	—	—	√	√	√	—

From Nancy Marshall, "Discourse Analysis as a Guide for Informal Assessment of Comprehension," in *Promoting Reading Comprehension*, edited by James Flood, p. 86. Copyright 1984 International Reading Association. Reprinted with permission of Nancy Marshall and the International Reading Association.

2. Determine whether response will be recognition (as in multiple choice), recall (who, why, or what questions), or production (recall, reorganization, and application of information to a new situation).
3. Write question stem in paraphrase form.
4. Make sure the answer is dependent on information in the passage, rather than on the respondent's prior knowledge.

Skills assessed. Many comprehension skills may be assessed through questioning: grasp of main idea and details, sequencing, summarizing, stating conclusions, vocabulary, predicting, making inferences, and interpreting mood. A student's understanding of text structure can also be assessed, as Marshall (1984) has shown.

MULTIPLE-CHOICE ASSESSMENT

The majority of teachers use achievement survey tests as a source of information about their students' comprehension abilities. Such tests usually provide a subtest score of reading comprehension, using such data as raw score, stanine, standard score, percentile, and grade equivalent to report the students' scores. Chapter 6 provides extended information on testing.

Comprehension is usually measured on achievement tests in a multiple-choice format. Typically, a short reading passage is provided, followed by a statement that requires a choice among several alternatives. This format involves a recognition type of response, as the answers are available to the reader.

Multiple-choice formats may be used to assess the student's ability to specify the main idea and details in a passage, to make inferences, and to understand vocabulary and word meanings. A caution concerning multiple-choice testing is that students may merely make wild guesses at the alternatives.

RETELLING OR RECALLING

Retelling is currently receiving increased attention as a way to assess a student's comprehension of a reading passage. The student is simply directed to retell the story or contents from a passage he has read. If a teacher wants to make a careful assessment, she might tape the student's retelling of the story; at other times, the teacher may ask the student to write down his recollections. Assessment of recall is usually determined by the amount and quality of information recalled.

The IRI of the Bader Reading and Language Inventory (1983) uses retelling as part of comprehension assessment (see Fig. 10.2). The teacher records in the blanks beside the recalled units the sequence in which units were recalled. The questions are used to prompt the student's recall of information that was not given in the retelling.

While recall seems to be a worthwhile way to assess comprehension of a story, it is difficult to determine the scoring for materials developed by the teacher. Clark (1982) has developed a technique for assessing taped free recall. He uses the following steps in preparing the text:

1. Place slashes at points in the text where a good reader would normally pause during oral reading. Such points are usually at punctuation marks and at connectives such as "and," "but," and "because"
2. List each unit between slashes sequentially on a sheet of paper
3. To the right of each unit, write a 1, 2, or 3 to indicate its relative importance to the text (1 = most important, 2 = moderately important, 3 = least important)

As the teacher plays back the taped recall, she puts a number (in sequential order) to the right of each unit that has been remembered. A 1 goes beside the unit that was remembered first, a 2 beside the second unit, and so on. A unit is scored if the student recalls the essence of the unit, not a word-for-word recall.

Figure 10.2. Bader's IRI Using Retelling for Comprehension Assessment

Here is a story about turtles.   **P C/A** (p. 127)

TURTLES AT HOME

Turtles are always at home.

If they visit the sea, they are at home.

If they go to the high hills, they are at home.

If they go far away, they have a home.

Turtles carry their homes with them.

Their shell is their house.

Turtles stay in their shells.

That is why they are always at home.   (58 words)

GRADED
PASSAGES:
EXAMINER'S
COPY

Unprompted Memories

Please retell the story.

_____ turtles at home

_____ visit sea, at home

_____ go to hills, at home

_____ go far away, have a home

_____ carry their home

_____ shell is house

_____ stay in their shell

_____ why always home

Comprehension Questions

_____ When are turtles at home? (always at home)

_____ Where do turtles visit? (high hills)

_____ (sea)

_____ (far away)

_____ What do the turtles carry all the time? (their own house/home)

_____ Where is the turtle's house? (on his back — his shell)

_____ Why are the turtles always at home? (because they stay in their shells)

Interpretive question: Why don't turtles leave their shells?

Acceptable answer: _____ Yes _____ No

Memories: _____ Unprompted _____ Prompted Organized retelling: _____ Yes _____ No

From Lois A. Bader, *Bader Reading and Language Inventory*, p. 57. Reprinted with permission of Macmillan Publishing Company, Inc. Copyright © 1983 by Lois A. Bader.

Clark has stated that examination of the recall data allows the teacher to assess the number of units recalled, their sequence, and their levels of importance.

In summary, retelling enables assessment of sequencing skills, making inferences, recalling main ideas and details, and understanding text structure.

CLOZE TECHNIQUE

One purpose in using the cloze technique is to assess reading comprehension. Cloze involves the deletion of certain words in a reading passage. The reader supplies the missing words as she reads the passage. Chapter 5 provides details on how to construct a typical cloze passage.

The cloze technique is said to give some indication of processing during reading, as comprehension is occurring. It is particularly helpful in assessing children's use of prior experiences, prediction, and understanding of sentence patterns.

MISCUE ANALYSIS

Miscue analysis (Goodman 1965; Goodman and Burke 1972) can provide insight into a student's comprehension. Chapter 14 contains a description of miscue analysis. The oral miscues of the reader can be examined in an attempt to understand her reading strategies. The student's efforts to self-correct and maintain text consistency (such as making subject and verb agree) can show whether she is monitoring comprehension. For example, the sentences below show how a reader, trying to maintain consistency, changed both the subject and verb.

The boy was running down the street. (sentence)
The boys were running down the street. (sentence as read by student)

In miscue analysis, comprehension is also assessed through retelling, with some prompting questions.

ASSESSMENT RELATED TO BASAL READERS

Durkin (1978–79, p. 490) has defined comprehension assessment by the teacher as follows:

Teacher does/says something in order to learn whether what was read was comprehended. Efforts take a variety of forms—for instance, orally posed questions; written exercises; request for picture of unpictured character in a story.

She found that teachers spend a considerable portion of time assessing comprehension in their daily reading lesson. Much of this assessment is done using questions in the directed reading lesson and workbook pages that accompany the basal reading texts. Workbook pages assess many types of comprehension skills: main idea, details, sequencing, summarizing, stating conclusions, inferring, and so on.

PROBLEMS IN COMPREHENSION ASSESSMENT

Three prevailing problems in comprehension assessment are passage dependency, the influence of memory, and background bias. Much more attention needs to be devoted to this area of assessment. There are some issues currently receiving attention of which classroom teachers should be aware as they assess students' problems.

Passage dependency. Students can sometimes get an item correct without reading the passage; the answer is not dependent upon the information in the passage. Since the purpose of comprehension assessment is to determine how much the student learned from reading the passage, a problem develops when questions can be answered without reading it.

In an examination of the passage dependency of four commonly used diagnostic tests, researchers found that a high percentage of the items were passage-independent (Allington et al. 1977). Many items could be answered on the basis of the student's past experience.

Testing memory. Most reading tests measure memory as well as comprehension. Since most testing is a measure of the product of comprehension, it is done after comprehension has occurred. A reader's memory may determine her success on many comprehension tests.

Johnston (1983) has pointed out that memory seems to determine how successful a reader will be on product assessment, or assessment after reading. If comprehension is seen as a process, then assessment should occur as comprehension is taking place. As noted, however, few measures are available to assess process comprehension.

Kender and Rubenstein (1977) have asserted that "a reader should be allowed to reread or reinspect the passage before answering comprehension questions—otherwise we are emphasizing memory factors" (p. 779). Their study showed significant differences in comprehension between readers who were allowed to reread or reinspect and readers who were not allowed to do so. They have argued that reinspection "eliminates an important source of error—namely, dependence on memory for sentence content" (p. 777).

Bias due to background. Problems with bias in assessment can occur due to differing levels of background knowledge. Because prior experiences have such an impact on comprehension, students who have had extensive backgrounds may score higher on comprehension tests than those whose backgrounds are more meager.

Since readers use their existing schemata as a framework for making inferences, fitting new information into that which already exists, the reader with the fullest framework should be able to make the best inferences.

In order to minimize the influence of background factors on comprehension assessment, Johnston (1983, p. 33) has made three recommendations to teachers:

1. Carefully select texts and questions so as to eliminate those which might contain "biases."
2. Assess in the language appropriate to the reader's subculture as well as in the standard language.
3. Assess in various contents and language structures, but include assessment that will discriminate between background knowledge-induced problems and others.

INFORMATION TO CONSIDER

1. Product assessment of comprehension can be done through questioning, multiple choice, and retelling/recalling.
2. Process assessment of comprehension can be accomplished using miscue analysis and cloze procedures.
3. According to Durkin, teachers may spend too much time in comprehension assessment.
4. Problems in comprehension assessment relate to passage dependency, testing memory, and bias due to background.

Instructional Activities

QUESTIONS TO GUIDE READING

Recall Questions
1. According to Durkin, how can the teacher facilitate comprehension?
2. What activities can a teacher use to improve vocabulary/word meaning? Main ideas and details? Sequence skills? Self-questioning? Prediction? Imagery? Inference? Text structure? Comprehension monitoring? Interpreting mood?

Thinking Questions
1. What additional activities can a teacher use for improving each skill identified in this section?
2. How can parents help with any of these activities?

As a result of the extensive research in the area of comprehension in recent years, reading specialists have been able to recommend activities that teachers can use to improve their students' comprehension. In the past, attempts to improve comprehension seemed to focus more on *product*—responses to questions—than on process (McNeil 1984). Today, instructional activities need to focus more on the *process* of comprehension.

Durkin (1978–79) has stated that comprehension instruction should help the student work out or understand text. The teacher can facilitate comprehension by:

- helping students understand the meaning of certain words in a printed passage
- pointing out the importance of certain key terms in a reading passage
- helping students understand that certain words provide clues to sequence in a passage
- encouraging students to form mental pictures of what is happening in the text
- asking students to find an answer to a question and then to verify that this is the appropriate response
- helping a student summarize a passage into its main idea

In this section will be outlined several activities to facilitate comprehension skills. Activities are organized by skill area so that teachers, after identifying which skills(s) their students may need to focus upon, may use the specific activity that seems most closely related to the individual student's problem.

ACTIVITIES FOR IMPROVING VOCABULARY/WORD MEANING SKILL

Activity: Develop two sets of index cards, one containing base words and the other showing prefixes that could be used with the base words. Ask students to combine a prefix card with a base word card to form a new word. Ask students to explain the change in the word when the prefix is added and to use the new word in a sentence. The same procedure could be used with suffixes.

Activity: Ask students to note one new word each night as they watch television, read the newspaper, or read a book. They must write down the sentence in which the word appeared. In the case of television, they should jot down the sentence as completely as possible, spelling the word as it sounds. Students then use a dictionary to determine the meaning of the new word. The teacher encourages students to become aware of new words and how they affect their comprehension in both reading and listening.

ACTIVITIES FOR IMPROVING SKILL IN MAIN IDEA AND DETAILS

Activity: Ask students to develop captions for pictures, describing what is happening in the picture; that is, the main idea. In a variation of the same activity, students can develop headings for untitled paragraphs.

Activity: Use a model recommended by Moldofsky (1983) for helping students to identify the main idea in fiction works. Moldofsky has concluded that "most fiction revolves around a central problem and it is this central problem that gives coherence to the story" (p. 741). To help in determining the central story problem, she has provided a format that includes four clue items:

1. Who is the main character?
2. What does he or she want, need, feel, or think?
3. Check: Does this fit all the important things that happen in the story?
4. Statement: The central story problem is that
   (who?)_____(pick one:) wants/needs/feels/thinks
   (what?)_____(pick one:) but/because_____.

Moldofsky has advocated that teachers use this model and then encourage students to use the same clue items, as their model.

Activity: Use underlining as an instructional strategy for teaching comprehension, as outlined by Poostay (1984):

1. The teacher underlines 5 to 7 key concepts in a 100- to 150-word passage. Words or phrases may be underlined.
2. Copies of the marked phrases only are provided to the students.
3. As the teacher reads aloud those underlined words or phrases, students point to them.
4. Using group discussion, the teacher explains what each underlined word or phrase means, why she underlined it, and how an underlined unit relates to a previous one.
5. After reading the underlined words and phrases again, students are asked to predict what the passage will be about, using only the underlined words and phrases as clues.
6. The teacher collects the underlined passages, hands out the original unlined passage, and asks students to read silently the original passage.
7. The teacher checks students' comprehension by asking questions about the passage.
8. The teacher encourages students to do their own underlining.

ACTIVITIES FOR IMPROVING SEQUENCING SKILLS

Activity: Provide pictures, sentences, and paragraphs for students to sequence.

Activity: Help students to understand textual clues to sequencing events, such as "then," "next," "until," and "afterward."

ACTIVITIES FOR IMPROVING SELF-QUESTIONING

Activity: Help students to model questioning using five clusters of questions developed by Crowell and Au (1981). The questions range in difficulty from easy (1) to hard (5), as follows:

1. *Association:* "What was the story about?" Any information recalled from the story is an acceptable answer.
2. *Categorization:* "Did you like_____[a certain character in the story]? Why or why not?" The response must be justified with information given in the story.
3. *Seriation:* "What happened first? What happened next? And then what?" At least three events in correct order are necessary to achieve this level.
4. *Integration:* "What was the problem in this story?" The student is expected to give the main idea or be able to summarize the story.
5. *Extension:* "Tell me another way the story could have ended." The ending must be different and also plausible, given the events of the story.

ACTIVITIES FOR IMPROVING PREDICTING SKILLS

Activity: Use book covers to let students predict what a book will be about. Make sure they justify their predictions; encourage them to verbalize their reasoning.

Activity: Either read or provide a printed copy of the beginning of a story to students. Ask students to tell or write two endings to the story: one that is reasonable and one that is not reasonable.

ACTIVITIES FOR USING IMAGERY

Activity: Ask students to use visual imagery as you describe a scene in a story. Then allow students to recall the description of the scene.

Activity: Write vivid descriptors, such as "tall brown building," "bright sun," "bright blue sea," on small slips of paper. Ask students to draw one of the slips of paper, read it, and then use imagery to think about the picture the words describe. They can then describe their image to another student.

ACTIVITIES FOR IMPROVING INFERENTIAL SKILLS

Activity: Omit the adjectives in a story. Let the students, using context, guess what the adjectives are.

Activity: Ask students to infer character traits in stories that are read.

Activity: Show students a book jacket from a new book with the title covered. Ask them what they think the title should be.

ACTIVITIES FOR UNDERSTANDING TEXT STRUCTURE

Activity: After reading a story to the children, ask them to discuss the pattern of the story. Then have them create a new story using the same pattern.

Activity: Use story components (setting, beginning, reaction, attempts, outcome, ending) in a cloze-type activity as described by Whaley (1981). Instead of deleting single words, a whole story category is deleted. Blank lines are drawn to show where the material was deleted, and students are asked to fill in the missing element of the story. There is a wide range of possibilities for the missing information.

AN ACTIVITY FOR IMPROVING COMPREHENSION MONITORING

Activity: Use an activity recommended by Fitzgerald (1983). Ask students to read a passage that is difficult for them to understand. Have students write answers to questions about the passage, rating their confidence that each answer is correct on a scale of 1 to 5. Discuss students' answers and ratings to help them understand their awareness of what they comprehend.

ACTIVITIES FOR INTERPRETING MOOD

Activity: Provide paragraphs that imply certain feelings; ask students to infer and name the feelings. Example: "The man lifted the large pail of water. He walked wearily to the house, wondering what other chores he must do before he could rest." The man was____because____.

Activity: Have students describe the mood of someone shown in a picture. Ask them to justify their reasons for assessing the person's mood as they did: facial expressions, movements or actions, or other clues.

Suggestions for Parents

Parents of corrective or remedial readers can provide help to their children in the area of comprehension. Often, however, parents do not realize that the emphasis in reading should be on meaning; they view reading primarily as a decoding activity. To encourage parents to focus activities on meaning, teachers can make the following suggestions:

1. Encourage your child to read materials found around the house. Examples are consumer products such as cereal boxes or toothpaste tubes, catalogues of various types, television guides, newspaper comics, and plant seed envelopes.
2. Point out to your child what kinds of information are typically found on household materials. For example, most packaged foods list the name of the product, how much it weighs, the ingredients, and how to cook or prepare it.
3. Help your child predict what words or ideas would be written on various reading materials around the house.
4. Encourage your child to retell a story that you have read to her.

The home environment offers many items to be read for a purpose, such as cooking recipes, directions for various home projects, grocery item labels, catalogues, or letters from relatives. In engaging in these activities, children can gain a sense of what is involved in comprehension.

The idea of text structure is well illustrated by reading materials in the home. A recipe has a certain format; directions on home care products and food labels follow a predictable structure; and catalogues are arranged in similar ways. Parents can help their children to predict formats or structure by discussing the types of information found in reading materials in the home: what ingredients will be listed on a box of gelatin or what the letter from Aunt Mary will say. Parents can ask their children why they made a certain prediction.

Retelling stories that parents read to them, either to the parents or to younger siblings, can afford children opportunities in sequencing information and recalling main ideas and details. Parents should encourage children to remember what happened first, second, and last.

INFORMATION TO CONSIDER

1. Parents can use materials found in the home environment to help their children predict and learn about how various reading materials are structured.
2. Parents should encourage their children to retell stories they read to them.

Summary

This chapter has attempted to help teachers in understanding comprehension as it relates to reading by providing information about theories and models of comprehension. Schema theory, metacognition, psycholinguistic theory, affective dimensions, and vocabulary have been discussed as they relate to reading comprehension. *Schema theory* points to the role of organization of ideas in comprehension; *metacognition* illustrates the need for the student's awareness of his comprehension processing; *psycholinguistic theory* addresses the importance of reconstructing meaning in text through the use of language; *affective dimensions* reveal the impact of attitude and motivation on comprehension; and the role of *vocabulary* shows that knowledge in this area is critical to comprehension.

Five categories of skills needed in comprehension have been presented and discussed: (1) *organizing information*, which includes determining main ideas and details, sequencing, summarizing, stating conclusions, and vocabulary and word meaning; (2) *self-monitoring/self-directing*, which includes setting purposes, self-questioning, using imagery, and correcting miscomprehension; (3) using *prior experiences and language*, which includes predicting, making inferences, understanding sentence patterns, and understanding punctuation; (4) *understanding text structure*; and (5) using *affect*.

Also presented in this chapter were procedures for measuring both product and process comprehension, including questioning, multiple-choice activities, retelling, cloze, and miscue analysis.

Instructional activities were suggested in this chapter for both teachers and parents of corrective and remedial readers. The use of a model of direct instruction was advocated.

Questions for Further Thought

1. What would stimulate teachers to provide more comprehension instruction than comprehension assessment?
2. Does your observation in schools suggest that teachers of corrective and remedial readers focus on comprehension assessment more than comprehension instruction? Justify your answer.
3. What percentage of a teacher's questions should be at the nonliteral level for corrective and remedial readers?
4. Are all comprehension skills equally important for the poor reader?
5. What is the best assessment measure for corrective and remedial readers? Why?
6. How much responsibility do the writers of children's stories have to write their materials in a structure to facilitate comprehension? Does this infringe on their creativity?

Activities and Projects

1. Conduct a survey of teachers to determine what they feel is included in comprehension instruction.
2. Using Sanders's levels of questions, write a sample of questions for a particular story to be used with a corrective or remedial student.
3. Examine several stories in a basal reading series to see how well they follow Mandler and Johnson's six major story elements.
4. Ask a group of corrective or remedial readers to develop a series of questions about a story. Determine whether they asked more literal or nonliteral level questions.
5. Use the list of questions and checklist developed by Marshall to assess a corrective or remedial reader's comprehension of a story.
6. Use Clark's technique for assessing taped free recall with a poor reader.

11

Study Skills and Content Reading

Students in our schools not only read for pleasure and entertainment, but also to gain knowledge in various courses or content areas, such as math, science, and social studies. Corrective and remedial readers often have great difficulties in learning content, partly because they have poor study skills and partly because they lack the reading skills needed with content-type materials. Content reading and study skills are inextricably linked because proficiency in content reading depends on effectiveness in study skills.

Rogers (1984) describes study skills (what he terms "study-reading skills") as "deliberate procedures for retaining or applying what is read"; such skills "permit people to complete tasks which they would not do as successfully if they read only casually" (p. 346). A study-reading skill, he says, requires "effort beyond that usually expended while reading casually" (p. 347). Graham and Robinson (1984) define study skills as "specific abilities which students may use alone or in combination to learn the content of the curriculum" (p. 3).

Studying is "a special form of reading," according to Anderson and Armbruster (1984, p. 657). They state that "studying is associated with the requirement to perform identifiable cognitive and/or procedural tasks" such as "taking a test, writing a paper, giving a speech, and conducting an experiment" (p. 657).

Graham and Robinson (1984, p. 23) suggest that study skills allow students to have certain capabilities:

- generate clearly defined purposes for reading
- acquire sufficient experiences in order to anticipate both the content of the reading material and the process by which the writer conveys the content
- conduct an active dialogue with the writer, resulting in adequate comprehension in relation to the purposes for reading

These definitions and ideas suggest that study skills (or "reading-study skills" or "study-reading skills") have the following characteristics:

1. Reading-study skills are applied deliberately. The reader intentionally uses these skills as he reads in a conscious attempt to make his reading more meaningful.
2. The reader may use one or more reading-study skills during his study time, either separately or in combination.
3. Reading-study skills facilitate learning of content-type materials. Their use allows the reader to make these materials meaningful and purposeful.
4. Reading-study skills help the reader retain the information she gains from reading content materials, so that she can complete such tasks as taking tests or preparing written assignments.
5. Reading-study skills are not used in casual or recreational reading. The attention needed during reading-study times is focused, not spontaneous.
6. Reading-study skills are used to organize information and ideas gained from content reading in ways that facilitate their application and usage.
7. Reading-study skills help the reader set specific purposes for reading, as opposed to just a vague idea of "reading a chapter in the text."
8. Reading-study skills help the reader understand how various content materials are arranged and organized. This facilitates understanding of the ideas the author presents to the reader.

Several writers emphasize the importance of teaching reading-study skills in the early years of school. Salinger (1983) believes that study skills should be taught from first grade on, so that they "become natural parts of the learner's reading behavior" (p. 334). Schilling (1984) also emphasizes the same point when he questions the commitment of intermediate teachers to teaching study skills. He feels intermediate teachers are committed to teaching reading, language arts, and math skills, but not to teaching study skills as much as they should be.

Layton (1979) also emphasizes that content-area reading is not just for secondary and college students but should be stressed at every educational level. He cites three reasons that students may be unsuccessful with reading-study tasks: teachers' unenthusiastic attitudes and resistance to implementing structured procedures; students' regard of the procedures as too time-consuming; and lack of cooperation between teachers and students in incorporating the procedures into daily, ongoing activities in subject-matter materials (p. 200).

This chapter focuses on reading-study skills as they are used in content-area reading. While some students may have a basic level of proficiency in word-recognition skills, they may lack adequate reading-study skills. Corrective and remedial readers need instruction in reading-study skills as well as word-recognition skills. They need to know how to read content materials effectively. This chapter addresses five areas of importance to the classroom teacher as he works with problem readers in improving their reading-study skills:

- helping students organize their reading-study activities
- helping students understand reference materials
- helping students understand content-area materials
- helping students organize their ideas during reading-study time
- assessing students' proficiency in reading-study skills

Corrective and remedial readers often have little metacognitive awareness of how they can improve their overall learning environment. There is much that they can do regarding goal setting, times to study, and proper environment that will assist them in their reading and study activities. Efforts that teachers devote to helping these students organize their reading-study endeavors can be time well spent, resulting in improved study habits in students.

Students must have an understanding of materials used to gain information if they are to be efficient as they study. Poor readers often have little awareness or concern about the purpose of the materials or how the writer has organized the material. Such knowledge would be helpful to the poor reader as she searches for information on a particular topic. Both reference and content materials are organized in specific ways. However, lack of awareness can inhibit the reader's comprehension of these special materials.

As students read informational materials, the ideas they encounter must be organized in some way so that they can be remembered, and so that they can use the information in preparing for tests or writing papers.

Teachers must assess whether their students are knowledgeable about reading-study skills and can use the skills to make learning more efficient. The teacher must determine if her corrective or remedial readers have particular reading-study skills that can be used or whether she will need to help the student in attaining such skills.

Organizing Reading-Study Activities

QUESTIONS TO GUIDE READING

Recall Questions
1. What two questions should students ask themselves as they set goals for their reading-studying?
2. What types of activities interfere with students' reading-study time?
3. What factors may promote effective reading-study time?
4. What steps should students use in evaluating their reading-study time?

Corrective or remedial readers are often unable to determine exactly what they are expected to do or to learn with regard to classroom activities or assignments. They are vaguely aware that they must prepare for a test, write a paper, or complete other tasks of this nature; however, they fail to understand the purposes for such tasks, and tend to study haphazardly to prepare themselves for the assignment. Teachers can help such students set goals for their study activities, organize their daily schedules to include time for study, determine what factors provide an appropriate learning environment, and evaluate their reading-studying. Parents can also be of valuable help in establishing effective reading-study times for their children.

GOAL SETTING FOR READING-STUDYING

After reviewing research on the topic, Anderson and Armbruster (1984) have concluded that the more specific the knowledge that students have about a criterion event (test, written paper, or assignment), the more effective their studying for it. Therefore, students should first be aware of the task for which they are preparing themselves: their purpose for studying.

Teachers may lead corrective or remedial readers to formulate answers to two questions concerning an assignment or test:

What does the teacher want me to know?
Why do I need to know this?

For example, the student may be studying a unit on punctuation. Her response to the two questions listed above might look like this:

What does the teacher want me to know?	Why do I need to know this?
1. A sentence may end with a period, a question mark, or an exclamation mark.	1. I, as a writer, must let my reader know when I finish an idea.
2. A period is used at the end of a statement.	2. My reader will know this is a statement, not a question.
3. A question mark is used at the end of a question.	3. I can show my reader I am asking a question by using this mark.
4. An exclamation mark shows a statement is emphasized or is an exciting one.	4. I can show the reader that I am really excited about something I am writing if I use this mark.

As corrective or remedial readers begin to write down *what* and *why* they are reading-studying, they should become more adept at questioning the teacher about classroom assignments and tasks. Teachers are often largely responsible for students' inability to understand their tasks. When a teacher comes into the classroom and writes down an assignment such as "Read pages 45–53 in your science book and do the activities on page 53," she has done little or nothing to provide students with the *what* and *why* of the assignment.

Teachers must be aware that their responsibility is to set the stage for instruction. They should explain to the student *what* is to be learned, and relate this new learning to experiences with which the student is familiar. For instance, the teacher explains: "Today you're going to write a sentence that asks a question." The teacher explains that the question mark can help someone who reads the student's letter or paper to know when he is asking for a response. The teacher provides several examples of using question marks to ask for a response; students then provide additional illustrations. After this, when the teacher assigns pages 45–53, students know *why* they're studying and *why* the activities on page 53 are important.

Lees (1976) recommends that every assignment "should have some time devoted to explaining the how, what, why and when of the assignment. Students can greatly benefit from knowing how to approach the assignment, what to look for, why they are doing it, and when it is due" (p. 625). Teachers must help the poor reader by carefully explaining these requirements and making sure they are understood.

Goal setting should be encouraged as an accompaniment to learning in school, not as something students do immediately before a test. Developing the habit of goal setting may take some time to establish. However, if students use this technique for a period of time, it can assist them in thinking through a task.

As corrective or remedial readers list *what* they are to learn, they begin to focus on the main points in a reading assignment. This will help them later as they organize their ideas by outlining or summarizing. Establishing *what* is to be learned develops thinking skills in corrective and remedial readers. They can no longer be passive learners; they must be actively involved in communication with the teacher about *what* she is presenting during instructional time.

The *why* of goal setting allows students to think about the purpose of their learning activities. Students all too frequently study a chapter only because the teacher has assigned it. They fail to see any purpose for the study or any relevance of the ideas expressed in the material to their lives. The teacher often fails to make the relevance clear, which may leave the student feeling that he is wasting his time.

Specifying the *why* should help not only the student but the teacher. The teacher should be able to justify what she is asking students to learn; if it has no relevance to students' present or future needs, perhaps the material is not worth the time the teacher or student is supposed to devote to it. If historical or scientific events can be shown to be relevant to students' lives, they become easier for students to learn because they can associate them with past and future experiences.

TIME FOR READING-STUDYING

Corrective and remedial students must realize that reading-studying takes time. It must be part of their daily activities, just as brushing their teeth and exercising their bodies. Their job is to be students, just as their mother's or father's job is to work at an office or store. Since their parents must devote time to their jobs, students must recognize that they, too, must spend time in their job of reading-studying. Some of this is done at school, and some must be done at home. The corrective or remedial student, especially, must consistently devote this special time to his studies.

There are several hindrances to students' reading-study times. Chief among these are the numerous activities in which they are involved, such as Girl Scouts, music lessons, and baseball practice. Television also claims inordinate amounts of their time. In one study, students reported that they would read more if they had time (Heathington 1979). They cited involvement in a multitude of activities as reasons that they had little time for reading.

Most of the activities in which students are involved are worthwhile. It is important that they participate in sports, church activities, hobby clubs, and other recreational pursuits. However, time should also be planned for reading-studying. This time must be as consistently observed as music lessons or sports practice, and should be kept free of interruptions.

Teachers will find that parents can aid them in their efforts to encourage studying by helping corrective or remedial readers plan their daily activities. One of the easiest ways to ensure daily reading-studying is to set aside a specific time for it in the home. This means the television set must be turned off for at least some portion of the evening hours. Most teachers have found sustained silent reading, in which everyone in a classroom reads, uninterrupted, for a specified period of time, to be successful. This practice can be equally valuable in a home situation: a specified period of quiet time in the evening allows everyone—mother, father, and children—to spend some time reading and studying.

Reading-study time does not have to consume all of a student's free time. Efficiency and success in reading-study time is dependent on the student's understanding of the *what* and *why* questions discussed earlier. Anderson and Armbruster state (p. 664):

> The more specific students' knowledge of the criterion task, the more able and likely they are to focus attention on relevant material and engage in processing activities appropriate to performing that task.

Thus, the student who more clearly understands what she is to do will have to spend less time studying than the student who cannot clearly focus on what is to be done.

Students should also learn to focus attention during reading-studying times. Moore, Readence, and Rickelman (1982, p.11) state:

> Because of limited capacities, readers need to select important bits of information in text and disregard less important information. Otherwise, all words, phrases, sentences, and paragraphs appear to have equal importance, and the barrage of information becomes overwhelming. Readers must face the problem of determining what merits attention.

This is why the teacher's time and effort in teaching corrective or remedial readers how to study is worthwhile. By showing them how to select the important, relevant information from a reading selection, students can improve their efficiency in study.

FACTORS THAT AFFECT READING-STUDYING

There are several factors that may help corrective and remedial students as they read and study. Teachers should consider these as they help their students to determine the best environment for reading-studying, and should also counsel parents about arranging these factors for their children's benefit. The following factors may be of importance for studying in the home environment:

- time of study
- distractions
- study equipment
- interactions with others

Time of study. Some students study best immediately when they get home from school; they accomplish their tasks and then have the evening free for recreation. These students cannot study effectively later in the evening; they may be sleepy or otherwise unable to concentrate. Another child may need a period of relaxation in outside play before reading-studying. Parents must learn to recognize when their child's efficiency is at its peak and ensure that this is the time set aside for study.

Distractions. Easily distracted children must have a study environment free of noise. Any talking, music, or similar sounds make it difficult for them to focus attention on what they are reading. Noise or other distractions may come from brothers or sisters and their friends as they talk and play. If a child needs absolute quiet time to study, parents must arrange family activities to accommodate this need. Conversely, some children study better when a radio is playing; they need a steady background sound to attend to the task at hand. Parents must observe their child to determine which atmosphere is best for facilitating her reading-studying.

Study equipment. As simple as it may seem, parents often don't realize that children vary regarding the furniture and equipment they need during reading-study time. Some children are able to study more efficiently at a desk, while others can study better sprawled in a cozy armchair. A hard chair with a straight back is just what some children want, even though it may seem uncomfortable to others. Some children want to write using a lap pad, while others need a large desk or table to spread out all their materials. Parents should realize that just because their child seems to be lost in the depths of a huge armchair does not mean that he is not studying efficiently.

Interactions with others. Some students want to be left completely alone to study and read; others like to have their parents and siblings assist and prompt them. One child may easily pursue a task to the end, while another will need parental encouragement and monitoring. Again, parents must determine which type of environment works best for their child. If assistance from others is needed, brothers, sisters, or parents may all serve to help the student. For some children, however, parents may be the best helpers, while siblings are better able to relate to other children's needs.

Teachers must make parents aware that they should examine these factors so that study time can be handled more efficiently. The factors discussed above can influence the reading-studying of corrective and remedial readers. Individuals have preferences for certain environments that they feel are more suitable for learning.

EVALUATING READING-STUDYING TIME

Students can be encouraged to evaluate their reading-studying time through the following questions:

1. How much time was focused on reading-study activities? Was a substantial portion of the time devoted to daydreaming, sharpening pencils, doodling on notepaper, or other nonstudying activities?
2. How much information was organized in some way, such as outlining or summarizing? Often reading itself will not suffice. Studying implies using strategies beyond reading.
3. Were assignments completed? If the child had specific activities to perform that evening, were those tasks accomplished? Those children who seem never to finish assignments are usually failing to use their time wisely.
4. How well did the students perform on tests or written papers? If the student failed the test or received a poor grade on a written paper, he is not reading-studying effectively. If the student was unsuccessful in his efforts, the teacher may want to help him examine his reading-studying activities. Two strategic questions may be asked:

- Did the student's list of *what the teacher wants me to know* correspond with items on the test? The student may have spent reading-study time on details when the teacher was interested in the main ideas. The student should compare items that he missed on the test with his *what* list. Are all items covered on the *what* list?
- For each item that he did not have on his *what* list, the student should establish a *what* and *why*. Although it may be too late for the test just taken, the student will benefit from the processs and be more aware of what he should do for the next reading-study time.

PARENTS AS AIDES

Parents can be valuable aides in helping their child establish appropriate reading-study strategies. Teachers should enlist parents' help in:

- encouraging their child to relate the purpose for his study or *what* she is to learn and *why*
- setting aside a special time for their child to study
- monitoring the study time to see if it is effective

- arranging factors (time of study, distractions, study equipment, and interactions with others) to promote effective reading-studying
- discussing grades on tests and assignments to determine whether reading-study activities have been successful

INFORMATION TO CONSIDER

1. Corrective and remedial students' reading-study activities are more effective if they have a well-defined goal or purpose.
2. Teachers must be aware of their responsibility to help students understand the purpose of reading-study activities.
3. It is important that teachers and parents help corrective and remedial readers establish a time for studying.
4. The time of study, distractions, study equipment, and interactions with others are four factors that can influence the effectiveness of students' reading-study activities.
5. Corrective and remedial readers should be encouraged to evaluate their reading-study activities.

Understanding the Organization of Reference Materials

QUESTIONS TO GUIDE READING

Recall Questions
1. What are the four principles specified for teachers as they provide instruction to poor readers in the area of reference materials?
2. What are the six types of reference materials with which corrective and remedial students should be familiar?
3. What skills are necessary for using reference materials?
4. When should instruction in reference materials begin?

Thinking Questions
1. What other principles should be specified for helping corrective and remedial readers understand the organization of reference materials?
2. What other reference materials could be used by poor readers for studying?
3. What portion of a corrective or remedial reader's instructional time should be devoted to study of reference materials?

Some of the primary materials that students should use in reading-studying are *reference materials*, such as the dictionary, encyclopedia, and card catalog. A table of contents, glossary, and index also can provide valuable information. An understanding of these materials allows the reader to be more efficient in her reading-study activities.

Teachers often focus activities for corrective and remedial readers almost exclusively on word-recognition drills. However, many of these students also need to learn how to use reference materials, as they can be an aid to informational reading. Students do not need complete proficiency in "learning-to-read skills" before engaging in "reading to learn." Instruction in reference skills may begin during the earliest stages of learning to read. For example, students can begin to use picture dictionaries during the early school years, thereby becoming familiar with the organization of such materials.

The following section addresses some of the predominant types of reference materials, their purposes and organization, and the skills needed to use them effectively. The focus is on helping poor readers become more proficient in their reading-studying activities—especially older students, who often need to use reference materials to complete school assignments or tasks.

Four principles should guide teachers as they provide instruction in reference materials:

1. Make sure the corrective or remedial reader understands the uses of the various materials. He should know how each type of material can help him in his reading-study activities, and when to use a particular material.
2. Assess whether the student has the skills necessary for using the various materials. For example, a student must understand alphabetical order before she can use even a beginning dictionary.
3. Help the student understand how each material is organized. The student should be provided with diagrams of the parts of a dictionary or an outline of the Dewey decimal system.
4. Provide practical experiences with the materials as much as possible. The student should research a topic of interest to him, one about which he actually wants to secure information, rather than an artificial problem created by the teacher using dittos instead of actual reference materials.

DICTIONARY

The dictionary is a reference source that students begin to use early in school. Teachers need to remind corrective or remedial readers that the dictionary can help them in several ways:

- to find out what a word means
- to find out how to pronounce a word
- to determine the parts of speech of a word
- to determine a word's origin
- to find synonyms of a word

The teacher should not assume that the student with a reading problem has the necessary skills to use the dictionary for the purposes mentioned above. She may need to focus on the skills the student will need to find a particular word in the dictionary, such as alphabetical order, pronunciation and accent rules, and the use of guide words.

Teachers can plan activities for corrective or remedial readers that will emphasize the important aspects of the dictionary as a resource. Endless dittos on using the dictionary are less effective than practical applications such as the following activities:

1. Ask students to jot down unknown words as they read content or recreational materials, newspapers, or magazines. Students should always note the context of the unknown word, perhaps by copying the sentence in which the word is found, so that each word is placed in a meaningful setting. Arrange times for students to look up the words and explain their pronunciation and meanings to others.
2. Ask students to make their own dictionaries, using words from language experience stories or content materials.
3. Using words students have identified in the first exercise above, let a small group find "John's word" or "Mary's word" in the dictionary.
4. Bring in package labels from cereal, green beans, and other products children normally eat. Students can find words on the package that they do not know and then look them up in a dictionary.
5. Using words corrective or remedial readers have brought to class, ask them to determine which of the multiple definitions of a word in the dictionary is appropriate for the particular sentence in which it was found.

ENCYCLOPEDIA

Corrective and remedial readers may have limited exposure to the encyclopedia because of their inability to read such materials fluently. Like all children, however, they have certain topics about which they want to learn more. The encyclopedia provides in-depth information about these topics. Teachers should focus on the benefits of the encyclopedia:

- it provides detailed information about a wide range of topics and people
- it has pictures, illustrations, and charts to make learning easier

• it can aid study by providing background or extended information about people and events with which the student should be familiar

As with the dictionary, the corrective or remedial reader may not have the necessary skills for using the encyclopedia. He may need instruction in the use of alphabetical order and the use of guide words.

Activities using the encyclopedia should be interesting to the corrective or remedial reader. Use children's encyclopedias if the student's reading level is low; this will give the student greater facility in the use of the material. However, teachers should not overlook the benefits to students at a low reading level from looking at pictures and graphs in a standard encyclopedia. For example, after they have heard about the Rough Riders in social studies class, they may be curious to see a picture of Teddy Roosevelt in an encyclopedia.

The encyclopedia also offers material to be read to the student. When students are particularly interested in a topic, such as Abraham Lincoln, the teacher may read out loud to students a section from the encyclopedia about Lincoln. This allows them to see the encyclopedia as a source of interesting information.

The teacher can ask each student in a group to become an authority on a certain topic; e.g., the aardvark, the Civil War, the Amazon River, or any other topic of interest to him at a particular time. As a specified group of students meets once a week, members may ask questions of the "authority" on his specialized topic. If he does not know the answer, he is to search through the encyclopedia to find the answer by the next meeting time.

Teachers must constantly be scouting for ways to encourage students to use the encyclopedia as a reference source. Even corrective and remedial readers can become "hooked" on reference materials.

CARD CATALOG

To use all types of library materials, the student needs to be knowledgeable about the card catalog. This reference material lists a library's holdings by subject, author, or title, enabling students to find a particular book or information about a certain topic. The card catalog, then, becomes a key link between the corrective or remedial reader and the information she wishes to find.

The primary skills students need to use the card catalog are in the use of alphabetical order and the Dewey decimal system or Library of Congress system. Students should recognize how books are arranged in the library. Teachers should assess whether their students understand the Dewey decimal system or Library of Congress system and then make sure that students have access to a copy for reference as they use the library.

Corrective or remedial readers should become familiar with the Dewey decimal system or Library of Congress system by using it as they study. They should always have the organizational charts available, and teachers should be willing to help them determine which section is appropriate for the topic they are researching.

An activity that teachers may use is to provide an overview of typical topics in a certain division, such as "science." Each student should then designate an interest area within the specified division and gather information about her area of interest.

TABLE OF CONTENTS

Poor readers often have difficulty in grasping the overall contents of a book or a chapter. The table of contents can help them understand the ideas that will be included in the book. They should realize that the table of contents lets the reader know what topics or ideas will be presented in the book; shows the reader on which pages the topic or ideas are discussed; and usually contains a list of subtopics under each major topic. The table of contents plays a major role in all content materials used by corrective and remedial students in their reading-study time. This important part of a book provides the quickest assessment of what will be included in a book, and allows the reader to make a rapid inspection of the topics and ideas to be covered.

The primary skill students need in using a table of contents is an understanding of major headings and subheadings. A table of contents has major headings, which are the primary ideas to be explored, and subheadings, which are the details under each major topic.

Most tables of contents are divided into chapters, but they may be arranged in a variety of ways. The corrective or remedial reader should become familiar with various formats. Teachers should use all types of books, such as science, social studies, or math, to illustrate how to use a table of contents.

Teachers can use games or other activities to increase the corrective or remedial reader's awareness of the table of contents as an overall guide to a book. For example, using the table of contents of a math book, the teacher could challenge students to be the first to find the page that discusses bar graphs.

GLOSSARY

An understanding of a glossary can aid the corrective or remedial reader in understanding specialized terms he finds in a book, which is especially important in content areas such as science. Numerous technical words in a text make reading difficult; the glossary provides a quick way to find the meaning of such words. The student should be aware that the glossary is a specialized type of dictionary for that book, and that it:

- is usually found in the back of a book
- contains specialized words found in the book
- has the specialized words arranged in alphabetical order
- defines the specialized words

As with several other common reference materials, to use a glossary the reader needs facility in finding words in alphabetical order.

Teachers should refer to the glossary often as they explain material to corrective or remedial readers. They should encourage students to use the glossary by asking them the meaning of certain technical words. Students with reading problems can benefit from creating their own glossary for a book that does not contain one. By actually constructing a glossary themselves, they will be more aware of its purpose, location, and organization.

INDEX

The index has a primary use that will help the reader: it allows the reader to determine quickly on exactly which page of a book a certain topic is discussed. Moreover, the index lists all occurrences of the topic, not just the major section where it is discussed. Corrective and remedial readers need to learn that they need not go through an entire chapter to find specific information about a topic they wish to read about.

Students need skills in finding words in alphabetical order to use the index. They must also recognize the hierarchical alphabetical arrangement of subheadings. Corrective and remedial readers need to know the following organizational features of a typical index:

- It is located at the end of a book.
- The words in the index are topics covered in the book. They are arranged in alphabetical order.
- Beside each words or topic are page numbers, indicating on what page(s) the topic is discussed in the book.
- A topic may have subtopics, which are treated similarly within a topic heading.

Teachers can ask students with reading problems simply to list all the pages in a book that discuss a particular topic. She can then quickly assess whether these students are using the index. The teacher can help students with problems by discussing a particular topic, using the index as a reference to find all the pages noted.

Understanding the Organization of Content Materials

QUESTIONS TO GUIDE READING

Recall Questions
1. How do content materials differ from recreational reading books and basal readers?
2. What problems are encountered by readers of content materials?
3. What four approaches to content instruction are presented by Moore and Readence?
4. What general strategies can be used to help students use content materials?
5. What are specific problems related to science texts? Social studies texts? Math texts?
6. What are ten guidelines teachers can use in planning activities for reading in content materials?

Thinking Questions
1. What are the advantages to students of using both basal materials and content materials for instruction?
2. Why would corrective or remedial readers have special problems in using content materials?
3. Which one of the four approaches described by Moore and Readence do you think is used most often in classrooms? Why do you think this approach is most often used?
4. Why are prediction strategies effective in reading-study activities involving content materials?
5. Which content-area material do you think would cause more problems for the poor reader: science, social studies, or math? Why?
6. What other guidelines could be used in planning activities for corrective and remedial readers in content materials?

Content materials, such as science, math, and social studies textbooks, are a primary source of reading-study activities for corrective and remedial readers. Content materials are used to learn about many technical subjects and disciplines. They differ from recreational reading materials and basal readers in several ways:

- They have a technical vocabulary with which students have often had little experience.
- They have a concept load that is much higher than basal readers or recreational materials.
- They often have a high readability level, due in part to the technical vocabulary, which is often multisyllabic.
- They are not written in the traditional narrative style with which students are familiar; instead, they are expository, with each type of content material having a particular style.

PROBLEMS IN CONTENT MATERIALS

Content materials as a group present problems for any student, especially for the corrective and remedial reader. The following usually concern students:

1. The technical vocabulary is unfamiliar. The words are often unique to a subject area or have a different meaning from when they are used outside the content area.
2. The concept load is heavy in content materials; many words have abstract meanings.
3. Content materials often contain maps, graphs, or charts, which must be interpreted in order to understand the text.
4. Students often fail to understand why they are to read and study a particular content-area reading selection; they do not see the task as a meaningful one. After analyzing events in four content classrooms, Smith and Feathers (1983) concluded that most students viewed their content-area reading as neither meaningful nor necessary. The only purpose that students saw in reading was "to locate specific answers to literal questions" (p. 266). There seemed to be little attempt to "link classroom activities with the students' lives elsewhere" (p. 267).

The classroom teacher cannot assume that students understand how to read content-area materials. For all students, especially the corrective or remedial reading student, instruction in the use of content materials is essential; without it, poor readers will have great difficulty in reading content texts.

APPROACHES TO CONTENT INSTRUCTION

Moore and Readence (1983) have described four approaches to content-area reading instruction:

1. Skills that could be associated with content reading are presented in isolation. For example, students learn how to outline, but do not apply this skill to content materials.
2. Content alone is the focus. Students are asked to find information in content materials, but are not given assistance in how to find the information.
3. The emphasis is still on content, but students are provided guidance in acquiring teacher-specified information.
4. Skills are presented in conjunction with content. Students are shown how to read content materials as they acquire information.

The fourth approach, in which content and skills are presented concurrently, seems to provide the best alternative for corrective or remedial readers. This approach should overcome some students' feelings that reading-study activities have no purpose. If the teacher clearly presents the purpose of studying a particular selection, students should perform with more efficiency.

STRATEGIES TO USE WITH CONTENT MATERIALS

Several general strategies may help corrective or remedial readers with content materials. The strategies described below focus on *monitoring* and *predicting* as ways to aid reading-study activities involving content materials.

Smith and Dauer (1984) describe a strategy designed to help students monitor their comprehension as they read content-area materials, by which students use a code to record their cognitive and affective responses to a particular selection. This strategy should be especially helpful to poor readers, because they rarely monitor their comprehension as carefully as proficient readers. Smith and Dauer provide an example of a code for reading a social studies selection:

A = Agree
B = Bored
C = Confused
D = Disagree
M = Main Idea

As they read, students monitor their responses to the selection, writing the appropriate code letters on strips of paper attached to the pages. They then participate in postreading discussions to clarify their thinking and discuss the feelings they had while reading the selection.

Another strategy that can be used to help corrective and remedial readers focus on the content of materials is prediction, or anticipation. Nichols (1983) encourages teachers to help their students use prediction to increase skills in content-area reading by directing them through several steps:

1. First, students are asked to skim or preview a reading selection.
2. Next, they are asked to predict what is to be learned from the selection.
3. Finally, students are encouraged to read, view, or listen carefully to the materials to determine if their predictions were correct.

Nichols (1983) also recommends using prediction guides. The teacher prepares a written guide such as a list of statements about a reading or viewing selection, and then asks students to check off which statements they believe will be proven true in the selection. After reading or viewing the selection, they then check those statements which were actually proven correct.

Another guide Nichols recommends is for the teacher to write the first major heading or section title of a chapter on the blackboard and ask students to construct five to ten questions about the heading that they predict will be addressed in the reading selection. Students then read to see if the questions they identified were actually answered.

Kaplan and Tuchman (1980) present several strategies for helping students with the specialized vocabulary of content-area reading:

1. After students scan a chapter title and headings, they predict what words will be included in the chapter. The words are listed on the chalkboard and later discussed to verify their inclusion.
2. The teacher begins a discussion by saying something like, "When I think about the environment, it reminds me of *pollution.*" The word "pollution" is written on the chalkboard. Then the teacher asks someone what the word "pollution" reminds them of, and writes that word on the board. Another student responds, and another, until about ten words are listed on the chalkboard.
3. The teacher writes a word on the chalkboard. Students are given two minutes to write down as many words as they can think of that relate to the given word.

SPECIFIC CONTENT MATERIALS

Content-area materials vary in specific characteristics, and so do the specialized skills needed for reading-studying each type of material. The content areas of science, social studies, and math are discussed in the following section. Activities are suggested for each content area.

SCIENCE TEXTS

Weidler (1984) states that science materials are characterized by:

- a specialized vocabulary
- information presented as a cause-effect relationship
- passive verbs
- terse and exact language

Specialized vocabulary. The unique vocabulary of science can be a particular concern to corrective and remedial readers, who often have difficulty enough in reading words normally found in verbal exchanges. When they must face the added problem of reading words of a technical or specialized nature, reading becomes an even more difficult task. Teachers must help them use the dictionary and glossary to unlock some of these difficult words. Students can make files of words unique to the field of science. At times, a teacher may want to tape a particular science selection from the text so that the poor reader can hear as well as see the specialized vocabulary.

Cause and effect relationship. Because the corrective or remedial reader may have problems in comprehension, the cause and effect relationship presented in science materials may be difficult. The teacher can provide an activity to help such students: using daily events, the teacher writes down a number of "effects" for which the student must supply "causes." For example, the following "effects" might be listed: water becomes ice; the water in a pan disappears; the baby cries. The student might list the following "causes":

Effect	Cause
Water becomes ice.	The temperature drops below freezing.
The water in a pan disappears.	The sun evaporated the water.
	The water evaporated as it boiled on the stove.
The baby cries.	The baby is hungry.
	The baby is cold.
	The baby is hurt.
	The baby is lonely.

This activity can prompt poor readers to look for cause and effect relationships, making science materials more meaningful.

Terse language. The terse language of science materials creates problems for readers accustomed to narrative writing. The teacher has little control over the writing style of authors of science texts, but he can work with the student in developing inferential reading skills.

An activity that can be used with a poor reader is to ask him both to expand brief, concise sentences and to reduce regular sentences to the bare essentials. As the teacher instructs the student, she will help him see that the writer often omits words that the reader must supply.

Passive verbs. Basal materials often contain active verbs, while science texts contain many passive verbs, which can make the material boring. As much as possible, the teacher should use active descriptions when instructing the students using science tests. In fact, students can even transform some of the passive sentences into active ones. While the teacher can do little about the author's use of passive verbs, he can be aware of this as a potential problem with content materials.

SOCIAL STUDIES TEXTS

Social science writing is characterized by main idea and supporting details, sequence, facts versus opinion, and flexibility in rate. These unique characteristics also pose problems for the student with low reading skills. To read social studies materials effectively, the student must be aware of these four elements.

Main idea and supporting details. Students must be able to determine the main idea that is being presented in a social studies reading passage, and also see how supporting details relate to the main idea. A more comprehensive discussion of main idea and supporting details is found in Chapter 10, in the context of comprehension. Students must be able to apply this comprehension skill to the area of social studies, since main idea and supporting details provide the basis for understanding this type of material.

Sequence. History and the study of the human race are characterized by a sequence of events. If the reader cannot sequence events, she will fail to achieve many of the understandings necessary for success in reading social studies materials. Time lines and major events become focal points in studying events and people in social studies. The teacher must constantly emphasize this characteristic of social studies materials to corrective and remedial readers. If concrete forms such as time lines are not used, the poor reader may see no relation of past events to current ones. Cause and effect can be added to sequencing to help the student see the development of society and its effects on her today.

Facts versus opinion. Perhaps no other thinking skill in social studies is more important than the ability to distinguish between fact and opinion. The tendency to believe that anything in print is true is prevalent among many students; corrective and remedial readers are no exception.

From the beginning of their schooling, students must question the authority of the printed word. Today's media makes the study of fact and opinion a rich field for students. Using newspaper and magazine advertisements and television commercials, the teacher can begin to urge children to question statements that are presented to them. They must learn to recognize the typical biases in advertising. From an appraisal of fact and opinion in advertising, students can easily move to an examination of an author's bias in writing about both historical and current events. Students must learn to separate factual statements from opinion, and to support their own statements with data based on events and numbers.

Flexibility in rate. Patberg and Lang (1983) define a flexible reader as "one who has the ability to successfully set his speed by integrating two important variables in the reading act: (1) the nature and difficulty of the material being read, and (2) the purpose for reading" (p. 246). At times, reading in social studies may be very fast—skimming and scanning the contents. At other times, reading must be slow and precise. Social studies offers excellent opportunities for corrective and remedial readers to practice varying rates of reading.

To determine rate, students must firmly grasp the purpose for reading. Is it merely to find the date that a certain event occurred? Or is it to understand an abstract concept, such as "freedom" or "liberty"? These two reasons for reading will require very different rates. Poor readers have often developed the habit of word-by-word reading; they must be shown that for some purposes, one does not read every word in a reading selection. Teachers may demonstrate the necessity of varying rates by having students read a single selection for two different purposes: to find the main idea of the passage and to summarize the passage. To find the main idea, the teacher will encourage students to read only the chapter headings and, perhaps, the first sentence in each paragraph. For the second purpose, to summarize the entire passage, the teacher will suggest that students read every sentence in each paragraph. The teacher can time each activity, and then lead a discussion of how reading rates vary depending on the purpose for reading.

MATH TEXTS

Nolan (1984) specifies the following characteristics of math texts that make such materials difficult for students:

- symbols
- specialized vocabulary
- terse style with few verbal context clues

Symbols. Students must memorize various symbols to succeed at math. They must recognize instantly such symbols as, $-$, $\times$, and $+$, and know what they signify. Corrective and remedial readers can benefit from activities that associate math symbols with words. Teachers may construct cards that allow students to match words with symbols, such as the following:

Specialized vocabulary. As with science and social studies, math has a specialized vocabulary. Students must learn specialized words such as "multiply," "root," and "square". To complicate learning further, they must realize that a word like "root" has a different meaning in math from what is normally used in ordinary language. Students can use the glossary provided in the text to help in understanding specialized vocabulary, or develop their own.

Style of writing. Many writers of math texts use a very terse writing style; this poses a difficulty in word problems. Nolan (1984) cites research that shows that rewriting word problems to "make them easier to read and to pattern them after oral language of students seems to be an efficient strategy for facilitating problem solving" (p. 30).

Coulter (1972) has made certain suggestions for helping students understand the general organization of math materials:

1. Provide students with a general description of the text, including the author's background.
2. Give students an overview of the organization of the text, perhaps comparing it with another arithmetic text or with a science or social studies text.
3. Show students how to examine the table of contents.
4. Point out the distinctive characteristics of text, such as the emphasis on quantitative concepts or the necessity to identify key words.
5. Discuss with students special features of the text; index, reference information, glossary of terms, or footnotes.

GUIDELINES FOR ACTIVITIES IN CONTENT MATERIALS

The teacher will need to adjust activities in the content area for corrective and remedial readers in her classroom. These students will find the reading materials typically used in content reading at their grade level to be very difficult. The classroom teacher must give special consideration to this problem, or the students will learn little and instead develop negative attitudes toward content material. The classroom teacher can use the following guidelines in planning activities for corrective and remedial readers in content materials:

1. Have more than one textbook available on the topic being studied. These texts should be on different reading levels, so that the student who is reading below grade level can gain information about the topic as he reads in a lower-level book.
2. Make resources such as films and tapes available to corrective and remedial students. Many ideas about a topic can be gained through this visual display that could not be attained through reading alone.
3. Have extensive picture files of the various content-area topics. Students can learn much from these pictures, although the teachers may need to label parts of the illustration.
4. Assign only the general concepts to be learned; let students select where they will learn them. They could use a wide variety of materials, such as different grade level textbooks, trade books, or films to master the assigned materials.
5. Tape important information from textbooks. The teacher does not have to do all of the taping; students who read well can do much of it. The corrective or remedial reader can listen to the tapes to learn material in the content texts.
6. Have corrective or remedial readers make vocabulary cards of important technical terms in the various content materials. They can take the cards home to explain to their parents what they are learning about in a certain text.
7. Use games, such as word bingo, that draw on technical vocabulary from content textbooks. The corrective and remedial reader needs added exposure to this vocabulary.
8. Use matching activities, especially in math, to link words to symbols. This will help the corrective and remedial reader recognize some of the technical vocabulary in the math textbook.
9. Pair a corrective or remedial reader with a student who reads well. The good reader can be a resource for pronunciation and definition of words, and can tape material for the corrective and remedial reader. The pairing, of course, must feel acceptable and worthwhile to both students.
10. Read content materials to students, just as you read them recreational materials. It may be of particular help to read a paragraph to a poor reader who is having trouble understanding a concept contained in the passage.

These guidelines can be used by classroom teachers as they plan activities in the content area for corrective and remedial readers. Special attention must be given to the student who has reading problems. He will find content materials difficult; it is the teacher's responsibility to ease his difficulty so that he can learn.

INFORMATION TO CONSIDER

1. Content materials and basal readers differ in several important ways.
2. The technical vocabulary; concept load; maps, graphics, or charts; and writing style are elements of content materials that may cause problems for corrective or remedial readers.
3. In teaching content, teachers may present skills in isolation, focus on content alone, emphasize content but provide guidance in acquiring information, or present skills and content concurrently.
4. Prediction and monitoring strategies may be used effectively with content materials.
5. Various content materials have specific characteristics that may cause problems in reading-study activities.
6. Classroom teachers can follow certain guidelines in planning activities in content areas for corrective and remedial readers.

Organizing Ideas Gained from Reading

QUESTIONS TO GUIDE READING

Recall Questions
1. What are the seven organizational strategies suggested as ways to organize ideas during reading-studying?
2. What are the suggestions McAndrew makes for underlining? For note taking?
3. What are the six steps in the new SQ4R technique?

Thinking Questions
1. Which organizational strategy would be the most beneficial for science materials? Social studies materials? Math materials?
2. What factors would influence the organizational strategy used by a particular reader?
3. Why would organizational strategies be especially beneficial to corrective and remedial readers?
4. Should parents be familiar with the seven organizational strategies? Why or why not?
5. Which organizational strategy should be taught first? Why?

Corrective and remedial readers must not only know how to read various reference and content materials, but must also be aware of strategies for organizing ideas as they read. Underlining, outlining, notetaking, mapping, questioning, summarizing, and SQ4R are some of the strategies that they can use in organizing their ideas during reading-studying.

UNDERLINING

Underlining is a very popular strategy used in studying. After reviewing research on underlining, Anderson and Armbruster (1984) state that it is probably no more effective than other study strategies; they find its major benefit to be that the student himself generates the underlining. This forces the student to make decisions about what to underline and, therefore, to play an active role in studying.

McAndrew (1983, p.107) provides some suggestions based on research for using underlining in the classroom. Among these suggestions are:

> Students should be given training in effective underlining.
> Encourage students to underline superordinate general ideas.
> Remind students that with underlining, less is more.
> Students should use the time saved by underlining to study the material.
> Students should know when to use some techniques other than underlining.

Part of the responsibility for effective underlining lies with the teacher. He should specify what the purpose for reading is to be, perhaps writing it on the chalkboard. Then, when students have completed their underlining of a passage, they should determine if everything that was underlined was relevant to the purpose for reading. Was too much underlined? Was enough underlined to satisfy the purpose for reading? This activity will help students see that underlining is not a haphazard activity.

OUTLINING

Outlining is a way of hierarchically organizing ideas and events that have been presented in a reading selection. The student must have skills in recognizing the main ideas and subordinate ideas in a reading passage.

The student usually is taught to use Roman and Arabic numerals and letters to outline material, in a pattern such as the following:

I.
  A.
  B.
    1.
    2.
      a.
      b.
        (1)
        (2)
 II.
III.

The teacher will initially want to encourage corrective and remedial students to use a simple outline of their ideas in a particular content reading selection. Harris and Smith (1980) suggest a series of steps in which a completed outline is first presented, then a partial outline, and finally, only the skeleton with numbers and letters. Each time the student is asked to fill in the missing parts of the outline. As each step progresses, he must supply more of the missing information.

The teacher can easily illustrate an outline by showing corrective or remedial readers tables of contents from various texts. She should provide many demonstrations and directed practice of outlining before asking the student to do independent outlining.

Because corrective and remedial readers often have difficulty in seeing reading as a meaningful process, they often fail to see how the various paragraphs or sections of a reading selection relate to each other. The teacher must help students to see the overall framework or outline of the passage.

NOTETAKING

McAndrew (1983, p. 107) provides the following suggestions for notetaking:

- Students should realize that the external storage function of notes is more important than the act of taking the notes.
- Instructors should try using a spaced lecture format.
- Instructors should insert questions or verbal and nonverbal cues into lectures to highlight structure.
- Instructors should write material on the blackboard if they want to be sure students will record it.
- When using transparencies or slides, instructors should compensate for possible information overload.
- Instructors should tell students what type of test to expect.

- Instructors should use handouts, especially with poor notetakers.
- Instructors should give students handouts with both full notes and space for student notes.

Schilling (1984) reports success in using a special type of notetaking with his sixth-grade students: he taught them that notetaking should be directed at helping them pass a test. He had his students formulate possible test questions and write the answers as notes. To reinforce taking notes for this purpose, Schilling provided time for team contests before an exam, in which students used only their notes to ask questions of the opposing team and to answer their opponents' questions.

MAPPING

Mapping organizes information in a visual, hierarchical, associative manner. Semantic mapping is described by Johnson, Pittelman, and Heimlich (1986, p. 1) as "structuring of information in graphic form." It relates to schema theory (see Ch. 10) in that the reader takes information from the text and integrates it with his prior knowledge. Johnson, Pittelman, and Heimlich recommend semantic mapping as a study skill strategy to guide the processing of textbook material. They cite Hanf's three basic steps for designing a semantic map of information from a textbook:

1. Identification of main idea. The main idea is written down on paper and a shape (perhaps a circle) is drawn around it.
2. Secondary categories. The principal parts of the textbook chapter form the secondary categories. Lines are drawn from the main idea. Secondary categories are written at the end of the lines.
3. Supporting details. Details for each secondary category are then listed underneath each category.

QUESTIONING

Using this technique, students generate questions about the particular content-area material they are reading. This method may be successful because the student encodes the information from the text and paraphrases it in some way or makes some other transformations on it (Anderson and Armbruster 1984). In a research study, André and Anderson (1978-79) found that students who had been taught to generate their own questions during study had greater learning outcomes than those who used rereading during study.

To use the questioning strategy effectively, students need to be well aware of the various levels of questions (see p. 304). They should use a variety of levels as they develop questions about a particular reading selection.

Students can benefit from developing their own test questions for content materials. As they decide what questions should be asked, they will be making judgments about what they consider to be the main ideas of the reading material.

SUMMARIZING

Summarizing is a way for corrective and remedial readers to assess their understanding of the materials they have read. They can prepare for a test by summarizing what they have read; their ability to summarize the material will be an indication of how well they have understood it.

In order to summarize material, corrective and remedial readers must be able to:

- identify the main idea in a passage
- relate how the details are associated with the main idea
- sequence the material correctly

Science experiments are an excellent way for teachers to demonstrate summarizing. After watching her conduct an experiment, students can then assist the teacher in writing a summary of what happened. This procedure can then be extended to an experiment that students conduct, and finally to an experiment that students merely read about in their science book.

SQ4R

The corrective or remedial reader can benefit from an organizational strategy known as the SQ4R. Pauk (1984) presented what he termed "the new, action-packed SQ4R" as an aid for students, consisting of six steps:

1. *Surveying.* This gets the reader started as he surveys chapter or unit headings and subheadings.
2. *Questioning.* This captures the reader's attention. Headings and subheadings are turned into questions.
3. *Reading.* This promotes concentration. The reader must read to answer the questions posed in Step 2.
4. *Recording.* This elicits ideas, facts, and details from the reader as he writes them in the margins. He must be selective in what he records.
5. *Reciting.* This forces the reader to think as he recites aloud the answers to his questions. (Pauk suggests that the reader cover the page, leaving only his notes uncovered. He uses these notes to recite.)

6. *Reflecting.* This step prompts the reader to reflect on what he has read by asking: "What are these ideas and facts based on?" "How can I use them?"

INFORMATION TO CONSIDER

1. Corrective and remedial readers need to be aware of strategies for organizing ideas as they read and study.
2. Underlining, outlining, notetaking, mapping, questioning, summarizing, and SQ4R are some of the strategies that may be used to organize ideas during reading-studying.

Assessing Students' Reading-Studying Skills

QUESTIONS TO GUIDE READING

Recall Questions
1. How may reading-studying skills be assessed?
2. What types of reading-studying skills are assessed on Rogers' checklist?

Thinking Questions
1. Would teachers share the results from an assessment of reading-study skills with parents? Why or why not?
2. Should reading-study skills of corrective and remedial readers be assessed more often than those of the normal achieving reader? Why or why not?
3. What are the advantages of using a test of reading-study skills? A checklist?

Reading-study skills may be assessed through both formal tests and informal checklists. Both types of assessment can provide the teacher with important information about the student's skills in reading-study activities.

STUDY SKILLS TEST

Teachers can obtain commercial tests for assessing their corrective and remedial readers' reading-studying skills, such as the *Wisconsin Design Test of Reading Skills Development.* Seven levels of the test are available:

Level A: kindergarten to grade 1
Level B: grades 1–2
Level C: grades 2–3
Level D: grades 3–4
Level E: grades 4–5
Level F: grades 5–6
Level G: grades 6–7

The test is criterion-referenced, with an 80 percent mastery level suggested. Many of the study skill areas mentioned in this chapter are covered in the test: symbols, alphabetizing, table of contents, indexes, guide words, headings and subheadings, fact and opinion, Dewey decimal system, reference materials, outlining, and card catalog. Illustrations of actual materials are often used in the testing, making the test more relevant to students.

INFORMAL CHECKLIST

Teachers will often find that an informal checklist provides the information they need about a student's reading-study skills. Rogers (1984) has developed an especially comprehensive one (see Fig. 11.1), covering skills related to:

- rates of reading
- parts of a book
- index, glossary, and table of contents
- reference materials (guide words, pronunciation key, word origins)
- encyclopedia
- card catalog
- underlining
- study habits (study time and organization)
- notetaking
- summarizing
- outlining

The checklist allows the teacher to record the degree of the student's skill—high, low, or absent—as noted through observation.

INFORMATION TO CONSIDER

1. Assessment of reading-study skills may be made by means of tests and checklists.

Figure 11.1. Rogers's Reading-Study Skills Checklist

	Degree of skill		
	Absent	Low	High
I. Special study-reading comprehension skills			
A. Ability to interpret graphic aids			
Can the student interpret these graphic aids?			
1. maps			
2. globes			
3. graphs			
4. charts			
5. tables			
6. cartoons			
7. pictures			
8. diagrams			
9. other organizing or iconic aids			
B. Ability to follow directions			
Can the student follow…			
1. simple directions?			
2. a more complex set of directions?			
II. Information location skills			
A. Ability to vary rate of reading			
Can the student do the following?			
1. scan			
2. skim			
3. read at slow rate for difficult materials			
4. read at average rate for reading level			
B. Ability to locate information by use of book parts			
Can the student use book parts to identify the following information?			
1. title			
2. author or editor			
3. publisher			
4. city of publication			
5. name of series			
6. edition			
7. copyright date			
8. date of publication			
Can the student quickly locate and understand the function of the following parts of a book?			
1. preface			
2. foreword			
3. introduction			
4. table of contents			
5. list of figures			
6. chapter headings			
7. subtitles			
8. footnotes			
9. bibliography			
10. glossary			
11. index			
12. appendix			
C. Ability to locate information in reference works			
Can the student do the following?			
1. locate information in a dictionary			
a. using the guide words			
b. using a thumb index			
c. locating root word			
d. locating derivations of root word			
e. using the pronunciation key			
f. selecting word meaning appropriate to passage under study			
g. noting word origin			

From Douglas B. Rogers, "Assessing Study Skills," *Journal of Reading*, January 1984, pp. 353–354. Copyright 1984 International Reading Association. Reprinted with permission of Douglas B. Rogers and the International Reading Association.

Summary

Reading-study skills are very important to corrective or remedial readers. These students, who are often at grade levels where content reading is necessary, should not be limited to reading instruction in word recognition using basal reading materials. They should be taught effective study techniques and given the opportunity to incorporate these techniques into their reading-study activities. These students need to be able to set goals, establish a time for reading-studying, and structure certain factors in their environment for optimally effective reading-studying. Students can also learn to evaluate their own reading-studying time.

Corrective and remedial readers should be actively involved in using many types of reference materials, such as the dictionary, encyclopedia, card catalog, table of contents, glossary, and index. With the corrective and remedial reader, the teacher may need to focus on the basic skills needed to use these materials. Activities should be purposeful, with the student actually using the reference materials rather than workbook sheets or dittos.

Content materials differ from basal readers and recreational reading materials. Content materials are often more difficult for students, especially the corrective or remedial reader, because of the technical vocabulary, concept load, graphic material, and author's writing style. Students should be aware of specific characteristics of the various types of content materials.

Corrective and remedial reading students need to organize the ideas they gain from reading, using organizational strategies such as underlining, outlining, notetaking, mapping, questioning, summarizing, and SQ4R.

Teachers may want to use a formal test to assess their corrective and remedial readers' reading-studying skills or they may choose an informal checklist that outlines the various skills needed for effective reading-studying.

Questions for Further Thought

1. Can reading-study activities be enjoyable times for students? Why or why not?
2. How can the microcomputer be used in encouraging reading-study activities?
3. Do you agree that some reading-studying should be done at home? Why or why not?
4. What can be done to make content text writers be more aware of students' needs related to writing style of the texts?
5. What can be done to help the content-area teacher appreciate the problems of corrective and remedial readers in reading-study activities involving content materials?

Activities and Projects

1. Develop a scope and sequence chart for teaching corrective and remedial readers to use the dictionary, the encyclopedia, or the card catalog.
2. Develop a checklist for corrective and remedial readers to use in evaluating their reading-study activities.
3. Develop four content reading lessons, one for each of the four approaches to content instruction suggested by Moore and Readence. Discuss the differences in the lessons.
4. Use the content reading strategy of Smith and Dauer with a group of students. Discuss students' reactions to the strategy.
5. Use the SQ4R technique to study this chapter.
6. Use the Rogers reading-study skills checklist to assess the proficiency of a corrective or remedial reader.

12

Materials for Corrective and Remedial Readers

Many classroom teachers have questions about materials for their corrective and remedial reading students. Their concerns include the following:

- What criteria should I use in selecting materials for students who are having difficulty in reading?
- What types of materials should I use with corrective and remedial readers in my classroom?
- How can I organize materials in my classroom for corrective and remedial readers?
- What recommendations should I make to parents of corrective and remedial readers about reading materials for their children?

Four basic criteria are established in this chapter for selection of classroom materials for the corrective and remedial reader. The teacher should choose materials that will motivate the student, that are at the appropriate level, that have a purpose for the student, and that expand his reading skills.

Eight types of materials are discussed in this chapter as appropriate for corrective and remedial readers: reading programs, computerized reading materials, taped and talking books, magazines, high interest/low vocabulary books, skill books, games, and newspapers. The reading skills promoted by each type of material are outlined. This section should be read in conjunction with Appendix E, which contains expanded lists of all eight types of materials, for a more comprehensive review of materials appropriate for corrective and remedial readers. The teacher should refer often to Appendix E as she reads this section.

Another section of this chapter provides recommendations to the classroom teacher about how to organize reading materials for the corrective or remedial reader. Because the classroom teacher has developmental as well as corrective and remedial readers in her class, she must organize instruction and materials in such a way to promote access and use by the students who are having difficulties in reading.

The last section covers recommendations to the classroom teacher for working with parents relative to materials for their children who have problems in reading. Many parents can play a prominent role in selecting materials for their children, once they know how; other parents may be unwilling or unable to help. The classroom teacher must be able to work within either framework in meeting the need for materials for these corrective and remedial readers.

Criteria for Selection of Materials

QUESTIONS TO GUIDE READING

Recall Question
1. What are the criteria suggested for materials for corrective and remedial readers?

Thinking Question
1. In what priority ranking would you place the various criteria for selecting materials? Why did you rank the various criteria as you did?

Previous chapters have already discussed many of the criteria for selecting materials. However, a review of some of these criteria seems appropriate. For this chapter, criteria have been organized into four major headings:

- Materials should be highly motivating.
- Materials should be on the appropriate level for the student.
- Materials should serve a worthwhile purpose.
- Materials should expand the student's reading skills.

MATERIALS THAT MOTIVATE

Most children seem eager to start the reading process; they are motivated to read. However, when students encounter problems in reading, they may become less motivated to engage in what is often a frustrating experience for them. The classroom teacher's task is to provide materials that will motivate sutdents who are "turned off" to reading.

How does the teacher provide materials that motivate students? A careful review of three of Mathewson's (1976, p. 657) motives for reading provides some guidance:

- *Curiosity*. Teachers can use the student's curiosity as motivation. Students who have been exposed, unsuccessfully, to the same type of materials—usually basal readers with accompanying workbook pages—for several years may need a complete change of pace. The teacher may need to switch to a totally different type of material, such as computer games involving reading, wordless books, or survival materials (described below). Hopefully, the student will become curious about the new materials and feel less threatened by them. His curiosity may motivate him to become involved with these materials.
- *Self-Actualization*. Students have ideals of what they want to be. Perhaps one student wants to be a great baseball player. This student may be motivated to read biographies about baseball stars, study a handbook of baseball techniques, or collect baseball cards describing facts about various players. Many types of materials on the topic of baseball may be motivating to the student. Teachers of corrective and remedial readers must be sensitive to the use of self-actualization as motivation.
- *Activity*. Materials should be available to the problem reader whenever he wants to read simply to have something to do. The teacher can help the student plan to have something to read during free time, while waiting for a bus, or numerous other times when the student would be receptive to reading. Many students who love to read keep books in various stages of completion in strategic places such as the breakfast table, the family room, or their bedroom. Forming the habit of reading may require special teacher attention and monitoring with the problem reader. The teacher may need to encourage the student to tuck into a pocket a small magazine, brochure, or book on a topic of interest to her. This provides the student with something to do while waiting for a haircut, for parents to pick her up from school, or other idle moments.

Students may already have some preconceived ideas about certain materials: basals are frustrating, worksheets are dull, and so on. Whether or not these beliefs are valid is immaterial; if the corrective or remedial reader has negative feelings toward certain materials, they will affect her desire to read. The teacher should plan to use materials that are acceptable to the corrective or remedial student for a major part of the student's reading program. In the initial stages, the primary goal is to kindle a desire in the student to approach reading materials. As the student gains confidence in her ability to read and develops a love of reading, she may find that the materials she had avoided are no longer unappealing.

Reading should be enjoyable. Materials can play a large role in the student's beliefs and feelings about reading. He may complain about "silly stories," "boring topics," or "baby books." His concerns are real and must be acknowledged by the classroom teacher, because they affect the student's desire to approach reading materials. Many teachers are concerned about whether or not a certain basal reader is completed within a specified time period; but they should really be much more concerned about the feeling the students are developing toward reading. The classroom teacher has the responsibility of nurturing positive feelings toward reading.

Classroom teachers must be especially attentive to the interests of students who are experiencing difficulty in reading. Materials should be selected with careful consideration of their interests, guided by the following questions:

- What topics interest the student? If only one topic seems to be of interest in the initial stage, the teacher should focus on that interest. Gradually, other topics may be introduced as the student broadens his areas of needs and interests.
- What formats are of interest to the student? It may be paperback books, or magazines, or newspapers. One format may be less threatening than another.
- What style of writing is of most interest to the student? She may want to read only mysteries, or poetry, or some other particular type of material.
- Does a book with lots of pictures or illustrations interest him? The student may well feel more comfortable with a book that has many pictures to help him interpret the printed passages. Just "reading" the pictures can be a worthwhile activity for such a student. The teacher should gradually encourage the student to read one or two words in a caption or to read a few sentences explaining what is happening in the pictures.

A multitude of activities compete for the attention of students. Reading is only one of them; television, sports, music, and play are also vying for their attention. The habit of reading must often be formed. If it is formed in childhood as a positive experience, it will usually extend into adulthood. Adults who read extensively consider the time spent worthwhile enough to let reading be a part of their daily activities.

The classroom teacher must consider reading materials that complement the "reading habit." For example, if the student is encouraged to check out library books, he may establish a pattern of going to the library once a week to select books. If the student reads a portion of the daily newspaper, she may form a habit of keeping up with current events in news periodicals. Materials that contribute to a lifelong pursuit of reading should play a role in a student's instructional reading program.

Parents can also help in forming the reading habit by reading themselves at home after dinner or before bedtime. If the classroom teacher can promote the idea of a family reading time, the corrective or remedial reader may get into the habit of reading for a few minutes each day. The teacher-parent conference is a perfect place to discuss which types of materials best lend themselves to family reading times.

Much has been written about the readability of books. Many educators stress that reading materials should not be so difficult that the student cannot read with the fluency she needs to comprehend the reading passage. Finding a book on the appropriate level for the corrective or remedial reader is often a difficult task for the classroom teacher. Various readability formulas have been proposed to guide teachers in their selection of materials, several of which will be mentioned in this section. Most readability formulas use difficulty of vocabulary, number of syllables in a word, sentence length, or word length as indicators of the reading difficulty of a passage. Inadequacies in predicting the exact grade level of materials are inevitable; however, the authors believe that as long as teachers recognize their limitations, these formulas can be of aid in the selection of materials for students.

Perhaps the most frequently used formula is the Fry Readability Graph. As shown in Figure 12.1, this formula uses average sentence length and

Figure 12.1. Fry Readability Graph

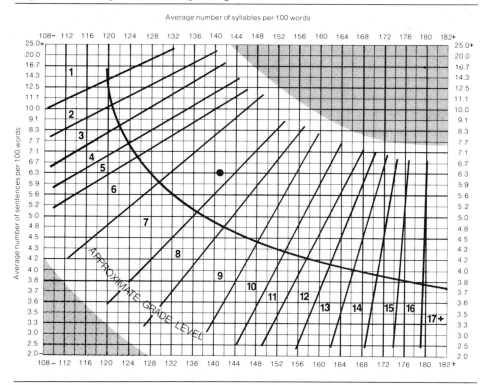

From Edward Fry, "Fry's Readability Graph: Clarifications, Validity, and Extensions to Level 17," *Journal of Reading*, December 1977. Copyright © 1977 by Edward Fry. Reprinted with permission of the author.

average number of syllables as measures of reading difficulty. It has the advantage of spanning a wide range of grade levels: from grade 1 through grade 17.

Other tests of reading difficulty that the classroom teacher may consult are the following:

1. FOG Index (Gunning 1968). Recommended for grade levels 4–12. Uses words per sentence and number of syllables to predict reading difficulty.
2. Spache Readability Formula for Primary Grade Reading Materials (Spache 1974). Recommended for grade levels 1–4. Uses sentence length and a listing of "hard" words as indicators of the difficulty of materials.
3. Flesch Reading Ease Score (Flesch 1948). Recommended for "very easy" to "very difficult" levels. Uses average number of syllables and average sentence length per sample to estimate readability.
4. SMOG Graded Reading Formula (McLaughlin 1969). Recommended for grades 4 and above. Words of three or more syllables are used to assess difficulty.
5. Dale-Chall Readability Formula (Dale and Chall 1948). Recommended for grade levels 3–12. Uses percentage of unfamiliar words (those outside a list of 3,000 words) and average sentence length to predict readability.

Klare (1974–75, p. 98) states that such formulas provide the classroom teacher satisfactory predictions for most purposes and can be used as one index of readability. Knowledge of learners (such as their interests and background of experience) and textual factors (such as concept density and writing style) should be considered also.[1]

WORTHWHILE PURPOSE

The teacher must constantly question, "Does the student understand the purposes of the materials that have been selected for instructional purposes, or does he think they only serve the teacher's purposes?" Interest and purpose are tied together. If a student is interested in a particular material, he usually feels that it has a purpose for him: it answers a question, entertains him, or provides him with desired information.

Often corrective and remedial reading students will not overtly resist materials that the teacher has selected for them—but they won't read them either. They procrastinate, dawdle, or otherwise avoid the prescribed reading, because they may not see a worthwhile purpose in reading the materials.

Sometimes the teacher attempts to set the purpose for the student's reading by saying something like, "Read this story to find out how the

[1]Further information regarding text/reader-based procedures can be found in *Teaching Reading*, 3rd ed., ed. J. Estill Alexander, (Scott, Foresman, 1988).

butterfly got its wings," or "Read this story to see what happened when Tom went to the county fair." The student may or may not accept the teacher's stated purpose for reading the story. He may not care how the butterfly got its wings or what happened when Tom went to the fair; his purpose in reading the story may be simply to satisfy the teacher. This purpose may not be strong enough to maintain his interest in some reading materials.

For the corrective or remedial reader, the teacher may need to attend more carefully to the student's expressed purposes for reading. A special understanding of the student and his needs and interests is needed to predict accurately his purposes for reading.

Parents often set purposes for reading without considering those of the child. A parent may intend, for example, to improve the child's reading ability; this may not be an equally acceptable purpose for the child.

Both parent and teacher should consider carefully the child's role in setting purposes for reading. While adults may be able to establish a reading purpose for the child, they must be sensitive to whether the student accepts their purpose for reading, or whether the child's avoidance of reading passages reveals his rejection of the purpose set for him.

READING SKILLS

The classroom teacher must constantly question what reading skills are facilitated by materials used with the corrective and remedial reader. Especially when many workbook practice pages are used, the teacher must assess whether the workbook activities actually promote the skill in question. Several questions about the selection of skill materials must be asked:

- Is the skill identified? The skill that is being practiced should be clearly evident to the student. If the student is to practice recognizing word parts, the purpose statement should state this clearly.
- Does the student understand why this particular skill is needed? For example, does he realize how recognizing word parts will enable him to identify unknown words in the future? All too often directions in workbook materials do not explain the importance of the skill to the student. It then becomes the teacher's responsibility to identify the importance of the skill. If she cannot do so, the student may easily find the practice irrelevant.
- Are there safeguards to ensure that the student is practicing a skill correctly? The workbook practice page should give an example, allow the child to respond, and then provide verification so that the child knows that he is practicing the skill properly.
- Does the practice page really help the student master the skill specified? For example, if the sheet is to practice finding the main idea, the student should have a firmly established strategy for finding the main idea after he has completed the assignment.

Types of Materials

Many types of materials may be used with corrective and remedial reading students. The classroom teacher should select those which are most appropriate for a particular student. In this section, eight types of materials are recommended:

- reading programs
- computerized reading materials
- taped and talking books
- magazines
- high interest/low vocabulary books
- skill materials
- games
- newspapers

Appendix E contains an extensive list of materials organized in these eight categories. After reading general information about each type of material in this chapter, the reader should examine the entries under that category in Appendix E.

READING PROGRAMS

Some publishers have recognized that special reading programs are needed for the corrective or remedial reader. These materials are often an extension of the basal reading program. They are beneficial to the student because they have controlled vocabulary and established readability levels, and offer the student continued practice in sight words, phonics, and comprehension activities.

The advantages of such materials are the following:

- The controlled vocabulary enables corrective and remedial readers to have basic vocabulary words repeated in the various levels of the materials.
- The leveling and labeling of the materials enable the teacher to be more precise in the level of materials in which she places the corrective or remedial reader. While there is some variability of readability in basal materials, they are more consistent than other materials such as newspapers or magazines.
- The materials in a reading program are extensive enough to provide activities over an extended period of time.
- The planned scope and sequence of such materials allow the teachers more confidence that skills in which the corrective and remedial reader may be deficient will be covered.

The disadvantages of these reading materials include the following:

- The corrective or remedial reader usually has been exposed to basal reading materials for several years, often without much success. Simply because they are the same type of book with which he has experienced problems, these materials may not appeal to the corrective or remedial reader.
- The corrective or remedial reader may not need all of the skills included in these reading programs; at this point in her development, she may have very specific skill needs. The classroom teacher must carefully monitor the materials in a reading program, selecting only those needed by the student.

COMPUTERIZED READING MATERIALS

Computers may be used in a variety of ways in reading instruction for corrective and remedial students. Mason and Blanchard (1979) suggest three types of programs of instruction available on the computer:

1. *Tutorial programs*, which are self-contained; that is, students do not need an instructor.

2. *Drill and practice,* in which instruction initially presented by the teacher is supplemented by drill and practice on the computer.
3. *Programs with dialogue,* which require that the student read the instructions in order to perform the various functions and routines of the program.

Albert Shannon (1985) suggests that almost any computer software with dialogue can be used as reading materials. If the corrective or remedial reader is interested in the program and reads the dialogue while performing the tasks, reading fluency can be promoted. Shannon cautions, however, that some teachers have become too concerned about such programs and overly specific about what criteria such materials should meet. They often provide too many follow-up activities when using the programs. Shannon cautions (p. 825) that too much concern may not be advisable:

> Software disks, after all, are very much like books: some are to be tasted, some chewed, and others thoroughly digested. Since we constantly provide students with literature and allow them to read unfettered by objectives, comprehension questions, book report forms and mandates for educational outcomes, it seems logical to suggest the same for using software.

Dudley-Marling (1985, pp. 388–89) advocates the use of commercial microcomputer programs that "were not written to teach reading but require its use." He recommends computer mystery games that require the reader to follow written clues; stories that give written directions to solve problems within the tale; and a type of narrative he terms "participa-story," in which the reader not only helps solve a mystery but "actively takes part in the story, making frequent decisions that alter the story's course."

Not only can students use software as reading materials, but teachers can use the computer in selecting books for students. Cunningham (1981) stresses the critical importance of finding "just the right book" to make reading an integral part of one's life. She describes a computer system, *Bookmatch,* which attempts to match a student with just the right book. Students complete an interest inventory, which is compared with the books in the computer's files; a printout of suggested books for a student is then provided. *Bookmatch* could be especially useful to the classroom teacher in selecting materials for corrective and remedial readers because it also sorts books according to reading level.

Computerized reading materials can provide overall practice in reading; however, there are a number of programs on the market that offer specialized practice in skills such as sight words, phonics, and structural analysis. These programs could be especially helpful to the classroom teacher in working with corrective or remedial readers.

Computerized reading materials for the corrective or remedial reader have the following advantages:

- The materials may be highly motivating because they provide the corrective or remedial reader with a new format.
- The materials require the active involvement of the learner; responses are required as the program moves along.
- The materials lend themselves to individualized use in the classroom, which is helpful for the student who reads at a different grade level from her peers.

Disadvantages of computerized reading materials include:

- The teacher must spend time reviewing computerized materials, which are somewhat new in the reading market and may not be familiar to her.
- As with other materials, students may tire of using computers on a regular basis. The classroom teacher must remember that the corrective or remedial reader needs a variety of materials to hold his interest in reading.

TAPED AND TALKING BOOKS

Gamby (1983) distinguishes between a talking book and a taped book. He describes a *taped book* as one "recorded at a slow rate of reading in order to give the pupil reading practice" (p. 366). As the student listens to a taped book, she points to the words in the book, matching the spoken word with the printed one. This is a particularly good exercise for students who need to acquire a basic sight vocabulary.

Teachers can record almost any book to make it a taped book. The teacher should be careful to record at a rate slow enough for the student to follow along and yet maintain the speech rhythms of natural language. Books that have a great amount of repetition are ideal for taping.

Advantages of taped books include the following:

- The corrective or remedial reader does not have to depend on his own ability in determining the words; he has an auditory confirmation of the word.
- The taped book is an appropriate activity for an individual student in a classroom. The corrective or remedial reader must often work on material at a different level from her classmates, and the taped materials are readily available for individual use.

- The corrective or remedial reader may not have been exposed to taped books; therefore, their novelty may be highly motivating.
- Tapes can be easily made of many different books in the classroom. The classroom teacher can even take advantage of superior readers in his class to do some of the taping.

Disadvantages of taped books include:

- A large amount of equipment may be needed in order to accommodate several corrective or remedial readers in the classroom.
- Tapes require time and planning by the classroom teacher in her already busy schedule.

A *talking book* is a "book recorded on tape at a normal rate of reading" (Gamby 1983, p. 366). The student's purpose in using a talking book is to acquire information, or to enjoy hearing a book read to her just as she would enjoy someone reading a story aloud to her. The student may have a copy of the book to follow along, or may simply listen to the recording.

For the student experiencing difficulty in content-area materials, talking books may be beneficial. Through them corrective or remedial readers can acquire information that they could not read themselves in content textbooks. Classroom teachers can have students who read well tape various parts of content-area texts.

Gamby (1983) gives three advantages of talking books:

- As the student engages in the language experiences of the book, he can gain concepts and vocabulary.
- The student hears the correct pronunciation of words.
- If the printed material is made available to the student, he can gain an understanding of the transition from spoken language to written language.

Disadvantages of talking books may be:

- The classroom teacher will need certain basic equipment to use talking books, including a tape recorder and one or more sets of headphones.
- The teacher must spend time planning for and making the talking books.

CHILDREN'S MAGAZINES

Children's magazines are another material that the classroom teacher may want to use with corrective and remedial readers. For children with negative attitudes toward reading, the timeliness of magazines may turn reading them into a positive experience. The teacher may also use magazines to work on general comprehension skills by asking students to relate the main ideas they gained from reading various articles.

Advantages of using children's magazines for reading include:

- Their format (size, illustrations, varied print styles) may motivate students who have been unsuccessful in traditional materials, such as basal readers.
- The brevity of stories may encourage corrective or remedial readers who have difficulty in reading longer passages.
- The variety of stories may allow students to find a topic of interest to them.
- Crossword puzzles and other types of activities often found in magazines are interesting ways to involve students in reading.

Disadvantages of magazines included the following:

- The classroom teacher may not have such materials in her classroom.
- Corrective and remedial readers may look only at the illustrations and pictures, and thereby get little practice in reading.

HIGH INTEREST/LOW VOCABULARY BOOKS

High interest/low vocabulary books are particularly useful as materials for readers below grade level. An increasing number of these materials have become available in recent years. These materials have generally received praise from educators, although some cautions have been cited. Teachers should know how to use these materials effectively.

Mason (1980) provides an excellent historical review of high interest/ low vocabulary books, tracing them from the 1940s to the present. He states that they were developed for older remedial readers, whose interests differ from those of younger students who read at the same level. These older students needed materials on an easy level yet written from a mature point of view.

High interest/low vocabulary books have the following advantages:

- They are written at a readability level that should be appropriate for the poor reader.
- They are interesting to older students who read at below-average levels.
- They are often in a small book format, which may be appealing to students.
- They are available on a number of topics of interest to both boys and girls.

Disadvantages or limitations of these materials are listed by Mason (1980):

- The materials are sometimes choppy and disjointed due to the short sentences they use.
- Because short words with many meanings are sometimes overused in high interest/low vocabulary materials, students may have trouble determining exactly which meaning is appropriate, with a corresponding effect on comprehension. To help alleviate this problem, teachers should look for books with a limited number of concepts.
- High interest/low vocabulary books often lack the natural patterns of language found in other reading materials, making it difficult for students to anticipate or predict words using their knowledge of the structure and flow of the language. The teacher may need to provide supplementary activities to give corrective and remedial students exposure to natural language patterns.

Although high interest/low vocabulary books have some problems, they are recommended as alternatives to books that do not meet the interests of the more mature student.

SKILL BOOKS

At certain times, when the classroom teacher wants to focus the corrective or remedial reader on specific skills that will improve her word recognition or comprehension, specific skill books can be of great value. These materials are often in a workbook format and are usually arranged by type of skill, such as consonant sounds, main idea, or root words. This allows the classroom teacher to select only those pages from the workbook which are applicable to a particular corrective or remedial reader.

Advantages of skill books include:

- They can be used to focus on a particular skill need.
- They are usually comprehensive enough to provide practice in most of the skills a student would need in reading.
- They lend themselves to individualized instruction because the workbook pages can be completed independently.
- They are commercially prepared, and therefore save the teacher time in preparing such materials.

Disadvantages of skill books include:

- They may be overused, and become boring to the corrective or remedial reader.
- They often provide little reading in context.
- They are sometimes seen as isolated activities that have little relevance to overall reading. The classroom teacher must make sure that the

corrective or remedial reader sees the application of such skills as relating to improving his overall reading in context materials.

GAMES

Games can be good motivational materials for corrective or remedial readers. Games may be used to teach a skill or, more often, to reinforce a previously taught skill. Brown (1985) lists tips on using games effectively:

- Use games that help meet your instructional goals.
- Match students to each other and to the game materials as well as you can.
- Encourage self-competition (have students compare their scores with their own previous scores).
- Have students correct their own mistakes as they occur.
- Analyze student responses. Identify error types and patterns and use this information for future practice.

Games can be used to help develop several skills in corrective and remedial readers. They are especially useful for students who need additional practice in sight words. By seeing the words again and again in a game situation, the corrective and remedial reader can add some of these words to her sight vocabulary.

Advantages of games include the following:

- They are highly motivating.
- They provide practice exercises in an interesting format.
- They enable the corrective and remedial reader to interact with other students in a game situation.
- They can be used in a classroom setting where there are many students reading at various reading levels.

Disadvantages of games include:

- They may place the corrective or remedial reader at an unfair disadvantage if he is not allowed to compete with those with reading abilities similar to his.
- They often do not provide words in context.

NEWSPAPERS

Cheyney (1984) points out that older unsuccessful readers are often turned off to basal readers and phonics materials. Such students are more receptive to reading newspapers because "the newspaper does not have to be read in the formal sense of reading a book in class" (p. 6). He says that students may not view newspaper reading as "reading instruction." Likewise, Beals (1983) views the newspaper as a way to "bridge the gap between the curriculum of the school and the real world in which the student lives and to which he relates" (p. 69).

The newspaper offers many ways to promote reading skills. For one, it is an excellent way to develop the vocabulary of the corrective or remedial reader. Cheyney (1984) cautions, however, that two standards must be kept in mind when using the newspaper for vocabulary activities:

> First, the activity must be high interest and low learning difficulty. If students are not intrigued by the activity or if they find it extremely difficult, they probably will not benefit appreciably. The activity should be so constituted as to give the students opportunities for meaningful practice so that carryover into the day-to-day language patterns is assured. Second, the activity must not present too many new words at one time.

Cheyney (1984) urges teachers to read the newspaper daily to remedial and corrective readers. According to him, this accomplishes several purposes:

- The student can learn that interesting material is to be found in the newspaper.
- The student can see the newspaper as a source of information about current events relevant to her daily life.
- The student can have a model of daily newspaper reading.
- The student may be motivated to seek out the newspaper for his own reading.
- The student can hear the language of written words.
- The student's concepts and vocabulary can be increased through indirect experiences written about in the newspaper.

Beals (1983) has cited advantages of the newspaper for corrective and remedial readers:

- Newspapers can be adapted to individual needs.
- They appeal to varied interests of students.
- The reading material is of proper maturity level.
- They are inexpensive.
- They are easily obtainable.

Disadvantages of the newspaper include:

- Their readability level is often higher than the corrective reader can manage for independent reading.

- They do not have the controlled vocabulary that the corrective or remedial reader may need.

OTHER MATERIALS

Although not included in Appendix E, several other types of materials may be used by the classroom teacher in working with students who have reading problems. Such materials include books with movable parts, wordless picture books, survival learning materials, dialogue journals, and comic books.

Books with movable parts. McGee and Charlesworth (1984) recommend books with movable parts for children who have experienced repeated failure in learning to read. They describe these books as follows (p. 853):

> Popularly known as pop-up books, peek-a-books, surprise books, puppet books, activity books, and revolving picture books, movable books are distinguished by text or illustrations that the reader can move. When the reader opens specially constructed pages, rotates disks, pulls tabs, raises lift-up flaps, turns wheels, or looks through a special magnifying glass, scenes spring off the page, characters perform actions, objects disappear, or hidden pictures and text appear.

McGee and Charlesworth find several advantages in movable books:

- They are highly motivating.
- Children deal with books in an interactive manner.
- Dialogue can be encouraged as readers manipulate movables, thus facilitating oral language.
- The books can stimulate the interactions of reading, writing, and art.
- The unique aspects of the books can be used as a stimulus to discuss books in greater detail.
- The movable parts may encourage interest in books in general.

Wordless picture books. Wordless picture books are often recommended for corrective or remedial readers. Some students who have become fearful of the printed word may be more comfortable with such books. Ellis and Preston (1984) summarize advantages of wordless picture books:

- The books can be used to enhance the reading and writing process. Children may be encouraged to provide a written label or description about the pictures.
- Children can learn how to handle books.
- Children can expand their oral language skills, if the teacher uses the materials in the proper way.

- Children can have successful, nonthreatening reading experiences.
- Children can learn to draw inferences.
- Children can learn to evaluate a character's actions.
- Children can increase their oral vocabulary.

Ellis and Preston discuss a cross-age tutoring program, in which fifth graders worked with first graders using wordless picture books. The fifth graders were instructed to use strategies such as: "sequencing, prediction, vocabulary development, determining cause and effect, expanding sentences, repetition of patterns, determining main idea, making judgments, and retelling the story" (p. 696).

Survival learning materials. Wilson and Barnes (1974, p. 1) define survival reading materials as "those materials related to the needs of an adult society which expects everyone to read certain labels, directions, signs, etc." They point out that teachers and parents often feel that children should "be prepared for the demands that will be imposed upon them by the real world as well as the academic world."

Examples of such survival materials include:

toothpaste labels
frozen food labels
do-it-yourself kits
aspirin labels
magazine subscriptions
record club materials
maps
travel brochures
fast-food menus
seed catalogues

Wilson and Barnes (1974) cite several positive points about using survival materials:

- Children are enthusiastic about using them.
- Children see the relevance of the materials.
- Children want to gain the skills needed to read these materials.

Dialogue journals. Gambrell (1985) advocates the use of a dialogue journal, a basic notebook in which the student writes anything he wants to share with the teacher. The teacher then reads the student's journal and responds in writing.

Gambrell provides several guidelines for using dialogue journals:

- The focus should be on communication. Therefore, the teacher should not correct children's entries. The teacher's modeling of correct spelling is used to teach the child correct spelling.
- Teachers must structure their writing to elicit more writing from the student. Such phrases as: "Tell me more about . . ."; "Describe . . ."; or "I'd like to know more about . . ." may be used by the teacher to elicit more details from the student about certain events or people.
- Dialogue journals should be held in confidence. Teachers should share comments from the journal only if the child gives permission.

Comic books. Koenke (1981) believes that comic books should be on the "useful list" of reading materials. He does not recommend them as the whole reading program, but rather as a "first step for children who do not like to read or have a fear of failure" (p. 592). He cautions teachers to examine their readability levels, which have been shown to vary from one comic book to another. Teachers should choose the content carefully, using students' interests as guides.

Koenke summarizes his discussion of comic books by stating: "Obviously, comic books are not recommended because they are great literature." However, he emphasizes that a creative teacher can use them occasionally as effective instructional materials.

USING SPECIAL MATERIALS

The list of materials presented in this section is certainly not complete; many others could be used effectively with corrective and remedial readers. The teacher should first consider the general criteria for materials as she tests the appropriateness of a particular material. After using a variety of materials, she can assess which ones seem to be of most interest and benefit to students.

INFORMATION TO CONSIDER

1. Teachers may select from a wide variety of reading materials for corrective and remedial readers.
2. Reading materials other than traditional, textbook-type readers are often less threatening and more appealing to corrective and remedial readers.
3. Teachers should try a variety of materials with corrective and remedial readers to determine those which seem to be of most interest to students.

Organizing Materials for Reading

One of the most difficult jobs of a teacher is to select appropriate materials for each corrective and remedial reader in his class. A great amount of assessment and planning time is required to establish and give consideration to each student's interests, purposes, and reading level.

There are times when a student's interests and skill needs are so specific that only individualized instruction is possible. In this case, the teacher will usually work individually with the student, although a volunteer tutor may also work with the student on a one-to-one basis. Sometimes the student may read independently, without the assistance of either the teacher or the tutor.

There are times, however, when the classroom teacher may want to instruct corrective and remedial readers in pairs or small groups, perhaps because certain materials lend themselves well to group use. Parents or siblings may also serve as a type of grouping for students. Either or both parents and one or more siblings may engage in reading activities with the corrective or remedial reader. Some of the materials discussed earlier in this chapter are especially appropriate for use by the student in the home environment.

The following section addresses the groupings mentioned above. For each grouping, materials mentioned earlier are suggested where they are especially appropriate for the specified grouping. Teachers may want to consider using a variety of groupings; as each new type of material is planned for the student, the teacher should consider which type of grouping will make the material most effective.

INDEPENDENT READING

At times, students should read independently, using materials chosen for their specific interest to a particular child. Such materials must be on the appropriate reading level of the child, easy enough to handle and promoting fluent reading. Several materials may be used for independent reading. Computer programs, either tutorial or dialogue type, lend themselves to independent reading. The child can interact directly with the computer, exchanging information and moving from step to step as directions are provided.

Talking or taped books are also an excellent source for independent reading. The talking book provides oral reading, which might otherwise be done by the teacher or parent. Since the teacher does not have adequate time to read orally to individual students, the talking book provides a way for a student to hear a book she especially wants to hear. The taped book serves a similar purpose, with the added advantage that the student can read along with the tape. In this way, a child may enjoy a favorite book over and over again, even though other children in the class may not share her great interest in that particular book.

TEACHER OR TUTOR WORKING WITH STUDENT

The teacher may at times listen to an individual child read a passage from a book, suggesting that the child choose her favorite passage or the most exciting part to read aloud. High interest/low vocabulary books are well suited for this situation. They are often on a fairly consistent readability level, which makes it easier for the child to practice the part she will read to the teacher. A tutor may listen to the child read the passage; in fact, often the tutor has more time to listen to the child read orally than does the busy classroom teacher.

Dialogue journals are a perfect material for the teacher or tutor to use on a one-to-one basis with the corrective or remedial reader. They can be the means of a very private exchange between the two. The student can share information and ideas with the teacher or tutor in written form, which there is often little time to do verbally.

PAIRING

Pairing as used here refers to an exchange between two students in a classroom. Wordless picture books are excellent materials for use with a pair of students. One student may use a wordless picture book to "read" a story to a partner; in turn, the partner can "read" another book to the other child. This provides an excellent opportunity for students to use a great amount of language and creativity. Since there are only two students to share the time, each one gets to "perform" a lot.

Games may also be used effectively with a pair of students. Once the students understand the rules of a particular game, they can function without the aid of the teacher or tutor. Either the students should know the words in a game, or the teacher should establish a system whereby they can ask for assistance from others.

SMALL GROUP

Several students together may benefit from the use of certain materials. For example, the newspaper may be read by the teacher to a small or large group of students. Discussion among students may lead to improved concepts. Interests in shared topics of current interest in the community or city may promote discussion among students and inspire extended reading.

A small group of students may also use common high interest/low vocabulary books for a reading session or a directed reading lesson.

Survival materials provide another possibility for reading in a small group. The reading level of such materials may be uneven or too high, but the teacher is available for assistance. Each student may bring a survival material in which he is particularly interested to share with the others in the small group, reading a portion of the material to the group.

PARENTS OR SIBLINGS

Certain materials, such as books with movable parts, may be best used in the home by parents or siblings. Teachers must be alert to informing parents of corrective and remedial readers about such materials. Using such materials before bedtime provides an excellent end to the day. In general, they can be a pleasant way to establishing reading and books as part of the home activity.

Magazines may be an appropriate source of reading material in the home. A gift subscription of a child's magazine may be a perfect birthday present for a child, especially if it has stories on topics of particular interest to him. The magazine can serve as his very own reading material, although parents and siblings may at times read portions of the magazine to or with the child. Such magazines often have other activities aside from reading that will be of interest to the child.

Comic books may also be used in the home (although parents must be encouraged to have other reading materials in the home in addition). Teachers can help parents in selecting those of most interest to the child. Parents and siblings may encourage the corrective or remedial reader to read portions of the comic book to them, so as to avoid the tendency for the child to rely only on the pictures.

INFORMATION TO CONSIDER

1. Various reading materials may lend themselves to certain types of groupings.

2. The classroom teacher should consider grouping corrective and remedial readers for portions of their reading instruction.
3. The classroom teacher should use a variety of groupings and materials for instruction.

Working with Parents

QUESTIONS TO GUIDE READING

Recall Questions
1. What recommendations can teachers make to parents of corrective or remedial readers about reading materials?
2. How may the classroom teacher educate parents about reading materials for their children?

Thinking Questions
1. Why do some parents have environments without reading materials?
2. Can a teacher have any influence on parents' beliefs and values concerning reading materials in the home?

Teachers of corrective and remedial readers can provide guidance for parents of corrective and remedial readers in selecting materials for their children, including the following suggestions:

1. Choose materials on topics that interest your child. Is he curious about the types of dinosaurs that lived during certain periods, or about how bird nests are made? Help him find stories or books about these topics. He may only look at the pictures or read the captions in these books, or he may ask you to read the book to him. Don't pressure him to read unless he chooses to do so.
2. Discover what goals your child wants to accomplish. Does she want to become a good tap dancer or chess player? Help her find materials that will help her reach her goals.
3. Select materials that can be used in a variety of places, and keep a record of when and where your child has spare time that he could spend reading. Does he wait for a friend to walk to school? Does he wait while you shop for groceries? Does he wait for a piano lesson to begin? If you, as a parent, can select materials which can be easily transported to these places, your child will be more likely to read. No *one* type of reading material is the answer to all of your child's reading needs; the important thing is to select materials that are easily accessible to your child when he has time available for reading.

4. Choose materials your child enjoys. Don't force him to read materials he says he doesn't like. The materials should not be "baby books," even if his reading level is very low.

5. Choose materials your child *can* read. When reading is a struggle to figure out too many words, your child may not view it as a pleasurable act. A quick way to determine whether material is too difficult is to have your child read a selection of about fifty words. She should be able to identify approximately 90 to 95 percent of the words correctly, that is, missing only about two to five words in the passage.

6. Select reading materials that serve a purpose for reading for your child, rather than for you. You will need to assess how your child feels about certain materials. If she is reading them only to satisfy you or a teacher, her enthusiasm may not be genuine.

7. Select materials that can be read during a regular family reading time. The habit of family reading is certainly to be encouraged. Your child's participation can be developed through a routine of weekly or monthly library visits so that he will have materials available for family reading time.

8. Let your child's teacher concentrate on skill development in reading. As a parent, you should concentrate on helping your child select materials that are enjoyable. Don't spend family reading time working with word cards or workbook pages; instead, use materials that contain interesting stories. If your child constantly works on reading skills through drill and word card activities, he may miss the point that reading is a language and meaning encounter. Parents should concentrate on the "magic" found in good stories and literature for their child.

Teachers must not leave it to chance that parents will follow the guidelines outlined above in selecting materials for their children. Teachers must become involved actively in educating parents. This may be done in several ways:

1. Teachers can provide workshops for parents on book selection. The teacher can demonstrate how to read a book to a child, how to select a book on the appropriate topic and reading level for the child, and how to set aside a family reading time. Parents may be intrigued by such topics as:
   - "Knowing How Much Television Your Child Should Watch"
   - "Helping Your Child Be a Better Reader"
   - "Family Reading Habits Can Be Formed"
   Workshops can be scheduled after school or during an open house visitation night.

2. Since some parents will not or cannot come to workshops held at school, teachers also may want to devise ways to disseminate information through printed materials sent to the home. Brief descriptions of the topics outlined above can be duplicated for distribution to parents.

3. Many parents are interested in receiving book lists, especially on specific topics. Seasonal lists, revolving around Halloween, Christmas, and other holidays, may serve as a focus for getting information to parents about designated books. Teachers should be careful to recommend books that can be found in local book stores or can be ordered through book clubs. The teacher must also consider the readability of the various books she recommends for corrective or remedial readers.
4. Parent conferences are another means of providing parents with information on selecting reading materials for their children. All of the suggestions made in this section can be shared with parents in a parent-teacher conference.

The teacher's role should be an active one, initiating parent training and providing parents with information about reading materials.

INFORMATION TO CONSIDER

1. The classroom teacher can make certain recommendations to parents of corrective and remedial readers about reading materials for their child.
2. The classroom teacher should play an active role in suggesting materials for corrective and remedial readers to their parents.

Summary

Materials are an important consideration in the reading program of the corrective and remedial reader. The classroom teacher should be familiar with a variety of materials so that she may select the most appropriate one for each student. Various criteria for selecting materials can help the teacher as she approaches the day-to-day task of guiding students in their selection of materials. Certain criteria are especially important for the student who is experiencing difficulty in reading. Various types of materials may be threatening or unappealing to the problem reader. The selection of alternative materials may set the stage for a more relaxed involvement with the reading task.

The classroom teacher must consider both the type of material and the type of grouping to use with it. Certain materials may lend themselves to particular types of groupings.

Parents should be encouraged to select materials for their corrective or remedial reader, with the assistance of the classroom teacher.

Questions for Further Thought

1. How can the classroom teacher with a limited budget acquire some of the special materials described in this chapter?
2. How can the teacher handle the situation of a child who has no reading materials in the home?
3. When would it be appropriate to refuse to let a student read a comic book or look at a wordless book during free time?
4. Is the use of computer materials for reading being promoted too much?

Activities and Projects

1. For a particular student, use the criteria given in this chapter to select reading materials for a one-week period.
2. Select a wordless picture book, a book with movable parts, and a children's magazine to share with others.
3. Check the readability of several comic books.
4. Review several tutorial computer programs.
5. Develop a list of essential reading materials you feel should be available in every home.
6. Develop an extended list of materials that may be used with corrective or remedial readers.

13

Putting It All Together: The Instructional Program in Classrooms for the Corrective or Remedial Reader

The preceding twelve chapters should serve as a knowledge base for the classroom teacher of children who have reading problems. Information has been presented about types of reading problems, possible contributing causes, assessment procedures, and corrective strategies. This chapter will focus on how the classroom teacher can put all this information together in the instructional program of a given corrective or remedial reader in her classroom. For the corrective reader, she will play a primary role in planning, implementing, and evaluating instruction as the corrective reader usually stays in the classroom and the classroom teacher is responsible for all instruction. For the remedial reader, the classroom teacher will need to monitor and provide input into the student's overall program, because this student may receive supplementary instruction from reading specialists, clinicians, tutors, and others.

This chapter focuses on three questions:

1. How does the classroom teacher identify a student who has a reading problem?
2. How does the classroom teacher shape the instructional program of the corrective reader?
3. How does the classroom teacher help shape the instructional program of the remedial reader?

The identification of a problem reader is the classroom teacher's first task. Certain techniques and step-by-step methods are presented in this chapter for determining whether or not a student should be considered a corrective or remedial reader.

With the corrective reader, the classroom teacher is usually responsible for the total instructional program: planning, implementing, and evaluating. This chapter presents guidelines for the classroom teacher to use in determining what instruction is needed, what plans are to be made, and how records may be organized.

Suggestions are also presented in this chapter about planning a program for the remedial reader. The classroom teacher should consider several factors: who will be involved in the planning, what information will be considered, and what type of plan will result. The classroom teacher recognizes that others will be involved in the remedial reader's instruction; she may want to set up a system to monitor the reader's overall program.

The final section of this chapter addresses the skills the classroom teacher needs in communicating with parents and others who work with corrective and remedial readers.

Identifying Problem Readers

QUESTIONS TO GUIDE READING

Informational Questions
1. What are four ways to identify problem readers?
2. What are the limitations of expectancy formulas?
3. What steps should a teacher follow to determine problem readers?

Thinking Questions
1. What other indicators could be used by the teacher in determining reading potential?
2. How would you decide whether or not to use an expectancy formula?
3. Which formula would you use? In what circumstances?

To identify problem readers, the classroom teacher may use four methods or techniques: (1) examining past history, (2) observation, (3) assessing listening comprehension, and (4) reading expectancy formulas. No single method or technique has sufficient validity to be used alone; the "expectancy" for a given reader should be based on as many indicators as possible.

PAST HISTORY

Past history often helps the classroom teacher identify a problem reader. Cumulative records, which contain achievement data and comments from previous teachers, may indicate that the learner has not been functioning to full potential. Records may show progressively declining achievement. Other diagnostic information may be found in school records: absenteeism, number of school transfers, grades repeated, standardized performance in reading compared to performance in math, and health problems. Former teachers may also have expressed opinions that the student was not reading at an appropriate level. Of course, teacher judgment may be biased, so statements from previous teachers should be used as only one indicator that a student may have a problem.

OBSERVATION

The classroom teacher can use observation as a valuable tool in assessing whether a reading problem exists, especially if the observation is structured and patterns of behavior are noted over time. Areas of observation must be well defined. The behaviors manifested by the student should be below the expected performance level given the student's prior instruction and perceived abilities. Suggestions for behaviors that should be observed can be drawn from the material in Chapter 5 and Chapters 7–12.

Observations done over a period of time have the advantage of greater representativeness over data from a single test. Observation, however, is only as good as the skill of the teacher in identifying and assessing valid behaviors.

LISTENING COMPREHENSION

When a student's listening comprehension is superior to his silent or oral reading comprehension on materials at a given level, a reading problem may exist. Such a comparison can be made in informal and formal ways. One informal way is through the use of an IRI (see Ch. 5), in which listening levels and instructional levels are compared on graded materials. Alternatively, the teacher may use a more formal commercially available test with a section designed to assess listening comprehension (see Ch. 14). When a student's listening comprehension is superior to his silent or oral reading comprehension, it is an indication that if the student could read the words, he could understand them at that level.

However, listening level should not be the only criterion, as the listening score may be affected by other factors such as language competence (concepts, syntax, word meanings) and the child's disposition to listen attentively. Some students may not have had as much opportunity to develop language fluency as others. As with other indicators, listening comprehension should not be used as the only indicator of reading problems.

EXPECTANCY FORMULAS

The classroom teacher should be aware of reading expectancy formulas as determinants of possible reading problems. The use of expectancy formulas for predicting reading potential has been frequently cited in the literature. However, at best, the formulas are estimates. Many of them are developed from normal population (Lavine and Putnam 1976) and are simplistically based on mental or chronological age, failing to take into account such influences as opportunity to learn and language fluency.

The use of an IQ score in these formulas also raises several concerns. One such concern is that bright children who have not had adequate educational experiences may not read at a level commensurate with their mental age. A second concern is that IQ tests may be culturally oriented to certain groups of children, and may yield a score for other groups that is lower than the true level of their mental functioning. Another concern is with the level of reading achievement needed to take a group test of mental ability involving reading. Neville (1965) concluded that a 4.0 reading achievement level was a critical minimum for obtaining a valid score on a group verbal intelligence test. Some reading educators prefer to use a performance IQ test rather than a verbal test, as these tests do not require reading per se. However, there is some question as to whether these tests are measuring the same kinds of abilities as are needed for verbal tasks.

The classroom teacher should try to approximate the student's reading expectancy, using reading expectancy formulas if desired to confirm or challenge that approximation. When there is general agreement with other indicators, the teacher may feel more confident about her own analysis of the student's reading problems. The *Bond and Tinker Expectancy Formula*, a widely used formula that is relatively simple for the classroom teacher to use, is presented below:

$$(IQ/100 \times \text{years of reading instruction}) + 1.0 = \text{R.E.}$$

Examples using the formula follow:

Kevin, whose IQ is 130, is entering the fourth grade, and his reading achievement is 4.5. Applying the formula, we find his reading expectancy to be 4.9 [(130/100 $\times$ 3) + 1.0 = 4.9]. Thus he is achieving close to, but not quite up to, his potential.

Don is also an entering fourth grader with an IQ of 80. His expectancy is (80/100 $\times$ 3) + 1.0 = 3.4. Don scored 2.1 on the reading achievement test and is therefore 1.3 years below expectancy. He would thus be classified as having a reading problem, even though his IQ is low to begin with.

A basic assumption underlying the Bond and Tinker formula is that IQ is an index of rate of learning and that the IQ score utilized is valid. The formula tends to rate too highly a learner who is low in ability and to expect too little of the gifted student. This finding corresponds with the statement by Bond et al. (1984, pp. 42–43) that the formula is considered accurate in estimating the reading potential for typical children. They suggest bearing the following considerations in mind:

1. The time of reading instruction should be the years and months in school beginning from the time systematic reading instruction was started. This typically begins with first grade, but some slow-learning children may have a delay of a year or so in starting to learn to read.
2. Readiness training in kindergarten is not counted, even though such instruction does much to diminish the chances of problems occurring once reading instruction has started.
3. If an IQ obtained from a Binet or Wechsler Intelligence test is not available, it is suggested that a Slosson Intelligence Test given by the teacher or a group performance intelligence test score be substituted temporarily.

According to Rodenborn (1974), the Bond and Tinker formula ignores the effects of high or low intelligence during the years before the child begins school and considers that all readers begin with an expectancy of 1.0. He also states that the Bond and Tinker formula ensures that more children of lower IQ levels and fewer high IQ level children will be included in classes for problem readers. For the low IQ student, he feels this is justified, since many poor readers do poorly on many intelligence tests.

DETERMINING POTENTIAL

In summary, the classroom teacher should use measures of reading potential cautiously and only in conjunction with other indicators. He might consider the following steps when evaluating the reader who has apparent reading problems:

Step 1. Consider past history. Has the learner progressed as well as could be expected based on past teacher judgment and test data? Are physical handicaps noted? Is the student motivated to read? Is he on medication?

Step 2. Consider listening comprehension. Administer an IRI (Informal Reading Inventory) or a comparable test (see Chapters 5 and 14). Was there a wide discrepancy between listening comprehension and reading level? Are data available from some other test that assessed listening level?

Step 3. Use a simple expectancy formula. Are the findings consistent with past histories and listening levels?

Step 4. Make observations over time. Is the student's reading behavior below performance in other areas? Is the student verbally mature yet has a reading problem? What are his current motivational levels? Are there continuing physical handicaps?

The classroom teacher should review the definitions of corrective and remedial readers given in Chapter 1. If the student is determined a corrective reader, the classroom teacher alone will usually plan appropriate classroom activities, implement those plans, and evaluate the student's program. If it is determined that the student has reading problems severe enough for outside remediation, the classroom teacher will plan with others and then monitor the progress of the remedial reader.

Instructional Program for the Corrective Reader

At this point, the classroom teacher has observed that a particular student is experiencing difficulty in reading, and has identified him as a corrective reader. The teacher usually has several indicators of such difficulties: observations, test scores, and records of past history of reading problems. Her professional judgment leads her to believe that the student's current reading program is inadequate; he needs special attention, strategies, and planning. What steps does the classroom teacher take to arrive at an instructional plan for the student? Three steps are recommended:

1. Accumulate and examine data from several sources about the corrective reader's reading progress.
2. Develop plans for working with the corrective reader in the classroom.
3. Monitor and evaluate the corrective reader's progress.

EXAMINING SOURCES OF DATA

Numerous sources of data are available to give information about a student's current reading level, such as: criterion-based and standardized tests, IRIs, basal placement tests, basal unit tests, and school records. Details about various tests have been presented in previous chapters. All data sources should be gathered into a file and the information compiled in some organized way, perhaps using the Summary Test Data Sheet (see Fig. 13.1) to assess their consistency.

Figure 13.1. Summary Test Data Sheet for the Corrective Reader

Name _____   Date _____

Birth Date _____   Grade _____

Areas					
Readiness	Source: ____ Date: ____*	Source: ____ Date: ____	Source: ____ Date: ____	Source: ____ Date: ____	Source: ____ Date: ____
Vocabulary	Source: ____ Date: ____	Source: ____ Date: ____	Source: ____ Date: ____	Source: ____ Date: ____	Source: ____ Date: ____
Word Recognition	Source: ____ Date: ____	Source: ____ Date: ____	Source: ____ Date: ____	Source: ____ Date: ____	Source: ____ Date: ____
Comprehension	Source: ____ Date: ____	Source: ____ Date: ____	Source: ____ Date: ____	Source: ____ Date: ____	Source: ____ Date: ____
Study Skills	Source: ____ Date: ____	Source: ____ Date: ____	Source: ____ Date: ____	Source: ____ Date: ____	Source: ____ Date: ____

*This is the date the test was administered.

In Figure 13.1, the five spaces to the right of each area could be used to summarize data from formal or informal tests or observations. For example, five sources relating to *reading vocabulary* could be (1) data from an IRI, (2) an achievement test, (3) a basal reader placement test, (4) a sample of workbook pages from a basal reading series, and (5) teacher observations. The data from these multiple sources would be examined for agreement or disagreement on the status of the student's reading vocabulary.

The five sources named are only a sample; a review of previous chapters can provide the classroom teacher with further possibilities. If sufficient data are not available, the classroom teacher should make arrangements to collect more.

A second body of information (see the Summary Interview Data Sheet, Figure 13.2) could be obtained from interviewing. On the right, information may be entered from several interview sources—parents, the student, former teachers, and others—relative to each area on the left-hand side of the data sheet.

While interviewing is time-consuming, it is often the most reliable way to secure information from parents and from the students themselves. Information from interviews is extremely helpful to the classroom teacher as she plans the corrective reader's instructional program.

Interviewing allows the current teacher to find out from other teachers previously perceived problems, instructional strategies, information on affect, and what oportunities the student has had to practice or apply the skills she has learned. Parents can offer data on their own concerns and attitudes, the student's health and personal or social problems, study habits, and previous special tutoring programs. From students can be obtained information about their own perceptions of their ability, their interests and attitudes, what they think about their reading environment at home and at school, and what kinds of approaches and materials they like or dislike.

PLANNING, IMPLEMENTING, AND EVALUATING

After compiling data on the student's status in reading as shown in Figures 13.1 and 13.2, the classroom teacher must then develop an instructional plan. The type of plan may vary from teacher to teacher, but it always includes activities (implementation) and evaluation. An example is provided in this section to illustrate how a plan is developed.

A third sheet (Fig. 13.3) is recommended for the corrective reader's folder in addition to the ones modeled in Figures 13.1 and 13.2. The sheet should be kept as simple as possible; therefore, only four major categories are recommended: goals, objectives, activities, and evaluation.

The classroom teacher should decide what is the overall, most pressing need of the corrective reader. This becomes the *goal statement*. (If more

Figure 13.2. Summary Interview Data Sheet for the Corrective Reader

Area	Individuals' Comments			
Attitudes	Source: _____	Source: _____	Source: _____	Source: _____
Self-Concept	Source: _____	Source: _____	Source: _____	Source: _____
Work Habits	Source: _____	Source: _____	Source: _____	Source: _____
Interests/ Motivations	Source: _____	Source: _____	Source: _____	Source: _____
Language	Source: _____	Source: _____	Source: _____	Source: _____
Physical Characteristics (such as sight and hearing)	Source: _____	Source: _____	Source: _____	Source: _____
Emotional Characteristics	Source: _____	Source: _____	Source: _____	Source: _____
Social Environment	Source: _____	Source: _____	Source: _____	Source: _____
Approaches/ Strategies/ Materials Used Previously	Source: _____	Source: _____	Source: _____	Source: _____

than one goal is defined, two sheets may be needed.) Information from the sheets shown in Figures 13.1 and 13.2 should be used as the basis for determining the goal statement. In surveying the areas shown in Figures 13.1 and 13.2, the classroom teacher may want to direct attention first to the affective data. Does the student have a poor reading self-concept? Does he have negative attitudes toward reading? Does he lack motivation for reading? If a problem is identified under affect, then the goal statements should be focused on this area. Next, the areas of readiness, word recognition, comprehension, and study skills should be examined to determine if there is an identified need under any of these headings. A goal statement may need to be established in two or more areas.

Figure 13.3. Planning Sheet for the Corrective Reader

Name _____ Date _____

Goal _____

Objectives	*Activities*	*Evaluations*
1.	1.	1.

After specifying a goal statement, the classroom teacher should determine the objectives that will enable the corrective reader to reach the goal. Several objectives will likely be specified. Activities are then planned to promote the accomplishment of the objectives, and responsibility for accomplishing each activity is assigned. Several activities may be planned for each objective. The final step is to determine how each activity will be evaluated.

The following example illustrates the use of the planning sheet shown in Figure 13.3, focusing on the affective domain:

After examining the data collected on record sheets such as those shown in Figures 13.1 and 13.2, the classroom teacher realizes that Tom has a very serious problem relating to his reading self-concept, specifically to his perceptions of himself as a reader and of how others view his reading (see Ch. 7 for a review of these two aspects of reading self-concept).

As illustrated in Figure 13.4, the plan for Tom's instructional reading program will center on building a positive reading self-concept (goal statement). Two objectives have been set, one in each area of the reading self-concept. One sample activity is illustrated for each objective, although it is likely that more activities would be planned to accomplish each objective. It is important for the classroom teacher to link goals, objectives, activities, and evaluation.

Planning is the beginning and key element in a corrective reader's instructional reading program. Effective planning requires time and commitment from the busy classroom teacher. However, time for planning is

Figure 13.4. Sample Planning Sheet for a Corrective Reader

Name ___Tom_____   **Date** _____

Goal For Tom to have a positive reading self-concept.

Objectives	*Activities*	*Evaluations*
1. To improve Tom's perceptions of himself as a reader.	1.1 Use repeated reading technique with a favorite book on Tom's reading level.	1.1 Have Tom chart his time on the repeated reading over several days. Discuss his progress with him.
2. To improve Tom's perceptions of how others view his reading ability.	2.1 Have Tom read the favorite book practiced in 1.1 to his mother.	2.1 Ask for feedback from his mother on Tom's reading and affect. Ask Tom how his mother liked his story. How did he feel he read?

time well spent; it can help the teacher as she implements and evaluates the corrective reader's problems.

INFORMATION TO CONSIDER

1. The classroom teacher should examine several sources of data on the corrective reader's performance in reading.
2. A corrective reader's plan should address goals, objectives, activities, and evaluation.

Instructional Program for the Remedial Reader

QUESTIONS TO GUIDE READING

Recall Questions
1. What individuals may be involved in the remedial reader's instructional program?
2. How may the classroom teacher monitor activities provided by special teachers of the remedial reader?

3. What interpersonal and conferencing skills does the classroom teacher need in working with others involved in the remedial reader's program?

Thinking Questions
1. Who should provide primary leadership in the instructional program for the remedial reader?
2. How can the classroom teacher find time to monitor the activities of the remedial reader?
3. What other interpersonal and conferencing skills does the classroom teacher need?

The instructional program for the remedial reader varies from that of the corrective reader in that others are usually involved in the instruction of the student. However, for her own work with the remedial reader, the classroom teacher may want to employ the steps described for the corrective reader.

The classroom teacher must be aware of the services others may provide for the remedial reader, and know how to monitor the student's instructional program. Because she does have the remedial reader in her classroom, she will want to be aware of his progress with others.

PERSONNEL INVOLVED IN THE INSTRUCTIONAL PROGRAM

Many people may be involved in planning, implementing, and evaluating the instructional program for a remedial reader such as the special teacher of reading, Chapter I teacher, classroom aide, tutor, clinician, psychologist, school nurse, and parents. Of course, not all of these individuals will be involved in every student's instructional program. Not every school will have a reading specialist or Chapter I teacher; one school may have classroom aides, while another will not; the student's parents may have arranged to have a private tutor or to send their child to a reading clinic. The point is that each student's circle of individuals who should be involved in planning, implementing, and evaluating varies, but all who do play a role must be aware of the overall plan for the student and how each person's efforts fit into it. Some of the specialists or persons who may be a part of the remedial reader's program are described below.

Special teacher of reading. Many schools hire special teachers of reading, who usually work in one of two ways: (1) with small groups of students who are experiencing difficulties in reading, or (2) with teachers to provide special advice on working with problem readers (Bean and Wilson 1981). The classroom teacher should consult the special reading teacher. If the reading teacher provides direct services to students, the classroom teacher should assess whether her student qualifies for such instruction, usually using reading potential or expectancy scores as indicators of problems. If the reading teacher provides consultation only, he can examine the data already compiled by the classroom teacher and make recommendations either for further testing (often by the special reading teacher) or for remediation. Chapters 14 and 15 concentrate on the services provided by the special teacher of reading.

Chapter I teacher. Starting with Title I legislation in the 1960s, the federal government has provided financial resources to establish special instruction for disadvantaged students who are not achieving normally. Title I classes are now called Chapter I classes, but the intent is still the same. Because low reading achievement is correlated with low socioeconomic status, the federal government allots specified amounts of money to a school district according to the number of disadvantaged students in the system. Chapter I teachers work with small groups of students, often on reading and math. A wide range of reading materials is often available in Chapter I classrooms. By working together, the classroom teacher and the Chapter I teacher can coordinate their instruction for the student's maximum benefits.

Classroom aide. Some classrooms have paraprofessionals who work as aides. These individuals can be extremely effective in working with remedial readers in the classroom. Because the classroom teacher is responsible for the instruction of twenty or thirty students, he often lacks the time to work in a one-to-one situation with a student; the classroom aide has the flexibility to do so. The classroom teacher should involve the aide in the planning process, as she needs to be aware of the student's skills and needs. The aide should understand why the student is performing certain tasks and how they relate to the overall plan for the student.

Tutor. Some parents who are financially able to do so may employ a private tutor to work with their child. Some schools may have special programs in which adults come into the schools to tutor a child who is having problems in reading. Tutors, like classroom aides, have the special advantage of being able to work with a student on a concentrated one-to-one basis. Some tutors may have extensive knowledge in the area of reading; while others will have very limited information. The classroom teacher must be aware of the tutor's knowledge of reading and take this into consideration as plans are developed. The tutor can be of great assistance to the classroom teacher in helping the student reach her goals in reading.

Clinician. Parents may be sending their child to a private or university-associated reading clinic, which usually performs extended diagnostic procedures and offers intensive one-on-one remedial instruction. The classroom teacher can benefit from mutual planning with the clinician, especially by comparing diagnoses and remedial strategies. Each educator can be aware of the other's role in helping the student overcome reading problems. Chapters 14 and 15 focus on diagnostic and remedial services provided by reading clinics. Teachers whose students are seen in clinics should know about the procedures used there.

Psychologist. If emotional problems seem to be a part of the student's problem in reading, the classroom teacher may solicit the help of a school psychologist. In planning sessions, the psychologist can provide insight into the effects certain plans may have on the emotional state of the student. Specialized tests, which only a trained person such as a psychologist can administer, may provide considerable direction as plans are made for the student's instructional reading program.

School nurse. If health or physical issues seem to be a contributing factor to reading problems, the school nurse may be consulted. The nurse may make recommendations for timing activities to correspond to the child's peak physical levels. If inadequate nutrition or sleep patterns are affecting the student's reading performance, the nurse may provide input into group planning, especially when the teacher meets with the child's parents. The nurse may also check for vision and hearing problems.

Parents. A valuable resource would be overlooked if parents were not included in the planning process. It is difficult, if not at times impossible, to involve some parents in the planning process, as they simply will not make themselves available. However, many parents are interested in doing all they can to help their child overcome his problems in reading. The classroom teacher should involve parents in the child's instructional program if at all possible. Parents have a special understanding of their child, which can help the classroom teacher and others.

How plans are made for the remedial reader may vary from one school to another. A group planning process may be employed, or a simple one-to-one informal planning system may develop. Whatever method is used, it is important that communication between individuals be maintained.

AWARENESS OF SCHEDULE

The classroom teacher should be familiar with a remedial reader's instructional program. She should be aware of what various instructional activities have been specified, where and when they are to take place, and who is responsible for each one. The classroom teacher may construct a schedule of the remedial reader's instructional program, to be placed in the student's folder. Figure 13.5 shows how such a schedule might look for a remedial student named Susan.

As shown in the illustration, plans have been made for Susan to work

Figure 13.5. Weekly Schedule for a Remedial Reader

Name___Susan_____   Date _____

Day	Time	Teacher/Resource Person	Location
Monday	10:00–10:30 A.M.	Classroom Aide	Classroom
Tuesday	9:00–10:00 A.M.	Special Reading Teacher	Reading Center
Wednesday	10:00–10:30 A.M. 7:00–7:30 P.M.	Classroom Aide Father	Classroom Home
Thursday	9:00–10:00 A.M.	Special Reading Teacher	Reading Center
Friday	10:00–10:30 A.M.	Classroom Aide	Classroom

with three persons. On Monday, Wednesday, and Friday, Susan meets with a classroom aide; on Tuesday and Thursday she goes to a special reading teacher; and once a week Susan's father is to listen to her read.

Such a schedule may extend over several weeks, and at times others may be involved in Susan's program. The classroom teacher can monitor the activities as the classroom aide, the special reading teacher, and the father work with Susan.

INTERPERSONAL SKILLS

Needless to say, one of the primary problems involved in remedial reading programs is the potential for disagreements and confrontations between those involved in delivery of a program about what is best for the student and how to achieve it.

Bean and Wilson (1981) provide six interpersonal characteristics needed by reading specialists. These characteristics can be equally important for the classroom teacher as he works with all those involved in a student's program:

1. *Acceptance*—the ability to work with many people with divergent views.
2. *Realness* or *genuineness*—a true concern for students and other professionals and an honesty in working relationships so that something is not promised that cannot be delivered.
3. *Sensitivity*—awareness of the feelings and beliefs of the various individuals with whom they work.
4. *Empathy*—the ability to "feel with" those with whom they work when these individuals are facing a difficult situation.
5. *Assertion*—the willingness to assume responsibility and to volunteer for opportunities to make improvements in the reading program.
6. *Initiative*—the ability to sense an opportunity and follow through on it.

These six characteristics indicate that the classroom teacher must have an overall awareness of what is happening in a student's reading program: who is having problems, what these problems are, what solutions are possible, and how the various individuals are reacting to these situations.

CONFERENCING SKILLS

In conferring with parents, classroom teachers can be guided by the same characteristics outlined above by Bean and Wilson (1981) for special teachers of reading:

- Be accepting of the views of parents, even though they may vary from yours.
- Have a genuine concern for what is best for the student and what progress he can realistically be expected to make.
- Be sensitive to parents' feelings about their child.
- Be able to "feel with" parents regarding their efforts to adjust to a child with a reading problem.
- Assume responsibility for giving suggestions to parents on ways they may help their child.
- Have the initiative to contact parents, and gain insights from them about ways they can assist in their child's reading program.

INFORMATION TO CONSIDER

1. Several individuals may be involved in the remedial reader's program.
2. The classroom teacher may use a scheduling form to monitor where and with whom the remedial student is working.
3. The classroom teacher needs certain interpersonal and conferencing skills to work with others.

Summary

In this chapter, suggestions have been made concerning how the classroom teacher uses the information presented in the first twelve chapters in an instructional program for the corrective or remedial reader. In "putting it all together," the classroom teacher must be knowledgeable about types of reading problems, possible contributing causes, assessment procedures, and corrective strategies.

Four ways to determine if a student has a problem in reading were presented: past history, observation, listening comprehension, and reading expectancy formulas. No single indicator of a problem should be used on its own; multiple indicators are recommended. A decision must be made about whether the student can be instructed in the classroom (corrective) or whether outside assistance (remedial) must be secured if it is available.

If the teacher decides that the student is a corrective reader whose problems can be handled in the classroom, she must plan, implement, and evaluate his progress in the instructional program. An organized record system may benefit the teacher in working with the corrective reader.

For the student who is considered a remedial reader, assistance is arranged outside the classroom for specialized services. Several individuals may be involved in the remedial reader's instructional program: a special teacher of reading, Chapter I teacher, classroom aide, tutor, clinician, psychologist, school nurse, and parents. The classroom teacher should be aware of the schedule of the remedial reader and who is providing services. She should be involved in planning and monitoring the student's progress. The classroom teacher needs special interpersonal skills in working with others and conferencing skills to report to parents about the remedial reader's progress.

Questions for Further Thought

1. What can a classroom teacher do to make more resource personnel available for a student's reading program?
2. What strategies can a classroom teacher use if agreement cannot be reached by the various resource people about priorities for a student's reading program?
3. How can a classroom teacher improve his interpersonal skills?
4. Should parents meet only with the classroom teacher in a conference or should they meet with all resource people? Why or why not?
5. How can a classroom teacher best convey the needs of the student to the student's next teacher?

Activities and Projects

1. Select one student from a classroom and use the various forms recommended in this chapter to plan a reading program for that student.
2. Critique the various forms recommended in the chapter.
3. Use the reading expectancy formula mentioned in this chapter with several students. Discuss the results.
4. Talk to a sample of classroom teachers about their views on effective characteristics needed by classroom teachers as they work with parents and other resource people.

IV
Extended Diagnosis and Remediation

Some students have reading problems so severe that they need specialized individual assistance that the classroom teacher does not have the time or expertise to provide. Such students are often referred outside the classroom for help, either to a special teacher of reading or to a private or university reading clinic.

When students are referred to outside help, teachers should be aware of the diagnostic and remediation procedures used and of how information about these procedures is reported back to them and to parents. This section of the book provides information on developing such awareness.

Chapter 14 addresses extended remediation, that done outside the classroom by a specialist. Information is provided on widely used mental ability tests and reading ability tests, and also on physical, emotional, and language assessments.

Chapter 15 presents information on methods, programs, and materials that may be used in extended remediation. This knowledge is important to the classroom teacher so that she may reinforce the outside instruction. Many of the methods, programs, and materials may be familiar to classroom teachers; others may not. At times, similar strategies are used in both classroom and extended settings.

This part also includes information on how to evaluate a diagnostic report and progress report, examples of which are given in Appendix B.

14
Extended Diagnosis

Assessment in classrooms generally focuses on the determination of reading levels, skill attainment, and affect. However, some children have problems severe enough to merit a more extensive evaluation, which may be beyond the classroom teacher's resources of time or expertise. For children with major problems, an evaluation may need to be done outside the classroom setting, either by a special teacher of reading within the school system or by a reading clinician in a private or university-based clinic. In this chapter we shall refer to such evaluation as *extended diagnosis*.

A basic goal of extended diagnosis is to obtain information on the strengths and weaknesses of children in order that they may be helped to read better. Attention is also given to the reasons that children may not be reading as well as they should. Children in need of extended diagnosis are classified as remedial readers.

Extended diagnosis has several characteristics:

1. Diagnosis is generally more individualized, involving personal interviews and tests of the student's mental functioning and reading skill, given on a one-to-one basis.
2. Diagnosis is intensive; that is, the evaluation procedures are concentrated in a short period of time.
3. Diagnosis is generally done by a professional with special training, such as a reading specialist or a clinician.
4. Diagnosis enables the teacher to obtain detailed, specific information about a student's reading ability.
5. Diagnosis in a special setting extends the information available from classroom assessment; it may be based in part on information supplied by teachers and parents.
6. Diagnosis may cover a variety of areas that affect skill in reading—affective, cognitive, language, cultural, physical, and educational.
7. Diagnosis is often done in a setting different from the classroom, and thus may generate types of responses not always found in the classroom. Factors specific to the classroom that may bear on the reading problem are not assessed.

8. Diagnosis facilitates the formation of hypotheses about reading problems and their causes. The validity of these hypotheses should be verified over time in the classroom setting.
9. Diagnosis may involve a number of professionals other than reading specialists, including school psychologists, speech and hearing clinicians, and other health care professionals.

Chapter 13 discussed reasons and procedures for referring children for extended diagnosis. The specialist performing the extended diagnosis generally prepares an extensive written report for parents or the classroom teacher.

The purpose of this chapter is to provide classroom teachers with information on extended diagnosis, the reports provided for teachers, and some of the tests, procedures, and report formats that may accompany extended diagnoses. No attempt is made to provide all the information a reading educator would need to do an extended diagnosis herself, nor is there room here to cover all the varied tests and procedures that may be done in an extended diagnostic setting. The information included is based on studies by the International Reading Associaton and the College Reading Association. These organizations of reading educators have a strong interest in clinical reading and have provided information on the tests and procedures most often found in reading clinics. At the outset, it should be noted that many of the tests and procedures presented in Chapters 5 and 6 and in the skill development chapters are also appropriate in extended diagnosis.

Gathering Preliminary Data

QUESTIONS TO GUIDE READING

Recall Question
1. What kinds of preliminary data are appropriate to consider in extended diagnosis?

Thinking Question
1. How could other sources of data not mentioned in this section be appropriately used in extended diagnosis?

Referral reports that classroom teachers send to special teachers of reading and to clinicians often include data that are important in extended diagnosis, such as general school records, history of reading performance, results of reading achievement and school ability tests, health information, interest records, records of physical disabilities, and reports from other agencies such as psychological clinics and speech and hearing clinics. Some of the data may be provided by parents.

When the kinds of data mentioned above are not available, the professionals doing the extended diagnosis may need to gather the information themselves, often through conferences with parents or teachers. When personal conferences are not possible, information sheets may be sent to the school or to the parents. Two sample forms are shown in Figure 14.1, a school referral form appropriate for a university reading center, and Figure 14.2, a parent information form used by a university reading clinic.

INFORMATION TO CONSIDER

1. Information valuable in the extended diagnostic process can be obtained from the child's school and from his or her parents.

Figure 14.1. School Referral Information

Child's Name _____ Date of Birth _____

School _____ Grade _____

School's Address _____

Principal _____ Teacher _____

Reason for Referral _____

_____

Most Recent Reading Achievement Test _____

  Date Administered _____ Test Score _____

Informal Reading Inventory Scores:

Potential Level _____ Independent Level _____ Instructional Level _____

  Frustration Level _____

Basal Reader Placement Test Scores _____

Basic Skills Test Scores _____

Has the child ever been referred for a psychological evaluation? _____

  When? _____ Where? _____

  Why? _____

continued

Figure 14.1. *(continued)*

Does the child attend a special reading program at school? _____

   For how long has he/she attended? _____

Does the child attend a Resource Room? _____

Has the child been tutored privately? _____

   When? _____ By whom? _____

Student Characteristics:

   The following is a list of characteristics which we can often observe in youngsters *if we have the opportunity for observation.* Please circle those which you think fit the child.

Classroom behavior: quiet   normal interaction   talkative

Attitude toward reading: very positive   somewhat positive
   somewhat negative   very negative

Educational interest span: very good   good   poor   very poor

Finishes required work: always   usually   once in a while   never

Popular with pals: always   usually   once in a while   never   don't know

Are there any other behaviors which affect classroom learning? _____

   If so, please explain: _____

_____

Which subject does student appear to like best? _____

In which subject is achievement the highest? _____

Which subject does student appear to like least? _____

In which subject is achievement the lowest? _____

What are the child's favorite hobbies and interests? _____

_____

What strategies have you found to be most effective in guiding this child?

_____

Least effective? _____

What appear to be the child's greatest strengths in reading? _____

_____

What appear to be the child's specific weaknesses in his reading achievement?

_____

Figure 14.1. *(continued)*

What reading book(s), materials, instructional methods are being used with the child to help alleviate this problem?

Basal: _____

Other instructional materials: _____

_____

Instructional methods: _____

_____

How is the student grouped for reading? _____

_____

Reading Behaviors: Please check any behaviors listed below which apply to the child:

Silent Reading Behaviors

_____ moves lips, whispers

_____ is comfortable, relaxed

_____ attentive (stays on task)

_____ reads at an appropriate pace

Oral Reading Behaviors

_____ word caller

_____ uses appropriate phrasing

_____ uses phonics skills effectively

_____ knows sight words appropriate to level

_____ comfortable, relaxed

Comprehension

_____ uses context clues effectively

_____ discusses material read

_____ makes appropriate inferences

_____ makes judgments about reading material

_____ relates reading material to personal experiences

Developed by Barbara Cary, Mary J. R. Herzog, Linda Irwin, and Debbie St. Clair-Wolf of the University of Tennessee Reading Center. Reprinted with permission.

Figure 14.2. University of Tennessee Reading Center

Confidential

Date this form filled out _____

Background Information

Student's Name: _____ Sex _____ Date of Birth _____

Address: _____ Telephone: (home) _____

_____ ZIP Code _____ Telephone: (work) _____

Father's Name _____ Occupation _____

  If working, hours on job (e.g., 9–5; 12–8) _____

Mother's Name _____ Occupation _____

  If working, hours on job (e.g., 9–5; 12–8) _____

Other children in family:

Name	Age	Living at home	If not, occupation
_____	_____	_____	_____
_____	_____	_____	_____
_____	_____	_____	_____
_____	_____	_____	_____

Last grade level father completed _____

Last grade level mother completed _____

Parents' marital status: Married _____ Separated _____ Divorced _____

  If divorced, age of child when this occurred _____

  Age of child when a new parent was introduced into home _____

Parents deceased: Father _____ Mother _____ Age of child at this time _____

Is this child adopted? _____ If so, does he/she know this? _____

What language is spoken in the home? _____

List everyone other than children who lives in the home.

Name	Age	Relationship
_____	_____	_____
_____	_____	_____
_____	_____	_____

List magazines in the home (e.g., *Time, Redbook,* etc.) _____

Figure 14.2. *(continued)*

How many hours per day does the child watch TV? _____

Does the child have a library card? _____

How much time does the child spend reading for pleasure? _____

Developmental and Medical History

Birth weight of child _____

Term of pregnancy _____

Was the child in an incubator? _____ How long? _____

At what age did the following occur:

   Single words _____ Simple sentences _____

Does your child have a speech defect? _____

   If so, has any attempt been made to correct it? _____

   Has anyone ever attempted to change the child's handedness? _____

Has your child had any serious accidents, operations, or unusual illnesses? _____

Illness	Hospitalized?	Age of child at time
_____	_____	_____
_____	_____	_____
_____	_____	_____

Does your child have any physical problems at this time? _____

_____

_____

Have you noticed any difficulty with your child's vision? _____

   If so, explain: _____

Have you noticed any difficulty with your child's hearing? _____

   If so, explain: _____

Does your child have any allergies? _____

Is he/she undergoing treatment for an allergic condition? _____

Was medication to control the child's behavior suggested? _____

   What? _____ Who prescribed? _____

Was medication to control behavior used? _____ For how long? _____

continued

Figure 14.2. *(continued)*

Was the child ever referred for a psychological evaluation? _____

By whom? _____

Why? _____

What time does the student go to bed? _____

What time does the student get up? _____

How many absences/month from school approximately? _____

Chores your child has in the home: _____

School Adjustment

Schools your child has attended:

Name	Location	Grade Level
_____	_____	_____
_____	_____	_____
_____	_____	_____
_____	_____	_____

Child's general achievement in school:

Grade Level	Very Poor	Poor	Average	Above Average
_____	_____	_____	_____	_____
_____	_____	_____	_____	_____
_____	_____	_____	_____	_____

What is your child's attitude toward school? _____

_____

_____

_____

Child's general attitude toward teachers? _____

_____

What are your child's interests outside of school? (Sports, hobbies, animals, etc.)

_____

_____

Did your child ever have a rapid turnover of teachers in one grade or one subject? _____

If so, what grade? _____ Subject? _____ How did you child react to this?

_____

Figure 14.2. *(continued)*

Describe any incidents when your child had a great deal of difficulty with a teacher:

_____

_____

_____

Subject child likes most _____

Subject child likes least _____

Subject child does best in _____

Subject child does worst in _____

Has your child ever failed a grade? _____ If so, what level? _____

Has your child ever received special tutoring in school subjects? _____

  In what? _____

_____

Has your child ever exhibited any fear of school or teachers? _____

When did you first notice that your child was having difficulty reading? _____

_____

_____

Who referred you to the Reading Center? _____

Are there any other conditions that you feel may have contributed to your child's reading

problem? _____

_____

Mental Ability Tests

QUESTIONS TO GUIDE READING

Recall Questions
1. What are two mental ability tests that are considered highly valid for use in extended diagnosis?
2. What are Searls's do's and don't's for interpreting IQ scores?

Thinking Questions
1. Why do you think the WISC-R is so widely used?

Some assessment of ability to perform academic tasks is generally done in extended diagnosis, sometimes through the PPVT or SIT (see Ch. 6). These tests do not require special training in psychometrics and are acceptable as a general measure of mental ability.

When a more precise level of mental functioning is desired, more sophisticated tests are used. Two widely used, individually administered mental tests are considered highly valid and reliable measures of mental functioning: the *Wechsler Intelligence Scale for Children–Revised,* or WISC–R (Psychological Corporation 1974) and the *Stanford–Binet Intelligence Scale,* 4th ed. (Riverside 1985). As classroom teachers may receive reports of extended diagnoses that have included one of these tests, they should have some knowledge of them.

WECHSLER INTELLIGENCE SCALE FOR CHILDREN–REVISED

The Wechsler Intelligence Scale for Children–Revised (WISC–R) is a classified psychological test that must be administered by a person who has had special training in giving and interpreting the test, such as a school psychologist. The test is individual in nature, and yields verbal, performance, and full-scale scores. Designed for ages 6 years through 16 years 11 months, the test requires fifty to seventy-five minutes to administer. It is more frequently used than the Stanford–Binet and is generally considered a standard by which to judge other tests of its kind.

The WISC–R verbal subtests are: Information, Similarities, Arithmetic, Vocabulary, Comprehension, and Digit Span. The performance subtests are: Picture Completion, Picture Arrangement, Block Design, Object Assembly, Coding (or Mazes), and Mazes (seldom used).

Full Scale, Verbal, and Performance IQs have split-half reliability coefficients that are satisfactory for the assessment of individuals. Some subtest scaled scores do not meet this criterion, however. The standard error of measurement for the Full Scale IQ (considering all eleven levels) is 3.19 IQ points. For the Verbal Scale the standard error is 3.60; for the Performance Scale, 4.66 (Wechsler 1974).

Teachers and clinicians should know that much has been written about the value of WISC–R scores in relationship to poor readers. Searls (1985, pp. 37–38) states that the WISC–R can help teachers "gather information about a student's cognitive abilities, generate hypotheses about a student's strengths and weaknesses, and plan appropriate educational intervention." She notes (p. 2) that the global score (WISC–R Full Scale IQ) is probably the "least important piece of information the test yields for the teacher working with the student on a daily basis" because it does not give clues as to students' strengths or weaknesses in particular types of tasks. This is particularly true if the IQ falls within the average range. It is the difference in the subtest scores that provides clues; scores that differ from the student's mean by 3 or more points are considered statistically significant (Kaufman 1979).

Subtest scores should be reported to teachers and explained. If no explanation is provided or if the teacher does not fully understand what individual scores really mean, she should consult the school psychologist, if one is available. If not, an explanation should be sought from the person who administered the WISC–R. Searls's monograph should also be of considerable help to teachers. Chapter 4 contains an analysis of WISC–R scores, including the interpretations of full-scaled scores, verbal- and performance-scaled scores, and subtest-scaled scores. She provides information on how to make comparisons among scores in language easily understood by teachers.

Searls cites research that suggests the following consistent findings for students with a reading disability (p. 2): "(1) Groups of disabled readers tend to score higher on the Performance than on the Verbal Scale, and (2) they tend to score lower on 5 of the subtests—Information, Arithmetic, Digit Span, Coding, and sometimes Vocabulary."

After discussing how to interpret the WISC–R scores in some depth, Searls (p. 38) provides reminders, which are appropriate for teachers to consider:

> *Don't* think of the IQ as some mystical number to be entered forever on the student's cumulative record.
>
> *Do* remember that the WISC–R, although one of the best IQ test instruments available, is still imperfect and measures only a small part of what constitutes human intelligence.
>
> *Don't* forget that it is a waste of time and money to have the WISC–R administered if the results are not used or are misused.
>
> *Do* become familiar with the behaviors sampled by the WISC–R and the abilities necessary to perform the tasks successfully.
>
> *Don't* be satisfied with reports only of the Full Scale and Verbal and Performance IQs.
>
> *Do* insist on a report of the subtest scaled scores; look for highs and lows of a student's performance.
>
> *Don't* make the mistake of thinking that the WISC–R will tell you everything you need to know about the student's learning abilities; use information from all available sources.
>
> *Do* carry out further informal testing as you work with the student in order to determine more specifically where the deficiences lie.

STANFORD–BINET INTELLIGENCE SCALE

The *Stanford–Binet Intelligence Scale,* 4th ed. (1972 norms) is described by the publisher (Riverside 1985) as a multiscore adaptive ability test. The test levels range from below-average two-year-old children to superior adults. The test is designed to be administered by a professionally trained, certified examiner.

Four areas are tested: verbal reasoning, quantitative reasoning, abstract/visual reasoning, and short-term memory. The publisher states that the score in each area reflects in part a "general ability factor" that is common to all four areas. A composite score is also provided that is stated to be a reliable assessment of the general ability factor. Norms are provided for each area and for all combinations of areas. Figure 14.3 illustrates the factors appraised in the current edition.

According to the publisher, the 1986 edition maintains historical continuity with the 1937 and 1960 editions in that it retains contemporarily useful item types, but the new edition incorporates the latest psychometric approaches and extensive statistical analyses. Kuder-Richardson Formula 20 indices of internal consistency for raw scores show a range of coefficients on subtests from .74 to .93 for ages 6 to 12.

Additional tests of mental ability may be found in Appendix C.

INFORMATION TO CONSIDER

1. Two tests with established validity for assessing mental ability are the WISC–R and the Stanford-Binet. Both tests require special training to administer.
2. Subscores on the WISC–R are more useful for reading teachers than global scores, as they give clues to students' strengths and weaknesses at particular types of tasks.

Tests of Reading Ability

QUESTIONS TO GUIDE READING

Recall Questions
1. Based on the International Reading Association's study, what are the most widely used diagnostic reading tests?
2. Based on the College Reading Association's study, what are the tests most widely used in clinics for measuring comprehension?

Figure 14.3. Cognitive-Abilities Factors Appraised in the Stanford–Binet: Fourth Edition

Crystallized Abilities		Fluid-Analytic Abilities	Short-Term Memory
Verbal Reasoning	Quantitative Reasoning	Abstract/Visual Reasoning	
Vocabulary	Quantitative	Pattern Analysis	Bead Memory
Comprehension	Number Series	Copying	Memory for Sentences
Absurdities	Equation Building	Matrices	Memory for Digits
Verbal Relations		Paper Folding and Cutting	Memory for Objects

3. Which tests (or subtests) meet the .90 reliability requirement felt to be necessary for tests are administered to individuals?

Thinking Questions
1. How would you account for the difference in the reviews of Spache's *Diagnostic Reading Scales* by Lida and by Mosenthal and Jackson?
2. On what basis would you choose any one of the tests discussed for a given remedial reader?
3. How does an RMI differ from an IRI?

Many of the tests of reading ability used in classroom assessment are also used in extended diagnostic settings. Recall that the basic goal is the same; it seems logical, then, that there should be some overlap. There is a major difference, however: most reading tests administered in extended diagnosis are administered individually, and some require special skill in administration and scoring. Persons who have taken practicum courses in the diagnosis of remedial reading problems generally have sufficient training to administer most tests of reading ability.

The most commonly used tests for extended diagnosis that have not been discussed in previous chapters are presented here. The tests were selected for inclusion in this section on the basis of two research studies under the direction of the International Reading Association and the College Reading Association.

In the International Reading Association study, reported by Schell (1981), a list of thirty-four diagnostic tests (group and individual, norm- and criterion-referenced) was sent to directors of reading in thirty-five cities in twenty-five states with populations of at least 250,000. The respondents were asked to check the ten to fifteen tests they felt should be reviewed by the International Reading Association's committee on evaluation of tests. The committee arbitrarily decided to review the twelve most frequently mentioned tests. Some of these tests were presented in Chapter 6; the remaining tests will be discussed in this chapter. The tests were:

- *Botel Reading Inventory*
- *Classroom Reading Inventory*
- *Diagnostic Reading Scales*
- *Durrell Analysis of Reading Difficulty*
- *Gates–McKillop Reading Diagnostic Tests*
- *Gilmore Oral Reading Tests*
- *Peabody Individual Achievement Test*
- *Sucher-Allred Reading Placement Inventory*
- *Woodcock Reading Mastery Tests*
- *Individualized Criterion-Referenced Tests*
- *Prescriptive Reading Inventory*, Levels A and B
- *Stanford Diagnostic Test*

The second study was done in 1982 by a committee of the College Reading Association, chaired by Myrna Ehrlich. A primary purpose of this study was to survey clinics regarding the methods of assessing reading comprehension. Thirty-six clinics from nineteen states were included in the final study. In assessing reading comprehension, 47.2 percent of the clinics reported that they used standardized tests; 30.6 percent used informal reading inventories; 27.8 percent used teacher-made tests; 16.7 percent used the Diagnostic Reading Scales; 13.9 percent used cloze techniques; 11.1 percent used the Reading Miscue Inventory; 8.3 percent used the Durrell Analysis of Reading Difficulty; 8.3 percent used the Classroom Reading Inventory; and 8.3 percent used the Analytical Reading Inventory (Ehrlich et al. 1984–85).

Based on a synthesis of these two studies (and excluding the tests discussed in Chapters 5 and 6), the following tests are briefly described (where a new edition has been published since the studies were completed, we will discuss the latest version):

- *Diagnostic Reading Scales* (CTB/McGraw-Hill 1981)
- *Durrell Analysis of Reading Difficulty* (Psychological Corporation 1980)
- *Gates–McKillop–Horowitz Reading Diagnostic Tests* (Teachers College Press 1981)
- *Gilmore Oral Reading Test* (Psychological Corporation 1968)
- *Peabody Individual Achievement Test* (American Guidance Service 1970)
- *Woodcock Reading Mastery Tests* (American Guidance Service 1973)
- *Gray Oral Reading Tests—Revised* (Pro-Ed 1986)
- *Reading Miscue Inventory* (Macmillan 1972)

In citing reviews, primary attention has been given to those done by the Evaluation of Tests Committee of the International Reading Association (Schell 1981). Teachers may also wish to check reviews of tests in the

Mental Measurement Yearbooks, edited by Oscar Buros and published by Gryphon in Highland Park, NJ.

DIAGNOSTIC READING SCALES

The 1981 revised edition of the Diagnostic Reading Scales (DRS) is an individually administered set of tests for reading levels at grades 1–7. It is intended to evaluate oral and silent reading, auditory comprehension, and phonic and word-analysis skills. The entire battery requires about one hour to administer.

The DRS contains three word-recognition lists, twenty-two graded reading selections, and twelve phonic and word-analysis tests. The word lists sample vocabulary from preprimer level to grade 5. Word list 1, containing fifty words, is most appropriate for nonreaders through first-grade level. Word list 2 consists of forty words and is suitable for students functioning on second- and third-grade levels. Word list 3 is for students reading at fourth- and fifth-grade levels; it consists of forty words. As with an IRI, the word lists serve the function of determining where to begin the reading of the graded passages.

The graded reading passages span preprimer through grade 7 levels and contain material from the natural, physical, and social sciences, history, and children's literature. The primary grade materials are narrative, while the intermediate grade level materials are either expository or descriptive. Each passage is followed by seven or eight comprehension questions: six focus on recall of facts; the others are inferential or interpretative. There are two sets of reading selections. One is used for initial testing; the other may be used for posttesting, or retesting if the clinician feels that the first administration was invalid for some reason.

The phonic and word analysis tests include initial consonants, final consonants, consonant digraphs, consonant blends, initial consonant substitution, initial consonant sounds recognized auditorily, auditory discrimination, short and long vowel sounds, vowels with *r*, vowel diphthongs and digraphs, common syllables or phonograms, and blending. The response mode is oral for all tests; no writing is involved. All tests use real words, and most require the student to pronounce the sound represented by the given symbols. Raw score data only may be obtained from the phonic and word analysis tests; no normative or grade equivalent norms are provided.

The DRS assesses three reading levels—instructional, independent, and potential. The instructional and independent levels are defined somewhat differently from what teachers are accustomed to when administering an IRI. The *instructional level* is based on oral reading comprehension, and the *independent level* is based on silent reading. Silent reading passages begin at the level above the one at which oral reading was stopped. This should be the point at which the child exceeds the acceptable number of miscues of words and fails to answer 60 percent of the comprehension questions correctly. Silent reading passages are continued until the child can no longer answer 60 percent of the comprehension questions correctly. The *potential level* testing begins one grade level above the failure level on silent reading, and continues until the student answers fewer than 60 percent of the questions. This test is similar to the IRI in that it is a measure of auditory comprehension.

A checklist of reading ability is also provided to assist in diagnosis: it is reproduced in Figure 14.4.

The standardization data from earlier editions (1963; 1972) still apply, since the word lists remain the same and the passages contain no major changes in content. In reviewing the 1972 edition for the Evaluation of Tests Committee of the International Reading Association (IRA), Mosenthal and Jackson (1981) stated that the scales are relatively well constructed, although not quite as rigorously as typical group reading achievement tests. They found the 1972 version to be "one of the more reliable oral reading tests available, reliable enough to use before and after instruction to measure growth" (p. 26). They considered the content validity of the passages to be adequate. The test was said to have more concurrent validity data than any similar test, but the reviewers saw the data as approximate rather than conclusive. They say that the test would more accurately place children in instructional material than silent reading tests would. As with an IRI, it should be noted that the "levels" are only approximations. Teachers should also recall the difference between Spache's definition of levels and definitions of typical IRIs.

Lipa (1985) reviewed the 1981 version. She finds that the scoring continues to be liberal, especially in comprehension. She feels the test is better as a diagnostic instrument than for determining placement in materials, and concludes that the test has no real advantage over published IRIs.

Durrell Analysis of Reading Difficulty

The third edition of the Durrell Analysis of Reading Difficulty (DARD), designed for grades 1–6, was developed by Donald D. Durrell and Jane H. Catterson. The individually administered test, which is untimed but usually takes 30 to 45 minutes, includes observations and evaluations of oral

Figure 14.4. Checklist of Reading Ability

Fill in the checklist upon completion of testing for the instructional and independent levels.

Sight-Word Vocabulary
_____ limited
_____ adequate
_____ good

Word Recognition
_____ slow, fumbling
_____ average
_____ quick, easy

Figure 14.4. *(continued)*

Oral Reading

Vocal Qualities	Errors	Few	Average	Excessive
_____ pitch quite low	omissions	_____	_____	_____
_____ pitch quite high	repetitions	_____	_____	_____
_____ monotone	substitutions	_____	_____	_____
_____ read too loudly	additions	_____	_____	_____
_____ read too softly	reversals	_____	_____	_____
_____ had difficulty articulating	self-corrections	_____	_____	_____

Reading Fluency	Oral	Silent
slow	_____	
average	_____	
rapid	_____	
too rapid for accuracy	_____	
word-by-word	_____	
poor phrasing	_____	
some phrasing	_____	
largely by phrases	_____	
skips over unknown words	_____	
needs frequent prompting	_____	_____
fumbles, repeats often	_____	
ignores punctuation	_____	
points to words	_____	_____

General Observations	Oral	Silent
moves lips, whispers	_____	_____
makes excessive head movements	_____	_____
booklet held closer than 14 inches	_____	_____
booklet held further than 18 inches	_____	_____
ill at ease, tense	_____	_____
indifferent	_____	_____
disliked reading	_____	_____

Reading Comprehension	Oral			Silent		
	Weak	Average	Strong	Weak	Average	Strong
recall of facts	_____	_____	_____	_____	_____	_____
inferences, conclusions	_____	_____	_____	_____	_____	_____

reading, silent reading, listening comprehension, listening vocabulary, word recognition/word analysis, sounds in isolation, spelling, phonic spelling of words, visual memory of words (primary and intermediate), identifying sounds in words, and prereading phonics abilities. The test package also includes a profile chart, a checklist of instructional needs, a general history data form, and suggestions for supplementary tests and observations. Figure 14.5 reproduces the profile chart.

The reader's instructional level, independent level, and level of listening comprehension are among the assessments that may be obtained. Instructional level is determined from oral reading paragraphs: five are available at the primary level and three at intermediate grade level. Each passage is followed by five to nine questions, which are primarily factual. Reading time is a basic criterion for the determination of instructional level, with some consideration being given to the comprehension.

Testing of the student's independent reading level also uses five primary and three intermediate grade level passages, this time read silently. The criteria for determining this level are based on reading time and on the retelling of the pasages.

There are six passages (grades 1–6) for measuring listening comprehension, each passage followed by seven or eight questions. The student's grade level is set at that of the highest passage on which he missed no more than two of the questions asked. One purpose of these tests is to estimate the child's reading capacity (recall that a child's listening level is one indicant of his reading potential).

The Word Recognition/Word Analysis test contains four word lists of fifty words each (one for grade 1 and three for grades 2–6). There are separate norms and checklists for quick sight recognition and for word analysis. Words are first flashed for sight recognition; unknown words are then shown untimed for analysis.

There are five word lists of fifteen words each in the Listening Vocabulary test. This test may also be used as an estimate of potential, as it permits a direct comparison of the number of words recognized through listening with the number of words recognized in reading. When more words are recognized through listening than through reading, it may be hypothesized that the child's reading potential is higher than his performance.

The Sounds in Isolation test is designed to assess the child's mastery of sound-symbol associations that are useful in reading, such as letters, blends, digraphs, phonograms, and affixes. It is appropriate for use from the beginning stages to about grade 5.

The Spelling test comprises two twenty-word lists—one for primary and one for intermediate grades. Its relationship to reading is not specified. The Phonic Spelling of Words test is intended to assess whether children can spell words (real and nonsense) as they sound and is intended for those children whose instructional level is between grades 4 and 6. The Visual Memory of Words tests include an identification test for primary grades

Figure 14.5. Individual Record Booklet

NAME _____ DATE _____
  Mo/Day/Yr

SCHOOL _____ EXAMINER _____

_____ REPORT TO _____

  PHONE _____ ADDRESS _____

AGE ____ GRADE _____ _____

DATE OF BIRTH _____ PHONE _____
  Mo/Day/Yr

Profile Chart

READING ANALYSIS TESTS

GRADE		Oral Reading	Silent Reading	Listening Compre-hension	Listening Vocabulary	Word Recognition	Word Analysis	Spelling
6	H M L							
5	H M L							
4	H M L							
3	H M L							
2	H M L							
1	H M L							
SCORES								

ADDITIONAL TESTS

Title	Date of Testing	Scores		

(intended for children at an instructional level of grade 3 or below) and a writing from memory test at the intermediate level (grades 3–6).

The Identifying Sounds in Words test is designed to assess a child's ability to discriminate phonemes in words along with graphemes used to represent them. The test is appropriate for children whose instructional level is grade 3 or below.

The DARD battery also includes Prereading Phonics Abilities Inventories, which are designed for nonreaders, children who have difficulty in learning to read, and kindergarteners who need this aspect of readiness assessed. These tests assess relationships between reading and speaking, such as syntax matching, identifying letter names in spoken words, identifying phonemes in spoken words, naming lowercase letters, writing letters from dictation, writing from copy, naming uppercase letters, and identifying letters named.

Schell and Jennings (1981), writing for IRA, note that the test developers focus on the observation of the children's behavior as they take the test. A Checklist of Difficulties, in which the examiner records his observations, follows several of the subtests. Durrell and Catterson view the observations as more important than the scores themselves. Teachers and clinicians as well should understand the importance that the test developers place on observational data.

The DARD is difficult both to give and to interpret. Special training is suggested by the test developers. Schell and Jennings (1981) note a problem in interpreting the grade-equivalent scores from this test: while the reliability coefficients of the tests are fairly satisfactory (ranging from .63 to .97, with a median of .81), no information about standard error is available; thus grade-equivalent scores may not be precise enough for placing children in reading materials. Another limitation is that retesting is impossible, as a second set of graded passages is not provided for this purpose.

GATES–McKILLOP–HOROWITZ READING DIAGNOSTIC TESTS

The Gates–McKillop–Horowitz Reading Diagnostic Tests are individually administered tests designed for disabled readers in grades 1–6. It is not intended that any one child be given the entire test battery; the manual helps examiners choose the most appropriate tests for a particular child. The test developers declare that although the units are labelled "tests," they are not primarily designed to compare the performances between children; their main function is rather to assess strengths and weaknesses in reading and related areas. There are, however, interpretation tables by which a child's grade scores may be rated as high, medium, low, or very low in comparison with her actual grade placement.

Oral reading is measured through seven graded paragraphs, with word-recognition errors being the criterion used to determine levels of performance; comprehension questions are not used. A reading sentences test contains four sentences to be read orally, with the criterion again being word recognition. Two tests of word recognition are also provided—Words: Flash and Words: Untimed. The same words are used for both tests.

The battery also includes the following tests: Knowlege of Word Parts:

Word Attack (Syllabication, Recognizing and Blending Common Word Parts, Reading Words, Giving Letter Sounds, Naming Capital Letters, Naming Lowercase Letters); Recognizing the Visual Form of Sounds (Vowels); Auditory Tests (Auditory Blending and Auditory Discrimination); and Written Expression (Spelling and Informal Writing Sample).

Six hundred children in ten different private (65 percent) and public (35 percent) were used to collect validity and reliability data. The schools were located in both rural (17 percent) and urban (83 percent) settings. Fifty-one percent of the children were males; 32 percent were black. The test-retest coefficient for the Oral Reading test was .94. correlations with the Gates–McGinitie Reading Tests and with the Metropolitan Achievement Tests ranged from .68 to .96, with the higher correlations appearing at lower grade levels.

In reviewing the previous edition for IRA, Gable and Santa (1981) suggested that the test is best used (1) as an informal assessment tool, ignoring norms, (2) to study response patterns for the development of possible remediation plans, and (3) in conjunction with other assessment tools to generate a comprehensive evaluation of reading strengths and weaknesses. We feel these comments apply to the present edition as well.

GILMORE ORAL READING TEST

The Gilmore Oral Reading Test is an individually administered oral reading test designed for grades 1–8. It measures three aspects of oral reading— accuracy, comprehension, and rate. The test has two alternate and equivalent forms, C and D, each form containing ten graded passages. Five literal recall questions to assess comprehension follow each of the passages. Stanines and grade-equivalent scores are provided for reading accuracy and comprehension, as are percentile ranges and a performance rating of poor, below average, average, above average, or superior. The test is untimed, but generally takes 15 to 20 minutes to administer.

The Gilmore Oral Reading Test is primarily a test of oral reading, recording such errors as: substitutions, mispronunciations, words pronounced by the examiner, disregard of punctuation, insertions, hesitations, repetitions, and omissions. Ryder and Walmsley (1981), reviewing for IRA, judged that the test probably measures adequately the accuracy of oral reading of material that is meaningful to the student.

Norms were based on 4,455 children in six school systems, representing a range of backgrounds and sections of the country. The reliability, based on alternate-form correlations, was .94 for third graders on accuracy and .84 for sixth graders; comprehension coefficients were .60 for third graders and .60 for sixth graders. Coefficients for third graders on rate were .70; for sixth graders, .54. According to Ryder and Walmsley (1981) these scores generally fall below accepted standards. Ryder and Walmsley also find a technical weakness of the Gilmore test in the absence of concurrent and content validity evidence. Further, they state that there is no evidence that the test correlates well with silent reading.

PEABODY INDIVIDUAL ACHIEVEMENT TEST

The Peabody Individual Achievement Test is an individual test designed as a screening instrument for grades K–12. It does not purport to be a diagnostic instrument. The total battery consists of Mathematics, Reading Recognition, Reading Comprehension, Spelling, and General Information. The testing time is between 30 and 40 minutes. Each subtest has eighty-four items, with the exception of Reading Comprehension, which has sixty-six. Training is needed for accurate administration. The first eighteen items on the Word Recognition subtest focus on naming letters; the remaining sixty-six items are single words, which the child is to pronounce aloud one by one. The Reading Comprehension subtest is composed of sixty-six sentences that are to be read silently. Each sentence is followed by four line drawings; the child is to choose the picture that best illustrates the meaning of the sentence. Only literal level comprehension is sampled.

Test items are sequenced in ascending order of difficulty, so that individual students are tested on a range of items appropriate for them (from a basal level to a ceiling level). Grade equivalents, age equivalents, percentile ranks, and standard scores are available.

The norms were developed on 2,889 cases in twenty-seven representative communities across the United States. Reliability data for the Reading Recognition subtest appear adequate based on a one-month testing interval. The correlations are generally in the high .80s. Reliability data for the Reading Comprehension subtest are lower, with a median of .64. According to the publisher, validity is based on the position that items on the subtests were written to be representative of courses of study across the United States. The focus was on measuring skills and knowledge rather than content and vocabulary, which might be considered representative of a particular curricular approach or geographical region.

In their review for the IRA, Hansen and Peterson (1981) questioned the validity of the comprehension subtest because of the narrow definition of comprehension. They also concluded that educators should be cautious in attempting to make decisions about reading achievement based on this test because of the poor validity and reliability of the subtests. They further recommended that other measures be used if more than initial gross screening is desired.

WOODCOCK READING MASTERY TESTS

The Woodcock Reading Mastery Tests are designed for grades K–12; there are two forms, each consisting of five individually administered reading tests: Letter Identification, Word Identification, Word Attack, Word Comprehension, and Passage Comprehension. The tests also yield a total score. Administration time is 30 to 50 minutes. The tests claim to be especially useful for clinical and research purposes.

The Letter Identification Test, which measures the child's ability to name English letters, contains 45 items arranged in order of difficulty. The test uses a variety of letter styles. The Word Identification Test consists of 150 words, ranging in difficulty from beginning level to twelfth grade. The Word Attack Test is a 50-item test that measures the reader's ability to identify nonsense words, using phonic and structural analysis skills. These items also are said to be arranged in order of difficulty. The Word Comprehension test has 70 items, which measure word meanings through an analogy format. The Passage Comprehension Test is a silent reading test that utilizes 85 items in a modified cloze procedure: the reader tells the examiner the missing words.

Raw scores for the Woodcock Tests may be converted into grade-equivalent scores, age scores, percentile ranks, and standard scores. According to Haggard and Smith's (1981) review for IRA, norming procedures were exceptionally thorough, with 36,000 children in grades K–12 involved in calibrating the individual items. The complete Forms A and B were administered to 5,252 students in fifty school districts representing a distribution of geographic locations and socioeconomic variables.

Both split-half and test-retest, alternative-form reliabiltiy data are available, based on 100 second graders and 100 seventh graders. Split-half reliabilites are generally high—in the .90–.99 range (with the exception of Letter Identification and seventh-grade Word Comprehension). Alternative-form reliabilites range from .84 (Letter Identification) to .97 (Total Reading). Haggard and Smith suggested exercising care when interpreting scores for older children because of low reliability scores at the seventh-grade level.

Haggard and Smith also questioned the adequacy of the validity evidence. The test developer states that the items represent tasks taken from the domain of reading, but no effort is made to compare them either to tasks found in materials that students use or to other tests. The reviewers feel that users are "left on their own to determine the validity of these tests" (p. 61).

Haggard and Smith stated that the tests have greatest usefulness below grade 6. They questioned the format of the Word Attack (use of nonsense words), Word Comprehension (analogy format), and Passage Comprehension (modified cloze format) tests: students who are familiar with these response formats may score higher than those who are not. The reviewers concluded: "The tests seem best suited as a global screening measure, particularly for identifying children experiencing difficulty in learning to read. The user must collect additional data from other sources before developing diagnostic prescriptions."

GRAY ORAL READING TESTS—REVISED

The Gray Oral Reading Tests—Revised (GORT–R) are designed to identify readers who are reading less well than their peers, and to pinpoint individual strengths and weaknesses. The tests measure the speed and accuracy of oral reading; they are not designed as substitutes for silent reading tests. There are two forms, each containing thirteen graded oral reading passages. Each passage is followed by five multiple-choice questions, which include literal, inferential, critical, and affective viewpoints. The GORT–R yields a passage score based on miscues, and also a comprehension score, even though it is not designed as a comprehension test. An Oral Reading Quotient, which combines passage and comprehension scores, is also provided. There are no grade-equivalent scores. Test administration time is 15 to 30 minutes.

In reviewing the test, Radencich (1986) found that the norming of the GORT–R was more extensive than for the previous edition. The revised edition used a random sampling of 1,401 students aged 7 to 17. Internal consistency reliabilities are in the .80s; alternate-form reliabilities are higher—in the .80s and .90s. One explanation of the low reliability is that passage-independent questions are used. Construct validity, according to Radencich, is weak, with no smooth progress in readability evident from grade level to grade level.

READING MISCUE INVENTORY

The Reading Miscue Inventory (RMI) was developed by Goodman and Burke (1972). Using sophisticated assessment procedures, it involves an in-depth, qualitative analysis of a child's reading performance, through both oral reading miscues and comprehension. The inventory uses both oral and silent reading passages. It takes about one hour to administer, and has an elaborate record-keeping system.

For an analysis of oral reading miscues (errors), RMI uses passages that are one level above the child's instructional level. This is necessary because at least twenty-five miscues are needed in order to do an analysis. The teacher tapes the oral reading and marks miscues on a worksheet. No help is given to students as they read orally, even if they fail to pronounce a word.

The major miscues marked are substitutions, omissions, insertions, reversals, and repetitions. Additional oral reading behaviors marked are producing partial words, nonword substitutions, dialect variations, and intonation shifts within words. Artificial pronunciations (separating words into a series of syllables) and very long pauses are optional markings that may be useful in analyses.

In analyzing each miscue, nine questions are asked:

1. Is a dialect variation involved in the miscue?
2. Is a shift in intonation involved in the miscue?
3. How much does the miscue look like what was expected?
4. How much does the miscue sound like what was expected?
5. Is the grammatical function of the miscue the same as the grammatical function of the word in the text?
6. Is the miscue corrected?
7. Does the miscue occur in a structure which is grammatically acceptable?
8. Does the miscue occur in a structure which is semantically acceptable?
9. Does the miscue result in a change of meaning?

The analysis of oral reading data differs from an IRI and from the analyses of oral reading passages that are parts of the tests previously described in this section in that the quality and variety of miscues are analyzed rather than merely counting the number of errors. Comprehension is also assessed differently from other tests discussed in this section. In the RMI, children are asked to retell stories, reviewing the material in their own words. The examiner does not interrupt the reader or interpret for the child at this point. Story retelling may be used for passages read orally or silently. For narrative material the recall would be evaluated in terms of character analysis (recall and development), events, plot, and theme. With informational material, the recall would be evaluated in terms of specifics, generalizations, and major concepts. Goodman and Burke suggest a point value for each of these categories.

Following the unaided retelling of the story, the examiner may ask questions that stimulate the reader to expand the retelling. These questions should focus on elements of the examiner's story outline that were either omitted or covered insufficiently, and should adhere to specific guidelines suggested by Goodman and Burke (1972, p. 25).

The 1972 version of the RMI lends itself better to a clinical setting than to the typical classroom situation. Teachers or clinicians should study the RMI manual carefully before using the procedure.

A revision of the RMI, authored by Yetta M. Goodman, Dorothy J. Watson, and Carolyn L. Burke and scheduled for publication in 1987 by Richard C. Owen Publishers, Inc., will contain alternative procedures designed to make the instrument more attractive for general use. Four procedures that investigate and describe students' reading will be included. The procedures vary in amounts of time needed for analysis, with the less time-consuming procedures providing more general than specific knowledge. The quickest procedure is designed for use with readers during individual reading conferences.

Other Frequently Assessed Areas

Areas other than mental ability and reading ability are frequently assessed in extended diagnosis. Physical problems receive considerable attention. Most clinics screen for visual and hearing problems, as do schools. Many clinics also screen for speech and general health problems; some may offer psychological services. Oral language and affect—attitudes and interests—may also be assessed.

In this section, physical screening, psychological and emotional screening, and psycholinguistic and oral language assessment are discussed. For a review of affective assessments, see Chapter 7.

Most extended diagnosis involves physical screening. This is certainly true with clinics: according to a study by Ehrlich et al. (1984–85), 94.4 percent of clinics provide both auditory and visual screening, 41.7 percent provide speech screening, 38.9 percent collect medical histories, and 25 percent collect nutritional data.

Visual screening. Recall from Chapter 2 that the incidence of visual problems in children who have reading problems is high. Visual screening in schools is a priority, and so data on vision for children referred to clinics may often be obtained from the school.

Virtually every elementary school has a visual screening program (Mangieri and Ingram 1982), but the frequency of visual screening in schools varies widely. About half the students in Mangieri and Ingram's study received a vision test on entering a school district; once enrolled, they received periodic tests, with the intervals ranging from twice per school year to once every six years.

According to Mangieri and Ingram's study, the most frequently used screening devices in schools are the Snellen Chart (the most widely used tool), the Titmus School Vision Tester, and the Visual Survey Telebinocular. Only 19 percent of the respondents reported using a checklist to help teachers detect visual problems. Ehrlich et al. (1984–85) found the most popular visual screening instrumentation to be the Keystone Telebinocular, Titmus Orthorater, Beery VMI, and the Slosson Visual–Motor, and informal observation.

Visual screening serves several purposes: (1) to identify pupils who may have problems seeing effectively, (2) to aid in securing adequate vision care for students, and (3) to alert teachers to the possibility that given students may have vision problems that interfere with learning (Jobe 1976, p. 26).

There are two general types of screening devices: true distance tests and simulated distance tests. The classroom teacher's observations may also be considered. Both tests and observation have limitations: vision tests may not be given at the most favorable time, and observation may not generate the most reliable symptoms. A combination of screening devices and observation is recommended; each supplements the other and reduces the chances of overlooking a serious eye problem (Jobe 1976, p. 26).

The list of symptoms from the National Society to Prevent Blindness (see Fig. 14.6) will help teachers in their observation process:

True distance tests. The true distance test most often used is the Snellen Chart test, which measures central visual acuity. The Snellen Chart, placed twenty feet from the child, contains rows of square-shaped symbols of

Figure 14.6. Symptoms of Visual Problems

1. Eyelids
   a. crusts on lids among lashes
   b. red eyelids
   c. recurring styes or swollen lids
2. Other
   a. watery eyes or discharges
   b. lack of coordination in directing gaze of the two eyes
   c. reddened conjunctiva
   d. sensitivity to light

Behavior and Complaints
1. Rubs eyes frequently
2. Attemps to brush away blur
3. Has dizziness, headaches, or nausea following close work
4. Is inattentive in chalkboard, wall chart, or map lessons
5. Complains of itchy, burning, or scratchy eyes
6. When looking at distant objects
   a. holds body tense
   b. contorts face in attempt to see distant things clearly
   c. thrusts head forward
   d. squints eyes excessively
7. When reading
   a. blinks continually
   b. holds book too far from face
   c. holds book too close to face
   d. makes frequent change in distance at which book is held
   e. is inattentive during lesson
   f. stops after brief period
   g. shuts or covers one eye
   h. tilts head to one side
   i. tends to reverse words or syllable
   j. tends to look cross-eyed
   k. tends to lose place on page
   l. confuses the following in reading or spelling: o's and a's; e's and c's; n's, and m's; h's, n's, and r's; f's and t's

Reproduced by permission from *Guide for Eye Inspection and Testing Visual Acuity of School Age Children*, published by the National Society to Prevent Blindness, 500 East Remington Road, Schaumburg, IL 60173-4557.

specified sizes. Teachers should remember, however, that the test measures monocular farpoint vision only. Nearpoint binocular coordination, which is critical in reading books and other printed materials at a distance of fourteen to sixteen inches, is not measured. A satisfactory performance on the Snellen may therefore mislead teachers into thinking that the child has no visual problems. This test should be used only in combination with other measures, such as observation and simulated distance tests involving binocular vision.

Simulated distance tests. These tests use a stereoscope, which places test objects at various distances from the child by optical means. The two most widely used such tests, according to Mangieri and Ingram, are the Keystone Visual Survey Tests and the Titmus School Vision Tester. Other tests of this type are the American Optical Company's Sight Screener and Bausch and Lomb's School Vision Tester. (See also Appendix C.)

The Keystone Visual Screening Test (1971), designed for grade 1 and up, uses fifteen stereographs to measure binocular nearpoint and farpoint acuity, muscle balance, depth perception, fusion, and color vision. The Titmus Vision Tester (1969) has a School Unit for grades 1–5 and a General Testing Unit for grades 1–12.

All stereoscopic visual screening tests have usage manuals, which must be followed scrupulously for meaningful results. The tests are useful screening devices but also have limitations, such as the "instrument effect." This is a tendency "to accommodate and to converge somewhat, simply because it is obvious that the target is not twenty feet away but quite near. The effects of the stereoscopic instrument on the examinee are a possible reduction in apparent visual acuity and a change in the phoria scores" (Jobe 1976, p. 37). If results seem doubtful, testing may be repeated on another day before a referral is made.

Auditory screening. Both auditory acuity and discrimination are felt to be important in the acquisition of reading skills, and both will usually be assessed in extended diagnosis. Ehrlich et al. (1984–85) found that 94.4 percent of clinics screened for such auditory difficulties, using a variety of instrumentation such as Maico and Beltone audiometers, the Goldman–Fristoe–Woodcock Test of Auditory Discrimination, the El Paso Phonics Test, and the Wepman Test of Auditory Discrimination, and also informal tests and observation.

Classroom teachers frequently use observation to assess potential hearing difficulties. Clinicians do have some opportunity for observation, but it may not be as reliable as that of the classroom teacher, whose observations usually occur over time. Signs of possible hearing problems may also be symptomatic of other problems; observation over time is needed to verify the hearing loss. Teachers and clinicians may be guided in the observation process by the following checklist of symptoms:

1. Inattention to those speaking.
2. Frequently asks for instructions to be repeated.
3. Complains of hearing noises in the head.
4. Exhibits faulty pronunciation of words.
5. Reads or speaks in a monotone.
6. Has discharges from the ears.
7. Complains of earaches or sinusitis.
8. Picks at the ears.

9. Breathes through the mouth.
10. Does not follow oral directions well.
11. Tilts an ear toward those speaking.
12. Seems to be lazy or indifferent.

The most common screening for auditory acuity problems in extended diagnosis is done with audiometers, Belltone and Maico being among the most widely used types. These devices function by producing tones that vary in intensity and in cycles per second, so that low, medium, and high tones can be measured. A high-tone loss is more likely to affect a child's ability to hear consonant sounds; a low-tone loss is more likely to affect his ability to hear vowel sounds.

Some authorities recommend informal screening devices, such as the whisper (or low-voice) test or the watch tick test, when an audiometer is not available (Kennedy 1977, p. 389). Given the high potential for inaccuracy with these tests, teacher observation is recommended instead.

Auditory discrimination may be assessed through reading skill tests, which are a part of several test batteries, and by teacher-made tests. In extended diagnosis, auditory discrimination tests are often given to students who do poorly on phonics tests.

Brief descriptions of some of the auditory discrimination tests found in frequent use by Ehrlich (1984–85) are presented below:

1. The *Goldman–Fristoe–Woodcock Test of Auditory Discrimination* (American Guidance Service 1970) is an individual test that measures ability to discriminate speech sounds, both in quiet situations and in noise. It is designed for ages 4 to adult. The response required of children is to point to one of four pictures whose names differ in one sound.
2. The *Wepman Auditory Discrimination Test* (Western Psychological Service 1973), designed for ages 5–8, tests children's ability to determine whether two words presented orally are the same or slightly different.
3. The *El Paso Phonics Survey*, a part of the *Ekwall Reading Inventory* (Allyn & Bacon 1986), measures recognition of initial consonant sounds; ending consonants; initial consonant clusters; and vowels, vowel teams, and special letter combinations. The first fifty-nine items focus on consonant letters; children are asked to name the letter(s) in column 1 of the test, then to name the word in the middle column that contains the letter(s), and finally to pronounce a nonsense word that contains the letter(s). The remainder of the test focuses on vowels and vowel combinations. Here the child must say the sound for a "short a" for *a*, for example, and pronounce the nonsense word that follows.

Speech screening. According to the study by Ehrlich et al. (1984–85), screening for speech disorders is done in 41.7 percent of reading clinics. Observation was the tool most often mentioned for this purpose, although various word recognition tests and the Goldman–Fristoe–Woodcock test are also used.

Informal checklists of pronunciation frequently provide sufficient basis for referral to a specialist. It is important to remember that one symptom alone does not indicate a problem; only when several symptoms are present or when there are noticeable problems with speaking should a referral be made. Kennedy (1977, p. 395) has developed a checklist of symptoms that may suggest a speech problem (see Fig. 14.7).

Medical history and nutritional data. The study by Ehrlich et al. (1984–85) reports that 38.9 percent of the responding clinics obtained medical history data, and 25 percent obtained nutritional data. Either type of data may be obtained from parent conferences, questionnaires, physician's reports, and observation.

PSYCHOLOGICAL OR EMOTIONAL SCREENING AND SERVICES

About half of the reading clinics Ehrlich surveyed supply some sort of psychological services. Some clinics merely make referrals to a private or university-based psychological clinic. Other clinics perform their own as-

Figure 14.7. Symptoms That May Suggest a Speech Problem

1. Refuses to talk.
2. Exhibits unusual movement of the head when talking.
3. Shows persistent delay in uttering words or speech sounds.
4. Is unable to imitate sounds.
5. Mispronounces particular patterns of words.
6. Has trouble getting the lips in shape to form words.
7. Cannot articulate some speech sounds.
8. Has unusual difficulty in learning specific phonetic units.
9. Stutters and stammers when trying to talk.
10. Talks in a high-pitched voice.
11. Speaks with too much volume.
12. Speaks with too little volume.
13. Cannot sound certain letters in the alphabet.
14. Slurs sounds until they are not recognizable.
15. Speaks too rapidly for proper articulation.
16. Lacks inflection of voice when speaking.
17. Voice lacks tonal quality.
18. Voice has an indefinable unpleasantness.
19. Has poor rhythm—does not phrase properly.
20. Seems to get "out of breath" when speaking.

From Eddie C. Kennedy, *Classroom Approaches to Remedial Reading* (Itasca, IL: F. E. Peacock Publishers, Inc., 1977), p. 395. Reprinted with permission.

sessments, on the basis of observation, attitude scales, and school or parent reports; two clinics in the Ehrlich study used the WISC–R for this purpose.

Cooperation among schools, parents, and clinics in obtaining psychological data is essential. The data should include information on at least three areas—the home setting, the school setting, and peer relationships—as problems in any of these areas may affect learning.

The reader is urged to return to Chapter 3 to review the relationship of personality and emotional problems to reading disability. The incidence of such problems in reading disability cases is high. Cause-effect relationships are often difficult to determine, but it is clear that learning is affected by emotional distress. When a teacher or clinician finds an emotional problem in a student, adjustments should be made to the student's instructional program so as to minimize the effects of such problems. Whenever a teacher or clinician suspects that a problem may exist, a referral may be in order.

One way of investigating emotional tests is through paper-and-pencil questionnaires, which often take the form of incomplete sentences. Information from such questionnaires should be interpreted with caution. Children often do not respond as they really feel; or they may respond with an impulsive answer that is not indicative of a broader pattern of feelings or behavior; or events or feelings specific to a given day may color their responses.

A potential major problem with any test that involves reading is that the child may not be able to read it. It is important that patterns of behavior over time be considered before referrals are made or changes are carried out in instructional programs.

Information should be sought about the home situation. Parents are of obvious importance in supplying such information; unfortunately, much valuable information may be withheld by parents who are hesitant to discuss home conditions and emotional problems candidly. There is also a possibility in some cases that child abuse may be involved. When abnormal conditions are suspected, appropriate personnel such as social workers should be alerted.

Observation is probably the most effective way to determine the presence of emotional problems, but it is time-consuming. To be reliable, observation should focus on patterns of behavior that are linked to emotional problems. All behaviors that deviate markedly from those typical of age/grade peers are potentially important for consideration. Observation should occur in a variety of situations, including classroom instruction, play settings, peer relationships, and test situations.

Harris and Sipay (1985, pp. 313–16) have identified a set of emotional problems that may contribute to reading problems. Their list may be used as a basic guide for observation:

1. Conscious refusal to learn.
2. Overt hostility.

3. Negative conditioning to reading.
4. Displacement of hostility.
5. Resistance to pressure.
6. Clinging to dependency.
7. Quick discouragement.
8. Feeling that success is dangerous.
9. Extreme distractibility or restlessness.
10. Absorption in a private world.
11. Depression.

When analyzing data from such observations, teachers and clinicians should remember that responses may be situation-specific. A lone symptom, such as "absorption in a private world," may not stem from emotional problems but rather from other pressures in the child's life, or from a health problem. When several symptoms exist, however, and when they can be termed "excessive," then the teacher or clinician may wish to include such information in a diagnostic report, make a referral to a school psychologist, or recommend that the parent secure professional help.

Referral decisions should be made with caution and with the full understanding of the parents. Parents tend to be much more sensitive about emotional difficulties than about physical problems such as vision or hearing.

Psycholinguistic and Oral Language Assessment

Selected aspects of expressive and receptive language (speech and auditory discrimination) have already been discussed earlier in this chapter. In extended diagnosis, additional language abilities are often assessed.

Psycholinguistic abilities. Psycholinguistic abilities—the child's use of language—are sometimes assessed through the Illinois Test of Psycholinguistic Abilities–Revised (ITPA) (Western Psychological Services). The ITPA is an individually administered test for ages 2–10 that assesses three language dimensions: channels of communication, psycholinguistic processes, and levels of organization. There are twelve subtests: auditory reception, visual reception, auditory-vocal association, visual-motor association, verbal expression, manual expression, grammatical closure, visual closure, auditory closure, sound blending, auditory sequential memory, and visual sequential memory.

There has been little support for the use of this test in extended diagnosis of children with reading problems. Newcomer and Hammill (1975) state that, from a review of 28 studies involving the earlier edition of the ITPA, only sound blending was correlated with reading ability. They also report that no subtests consistently distinguished between reading disability and nonreading disability cases. Teachers should view diagnostic reports that base recommendations on the ITPA with caution.

Oral language. The importance of oral language abilities was discussed in Chapter 3. Children who are slower than normal in language development may encounter problems with reading. In some extended diagnoses, an effort may be made to measure oral language abilities. Certainly they should be assessed in children who speak little English. It is also important to recall the distinction between language competence and language production; simply because a child does not *produce* oral language correctly does not mean that she does not *understand* it.

Linguists seem to agree on the importance of three dimensions of language: the sound system, the grammatical system (syntax), and a knowledge of meanings (semantics). Many tests described above focus on the child's ability to produce selected sounds and to pronounce given common words; these deal with the sound system of English. Many other tests (both achievement and mental ability tests, such as the PPVT) deal with knowledge of words. Less frequently do we find tests that assess English syntax.

Silvaroli, Kear, and McKenna (1982, p. 13) note two characteristic features of oral language tests: the use of pictures and/or oral questions to elicit oral responses, and the assessment of children's ability to produce sounds and/or syntactic patterns. Below we will briefly discuss a rare example of a test of English syntax, developed by Silvaroli, Skinner, and Maynes (1977).

The test is designed for children who have little or no command of the English language. It contains six areas of assessment: Labeling; Basic Sentences (structures); Language Expansion; Connecting, Relating, and Modifying; Storytelling—"concrete" or "simple"; and Storytelling—"abstract" or "complex." The authors provide stimulus situations for oral language and suggest how responses may be interpreted. Guidelines are offered for determining the suitability of beginning oral language training, more advanced oral language training, commercial reading programs, or reading taught along with continued oral language training.

A less formal way of assessing oral language is through a dictated language experience story. Teachers may note how distinctly the child speaks, whether he uses complete sentences, how large the child's vocabulary is, and whether the story makes logical sense.

INFORMATION TO CONSIDER

1. Several other factors besides mental ability and reading ability are important to consider for assessment in extended diagnosis: affect, vision, hearing, speech, emotional, and oral language.
2. Assessment tests and procedures for the factors mentioned above have strengths and limitations, of which teachers and clinicians should be aware.

3. Observation can be an effective assessment tool. Teachers and clinicians should use observational guides for assistance in noting relevant behaviors.

The Diagnostic Report

QUESTIONS TO GUIDE READING

Recall Questions
1. What are some cautions that teachers should be aware of as they read diagnostic reports?
2. What are ten criteria that may be used to evaluate diagnostic reports?

Thinking Questions
1. Are there other criteria that may be useful in evaluating diagnostic reports?
2. Does the diagnostic report included in Appendix B meet the suggested criteria?

A diagnostic report summarizes and interprets data obtained from the extended diagnostic procedures. Teachers should be aware that children's problems may have been interpreted in terms of the philosophy of the clinician or the special reading teacher. This philosophy may also have affected the selection of tests given: a reading teacher or clinician who believes that perceptual deficits contribute significantly to reading problems will tend to use tests that assess such deficits, whereas a teacher or clinician who believes that reading is primarily a decoding process will be more likely to assess discrete skills such as discrimination and phonic abilities. Another caution for teachers is that the data on which extended diagnoses are based are often, of necessity, drawn rapidly and from a limited base. The professionals doing the diagnostic work will probably not have had enough time to verify the hypotheses they generated based on the obtained data.

Clinicians or special teachers of reading may use the following criteria as they summarize and interpret data or evaluate diagnostic reports:

1. Diagnosticians must understand the functions of the tests or assessment techniques used and know whether the test or technique is both a valid and a reliable measure.

2. Interpretations of specific reading problems should be based on data from more than one source and at more than one point in time, if possible. If this is not possible, then limitations on the validity of interpretation should be mentioned in the report.

3. Interpretations should be based on patterns of behaviors, not on isolated data. When more than one method has been used to assess the same skill or possible cause of reading difficulty, the results from the tests or procedures should be compared. The format of the test and the specific stimulus situation should be described so the reader of the report can know *how* the information was obtained, since the stimulus situation often affects the results—and thus the interpretation—of the data.

4. There should be some distinction made between symptoms found and probable causes. Possible interrelationships among causal factors should be noted when appropriate.

5. The report should be accurately and clearly written. It should be understandable to parents as well as reading professionals.

6. The information in the report should be grouped or classified in a useful and uniform manner. That is, a child's proficiency in word recognition, comprehension, attitudes, and so on should be presented in categories so that the reader may obtain a clear picture of the findings. Possible interactions among areas should be noted when appropriate.

7. Samples of behaviors on which judgments are made should be included. This enables the reader of the report to know what was actually tested.

8. Strengths as well as weaknesses should be discussed.

9. The significance of the behaviors noted for remedial instruction should be stated.

10. A brief description of each test or procedure should be included.

A sample diagnostic report prepared at a university reading clinic may be found in Appendix B. As you read the report, note whether it meets the criteria listed above. (No attempt has been made to adapt the report to meet the criteria.) All names and dates have been changed. The test scores and behaviors mentioned were those of a nine-year-old boy.

INFORMATION TO CONSIDER

1. There are criteria by which extended diagnosis reports may be evaluated.
2. The examiner's biases may affect a diagnosis.

Summary

This chapter has focused on tests and procedures used in extended diagnosis. Extended diagnoses are individual in nature and are generally done by clinicians or special teachers of reading. While many of the tests and procedures used by classroom teachers are also relevant, there are some differences: tests given in extended diagnosis often require special preparation and must be administered on an individual basis. Valuable diagnostic information also comes from classroom teachers and from parents.

In this chapter, information was presented on selected mental ability and reading ability tests used in extended diagnosis. Attention was also given to physical and language assessments. An example of a diagnostic report based on extended diagnosis has been included in Appendix B. Diagnostic reports are normally prepared for parents or schools; criteria were offered for evaluating such reports.

Questions for Further Thought

1. What additional tests and procedures may be considered for use in extended diagnosis?
2. Should separate reports be prepared for parents and schools? Why or why not?
3. What other formats may be used in writing diagnostic reports?

Activities and Projects

1. Visit a reading clinic, and ask what diagnostic tests and procedures are used. Ask why in each case.
2. Visit a special teacher of reading. Ask the same questions as above. Describe the similarities and differences in the answers obtained.
3. Obtain copies of several of the tests discussed in this chapter. Take these tests yourself. Do you think they measure what they claim to measure? Would you include them in a set of diagnostic tests you planned to use?
4. Read *How to Use WISC–R Scores in Reading/Learning Disability Diagnosis* by Evelyn F. Searls (Newark, Del.: International Reading Association, 1985). List the information you feel is important for classroom teachers. Do the same for clinicians.

15

Extended Remediation

$\mathbf{I}$n the history of reading instruction, several methods have been developed specifically to help readers with severe problems. Pelosi (1982), reviewing the major remedial methods used over the last fifty years, has found many similarities between current and earlier techniques. One major difference, however, is that many earlier methods were designed to be used with individuals rather than groups. Adaptations of many of these methods are often used by classroom teachers and special reading teachers today.

When teachers refer children for extended remediation, they should not expect that the children will be taught by an entirely new set of methods. This is not to say that there are no differences. An important distinction between a clinical or Chapter I setting and the classroom is that remedial instruction places emphasis on matching a particular method to the specific needs of the child. This is not always possible in classrooms because teachers must deal with larger numbers of children, which usually necessitates some form of group instruction. Most of the strategies presented in Chapters 7–12 may also be used in extended remediation. Teachers who receive progress reports of children's performance from special reading teachers or clinicians may expect this similarity, and therefore find follow-up in classrooms easier.

One purpose of this chapter is to describe selected methods designed for remedial readers. It is not possible in one chapter to be comprehensive, either in scope or in depth of presentation. The methods selected show a representative range of focus. A grasp of the basic components of these methods will help classroom teachers understand important trends in extended remediation and will aid them in providing follow-up in the classroom setting.

This chapter also aims to identify some of the programs and materials used in extended remediation. Our selection is based on a review of texts that describe such programs and materials for remedial readers. Some are more widely used than others, but teachers should be familiar with all the basic types.

The first section of this chapter focuses on criteria for evaluating special remedial methods. Next, descriptions of some specific remedial reading methods are presented. These methods are categorized into four groups based on descriptors frequently found in reading education literature: multisensory, language-based, auditory emphasis, and neurologically based. The reader will note that this classification scheme is somewhat arbitrary, as elements of one method often appear in another; for example, the VAKT method has a heavy language-based component.

Mention will also be made of selected other programs and materials often mentioned in the literature: perceptual, linguistic, programmed, modifed alphabets, behavior management, and psychological or counseling techniques. The chapter will conclude with a discussion of reports that teachers may receive from extended remediation.

Criteria for Evaluating Extended Remedial Methods

QUESTIONS TO GUIDE READING

Recall Question
1. What are seven criteria by which a teacher may evaluate a special remedial method?

Thinking Question
1. Are there other criteria that should be applied to special remedial programs? What are they? Why do you think they should be considered?

The ultimate goal of extended remediation is to improve the reading ability and affect of the problem reader. The following criteria are intended to help teachers evaluate methods used in extended programs and to help clinicians or special teachers design such programs. The authors have found these criteria to be effective in working with teachers and in a clinical setting.

1. The remedial method should take the learner's strengths and weaknesses into consideration. If the special method bears little relationship to these strengths and weaknesses, then it should not be used. For example, if the assessment indicates that the student has a fairly good knowledge of sound-symbol relationships, the auditory emphasis method would help the child build on his strengths. Other methods or programs would be needed, however, to address the child's weaknesses.

2. Whenever possible, the special method should have potential for use in conjunction with materials the child is interested in. Some programs require the use of specific commercial materials; for example, some specific linguistic materials involve heavy vocabulary controls through spelling patterns. If the student is not interested in the type of content that such controls necessitate, then it is best not to use these programs.

3. The special method should enable the child to make short-term gains in the program and to see his success. No method should be used for which the child does not already have the prerequisite readiness skills. For example, a child lacking auditory skills should not be immersed immediately into an intensive phonics program.

4. The method should facilitate the transfer of learned skills to a classroom situation. If there is no suggestion in a remediation progress report of how the learning in the program can be practiced in the classroom, the teacher should consider whether the method will actually have helped the child. Certain perceptual programs, for example, have not been found to transfer to regular instruction.

5. The method should foster positive affect as well as skill development. Teachers should ask the question, "Has the method [or program] fostered interest in and more positive attitudes toward reading?"

6. The method should help overcome major areas of a student's weaknesses that affect classroom performance. A program that focuses primarily on word recognition is not appropriate for a child who has many word recognition skills but lacks adequate comprehension.

7. The method should ensure the active involvement of the child. One such program is the language experience approach, which involves the child in the preparation of the materials she is to use.

INFORMATION TO CONSIDER

1. Remedial methods may be evaluated against certain criteria.

Specific Remedial Methods

QUESTIONS TO GUIDE READING

Recall Questions
1. What are four possible categories into which remedial reading methods may be placed?
2. What is a characteristic of each?
3. What are the stages in Fernald's VAKT?
4. What are the six assumptions on which the language experience approach is based?
5. What are the "associations" in the Gillingham–Stillman method?
6. What are the procedures used in the neurological impress method?

For purposes of discussion, special remedial methods have been placed into four major categories—multisensory, language-based, intensive phonic (auditory emphasis), and neurologically based. It is important for the reader to note that the categories are not mutually exclusive; however, each one has a rationale or major emphasis, which should help teachers better understand other methods with a similar focus.

MULTISENSORY METHODS

Methods that utilize multisensory input have been popular for over fifty years. In fact, if frequency of appearance in the literature can be used as a criterion, these methods may be judged the most popular (Pelosi 1982).

A special characteristic of multisensory methods is that senses other than vision and hearing are used in teaching word recognition: specifically, the *kinesthetic* (related to motion) and the *tactile* (related to touch). The methods labeled VAK (visual, auditory, and kinesthetic) and VAKT (visual, auditory, kinesthetic, and tactile) are frequently associated with Grace M. Fernald.

The use of the kinesthetic and tactile senses helps the child focus on specific features of the word. (Recall from Chapter 2 that focusing attention on features of letters and words may be a key task for a reader with severe problems in learning to read.) This method also encourages individual initiative in learners by having them select the words they want to learn and write their own stories to read. This individual attention may help account for the success of the method.

The VAKT method was devised by Fernald and Keller (1921). It works by finding some means by which a child can learn to write words correctly, motivating such writing, and reading back what the child has written (Fernald 1936, p. 7; Fernald 1943, pp. 35–55). Ideally, children can move from inability to recognize the simplest of words to acceptable levels of reading performance. The specific stages in the method are as follows:

Stage I. The child learns by tracing a word with his finger as the word is pronounced, thus stimulating his tactile sense. This process is repeated as necessary until the child can both pronounce and write the word without looking at the exemplar. The child first writes the word on scrap paper and later incorporates it into his own "story." After a story has been written, the words that the child has studied are entered into a word file.

Fernald (1943, pp. 37–39) notes the following important points at this stage: (1) actual finger contact is important in tracing; (2) the child should write the word without looking at a copy; (3) the word should always be written as a unit; and (4) the words being studied should always be used in context.

Stage II. Tracing (tactile sense) is omitted from the procedure as the child shows he can learn words without tracing. Fernald (1943, pp. 40–44) stipulates that : (1) the child must say the word either to himself or aloud as he writes it; (2) the material that the child writes must be typed for him within twenty-four hours so that he can read it while the story is still fresh in his mind; and (3) there should be no simplification of material, whether in vocabulary or complexity of subject matter, for children of normal and superior mental ability.

Stage III: The child now learns words by looking at them and saying them before writing them down himself; the teacher no longer copies out the word for the child. Fernald (1943, p. 51) finds that at this stage, the child generally wants to read from books. He should be allowed to read as much as he wishes; it is important, though, to check the words learned for retention.

Stage IV: The child is now able to recognize new words from their similiarity to words already learned. The child is generally eager to read, since he has been successful (Fernald 1936, p. 9), and should be allowed to read whatever materials interest him. In Fernald's method, children are not read to; they must do the reading. She also notes (1943, p. 53) that the child should never be made to sound the word out when he fails to recognize it; instead, the teacher tells him the word.

The VAK approach is essentially Stage II of the method described above. In actual practice, a number of teachers and clinicians find that many readers with even severe problems do not actually need to go through Stage I of the Fernald method.

The Fernald method is time-consuming, but has proved successful for many experienced teachers and clinicians. Gains with children who have severe reading problems do not come quickly with any method. The validity of this method and its variations has been supported by many writers (Witman and Riley 1978; Miccinati 1979; Peters 1981).

LANGUAGE-BASED METHOD

The language experience approach (LEA) is the most widely known language-based method for remedial readers that builds on the idea that the child's own language can be used as a foundation for reading instruction. The term "approach" will be used in this section since it is the descriptor most frequently found in the literature. In LEA the child writes or dictates, from her background of experience, the reading material that she will use in learning to read or improving her reading skill. The approach is based on four premises (Lee and Allen 1963):

1. What a child thinks about she can talk about.
2. What a child can talk about can be expressed in writing or some other form.
3. Anything a child writes can be read.
4. A child can read what she writes and what other people write.

Although the language experience approach involves listening, speaking, writing, and reading, oral language is the primary language base. Oral language is generally better developed than reading skills in children who have severe reading problems. LEA is based on six assumptions about language (Lee and Allen 1963, pp. 1–2):

1. There is a close interrelationship among speaking, listening, reading, and writing as language skills.
2. The background of experiences of the individual learner provides the meaning of the words for that learner.
3. Words have no inherent meanings in and of themselves; the experience of the learner provides the meaning.
4. When visual symbols are associated with known sound symbols, meaning occurs in the mind of the reader.
5. Spoken words comprise the sound symbols that a listener uses to signal meaning.
6. Reading is a process of developing meaning from patterns that one recognizes. Reading arouses meanings based on the experience of the learner; it does not provide the meanings.

In the early stages of LEA, students dictate stories to the teacher or clinician, who handwrites them as dictated. Children then use these stories in word-recognition activities and in oral reading. Specific procedures in using the language experience approach are covered in many introductory reading methods textbooks; as they are generally known to teachers, they will not be repeated here. The reader who seeks an in-depth treatment of LEA is referred to MaryAnne Hall's *Teaching Reading as a Language Experience*, 3rd ed. (Columbus, OH: Charles E. Merrill, 1981).

Many writers recommend the use of LEA with remedial readers (Hall 1981, pp. 19–20; Huff 1983, pp. 314–16). The method does indeed contain a strong psychological rationale in its use of learning principles that are important in working with remedial readers. Johnson (1966) lists five such important principles:

1. Learning begins with the known.
2. Learning proceeds from the concrete to the abstract.
3. Learning demands active participation.
4. Learning should be goal-directed.
5. Learning is an individual matter.

LEA fulfills these learning principles. Children begin with what they know from experience (which is generally concrete), and use their oral language patterns to express this knowledge. Certainly the approach involves the learner actively and is directed toward goals that are easily understood by the child. Although all LEA activities do not have to be on an individual basis, this is recommended with remedial readers.

One of the major reasons for using LEA with remedial readers has to do with the affective domain. The approach is motivational in that children write their own stories and experience success in learning to recognize words they already know. They can also take pride in ownership of the material they have written. The learner's interests may be tapped to the fullest, as the student will usually write about things that interest her.

The language experience approach places fewer cognitive demands on readers than some other methods, in that the child already knows the concepts about which he writes. The child's main task in the beginning is learning to decode what he has written himself; success is thus almost assured. When the child has gained skill in reading the stories he has written, he can begin to read other stories on the same subjects, containing many of the words he has written and learned. Words learned in LEA stories can be used as a basis for work on sight vocabulary, phonic knowledge, and structural analysis.

LEA should not be viewed as a panacea—no single method (or approach) should. While the approach works with many remedial readers, it may not appeal to all. There are some limitations in its use. There may need to be more repetition of basic sight vocabulary than LEA provides. Teachers would then have to provide this repetition, and have to know about sequencing skill development.

The time will come in remedial programs when the sole use of LEA will be restrictive. When a child gains skill in recognizing words, he should be given the opportunity to read materials written by others in order that the words learned may be recognized in contexts other than that which he has written. In addition, exclusive use of LEA would not provide the opportunity to refine concept development through meeting words in slightly different contexts nor will it provide the opportunity to extend learning through reading.

Intensive Phonics (Auditory Emphasis)

In this category, the methods discussed have a focus on sounding and blending. Basic characteristics of these methods are that learning is based on associating sounds with letters and that the sounds are blended to form words. In other words, these are *synthetic* phonic methods. Elements of these methods are commonly found in today's curricula that focus on basic skills.

One of the early advocates of a method that utilized intensive phonics was Samuel T. Orton. Today, the Orton Society exists to promote the use of this method. June L. Orton (1966, p. 144) characterizes the Orton method as teaching phonic units in isolation, with special training in blending. Consonants and short vowels are introduced first so that three-letter words may be built for reading and spelling. A kinesthetic element is also used to reinforce visual-auditory language associations and to establish left-to-right progression habits.

Orton (1937, pp. 157–58) wrote that each child presents an individual problem because of diverse environmental conditions and because the "relative part played by each of the three major functions entering into the language faculty—vision, audition, and kinaesthesis—varies markedly in different children as does the child's emotional reaction to his difficulty. The first step toward successful treatment therefore must be a careful evaluation of the extrinsic factors—economic, social, educational, etc.— together with an extensive analysis of the status of spoken language, graphic language, motor skills or limitations, and emotional reactions." Orton cautioned against using his procedures inflexibly, and noted that they should not be "looked upon as a routine method applicable to all cases of nonreaders" (p. 161).

Gillingham and Stillman (1966, pp. 39–71) present a detailed description of a method that involves both sounding and blending. Their method could also have been discussed in the previous section, as it also focuses on the visual and the kinesthetic. The description below, however, is meant to give the reader some understanding of sounding and blending techniques.

Although their method is frequently referred to as an intensive phonics method, Gillingham and Stillman regard the use of "grunt and groan" procedures as useless, if not dangerous, noting that a child who follows a consonant uttered in isolation with a prolonged vowel sound /ə/ will be hindered in pronouncing the word (that is, blending the sounds). They state that "the only way that giving the sounds of the letters in succession can suggest a word is to produce them so lightly and briefly that the series sounds like the word spoken slowly" (p. 39).

The Gillingham–Stillman method is "to teach the sounds of the letters and then build these letter sounds into words, like bricks into a wall. This method of word-building cannot be used as supplementary to that of learning words as sight units. The two concepts are mutually exclusive" (p. 40).

They view their method as "based upon the close association of visual, auditory, and kinesthetic elements forming what is sometimes called the 'language triangle' " (p. 40).

Their method involves three processes, referred to as associations among visual (V), auditory (A), and kinesthetic (K) records on the brain. They state:

Association I: This Association consists of two parts—association of the visual symbol with the name of the letter, and association of the visual symbol with the sound of the letter: also the association of the feel of the child's speech organs in producing the sound of the letter as he hears himself say it. Association I is V–A and A–K. Part b. is the basis of oral reading.

Part a. The card is exposed and the name of the letter spoken by the teacher and repeated by the pupil.

Part b. As soon as the name has been really mastered, the sound is made by the teacher and repeated by the pupil. It is here that most emphasis must be placed if the case is primarily one of speech defect. The card is exposed, the implied question being, "What does this letter (or phonogram) say?", and the pupil gives its sound.

Association II. The teacher makes the sound represented by the letter (or phonogram), the face of the card not being seen by the pupil, and says, "Tell me the name of the letter that has this sound." Sound to name is A–A, and is essentially oral spelling.

Association III. The letter is carefully made by the teacher and then its form, orientation, etc., explained. It is then traced by the pupil over the teacher's lines, then written from memory, and finally written again with eyes averted while the teacher watches closely. This association is V–K and K–V. . . . Now, the teacher makes the sound, saying, "Write the letter that has this sound." This association is A–K and is the basis of written spelling.

Gillingham and Stillman (1966, p. 41) state that certain other associations are basic in the method and should be formed as soon as possible, if they are not already known:

1. The most basic requirement of all is that the child should be taught the name of each letter, or the letters in each phonogram. This is done by showing the card and teaching the child to say the name.

2. If the child's production of sounds is faulty, there will have to be practice in echo speech, i.e., the teacher will produce the sound for the child to imitate. Very little of this drill may be needed, and then, perhaps, only for certain sounds. On the other hand, other children, who may be able to recognize and remember the sound correctly, will persist in rendering it incorrectly, so that practice with echo speech will have to be continued for a considerable period of time.

3. When the name of the phonogram has been acquired, and correct sounds of speech have been found to be largely dependable, the following drill will be found to be useful reinforcement: The teacher says the names of various phonograms, and the child responds with the related sound or sounds which he has learned.

4. Before he is asked to write there must be whatever practice is necessary in tracing, copying, and writing from memory to dictation, this last being sometimes carried out with the child's eyes averted. Except in tracing and copying, the teacher dictates the name of the phonogram. In all instances the child says the name of each letter as he writes it.[1]

Reading of connected text is discouraged while the child is progressing through the "associations" so as to eliminate guessing in word recognition. It is recommended that the child's teacher and parents not require the child to read while the Gillingham and Stillman method is being used.

An often used phonogram unit is initial sound plus vowel (/ba/ plus /t/ rather than /b/ plus /at/, for example). When the pupil can read and write three-letter, phonemically regular words, she is ready to combine the known words into sentences and stories. It is permissible to include some phonemically irregular words when necessary. These words are told to the child; she is not to attempt to decode them.

Bond et al. (1984, pp. 230–31) find intensive phonic methods rigid, drill-oriented, and time-consuming, albeit necessary for some severely disabled readers. Commenting specifically on the Gillingham–Stillman method, they feel the method should be recommended only for those "most severe cases of reading disability who have failed to establish fundamental phonics knowledge" (p. 231).

NEUROLOGICALLY BASED METHODS

Some remedial methods are presented by their developers as being neurologically based. Two such methods that use the descriptor "neurological" are those of Heckelman (1966) and Delacato (1966).

The Neurological Impress Method has a promising research base for use with remedial readers (Chompsky 1976; Hollingsworth 1978). The use of the term "neurological" may be misleading since the procedure does not seem to affect a student's neurological functioning any more than other remedial approaches discussed in this text (VAKT, for example). The method is not appropriate as a beginning technique with severely disabled readers because the student needs some sight vocabulary knowledge in order to follow the procedures.

The impress method has been used in remedial reading classes for several years. It probably has its roots in Huey's (1908) "Imitation Reading." Heckelman reported using the method beginning in 1961. While Heckelman has had positive results with children using the method, he does not believe that the approach is the answer to all students' reading problems.

[1]From Anna Gillingham and Bessie Stillman, *Remedial Training for Children with Specific Disability in Reading, Spelling, and Penmanship.* 7th ed. (Cambridge, MA: Educators Publishing Service, 1966), pp. 39–41. Reprinted by permission.

The impress method should be done on a one-to-one basis. Heckelman has recommended that the student and teacher use the method for about fifteen minutes daily, for a total period of eight to twelve hours. Heckelman believes that if gains have not been made in that amount of time, the strategy may not be appropriate for that student.

The impress method has the teacher and student read aloud in unison. The teacher should be seated very near the student so that they both can see the book. The teacher places his finger under the words as they are read; later, the student may assume this task.

For fifteen minutes, the teacher and student read as much material as possible, with no interruptions to sound out words, ask comprehension questions, or discuss what is being read. The teacher should establish a comfortable rate, reading a little louder than the student. The student should be urged to forget about mistakes, and the teacher should not point out any made by the student.

Establishing a proper pace may require practice. The reading should be fluent, not a word-by-word monotone, and the teacher should try to synchronize her finger movement to her voice. The student may have difficulty keeping up at times, but the teacher should not slow down to a reading pace that lacks expression.

The impress method allows remedial students to participate in fluent oral reading. Because much of their reading has been at a word-by-word pace, they often have not had the opportunity to read fluently so that they can view reading as a meaningful process.

The Delacato method, not well received by many reading educators, is based on the theory that problems result from the failure of the child to achieve neurological integration at the subcortical level of the brain. Remedial training involves the use of creeping and crawling exercises and sleeping in a particular position; Delacato feels that these exercises will help achieve the hypothetically desired neurological organization. Some children with reading problems do not have problems with subcortical integration. In these cases, Delacato hypothesized, the problem was the absence of a clear and consistent cerebral dominance. A major symptom in these instances is crossed eye-hand dominance, which Delacato attempts to eliminate through eye exercises. Spache (1976, pp. 347–48) summarizes research that indicates that the method has no effect on reading achievement. Teachers should view Delacato's procedures with a great deal of skepticism.

Additional Remedial Methods, Programs, and Materials

Additional methods, programs, and materials have been recommended in the literature for use with remedial readers. Many are already used by classroom teachers in regular instruction, and may be used with developmental, corrective, or remedial readers as appropriate. Among these options are: perceptual programs; linguistic materials; computer programs; programmed instruction using operant conditioning; changed alphabets and procedures for teaching phoneme/grapheme relationships; behavior management; and psychological or counseling approaches.

Perceptual programs. Some professionals who work with problem readers believe a major cause of severe reading problems to be perceptual deficits in the visual, auditory, or visual-motor areas. The relationship of perceptual factors to reading disability was discussed in Chapter 2. The general conclusion of research is that while perceptual skills are important in learning to read, perceptual learning is dependent on such factors as the child's attitudes and interests, innate mental and physical abilities, and experiential background. Thus, the specific contribution of a perceptual deficit per se is difficult to determine.

Visual perception is a perceptual area that has received considerable attention, including several recommended visual training programs and exercises. Two well-known programs for visual perceptual training are the Getman–Kephart programs and the Frostig program.

Getman–Kephart programs (Kephart 1971) involve training in areas such as laterality or body-image, directionality, and binocular and monocular motility and control. Spache (1981) has summarized research on programs that emphasize such visual-motor skills as laterality, directionality, form reproduction, ocular control, and body image as needing "more research to sort out its effective components." He notes, however, that "general training, as in the Kephart or Getman programs, in body image, directionality, form tracing, or hand-eye coordination, ocular control and motility . . . is relevant to readiness and reading . . . These types of training do benefit low socioeconomic or low intelligence children" (pp. 415–18).

The Frostig perceptual training program is a five-part program based on the results of the *Frostig Development Test of Visual Perception* (1966). The five subtests and the worksheets used in the program are based on the perceptual areas that the developers of the program feel have the greatest relevance for academic work: perception of position in space, perception of spatial relationships, perceptual constancy, visual-motor coordination, and figure-ground perception. Frostig and Horne (1964, p. 13) state that the exercises can benefit all children in kindergarten and first grade, and can be used in remedial programs for children of any grade level who need work in visual perceptual development. The program makes extensive use of worksheets, but also includes recommendations for preceding and supplementing the worksheets with exercises that involve the whole body.

Research on the Frostig method suggests that the program yields gains on the Frostig test itself, but finds that the effect on reading is generally nonsignificant (Spache 1981, pp. 420–23). Teachers are cautioned about the use of this method as a basic remedial program.

Linguistic materials. Linguistic materials, as used in the literature focusing on remedial readers, usually refers to a type of material that uses a high degree of phoneme/grapheme regularity (spelling patterns). One example of such material is the *Merrill Linguistic Readers* (Columbus, OH: Charles E. Merrill, 1980). The materials provide much repetition of regular spelling patterns (can, nan, Dan, tan, fan, etc.), but the teaching method differs from intensive phonic approaches in that sounds are not taught in isolation. A potential disadvantage to linguistic readers is that the sentences are more stilted than when a larger variety of words may be used.

Computer programs. Computers are found more and more in reading clinics and special programs. Software for computer programs continues to focus on the teaching of subskills of the reading process. Higher level comprehension skills are less well presented than word-recognition skills, yet programs continue to improve. (See Chapter 12 for a discussion of selected available computer programs.)

Computer programs may, through their visual displays, provide motivation for the remedial reader who has not had success with print materials. They lend themselves well to the need for instruction paced in small steps, with immediate feedback. Computers also offer the opportunity for additional practice of skills presented first through the print medium.

Programmed materials. The programmed procedure involves the presentation of small bits of information that require a specific response from the child. There is an opportunity for immediate feedback on the correctness of the response. The bits of information are self-instructional and are carefully sequenced so that the child may achieve success easily. The programs are based on the psychological principles of operant conditioning.

One example of programmed materials is *Programmed Reading*, developed by M. W. Sullivan and C. B. Buchanan (McGraw-Hill, 1973). The series consists of twenty-three programmed textbooks, plus a number of readers correlated with the programmed texts so that students can practice applying what they have learned in the texts. The materials use the spelling pattern approach to word recognition.

Modified alphabets. Modified alphabets are still mentioned in the literature on remedial and corrective programs, but they are not as widely used as they once were. Modified alphabets are based on the assumption that a major cause of difficulty in learning to read is the irregularity of the sound/symbol relationships of many words commonly found in beginning reading materials. Modifying the alphabet to make a one-to-one correspondence between sound and symbol is seen as one way to avoid this problem. The rationale for the use of modified alphabets with remedial readers is that it will speed their learning to read more conceptually complex material, since they presumably will have fewer problems with decoding.

There are problems with this rationale; for one, remedial students already have considerable experience with traditional orthography and may have difficulty dealing with a new set of symbols. Another problem is the dearth of available materials written in the modified alphabets.

The most commonly used modified alphabet is the Initial Teaching Alphabet (i/t/a), which has forty-four symbols, each representing one English sound. Another is UNIFON (International Phoneme Corporation), which uses forty symbols, all uppercase. Any type of text, approach, or method can be used with i/t/a. The system can be used with LEA or be incorporated into a basal series, such as the "Early-to-Read" program developed by Albert J. Mazurkiewicz and Harold Tanyzer (1964).

A second way to simplify the learning of sound-symbol relationships is to use color to signal different sounds, as is done in *Words in Color* by Caleb Gattegno (Educational Solutions, Inc., 1962). Each of the vowel sounds in *Words in Color* is coded to a specific color; so, to a somewhat lesser degree, are the consonants. Digraphs, both vowel and consonant, also have their own special colors. The method of word-recognition instruction is that of synthetic phonics.

Behavior management. Behavior-management techniques often involve the use of praise, the giving of stars or other tokens, and the charting of progress to improve the motivation and learning of remedial readers. Rooted in behavioral learning theory, these procedures include among key concepts the use of extrinsic and intrinsic reinforcement, contingency contracting, and management.

Some reading programs incorporate the principles of behavior management, including DISTAR (Science Research Associates 1983), which features direct instruction in reading. The emphasis is on programmed learning, with frequent drill and repetition. The program features highly structured, fast-paced instruction: simple reading tasks, a teacher-directed procedure with no deviations permitted, a strictly controlled sequence, and no allowance for creativity. Children respond to teacher questions in unison. The word-recognition aspect of the program is largely a synthetic phonics approach. The program has been said to be effective with students who have experienced school failure (Haring and Bateman 1977), and may also be helpful in working with children who are linguistically different.

Psychological or counseling approach. The purpose of psychological or counseling approaches is to ameliorate those emotional factors that may interfere with reading success. Interpersonal relationships between teacher and pupil are critical to these approaches. Counseling may occur prior to or concurrent with remediation. Many techniques have been used in working with remedial readers who need counseling: nondirective counseling, directive counseling, play therapy, counseling of parents, and bibliotherapy (Spache 1981, pp. 336–42).

Reporting the Results of Extended Remediation

Reporting to classroom teachers and to parents is essential if extended remedial programs are to be maximally effective in promoting reading growth. Teachers must understand what has been accomplished and must provide an opportunity for the child to use and refine the skills learned in the special remedial program. Classroom teachers and special instructors can frequently provide the dialogue needed in conferences, in both formal and informal settings.

When remediation occurs in a place physically removed from the school building (a private or university clinic, for example), a progress report is generally made available to the parent, and, with parental permission, to the teacher. It is essential that parents share this information with teachers.

The following criteria may be useful in preparing remediation reports and in evaluating the reports received:

1. The report should be complete; that is, it should contain enough information so that the parent and the teacher may know what was done and how effective the remediation was.
2. The report should be clearly written. Educational jargon should be avoided. Language that is easily understood by parents, as well as by teachers, should be used.
3. Such reports should contain the following minimum components:
   a. Complete demographic data, such as name, date of birth, age, grade, parents' or guardian's names, date of report, and the name of the individual providing the remediation.
   b. The instructional goals for the term.
   c. A statement of how well each of the instructional goals was met.
   d. A listing of the methods, materials, and strategies used.
   e. The results of any pretesting and posttesting.
   f. Recommendations to parents and/or teachers about the need for further special remediation.

An example of a progress report sent from a university clinic to a parent may be found in Appendix B. As you read the report, consider whether the report meets the criteria above. Also consider what additional information you would want as a parent or as a teacher.

INFORMATION TO CONSIDER

1. There are criteria against which reports of special remedial programs may be evaluated.

Summary

Several special methods, programs, and materials have been recommended for use in extended programs with remedial readers. Most of the special "methods" were first used decades ago; there are very few remedial methods that have been proposed recently.

For purposes of discussion, the special remedial methods were grouped into the following categories: multisensory, language-based, intensive phonics (auditory emphasis), and neurologically based. The categories are not mutually exclusive, as components in one category may be found in another. Also discussed were selected additional methods, programs, and materials that have been mentioned in the literature as appropriate for use with remedial readers. These include perceptual programs, linguistic materials, computer programs, programmed instruction, changed alphabets and procedures for regularizing sound-symbol correspondences, behavior management, and psychological or counseling approaches.

Many methods, programs, and materials used in extended remediation are also used by classroom teachers in regular instruction. One major difference is that the method or material must be matched with the specific needs of the learner who is having reading problems.

Questions for Further Thought

1. What are the overall advantages and limitations of each of the major categories of methods discussed in this chapter?
2. What criteria would you consider in selecting a remedial method, program, or material for a given child?

3. What are some additional remedial methods that may be found in the literature? What are their major characteristics?

Activities and Projects

1. Visit a university reading clinic. Ask what special remedial methods are used in that clinic and why. Do the same with a Chapter I reading teacher. What are the similarities and differences in their use of remedial methods?
2. Study Peter L. Pelosi's classification scheme for remedial reading methods in "A Method for Classifying Remedial Reading Techniques" (*Reading World* [December, 1982], pp. 119–28). Compare his classification scheme with that used in this text. List points of agreement and disagreement. Which do you consider more valid? Why?
3. Read *Teacher* by Sylvia Ashton-Warner (New York: Bantam Books, 1971). Compare her methods with the Fernald method and with the language experience approach.
4. Read MaryAnne Hall's *Teaching Reading as a Language Experience*, 3rd ed. (Colum-

bus, OH: Charles E. Merrill, 1981). Make a list of ideas that should be especially relevant for remedial readers.
5. Read Chapter VI of *Children Who Cannot Read* by Marian Monroe (University of Chicago Press, 1932). How does Monroe's method compare with the Gillingham–Stillman method presented in this text? List the strengths and limitations of the Monroe method. If you were to choose one method over the other, what would influence your decision?
6. Read Marianne Frostig's *Selection and Adaptation of Reading Methods* (San Rafael, CA: Academic Therapy Publications, 1973). Study her discussion of symptoms of reading problems observed in classrooms, possible underlying deficits, methods of evaluating deficits, suggested training methods, and suggested reading methods. Locate a teacher or clinician with experience in working with severely disabled

readers. Discuss with this person the applicablity of what you have read. You may also wish to compare Frostig's program with that of Kephart in *The Slower Learner in the Classroom*, 2nd ed., (Columbus, OH: Charles E. Merrill, 1971).

Appendix A
Constructing an Informal
Reading Inventory

This appendix is intended to help teachers construct an informal reading inventory (IRI). The construction of a set of IRIs involves several processes at each grade (or book) level. Generally, there should be as many IRI levels as there are levels in the graded materials under consideration for use. For example, a fourth grade teacher may need IRIs from beginning primary levels through upper elementary levels.

Each level requires a sight word list. Teachers should select two or three reading passages for each level, each accompanied by comprehension questions. They should also prepare sets of introductory background statements and instructions for reading. Finally, there should be a format for presenting word lists and graded passages to children and a record-keeping system.

SIGHT RECOGNITION WORD LISTS

Sight word lists may come from two sources. They may be prepared by using randomly selected words from the books from which the graded passages were taken; or already prepared graded word lists, such as the Dolch Word List, may be used.

Word lists prepared by teachers are usually constructed in one of two ways: by taking a random sample of the running words from the text, or by taking a sample of the "new" words in a teacher's manual for a basal or content text. Samples must be truly random and the same selection procedures should be used at each grade level. A list of twenty words at each level is adequate.

In making a random sample of a running text, teachers should decide in advance which pages are to be sampled and which words on those pages are to be chosen. For example, choosing the twelfth word on every twentieth page might be one way to create a list. Procedures should be identified for selecting an alternative word if the randomly selected word is a difficult proper name, or if it is a word that already appears at the level being sampled (or at a lower level). One way to attend to these potential problems is to select twenty-five words randomly, using the first twenty that are not repeats or difficult proper nouns. Words chosen from lists of "new" words may be made by selecting each Nth word; for example, each tenth word from a list of 200 words, or each fifth word from a list of 100. (The uses of sight word lists were explained in Chapter 5. Criteria for "new" and running word samples were also outlined.)

SELECTING GRADED PASSAGES

Several factors should guide the selection of passages from texts. In general practice, two passages are selected for each level—one for reading aloud and the other for silent reading. However, teachers may wish to select a third passage. The third passage could serve two purposes. First, it could provide an option to be used for assessing listening when both passages at a given level have already been read by a child being administered the IRI. Sometimes a student will be unable to comprehend satisfactorily by listening at the next level higher than the last passage that was read at the frustration level. In such instances the teacher may wish to assess listening at a lower level to obtain diagnostic information about a child's listening comprehension. A third passage also permits a check on either the silent or the oral reading at a later point in time.

Teachers should be aware that texts vary widely in readability, both within a given text and among tests designed for the same grade level. This means that samples must be chosen with care. Several considerations seem warranted when passages are selected. These include:

1. Passages should be cohesive. That is, they should make some overall sense to the reader, assuming the reader has the skills needed to comprehend. It is desirable for the oral and silent passages to come from the same story. Comparisons are more valid since concept density and passage interest are more likely to be similar.
2. The content of passages should be typical of the text. A poem from a text that is basically narrative would not be appropriate.
3. Passages should be within typical interest ranges. Passages deemed especially high or low in interest for the readers in the class should not be chosen. Students tend to comprehend better in an area of high interest.
4. Passages that have unusual proper nouns should be avoided unless such proper nouns are typical of the entire text.

5. Passages are generally appropriate when selected about one-fourth to one-third of the way through the text. Some materials are designed to be easier for review purposes in the early part of the text.
6. Passages from which it is possible to construct good comprehension questions should be chosen.
7. Passages written in dialect (respellings) should be avoided since these passages are typically difficult to read.
8. Passages should be of an appropriate word length.

Recommendations for passage length at given grade levels vary in the literature. The following passage length guide, which is meant to be suggestive and not absolute, seems reasonable.

Grade Level	Silent Reading/ Listening Level Passages	Oral Reading Passages
Pre-primer	30	30
Primer	50	50
Grade 1	75	75
Grade 2	100	100
Grade 3	125	100
Grade 4	150	100
Grade 5	175	100
Grade 6	200	100

Note that the length of passages to be read orally does not exceed 100 words at any grade level. This passage length is adequate when dealing with oral reading, especially when the reader approaches frustration level. It also makes the calculation of miscue percentages easy.

An additional consideration for selecting passages has been suggested by Savage and Mooney (1979, p. 93). They note that when IRIs are being constructed for general use (presumably when a match with materials proposed for use is not the main concern) the nature of the materials that have been used for instructional purposes in previous years should be considered. That is, if the materials used previously have had a sound-symbol relationship base (certain linguistic and phonic based materials), then these materials provide a fairer approximation of level than will material that differs (one that has a high incidence of phonemically irregular words, for example).

The actual format of the child's version of the graded passages may vary.

1. The teacher may give the child the actual text and indicate the portion to read. Care should be taken, however, that there are no comprehension questions that could be answered by looking at any accompanying pictures.

2. Passages may be typed on white paper. The type size should be as close as possible to the type generally used in texts. The use of a primer typewriter is advised for beginning levels. Length of lines should be similar to that generally found in texts.
3. Pages or portions of pages may be cut from texts, mounted on cardboard, and laminated. They could then be placed in a notebook binder to make a booklet.

INTRODUCTORY STATEMENTS

The statements made to readers prior to administering the graded passages can affect comprehension of the passages. Explicitly stated purposes can restrict comprehension of the purposes set. Unless comprehension questions are closely related to these explicitly stated purposes, comprehension as measured by the IRI may suffer, and an accurate determination of levels may be difficult. Often, it is best to tell children that they will be reading (or listening to) some passages and that they will be asked questions after they finish. Children generally attend more broadly when their thinking is not focused in a particular direction.

If a passage does not start at the beginning of a story, it may be necessary to provide an introductory statement or a brief synopsis of what has preceded so that the passage is understood in context. Care should be taken, however, that these comments do not provide answers or clues to answers to the comprehension questions asked.

CONSTRUCTING QUESTIONS

Good questions are critical to the determination of valid levels from an IRI. Different sets of questions can yield different results from the same passage (Peterson et al. 1978). Thus, questions should be carefully constructed. Two sets of guidelines that the authors have found useful are those of Valmont (1972), and of Johnson and Kress (1965).

It is important that questions following passages sample both literal recall and inferential thinking. Both are important, and some children do better on one than the other. This is important for teachers to know. The number of questions usually ranges from 4–5 at beginning levels to 8–10 at middle and upper grade levels.

Johnson and Kress (1965, p. 34) suggest that for five question sets the following types of questions be asked: two factual questions, two inferential questions, and one vocabulary question. Valmont (1972) has provided models for seven types of questions that sample both literal and inferential comprehension. These are main idea, detail, inference (general), drawing conclusions, organization (includes sequence), cause and effect, and vocabulary.

The following suggestions for selecting types of questions seem reasonable:

1. Four or five questions are appropriate for pre-primer level through grades 1 or 2. It is difficult to ask several good questions from short passages, however. Four questions make the calculation of instructional and frustration levels easy (using the Betts criteria).
2. The following four question types should be included at lower levels when possible: main idea, detail, inference, and vocabulary. When a fifth question is needed, an additional detail question may be added. At lower levels, it is sometimes difficult to ask good vocabulary questions that cannot be answered from general knowledge. When this happens, a balance of literal and inferential questions should be sought.
3. For grades 2 through 6, eight questions are appropriate. Again, this number makes the calculation of instructional and frustration level easy (Betts criteria). Ten questions are also appropriate for upper levels (grade 4 and up). Ten questions make the calculation of all levels easy. Longer passages are usually needed to yield ten good questions.

If eight questions are asked, two schemes are recommended, depending on how well the material lends itself to a given scheme.

The Schemes

	Set I	Set II
Main idea (literal or inferential)	1	1
Vocabulary	2	1
Literal (details, sequence)	2	3
Inference (variety of types)	3	3
	8	8

If ten questions are desired, another literal and another inferential question may be added.

Some cautions about types of questions are warranted. It may not be possible to utilize every question type listed above with every passage. It is more important that questions be good ones than that a specific number or type be asked. When a desired question type is omitted or an imbalance of question types occurs at a given grade level, the inequity can be corrected by selecting a passage that samples the desired question types at a level immediately above or below the level in question. This generally provides an opportunity for the reader to respond to all question types sometime during the administration of an IRI.

If IRIs are to provide for the best match between learner and material, then they should be reality oriented. That is, the types of questions asked on the IRI and the types of questions asked in daily instruction should be similar. This tells the teacher how the child will respond to types of questions that are typically asked in the instructional setting.

The following examples of appropriate question types are based on Valmont (1972):

1. Main idea
   a. What would be a good title for this passage? (This is a convenient but sometimes overworked question. When possible it is desirable to use a question similar to b.)
   b. What did Jill tell Janet to do? (The response to this question type should summarize what the passage is all about. Otherwise, it is just another detail question.)
2. Detail
   a. Where did Frosty go?
   b. What did Fred find at home?
      (Detail questions are generally literal, but not necessarily so. For example, the story may not have stated explicitly what Fred found at home. Instead, the story may have told what he did with what he found, which would give a rather clear notion of what the object was.)
3. Inference
   a. Why do you believe Janet was either happy or sad? (Note the general inference does not state which emotional state Janet was in. This wording helps reduce guessing.)
   b. What do you think Janet will do next? (This involves drawing a conclusion from previous information. There should be more than one bit of information in the text that would lead to a reasonable response.)
   c. Why was Mother in a hurry? (This is an example of a cause and effect inference question when the answer is *not* stated directly but must be inferred from something that happened previously in the story.)
4. Sequence (or organization)
   a. Name, in order, three things that Jill did after she found her room had been ransacked? (Asking for an answer in order is important in a sequence question since the sequence should be important to the story. If the sequence is not important, then this question is not a good question and should not be asked.)
5. Vocabulary
   a. What does "run" mean in this passage? (Note the phrase "in this passage." A word or phrase that may be defined from general knowledge is not a good item to use. Restricting word selection to words that have multiple meanings—but specific to the context of the passage—are more desirable.)
   b. What does "in the hopper" mean in this passage? (A vocabulary item may be a phrase as well as a single word.)

As teachers construct questions, they should ask themselves whether the questions are passage dependent or passage independent. A passage-independent question can be answered correctly from general knowledge. Passage-dependent questions cannot. The examples of vocabulary questions cited above are structured so that they relate to the specific passage.

Valmont (1972, p. 511) has suggested an excellent set of guidelines for evaluating IRI questions. These are:

1. Main idea questions should generally be asked first.
2. Other questions should generally be asked in the order in which answers occurred in the text.
3. Questions that are so broad that any answer is acceptable should be avoided.
4. Questions that test general knowledge should be avoided.
5. The syntax of the question should be as simple as possible for clarity. Questions should generally begin with question words (who, when, why, and so on).
6. Questions should be passage dependent.
7. Questions that can be answered by "reading" illustrations in the text should be avoided.
8. Negative questions should be avoided whenever possible.
9. Yes-no or multiple-choice questions should be avoided since a chance factor is involved in the answer.
10. Questions that ask children to construct lists should be avoided unless these are important sequence questions.

Appendix B
Diagnostic Report and Progress Report

The diagnostic report and progress report which follow are based on actual reports of a nine year old boy that were done at a university reading center.[1] The names and dates have been changed so that identification is not possible.

Wayne University
The Reading Center
Monticello, Kentucky 42633

Diagnostic Report

Name: Alex James   Date: April, 1986
Date of Birth: 2/7/77   Grade: 3
Parents: Levi and Bertha James   Age: 9
Address: 1931 Alfred Road   Examiner: Geneva Smith
          Bethesda, KY 42301   Supervisor: Chuck Fairchild

Appearance, Interview, and Test Behavior:

Alex is a well-behaved child who appears to be shy at first, but who warms up as he becomes familiar with new surroundings. Alex attends third grade at Bethesda Elementary School. He was seen two times at the Wayne University Reading Center for assessment purposes and was accompanied by his father to each session.

During tests requiring any type of reading, Alex was very nervous and would twist his fingers under the table, wiggle on his seat, or even stand up at times. He did try his best on each of the tests given, however. Therefore, the information given in this report is considered valid and can be used in planning a corrective program for Alex.

[1]Permission from the parents to use the reports as changed is on file.

Test Results:

A. Vision: Questionable
    Test: *Titmus T/O Tester*

B. Hearing: Normal
    Test: *Maico Audiometer*

C. Verbal Ability: Average for grade level peers
    Tests: *Slossen Intelligence Test for Children and Adults*
    Peabody Picture Vocabulary

D. Reading: Below average for grade level peers

Tests:	No. Correct/ No. Possible	Grade Equivalent
Diagnostic Reading Scales (DRS)		
Word Recognition, List 1	43/50	2.3
Word Recognition, List 2	12/40	2.8
Instructional Level	Beginning second gr.	
Independent Level	Beginning first gr.	
Listening Level	Not determined	
Consonant Sounds	21/21	
Vowel Sounds	2/10	
Consonant Blends and Digraphs	12/15	
Common Syllables	19/33	
Blending	4/10	
Letter Sounds	24/26	
Gates–McKillop Reading Diagnostic Tests, **Form 2**		
Words: Flashed	5/40	1.7
Words: Untimed	8/80	1.8
Phrases: Flashed	5/26	1.8
Recognizing and Blending Parts	8/23	1.8
Giving Letter Sounds	26/26	
Recognizing the Visual Form of Sounds	14/20	
Initial Letters	19/19	
Final Letters	13/14	
Vowels	9/10	
Auditory Blending	15/15	
Syllabication	4/20	
Gates–MacGinitie Reading Test, **Primary A, Form 1**		
Vocabulary	30/48	2.3
Comprehension	23/34	2.1

School Tasks:

Reader's Digest Skill Builders
Level 1, Part 1
  "The Camel" (Silent Reading)
  Comprehension: Fact-Recall   3/5
  "The Bus Stop" (Oral Reading)
  (17 errors on 95 words)

Reader's Digest Skill Builders
Level 2, Part 1
   "Trolley Cars" (Silent Reading)
   Comprehension: Fact-Recall   3/5
   "The Story of a Book" (Oral Reading)
   Invalid

Dolch Word Lists	
Pre-Primer	33/37
Primer	35/48
First Grade	31/50
Second Grade	23/50

Interpretation of Non-Reading Test Results:

Alex was tested with the *Titmus T/O Vision Tester*, a screening device for near- and farpoint visual acuity. He experienced difficulty with his right and left eyes on both far and near portions of the test. Further testing by an eye-care specialist is recommended.

Alex's hearing was tested with the *Maico Audiometer*. This is an assessment of ability to hear sounds at various levels of loudness and softness. The test results indicate that his hearing is within the normal range and that he has no auditory difficulties.

The *Slossen Intelligence Test for Children and Adults* was administered to Alex. This is a useful screening device to give an indication of a person's ability to solve problems, learn, judge, and retain knowledge. The questions asked included facts learned, math problems, definitions, comparisons, and repetitions of numbers. The test results indicate that Alex is within the normal range for his grade level peers.

The *Peabody Picture Vocabulary Test* (PPVT) was given to determine Alex's receptiveness (hearing and understanding) of Standard American English vocabulary. In this test, the examiner calls a word and the student points to a picture that depicts the word. On the PPVT, Alex's score indicates that his understanding of oral vocabulary is average when compared with his peers'.

Alex's listening potential was not determined from the administration of the *Diagnostic Reading Scales* because at the time this test was administered, he was very frustrated and did not wish to continue. Generally, this test indicates how much a child can comprehend when he listens. On this test, the examiner reads short passages at various levels of difficulty to the child. Then the child is asked questions to check his comprehension.

In summary, Alex's non-reading test results show that his hearing is within the normal range, but that he may be experiencing visual difficulty. His verbal ability is average when compared with his peers'. His listening potential could not be determined on the testing date.

Interpretation of Reading Test Results:

One of the first skills tested in the series of reading tests given to Alex was his sight word ability. Sight words are those words that a student recognizes at a glance without having to sound them out or to analyze them. A large sight vocabulary is a must for reading success. Without a good sight vocabulary, a child will have difficulty with comprehension and fluency in reading.

Sight word vocabulary was measured in isolation on the Word Recognition Lists of the *Diagnostic Reading Scales* (DRS). On these lists, the student is asked to call words with no time restrictions. Word List 1 was given first. On this list, Alex was asked to call 50 words at his own pace. He was able to call 43 of the 50 words correctly for a grade-equivalent score of 2.3. The words he did not know or failed to call correctly were: ball, eat, children, around, breakfast, rain, and girl. List 2 was given next. On this list, Alex was asked to call 40 words correctly at his own pace. He was able to call 12 of the 40 correctly for a grade-equivalent score of 2.8. Some of the words that he did not know were: quickly, turkey, handle, battle, bridge, and road.

The *Gates-McKillop Reading Diagnostic Tests* were also given to test Alex's ability to call sight words correctly. On subtest III, he was asked to call 80 words with no time restrictions. On this test, he was able to call 8 words correctly for a grade-equivalent score of 1.8. Some of the words that Alex did not call correctly were: men (which he called asman), train (which he gave as trim), and wagon (which he called when). Some of the words that he did not know at all were: ate, temple, torment, and respect.

To measure Alex's visual memory and the ability to read in phrases, Tests II and IV of the *Gates-McKillop* were administered. On test II, he was presented forty words using a flash presentation of one-half second each. Alex was able to call 5 of the 40 words correctly for a grade-equivalent score of 1.7. Some of the words that he did not attempt were: cruel, avenue, day, men, train, wagon, temple, torment, and respect. On Test IV, Alex was shown phrases of two to four words in length. The exposure time was one-half second. He was able to call 5 of the 26 phrases correctly for a grade-equivalent score of 1.8. Some of the phrases he did not attempt were: my train, one coat, color it, and go away.

The vocabulary test of the *Gates-MacGinitie Reading Test*, Primary A, Form 1 was then administered. This test measures the ability to recognize or analyze words in isolation. Forty-eight exercises (each consisting of four words and a picture illustrating the meaning of one of the words) are shown to the child. The child circles the word that best corresponds to the picture. The exercises are arranged so that the easier ones are pictured first. The child has 15 minutes to complete the test. Alex was able to circle the correct word on 39 of the 48 exercises for a grade-equivalent score of 2.3. Some of the words that he did not circle correctly were: walking, calf, pies, and railroad. (Normally, this form of the test is given to students who read on a first grade level.)

A knowledge of consonant and vowel sounds, tested in isolation on both the DRS and on the *Gates-McKillop*, is helpful in decoding and word attack. On these two tests combined, Alex was able to demonstrate a working knowledge of consonant sounds but had difficulty with vowel sounds. Those vowel sounds that he failed to call correctly were: long and short *a*, long and short *o*, long and short *e*, and long and short *u*. The vowel sounds that he called correctly were long and short *i*.

An assessment was made of Alex's use of beginning and ending sounds on *Gates-MacGinitie* subtests VI-2 and VI-3. On these tests a student must listen to a word and circle the sound he hears at the beginning of a word. Next the student listens to a word and circles the sound heard at the end of the word. Alex was able to circle correctly all the sounds he heard at the beginnings of words but failed to circle the sound of *d* that he heard at the end of a word.

A knowledge of consonant blends (or clusters) and digraphs is also important in decoding. A cluster refers to the reader's ability to say two consonant sounds closely together so that they are pronounced as a unit. A digraph is two consonant letters that together represent a single sound. Test 3 of the DRS was used to test Alex's knowledge of consonant blends and digraphs. On this test, he was able to give 12 of 15 consonants blends and digraphs correctly. Those that he did not give correctly were: *wh, ck,* and *fl.*

Test 4 of the DRS was given to assess Alex's knowledge of common syllables. A knowledge of syllables is an important aid to a reader in recognizing certain sound units instantly so that he does not need to depend on letter-by-letter decoding. On this test, Alex read a list of 33 common syllables such as *ail, est, ite,* and *ock.* He was able to call 19 of the 33 correctly. Some of the syllables that he did not know were: *ail, ter, ow, ake,* and *ent.* On Test 5 of the DRS, a student must read 10 nonsense words that are divided into syllables, and then blend the syllables back into the nonsense word. For example, the student must be able to give the sounds for "tr—est—ing" separately and then blend the parts into whole words. Alex blended four words correctly but failed to do so for the remaining six. These were: cl–ide, st–ain–ite, sp–ick–tion, te–est–ing, sh–ay–ter, and ch–ail–er.

Blending and recognizing word parts were also assessed using the *Gates-McKillop*. On this test, a child is asked to pronounce a nonsense word in its entirety. If he fails to do so, he is then shown the word parts separately and asked to blend the parts into a whole word. (For example: /sp/ /ack/ into spack.) On this test, Alex could correctly blend 8 of 23 nonsense words. Some of those missed were: whickle, glemp, twasp, plew, crell, and flark.

The ability to blend word parts auditorially is also tested on the *Gates-McKillop*. On this test, the examiner gives the sounds orally to the child. Then the child must blend the parts into a whole word. (For example: h + or + se = horse.) On this test, Alex was able to blend correctly all of the 15 sounds into whole words.

An additional measure of the *Gates-McKillop* is a test of a student's knowledge of the visual form of sounds. On this test, the examiner reads a nonsense word and the student must circle the word he hears. On this test, Alex was able to circle 14 of the 20 words correctly. Some of the words he missed were: dom, thispen, fandin, and inchitome.

Alex's comprehension was checked using the *Diagnostic Reading Scales,* which contain graded passages for a student to read. When the child has read a passage, he is then asked comprehension questions that deal with facts, main idea, and inference. Based on Alex's performance on these paragraphs, his instructional level was estimated to be about beginning second grade. This is the level at which he can function with a teacher's help in reading. This level was obtained by having him read the passages orally and then answer questions at an 80 percent level of accuracy. Alex's pattern of errors on the oral reading portion of the test consisted of self-corrections, repetitions, omissions of words he did not know (or calling them incorrectly), and insertions of words that did not belong. He also appeared to have a difficult time keeping his place as he read.

Alex's independent level on the DRS (the level at which he can work most comfortably alone) was estimated to be at the beginning first grade level. This was the level at which he could read paragraphs silently and answer questions with 90 percent accuracy.

Alex's comprehension was also tested using the *Gates-MacGinitie Reading Test,* Primary A, Form 1. Normally, this test is given to first graders. Since Alex fell below grade level on other tests given, this form was used to assess comprehension. In this test, a child is asked a question or presented a situation verbally, and then told to select a picture that best describes the statement. On this test, Alex correctly answered 23 of a possible 34 for a grade-equivalent score of 2.1.

School tasks were administered next. These are measures to see how a child performs in a school-like reading task. Given the time constraints, it was possible to sample only a few school-like tasks. The *Reader's Digest Skill Builders* and the *Dolch Word List* were used to evaluate his comprehension and word recognition respectively.

The beginning first grade level of the *Reader's Digest Skill Builders* was selected as the first school-like task. Alex was asked to read a short selection silently. He was then asked five fact recall questions. He was able to answer three of the five questions correctly. Next, he read a short selection orally. Once again, a pattern of word recognition errors was found. These were miscalling words, repetitions, self-corrections, and asking for help on unknown words. Following the oral reading, five fact recall questions were asked. Alex was able to answer three of the five correctly.

The second grade level of the *Reader's Digest Skill Builders* was then given to Alex. He was asked to read a short passage silently followed again by five fact recall questions. On this level, he was able to answer two of the five questions correctly. Again he was asked to read a passage orally. He read a few lines of the passage and then became so frustrated that he asked to stop.

The *Dolch Word List* was used to assess Alex's knowledge of commonly used words. The preprimer list was given first. On this list, he was asked to call 37 words such as: a, go, I, is, up, you, not, and to. He correctly called 33 of the 37 words. Those he did not call correctly were: get (which he called go), what (which he called went), and ride (which he called rid). Next the primer list was administered. On this list, he was asked to call 48 words such as: are, but, too, think, walk, and laughed. He called 35 of the 48 possible words correctly. Some of the words he missed were: take (which he called that), white (which he called which), new (which he called near), and seven (He asked, "What is this thing?"). Following the primer list, the first grade list was administered. On this list, Alex was asked to call a total of 50 words such as: sing, keep, soon, that, three, and were. He correctly called 31 of the 50 words. Some of the words he missed were: how (which he called hoe), let's (which he called list), over (which he called every), and soon (which he called son). Finally, the second grade list was given. On this list, he was asked to call a total of 50 words such as: or, tell, together, under, and wish. He called 23 of the 50 words correctly. Some of the words he missed were: tell (which he called stale), gave (which he called five), got (which he called go), and live (which he called love).

In summary, the tests administered and the school tasks used suggested that Alex's independent level is beginning first grade and his instructional level is beginning second grade.

Recommendations:

It is recommended that Alex receive sight word instruction. The *Dolch Word List* can be used as a starting point. Phonics instruction, which focuses on vowel sounds, will also be helpful. In addition, he needs help with word parts and syllabication, which will further help him unlock unknown words.

Alex also needs help with comprehension. He should be taught the meanings of words as he works with word recognition skills. Comprehension should be taught using teacher modeling in which the teacher explains how she answers comprehension questions.

Alex lacks self-confidence in reading. This problem can be lessened by placing him on his independent level for free reading and on his instructional level in classroom reading tasks. Praise and positive reinforcement should be used whenever possible. Comparisons of Alex's reading skills with those of his peers should be avoided.

Alex is a very pleasant child with a winning personality. It is recommended that he receive one-on-one tutoring until he is able to overcome reading skill deficiencies.

Wayne University
The Reading Center
Monticello, KY 42633

Progress Report

Name: Alex James
Parents: Levi and Bertha James
Address: 1931 Alfred Road
         Bethesda, KY 42301

Date: December, 1986
Grade: 4
Age: 9
Tutor: Geneva Smith
Supervisor: Chuck Fairchild

General Impressions:
Alex is a pleasant boy who is somewhat shy. He attended all of the sixteen individualized tutoring sessions and was agreeable to most of the tasks asked of him. He generally completed each task he tried.

Materials Used:
Flash Cards
Comprehension: *Finding the Main Idea and Supporting Details*, Developing Reading Comprehension Skills Series, Book A, pp. 1–20 (Oceana Educational Communications).
Comprehension: *Main Idea*, Book A, Specific Skill Series, pp. 1–10 (Barnell Loft).
Butternut Bill and the Little River (completed book) (Benefic Press). Primer reading level.
Butternut Bill and His Friends, pp. 1–22 (Benefic Press) Reading level 1

Goals and Assessment of Goals:
1.   Alex will increase his sight word vocabulary by 10 words. He will correctly call each word five times in a row.
Alex has done extremely well in meeting and exceeding this goal. He learned 34 new words this term. According to the *Gates-MacGinitie Reading Test*, Primary A, form 1 given in April, 1986, Alex obtained a grade-equivalent score of 2.3 in vocabulary. Form 2 of this test was given on November 11, 1986. His grade level equivalency score on this test was 3.3. It must be noted that the form of the test Alex took is not on his current grade level. However, it is apparent that there has been growth in vocabulary development.
2.   Alex will increase his confidence in reading through the use of Language Experience stories (LEA).
Based on tutor observations, Alex has made significant gains in this area. He now shows a willingness to cooperate on writing LEA stories and expresses an eagerness to do other reading tasks.
3.   Alex will increase his comprehension of fact recall and main idea to the 75 percent accuracy level.
Based on *Gates-MacGinitie Reading Test* scores, Alex has not made significant gains in comprehension. According to test results in April, 1986, his comprehension grade equivalency was 2.1. In November, 1986, he scored 2.3. However, the tutor feels that he has done much better than the test results indicate, especially in his attitude toward reading.
Alex does very well on main idea tasks. By listening to short paragraphs read by the tutor (and by listening to a list of possible main ideas for the paragraphs), he can select the main idea three times out of four for a 75 percent accuracy level. He is beginning to apply this skill in his other reading activities. Alex was also able to answer three of four fact recall questions during tutoring sessions.

Teacher modeling was used to help him understand the process of comprehension. Although Alex is a bit hesitant to answer at times, he is usually correct when he does answer. The tutor feels that he needs to gain more confidence in his ability to comprehend.

Recommendations:

It is recommended that Alex continue his one-on-one tutoring at the Wayne University Reading Center. It is further recommended that LEA be used to help increase his confidence with the reading act. Alex should receive lots of encouragement. Teacher modeling should be used to help Alex understand how one comprehends text.

Appendix C
Terms and Concepts for Understanding Tests

In selecting and interpreting texts, an understanding of certain terms and concepts is most important. The terms and concepts that follow will aid teachers in this understanding.

Age-equivalent scores. A type of derived score that represents the age for which a given score is the real or estimated average score.

Assessment. The act of gathering data in order to better understand an area of concern. In this text, assessment refers to data gathering through such means as observation, interviews, tests, and so forth.

Correlation, coefficient of (r). A measure of the degree of relationship between two variables, test scores, or sets of data. This relationship is expressed numerically from $+1.00$, which is a perfect relationship, to -1.00, which is a completely negative relationship. The existence of a high positive correlation means, for example, that an individual who scores high on one measure will score high on another measure. In a high negative relationship individuals who score high on one measure will score low on the other. It should always be kept in mind that correlation does not imply causation, merely that certain scores were obtained. Teachers must determine the type and meaning of the relationship. The question of how high a correlation must be in order to be meaningful is complex. It depends on the measure used and on the assessment situation. As a general guide, Garrett and Woodworth (1966) have suggested the following: 0.20–0.40, low correlations; 0.40–0.70 moderate correlations; 0.70 and above, high correlation.

Criterion. A standard by which a test may be judged or evaluated. It is the level of performance considered acceptable. For example, a correct response rate of 90 percent may represent an acceptable level of performance on a given test.

Criterion-referenced reading test. A measure of the extent to which a student can achieve a desired reading level. Students are not compared with other students; rather, their performance is compared with a standard, or criterion, deemed to represent satisfactory performance.

Deviation IQ. A standard score in which the mean is given a score of 100 and a standard deviation is given a score of 15. Thus, a score one standard deviation above the mean would be 115; a score two standard deviations above the mean would be 130.

Diagnosis. A form of evaluation based on multiple assessments of reading or reading-related behaviors. These assessments may be tests, observations, or any other procedures that yield information. Diagnosis involves making judgments about the adequacy of performance and the factors that impinge on this performance. It involves data gathering and hypothesis generation procedures.

Diagnostic reading test. A test that measures discrete reading skills. Examples include such skills as auditory discrimination and literal comprehension. A separate score is obtained for each skill through subtests. These tests help reading educators spot important reading skill strengths and weaknesses.

Extrapolation. The process of estimating the value of a variable beyond its known range based on the available data. In norming tests, extrapolation refers to the statistical process of estimating scores, such as grade-equivalent scores, at age and grade levels beyond the limits of observed data. This extension makes interpretation of extreme scores possible. For example, a test may contain grade-equivalent scores at the eighth grade level, when the highest grade level on which the test was normed was grade six.

Grade-equivalent score. An indicant of the grade level, expressed in months, at which the average reader in a norming population scored a given number of items correctly. It is the grade level for which a given score is the real or estimated average. Assume that a reader obtains a grade-equivalent score of 4.5. This means that this reader can answer as many questions right as the average fourth grader in the fifth month of school. It does not indicate what kinds of tasks the reader can do well or that he can handle materials designed for average fourth graders.

Some tests are only normed during one month of school; thus, most grade-equivalent scores are statistically determined and are estimates. Such estimates assume that progress between grade levels is uniform and that change does not take place during the summer. Both assumptions are false.

Group test. A test that can be administered to several examinees at one time by one examiner. Individual attention to given students on the part of the examiner is not necessary.

Individual test. A test administered to only one examinee at a time. Individual attention to the examinee is required throughout the test.

Interpolation. A statistical process in which values that fall between known points are inferred. For example, grade equivalent scores such as 3.5 and 3.8 are inferred when the students who took the norming instrument were actually in the first month of the third grade and in the first month of the fourth grade. Values (grade equivalents) between 3.1 and 4.1 have been inferred from those data actually obtained.

Mean. A descriptive statistic that is obtained by adding all given scores on a measure and dividing by the number of scores. It is the arithmetic average.

Median. The score above which and below which 50 percent of the scores on a test fall. It is the middle score of a set of test scores.

Mode. The score that occurs most frequently in a set of scores resulting from a given test administration. A set of test scores may have more than one mode. That is, there may be more than one score tied for the highest frequency of cases.

Norm-referenced test. A test that enables a given reader's performance to be described in relation to that of a reference group. Standardized achievement tests and intelligence or school ability tests are examples of this type of test.

Normal curve. A distribution of scores or measures that has a bell-shaped appearance when displayed in graphic form. Scores or measures are distributed symmetrically about the mean, with as many scores at various distances above the mean as at equal distances below the mean. Scores concentrate near the mean and decrease in frequency as one departs from the mean. (See Fig. 1.)

Normal curve equivalents (NCE)—Scores derived from percentile ranks. NCE scales are constructed so that NCEs of, 1, 50, and 99 correspond to percentile ranks of the same value. NCEs are used mainly for research purposes.

Percentile rank. A score that indicates the percentage of examinees in the norming group who scored below the score made by a given examinee. For example, a percentile rank of 86 indicates that the examinee scored higher than 86 percent of the subjects on whom the test was normed. The percentile range is from 1 to 99.

Power test. A test that permits the examinee to take as long as he desires in attempting to answer as many of the test items as possible.

Reliability. A measure of the extent to which test scores are consistent. It has three important dimensions: the consistency of test scores from one administration to another, the consistency of items in a given test, and consistency across different forms of a given test. Reliability is expressed as a reliability coefficient in a norm-referenced test. This coefficient is expressed in the same terms as the coefficient of correlation.

There are several ways to estimate reliability that correspond to the types of consistency mentioned above. In the *test-retest procedure,* the same measure is administered to the same set of subjects on two different occasions. *Alternate form reliability* is determined from the administration of a second test, similar to the original test, to the same set of subjects. *Split-*

Figure 1. A Bell Curve

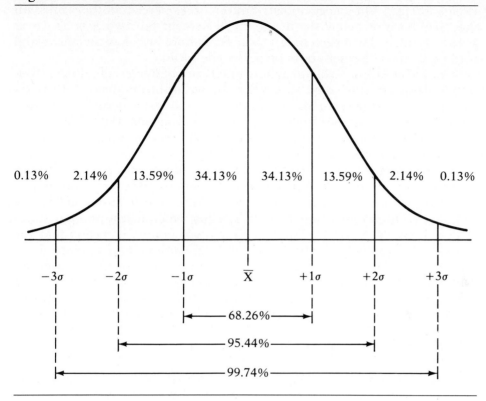

half reliability is determined by comparing two halves of a given test. Split-half reliability usually involves scoring the odd and even numbered items separately. Kuder-Richardson formulas estimate reliability from a single test administration by utilizing information about the individual test items, or from the mean score, standard deviation, and number of items in the test. Kuder-Richardson formulas are not appropriate for speed tests.

Scaled scores. Scaled scores are transformed scores that permit ease of interpretation and comparability among levels or forms of a given test. Such scores are formed on a continuous scale, and are comparable from battery level to battery level, as well as from form to form. A scaled score of 280, for example, on one level of a given test would have the same meaning as a scaled score of 280 on another form or level of the same test. Scaled scores from two different commercial tests have no inherent meaning and should not be compared.

Speed test. A test that places emphasis on the number of tasks completed in a specified time period.

Standard deviation. A measure of variability or dispersion of a set of scores from the mean. Standard deviation (SD) varies with the range of a set of scores. The greater the range, the larger the standard deviation. (Refer to Fig. 1.) In a normal distribution, 34.13 percent of the scores fall one SD above or below the mean, 13.59 percent fall two SDs above or below the mean, 2.14 percent fall three SDs above or below the mean, and 0.13 percent are farther above or below the mean.

Standard error. An estimate of how much an obtained score differs from a hypothetically true score. Differences between the obtained score and a hypothetically true score may occur because the test generates "relative" data since it compares a student's performance against that of other students and does not address the student's specific skill strengths and weaknesses. In addition, differences in an individual's obtained scores may vary from the hypothetical for a number of other reasons—how he felt on a given day, his interests, his attitudes toward school or the test, for example.

Standard error indicates the percentage of the time an individual's score falls between certain points or scores. Thus, when a test manual states that the standard error (SEm) is 6 raw score points, it means that the examinee's hypothetically true score will fall between 6 raw points above and 6 raw points below the obtained score 68 percent of the time. In addition there is a 32 percent chance that the hypothetically true raw score will deviate by more than 6 points from the obtained score. Standard error is related to the reliability of a test. Generally, the higher the reliability, the smaller the SEm.

Karlsen (1980, p. 155) has devised a table that shows an interpretation of SEm of an achievement test and an IQ test. (See Table 1.)

Standard scores. Derived scores that express the testee's distance from the mean in terms of the standard deviation of the distribution. Stanines, deviation IQs, and Z-scores are examples of standard scores.

Stanine. A score that places examinees in one of nine groups based on performance of a norming population. Stanines are related to the normal curve. The stanine groups and the percentages that comprise them are as follows:

9—top 4 percent of norm group
8—next 7 percent of norm group
7—next 12 percent of norm group
6—next 17 percent of norm group
5—middle 20 percent of norm group
4—next 17 percent of norm group
3—next 12 percent of norm group
2—next 7 percent of norm group
1—bottom 4 percent of norm group

Stratified random sample. A sample that is selected from a population that has been divided into categories. A stratified sample contains testees in each category in approximately the same proportion as they exist in the entire population. For example, the stratified sample would contain

Table 1. Interpretation of Standard Error of Measurement

If standard error of measurement is	the probability is about	that a score of	could fluctuate by chance from
.4 years	68%	grade 5.5	5.1 to 5.9
.4 years	95%	grade 5.5	4.7 to 6.3
.4 years	99%	grade 5.5	4.3 to 6.7
5 points	68%	IQ 90	85 to 95
5 points	95%	IQ 90	80 to 100
5 points	99%	IQ 90	75 to 105

proportional numbers of testees in terms of gender, ability levels, socio-economic levels, geographical areas, etc.

Statistical significance level. A level that suggests that an observed phenomenon represents a significant departure from what might be expected by chance. The significance levels most often reported are .01 and .05. The .01 level means that there is one chance in 100 that the difference in two observable events occurred by chance. The .05 level means that there is one chance in twenty that the difference can be accounted for by chance.

Survey test. A test that may measure a variety of reading skills, yet yield only an overall score. Most survey tests measure a limited number of broadly defined reading skills, such as word recognition or vocabulary and comprehension. The focus is more on the status of a group than on the proficiency of individuals. Such tests are appropriate for pre- and post-comparisons of groups or for comparing one group with the population on which the test was normed.

Validity. An indicant of how well a test measures what it is supposed to measure. Validity is concerned with the usefulness of a test for a given purpose. Validity may be divided into four major types (Pyrczak 1979):

1. *Construct validity:* is a test measuring a psychological quality that theory and common sense assumes to exist? Intelligence, anxiety, and comprehension are examples of constructs.
2. *Content validity:* how appropriate are the content or skills covered by the tests?
3. *Criterion validity:* to what extent do the scores obtained correlate with some other independent measure? There are two types of criterion validity—concurrent and predictive. *Concurrent validity* refers to how well performance on a given test compares with another measure that is assumed to be valid. *Predictive validity* refers to how well the test predicts future behavior.
4. *Face validity:* does the test appear to be measuring visually what it is intended to measure?

Z-scores. Derived scores for which the mean is set as 0 and a standard deviation is given a value of 1. For example, a Z-score of 2.5 means that the testee's obtained score is 2.5 standard deviations (SDs) above the mean.

Appendix D
Selected Tests*

This appendix includes the tests mentioned in this text that are currently available, and selected other assessment tools which are likely to come to the attention of teachers. The tests are organized in the following categories: attitudes; reading achievement (a) norm referenced, (b) criterion referenced; reading diagnostic (a) group, (b) criterion referenced; reading diagnostic (a) group, (b) individual; school ability/intelligence (a) group, (b) individual; reading readiness; vision and hearing screening; informal reading inventories; language; and perceptual. Information was sought from publishers on the tests included. The descriptions reflect the information received. An attempt has been made when possible to include the following: name of test, publisher, copyright date, forms or scales available, administration time, and a description of the test and its uses. No attempt to be comprehensive about the testing field has been made. For more comprehensive lists consult the ERIC Clearinghouse on Tests.

Publishers' addresses are in Appendix F.

1. Attitudes

Estes Attitude Scales. 1981.
Pro-Ed.
Two Forms: Elementary (3 scales: grades 2–6), and Secondary (5 scales: grades 7–12).
Grades 2–12.
Elementary form measures attitudes toward reading, science, and math; secondary form measures reading, science, math, English, and social studies.

Heathington Intermediate Attitude Scale.
1976. In *Attitudes and Reading* by J. Estill

Alexander and Ronald C. Filler. International Reading Association.
Uses the Likert type response format; 24 items assess free reading in the classroom, organized reading in the classroom, reading in the library, reading at home, other recreational reading, and general reading.

Heathington Primary Attitude Scale.
1976. In *Attitudes and Reading* by J. Estill Alexander and Ronald C. Filler. International Reading Association.
Uses the Likert type response format, 20

*Compiled with the assistance of Laura Rule Hendricks.

items assess free reading in the classroom, organized reading in the classroom, reading in the library, reading at home, other recreational reading and general reading.

Measuring Attitudes Toward Reading. 1980. ERIC Report 73.
Among attitude scales included are the following: *San Diego County Inventory of Reading Attitudes; Incomplete Sentence Projectial Test* by Thomas Boning and Richard Boning; *Primary Reading Attitude Index* by Arnelle Powell; *A Scale of Reading Attitude Based on Behavior* by C. Glennon Rowell; *The Reading Attitudes Inventory* by Harry W. Sartain; and *Reading Attitude Scales* by William H. Teale and Ramon Lewis.

Mikulecky Behavioral Reading Attitude Measure.
School of Education, Indiana University. Monographs in Reading and Learning #2. Consists of 20 descriptions; examinees respond by indicating how much the descriptions are like or unlike themselves.

Primary Pupil Reading Attitude Inventory. Kendall/Hunt.
Consists of 34 forced choice stimuli situations in both a boy's and a girl's version; the focus is on reading activities paired with other recreational activities.

II. Reading Achievement
A. Norm referenced

Assessment of Reading Growth.
Jamestown Publishers.
Three levels:
    Level (Age) 9—Grades 2, 3, 4;
    Level (Age) 13—Grades 6, 7, 8;
    Level (Age) 17—Grades 10, 11, 12, Adult.
Grade 2–adult
Determines silent reading comprehension; assesses literal and inferential comprehension; uses items released by National Assessment of Educational Progress.

California Achievement Tests: Reading. 1985.
CTB/McGraw-Hill.
Forms E–F, 11 levels (Level 10 through Level 20).

Grades K.0–12.9.
Measures vocabulary and comprehension at all levels. Sound recognition and visual recognition at Level 10 and Word Analysis at Levels 11–16.

Comprehensive Tests of Basic Skills: Reading. 1985.
CTB/McGraw-Hill.
Forms U and V.
Grades K.0–12.9.
Administration time: 45–70 minutes.
Measures word attack, vocabulary, and comprehension, and includes visual and sound recognition of letters, words, vowels, and consonants, categories and definitions, same meaning words, and word affixes, understanding sentence meaning, passage details, character analysis, main ideas, generalizations, written forms, and author techniques.

Gates-MacGinitie Reading Tests. 1978.
Riverside Publishing.
Two forms: Levels Basic R and A–F. Levels D and E for grades 4–9 have 3 Forms.
Grades 1–12.
Administration time varies: 55–65 minutes.
Measures reading comprehension and vocabulary development; available with out-of-level norms.

Iowa Tests of Basic Skills. 1982.
Riverside Publishers.
Primary Battery, Forms 5–8;
Multilevel Edition, Forms 9–14.
Grades K–9.
Administration time for primary battery is 1 hour and 55 minutes; for the multilevel edition, it is approximately 4 hours. Measures the basic skills: listening, word analysis, vocabulary, reading comprehension, language, spelling, capitalization, punctuation, usage, reference materials, mathematics, mathematics concepts, mathematics problem solving, mathematics computation.

Metropolitan Achievement Tests (MAT 6): Reading Instruction Tests. 1986.
The Psychological Corporation.
Two forms with 8 overlappng levels.
Grades K.5–12.9.
Levels spanning K.5–4.9 measure word rec-

ognition, vocabulary, and comprehension, while levels 5.0–12.9 measure vocabulary and comprehension; determination of instructional reading levels also possible.

Stanford Achievement Test Series. 1984.
The Psychological Corporation.
Includes *Stanford Achievement Test* 7th Edition; *Stanford Early School Achievement Test* (SESAT) 2nd Edition; and *Stanford Test of Academic Skills (TASK)* 2nd Edition.
Two alternate and equivalent forms, E and F for Primary 2 through TASK 2. SESAT 1 and 2 each have one form, E. Primary 1 has three forms: two alternate and equivalent forms, E and F, and a third form, G, that combines in one booklet the reading tests of Primary 2, Form F and the remaining subtests of Primary 1, Form F. There are 10 Battery Levels, Grades K–13.
Administration time varies according to which and how many subtests are given: 15–35 minutes each.
Students may be tested out of level. Reading test booklets include word study skills, reading comprehension, and vocabulary subtests.

Test of Reading Comprehension. 1978.
Pro-Ed.
Ages 6½ to 17 years.
No administration time given.
A multidimensional test of silent reading comprehension; the aspects of comprehension are combined to determine a basic comprehension core expressed as a Reading Comprehension Quotient (RCQ); tests the ability to identify words that are related to a common concept, the understanding of sentences similar in meaning but syntactically different, and the ability to answer questions related to paragraphs. Supplementary subtests measure the students' abilities in reading the vocabularies of math, science, and social studies. There is a special subtest for younger and remedial students.

Wide Range Achievement Test. 1984.
Jastak.
Forms Level 1 and Level 2.
Ages 5 years and up.
Focuses on decoding skills: reading (recognizing and naming letters, pronouncing printed

words); spelling (copying marks resembling letters, writing names, printing words); and arithmetic (counting, reading number symbols, oral and written computation). Used in diagnosing learning disabilities in reading, spelling, and arithmetic; measures the development of basic academic codes over time when intervention techniques are attempted; used for studying the relationships between reading and arithmetic and behavioral disabilities of verbal and numerical comprehension and problem solving; also checks school achievement for vocational assessment, job placement, and training.

B. Criterion referenced

Brigance Diagnostic Comprehensive Inventory of Basic Skills. 1983.
Curriculum Associates.
Forms A and B.
Grades pre-K–9.
No administration time given.
Measures: readiness, speech, word recognition, grade placement, oral reading, reading comprehension, listening, functional word recognition, word analysis, reference skills, graphs and maps, spelling, writing, math grade placement, numbers and number facts, whole number computation, fractions and mixed numbers, decimals, percentages, word problems, metrics, and math vocabulary.

Decoding Inventory. 1979.
Kendall/Hunt.
Levels: readiness, basic (grades 1–3), and advanced (grade 4 and above).
Group screening; assesses student performance in auditory and visual discrimination, phonics, structural analysis, and use of context clues; ascertains students' abilities to pronounce synthetic words that include common phonic and structural elements found in real words.

El Paso Phonics Test. 1979.
Allyn & Bacon.
A part of the *Ekwall Reading Inventory;* measures initial consonant sounds, ending consonants, initial consonant clusters, and vowels, vowel teams, and special letter combinations.

Fountain Valley Reading Skills Tests.
Zweig.
Grades 1–12.
Seventy-seven one-page tests for grades 1–6; covers 367 objectives measuring phonic and structural analysis, vocabulary, comprehension, and study skills; test for grades 7–12 measures vocabulary, comprehension, and study skills.

Group Phonics Analysis Test. 1971.
Jamestown Publishers.
Grades 1–3.
Measures knowledge of number and letter reading, hearing consonants, alphabetization, recognition of vowels, vowel digraph rule, final *e* rule, open and closed syllables, and syllabication.

Library Skills Test. 1980.
Scholastic Testing Service.
Grades 7–13.
Measures strengths and weaknesses in working with library materials, including terminology, card catalog classification system, filing, parts of a book, indexes, reference tools, and bibliographic forms.

PRI Reading Systems. 1980.
CTB/McGraw-Hill.
5 Levels.
Grades K–9.
Untimed.
Includes four skill clusters: oral language, word attack and usage, comprehension, and applications; a total of 171 specific reading objectives may be assessed across the five levels. Three types of assessment are possible: broad reading skills, terminal reading objectives, and specific reading skills; may be used to place students in instructional levels, and to diagnose strengths and needs.

Reading Yardsticks. 1981.
Riverside Publishing.
Nine levels.
Grades K–8.
Measures decoding, vocabulary, comprehension, and reading rate; skill emphases vary from level to level. The number of subtests in a skill area ranges from 4 to 8; the number of specific objectives range from 17–46.

San Diego Quick Assessment.
Ramon Ross.
Grades 1–11.
Measures ability to recognize and pronounce words presented in isolation.

Sipay Word Analysis Tests. 1974.
Stoelting and Educator's Publishing Service.
Grades 1–6.
An individual test that measures skills and pinpoints specific strengths and weaknesses in three basic areas: visual analysis, phonic analysis, and visual blending. Used to diagnose word analysis difficulties, assess learner progress, or evaluate program effectiveness.

Slosson Oral Reading Test. 1981.
Slosson.
Grades primer–high school.
Administration time: 3–5 minutes.
Provides a quick measure of reading ability and is most useful in identifying reading handicaps; based upon the ability to pronounce words at different levels of difficulty; can be used at frequent intervals to measure a child's progress in reading, providing no specific coaching with these particular words has been given.

Wisconsin Design Tests of Reading Skill Development. 1972.
Learning Multi-Systems.
Two parallel forms, seven levels.
Grades K–6.
No time limit.
Identifies and describes essential reading skills, assesses pupils' reading skill development and monitors pupils' progress in the areas of word attack (grades K–3), comprehension (grades K–6), and study skills (grades K–6).

III. Reading diagnostic
A. Group

Diagnostic Reading Tests.
Committee on Diagnostic Reading Tests.
1974 Edition (percentile norms for 1979).
Eight forms for the survey test component.
The Diagnostic Battery, Lower Level (Grades 4–8), tests word recognition and comprehension; vocabulary; rate of reading; and word

attack (oral and silent). Oral tests are individually administered.

Doren Diagnostic Reading Test of Word Recognition Skills. 1973.
American Guidance Service.
Administration time: 1–3 hours.
Measures word recognition: letters, beginning sounds, whole word recognition, words within words, speech consonants, ending sounds, blending, rhyming, vowels, discriminate guessing, spelling, and sight words.

Stanford Diagnostic Reading Test. 1984.
The Psychological Corporation.
Forms G and H with four levels: Red, Green, Brown, and Blue.
Grades 1.5–12.
Administration time: 15–40 minutes per subtest.
Red level (grades 1, 2, and extremely low 3) assesses auditory discrimination, phonetic analysis, auditory vocabulary, word recognition, and comprehension of short sentences and paragraphs. Green level (grades 3, 4, and very low 5) assesses auditory discrimination, phonetic and structural analysis, auditory vocabulary, and literal and inferential comprehension. Brown level (grades 5–8 and very low high school) assesses phonetic and structural analysis; auditory vocabulary; literal and inferential comprehension of textual, functional, and recreational material, and reading rate. Blue level (grade 8 through community college) assesses phonetic and structural analysis; knowledge of word meanings and word parts; reading rate, including skimming and scanning; and literal and inferential comprehension of textual, functional, and recreational materials.

B. Individual

Botel Reading Inventory. 1978.
Modern Curriculum Press.
Forms A and B.
No time limit.
Checks skills in decoding, word recognition (Forms A and B for oral reading ability), spelling, and word opposites (Forms A and B for reading comprehension); (word opposites may be administered to groups); test is scaled in order of difficulty and is used for placement at the beginning of the school year, measuring progress throughout the school year, and for placing new students.

Diagnostic Reading Scales. Revised. 1982.
CTB/McGraw-Hill.
Form DRS-81.
Grades 1–7.
Administration time: 60 minutes.
Consists of three word recognition tests, 22 graded passages, and 12 phonic and word analysis tests; identifies strengths and weaknesses that affect reading proficiency at grade levels in which reading is normally taught by evaluating oral and silent reading, auditory comprehension and phonic and word analysis skills; assesses instructional, independent, and potential reading levels.

Durrell Analysis of Reading Difficulty. 1980.
The Psychological Corporation.
Grades 1–6.
Administration time: 30–45 minutes.
Includes observations and evaluations of oral reading, silent reading, listening comprehension, listening vocabulary, word recognition and word analysis, spelling, auditory analysis of words and word elements, pronunciation of word elements, visual memory of words, and prereading of phonics abilities.

Gates–McKillop–Horowitz Reading Diagnostic Tests. 1981.
Teachers College Press, and Western Psychological Services.
Grades 1–6.
Administration time: approximately 1 hour.
Examines oral reading using graded passages, sentence reading, and word recognition (flash and untimed). Tests word attack, recognition of visual form of words, auditory blending and disorientation, and written expression (spelling and informal writing sample).

Gilmore Oral Reading Test. 1968.
The Psychological Corporation.
Forms C and D.
Grades 1–8.
Untimed, approximately 15–20 minutes.

Consists of graded reading passages; measures three aspects of oral reading: accuracy, comprehension, and rate.

Gray Oral Reading Tests. Revised. 1986.
Pro-Ed.
Forms A and B with 13 graded oral reading passages in each.
Administration time: 15–30 minutes.
Measures oral reading; designed to identify readers who are reading more poorly than their peers, and to identify individual reading strengths and weaknesses.

Peabody Individual Achievement Test (PIAT). 1970.
American Guidance Service (AGS).
Grades K–12 and adults.
Administration time: 30–50 minutes, five subtests in two volumes.
Designed for screening; measures mathematics (Volume I), reading recognition (Volume I), reading comprehension (Volume II), Spelling (Volume II), and general information (Volume II): science, social studies, fine arts, and sports.

Reading Miscue Inventory. 1972.
Macmillan.
(2nd edition to be published in 1987 by Richard C. Owen Publishers.)
Administration time: 1 hour
Provides an in-depth, qualitative analysis of oral reading performance and comprehension.

Roswell-Chall Diagnostic Reading Test of Word Analysis Skills. 1978.
Essay Press.
Forms A and B.
Grades K–4.
Administration time: 10–15 minutes.
Measures sight recognition of high frequency words, capital and lower case letters, consonant blends and digraphs, short vowels, long vowel with *e*, long vowel combinations, writing and spelling CVC words.

Woodcock Reading Mastery Tests. 1973.
American Guidance Service.
Forms A and B.
Grades K–12.

Administration time: 30–45 minutes.
Provides for detection of reading problems; facilitates grouping students for instruction and evaluates school reading programs by testing for letter identification, word identification, word attack, word comprehension, and passage comprehension.

IV. School ability and intelligence
A. Group

Cognitive Abilities Test. 1982.
Riverside Publishing.
An integrated series for K–12.
Primary Battery—Levels 1 and 2 for grades K–3; and Multilevel Edition—Levels A through H for grades 3–12. Administration time of primary battery approximately 55 minutes. Administration time of multilevel edition is 98 minutes. Measures verbal, quantitative, and nonverbal abilities.

Culture Fair Intelligence Tests. 1973.
Western Psychological Service.
Scale 1 is for ages 4–8 years and mentally defective adults, and takes 30 minutes to administer. Scale 2 is for ages 8–14 years and average adults, and takes 15 minutes to administer to a group; has two equivalent forms, A and B. Scale 3 is for ages 14 years through superior adult and takes 15 minutes to administer to a group. There are two equivalent forms, A and B.

Measures intelligence not influenced by cultural background, scholastic, or verbal training and is used for work with the culturally and educationally deprived.

Detroit Tests of Learning Aptitude.
Pro-Ed.
Ages 6–17.
Used in diagnosing learning disabilities and mental retardation; isolates special individual strengths and weaknesses; identifies students deficient in general or specific aptitudes; serves as standardized instrument in research; provides a profile of a student's abilities and deficiencies. Abilities measured are: vocabulary, grammar, following commands, repeating words, story telling, drawing from memory, order recall, reasoning,

relationship knowledge, gestalt-closure function, and order recall.

Henmon-Nelson Test of Mental Ability. 1973.
Riverside Publishing.
Grades K–12.
Untimed (approximately 25–30 minutes for K–2; and 30 minutes for grades 3–12).
Aims to provide a quick and reliable measure of cognitive ability; tests vocabulary, sentence completion, opposites, general information, verbal analogies, verbal classification, verbal inference, number series, arithmetic reasoning, and figure analogies for grades 3–12. The primary battery tests listening, picture vocabulary, size, and numbers.

Kuhlman-Anderson Tests. 8th Edition. 1982.
Scholastic Testing Service.
Grades K–12; nine levels.
Administration time: 50–75 minutes.
Measures cognitive tasks that assess verbal and nonverbal capacity.

Nonverbal Test of Cognitive Skills. 1981.
Charles E. Merrill.
Grades K–7.
Administration time: 25–35 minutes.
Measures aspects of reasoning, rote memory, recognition and memory of patterns, visual memory, discrimination, space and spatial relationships, conceptual thinking, recognition of and ability to deal with quantities, quantitative memory, and visual motor perception.

Otis-Lennon School Ability Test. 1982.
The Psychological Corporation.
5 levels in two forms, R and S.
Grades K.5–12.
Untimed.
Designed to predict success in cognitive, school-related activities; measures abstract thinking and reasoning.

School and College Ability Tests, Series III.
1980.
CTB/McGraw-Hill.
Alternate forms for each of three levels: elementary (grades 3–6), intermediate (grades 6–9), and advanced (grades 9–12). Grades 3.5–12.9.

Administration time: 40 minutes.
Measures basic verbal and quantitative abilities (the understanding of words and the understanding of quantitative comparison items.)

Test of Cognitive Skills. 1981.
CTB/McGraw-Hill.
Five levels (one for grades 2–3; two for grades 3–5; three for grades 5–7; four for grades 7–9; five for grades 9–12); each level has four tests (sequence, memory, analogies, and verbal reasoning).
Grades 2–12.
Approximate testing time per subtest is 6–10 minutes.
Designed to test level of aptitude attained by students; emphasis is on abilities of a relatively abstract nature that are important for school success.

B. Individual

Kaufman Assessment Battery for Children.
1983.
American Guidance Service.
Ages 2½–12½.
Administration time varies from 35 minutes to 1 hour, 25 minutes.
Measures the ability to solve problems using simultaneous and sequential mental processes. Also measures acquired knowledge, including skills in reading and arithmetic; yields four global scores; sequential processing, simultaneous processing, mental processing composite, and achievement.

Peabody Picture Vocabulary Test, Revised.
1981.
American Guidance Service.
Forms L and M.
Ages 2 ½ to adult.
Administration time: 10–20 minutes.
Measures receptive (hearing) vocabulary. Used to screen for mental retardation and giftedness; to evaluate pupils for remedial education services; to assess English hearing vocabulary of non-English-speaking students; to screen for jobs requiring good comprehension of aural vocabulary; to aid in the selection of occupations for handicapped adults; and to measure adult verbal ability.

Slosson Intelligence Test, Revised. 1984.
Stoelting and Slosson Educational Publications.
All ages from infants to adults.
Administration time: 10–20 minutes.
Assesses mental ability; used to predict reading achievement and to screen students who have reading problems.

Stanford–Binet Intelligence. Fourth Edition. 1985.
Riverside Publishing Company.
Forms L and M.
Ages 2 to adult.
Untimed.
Measures verbal reasoning, quantative reasoning, abstract, visual reasoning, and short-term memory.

Test of Nonverbal Intelligence. 1982.
Slosson and Pro-Ed.
Forms A and B.
Ages 5.0 through 85.11 years.
A measure of intelligence and reasoning completely free of reading, writing, and verbalization as the examiner pantomimes the instructions and the subject responds by pointing; used to evaluate the intellectual capacity of subjects suspected of having difficulty in reading, writing, speaking, or listening, including people who are mentally retarded, speech or language handicapped, learning disabled, deaf, or victims of stroke or brain injury (as well as bilingual and non-English-speaking people).

Wechsler Intelligence Scale for Children. Revised. 1974.
The Psychological Corporation.
Ages 6 years and 0 months–16 years and 11 months.
Administration time: 50–75 minutes.
A classified test that measures the individual's capacity to understand and cope with the world; yields verbal, performance, and full-scale scores. Verbal subtests include information, similarities, arithmetic (timed), vocabulary, comprehension, and digit span; performance subtests include picture completion, picture arrangement, block design, object assembly, coding, and mazes.

Wechsler Preschool and Primary Scale of Intelligence. 1967.
The Psychological Corporation.
Ages 4–6½.
Administration time: approximately 1 hour.
Measures the child's capacity for intelligence; subtests are information, vocabulary, arithmetic, similarities, comprehension, and sentences; uses mazes, geometric designs, block designs, and picture completion.

Woodcock-Johnson Psycho-Educational Battery.
DLM Teaching Resources.
Ages 3–80.
Administration time: 2 hours.
Measures cognitive ability, scholastic aptitude, academic achievement and interest level; tests visual matching, auditory blending, concept formation, reasoning with analogies, reading achievement, mathematics achievement, written language, knowledge, level of preference for participating in certain scholastic and nonscholastic activities, and adaptive behavior.

V. Reading readiness

Basic School Skills Inventory—Screen. 1983.
Pro-Ed.
Ages 4.0–6.11.
Administration time: 5 to 8 minutes.
Locates children who are "high risk" for school failure, who need more in-depth assessment, and who should be referred for additional study, as well as estimating children's overall readiness for school.

Beginning Assessment Test for Reading. 1975.
Lippincott.
Grades K–1.
This criterion-referenced comprehensive test measures 19 objectives with 2–6 items, each including an understanding of spoken words, visual and auditory discrimination, classification, rhyming, sequencing, riddles, letter names, sound-symbol associations, picture-word and picture-sentence matching, spelling, sentence completion, oral production and comprehension, and color naming.

Brigance K & 1 Screen. 1983.
Curriculum Associates.
Grades K–1.
Administration time: 12 minutes.
Measures personal data response, color recognition, picture vocabulary, visual and auditory discrimination, visual motor, gross motor, rote counting, identification of body parts, following of verbal directions, numeral identification, syntax and fluency, and the ability to draw a person, to recite the alphabet, and to recognize letters and place numerals in sequence.

Clymer-Barrett Readiness Test. 1983.
Chapman, Brook & Kent.
Forms A (advanced) and B (beginning or basic).
Grades K–1.
Administration time is 3 separate periods of 30 minutes each. Measures visual discrimination (the recognition of letters and matching of words), and auditory discrimination (beginning and ending sounds), as well as the ability to complete shapes and copy sentences.

Concepts about Print Test: Sand. 1972; *Stones.* 1979.
Heinemann.
Ages 5–7.
Measures the individual child's concepts about book orientation; whether print or pictures carry the message; directionality of lines of print, words, and page sequence; relationships between written and spoken language; words, letters, capitals, space, and punctuation.

First Grade Screening Test. 1969.
American Guidance Service.
Two forms: girl's (U1101) and boy's (U1192).
Grades K–1.
Administration time: 45 minutes for kindergarten, and 30 minutes for first grade.
Identifies children likely to experience significant difficulty during their first year of school and those who may need individual assessment and compensatory or remedial attention; assesses vocabulary, general knowledge, body image, and emotional maturity.

Linguistic Awareness in Reading Readiness Test. 1983.
Nelson.
Two forms.
Ages 5–6.
A group administered test containing three subtests. One measures recognizing literacy behavior (the extent to which the child can recognize the kinds of activities involved in reading and writing); one measures the understanding of literacy functions (the understanding of varied purposes of reading and writing); and one measures the technical language of literacy (knowledge of technical terms such as letter, word, and top line).

Metropolitan Readiness Tests. 1976.
Psychological Corporation.
Forms P and Q; two levels: Level I for K and Level II for K–1.
Grades K–1.
Administration time: 80 to 100 minutes.
Measures cognitive development, auditory discrimination, visual discrimination, language comprehension, and quantitative concepts.

Roswell-Chall Auditory Blending Test. 1963.
Essay Press.
Grades 2–6.
Administration time: 5 minutes.
Measures ability to blend sounds to form words.

Search. 1981.
Walker and Company.
Ages 5–6 years; grades K–early 1st grade.
Administration time: about 20 minutes.
Measures visual perception such as matching, recall, and visual-motor, auditory discrimination and sequencing, articulation, initial consonants, and body-image, such as directionality, finger schema, and pencil grip.

Test of Early Reading Ability. 1981.
Pro-Ed.
Preschool, kindergarten, and primary level.
Measures the actual reading ability of preschool, kindergarten, and primary level students; documents early reading ability; diagnostic information available about three areas related to early reading: knowledge of

the alphabet, comprehension, and conventions of reading, for example, book orientation and format.

VI. Vision and hearing screening

A O Sight Screener. 1956.
American Optical.
Administration time: 4 minutes or less.
Measures visual acuity, fusion, depth, color perception, heterophoria (eye imbalance), and horizontal field vision.

Beltone Model 109 and Model 119.
Beltone Special Instruments.
All ages.
Provides for full testing range of -10 to $+110$dB and 125Hz to 8,000Hz.

Keystone Complete School Vision Screening Program. 1971.
Keystone.
Grades 1 and up.
A complete school vision screening program including testing for farsightedness, lateral peripheral (side) vision, tunnel vision, and hand-eye coordination, as well as muscle balance, depth perception, fusion, and color vision.

Maico Audiometer Systems (Models 39 and 40).
Maico Hearing Instruments Company.
All ages.
Model 39 measures air conduction; Model 40 measures air conduction with bone and masking; testing range of 125Hz to 8,000Hz and -10 to $+100$dB.

Ortho-Rater. 1958.
Bausch & Lomb.
Grades 1 and up.
Uses a stereoscopic instrument and accompanying stereographic slides; measures binocular near- and farpoint acuity, depth perception, visual discrimination, and color vision.

School Vision Tester. 1974.
Bausch & Lomb.
Grades K and up.
Tests for tumbling E acuity in each eye, farsightedness in each eye, and muscle balance both far and near.

Spache Binocular Reading Test. 1955.
Keystone.
Test 1—for non-readers to grade 1;
Test 2—grade 1.5–2;
Test 3—grade 3–adult.
Measures intermittent suppression, wide heterophoria, and lack of good fusion at nearpoint; shows whether a student tends to read more with one eye than the other; can indicate possible cause of interference.

Titmus II Vision Tester—pediatric model—preschool and primary. 1969.
Titmus and Falvey Company.
All ages.
Administration time: 5 minutes.
Detects common vision problems: binocularity, acuity of both eyes, heterophorias, color perception, lateral phoria, and vertical phoria.

VII. Informal reading inventories

Analytic Reading Inventory. 3rd ed. 1985.
Charles E. Merrill.
Three forms.
Grades: primer through 9.
Consists of graded passages for determining reading levels in the general area of reading content; both qualitative and quantative evaluations are possible.

Bader Reading and Language Inventory. 1983.
Macmillan Publishing.
Grades: preprimary through adult.
Designed to place students in instructional materials through three sets of graded passages: one for preprimary through 11th to 12th grades; one for use with children, adolescents, or adults; and one for adults who are beginning to read. Specific tests are included for reading skills.

Basic Reading Inventory. 3rd ed. 1985.
Kendall/Hunt.
Three forms.
Preprimer through 8th grade.
Contains graded word lists and graded reading passages; determines strengths and weaknesses in word attack and comprehension.

Classroom Reading Inventory. 5th ed. 1986.
Wm. C. Brown.
Forms A (grades 1–6), B (grades 1–6),
C (jr. high), and D (high school and adult).
Grades 1–adult.
Administration time: 12 minutes or less.
Includes graded passages; measures individual reading capabilities of children and adults; aids in creating individualized reading programs.

Content Inventories for English, Social Studies, and Science. 1979.
Kendall/Hunt.
Grades 4–12.
A series of ready-to-use informal tests for content teachers; includes cloze placement inventory, group reading inventories, and tests for determining the ability to use reading and study strategies in content-area subjects.

Ekwall Reading Inventory. 2nd ed. 1986.
Allyn & Bacon.
Four forms (two oral and two silent).
Grades: preprimer through 9th grade.
Consists of graded passages for determining reading levels with general content; sight words and phonics surveys are also included.

Individual Evaluation Procedures in Reading. 1983.
Prentice-Hall.
Two forms.
Grades: primer through 10th grade.
Designed for diagnosis and prescription for typical and exceptional children; consists of graded passages for determination of general content reading levels; visual tests, auditory tests, and special word analysis and vocabulary tests are also included.

Informal Reading Inventory. 2nd ed. 1985.
Houghton Mifflin.
Four forms.
Grades: primer through 12th grade.
Consists of graded passages; measures general content.

Oral Reading Criterion Test. 1971.
Jamestown Publishing.
Grades 1–7.

Consists of graded passages for determining a student's independent, instructional, and frustrational reading levels; is useful for placing new students and monitoring individual progress.

Reading Diagnosis: Informal Reading Inventories. 1981.
Jamestown Publishing.
Grades 1–6, and remedially with older students.
Determines students' abilities in oral reading, silent reading, comprehension, phonics, sight word vocabulary and vocabulary size, word meaning, letter and number recognition, spelling, handwriting, vision, and hearing.

The Sucher-Allred Reading Placement Inventory. 1981.
Economy.
Forms A and B.
Grades 1–6.
Includes placement inventory for grades 1 to adult; reading skills survey for grades 2–9; and *Lane Diagnostic Test of Word Perception Skills* for grades 4–12.
Measures independent, instructional, and frustrational reading levels, word recognition, and oral reading skills.

VIII. Language

Illinois Test of Psycholinguistic Abilities. 1969.
University of Illinois Press, Western Psychological Service, and Slosson.
Ages 2 to 10.
Twelve subtests delineate specific abilities and disabilities for remediation; provides a comprehensive evaluation of abilities in channels of communication, psycholinguistic processes and levels of organization; and provides a composite psycholinguistic age, an estimated mental age, and IQ by measuring auditory reception, visual reception, auditory association, visual association, verbal expression, manual expression, grammatic closure, visual closure, auditory sequential memory, visual sequential memory, auditory closure, and sound blending.

Language Assessment Battery. 1977.
Riverside Publishing Co.
Grades K–12.
Administration time: approximately 41 minutes for each edition. Measures achievement of basic reading, writing, listening, comprehension, and speaking skills in Spanish and English.

Oral Language Evaluation. 1977.
EMC Corp.
Six levels of assessment—labeling, basic sentence (structures), language expansion, connecting, relating, and modifying, story telling, concrete, and story telling, abstract; designed to help teachers assess, diagnose, and prescribe for the oral language needs of children; intended for children who have little or no command of English; guidelines are provided for determining whether beginning oral language training is needed, whether more advanced oral language is needed, whether commercial reading programs are appropriate, and whether reading is advisable with continued oral language training.

Test of Language Development (TOLD). 1982.
Pro-Ed.
Ages 4 to 12.
Forms P (for ages 4–8) and I (for ages 4–12). Measures different components of spoken language, assesses the understanding and meaningful use of spoken words, differing aspects of grammar, and the abilities to say words correctly, and to distinguish between words that sound similar.

IX. Perceptual

Auditory Discrimination Test. 1978.
Western Psychological Services.
Forms 1, 1A, 2, and 2A.
Ages 5–8.
Administration time: 5 minutes.
Determines a child's ability to recognize the fine differences that exist between the phonemes used in English speech; measures the ability to hear accurately and requires no visual ability. Identifies young children who are slow in developing auditory discrimination; identifies those who are likely to have

difficulty learning to use the phonics necessary for reading. Used for differential diagnosis of reading and speech difficulties.

Bender Visual Motor Gestalt Test. 1946.
American Guidance Service; Psychological Corporation.
Ages 4 to adult.
Untimed.
Indicates the maturation level of visual motor perceptions: testee reproduces a series of designs that are interpreted in terms of Gestalt laws of perception and organization.

Benton Revised Visual Retention Test. 1974.
Psychological Corporation.
Forms C, D, and E.
Ages 8 to adult.
Administration time: 5 minutes.
Measures visual perception, visual memory, and visuo-constructive abilities.

Developmental Test of Visual-Motor Integration (Beery and Buktenica). 1983.
Modern Curriculum Press.
Short form for ages 2–8;
Long form for ages 2–15;
Two levels.
Assesses visual-motor integration skills; consists of a set of stimulus cards used in remedial work; assessment and remediation worksheets available.

Frostig Developmental Test of Visual Perception. 1966.
Consulting Psychologists Press, Inc.; Modern Curriculum Press; Stoelting.
Ages 4 to 8.
Grades: preschool to 3rd grade.
Aims to evaluate perceptual skills of young children in five different perceptual areas: visual-motor coordination, figure-ground, constancy of shape, position in space, and spatial relationships.

Goldman-Fristoe Test of Articulation. 1972.
American Guidance Service.
Ages 2 to 16+.
Grades 1–12.
Administration time: 10–15 minutes for the Sounds-in-Words subtest. Time varies for the

other two subtests. The full test is administered in two sessions.
Measures the individual's articulation of consonant sounds.

Goldman-Fristoe-Woodcock Auditory Skills Test Battery. 1976.
American Guidance Service.
Ages 3 to adult.
Administration time: 15 minutes per test.
Measures a broad spectrum of skills, ranging from simple auditory attention and discrimination to complex association of sounds with symbols in written language; provides diagnostic information needed for instructional planning.

Goldman-Fristoe-Woodcock Test of Auditory Discrimination. 1970.
American Guidance Service.
Ages 4 and above.
Administration time: 20–30 minutes.
Measures speech-sound discrimination.

Screening Test for Auditory Perception. 1981.
Slosson.
Grades 1 to 6, and those in remedial classes.
Administration time: 45 minutes.
Assesses weaknesses rather than strengths in auditory perception; assists in identifying students who are performing significantly below their grade or age level in the five areas considered when testing to determine the student's ability to discriminate among long versus short vowels, single versus blend initial consonants, rhyming versus nonrhyming words, same versus different rhythmic patterns, and same versus different words.

Visual Discrimination Test. 1975.
Western Psychological Services; Stoelting.
Ages 5 to 8.
Measures ability to discriminate between similar visually perceived forms in assessing skills needed prior to learning to read.

Visual Memory Test. 1975.
Stoelting; Western Psychological Services.
Ages 5 to 8.
Assesses a child's ability to recall unfamiliar forms that cannot readily be named (a forerunner to learning to read).

Wepman Auditory Discrimination Test. 1973.
Stoelting.
Forms 1 and 2.
Ages 5 to 8.
Administration time: less than 1/2 hour.
Used to establish the basis for articulatory accuracy in speech and readiness for reading instruction by the phonic approach, and in determining the cause of specific auditory learning disabilities.

Appendix E
Selected Materials for Corrective and Remedial Readers
Developed by Sabiha Tufail Aydelott

The materials in this appendix may be helpful to teachers as they work with corrective and remedial readers in the classroom. The categories are reading programs, computerized reading materials, taped and talking books, magazines, high interest/low vocabulary books, skill materials, games, and newspapers.

Addresses of publishers may be found in Appendix F.

Reading Programs

1. ROOKIE READER
   Children's Press
   grade level: preprimer–2
   This program consists of supplementary readers to help develop sequential reading skills. The books focus on different aspects of language usage. The activities are designed to motivate young readers.

2. FOCUS
   Scott, Foresman & Company
   grade level: kindergarten–grade 8
   This series is designed as a complete, traditionally organized reading program for students who are reading below their grade levels. The program presents the sequence of skills at a pace that is appropriate to the needs of students who are behind in reading skills.

3. THE WONDER STORY BOOKS
   Scribner Educational Publishers
   grade level: 1–6
   Designed for use as a supplementary reading program, this series has stories that introduce children to literature while helping them to develop and enrich their comprehension skills and vocabulary.

4. CONTENT READERS
   Scribner Educational Publishers
   grade level: 1–6
   The emphasis in this series is on helping students to read more effectively in science, social studies, math, and literature. Comprehension and study skills are stressed while basic skills are reinforced.

5. QUEST: A SCHOLASTIC READING IM-
PROVEMENT SERIES
Scholastic Inc.
grade level: 4–8
This series is a combination of "great" stories and effective strategies. The six the-
matic units in each text focus on themes
and topics that help students acquire vocabulary and build up comprehension and
knowledge systematically.

6. QUEST EXTENDERS
Scholastic Inc.
grade level: 4–6
This is a companion to *Quest: A Scholastic
Reading Improvement Series.* The program
is designed to allow students to apply skills
and strategies that they have developed
earlier and to extend their knowledge of
theme, skills, and activities already begun.

7. BEYOND BASICS
Jamestown Publishers
grade level: 4–12
This is a graded developmental reading
program which is designed to develop reading skills that students need in order to
"comprehend and make judgments" about
a variety of reading materials: textbooks,
fiction, nonfiction, periodicals, reference
works, and graphics.

Computerized reading materials

1. ALPHABET BEASTS AND COMPANY
Reader's Digest
for Apple and Commodore 64 systems
grade level: preschool–2
This readiness program uses sounds to introduce new words to the learner. The
concepts are presented with moving
graphics and sounds corresponding to the
beasts appearing on the screen.

2. ALPHABET ZOO
Spinnaker Software
for Apple, Atari, Commodore 64, and IBM
systems
grade level: preschool–2
Alphabet Zoo is designed to help children

strengthen their letter recognition skills
as they learn to associate letters of the
alphabet with the sounds they represent.
It also helps a child's spelling skills.

3. SPELLER BEE "TALKING NOTEBOOK
SERIES"
First Byte
for Apple Macintosh
grade level: preschool–junior high
With this program, the student is provided visual as well as spoken clues to help
master the spelling of each word. It is one
of the first educational software programs
to use speech in order to improve spelling
skills.

4. VISUAL VOCABULARY
C. F. Software
for Apple
grade level: kindergarten–2
The focus of this program is on helping
students associate objects with words. The
content, pace, and presentation are suitable for younger students, as well as ESL
and special education students.

5. CUSTOMIZED FLASH SPELLING
Random House
for Apple and TRS-80
grade level: 2–6
As its name implies, this program is designed to introduce spelling by flashing
words on the screen. If the student can
spell the word correctly, another word is
flashed on the screen but for a shorter time.
If the answer is incorrect, the word flashes
on the screen again and the student must
respond correctly before proceeding.

6. CUSTOMWARE SPELLING—SPELLING
DEMONS: CREATION PACKAGE
Random House
for Apple and TRS-80
grade level: 3–6
Introducing spelling and vocabulary, this
program first shows the word in the middle of the screen, then in context. Finally,
the student is asked to spell the word. The
lesson continues only if the correct word
is typed.

7. CAPITALIZATION PRACTICE
Hartley
for Apple, IBM PC, and IBM PC Jr.
grade level: 3–8
Practice on seven topics is offered in this program: first word in sentences and I; proper personal names; days of the week and month; holidays, AM and PM; proper place names; titles; and miscellaneous—a mixture of the others.

8. STORY TREE
Scholastic Wizware
for Apple, Commodore, IBM PC, and IBM PC Jr.
grade level: 3–middle school
Designed as a tool for the reading and language arts classroom, this program provides opportunities for reading and creative writing. Students can create stories, change them in various ways through the use of the word processor, and print them out for rereading later.

9. HIDE 'N SEQUENCE
Sunburst Communications
for Apple and Commodore 64
grade level: 4–6 and 6–9
The focus of *Hide 'N Sequence* is to increase student involvement and encourage students to read the complete books from which the excerpts are taken for the program. Students are helped to organize and sequence ideas while they become familiar with four kinds of discourse—narration, exposition, description, and persuasion.

10. VOCABULARY BASEBALL
J. & S. Software
for Apple
grade level: 4–8
Emphasizing word meaning, this program is set up as a game with "four leagues: easy, hard, very hard, or mixed." The program comes with a word bank of 900 words randomly presented. Teachers may add words and modify definitions.

11. CAPITALIZATION PLUS!
Microcomputer Workshops
for Apple

grade level: 5–12
This program allows teachers to personalize their lessons by entering their own sentences, student-created sentences, and places around school. It also contains a diagnostic test that students can use to determine which topics to study prior to working on the exercises.

12. HOW CAN I FIND IT IF I DON'T KNOW WHAT I'M LOOKING FOR: LIBRARY SKILLS
Sunburst Communications
for Apple II, IIc, and IIe
grade level: upper elementary–high school
The purpose of this program is to encourage students to work independently to find a variety of reference books. The software can be customized by librarians to include the reference materials available to them, saving students hours of aimless searching.

13. NOTE CARD MAKER
Grolier Electronic Publishing Inc.
for Apple, Commodore, IBM
grade level: upper elementary–high school
Note Card Maker demonstrates how to prepare note cards. Using key words, source codes, and notes, students can collect information needed and arrange it in the order they want.

14. FRIENDLY FILER
Grolier Electronic Publishing Inc.
for Apple and IBM
grade level: all grades
Providing instruction in the use of database management, this program introduces students of all ages to database management, and has possibilities for the classroom as well as the home. The program consists of four instructional parts; the fifth option is to quit.

Taped books/talking books

1. THE ABC BOOK: Read Alongs—A Talking Book
Peter Pan Industries
grade level: preschool–1
This book is designed to capture the child's

interest while introducing the alphabet to the beginner. It is also reinforcing for those who are beyond the beginning stage.

2. TEN LITTLE INDIANS: Read Alongs—A Talking Book
   Peter Pan Industries
   grade level: preschool–1
   The book and tape are designed to help children to count as well as read as they follow the book while listening to the tape.

3. TALK-ALONG BOOKS
   Children's Press
   grade level: preschool–2
   This set consists of three titles. It is designed to encourage student participation and involvement. The read-aloud format changes when students are asked to supply the final rhyming word on each page.

4. FAR-FETCHED PETS READ ALONGS
   Children's Press
   grade level: preschool–3
   This series has a word-for-word reading of the test plus realistic sound effects, multiple voices, and humorous dialogue to dramatize the illustrations. The series is designed to develop basic listening and comprehension skills as well as vocabulary.

5. FLUTTERBY
   Society for Visual Education, Inc.
   grade level: primary
   Designed to hold the interest of the reader/listener while reading the book and listening to the tape, this book is also easy to read.

6. THE GNOME FROM NOME
   Society for Visual Education, Inc.
   grade level: primary
   The reader will find this story easy to follow because it is interesting and uses an accompanying tape. The book follows the cassette word for word.

7. THE GOOSE GIRL: A TALE FROM THE BROTHERS GRIMM
   Society for Visual Education, Inc.
   grade level: primary
   This "talking book" makes it easier for the reader to follow one of the many tales collected by the brothers Grimm. Listening to the tape, looking at the illustrations, and reading the printed word are all designed to help the child develop an interest in reading.

8. THE WATER OF LIFE: A TALE FROM THE BROTHERS GRIMM
   Society for Visual Education, Inc.
   grade level: primary
   The printed and spoken word, combined with pictures, are used to motivate the child to read.

9. WALT DISNEY READ-ALONG LIBRARIES
   Walt Disney Educational Media Co.
   grade level: primary
   These libraries—a total of eight, each containing six titles—are designed to encourage students to develop, improve, and reinforce reading skills. They aim to build vocabulary through hearing and seeing new words in context; to provide individualized practice with paced reading; to illustrate the importance of inflection, emphasis, and voice pitch; to make children familiar with children's literary classics; and to build confidence in reading.

10. THE THREE LITTLE PIGS: Read Alongs—A Talking Book
    Peter Pan Industries
    grade level: primary
    In this book, the child is introduced to the world of reading through the children's all-time favorite story. The fully colored book follows the cassette word for word. A signal tells the reader when to turn the page.

11. HANS CHRISTIAN ANDERSEN
    Society for Visual Education, Inc.
    grade level: primary
    The four titles in this series are designed to introduce the reader to the humor, action, and folk wisdom of Hans Christian Andersen's tales.

12. AESOP'S FABLES
    Society for Visual Education, Inc.
    grade level: primary

The set includes five titles that revolve around Aesop's heroes who demonstrate human strengths and weaknesses. With simple language and colorful illustrations, they are designed to hold the interest of beginning readers.

13. WORLD OF JUST-SO STORIES
Society for Visual Education, Inc.
grade level: primary
Consisting of four titles, this set has a verbatim cassette narration designed to stimulate general reading interest while developing reading skills.

14. ADVENTURES OF WILD ANIMALS
Society for Visual Education, Inc.
grade level: upper primary–intermediate
This set consists of six titles, depicting true-to-life portrayals of animals in the wild of three continents—Africa, Australia, and Antarctica.

15. WILDLIFE STORIES
Society for Visual Education, Inc.
grade level: upper primary–intermediate
The six stories are designed to help students build reading skills and increase vocabulary. Students also learn about the development of animals from birth to adulthood.

16. COMIC BOOK READ-ALONGS
Walt Disney Educational Media Co.
grade level: intermediate
Used with their accompanying cassettes, these books are designed to improve reading comprehension skills, to promote vocabulary development, and to encourage independent reading.

17. HERO LEGENDS
Society for Visual Education, Inc.
grade level: intermediate–junior high
In this set of six titles, stories focus on the deeds of legendary heroes from England, Switzerland, Greece, and Arabia. These tales are designed to serve as "samplers" so that students will be motivated to read more.

18. AUDIO LANGUAGE STUDIES READ-ALONG SERIES
ALS Audio Language Studies, Inc.

These series are presented in four categories.

a. Children's—including the following titles:
Grimms' *Fairy Tales*   grade level: 3–5
The Jungle Book   grade level: 6–8
Heidi   grade level: 5–7
Treasure Island   grade level: 6–8
Pinocchio   grade level: 4–6

b. Young People's—includes the following titles:
The Adventures of Huckleberry Finn   grade level: 5–7
Black Beauty   grade level: 4–6
The Wind in the Willows   grade level: 3–5
Little Women   grade level: 5–7
The Railway Children   grade level: 6–8
Kidnapped   grade level: 7–9
The Secret Garden   grade level: 5–7
Alice in Wonderland   grade level: 5–7
Through the Looking Glass   grade level: 5–7
Kim   grade level: 7–9

c. Mystery and Horror—includes the following titles:
The Hound of the Baskervilles   grade level: 7–9
The Sign of Four   grade level: 5–7
A Study in Scarlet   grade level: 5–7

d. Classics—includes the following titles:
Jane Eyre   grade level: 6–8
The Time Machine   grade level: 7–9
A Christmas Carol   grade level: 6–8
Oliver Twist   grade level: 7–9
The Lost World   grade level: 6–8
The Hunchback of Notre Dame   grade level: 6–8
The Red Badge of Courage   grade level: 6–8
The Prisoner of Zenda   grade level: 7–9
The Man of Property   grade level: 7–9
The Picture of Dorian Gray   grade level: 6–8
Wuthering Heights   grade level: 7–9
This series claims to be a major breakthrough in reading comprehension with titles that are designed to spark the imagination and enthrall the listener/reader.

19. TALES OF WINNIE THE WITCH
Society for Visual Education, Inc.
grade level: upper primary–intermediate
The focus in the six titles is on the adventures of Winnie the Witch and her companions. These tales are designed to help students develop and reinforce basic reading skills, and to start them to read independently.

Magazines

1. PEANUT BUTTER
Scholastic Inc.
age level: 4–7 years
This magazine is designed to help young children build their language arts skills. The "builders" for the children are the activities used.

2. MY WEEKLY READER SURPRISE
Xerox Education Publications
grade level: kindergarten
This is a four-page newspaper for kindergarteners. Illustrated activities of certain animals are presented which are intended to elicit stories of the pictures from the "readers." Contents cover science, social studies, and language arts.

3. SCHOLASTIC LET'S FIND OUT
Scholastic Inc.
grade level: kindergarten
Designed to interest the child with a rapidly expanding world, this magazine includes read-to-me stories, classroom calendars, games, and activities that encourage a child to use his senses to learn. The magazine is pictorial and the text is designed for the adult to read aloud to the child.

4. CHILDREN'S TELEVISION WORK-SHOP
a. *Sesame Street Magazine*
age level: 2–6 years
b. *The Electric Company Magazine*
age level: 6–10 years
c. 3-2-1-*CONTACT*
age level: 8–14 years

Children's Television Workshop
Prepared in conjunction with the television programs of the same names, these magazines are designed to present innumerable ways of how children might, with pleasure and enjoyment, improve their reading, math, and thinking skills.

5. BUDDY'S WEEKLY MAGAZINE
Xerox Education Publications
grade level: 1
This four-page magazine brings a message from "Good Citizen" to first graders, as well as a puzzle page that allows them to use their beginning thinking skills. All reports are planned to help children observe, discover, and understand basic science concepts.

6. CHICKADEE
Young Naturalist Foundation
age level: under 8 years
Aimed at interesting children under eight "in their environment and the world around them," each issue of this magazine has a read-to-me story. The activities and games included are to be filled in or cut out. The contents cover fiction and nonfiction stories and articles.

7. CHILDREN'S DIGEST
Children's Better Health Institute
age level: 8–10 years
This is a health-oriented publication. Fiction, nonfiction, poetry, games, puzzles, activities are all concerned with the well-being of children. Different writing forms are used: realistic stories, adventure, mysteries, and science fiction. The contents also cover nature, science, sports, history, and biography.

8. CRICKET
Open Court Publishing Co.
age level: 6–12 years
The contents of the magazine are varied and include poetry, folktales, biography, and nonfiction articles; fantasy, science fiction, historical fiction, and modern realism; and the mysterious, the humorous,

and the suspenseful. Each issue includes reprints from highly regarded books as well as original submissions.

9. BOY'S LIFE
    Boy Scouts of America
    age level: 8–18 years
    Sports and recreation are the central contents of this magazine. The emphasis on outdoor life encompasses science while channeling the various and numerous interests of boys united by the rules and tenets of an organization. An addition is available in braille from Volunteer Services for the Blind.

10. EBONY JR!
    Johnson Publishing Co., Inc.
    age level: 6–12 years
    This magazine focuses on "the hopes, ideals, and accomplishments of Black children throughout the world." It is intended to encourage reading and the development of other related skills. The contents range from highly informative articles to exercises masked as puzzles.

11. RANGER RICK
    National Wildlife Federation
    age level: 5–12 years
    This periodical aims to teach children "about wildlife; natural history and natural science; and about the environment in an entertaining, lively framework." The articles are informative and clearly written. Nature projects are suggested and explained so that children might do them on their own or with some help.

12. STONE SOUP
    Children's Art Foundation
    age level: 8–13 years
    The stories, poems, book reviews, and pictures are submitted by children aged 5–12. The publications are designed to spotlight the imagination and interests of creative children. They are based on the children's personal experiences and on their observations of people and places.

13. SEEDLING SERIES: SHORT STORY INTERNATIONAL
    International Cultural Exchange
    grade level: 4–7
    This quarterly publishes about eight stories in each issue and gives an 'international flavor' to the children's reading. The contents list the countries from which the stories come or in which they have been set. Folktales are among the kinds of stories presented in the periodical.

14. SCHOLASTIC SPRINT
    Scholastic Inc.
    grade level: 4–6
    This magazine aims at those students who are reading at the second and third grade levels. It presents topics and activities of interest to children within a limited vocabulary. This magazine is designed to develop positive reading attitudes, along with needed skills.

15. READ
    Xerox Education Publications
    grade level: 6–10
    Emphasizing the language arts, this magazine's contents are designed to appeal to junior high students. Over a period of time students have the opportunity to sample a variety of genres—short fiction, narrative, essay, expositive—and to read from the works of well-known writers. The readability level is at the 5–7 grade level.

16. JUNIOR SCHOLASTIC
    Scholastic Inc.
    grade level: 6–8
    This biweekly publication is designed to help junior high readers explore their country, the world, and the nation's history in pictures, maps, and articles written to appeal to their point of view.

17. CURRENT SCIENCE
    Xerox Education Publications
    grade level: 6–10
    Focusing on the latest advances in science and technology, this magazine has materials that may be too recent to be in textbooks. Each issue covers subjects in the

life sciences, physical sciences, earth sciences, and general science. The writing is clear and precise; there is a scoreboard of new terms introduced.

18. CURRENT EVENTS
Xerox Education Publications
grade level: 6–10
Current Events presents coverage of national and world events, and the people behind those events, in a vocabulary and style appropriate to children in grades six to ten. The reading level is between fifth and seventh grade. The back page is full of vocabulary and comprehension exercises, as well as drills on maps, charts, and graphs.

High interest/low vocabulary

1. ANIMAL ADVENTURE SERIES
Benefic Press
grade level: preprimer–1
interest level: 1–4
These stories of the actions and adventures of animals are based on scientific knowledge and facts. The series is a collection of twelve stories.

2. BUTTERNUT BILL SERIES
Benefic Press
grade level: preprimer—1
interest level: 1–4
Stories are about the adventures of a young boy and his friends. The stories are set in the Ozark Mountains in the 1850s. The series is a collection of eight books.

3. TOM LOGAN SERIES
Benefic Press
grade level: preprimer—1
interest level: 1–4
The ten books that comprise this series deal with the adventures of a young boy growing to manhood. The stories are set in the Old West.

4. COWBOY SAM SERIES
Benefic Press
grade level: preprimer—3
interest level: 1–6
This series is designed to appeal to young boys. The content is western in nature.

5. MOONBEAM SERIES
Benefic Press
grade level: preprimer–3
interest level: 1–6
There are ten titles in the series. Each book is about the space-age adventures of a monkey, while the "costars" are adult multi-ethnic characters.

6. DAN FRONTIER SERIES
Benefic Press
grade level: preprimer–1
interest level: 1–6
There are ten books in the series, and each book depicts early pioneer life in the Midwest.

7. SIGHT READERS—ENDANGERED SPECIES
Schoolhouse Press
grade level: 1
interest level: K–3
The books focus on the problems of endangered species from all over the world. The easy-to-read stories are designed to nurture a "sense of caring" about animal life while developing reading skills.

8. FABLE PLAYS FOR ORAL READING
Curriculum Associates
grade level: 1–3 (remedial)
These plays are based on Aesop's Fables. They are designed for readers of varying reading skills.

9. MANIA BOOKS
Children's Press
grade level: 1
interest level: 1–5
The MANIA books include such diverse subjects as animals, clowns, and volcanoes. The series consists of sixteen books containing many full-page illustrations.

10. HELICOPTER ADVENTURE SERIES
Benefic Press
grade level: 1–3
interest level: 1–4
Six adventure stories are in the series. Some of these stories depict women in active roles.

11. **FIND OUT ABOUT BOOKS**
Benefic Press
grade level: 1–3
interest level: 1–6
Twelve books comprise the set. Each book investigates basic science facts and concepts.

12. **READY, GET SET, GO BOOKS**
Children's Press
grade level: 1–3
interest level: 1–6
This set of books deals with a variety of topics like dinosaurs, trucks, motorcycles, and dolls.

13. **FIRST READING BOOKS**
Garrard Publishing Co.
grade level: 1
interest level: 2–3
Subjects such as pets, birds, and wild animals are included in the books. The vocabulary used is based on the easier half of the Dolch Basic Sight Words and the ninety-five common nouns.

14. **PACESETTERS**
Children's Press
grade level: 1–4
interest level: 4–12
This series consists of twenty-four titles, which are adventure stories, suspense stories, science fiction, and mysteries.

15. **BASIC VOCABULARY BOOKS**
Garrard Publishing Co.
grade level: 2
interest level: 3–4
This is a set of books whose contents include Indian folklore, animals, and folk tales.

16. **FIRST HOLIDAY BOOKS**
Garrard Publishing Co.
grade level: 2
interest level: 3–5
The content of these books is based on folklore and legends, not only of America but also of other countries, interwoven into holiday stories.

17. **DISCOVERY**
Garrard Publishing Co.
grade level: 2–3
interest level: 4–6
This set of books consists of over sixty biographies of outstanding well-known women, scientists, reformers, humanitarians, explorers, and statesmen.

18. **READ ABOUT SCIENCE**
Raintree Publishers, Ltd.
grade level: 2–3
interest level: 4–6
There are fifteen titles in this set of books. The stories deal with topics such as space, light and color, time and clocks.

19. **INTRIGUE SERIES**
Benefic Press
grade level: 2–3
interest level: 4–12
The four stories in this series are tales of intrigue and mystery. The process of unravelling the plot helps to develop map and chart skills.

20. **JIM HUNTER BOOKS**
Fearon Education
grade level: 2–3
interest level: 6–adult
This series deals with the adventures and escapades of a secret agent of the caliber of James Bond. There are sixteen titles in all.

21. **SPORTSTELLERS**
Fearon Education
grade level: 2–3
interest level: 6–adult
Eight titles are in the set. Each book deals with a major sport, while the subplots deal with challenges and conflicts that today's athletes face.

22. **SPACE POLICE**
Fearon Education
grade level: 2–3
interest level: 6–adult
These six books focus on the concept of space-age "cops and robbers" or "good guys and bad guys."

23. INNER CITY SERIES
Benefic Press
grade level: 2–4
interest level: 2–7
The five titles that comprise this set focus on young people solving their own difficulties and problems. Imagination, humor, and determination are characteristics of the young people.

24. THE WILDLIFE ADVENTURE SERIES
Addison-Wesley Publishing Co.
grade level: 2–4
interest level: 3–7
These books focus on the "true-to-life" experiences of various wild animals.

25. THE MORGAN BAY MYSTERIES
Addison-Wesley Publishing Co. Inc.
grade level: 2–4
interest level: 3–8
These books—nine in all—are well illustrated. They are mystery books and are designed for remedial, supplementary, and individualized reading programs. They also include teenage characters.

26. HORSES AND HEROINES
Benefic Press
grade level: 2–4
interest level: 4–7
This set includes six titles focusing on the adventures of a young girl and her horse.

27. RACING WHEEL SERIES
Benefic Press
grade level: 2–4
interest level: 4–12
The twelve titles revolve around an inner-city boy and his friends. These boys learn all that is involved in auto racing—training, equipment, and driving techniques.

28. CHECKERED FLAG SERIES
Addison-Wesley Publishing Co.
grade level: 2–4
interest level: 5–12
The stories in this series are set at a fast-moving pace, which is combined with a racing setting full of intrigue and mystery, featuring different kinds of cars, races, and motorcycles.

29. THE DEEP SEA ADVENTURE SERIES
Addison-Wesley Publishing Co.
grade level: 2–5
interest level: 3–8
These stories revolve around mature characters, and are full of adventure and mystery involving the sea. The series consists of twelve titles.

30. SPACE SCIENCE FICTION SERIES
Benefic Press
grade level: 2–6
interest level: 4–12
The six titles in this series deal with space travelers who visit alien planets and come into contact with the inhabitants of those planets.

31. FOLKLORE OF THE WORLD
Garrard Publishing Co.
grade level: 3
interest level: 4–5
This is a set of fourteen books that focuses on folklore or folk tales from around the world.

32. INDIANS
Garrard Publishing Co.
grade level: 3
interest level: 4–6
Thirteen titles written from the American Indian's point of view are included in this set of books. The historical biographies are of both Indian heroines and heroes.

33. GOOD EARTH BOOKS
Garrard Publishing Co.
grade level: 3
interest level: 4–7
These books focus on scientific topics dealing with ecology and environmental education.

34. PLEASURE READING BOOKS
Garrard Publishing Co.
grade level: 4
interest level: 5–7
Books in this series are an adaptation of famous legends and stories. Some of the titles are Robinson Crusoe, Aesop, and Robin Hood. Folk tales and fairy tales are also included.

35. INCREDIBLE SERIES
Barnell Loft, Ltd.
grade level: 4–5
interest level: 7–12
This series consists of twelve short stories. Each story is about an unusual historic event.

Specific skills books

1. PHONICS PLUS
Schoolhouse Press
grade level: readiness–3
This is a program designed for those who need additional reinforcement in phonics skills. It provides for sequential development and extensive practice of phonics skills. Each book contains reviews of skills taught earlier. The program includes a systematic word attack strategy integrating skills used for phonics, context clues, prefixes, suffixes, syllabication, and the dictionary.

2. DISCOVERING PHONICS WE USE
The Riverside Publishing Co.
grade level: readiness–6
These workbooks are self-directed texts focusing on basic decoding skills and inductive instructional techniques to develop phonics generalizations. In addition to the phonics workbooks, the series contains crossword puzzles, word games, rhymes, riddles, a few stories, and cassette tapes and filmstrips.

3. EARLY SKILLS TREASURE CHEST
The Continental Press, Inc.
grade level: kindergarten–1
This series introduces young learners to beginning reading and thinking skills. Each book contains a progression of tasks providing meaningful reinforcement to students of varying abilities. Topics covered are: association and classification, patterns and sequences, rhyming, visual discrimination, and visual-motor skills.

4. BUILDING SIGHT VOCABULARY
Steck-Vaughn Co.
grade level: kindergarten–3
This is a sight-word program designed for beginning and remedial readers. Some of the features of the program are: sight words selected on the basis of recognized word lists and frequency of use, highly motivating games that introduce and practice vocabulary, and stories that deal with cultural diversity.

5. MERRILL READING SKILLTEXT SERIES
Charles E. Merrill Publishing Co.
grade level: kindergarten–6
This supplementary reading program is designed to improve the reading and study skills of students. The series blends story selections with skill activities. The development of skills is consistent.

6. MULTIPLE SKILL SERIES
Barnell Loft, Ltd.
grade level: preprimer–9
The focus in this series is to develop different reading skills. The high interest units progress gradually in difficulty. The multilevel approach is designed to be effective with all students, while four booklets at each level help to reinforce skills and help build basic sight vocabulary.

7. SPECIFIC SKILL SERIES
Barnell Loft, Ltd.
grade level: preprimer–12
Eight reading skills are emphasized in this series: working with sounds, following directions, using the context, locating the answer, getting the facts, getting the main idea, drawing conclusions. The series is designed to foster and maintain the reader's interest.

8. PATTERNS, SOUNDS, AND MEANING
Allyn & Bacon
grade level: 1–4
This is a program consisting of four books, designed for a diagnostic/prescriptive approach that utilizes a logical sequence of skills. The focus of the program is on phonics. These books are titled: *Clues to Consonants*, *Views on Vowels*, *Letters and Syllables*, *Syllables and Words*.

9. COMPREHENSION PLUS
Schoolhouse Press
grade level: 1–6
This is an elementary comprehension program, covering both literal and comprehension skills. Some of the features for the program are: a wide range of fiction and nonfiction reading selections, a range of reading comprehension skills for grades 1–6, vocabulary checks, response modes needed for taking tests, and study and survival skills.

10. STECK-VAUGHN CRITICAL THINKING
Steck-Vaughn Co.
grade level: 1–6
Designed to develop reading, thinking, and reasoning skills, this series assumes that students learn to think systematically and effectively, as it organizes thinking skills within the six stages of Bloom's Taxonomy of Educational Objectives.

11. SCHOLASTIC LISTENING SKILLS
Scholastic Inc.
grade level: 1–6
This is a systematic program of personal encouragement, practice, and reinforcement that is designed to develop and improve basic listening and reading comprehension. Each lesson is a taped segment plus a corresponding illustrated skills worksheet. The program is designed to motivate students to learn through a mix of radio-style story times and activities.

12. VOCABULARY SKILLS
Scholastic Inc.
grade level: 1–6
This program utilizes workbooks that provide instruction and practice in finding word meaning through structure and context. The books focus on experience, direct explanation, classifying synonyms and antonyms, summary clues, and inferences provided by the context to determine new word meanings.

13. READING FOR CONCEPTS
McGraw-Hill Book Co.
grade level: 1–6
The systematic development of reading skills through readings is the focus of the series. Some of the skills included are: factual recall, vocabulary, inference, identification of main idea, cause and effect, and concept recognition. A cassette program accompanies the first four levels, which is designed to help students follow the readings and relate their oral vocabulary to the words on the page.

14. NEW READING-THINKING SKILLS
The Continental Press, Inc.
grade level: 1–6
Designed to help students improve their critical reading and thinking abilities, the series focuses upon such skills as: inference, analogies, organization of ideas, relationships, classification, multiple meanings, and pronoun antecedents. The lessons are based on topics that aim to be of wide appeal and interest.

15. THE MCP PHONICS WORKBOOK PROGRAM
Modern Curriculum Press
grade level: 1–6
This program uses a logical development of decoding skills that introduces consonants before vowels, followed by the building of skills in word study, dictionary usage, syllabication, and more.

16. READER'S DIGEST
1. Reading Skill Building
grade level: 1–6
2. New Reading Skill Builder
grade level: 1–6
3. Advanced Reading Skill Builder
grade level: 7–9
Random House School Division
These books are based on articles selected from *Reader's Digest*, and are designed to help students develop comprehension, interpretation, and application skills. They also aid in building vocabulary and improving oral communication. They are designed for use in developmental reading programs, individualized programs, or as free reading.

17. SUPPORTIVE READING SKILLS
Barnell Loft, Ltd.
grade level: 1–9
This is a diagnostic/prescriptive reading

program, complementing and supplementing the *Specific Skills Series*. The program claims to develop and refine techniques that underlie eight major skill areas, which are divided into various levels.

18. CLUES FOR BETTER READING
Curriculum Associates, Inc.
grade level: 1–9
This is designed to be a research-based comprehension program. The activities are designed to develop, reinforce, and review basic reading comprehension skills. Each level strengthens comprehension skills, application of reading skills, independent study skills, critical thinking, and self-evaluation.

19. LISTENING COMPREHENSION SKILLS PROGRAM
Curriculum Associates, Inc.
grade level: 1–10
This program is designed to help students learn comprehension skills through oral reading and listening activities that provide for rate, level, and teaching and learning styles. The program can be used for the entire class or for team learning. The program offers intensive practice in eleven skill areas.

20. CAPITALIZATION AND PUNCTUATION
Barnell Loft, Ltd.
grade level: 1–9
Designed to help students develop capitalization and punctuation concepts, this program features the discovery of principles, and intensive practice, immediate application, frequent reviews, and built-in tests.

21. THINKING ABOUT READING
Modern Curriculum Press
grade level: 2–6
Focusing on story comprehension, this program aims to build higher level inference skills, expand vocabulary, and develop critical thinking ability. Some of the strategies employed to develop and foster comprehension skills are: the directed reading-thinking activities, the vocabulary self-collection strategy, and creative thinking-reading activities. Reading, thinking, and writing are integrated in this program.

22. VOCABULARY WORKS
Schoolhouse Press
grade level: 2–6
Included in this program are words from recognized word lists appropriate to the different levels of the program. It includes exercises in standard test formats. Riddles, crossword puzzles, and word searches are designed to provide fun and instructional reinforcement of vocabulary.

23. EXPLORING LANGUAGE WITH THE DICTIONARY
Schoolhouse Press
grade level: 3–6
This is a basic program for teaching dictionary and language arts skills. It is designed to help students use locational skills—such as guide words and entry words; functional skills—such as parts of speech; application skills—such as forms of adjectives and adverbs; and extension skills—such as illustrations and other reference materials.

24. STANDARDIZED TEST EXERCISE PROGRAM
Schoolhouse Press
grade level: 3–6
Designed to provide practice with standardized test-like materials, this program helps students become familiar with standardized reading comprehension test formats while improving their reading comprehension. The method used in the program is designed to enable students to search for information in their reading.

25. READING COMPREHENSION
Scholastic Inc.
grade level: 3–6
Children's literature is used to provide instruction and practice in literal, interpretive, and critical reading skills. The series consists of four sequential levels, with three different workbooks at each level.

26. SPRINT READING SKILLS PROGRAM
Scholastic Inc.
grade level: 4–6
A developmental reading program, consisting of four separate levels, the program is a combination of high-interest stories and controlled reading levels based on the revised Spache Readability Formula. In addition, it has a lot of graphics and skill exercises designed to capture students' interest.

27. COMPREHENSION TEST STRATEGIES
Scholastic Inc.
grade level: 4–6
The goal of this program is to prepare students for the reading comprehension section of standardized tests. The program claims that when it is used in conjunction with a reading and writing program, students acquire the understanding and confidence needed to get better scores on standardized tests.

28. SKIMMING AND SCANNING
Jamestown Publishers
grade level: 4–6
This program emphasizes developing faster, more flexible readers. Students are given instructions which help them to read about twice their average reading speed, and attain a comprehension score of 50% to 60%.

29. READING DRILLS
Jamestown Publishers
grade level: 4–6
This is a companion to *Skimming and Scanning* that combines the two attempts to 'create an effective program for building reading speed and comprehension.' The types of drills that follow the timed readings are: multiple-choice comprehension questions, subject-matter cloze, structure-word cloze, and a vocabulary exercise.

30. FADS: READING COMPREHENSION SERIES
Bowmar/Noble Publishers, Inc.
grade level: 4–6
Reading kits on a variety of topics are part of this series. These kits are designed to provide easy-reading material and to help students improve reading comprehension skills.

31. MAP & GLOBE SKILLS KIT
SRA
grade level: 4–6
The purpose of this kit is to provide materials to promote development of the skills and understanding needed to use maps and globes effectively. An effort has been made to create and use visual materials designed to teach map and globe skills.

32. STUDY SKILLS FOR INFORMATION RETRIEVAL SERIES
Allyn & Bacon
grade level: 4–8
This series focuses on skills needed to evaluate and organize information for all content areas. Dictionary use and library skills are also emphasized.

33. IN OTHER WORDS: A JUNIOR THESAURUS
Scott, Foresman and Co.
grade level: 7–8
The book is designed to help students get acquainted with the working of a thesaurus. The book presents 342 basic entry words grouped with their more than 2,600 synonyms, antonyms, and related words.

34. SCOTT, FORESMAN INTERMEDIATE DICTIONARY
Scott, Foresman and Co.
grade level: 7–8
The dictionary includes thirty-four pages of practical self-help exercises that are designed to aid students in dictionary use. Graphics are included, which helps to clarify meanings.

35. READING LABORATORY
SRA
grade level: 1–12
This is a multilevel, developmental reading improvement program. It is designed for individual reading instruction.

36. SCHOOLHOUSE COMPREHENSION PATTERNS
SRA
grade level: 3–8
This kit is designed to help students improve their sentence patterns by combining vocabulary, comprehension, and syntactic skills in a sequential arrangement.

37. BE A BETTER READER
Prentice-Hall, Inc.
grade level: 4–12
This program teaches comprehension and study skills that are needed in grades 4–12. Each lesson begins with instruction in social studies, science, math, or literature. Students learn to master and apply a skill. The program covers a variety of useful and important skills.

38. BASIC READING UNITS: MULTI-SKILLS KITS
The Continental Press, Inc.
grade level: 6–12
These kits are designed to prepare students for competency tests in basic reading skills. The kits feature high-interest lessons that reinforce one of four reading skills: main idea, facts and details, inferences and conclusions, and sequence.

Games

1. BLEND DOMINOES
Ideal School Supply Company
grade level: preprimer–3
This is a word game designed to develop and reinforce basic reading skills. It aims to interest and challenge children of diverse developmental levels.

2. SILLY SOUNDS—GAME OF INITIAL CONSONANTS
Ideal School Supply Company
grade level: kindergarten–2
The focus of this game is to teach consonants. Practice is provided in developing and improving vocabulary.

3. SEA OF VOWELS—LONG & SHORT VOWEL GAME
Ideal School Supply Company
grade level: 1–3
This game is designed to reinforce long vowel sound recognition and short vowel sound recognition. Through game play, basic vocabulary skills are developed.

4. INFERENCE GAME: THE FUN WAY TO LEARN
Comprehension Game Corp.
grade level: 1–4
As a reading comprehension board game, this game focuses on inference skills. The objective of the game is for the students to be able to make inferences after reading short stories.

5. SPACE FLIGHT NO. 2403: A GAME OF BLENDS
Ideal School Supply Co.
grade level: 1–3
This game is designed to increase and reinforce students' use and awareness of blends.

6. RHYMING ZIG ZAG NO. 2400: A GAME OF RHYMING WORDS
Ideal School Supply Co.
grade level: 1–3
As a game focused on rhyming words, this game also provides practice in developing vocabulary.

7. LINK LETTERS: IMPROVING STRUCTURAL READING SKILLS
Milton Bradley Co.
grade level: 1–4
Letter recognition, spelling, and sentence building skills are promoted in this game. It is a multi-purpose learning aid and it lends itself to a variety of uses.

8. INSTRUCTIONAL AID PACKS—VOCABULARY GAMES
Barnell Loft, Ltd.
grade level: 1–5
Described as a diagnostic and prescriptive decoding program, these games aim to increase vocabulary and word power. The

games can be used with an entire class, a small group, or even two students.

9. **WORD MASTERY WITH PUZZLES AND GAMES**
Scholastic Inc.
grade level: 1–6
These games are designed to help students develop and acquire greater verbal skills while reinforcing areas such as vocabulary, word recognition, spelling, alphabetizing, short vowel sounds, compound words, syllabication, and rhyming words.

10. **SCRABBLE: A CROSSWORD GAME**
Selchow & Righter Co.
grade level: 1–adult
Designed to increase word recognition skills and develop vocabulary, this game also helps develop and improve dictionary and reference skills.

11. **COMPREHENSION GAMES KIT: GETTING THE MAIN IDEA**
Comprehension Games Corp.
grade lcvcl: 2–adult basic education
A game approach is used to meet the needs for reinforcement materials in comprehension skills. The objective of the game is that the student will be able to match a story with a corresponding card that states the main idea of the story.

12. **FACT OR OPINION: A GAME FOR DEVELOPING CRITICAL READING SKILLS**
Comprehension Games Corp.
grade level: 2–3 and 3–4
Providing practice in distinguishing between fact and opinion is the focus of this game. The game consists of gameboard and story cards that are of high interest and easy to read.

13. **BASE WORD RUMMY**
The Judy Co. General Learning Corp.
grade level: 4 and up
This card game is designed to increase and reinforce students' awareness of word structure, readiness of parts of speech, pronunciation skills, and visual as well as aural vocabulary.

Newspapers—How to use newspapers in the classroom

This category consists of a list of books that are designed to help the teacher use the newspaper as a tool to encourage students to develop the ability and skills needed to read critically, intelligently, quickly, and for pleasure.

1. **AMERICAN NEWSPAPERS PUBLISHERS ASSOCIATION FOUNDATION**
This is a useful source of information regarding the use of the newspaper in teaching. It also helps to identify a newspaper educator in your area or region.

2. Cheyney, Arnold B. **TEACHING READING SKILLS THROUGH THE NEWSPAPER**
International Reading Association
Cheyney discusses the importance of the newspaper in education, specifically in the reading classroom. The major purpose of this book is to provide teachers with techniques for teaching reading skills using the newspaper as the medium. The suggestions and activities are designed for use with students at all levels of reading ability.

3. Heitzmann, William R. **THE NEWSPAPER IN THE CLASSROOM**
National Education Association
This book stresses the importance of the newspaper as a valuable teaching aid, as it helps in developing student skills and maximizing student abilities. Heitzmann points out that the newspaper can be used as a motivational device to develop basic skills and to promote learning in various subject areas. The newspaper helps students with skimming, vocabulary development, increasing reading speed, improving comprehension skills, and the ability to read critically.

4. **50 POLITICAL CARTOONS FOR TEACHING AMERICAN HISTORY**
J. Weston Walch, Publishers
This is a series that contains a 'careful' selection of editorial cartoons. Each of the series consists of background information as well as suggested teaching ideas.

5. Jacobs, Jo Ann. ELEMENTARY ACTIVITIES FOR USING THE NEWSPAPER
Detroit Free Press
A collection of 225 cards, covering various subject areas, can be used by students independently or with teacher help and involvement.

6. LEARNING ACTIVITIES FOR PRIMARY GRADES
Independent Press
Hints are provided for using the newspaper in a variety of fields. The ideas are focused on young students.

7. NEWSPAPER IN THE CLASSROOM
New York Daily News
This is a helpful and fairly comprehensive booklet, focusing on the tabloid format.

8. NEWSPAPER ADVERTISING BUREAU, INC.
The research department of the Bureau conducts a wide variety of research. It was under the Newspaper Readership Project that studies were done which resulted in:
1. Children and Newspapers: Changing Patterns of Readership and Their Effects
2. The Newspaper in Education: What It Does to Children's Civic Awareness and Attitudes Towards Newspapers

3. Guidelines for Conducting Newspaper in Educational Research: Assessing the Impact of NIE on Student Attitudes, Newspaper Reading, and Civic Awareness

9. NEWSPAPER UNIT: ELEMENTARY LEVEL
San Jose Mercury & News
Information and suggestions are provided for a two-week unit for younger students.

10. Partlow, Hugh. LEARNING FROM NEWSPAPER: READING
Canadian Daily Newspaper Publishers Association
The focus of the book is on the development of reading competence and skills through continued daily newspaper use.

11. Piercey, Dorothy, ed. NEWSPAPER IN EDUCATION
Arizona Republic & Phoenix Gazette
This is a series of booklets focusing on topics and subjects that are beneficial to elementary as well as secondary teaching.

12. VISUAL EDUCATION CONSULTANTS
A kit is provided with suggested activities for using the newspaper (as well as film strips of the previous week's news). This is accompanied by a teacher's guide covering materials for thirty-five weeks.

Appendix F
Publishers' Addresses

Addison-Wesley Publishing Company, Inc.
One Jacob Way
Reading, MA 01867

Allyn & Bacon, Inc.
160 Gould Street
Needham Heights, MA 02194

Allyn & Bacon, Inc.
Elhi Division
Link Drive
Rockleigh, NJ 07647

American Guidance Service
Publishers' Building
Circle Pines, MN 55014-1796

American Newspaper Publishers Association
Foundation
The Newspaper Center
11600 Sunrise Valley Drive
Reston, VA 20091

American Optical
Box 1
Southbridge, MA 01550

Arizona Republic & Phoenix Gazette
P.O. Box 1950
120 E. Van Buren St.
Phoenix, AZ 85110

Audio Language Studies, Inc.
One Colomba Drive
Niagara Falls, NY 14305

Barnell Loft, Ltd.
958 Church Street
Baldwin, NY 11510

Bausch & Lomb Optical Company
Rochester, NY 14602

Beltone Electronics Corp.
4201 West Victoria Street
Chicago, IL 60646

Benefic Press
1900 N. Naragansett
Chicago, IL 60639

Bowmar/Noble Publishers, Inc.
4563 Colorado Blvd.
Los Angeles, CA 90039

Boy Scouts of America
1325 Walnut Hill Lane
Irving, TX 75062

Wm. C. Brown Group
2460 Kerper Boulevard
Dubuque, IA 52001

C.F. Software
P.O. Box 2101
Huntington Beach, CA 92647

CTB/McGraw-Hill
Del Monte Research Park
Monterey, CA 93940

Canadian Daily Newspaper Publishers
Association
Suite 214
321 Bloor Street, East
Toronto, Ontario
M4W 1E7
Canada

Chapman, Brook & Kent
1215 De La Vina, Suite F
Santa Barbara, CA 93101

Children's Art Foundation
P.O. Box 83
Santa Cruz, CA 95063

Children's Better Health Institute
Benjamin Franklin Literary & Medical So-
ciety, Inc.
1100 Waterway Blvd.
P.O. Box 567
Indianapolis, IN 46206

Children's Press
1224 West Van Buren Street
Chicago, IL 60625

Children's Television Workshop
One Lincoln Plaza
New York, NY 10023

The Committee on Diagnostic Reading
    Tests, Inc.
Mountain Home, NC 28758

Comprehension Games Corporation
200 South Service Road
Roslyn Heights, NY 11577

The Consulting Psychologists Press, Inc.
577 College Avenue
Palo Alto, CA 94306

Continental Press, Inc.
520 East Bainbridge Street
Elizabethtown, PA 17022

Curriculum Associates, Inc.
5 Esquire Road
North Billerica, MA 01862-2589

DLM Teaching Resources
P.O. Box 4000
One DLM Park
Allen, TX 75002

Detroit Free Press
321 W. Lafayette
Detroit, MI 48231

Walt Disney Educational Media Company
500 South Buena Vista Street
Burbank, CA 91521

EMC Publishing
Changing Times Education Service
300 York Avenue
St. Paul, MN 55101

The Economy Company
P.O. Box 25308, N. Walnut
Oklahoma City, OK 73125

Educators Publishing Service, Inc.
75 Moulton Street
Cambridge, MA 02238

Essay Press
P.O. Box 2323
La Jolla, CA 92037

Falvey Company
1312 West 7th Street
Piscataway, NJ 08854

Fearon Education
19 Davis Drive
Belmont, CA 94002

First Byte
2845 Temple Avenue
Long Beach, CA 92647

Garrard Publishing Company
1607 North Market Street
Champaign, IL 61820

Grolier Electronic Publishing, Inc.
95 Madison Ave.
Suite 1100
New York, NY 10016

Hartley
P.O. Box 431
Dimondale, MI 48821

Heinemann Educational Books Inc.
70 Court St.
Portsmouth, NH 03801

Houghton Mifflin Company
One Beacon St
Boston, MA 02108

Ideal School Supply Company
Oak Lawn, IL 60453

Independent Press
P.O. Box 230
Long Beach, CA 90844

Indiana University Press
Tenth and Morton Sts.
Bloomington, IN 47405

International Cultural Exchange
6 Sheffield Road
Great Neck, NY 11021

International Reading Association
800 Barksdale Road
P.O. Box 8139
Newark, DE 19714-8139

J. & S. Software
1410 Reid Avenue
Port Washington, NY 11050

Jamestown Publishers
P.O. Box 6743
Providence, RI 02940

Jastak Associates, Inc.
1526 Gilpin Avenue
Wilmington, DE 19806

Johnson Publishing Company, Inc.
Box 990, 1880 S. 57 Ct.
Boulder, CO 80306

The Judy Company
General Learning Corporation
Minneapolis, MN 55401

Kendall/Hunt Publishing Company
2460 Kerper Boulevard
P.O. Box 539
Dubuque, IA 52001

Learning Multi-Systems, Inc.
340 Coyier Lane
Madison, WI 53713

J.B. Lippincott Company
East Washington Square
Philadelphia, PA 19105

Macmillan Publishing Company, Inc.
866 Third Avenue
New York, NY 10022

Maico Hearing Instruments Company
7375 Bush Lake Road
Minneapolis, MN 55435

Mast/Keystone
2212 East 12th Street
Davenport, IA 52803

McGraw-Hill Book Company
1221 Avenue of the Americas
New York, NY 10020

Charles E. Merrill Publishing Company
936 Eastwind Dr.
Westerville, OH 43081

Microcomputer Workshops
225 Westchester Avenue
Port Chester, NY 10573

Milton Bradley Company
443 Shaker Road
East Longmeadow, MA 01028

Modern Curriculum Press, Inc.
13900 Prospect Road
Cleveland, OH 44136

National Education Association (NEA)
1201 16th St. N.W.
Washington, DC 20036

National Wildlife Federation
1412 16th Street, N.W.
Washington, DC 20036

Thomas Nelson, Inc.
P.O. Box 14100
Nelson Place at Elm Hill Pike
Nashville, TN 37214

New York Daily News
New York News Inc.
220 East 42nd Street
New York, NY 10017

Newspaper Advertising Bureau, Inc.
485 Lexington Avenue
New York, NY 10017

Open Court Publishing Company
1058 Eighth St.
La Salle, IL 61301

Peter Pan Industries
145 Komorn Street
Newark, NJ 07105

Prentice-Hall, Inc.
Educational Book Division
Route 9 West
Englewood Cliffs, NJ 07632

Pro-Ed
5341 Industrial Oaks Blvd.
Austin, TX 78735

The Psychological Corporation
6277 Sea Harbor Drive
Orlando, FL 32821

Raintree Publishers International, Ltd.
330 Kilbourne Ave.
Milwaukee, WI 53202

Ramon Ross
School of Education
California State University
5402 College Avenue
San Diego, CA 92115

Random House
201 East 50 St.
New York, NY 10022

Reader's Digest
Pleasantville, NY 10570

Riverside Publishing Company
8420 Bryn Mawr Avenue
Suite 1000
Chicago, IL 60631

San Jose Mercury & News
750 Ridder Park Dr.
San Jose, CA 95190

Scholastic, Inc.
730 Broadway
New York, NY 10003

Scholastic Magazines, Inc.
902 Sylvan Avenue
Englewood Cliffs, NJ 07632

Scholastic Testing Service, Inc.
480 Meyer Road
P.O. Box 1056
Bensenville, IL 60106

Scholastic Wizware
730 Broadway
New York, NY 10003

Schoolhouse Press
13796 Prospect Road
Cleveland, OH 44136

Science Research Associates, Ltd.
259 East Erie Street
Chicago, IL 60611

Scott, Foresman & Company
1900 East Lake Avenue
Glenview, IL 60025

Charles Scribner's Sons
597 Fifth Avenue
New York, NY 10017

Scribner Educational Publishers
866 Third Avenue
New York, NY 10022

Selchow & Righter Co.
999 Quaker Lane St.
West Hartford, CT 06110

Slosson Educational Publications, Inc.
P.O. Box 280
East Aurora, NY 14052

Society for Visual Education, Inc.
1345 Diversey Parkway
Chicago, IL 60614

Spinnaker Software
215 First Street
Cambridge, MA 02124

Steck-Vaughn Company
P.O. Box 2028
Austin, TX 78768

Stoelting Company
1350 South Kostner Avenue
Chicago, IL 60623-1196

Sunburst Communications
39 Washington Avenue
Pleasantville, NY 10570

Teachers College Press
Teachers College
Columbia University
1234 Amsterdam Ave.
New York, NY 10027

Titmus
Ophthalmic Products Division
P.O. Box 191
Petersburg, VA 23804-0191

University of Illinois Press
54 East Gregory Drive
Champaign, IL 61820

Visual Education Consultants
P.O. Box 52
Madison, WI 53701

J. Weston Walch Publishers
321 Valley Street
Box 658
Portland, ME 04104

Walker and Company
720 Fifth Avenue
New York, NY 10019

Western Psychological Services
12031 Wilshire Boulevard
Los Angeles, CA 90025

Xerox Education Publications
245 Long Hill Rd.
Middletown, CT 06457

Young Naturalist Foundation
59 Front Street, East
Toronto, Ontario
M5E 1B3
Canada

Richard L. Zweig Associates, Inc.
20800 Beach Blvd.
Huntington Beach, CA 92648

Bibliography

Alexander, J. Estill. 1971. Relationship between personality and reading disability. *College Student Journal, 5* (November–December): 121–128.

Alexander, J. Estill. 1983. Affective dimensions. In *Teaching reading*, 2nd ed., ed. J. Estill Alexander, pp. 356–388. Boston: Little, Brown and Company.

Alexander, J. Estill, and Filler, Ronald C. 1976. *Attitudes and reading*. Newark, Delaware: International Reading Association.

Allington, Richard L. 1977. If they don't read much, how they ever gonna get good? *Journal of Reading, 21* (October): 57–61.

Allington, Richard L., Chodos, Laura, Domaracki, Jane, and Truex, Sharon. 1977. Passage dependency: Four diagnostic oral reading tests. *The Reading Teacher, 30* (January): 369–375.

Almy, Millie Corrine. 1949. *Children's experiences prior to first grade success in reading*. New York: Bureau of Publications, Teachers College Press, Columbia University.

Anastasiow, Nicholas J. 1964. A report of self-concept of the very gifted. *The Gifted Child Quarterly, 8* (Winter): 177–178, 189.

Anastasiow, Nicholas J. 1967. Sex differences in self-concept scores of high and low ability elementary students. *The Gifted Child Quarterly, 11* (Summer): 112–116.

Anderson, Billie V., and Barnitz, John G. 1984. Cross-cultural schemata and reading comprehension instruction. *Journal of Reading, 28* (November): 102-108.

Anderson, Linda M., Evertson, Carolyn M., and Brophy, Jere E. 1979. An experimental study of effective teaching in first grade reading groups. *The Elementary School Journal, 79* (March): 193–223.

Anderson, Richard C., and Freebody, Peter. 1979. *Vocabulary knowledge*. (Technical Report Number 136.) Urbana, Illinois: University of Illinois Center for the Study of Reading.

Anderson, Richard C., and Pearson, P. David. 1984. A schema-theoretic view of basic processes in reading comprehension. In *Handbook of reading research*, ed. P. David Pearson, pp. 225-292. New York: Longman.

Anderson, Thomas H., and Armbruster, Bonnie B. 1984. Studying. In *Handbook of reading research*, ed. P. David Pearson, pp. 657–679. New York: Longman.

André, Marli E.D.A., and Anderson, Thomas H. 1978–1979. The development and evaluation of a self-questioning study technique. *Reading Research Quarterly, 14* (Number 4): 605–623.

Armbruster, Bonnie B., and Brown, Ann L. 1984. Learning from reading: The role of metacognition. In *Learning to read in American schools: Basal readers and content texts*, eds. Richard C. Anderson, Jean Osborne, and Robert J. Tierney, pp. 273–281. Hillsdale, New Jersey: Lawrence Erlbaum Associates.

Asher, Steven R. 1977. Sex differences in reading achievement. (Reading Education Report No. 2) Champaign, Illinois: Center for the Study of Reading, University of Illinois.

Asher, Steven R., and Markell, Richard A. 1974. Sex differences in comprehension of high- and low-interest reading material. *Journal of Educational Psychology, 66* (October): 680–687.

Athey, Irene. 1983. Thinking and experience: The

cognitive base for language experience. In *Developing literacy: Young children's use of language*, eds. Robert P. Parker and Frances A. Davis, pp. 19–33. Newark, Delaware: International Reading Association.

Aulls, Mark W. 1982. *Developing readers in today's elementary schools*. Boston: Allyn and Bacon.

Babbs, Patricia, J., and Moe, Alden J. 1983. Metacognition: A key for independent learning from text. *The Reading Teacher, 36* (January): 422–426.

Bader, Lois A. 1980. *Reading diagnosis and remediation in classrooms and clinics*. New York: Macmillan.

Bader, Lois A. 1983. *Bader reading and language inventory*. New York: Macmillan.

Baker, Linda, and Brown, Ann L. 1984a. Metacognitive skills and reading. In *Handbook of reading research*, ed. P. David Pearson, pp. 353–394. New York: Longman.

Baker, Linda, and Brown, Ann L. 1984b. Cognitive monitoring in reading. In *Understanding reading comprehension*, ed. James Flood, pp. 21–44. Newark, Delaware: International Reading Association.

Baldwin, R. Scott, Johnson, Dale M., and Peer, Gary G. 1981. Self-report inventories: Are they valid? Paper presented at the National Reading Conference at Dallas, Texas.

Barnitz, John G. 1980. Black English and other dialects: Sociolinguistic implications for reading instruction. *The Reading Teacher, 33* (April): 779–786.

Bartel, Nettie. 1975. Assessing and remediating problems in language development. In *Teaching children with learning and behavior problems*, eds. Donald Hammill and Nettie Bartel, pp. 155–201. Boston: Allyn and Bacon.

Barton, Allen H. 1963. Reading research and communication: The Columbia-Carnagie Project. In *Reading as an intellectual activity*, ed. J. Allen Figurel, pp. 246–250. Newark, Delaware: International Reading Association.

Bauer, Gary W. 1982. Information processing as a way of understanding and diagnosing learning disabilities. *Topics in Learning Disabilities, 2* (July): 33–45.

Baumann, James F. 1984. Implications for reading instruction from the research on teacher and school effectiveness. *Journal of Reading, 28* (November): 109–115.

Beals, Paul E. 1983. The newspaper in the classroom: A rationale for its use. *Reading World, 23* (October): 69–70.

Bean, Rita M., and Wilson, Robert M. 1981. *Effecting change in school reading programs: The resource role*. Newark, Delaware: International Reading Association.

Beebe, Mona J. 1980. The effect of different types of substitution miscues on reading. *Reading Research Quarterly, 15* (Number 3): 324-336.

Belloni, Loretta Frances, and Jongsma, Eugene A. 1978. The effects of interest on reading comprehension of low-achieving students. *Journal of Reading, 22* (November): 106–109.

Benson, P. Frank. 1983. Brain processes and reading. In *Progress in learning disabilities*, ed. Helmer Mykelbust, pp. 3–25. New York: Grune and Stratton.

Benton, Arthur L. 1975. Developmental dyslexia: Neurological aspects. In *Advances in neurology*, ed. W.J. Friedlander, pp. 1–47. New York: Raven Press.

Berliner, David C. 1981. Academic learning time and reading achievement. In *Comprehension and teaching: Research reviews*, ed. John T. Guthrie, pp. 203–226. Newark, Delaware: International Reading Associaton.

Berliner, David C., and Rosenshine, Barak. 1977. The acquisition of knowledge in the classroom. In *Schooling and the acquisition of knowledge*, eds. Richard C. Anderson et al., pp. 375–404. Hillsdale, New Jersey: Lawrence Erlbaum Associates.

Betts, Emmett A. 1946. *Foundations of reading instruction*. New York: American.

Bingham, Grace. 1980. Self-esteem among boys with and without specific learning disability. *Child Study Journal, 10* (Number 1): 41–47.

Black, F. William. 1976. Cognitive, academic, and behavioral findings in children with suspected and documented neurological dysfunction. *Journal of Learning Disabilities, 9* (March): 182–187.

Blachowicz, Camille L. Z. 1978. Metalinguistic awareness and the beginning readers. *The Reading Teacher, 31* (May): 875–876.

Blum, Irene H., and Koskinen, Patricia S. 1984. Adapting repeated reading for use in the classroom. In *Reading: Process, instruction and assessment*, ed. Linda B. Gambrell, pp. 14–24. College Park, Maryland: The State of Maryland International Reading Association.

Boehnlein, Mary M., and Hager, Beth. 1985. *Children, parents, and reading*. Newark, Delaware: International Reading Association.

Bond, Guy L., and Dykstra, Robert. 1967. Final report of project no. X-001, contract no. OE-5-10-264. Minneapolis: University of Minnesota.

Bond, Guy L., Tinker, Miles A., Wasson, Barbara

B., and Wasson, John B. 1984. *Reading difficulties: Their diagnosis and correction*, 5th ed. Englewood Cliffs, New Jersey: Prentice-Hall.

Bougere, Marguerite B. 1981. Dialect and reading disabilities. *Journal of Research and Development in Education, 14* (Summer): 67–73.

Bradley, John M., Ackerson, Gary, and Ames, Wilbur S. 1978. The reliability of maze procedure. *Journal of Reading Behavior, 10* (Fall): 291–296.

Bransford, J.D., Stein, B.S., Shelton, T.S., and Owings, R.A. 1981. Cognition and adaptation: The importance of learning to learn. In *Cognition, social behavior, and the environment*, ed. J. Harvey. Orlando, Florida: Academic Press.

Brophy, Jere E. 1979. Advances in teacher effectiveness research. Paper presented at the American Association of Colleges for Teacher Education annual meeting. Chicago, Illinois (ED 170 281).

Brown, Ann L. 1978. Knowing when, where, and how to remember: A problem of metacognition. In *Advances in instructional psychology*, ed. R. Glasser. Hillsdale, New Jersey: Lawrence Erlbaum Associates.

Brown, David M. 1985. Five tips on using games effectively. *The Reading Teacher, 38* (April): 819–820.

Brown, Dorothea, Wallbrown, Fred H., and Engin, Ann W. 1979. Developmental changes in reading attitudes during the intermediate grades. *Journal of Experimental Education, 47* (Spring): 259–262.

Brown, Roger. 1973. *A first language/The early stages*. Cambridge, Massachusetts: Harvard University Press.

Bruckerhoff, Charles. 1977. What do students say about reading instruction? *The Clearing House, 51* (November): 104–107.

Bullen, Gertrude F. 1970. *A study in motivating children to read*. ERIC Document ED 040 018.

Burmeister, Lou. 1968. Usefulness of phonic generalizations. *The Reading Teacher, 21* (January): 349–356.

Canney, George. 1979. Organizing and applying test results. In *Reading tests and teachers: A practical guide*, ed. Robert Schreiner, pp. 53–71. Newark, Delaware: International Reading Association.

Carney, John. 1979. What research says about reading for the mentally retarded child. Paper presented at the April 1979 convention of the International Reading Association, Atlanta, Georgia.

Catterson, Jane. 1979. Comprehension: The argument for a discourse analysis model. In *Reading comprehension at four linguistic levels*, ed. Clifford Pennock, pp. 2–7. Newark, Delaware: International Reading Association.

Cazden, Courtney B. 1983. Adult assistance to language development: Scaffolds, models, and direct instruction. In *Developing literacy: Young children's use of language*, eds. Robert P. Parker and Frances A. Davis, pp. 3–18. Newark, Delaware: International Reading Association.

Ceprano, Maria A. 1981. A review of selected research on methods of teaching sight words. *The Reading Teacher, 35* (December): 314–322.

Chall, Jeanne S. 1978. A decade of research on reading and learning disabilities. In *What research has to say about reading instruction*, ed. S. Jay Samuels, pp. 31–42. Newark, Delaware: International Reading Association.

Cheyney, Arnold B. 1976. *Teaching children of different cultures in the classroom: A language approach*, 2nd ed. Newark, Delaware: International Reading Association.

Cheyney, Arnold B. 1984. *Teaching reading skills through the newspaper*, 2nd ed. Newark, Delaware: International Reading Association.

Chompsky, Carol. 1976. After decoding: What? *Language Arts, 53* (March): 288–296, 314.

Clark, Charles H. 1982. Assessing free recall. *The Reading Teacher, 35* (January): 434–439.

Clay, Marie M. 1979. *The early detection of reading difficulties: A diagnostic survey with recovery procedures*. New Zealand: Heinemann Educational Books.

Cleland, Craig J. 1980. Piagetian implications for reading models. *Reading World, 20* (October): 10–15.

Cleland, Craig J. 1981. Learning to read: Piagetian perspectives for instruction. *Reading World, 20* (March): 223–224.

Cohen, Elizabeth G., Intili, Jo-Ann K., and Robbins, Susan Hurevitz. 1978. Teachers and reading specialists: Cooperation or isolation? *The Reading Teacher, 32* (December): 281–287.

Cohn, Marvin, and D'Alessandro, Cynthia. 1978. When is a decoding error not a decoding error? *The Reading Teacher, 32* (December): 341–344.

Combs, Arthur, Avila, Donald L., and Purkey, William W. 1971. *Helping relationships: Basic concepts for the helping professions*. Boston: Allyn & Bacon.

Comer, James. 1980. *School power*. New York: Macmillan, The Free Press.

Cooper, J. David 1986. *Improving reading comprehension*. Boston: Houghton Mifflin Company.

Cooper, J. David, and Worden, Thomas W. 1983. *The classroom reading program in the elementary school*. New York: Macmillan.

Cooper, J. Lewis. 1952. The effect of adjustment of basal reading materials on reading achievement Unpublished doctoral dissertation, Boston University.

Copple, Carol E., and Suci, George J. 1974. The comparative ease of processing standard English and Black nonstandard English by lower-class Black children. *Child Development*, *45* (December): 1048–1053.

Coulter, Myron L. 1972. Reading in mathematics: Classroom implications. In *Reading in the content areas*, ed. James L. Laffey, pp. 94–126. Newark, Delaware: International Reading Association.

Crowell, Doris C., and Hu-Pei Au, Kathryn. 1981. A scale of questions to guide comprehension instruction. *The Reading Teacher*, *34* (January): 389–393.

Crowl, Thomas K., and MacGinitie, Walter H. 1974. The influence of students' speech characteristics on teachers' evaluations of oral answers. *Journal of Educational Psychology*, *66* (June): 304–308.

Cunningham, Patricia M. 1976–1977. Teachers' correction responses to Black dialect miscues which are non-meaning-changing. *Reading Research Quarterly*, *12* (Number 4): 637–653.

Cunningham, Patricia M. 1980. Applying a compare/contrast process to identifying polysyllabic words. *Journal of Reading Behavior*, *12* (Fall): 213–223.

Cunningham, Patricia M. 1981. Finding "just the right book." *The Reading Teacher*, *34* (March): 720–722.

Cunningham, Patricia M. 1983. Beginning reading without readiness: Structured language experience. In *Reading horizons: Selected readings*, ed. Ken Vander-Meulen, pp. 61–66. Kalamazoo, Michigan: Western Michigan University.

Dahl, Patricia R., and Samuels, S. Jay. 1977. Teaching children to read using hypothesis/test strategies. *The Reading Teacher*, *30* (March): 603–606.

Dale, Edgar, and Chall, Jeanne S. 1948. A formula for predicting readability. *Educational Research Bulletin*, *27* (February): 37–54.

D'Angelo, Karen, and Mahlios, Marc. 1983. Insertion and omission miscues of good and poor readers. *The Reading Teacher*, *36* (April): 778–782.

Dave, R. H. 1963. The identification and measurement of environmental process variables that are related to educational achievement. Doctoral disssertation, University of Chicago.

Davis, Frederick B. 1968. Research in comprehension in reading. *Reading Research Quarterly*, *3* (Summer): 449–545.

Davis, Patsy McLain. 1978. An evaluation of journal-published research on attitudes in reading, 1900–1977. Unpublished doctoral dissertation, University of Tennessee, Knoxville.

Dearborne, Walter F. 1939. The nature and causation of disabilities in reading. In *Recent trends in reading*, Supplementary Educational Monographs No. 49. Chicago: University of Chicago Press.

De Cecco, John, and Crawford, William. 1974. *The psychology of learning and instruction*, 2nd ed. Englewood Cliffs, New Jersey: Prentice-Hall.

Dechant, Emerald V., and Smith, Henry P. 1977. *Psychology in teaching reading*, 2nd ed. Englewood Cliffs, New Jersey: Prentice-Hall.

Delacato, Carol H. 1966. *Neurological organization and reading*. Springfield, Illinois: Charles E. Thomas.

Denby, Catherine. 1979. "Vision" problems and reading disability: A dilemma for the reading specialist. *The Reading Teacher*, *32* (April): 787–795.

DeStefano, Joanna S. 1978. *Language, the learner, & the school*. New York: John Wiley and Sons.

DeStefano, Joanna S. 1980. Research update: Enhancing children's growing ability to communicate. *Language Arts*, *57* (October): 807–813.

Doehring, D. G., Hosko, I. M., and Bryans, B. N. 1979. Statistical classifications of children with reading problems. *Journal of Clinical Neuropsychology*, *1*: 5–16.

Downing, John, and Leong, Che Kan. 1982. *Psychology of reading*. New York: Macmillan.

Downing, John, and Thackray, Derek V. 1975. *Reading readiness*. London: Hodder and Stoughton.

Downing, John, and Thomson, Doug. 1977. Sex role stereotypes in learning to read. *Research in the Teaching of English*, *11* (Fall): 149–155.

Dreher, Mariam Jean, and Singer, Harry. 1985. Parents' attitudes toward reports of standardized reading test results. *The Reading Teacher*, *38* (March): 624–632.

DuBois, Diane, and Stice, Carole. 1981. Comprehension instruction: Let's recall it for repair. *Reading World*, *20* (March): 173–184.

Dudley-Marling, Curtis C. 1985. Microcomputers, reading, and writing: Alternatives to drill and practice. *The Reading Teacher*, *38* (January): 388–391.

Duffy, F. H., Burchfiel, J. L., and Lombroso, C. T.

1971. Brain electrical activity mapping (BEAM). *Annals of Neurology*, 7 (May): 421–428.

Dunkeld, Cohn G. M. 1970. The validity of the informal reading inventory for the designation of instructional levels: A study of the relationships between children's gains in reading achievement and the difficulty of instructional materials. Unpublished doctoral dissertation, University of Illinois at Urbana-Champaign.

Dunn, Lloyd M., and Dunn, Leota M. 1981. *Manual, forms L and M: Peabody Picture Vocabulary Test—revised*. Circle Plains, Minnesota: American Guidance Service.

Durkin, Delores, 1978–1979. What classroom observations reveal about reading comprehension instruction. *Reading Research Quarterly*, *14*: 481–533.

Durkin, Delores. 1981. Reading comprehension instruction in five basal reading series. *Reading Research Quarterly*, *16*: 515–544.

Durost, Walter N. 1961. How to tell parents about standardized test results. *Test Service Notebook*, No. 26. New York: Harcourt, Brace, & World.

Earle, Richard A. 1976. *Teaching reading and mathematics*. Newark, Delaware: International Reading Association.

Early, Margaret, and Sawyer, Diane J. 1984. *Reading to learn in grades 5 to 12*. San Diego: Harcourt Brace Jovanovich.

Ehri, Linnea C. 1978. Beginning from a psycholinguistic perspective: Amalgamation of word identities. In *The recognition of words*, eds. Linnea C. Ehri, Roderick W. Barron, and Jeffrey M. Feldman, pp. 1–33. Newark, Delaware: International Reading Association.

Ehri, Linnea C., and Wilce, Lee S. 1980. Do beginners learn to read function words better in sentences or lists? *Reading Research Quarterly*, *15*: 451–476.

Ehrlich, Myrna et al. 1984–85. CRA survey of comprehension testing in clinics. *Journal of Clinical Reading*, *1* (Number 3): 14–21.

Ekwall, Eldon E., and Shanker, James L. 1983. *Diagnosis and remediation of the disabled reader*, 2nd ed. Boston: Allyn & Bacon.

Ellis, DiAnn Waskul, and Preston, Fannie Wiley. 1984. Enhancing beginning reading using wordless picture books in a cross-age tutoring program. *The Reading Teacher*, *37* (April): 692–698.

Emans, Robert, and Fisher, Gladys Mary. 1967. Teaching the use of context clues. *Elementary English*, *44* (March): 243–246.

Entwistle, Doris R. 1977. A sociologist looks at reading. In *Reading problems: A multidisciplinary perspective*, eds. Wayne Otto, Charles W. Peters, and Nathanial Peters, Chapter 4. Reading, Massachusetts: Addison-Wesley.

Epstein, Ira. 1980. *Measuring attitudes toward reading*. ERIC/TM Report 73, Princeton, New Jersey: ERIC Clearinghouse on Tests, Measurements, and Evaluation, Educational Testing Service.

Estes, Thomas H. 1971. A scale to measure attitudes toward reading. *Journal of Reading*, *15* (November): 135–138.

Estes, Thomas H., and Johnstone, Julie P. 1979. Twelve easy ways to make readers hate reading (and one difficult way to make them love it.) In *Motivating children and young adults to read*, eds. Jane L. Thomas and Ruth M. Loring, pp. 5–13. Phoenix, Arizona: Oryx Press.

Estes, Thomas H., and Vaughn, Joseph L., Jr. 1973. Reading interests and comprehension: Implications. *The Reading Teacher*, *27* (November): 149–153.

Estes, Thomas H., and Vaughn L., Jr. 1978. *Reading and learning in the content classroom*. Boston: Allyn & Bacon.

Estes, William H. 1970. *Learning theory and mental development*. New York: Academic Press.

Farr, Roger. 1969. *Reading: What can be measured*. Newark, Delaware: International Reading Association.

Farr, Roger, and Carey, Robert F. 1986. *Reading: What can be measured*, 2nd ed. Newark, Delaware: International Reading Association.

Fernald, Grace. 1936. *On certain language disabilities: Their nature and treatment*. Baltimore, Maryland: Williams and Wilkins.

Fernald, Grace M. 1943. *Remedial techniques in basic school subjects*. New York: McGraw-Hill.

Fernald, Grace M., and Keller, Helen B. 1921. The effect of kinesthetic factors in the development of word recognition. *Journal of Educational Research*, *4* (December): 355–377.

Fischer, Karen M. 1980. Metalinguistic skills and the competence-performance distinction. In *Language awareness and reading*, eds. Lynn H. Waterhouse, Karen M. Fischer, and Ellen Bouchard Ryan, pp. 23–37. Newark, Delaware: International Reading Association.

Fishbein, Martin, and Ajzen, Icek. 1975. *Belief, attitude, intention, and behavior: An introduction to theory and research*. Reading, Massachusetts: Addison-Wesley.

Fitzgerald, Jill. 1983. Helping readers gain self-control over reading comprehension. *The Reading Teacher, 37* (December): 249–253.

Flesch, Rudolph F. 1948. A new readability yardstick. *Journal of Applied Psychology, 32* (June): 221–223.

Frenzel, Norman. 1978. Children need a multipronged attack in word recognition. *The Reading Teacher, 31* (March): 627–631.

Frostig, Marianne, and Horne, David. 1964. *The Frostig program for the development of visual perception: Teacher's guide*. Chicago: Follett Educational Corp.

Fry, Edward. 1977. Fry's readability graph: Clarifications, validity, and extension to level 17. *Journal of Reading, 21* (December): 242–252.

Fry, Edward. 1980. The new instant word list. *The Reading Teacher, 34* (December): 284–289.

Frymier, Jack R. 1968. Motivating students to learn. *NEA Journal, 57* (February): 37–39.

Furth, Hans G. 1970. *Piaget for teachers*. Englewood Cliffs, New Jersey: Prentice-Hall, Inc.

Gable, Sherry, and Santa, Carol. 1981. Gates-McKillop Reading Diagnostic Tests. In *Diagnostic and criterion-referenced reading tests: Review and evaluation*, ed. Leo M. Schell, pp. 37–43. Newark, Delaware: International Reading Association.

Gambrell, Linda B. 1985. Dialogue journals: Reading-writing interaction. *The Reading Teacher, 38* (February): 512–515.

Gamby, Gert. 1983. Talking books and taped books: Materials for instruction. *The Reading Teacher, 36* (January): 366–369.

Garman, Dorothy. 1981. Language development and first-grade reading achievement. *Reading World, 21* (October): 40–49.

Garrett, Henry, and Woodworth, R. S. 1966. *Statistics in psychology and education*. New York: David McKay.

Gates, Arthur I. 1937. The necessary mental age for beginning reading. *Elementary School Journal, 37* (March): 497–508.

Geneva Medico-Educational Service. 1968. Problems posed by dyslexia. *Journal of Learning Disabilities, 1* (March): 158–171.

Gibson, Eleanor J., and Levin, Harry. 1975. *The psychology of reading*. Cambridge, Massachusetts: MIT Press.

Gilliland, Hap. 1974. *A practical guide to remedial reading*. Columbus, Ohio: Charles E. Merrill.

Gillingham, Anna, and Stillman, Bessie. 1966. *Remedial training for children with specific disability in reading, spelling, and penmanship*, 7th ed.

Cambridge, Massachusetts: Educators Publishing Service.

Golinkoff, Roberta Michnick. 1975–1976. A comparison of reading comprehension processes in good and poor comprehenders. *Reading Research Quarterly, 11*: 523–659.

Gonzales, Phillip C. 1980. What's wrong with the basal reader approach to language development? *The Reading Teacher, 33* (March): 668–673.

Good, Thomas L., and Beckerman, Terrill M. 1978. Time on task: A naturalistic study in sixth grade classrooms. *Elementary School Journal, 78* (January): 192–201.

Goodman, Kenneth S. 1965. A linguistic study of cues and miscues in reading. *Elementary English, 42* (October): 639–643.

Goodman, Kenneth S. 1976. Behind the eye: What happens in reading. In *Theoretical models and process of reading*, 2nd ed., eds. Harry Singer and Robert Ruddell, pp. 470–496. Newark, Delaware: International Reading Association.

Goodman, Kenneth S., and Buck, Catherine. 1973. Dialect barriers to reading comprehension revisited. *The Reading Teacher, 27* (October): 6–12.

Goodman, Yetta M., and Burke, Carolyn L. 1972. *Reading miscue inventory manual procedure for diagnosis and evaluation*. New York: Macmillan.

Gove, Mary K. 1975. Using the cloze procedure in first grade classrooms. *The Reading Teacher, 29* (October): 36–38.

Graham, Kenneth G., and Robinson, H. Alan. 1984. *Study skills handbook: A guide for all teachers*. Newark, Delaware: International Reading Association.

Graves, Michael, and Hammond, Heidi K. 1980. A validated procedure for teaching prefixes and its effect on students' ability to assign meaning to novel words. In *Perspective and reading research and instruction, 29th yearbook of the National Reading Conference*, eds. Michael L. Kamil and Alden J. Moe, pp. 184–188. Washington, D.C.: National Reading Conference.

Greaney, Vincent. 1986. Parental influences on reading. *The Reading Teacher, 39* (April): 813–817.

Greenewald, M. Jane, and Pederson, Carolyn. 1983. Effects of sentence organization instruction on the reading comprehension of poor readers. In *Searches for meaning in reading/language processing and instruction*, eds. Jerome A. Niles and Larry A. Harris, pp. 101–103. Rochester, New York: National Reading Conference.

Greenlaw, M. Jean. 1983. Reading interest research and children's choices. In *Children's choice:*

Teaching with books children like, eds. Nancy Roser and Margaret Frith, pp. 90–92. Newark, Delaware: International Reading Association.

Groff, Patrick. 1979. A critique of teaching reading as a whole-task venture. *The Reading Teacher, 32* (March): 647–652.

Groff, Patrick. 1981. Teaching reading by syllables. *The Reading Teacher, 34* (March): 659–664.

Gronlund, N. E. 1976. *Measurement and evaluation in teaching*, 3rd ed. New York: Macmillan.

Gross, Alice Dzen. 1978. The relationship between sex differences and reading ability in an Israeli kibbutz system. In *Cross-cultural perspectives on reading and reading research*, ed. Dina Feitelson, pp. 72–87. Newark, Delaware: International Reading Association.

Grossman, H.J. 1983. *Classification in mental retardation*, 1983 revision. Washington, D.C.: American Association of Mental Deficiency.

Gunning, Robert. 1968. *The technique of clear writing*. Revised edition. New York: McGraw-Hill.

Guszak, Frank J. 1978. *Diagnostic reading instruction in the elementary school*, 2nd ed. New York: Harper and Row.

Guthrie, John T. 1977. Research views: Story comprehension. *The Reading Teacher, 30* (February): 574–577.

Guthrie, John T. 1982. Metacognition: Up from flexibility. *The Reading Teacher, 35* (January): 510–512.

Guthrie, John T., Seifert, Mary, Burnham, Nancy A., and Caplan, Ronald I. 1974. The maze technique to assess, monitor reading comprehension. *The Reading Teacher, 28* (November): 161–168.

Guthrie, John T., Seifert, Mary, and Kline, Lloyd W. 1978. Clues from research on programs for poor readers. In *What research has to say about reading instruction*, ed. S. Jay Samuels, pp. 1–12. Newark, Delaware: International Reading Association.

Haggard, Martha Rapp, and Smith, Nancy. 1981. Woodcock Reading Mastery Tests. In *Diagnostic and criterion-referenced reading tests: Review and evaluation*, ed. Leo M. Schell, pp. 57–63. Newark, Delaware: International Reading Association.

Hall, MaryAnne. 1981. *Teaching reading as a language experience*, 3rd ed. Columbus, Ohio: Charles E. Merrill.

Hamachek, Don. E. 1975. *Behavior dynamics in teaching, learning, and growth*. Boston: Allyn and Bacon.

Hammill, D., Leigh, J., McNutt, G., and Larsen, S. 1981. A new definition of learning disabilities. *Learning Disabilities Quarterly, 4* (Number 4): 336–342.

Hansen, Jane, and Hubbard, Ruth. 1984. Poor readers can draw inferences. *The Reading Teacher, 37* (March): 586–589.

Hansen, Karen, and Peterson, Joe. 1981. Peabody Individual Achievement Test. In *Diagnostic and criterion-referenced reading tests: Review and evaluation*, ed. Leo M. Schell, pp. 49–52. Newark, Delaware: International Reading Association.

Hargis, Charles H. 1972. A comparison of retarded and non-retarded children on the ability to use context in reading. *American Journal of Mental Deficiency, 76* (May): 726–728.

Hargis, Charles H., and Gickling, Edward E. 1978. The function of imagery in word recognition development. *The Reading Teacher, 31* (May): 870–874.

Haring, N., and Bateman, B. 1977. *Teaching the learning disabled child*. Englewood Cliffs, New Jersey: Prentice-Hall.

Harris, Albert J. 1963. Intellectual and perceptual development. In *Readings on reading instruction*, ed. Albert J. Harris, pp. 47–52. New York: David McKay.

Harris, Albert J. 1979. The effective teacher of reading, revisited. *The Reading Teacher, 33* (November): 135–140.

Harris, Albert J., and Sipay, Edward R. 1985. *How to increase reading ability*, 8th ed. New York: Longman.

Harris, Larry A., and Smith, Carl B. 1980. Reading instruction: Diagnostic teaching in the classroom, pp. 314–317. New York: Holt, Rinehart and Winston.

Harris, Theodore L., and Hodges, Richard E. 1981. *A dictionary of reading and related terms*. Newark, Delaware: International Reading Association.

Harth, Robert. 1982. The Feuerstein perspective on the modification of cognitive performance. *Focus on Exceptional Children, 15* (November): 3–12.

Heathington, Betty S. 1975. The development of scales to measure attitudes toward reading. Unpublished doctoral dissertation, The University of Tennessee.

Heathington, Betty S. 1979. What to do about reading motivation in the middle school. *Journal of Reading, 22* (May): 709–713.

Heathington, Betty S. 1981. Reading interests of students in middle grades. *The Educational Catalyst, 11* (Fall): 37–39.

Heathington, Betty S., and Alexander, J. Estill.

1978. A child-based observation checklist to assess attitudes toward reading. *The Reading Teacher, 31* (April): 769–771.

Heathington, Betty S., and Alexander, J. Estill. 1984. Do classroom teachers emphasize attitudes toward reading? *The Reading Teacher, 37* (February): 484–488.

Heathington, Betty S., and Gambrell, Linda B. 1980. *Helping hands.* Knoxville, Tennessee: Applied Research Associates, Inc.

Hebb, D.O. 1955. Drives and C.N.S. (conceptual nervous system). *Psychological Review, 62* (July): 243–254.

Heckelman, R.G. 1966. Using the neurological impress method remedial reading technique. *Academic Therapy Quarterly, 1* (Summer): 235–239, 250.

Heilman, Arthur W. 1972. *Principle and practices of teaching reading,* 3rd ed. Columbus, Ohio: Charles E. Merrill.

Heimlich, Joan E., and Pittelman, Susan D. 1986. *Semantic mapping: Classroom applications.* Newark, Delaware: International Reading Association.

Helgren-Lempesis, Valerie A., and Mangrum II, Charles T. 1986. An analysis of alternate-form reliability of three commercially prepared informal reading inventories. *Reading Research Quarterly, 21* (Spring): 209–215.

Hiebert, Elfrieda H. 1980. The relationship of logical reasoning ability, oral language comprehension, and home experiences to preschool children's print awareness. *Journal of Reading Behavior, 12* (Winter): 313–324.

Hittleman, Daniel R. 1978. *Developmental reading: A psycholinguistic perspective.* Chicago: Rand McNally.

Hoffman, James V., and Rutherford, William L. 1984. Effective reading programs: A critical review of outlier studies. *Reading Research Quarterly, 20* (Fall): 79–92.

Hoffman, Stevie, and Fillmer, H. Thompson. 1979. Thought, language and reading readiness. *The Reading Teacher, 33* (December): 290–294.

Hollingsworth, Paul M. 1978. An experimental approach to the impress method of teaching reading. *The Reading Teacher, 31* (March): 624–626.

Hosslini, Jinoas, and Ferrell, William R. 1982. Measuring metacognition in reading by detectability of cloze accuracy. *Journal of Reading Behavior, 14* (Summer): 263–274.

Huck, Charlotte S. 1973. Strategies for improving interest and appreciation in literature. In *Elementary school language arts,* eds. Paul C. Burns and Leo M. Schell, pp. 203–210. Chicago: Rand McNally.

Huey, Edmund Burke. 1908. *The psychology and pedagogy of reading.* New York: Macmillan.

Huff, Phyllis. 1983. Language experience approach. In *Teaching reading,* 2nd ed., ed. J. Estill Alexander, pp. 303–323. Boston: Little, Brown.

Humphrey, Jack W. 1971. Remedial programs: Can they be justified? *Journal of Reading, 15* (October): 50–53.

Huus, Helen. 1972. Critical aspects of comprehension. In *Readings for diagnostic and remedial reading,* eds. Robert M. Wilson and James Geyer, pp. 223–231. Columbus, Ohio: Charles E. Merrill.

Ives, Josephine P., Bursuk, Lauren Z., and Ives, Sumner A. 1979. *Word identification techniques,* pp. 110–115. Chicago: Rand McNally.

Jacobs, H. Donald, and Searfoss, Lyndon W. 1977. *Diagnostic reading inventory.* Dubuque, Iowa: Kendall/Hunt.

Jerrolds, Bob W., Callaway, Bryon, and Gwaltney, Wayne. 1971. A comprehensive study of three tests of intellectual potential, three tests of reading achievement, and the discrepancy scores between potential and achievement. *Journal of Educational Research, 68* (December): 168–172.

Jobe, Fred W. 1976. *Screening vision in schools.* Newark, Delaware: International Reading Association.

Johns, Jerry L. 1975. Dolch list of common nouns— a comparison. *The Reading Teacher, 28* (March): 538–540.

Johns, Jerry L. 1983. Sight vocabulary in beginning reading. In *Reading horizons: Selected readings,* 2nd ed., ed. Ken VanderMeulen, pp. 81–88. Kalamazoo, Michigan: Western Michigan University.

Johnson, Barbara, and Lehnert, Linda. 1983. Learning phonics naturally: A model for instruction. In *Reading horizons: Selected readings,* 2nd ed., ed. Ken VanderMeulen, pp. 285–293. Kalamazoo, Michigan: Western Michigan University.

Johnson, Dale D. 1976. Cross-cultural perspectives on sex differences in reading. *The Reading Teacher, 29* (May) 747–752.

Johnson, Dale D., Pittelman, Susan D., and Heimlich, Joan E. 1986. Semantic mapping. *The Reading Teacher, 39* (April): 778–783.

Johnson, Marjorie S. 1966. Basic considerations in corrective instruction. In *Corrective reading in the classroom: Perspectives in reading, No. 7,* eds.

Marjorie S. Johnson and Roy A. Kress, pp. 64–68. Newark: Delaware: International Reading Association.

Johnson, Marjorie Seddon, and Kress, Roy A. 1965. *Informal reading inventories*. Newark, Delaware: International Reading Association.

Johnston, Peter H. 1983. *Reading comprehension assessment: a cognitive basis*. Newark, Delaware: International Reading Association.

Jones, Margaret B., and Pikulski, Edna C. 1974. Cloze for the classroom. *Journal of Reading, 17* (March): 432–438.

Jongsma, Kathleen S., and Jongsma, Eugene A. 1981. Test review: Commercial informal reading inventories. *The Reading Teacher, 34* (March): 697–705.

Kachuck, Beatrice. 1978. Black English and reading: Research issues. *Education and Urban Society, 10* (May): 385–399.

Kaluger, George, and Kolson, Clifford J. 1978. *Reading and learning disabilities*. 2nd ed. Columbus, Ohio: Charles E. Merrill.

Kaplan, Elaine M., and Tuchman, Anita. 1980. Vocabulary strategies belong in the hands of learners. *Journal of Reading, 24* (October): 32–34.

Karlin, Robert. 1973. Evaluation for diagnostic teaching. In *Assessment problems in reading*, ed. Walter H. MacGinitie, pp. 8–13. Newark, Delaware: International Reading Association.

Karlsen, Bjorn. 1980. Assessment and diagnosis of reading abilities. In *Teaching reading: Foundations and strategies*, eds. Pose Lamb and Richard Arnold, pp. 133–169. Belmont, California: Wadsworth.

Kaufman, Alan S. 1979. *The WISC-R and learning disabilities assessment: State of the art*. New York: John Wiley & Sons.

Kavale, Kenneth. 1979. Selecting and evaluating reading tests. In *Reading tests and teachers: A practical guide*, ed. Robert Schreiner, pp. 9–34. Newark, Delaware: International Reading Association.

Kavale, Kenneth. 1982. Meta-analysis of the relationship between visual perceptual skills and reading achievement. *Journal of Learning Disabilities, 15* (January): 42–51.

Kender, Joseph P., and Rubenstein, Herbert. 1977. Recall versus reinspection in IRI comprehension tests. *The Reading Teacher, 30* (April): 776–779.

Kennedy, Eddie C. 1977. *Classroom approaches to remedial reading*, 2nd ed. Itasca, Illinois: F. E. Peacock.

Keogh, Barbara K., and Margolis, Judith. 1976.

Learning to labor and to wait: Attentional problems of children with learning disorders. *Journal of Learning Disabilities, 9* (May): 276–286.

Kephart, Newell C. 1971. *The slow learner in the classroom*, 2nd ed. Columbus, Ohio: Charles E. Merrill.

Kiefer, Barbara Z., and DeStefano, Joanna S. 1985. Cultures together in the classroom: "What you sayin?" In *Observing the language learner*, eds. Angela Jagger and M. Trika Smith-Burke, pp. 159–172. Newark, Delaware: International Reading Association.

King, Glynn Travis, and Henk, William A. 1985. Renorming the SIT: Implications for teachers of reading. *Reading World, 24* (March): 28–33.

Kirk, Samuel A., Kliebhan, Sister Joanne Marie, and Lerner, Janet W. 1978. *Teaching reading to slow and disabled learners*. Boston: Houghton Mifflin.

Kirkland, Eleanor R. 1978. A Piagetian interpretation of beginning reading instruction. *The Reading Teacher, 31* (February): 497–503.

Kirsch, Irwin, and Guthrie, John T. 1977–1978. The concept and measurement of functional literacy. *Reading Research Quarterly, 13* (Number 4): 485–507.

Klare, George R. 1974–1975. Assessing readability. *Reading Research Quarterly, 1, 10*: 62–103.

Klein, Roslyn S., Altman, Steven D., Dreizen, Kathryn, Friedman, Robert, and Powers, Lois. 1981. Restructuring dysfunctional attitudes toward children's learning and behavior in school: Family-oriented psychoeducational therapy. *Journal of Learning Disabilities, 14* (January): 15–19.

Koenke, Karl. 1981. The careful use of comic books (ERIC/RCS). *The Reading Teacher, 34* (February): 592–595.

Kolczynski, Richard. 1973. Boys' right to read: Sex factors in learning to read. In *Literacy for diverse learners*, ed. Jerry L. Johns, pp. 39–45. Newark, Delaware: International Reading Association.

Kolker, Brenda, and Terwilliger, Paul N. 1981. Sight vocabulary learning of first and second graders. *Reading World, 20* (May): 251–258.

Krieger, Veronica K. 1981. Differences in poor readers' abilities to identify high-frequency words in isolation and context. *Reading World, 20* (May): 263–272.

Kurtz, John J., and Swenson, Esther J. 1951. Factors related to overachievement and underachievement in school. *School Review, 59* (November): 472–480.

LaBerge, David, and Samuels, S. Jay. 1985. Toward a theory of automatic processing in reading. In *Theoretical models and processes of reading*, 3rd ed., eds. Harry Singer and Robert B. Ruddell, pp. 689–718. Newark, Delaware: International Reading Association.

Labov, Walter. 1970. Language characteristics: Blacks. In *Reading for the disadvantaged: Problems of linguistically different learners*, ed. Thomas Horn, pp. 139–157. New York: Harcourt, Brace & World.

Ladd, Eleanor. 1961. A comparison of two types of training with reference to developing skill in diagnostic oral reading testing. Unpublished doctoral dissertation, Florida State University.

Lapp, Diane, and Flood, James. 1984. Promoting reading comprehension: Instruction which ensures continuous reader growth. In *Promoting reading comprehension*, ed. James Flood, pp. 273–288. Newark, Delaware: International Reading Association.

LaPray, Margaret, and Ross, Ramon. 1969. The graded word list: Quick gauge of reading ability. *Journal of Reading, 12* (January): 305–307.

Lavine, Stephen B., and Putnam, Lillian R. 1976. Predicting expected achievement in a remedial reading program. *Reading World, 15* (March): 176–182.

Layton, James R. 1979. *The psychology of learning to read*. New York: Academic Press.

Lee, Doris M., and Allen, Roach Van. 1963. *Learning to read through experience*, 2nd ed. New York: Appleton-Century-Crofts.

Lees, Fred. 1976. Mathematics and reading. *Journal of Reading, 19* (May): 621–626.

Lehman, Elyse Brauch. 1972. Selection strategies in children's attention to task-relevant information. *Child Development, 43*, part 1 (Number 1-2): 197–209.

Lehr, Fran. 1982. Cultural influences and sex differences in reading. *The Reading Teacher, 35* (March): 744–746.

Lepper, Mark R., Greene, David, and Nisbett, Richard E. 1973. Undermining children's intrinsic interest with extrinsic reward: A test of the "overjustification" hypothesis. *Journal of Personality and Social Psychology, 28* (October): 129–137.

Lerner, Janet W. 1985. *Learning disabilities: Theories, diagnosis, and teaching strategies*, 4th ed. Boston: Houghton Mifflin.

Leu, Donald J., Jr. 1982. Oral reader error analysis: A critical review of research and application. *Reading Research Quarterly, 17* (Number 3): 420–437.

Lewis, Ramon, and Teale, William H. 1980. Another look at secondary school students' attitudes toward reading. *Journal of Reading Behavior, 12* (Fall): 187–201.

Lipa, Sally. 1985. Test review: Diagnostic reading scales. *The Reading Teacher, 38* (March): 664–667.

Loban, Walter. 1976. *Language development: Kindergarten through grade twelve*. Urbana, Illinois: National Council of Teachers of English.

Lopardo, Genevieve S. 1975. LEA-cloze reading material for the disabled reader. *The Reading Teacher, 29* (October): 42–44.

Lucas, Marilyn S., and Singer, Harry. 1975. Dialect in relation to oral reading achievement: Recoding, encoding, or merely a code. *Journal of Reading Behavior, 7* (Summer): 137–148.

Lyle, J. G. 1970. Certain antenatal, perinatal and developmental variables and reading retardation in middle-class boys. *Child Development, 41* (June): 481–491.

MacGinitie, Walter H. 1967. Auditory perception in reading. *Education, 87* (May): 532–538.

Maehr, Martin L. 1969. Self-concept, challenge, and achievement. *Lutheran Education, 105* (October): 50–57.

Mangieri, John N., and Ingram, Richard. 1982. Visual screening: Present policies and procedures. *Reading World, 22* (October): 34–38.

Mangrum Charles T., II, and Forgan, Harry W. 1979. *Developing competencies in teaching reading*. Columbus, Ohio: Charles E. Merrill.

Manning, Gary, Manning, Maryann, and Wolfson, Bernice J. 1982. A study of the reading interests of fourth-grade students. Paper presented at the eleventh annual meeting of the Mid-South Educational Research Association, New Orleans, Louisiana.

Marshall, Nancy. 1984. Discourse analysis as a guide for informal assessment of comprehension. In *Promoting reading comprehension*, ed. James Flood, pp. 79–96. Newark, Delaware: International Reading Association.

Martin Luther King Junior Elementary School Children, et al. v. *Ann Arbor School District Board.* 1979. Civil Action No. 7-71861. Civil Action District Court, Eastern District of Michigan, Southern Division.

Mason, George E. 1980. High interest-low vocabulary books: Their past and future. *Educational Technology, 20* (October): 18–22.

Mason, George E. 1981. High interest-low vocabulary books: Their past and future. *Journal of Reading, 24* (April): 603–607.

Mason, George E., and Blanchard, Jay S. 1979. *Computer applications in reading*. Newark, Delaware: International Reading Association.

Masztal, Nancy B., and Smith, Lawrence L. 1984. Do teachers really administer IRIs? *Reading World, 24* (October): 80–83.

Mathewson, Grover C. 1976. The function of attitude in the reading process. In *Theoretical models and processes of reading*, 2nd ed., eds. Harry Singer and Robert Ruddell, pp. 655–676. Newark, Delaware: International Reading Association.

Mathewson, Grover C. 1985. Toward a comprehensive model of affect in the reading process. In *Theoretical models and processes of reading*, 3rd ed., eds. Harry Singer and Robert B. Ruddell, pp. 655–676. Newark, Delaware: International Reading Association.

McAndrew, Donald A. 1983. Underlining and note-taking: Some suggestions from research. *Journal of Reading, 27* (November): 103–108.

McCabe, Don. 1978. 220 sight words are too many for students with memories like mine. *The Reading Teacher, 31* (April): 791–793.

McCool, Mary. 1979. From the field: The ten commandments (or how to get students to hate reading). *Momentum, 10:* 11.

McDermott, R. P. 1985. Achieving school failure: An anthropological approach to illiteracy and social stratification. In *Theoretical models and processes of reading*, 3rd ed., eds. Harry Singer and Robert B. Ruddell, pp. 558–594. Newark, Delaware: International Reading Association.

McDonald, Kay A. 1980. Enhancing a child's positive self-concept. In *The self-concept of the young child*, ed. Thomas Daniels Yawkey, pp. 51–62. Provo, Utah: Brigham Young University Press.

McGee, Lea M., and Charlesworth, Rosalind. 1984. Books with movables: More than just novelties. *The Reading Teacher, 37* (May): 853–859.

McKenna, Michael. 1976. Synonymic versus verbatim scoring of the cloze procedure. *Journal of Reading, 20* (November): 141–143.

McLaughlin, G. Harry. 1969. Smog grading—a new readability formula. *Journal of Reading, 12* (May): 639–646.

McNeil, John D. 1984. *Reading comprehension: New directions for classroom practice*. Glenview, Illinois: Scott, Foresman.

McNinch, George H. 1981. A method for teaching sight words to disabled readers. *The Reading Teacher, 35* (December): 269–272.

Medley, Donald M. 1977. *Teacher competence and teacher effectiveness: A review of process-product research*. Washington, D.C.: American Association of Colleges for Teacher Education (ED 143 629).

Meisel, Stephen, and Glass, Gerald G. 1970. Volun-

tary reading interests and the interest content of basal readers. *The Reading Teacher, 23* (April): 655–659.

Miccinati, Jeanette. 1979. The Fernald technique: Modifications increase the probability of success. *Journal of Learning Disabilities, 12* (March): 139–142.

Moldofsky, Penny Baum. 1983. Teaching students to determine the central story problem: A practical application of schema theory. *The Reading Teacher, 36* (April): 740–745.

Moore, David W., and Readence, John E. 1983. Approaches to content area reading instruction. *Journal of Reading, 26* (February): 397–402.

Moore, David W., Readence, John E., and Rickelman, Robert J. 1982. *Prereading activities for content area reading and learning*. Newark, Delaware: International Reading Association.

Moore, Michael J., Kagan, Jerome, Sahl, Michelle, and Grant, Susan. 1982. Cognitive profiles in reading disability. *Genetic Psychology Monographs, 105* (February): 41–93.

Morine-Dershimer, Greta. 1982. Pupil perceptions of teacher praise. *The Elementary School Journal, 82* (May): 421–434.

Morris, Darrell, and Henderson, Edmund H. 1981. Assessing the beginning reader's concept of word. *Reading World, 20* (May): 279–285.

Morrison, Beverly S. 1979. One route to improved reading comprehension: A look at word meaning skills. In *Reading comprehension at four linguistic levels*, ed. Clifford Pennock, pp. 34–43. Newark, Delaware: International Reading Association.

Mosenthal, Peter, and Jackson, Shirley. 1981. Diagnostic Reading Scales. In *Diagnostic and criterion-referenced reading tests: Review and evaluation*, ed. Leo M. Schell, pp. 23–29. Newark, Delaware: International Reading Association.

Murray, Frank B. 1978. Implications of Piaget's theory for reading instruction. In *What research has to say about reading instruction*, ed. Jay Samuels, pp. 98–108. Newark, Delaware: International Reading Association.

Naiden, Norma. 1976. Ratio of boys to girls among disabled readers. *The Reading Teacher, 29* (February): 439–442.

Neilsen, Allan, and Braun, Carl. 1980. Informal assessment of comprehension: Guidelines for classroom and clinic. In *Disabled readers: Insight, assessment, instruction*, ed. Diane J. Sawyer, pp. 67–73. Newark, Delaware: International Reading Association.

Neisser, Ulric. 1976. *Cognition and reality: Princi-*

ples and implications of cognitive psychology. San Francisco: W. H. Freeman.

Neuman, Susan B. 1980. Why children read: A functional approach. *Journal of Reading Behavior*, 12 (Winter): 333–336.

Neuman, Susan B. 1981. Effect of teaching auditory perceptual skills on reading achievement in first grade. *The Reading Teacher*, 34 (January): 422–426.

Neville, Donald. 1961. A comparison of the WISC patterns of male retarded and nonretarded readers. *Journal of Educational Research*, 54 (January): 195–197.

Neville, Donald. 1965. The relationship between reading skills and intelligence test scores. *The Reading Teacher*, 18 (January): 257–262.

Newcomer, Phyllis L., and Hammill, Donald. 1975. ITPA and academic achievement: A survey. *The Reading Teacher*, 28 (May): 731–741.

Nichols, James N. 1983. Using prediction to increase content area interest and understanding. *Journal of Reading*, 27 (December): 225–228.

Nolan, James F. 1984. Reading in the content area of mathematics. In *Reading in the content areas: Research for teachers*, ed. Mary M. Dupuis, pp. 28–41. Newark, Delaware: International Reading Association.

Norton, Donna E. 1980. *The effective teaching of language arts*. Columbus, Ohio: Charles E. Merrill.

Norvell, George W. 1958. *What boys and girls like to read*. Morristown, New Jersey: Silver Burdett.

Nurss, Joanne R., Hough, Ruth A., and Goodson, Millie S. 1981. Prereading/language development in two day care centers. *Journal of Reading Behavior*, 13 (Spring): 23–31.

Nuttin, Joseph R. 1976. Motivation and reward in human learning: A cognitive approach. In *Handbook of learning and cognitive processes*, Vol. III, ed. W. K. Estes, pp. 247–281. New York: Erlbaum and Wiley.

Ofman, William, and Schaevitz, Morton. 1963. The kinesthetic method in remedial reading. *Journal of Experimental Education*, 31 (March): 319–320.

Oliver, Lin. 1977. The reading interests of children in the primary grades. *The Elementary School Journal*, 77 (May): 401–406.

Orton, June L. 1966. The Orton-Gillingham approach. In *The disabled reader*, ed. John Money, pp. 119–146. Baltimore: Johns Hopkins University Press.

Orton, Samuel T. 1937. *Reading, writing, and speech problems in children*. New York: W. W. Norton.

Otto, Wayne. 1973. Evaluating instruments for assessing needs and growth in reading. In *Assessment problems in reading*, ed. Walter H. MacGinitie, pp. 14–20. Newark, Delaware: International Reading Association.

Otto, Wayne, and Smith, Richard J. 1980. *Corrective and remedial teaching*, 3rd ed. Boston: Houghton Mifflin.

Past, Kay Cude, Past, Al, and Guzman, Shiela Bernal. 1980. A bilingual kindergarten immersed in print. *The Reading Teacher*, 33 (May): 907–913.

Patberg, Judythe, and Lang, Janell B. 1983. Teaching reading flexibility in the content areas. In *Reading horizons: Selected readings*, 2nd ed., ed. Ken VanderMeulen, pp. 245–253. Kalamazoo, Michigan: Western Michigan University.

Pauk, Walter. 1984. The new SQ4R. *Reading World*, 23 (March): 274–275.

Pearson, P. David. 1984. A context for instructional research in reading comprehension. In *Promoting reading comprehension*, ed. James Flood, pp. 1–15. Newark, Delaware: International Reading Association.

Pearson, P. David, and Johnson, Dale D. 1978. *Teaching reading comprehension*. New York: Holt, Rinehart and Winston.

Pelosi, Peter L. 1982. A method for classifying remedial reading techniques. *Reading World*, 22 (December): 119–128.

Pertz, Doris L., and Putnam, Lillian R. 1982. An examination of the relationship between nutrition and learning. *The Reading Teacher*, 35 (March): 702–706.

Pescosolido, John D. 1962. The identification and appraisal of certain major factors in the teaching of reading. Doctoral dissertation, University of Connecticut.

Peters, Michael. 1981. Dyslexia: Why and when the visual-acoustic-kinesthetic-tactile remedial approach might work. *Perceptual and Motor Skills*, 52 (April): 630.

Peterson, Joe, Greenlaw, M. Jean, and Tierney, Robert J. 1978. Assessing instructional placement with the IRI: The effectiveness of comprehension questions. *Journal of Educational Research*, 71 (May/June): 247–250.

Phillips, John L., Jr. 1969. *The origins of intellect: Piaget's theory*. San Francisco: W. H. Freeman.

Pickert, Sarah M., and Chase, Martha L. 1978. Story retelling: An informal technique for evaluating children's language. *The Reading Teacher*, 31 (February): 528–531.

Pikulski, John J., and Shanahan, Timothy. 1982. Informal reading inventories: A critical analysis. In *Approaches to the informal evaluation of read-*

ing, eds. John J. Pikulski and Timothy Shanahan, pp. 94–116. Newark, Delaware: International Reading Association.

Poostay, Edward J. 1984. Show me your underlines: A strategy to teach comprehension. *The Reading Teacher, 37* (May): 828–830.

Popham, W. J. 1978. *Criterion referenced measurement.* Englewood Cliffs, New Jersey: Prentice-Hall.

Powell, William R. 1970. Reappraising the criteria for interpreting informal inventories. In *Reading Diagnosis and Evaluation*, ed. Dorothy L. DeBoer, pp. 100–109. Newark, Delaware: International Reading Association.

Powell, William R. 1980. Measuring reading performance informally. *Journal of Children and Youth, 1* (Winter): 23–31.

Powell, William R., and Dunkeld, Colin G. 1971. Validity of IRI reading levels. *Elementary English, 48* (October): 637–642.

Pressley, Michael. 1977. Imagery and children's learning: Putting the picture in developmental perspective. *Review of Educational Research, 47* (Fall): 585–622.

Preston, Mary I. 1939. The reaction of parents to reading failure. *Child Development, 10* (September): 173–179.

Preston, Ralph C. 1962. Reading achievement of German and American children. *School and Society, 90* (October): 350–354.

Preston, Ralph C. 1964. Ability of students to identify correct responses before reading. *Journal of Educational Research, 58*: 181–183.

Pyrczak, Fred. 1979. Definition of measurement terms. In *Reading tests and teachers: A practical guide*, ed. Robert Schreiner, pp. 72–81. Newark, Delaware: International Reading Association.

Quandt, Ivan, and Selznick, Richard. 1984. *Self-concept and reading*, 2nd ed. Newark, Delaware: International Reading Association.

Radencich, Marguerite C. 1986. Test review: Gray Oral Reading Tests Revised, Formal Reading Inventory. *Journal of Reading, 30* (November): 136–139.

Ramsey, Wallace Z. 1962. An evaluation of three methods of teaching reading. In *Challenge and experiment in reading*, ed. J. Allen Figural, p. 153. Newark, Delaware: International Reading Association.

Ramsey, Wallace Z. 1967. The value and limitations of diagnostic reading tests for evaluation in the classroom. In *The evaluation of children's reading achievement*, ed. Thomas C. Barrett, pp. 65–77. Newark, Delaware: International Reading Association.

The reading report card. 1985. Princeton, New Jersey: Educational Test Service.

Reid, Jessie F. 1966. Learning to think about reading. *Educational Research, 9* (November): 56–62.

Rentel, Victor M., and Kennedy, John J. 1972. Effects of pattern drill in phonology, syntax, and reading achievement of rural Appalachian children. *American Educational Research Journal, 9* (Winter): 87–100.

Reynolds, Ralph E., Taylor, Marsha A., Steffensen, Margaret S., Shirey, Larry L., and Anderson, Richard C. 1982. Cultural schemata and reading comprehension. *Reading Research Quarterly, 17* (Number 3): 353–366.

Ribovich, Jerilyn K. 1979. A methodology for teaching concepts. *The Reading Teacher, 33* (December): 285–289.

Robeck, Mildred C., and Wilson, John A. R. 1974. *Psychology of reading: Foundations of instruction.* New York: John Wiley and Sons.

Roberts, Leslie Lewis. 1981. First graders' understanding of reading and reading instructional terminology. Unpublished doctoral dissertation, The University of Tennessee.

Roberts, Richard W., and Coleman, James C. 1958. An investigation of the role of visual and kinesthetic factors in reading failures. *Journal of Educational Research, 51* (February): 445–451.

Robertson, Jean E. 1968. Kindergarten perception training: Its effects on first grade reading. In *Perception and reading*, ed. Helen K. Smith, pp. 93–99. Newark, Delaware: International Reading Association.

Robinson, Helen M. 1946. *Why pupils fail in reading.* Chicago: University of Chicago Press.

Robinson, Helen M., and Weintraub, Samuel. 1973. Research related to children's interests and to developmental values of reading. *Library Trends, 22* (October): 81–108.

Rodenborn, Leo V. 1974. Determining, using expectancy formulas. *The Reading Teacher, 28* (December): 286–291.

Rodrigues, Raymond J., and White, Robert H. 1981. *Mainstreaming the non-English speaking student.* Urbana, Illinois: National Council of Teachers of English.

Rogers, Douglas B. 1984. Assessing study skills. *Journal of Reading, 27* (January): 346–354.

Rogers-Zegarra, Nancy, and Singer, Harry. 1985. Anglo and Chicano comprehension of ethnic stories. In *Theoretical models and processes of reading*, 3rd ed., eds. Harry Singer and Robert B.

Ruddell, pp. 611–617. Newark, Delaware: International Reading Association.

Roggenbuck, Mary June. 1977. Motivating farm children to read. *The Reading Teacher, 30* (May): 868–874.

Rosenshine, Barak V., and Furst, N. 1971. Current and future research on teacher performance criteria. In *Research on teacher education: A symposium*, ed. B.O. Smith. Englewood Cliffs, New Jersey: Prentice-Hall.

Rosenshine, Barak, and Stevens, Robert. 1984. Classroom instruction in reading. In *Handbook of reading research*, ed. P. David Pearson, pp. 745–798. New York: Longman.

Rosner, Stanley, Abrams, Jules, Daniels, Paul, and Schiffman, Gilbert. 1981. Dealing with reading needs of the learning disabled child. *Journal of Learning Disabilities, 14* (October): 436–438.

Rosso, Barbara Rok, and Emans, Robert. 1981. Children's use of phonic generalizations. *The Reading Teacher, 34* (March): 653–658.

Rouse, Michael W.., and Ryan, Julie B. 1984. Teachers' guide to vision problems. *The Reading Teacher, 38* (December): 306–317.

Rowell, C. Glennon. 1972. An attitude scale for reading. *The Reading Teacher, 25* (February): 442–447.

Ruddell, Robert B. 1985. Knowledge and attitudes toward testing: Field educators and legislators. *The Reading Teacher, 38* (February): 538–543.

Ruddell, Robert B., and Haggard, Martha Rapp. 1982. Influential teachers: Characteristics and classroom performance. In *New inquiries in reading research and instruction*, Thirty-first Yearbook of the National Reading Conference, pp. 227–231. Published by the National Reading Conference, Inc., edited by Jerome A. Niles assisted by Larry A. Harris.

Ruddell, Robert B., and Haggard, Martha Rapp. 1985. Oral and written language acquisition and the reading process. In *Theoretical models and processes of reading*, 3rd ed., eds. Harry Singer and Robert B. Ruddell, pp. 63–80. Newark, Delaware: International Reading Association.

Rumelhart, David E. 1980. Schemata: The building blocks of cognition. In *Theoretical issues in reading comprehension*, eds. Rand J. Spiro, Bertram C. Bruce, and William F. Brewer, pp. 33–58. Hillsdale, New Jersey: Lawrence Erlbaum Associates.

Rumelhart, David E. 1981. Schemata: The building blocks of cognition. In *Comprehension and teaching: Research reviews*, ed. John T. Guthrie, pp. 3–26. Newark, Delaware: International Reading Association.

Rumelhart, David E. 1984. Understanding understanding. In *Understanding reading comprehension*, ed. James Flood, pp. 1–20. Newark, Delaware: International Reading Association.

Rupley, William H. 1976. Effective reading programs. *The Reading Teacher, 29* (March): 616–623.

Rupley, William H., and Blair, Timothy R. 1983. *Reading diagnosis and direct instruction: A guide for the classroom*. Boston: Houghton Mifflin.

Rupley, William H., Wise, Beth S., and Logan, John W. 1986. Research in effective teaching: An overview of its development. In *Effective teaching of reading: Research and practices*, ed. James V. Hoffman, pp. 3–36. Newark, Delaware: International Reading Association.

Ryan, Ellen Bouchard. 1980. Metalinguistic development and reading. In *Language awareness and reading*, eds. Lynn H. Waterhouse, Karen M. Fischer, and Ellen Bouchard Ryan, pp. 38–59. Newark, Delaware: International Reading Association.

Ryan, Ellen Bouchard. 1981. Identifying and remediating failures in reading comprehension: Toward an instructional approach for poor comprehenders. In *Reading research: Advances in theory and practice*, eds. T. G. Waller and G. E. MacKinnon, pp. 223–261. New York: Academic Press.

Ryder, Randall, and Walmsley, Sean. 1981. Gilmore Oral Reading Test. In *Diagnostic and criterion-referenced reading tests: Review and evaluation*, ed. Leo M. Schell, pp. 44–48. Newark, Delaware: International Reading Association.

Sadow, Marilyn W. 1982. The use of story grammar in the design of questions. *The Reading Teacher, 36* (February): 518–522.

Salinger, Terry S. 1983. Study skills: A "basic" in elementary reading instruction. *Reading Improvement, 20* (Winter): 333–337.

Sampson, Olive C. 1966. Reading and adjustment: A review of the literature. *Educational Research, 8* (June): 184–190.

Samuels, S. Jay. 1976. Modes of word recognition. In *Theoretical models and processing of reading*, 2nd ed., eds. Harry Singer and Robert B. Ruddell, pp. 270–282. Newark, Delaware: International Reading Association.

Samuels, S. Jay. 1979. The method of repeated readings. *The Reading Teacher, 32* (January): 403–408.

Sanders, Norris M. 1966. *Classroom questions: What kinds?* New York: Harper and Row.

Sanders, Robbie S. 1981. Three first graders' concept of words and concepts about the language of literacy instruction. In *Directions in reading: Research and instruction*, ed. Michael L. Kamil, pp. 266–272. Washington, D.C.: National Reading Conference.

Sartain, Harry W. 1981. Research summary: Family contributions to reading attainment. In *Mobilizing family forces for worldwide reading success*, ed. Harry W. Sartain, pp. 4–18. Newark, Delaware: International Reading Association.

Savage, John F., and Mooney, Jean F. 1979. *Teaching reading to children with special needs*. Boston: Allyn and Bacon.

Schallert, D. L., and Kleinman, C. M. 1979. *Why the teacher is easier to understand than the textbook* (Reading Education Report No. 9). Urbana: University of Illinois Center for the Study of Reading (Eric Document Reproduction Service No. Ed 172 189).

Schell, Leo M., ed. 1981. *Diagnostic and criterion-referenced reading tests: Review and evaluation*. Newark, Delaware: International Reading Association.

Schell, Leo M. 1984. Test review: Comprehensive Test of Basic Skills (CTBS, Form U, Levels A-J). *Journal of Reading*, 27 (April): 586–589.

Schell, Leo M., and Hanna, Gerald S. 1981. Can informal reading inventories reveal strengths and weaknesses for comprehension subskills? *The Reading Teacher*, 35 (December): 263–268.

Schell, Leo M., and Jennings, Robert E. 1981. Test review: Durrell Analysis of Reading Difficulty (3rd Edition). *The Reading Teacher*, 35 (November): 204–210.

Schilling, Frank C. 1984. Teaching study skills in the intermediate grades—we can do more. *Journal of Reading*, 27 (April): 620–623.

Searls, Evelyn F. 1985. *How to use WISC-R scores in reading/learning disability diagnosis*. Newark, Delaware: International Reading Association.

Seng, Mark W. 1970. The linguistically different: Learning theories and intellectual development. In *Reading for the disadvantaged: Problems of linguistically different learners*, ed. Thomas D. Horn, pp. 99–114. New York: Harcourt, Brace and World.

Shannon, Albert J. 1985. Computer software as books. *The Reading Teacher*, 38 (April): 825–826.

Shannon, Patrick. 1985. Reading instruction and social class. *Language Arts*, 62 (October): 604–613.

Shavelson, Richard J., Hubner, Judith J., and Stanton, George C. 1976. Self-concept: Validation of construct interpretations. *Review of Educational Research*, 46 (Summer): 407–441.

Sheridan, E. Marcia. 1981. *Early reading in Japan*. South Bend, Indiana: Indiana University at South Bend.

Siegler, Hazel G., and Gynther, Malcolm D. 1960. Reading ability of children and family harmony. *Journal of Developmental Reading*, 4 (Autumn): 17–24.

Silvaroli, Nicholas J., Kear, Dennis J., and McKenna, Michael C. 1982. *A classroom guide to reading assessment and instruction*. Dubuque, Iowa: Kendall/Hunt.

Silvaroli, Nicholas J., Skinner, Jann, and Maynes, J. O. "Rocky". 1977. *Oral language evaluation teacher's manual*. St. Paul, Minnesota: EMC Corporation.

Sinatra, Richard. 1981. Using visuals to help the second language learner. *The Reading Teacher*, 34 (February); 539–546.

Singer, Harry. 1980. Sight word learning with and without pictures: A critique of Arline, Scott, and Webster's research. *Reading Research Quarterly*, 15: 290–298.

Smith, Donald E.P., and Fisher, Daniel. 1978. *More than you ever wanted to know about measurement and statistics: For reading specialists*. Ann Arbor, Michigan: Ulrich's Books.

Smith, Frank. 1983. *Essays into literacy*. London: Heinemann Educational Books.

Smith, Frederick R., and Feathers, Karen M. 1983. Teacher and student perceptions of content area reading. *Journal of Reading*, 26 (January): 348–354.

Smith, Lawrence L., Johns, Jerry L., Ganschow, Leonore, and Mastel, Nancy Browning. 1983. Using grade level vs. out-of-level reading tests with remedial students. *The Reading Teacher*, 36 (February): 550–553.

Smith, Richard J., and Dauer, Velma L. 1984. A comprehension monitoring strategy for reading content area materials. *Journal of Reading*, 28 (November): 144–147.

Smith, William Earl, and Beck, Michael D. 1980. Determining instructional level with the 1978 Metropolitan Achievement Tests. *The Reading Teacher*, 34 (December): 313–319.

Solomon, Daniel, and Kendall, Arthur J. 1976. *Final report: Individual characteristics and children's performance in varied educational settings*. Rockville, Maryland: Montgomery County Public Schools.

Spache, George. 1974. *Good reading for poor readers*, 9th ed. Champaign, Illinois: Garrard Press.

Spache, George D. 1976. *Investigating the issues of reading disabilities*. Boston: Allyn and Bacon.

Spache, George D. 1981. *Diagnosing and correcting*

reading disabilities, 2nd ed. Boston: Allyn and Bacon.

Spiegel, Dixie Lee, Reck, Miles H., and Fitzgerald, Jill. 1983. An investigation of a context-plus-phonics strategy for increasing second-grade students' use of context to aid word recognition. In *Searches for meaning in reading/language processing and instruction: Thirty-second yearbook of the National Reading Conference*, ed. Jerome A. Niles, pp. 231–237. Rochester, New York: The National Reading Conference.

Stanchfield, Jo M., and Fraim, Susan M. 1979. A follow-up study on the reading interests of boys. *Journal of Reading*, 22 (May): 748–752.

Stauffer, Russell G., Abrams, Jules C., and Pikulski, John J. 1978. *Diagnosis, correction, and prevention of reading disabilities*. New York: Harper and Row.

Steig, Janet. 1979. What can we learn from poor comprehenders? A review of recent research. *Reading World*, 19 (December): 124–128.

Steingart, Sandra Koser, and Glock, Marvin D. 1979. Imagery and the recall of connected discourse. *Reading Research Quarterly*, 15: 66–83.

Stewart, Robert S. 1950. Personality maladjustment and reading achievement. *American Journal of Orthopsychiatry*, 20 (April): 410–447.

Strang, Ruth. 1969. *Diaganostic teaching of reading*, 2nd ed. New York: McGraw-Hill.

Strange, Michael. 1980. Instructional implications of a conceptual theory of reading comprehension. *The Reading Teacher*, 33 (January): 391–397.

Sucher, Floyd, and Allred, Ruel A. 1973. *Teacher's manual: Sucher-Allred reading placement inventory*. Oklahoma City: The Economy Co.

Taylor, Nancy, and Waynant, Pricilla Pilson. 1978. Reading logs reflect students' real world reading needs. *The Reading Teacher*, 32 (October): 7–9.

Thonis, Eleanor Wall. 1976. *Literacy for America's Spanish speaking children*. Newark, Delaware: International Reading Association.

Tovey, Duane R. 1980. Children's grasp of phonic terms vs. sound-symbol relationships. *The Reading Teacher*, 33 (January): 431–437.

Trabasso, Thomas. 1981. On the making of inferences during reading and their assessment. In *Comprehension and teaching: Research reviews*, ed. John T. Guthrie, pp. 56–76. Newark, Delaware: International Reading Association.

Tuinman, Jaap. 1984. Book review-reading comprehension assessment: A cognitive basis. *Journal of Reading Behavior*, 16: 159–164.

Tuinman, Jaap, Rowls, Michael, and Farr, Roger.

1976. Reading achievement in the United States: Then and now. *Journal of Reading*, 19 (March): 455–463.

United States Office of Education. August 23, 1977. *Education of handicapped children*. Implementation of Part B of the Education for Handicapped Act. Federal Register, Part II. Washington, D.C.: United States Department of Health, Education, and Welfare.

Urell, Barbar. 1976. They call that reading. *Teacher*, 93 (January): 64–68.

Valmont, William J. 1972. Creating questions for information reading inventories. *The Reading Teacher*, 25 (March): 509–512.

Valtin, Renate. 1978–1979. Dyslexia: Deficit in reading or deficit in research. *Reading Research Quarterly*, 14 (Number 2): 202–221.

Vellutino, Frank R. 1977. Alternative conceptualizations of dyslexia: Evidence in support of a verbal-deficit hypothesis. *Harvard Educational Review*, 47 (August): 334–354.

Vernon, Magdalen D. 1969. *Visual perception and its relation to reading*. Newark, Delaware: International Reading Association.

Vogel, Juliet M. 1980. Getting letters straight. In *Some perceptual prerequisites for reading*, eds. Uta Frith and Juliet M. Vogel, pp. 20–42. Newark, Delaware: International Reading Association.

Vygotsky, L. S. 1962. *Thought and language*. Cambridge, Massachusetts: MIT Press.

Walker, Charles Monroe. 1979. High frequency word list for grades 3 through 9. *The Reading Teacher*, 32 (April): 803–812.

Waller, T. Gary. 1977. *Think first, read later! Piagetian prerequisites for reading*. Newark, Delaware: International Reading Association.

Warwick, B. Elley. 1978. Cloze procedure (Ebbinghaus completion method) as applies to reading. In *Eighth Mental Measurements Yearbook*, Vol. II, ed. O. K. Buros, pp. 1174–1176. Highland Park, New Jersey: Gryphon Press.

Wattenberg, William W., and Clifford, Clare. 1966. Relationships of self-concept to beginning achievement in reading. *Child Development*, 35, part 1 (June): 461–467.

Wechsler, David. 1974. *Wechsler Intelligence Scale for Children-Revised: WISC-R Manual*. New York: Psychological Corp.

Weidler, Sarah D. 1984. Reading in the content area of science. in *Reading in the content areas: Research for teachers*, ed. Mary M. Dupuis, pp.

54–65. Newark, Delaware: International Reading Association.

Weiner, Bernard. 1979. A theory of motivation for some classroom experience. *Journal of Educational Psychology*, *71* (Number 1): 3–25.

Weiner, Bernard, Frieze, I. H., Kukla, A., Read, L. Rest, S., and Rosenbaum, R. M. 1971. *Perceiving the cause of success and failure*. Morristown, New Jersey: General Learning Press.

Weintraub, Samuel. 1968. Research: Eye-hand preferences and reading. *The Reading Teacher, 21* (January): 369–373, 401.

Whaley, Jill Fitzgerald. 1981. Story grammars and reading instruction. *The Reading Teacher, 34* (April): 762–771.

Wigfield, Allan, and Asher, Steven R. 1984. Social and motivational influences on reading. In *Handbook on reading research*, ed. P. David Pearson, pp. 423–452. New York: Longman.

Wilson, LaVisa Cam, and Thrower, Jan. 1985. Early childhood reading educators' perceptions of reading readiness. *Reading Research and Instruction, 25*: 21–23.

Wilson, Robert M. 1981. *Diagnostic and remedial reading for classroom and clinic*, 4th ed. Columbus: Charles E. Merrill.

Wilson, Robert M., and Barnes, Marcia M. 1974. *Survival learning materials: Suggestions for developing*. York, Pennsylvania: Strine.

Winograd, Peter, Witte, Ray, and Smith, Lynne. 1986. Measuring attributions for reading: A comparison of direct and indirect locus and stability scores. In *Solving problems in literacy: Learners, teachers, and researchers*, eds. Jerome A. Niles and Rosary V. Lalik, pp. 387–394. Rochester, New York: Thirty-fifth Yearbook of the National Reading Conference.

Witman, Carolyn Cattron, and Riley, James D. 1978. Colored chalk and messy fingers: A kinesthetic-tactile approach to reading. *The Reading Teacher, 31* (March): 620–623.

Yawkey, Thomas Daniels. 1980. Creative thinking and self-concept in young children. In *The self-concept of the young child*, ed. Thomas Daniels Yawkey, pp. 151–163. Provo, Utah: Brigham Young University Press.

Yellin, David. 1979. Defining the relationship between language and cognition: A conundrum for our times. *Reading World, 19* (December): 157–167.

Name Index

Ackerson, Gary, 118
Ajzen, Icek, 21, 167, 169
Alexander, J. Estill, 21, 27, 73, 169, 170, 179, 184
Allen, Roach Van, 441
Allington, Richard L., 254, 310
Allred, Ruel A., 105, 109
Almy, Millie Corrine, 52
Ames, Wilbur S., 118
Anastasiow, Nicholas J., 26
Anderson, Billie V., 54
Anderson, Linda M., 77
Anderson, Richard C., 36, 287
Anderson, Thomas H., 37, 319, 322, 325, 344, 346
André, Marli E.D.A., 37, 346
Armbruster, Bonnie B., 38, 319, 322, 325, 344, 346
Asher, Steven R., 13, 24, 26, 28
Ashton-Warner, Sylvia, 452
Athey, Irene, 29, 35
Aulls, Mark W., 29, 43
Avila, Donald L., 70
Aydelott, Sabiha Tufail, 489

Babbs, Patricia J., 286
Bader, Lois A., 106, 115, 116–117
Baker, Linda, 36, 37, 38
Baldwin, R. Scott, 183
Barnes, Martha M., 370
Barnitz, John G., 49, 54
Bartel, Nettie, 44
Barton, Allen H., 53–54
Bateman, B., 449
Bauer, Gary W., 30
Baumann, James F., 71, 75
Beals, Paul E., 368
Bean, Rita M., 390, 393, 394
Beck, Michael D., 134
Beckerman, Terrill M., 75
Beebe, Mona J., 100
Belloni, Loretta Frances, 24
Benson, P. Frank, 60

Benton, Arthur L., 62
Berliner, David C., 71, 75
Betts, Emmett A., 92
Bingham, Grace, 26
Blachowicz, Camille L.Z., 46, 213
Black, F. William, 62
Blair, Timothy R., 149
Blanchard, Jay S., 361
Blum, Irene H., 269
Boehnlein, Mary M., 53
Bond, Guy L., 27, 44, 67, 383, 445
Botel, Morton, 109
Bougere, Marguerite B., 49
Bower, Gordon, 284
Bradley, John M., 118
Bransford, J.D., 37
Braun, Carl, 305–306
Brophy, Jere E., 68
Brown, Ann L., 36, 37, 38
Brown, David M., 367
Brown, Don A., 122
Brown, Dorothea, 169
Brown, Roger, 44
Bruckerhoff, Charles, 178
Buchanan, C.B., 448
Buck, Catherine, 49–50
Bullen, Gertrude F., 169
Burke, Carolyn L., 309, 422–423
Burmeister, Lou, 242, 264
Burns, Paul C., 109
Buros, Oscar, 413
Bursuk, Lauren Z., 260

Canney, George, 158
Carey, Robert F., 89, 90, 105, 115, 122, 125–126, 136, 146, 148, 160
Carney, John, 38
Catterson, Jane H., 284–285, 414, 418
Cazden, Courtney B., 214
Ceprano, Maria A., 235

Subject Index

Page numbers in bold refer to figures.

Incentive component of motivation, 23
Independent reading level, 91, 104
Independent reading, 372–373
Index, 333
Individual Evaluation Procedures in Reading, 109
Individualized programs, 76
Inferential skills
   activities for improving, 315
   role in comprehension, 295
Informal assessment
   in classroom, 85–124
   limitations, 120–121
   of reading studying skills, 349
   strengths, 119–120
Informal reading inventories. *See* Commercial IRIs; IRIs
Information organization as a comprehension skill, 289–292
Initial placement inventory, 111
Initial Teaching Alphabet (i/t/a), 449
Instruction, 379–395. *See also* Activities
   for corrective readers, 384–389
   diagnostic procedures, 76
   motivational techniques, 77
   -objectives assessment, 153
   planning, 386–389
   remedial readers and, 389–394
     personnel involved in, 390–392
   role in comprehension problems, 301
   sight words, 236–237
   strategies to improve negative attitudes, 178–179
   teacher-directed, task-oriented, 75
   test-teach-retest-reteach model, 75–76
   time, organizing, 74–75
Instructional reading level (IRL), 91, 104, 134
   determining appropriate, 73
   quick assessments for, 118
Instrumental hypothesis, and comprehension, 287
Intelligence, 38–39. *See also* IQ
Intensive phonics (auditory emphasis) for extended remediation, 443–445
Intensity deafness, 59
Interest(s), 166, 181–188
   Alexander Inventory, **184**
   assessment, 183–185
   categorizing, 182–183
   checklist, **186**
   effect on reading, 24–25
   for teachers, 180–181
   influences on, 25
   influence on comprehension, 183
   self-report instruments to assess, 183–184
Internal determinants of self-concept, 26
International Reading Association, 142, 400, 411
   Evaluation of Tests Committee, 412
Interpersonal skills needed by reading specialists, 393–394
Interpretive level of comprehension, 279
Interviewing, 386
   data sheet for corrective readers, 387
Intrinsic motivation, 190
Iowa Tests of Basic Skills, 133
IQ, 38–39

level of mental retardation indicated by (table), 10
   and reading achievement test scores, 38
   and reading expectancy formulas, 382
   and school ability indexes, 128
   scores, reporting to parents, 144–145
   tests, 39, 127, 130–133, 481–483
     and mental retardation, 14
IRIs (Informal reading inventories), 89–109, 412, 485–486
   administration of, 93–95
   to assess listening comprehension, 381
   behavior characteristics, 96, 103
   Bett's criteria for determining performance levels, **92**, 96, 98, 123
   commercial. *See* Commercial IRIs
   comprehension data
     interpreting, 102–103
     summarizing, **100**
   constructing, 93, 455–461
   criteria for determining performance levels, 91–93
   determining reading levels, 104–105
   graded passages for, 456–458
   interpreting, 98–105
   levels, 89
   miscues
     guidelines for scoring, 98
     recording and scoring, 96
     summary, **100**
     types and recording, **97**
   oral reading protocol, analyzing, 101–102
   performance levels, 91
   purposes, 90
   question probes to assess comprehension, 103
   questioning related to, 304
   reading rates, 103
   scoring criteria, **93**
   summarizing data, 96, 98, **101**
   for word recognition problems, 230

John's list of nouns, 234
Johnson and Lehnert's Instructional Model for Phonics, **244**

Kinesthetic perception, 34
Knowledge hypothesis and comprehension, 287

Language
   abilities, tests, 486–487
   -based method of extended remediation, 440–442
   bilingualism, 48–49
   characteristics of children age 3 months to 12 years, **45–46**
   correlates of reading problems, 42–51
   development, 43–46
   dialects, 49–51
   -different children, 11
   -different speakers and auditory discrimination, 34
   experience approach to teaching reading, 211, 440–442
   experience stories, 212–213, 251
   Language Instruction Register (LIR), 47
   metalinguistic awareness, 45–46
   registers, 47

evaluating and selecting, 148–151
face validity, 149–150
limitations, 145–148
machine scoring, 148
norming population, 150
percentile ranks, 128, 142
practicality, 150
predictive validity, 149
reliability, 150
school ability indexes, 128
scores, 137, 141–143
  grade-equivalent, 142, 147
  raw, 141
  reported to parents, 143–145
  scaled, 143
scoring ease, 150
stanines, 128, 143
types, 127–140, 127
validity, 148–150
Nutrition and learning, 63

Observation to identify problem readers, 381
Ophthalmologists, 57–58
Optometrists, 57–58
Oral language. *See also* Language
  abilities, 432
  assessment for extended diagnosis, 431–432
  relationship to reading, 44
Oral miscues. *See* Miscues
Oral reading protocol, **99**
  analyzing, 101–102
Organizing ideas from reading, 343–348
Orton Society, 443
Otis-Lennon School Ability Test (O-LSAT), 127–129
  norms for performance, **129**
  scores, 127
Out-of-level tests, 139–140
Outlining, 344–345
Pairing students in a classroom, 373
Parent(s). *See also* Family; Home
  and attitude formation, 21
  conferring with, 394
  information form, University of Tennessee Reading Center, **404–407**
  materials to use, 374
  NRT scores reported to, 143–145
  planning for remedial readers, 392
  reaction to reading classifications, 12
  role in
    comprehension skills improvement help, 316–317
    context, 252, 274
    interest assessment, 187
    language development of children, 214–215
    minimizing cultural differences, 55
    phonics, 273
    print awareness in child, 221
    promotion of thinking skills, 210
    reading achievement, 39, 52–53
    reading difficulties, 79
    reading-study skill development, 325, 327–328

self-concept improvement, 199–200
    setting purposes, 359
    sight words, 272–273
    structural analysis, 274
    word-recognition skills, 272–274
  as role models, 356
  teachers working with, 375–377
Part-whole concepts, 208
Passage dependency in comprehension assessment, 310
Past history in identifying problem readers, 380–381
Peabody Individual Achievement Test, 420
Peabody Picture Vocabulary Test–Revised (PPVT-R), 130–133
  communities included in standardization sample, 132
  stimulus training plate, **131**
Percentile ranks
  NRTs, 128, 142
    reported to parents, 144
Perception, 5, 31–34
Perceptual learning, 31. *See also* Perception
  and reading, 32
Perceptual programs of extended remediation, 447
Perceptual tests, 487–488
Personality problems
  affect on reading, 27–28
  and motivation for reading, 193–194
Personnel involved in instructional program, 390–392
Phenomenal determinants of self-concept, 26
Phonemic discrimination. *See* Auditory discrimination
Phonic families. *See* Word families
Phonics, 219, 224, 238–239
  activities for teaching, 242–246
  context-plus, method, 252–243
  generalizations, 242
  intensive, for extended remediation, 443–445
  overemphasis on, 251
  parents helping with, 273
  skills assessment, 239–241
  and structural analysis, 257
  teaching terminology, 241–242
Phonological systems of children, 44
Physical correlates of reading problems, 56–64
  health, 63–64
  laterality, 62–63
  neurological dysfunction, 61–62
  speech disorders, 60–61
Physical screening for extended diagnosis, 425–429
Picture(s)
  books, 214
    wordless, 369–370
  interpreting, 5
  and word distinctions, 217
Planning sheet for corrective readers, **388, 389**
Poor reading habits, behavioral characteristics associated with, 104
Powell IRI criteria, 93, 96, 98
Praise, use of, 77
Prediction skills
  activities for improving, 314
  role in comprehension, 294, 337

Predictive validity, NRTs, 149
Prefixes, 258–264
    increasing students' knowledge of, 292
    list, **260–261**
Preliminary data for extended diagnosis, 400–407
PRI Reading Systems, 153
    objective structure of, **154–155**
Primary materials. *See* Reference materials; specific
        sources
Print awareness, 35, 203, 216–222
    assessing, 221
    development of, 220–221
    relationship to other skills, 220–221
Print orientation, 217
Problem readers. *See also* Readers
    identifying, 380–384
Process assessment for comprehension, 304
Product assessment for comprehension, 304
Programmed materials for extended remediation, 448
Programmed Reading, 448
Progress report, example, 468–469
Psycholinguistic abilities, 431
Psycholinguistic assessment for extended diagnosis, 431–
        432
Psycholinguistic theory, 211–212, 286, 294, 299
Psychological approach to extended remediation, 449
Psychological integration level of comprehension, 279
Psychological screening, 429–431
Psychologists, 392
Public Law 94–142, 8, 10
Punctuation, role in comprehension, 296
Purpose of materials, 5, 358–359

Question(s)
    for IRI, constructing, 458–461
    probes, 103
Questioning, 346–347
    to assess comprehension, 304–306
    skills assessed by, 306
Quick assessment procedures for instructional level, 118

Raw scores, NRTs, 141
Readers, 6. *See also* Basal reader(s); Books; Corrective
        readers; Remedial readers; Student(s)
    causes of comprehension problems associated with, 299–
        300
    classification of, 7–12
    corrective, 7, 8
    developmental, 7
    disabled, 418
    evaluation of, 383–384
    problem, identifying, 380–384
    remedial, 7–8
Readiness for reading, 202–223
Reading
    ability
        checklist, **414**
    tests, 410–424
    achievement
        and the home, 52–53

    tests, 38, 133–136, 477–479
    attitudes toward, 166–179
    beliefs about, 4–5
    diagnostic tests, 479–481
    effect of dialects on learning, 49–50
    expectancy formulas, 382–383
    independent, 372–373
    interests, 24–25, 166, 181–188. *See also* Interest(s)
        categorization, 182–183
        checklist, **186**
    language acquisition linked to, 44
    levels
        cloze procedure scores, 116
        group procedures for estimating, 110–119
        individual procedures for estimating, 88–110
        initial placement inventory, **111**
        instructional, 73, 91, 104, 118, 134
            IRI-based, 91, 104
        quick assessment procedures, 118
    materials, selecting appropriate, 74, 357–358
Reading Miscue Inventory (RMI), 412, 422–423
    motives for, 355
    assessing, 194–195
    organizing ideas from, 343–348
    problems, 5–6
        affective correlates, 18–41
        auditory acuity correlated to, 59–60
        cognitive correlates, 18–41
        cultural correlates, 51–56
        and gender, 13–14,55–56
        health correlated to, 63–64
        the home correlated to, 52–53
        language correlates, 42–51
        laterality correlated to, 62–63
        neurological dysfunction correlated to, 61–62
        physical correlates of, 56
        preventing, 78
        related to thinking skills, 207–209
        socioeconomic levels correlated to, 53–54
        speech disorders correlated to, 60–61
        in the U.S., 13–16
        visual acuity correlated to, 57–59
    programs, 361
        context reading time, 268
    rates
        grades 2-6, **103**
        IRI, 103
    readiness, 202–223
        tests, 484–485
    recreational, 177
    relationship to oral language, 44
    repeated, 268–269
        rating sheet, **270, 271**
        technique for readers with inadequate decoding skills,
            300
    self-monitoring, 292–294
    setting purposes, 293
    skills and classroom materials, 359
    specialists, 9, 393–394
    -study skills, 319–328